3. 7. 9

The English Romance in Time

The English Romance in Time

*Transforming motifs from
Geoffrey of Monmouth
to the death of Shakespeare*

HELEN COOPER

OXFORD
UNIVERSITY PRESS

OXFORD

UNIVERSITY PRESS

Great Clarendon Street, Oxford OX2 6DP

Oxford University Press is a department of the University of Oxford.
It furthers the University's objective of excellence in research, scholarship,
and education by publishing worldwide in

Oxford New York

Auckland Cape Town Dar es Salaam Hong Kong Karachi Kuala Lumpur
Madrid Melbourne Mexico City Nairobi New Delhi Shanghai Taipei Toronto

With offices in

Argentina Austria Brazil Chile Czech Republic France Greece
Guatemala Hungary Italy Japan South Korea Poland Portugal
Singapore Switzerland Thailand Turkey Ukraine Vietnam

Oxford is a registered trade mark of Oxford University Press
in the UK and in certain other countries

Published in the United States
by Oxford University Press Inc., New York

© Helen Cooper 2004

British Library Cataloguing in Publication Data

Data available

Library of Congress Cataloging in Publication Data

Data available

ISBN 0-19-924886-9

5 7 9 10 8 6 4

Typeset by Hope Services (Abingdon) Ltd.
Printed in Great Britain
on acid-free paper by
Biddles Ltd., King's Lynn, Norfolk

Michael

Myn owne swete herte

Preface

This book is a study of romance motifs in England and their changing
uses from Geoffrey of Monmouth to the death of Shakespeare; or, to put
it another way, it is a study of the Tudor and early Stuart reception of
black-letter prints of Middle English romance. Just one later author was
reading these same romances and turning them into a work that itself
entered the canon of cultural literacy, and that is John Bunyan; so, for the
purposes of the book, he counts as an honorary Jacobean. The broad
argument of the book is that while the motifs of romance remain largely
the same, the usage and understanding of them changes over time, in the
same way that words themselves change meaning. This book traces a
comparable historical semantics of romance motifs. It therefore offers a
way to read, as evidence of a particular moment, stories of such longevity
or of such fantasy that they seem resistant to historical interpretation.
Romance emerges in the twelfth century in response to cultural
pressures, and had changed from an elite- to a mass-culture form by the
seventeenth century under new cultural pressures. The half millennium
in between constitutes the great age of romance, but not as a static phe-
nomenon. This book sets out to tell the story of those centuries, as a
process of change and reinvention that uses the materials of nostalgia,
fantasy, and social and religious ideals as vehicles of contemporary
concern.

My interest in romance and its development goes back many years, but
it is only recently that I have realized how closely many of the ways I have
approached it in the past coalesce to form a single story. Many of the
chapters therefore draw on the earlier articles cited in the notes. In most
instances these have been almost entirely reworked, but the core of
Chapter 3 will still be recognizable from my very first substantial article,
entitled, like the chapter itself, 'Magic that doesn't work', first published
in *Medievalia et Humanistica*.

My concern has been to write a study that will be accessible to as many
people working in the Middle Ages and early modern periods as possible,
whatever their level of expertise. Some passages will therefore no doubt
be over-explicit about matters that will be entirely familiar to medieval-
ists, but not so well known to early modernists, and *vice versa*: for these,

I apologize, but not very much. For the shorter romances, I have normally cited the most easily accessible anthologies. I have worked largely from modern editions so as to profit from their editorial material, though Early English Books Online has transformed the accessibility of early prints since I began the writing of this book, and I have supplemented the holdings of the Bodleian and Cambridge University Libraries by electronic means with increasing frequency. *Short-title Catalogue* reference numbers and further information about editions and the history of both the manuscript and printed versions of all the Middle English romances that crossed the 1500 divide are given in the appendix.

With the same aim of accessibility in mind, quotations from Middle English are glossed or translated where they present difficulty, and quotations from other languages are translated or given a close paraphrase. All translations are my own unless otherwise stated, though published translations of French and Anglo-Norman works that come under discussion are noted to enable the easier following-up of particular texts. In quotations, thorn and yogh are given their modern equivalents, and i/j and u/v are normalized in all cases except for the detail of bibliographical titles. Capitalization, typography, and punctuation have been modernized or made consistent unless there were some specific reason not to do so.

The book could not have been written without the award of a two-year Research Readership by the British Academy, and I owe them the greatest thanks. The Master and Fellows of University College, and most particularly Jon Mee, gave me generous support in my application and throughout the duration of the Readership. Many other friends have offered help and encouragement along the way. Andrew King, Matthew Woodcock, and Corinne Saunders not only took over my work to enable me to do the writing but read and commented on the book in draft, and Ruth Morse, most steadfast of readers, also read parts of it. It is all the better for their comments, and would be still better if I had incorporated more of them. I have profited in less visible ways from discussions over the years with my research students in romance and adjacent areas, Corinne, Andrew, and Matt foremost among them, but also Jane Bliss, Joyce Boro, Alexandra Gillespie, Helen Moore, Nicola McDonald, and Rachel Snell. The scholars and enthusiasts at the biennial conferences on the non-canonical Middle English romances have also been an inspiration. Many other people have answered queries or provided information, including Elizabeth Archibald, Kate Belsey, Roger Dalrymple, Jennifer Fellows, Linda Georgianna, Ralph Hanna, Susan Hurley, Elspeth

Kennedy, Paulina Kewes, Elizabeth Maslen, Alexander Murray, Rhiannon Purdie, Nicholas Rawlins, and Simon Walker. Bill Byrne provided me with quiet space. The staff of the Cambridge University Library and the Bodleian Library have been unremittingly helpful. My husband has, yet again, been unstinting in his support, and the dedication reflects my debt to him.

List of Contents

Abbreviations   xv

INTRODUCTION: 'ENTER, PURSUED WITH A BEAR'   1

   Replication across cultures: the meme   3
   Recognizing romance   7
   Exploiting the familiar   15
   Romance in England: a summary history   22
   Coda: The rise and fall of the knight   41

1. QUEST AND PILGRIMAGE: 'THE ADVENTURE THAT
   GOD SHALL SEND ME'   45

   Society and the solitary knight   50
   Mythic symmetries   57
   Quests without maps   67
   Questing westward   72
   Landscapes of desire and fear   77
   Seeking forgiveness   86
   The penitential quest at the Reformation   90
   The journey of the soul   98

2. PROVIDENCE AND THE SEA: 'NO TACKLE, SAIL, NOR
   MAST'   106

   Pollution, guilt, and the state   113
   'God is our pilot'   119
   From miracle to magic   128

3. MAGIC THAT DOESN'T WORK 137

    Non-functioning magic 144

    Non-replicating magic 152

    Magic in the web? 159

    Magic enacted 164

4. FAIRY MONARCHS, FAIRY MISTRESSES: 'I AM OF ANE
   OTHER COUNTREE' 173

    'Some uncouth tidings tell you me' 187

    'I love thee well by cause of the trouthe that is in thee' . . 197

    'We had thought indeed the Lake had been ours' . . 207

    'An elf-queen shall my lemman be' 211

5. DESIRABLE DESIRE: 'I AM WHOLLY GIVEN OVER UNTO
   THEE' 218

    The politics of women's desire 221

    Erotic thought: the Middle Ages 229

    Sanctifying sexuality 241

    Erotic thought: Spenser and Sidney 251

    'Quick, and in mine arms' 260

6. WOMEN ON TRIAL 269

    The calumny romance in Tudor England 274

    'I am falsely and without cause accused' 280

    If women be a good thing, or no 292

    'Do after the good and leave the evil' 300

    The adultery question 307

    Adultery in English romance 314

7. RESTORING THE RIGHTFUL HEIR: 'IF THAT WHICH
   IS LOST BE NOT FOUND' 324

    The foundling and the Fair Unknown 331

    The descent of the crown 340

Romance after Bosworth   344

Dangerous virginity   353

8. UNHAPPY ENDINGS: 'THE MOST ACCURSED, UNHAPPY,
   AND EVIL FORTUNED'   361

Questing towards death   367

Exposure on the seas   375

Diabolic magic   377

Fairies and fates   381

Desire   387

Accusation   396

From family romance to family tragedy   398

Appendix: Medieval romance in English after 1500   409

Notes   431

Bibliography   499

Index   533

Abbreviations

ANTS	Anglo-Norman Text Society
CFMA	Classiques français du moyen age
CT	*Canterbury Tales*
EETS	Early English Text Society
E.S.	Extra Series
O.S.	Original Series
S.S.	Supplementary Series
ELR	*English Literary Renaissance*
FQ	*Faerie Queene*
French and Hale	*Middle English Metrical Romances*, ed. W. H. French and C. B. Hale
MED	*Middle English Dictionary*
PMLA	*Publications of the Modern Languages Association*
Percy	*Bishop Percy's Folio Manuscript: Ballads and Romances*, ed. John W. Hales and Frederick J. Furnivall
Sands	*Middle English Verse Romances*, ed. Donald B. Sands
SATF	Société des anciens textes français
SR	*Stationers' Registers*
STC	*A Short-title Catalogue of Books printed in England, Scotland, and Ireland 1475–1642*
TLF	Textes littéraires français

Citations from Chaucer are taken from *The Riverside Chaucer*, general ed. Larry D. Benson (Boston: Houghton Mifflin, 1987).

Citations from Malory are taken from *The Works of Sir Thomas Malory*, ed. Eugène Vinaver, 3rd edn., rev. by P. J. C. Field, 3 vols. (Oxford: Clarendon Press, 1990); cross-references to the book and chapter numbering of Caxton's edition are given in parentheses.

Citations from Shakespeare are taken from *The Complete Works*, general eds. Stanley Wells and Gary Taylor (Oxford: Clarendon Press, 1986), unless otherwise stated.

Introduction:
'Enter, pursued with a bear'

Early in the 1590s, the Queen's Men required a bearsuit. They were about to stage a dramatized version of *Valentine and Orson*, a romance about an empress falsely accused of adultery who gives birth to twins in a forest, only to have one of them snatched away by a bear.[1] The text does not survive, but it would have been a big disappointment to the spectators if the bear had not put in an appearance: they knew the story already, and would have been waiting for it. Some of them would have read the source of the play, in the form of one of the reprints of a translation made most of a century earlier from a French prose version. That version was itself a reworking of a fourteenth-century verse original, which had in turn been compiled out of materials recycled from other romances, and which was to work its way across the languages of Europe as far as Sweden. Those playgoers who had not read the actual text still knew the story of its main characters, the hairy wild man, Orson, and his chivalric brother, Valentine. For centuries, they were as familiar as Cinderella is now, and by similar means: through oral retellings, through illustrations, by simply being around in the culture. They had figured in a street pageant for the coronation of Edward VI in 1549;[2] they were to get a mention—'play the Valentine with our wilder brothers, and bring them back with brotherly care to civilisation and happiness'—by John Forster in his *Life of Charles Dickens*, alongside Cinderella, with all the casualness that comes from the safe assumption of shared knowledge.[3] The omission of the bear on stage would have been sorely felt.

It would not have been difficult to acquire the materials to make the suit, if the company did not already have one in the property cupboard. Bearbaiting pits often doubled as venues for early plays, and several of the public theatres were clustered around the Beargarden on Bankside; a bearskin, even if somewhat damaged, could have been acquired and recycled for stage purposes as easily as the elements of earlier romances were recycled to make the original story. It must have been a bulky item to store, all the same, and once acquired, was crying out for good uses. More bears accordingly began to appear on the Elizabethan stage to occupy the empty suit. An anonymous romance play entitled *Mucedorus* gets its action off to a swinging start by having its heroine 'Enter . . . pursued with a bear'.[4] Other bears figured in an opening dumbshow, or in spectral form to terrify a murderer into suicide.[5] Some twenty years later, when Shakespeare wanted to call to his audience's minds the resonances and assumptions of romance, he combines a story of a queen falsely accused of adultery with a bear that chases (and, offstage, eats) the guardian of her baby at the moment when he abandons it in the wilds. The bearsuit, if it was the same one, was coming towards the end of its days by that time: motheaten, no doubt; the fur worn away, especially around the scars from its first occupant's life in the bearpit; and probably going mouldy too. *The Winter's Tale* was its last new appearance, as if to outface the developing estimate of romances as 'mouldy tales'.[6] It is appropriate that the stage direction for its bear should be not an entrance, but an exit.

'Exit, pursued by a bear' is notorious because to modern theatregoers it seems so random and meaningless: it is not prepared for by the previous action of the play. The preparation for it lies rather in the coding and resonances that the motif brought with it, still familiar to Jacobean spectators, but long lost to modern readers or audiences. An understanding of much of what is going on in Renaissance plays has disappeared along with a comprehension of the codes of romance and a sense of their resonance. The bear is the most famous example only because it is the most extreme, and therefore the one of which we are the most aware. The object of this book is to bring that extensive level of allusions, the context of understanding, back to the surface: to restore to modern readers the 'literary competence', in Jonathan Culler's phrase, that Renaissance and medieval readers brought as a matter of course to their reading or watching of romances.[7] Romance was itself the major genre of secular fiction for the five hundred years covered by this book: a time span that makes the novel appear the youngster that it is. Without such an understanding of romance, it is impossible to make sense of that half millennium of literature in which men and women of the Middle Ages and Renaissance fashioned themselves, their culture, and their ideals. The bear will serve as an emblem for the book: a motif that owes its birth and longevity to the fact that it is an enthralling story element, but which was used to tell a story about providence, the disruption and restoration of order and lineal succession, innocence accused and vindicated; and which, once invented, like the empty bearsuit waiting backstage, needed new meanings, new justifications, to fill it out and give it continued life.

REPLICATION ACROSS CULTURES: THE MEME

The abduction of a child by a bear or some other wild animal is an example of a romance motif: a unit within literature that proves so useful, so infectious, that it begins to take on a life of its own. There is a word for such things now: a 'meme', an idea that behaves like a gene in its ability to replicate faithfully and abundantly, but also on occasion to adapt, mutate, and therefore survive in different forms and cultures.[8] These motifs and conventions grew up with the genre of which they formed a part and which they helped to define. They were first developed in the twelfth century in romances written in French and the gradually diverging form of French spoken in England, Anglo-Norman; they moved across the language barrier into English in the thirteenth to fifteenth centuries, acquired a new and vibrant popularity when prints of medieval romances became the pulp fiction of the Tudor age, and underwent remarkable metamorphoses in the works of the great Elizabethan writers.[9] Their quality as memes, with their generous capacity to latch onto the mind and replicate, is wonderfully caught by one of the last authors to use medieval texts in an unbroken line of transmission, John Bunyan, in the later seventeenth century. He misspent his youth reading cheap prints of romances, not least the perennial favourite *Bevis of Hamtoun*: a work that owed much of its popularity to its density of the simplest and most colourful of such motifs, dragons and giants and grim prisons and healing balms. Such items came into their own when he realized how they could be used in the service of God, in the work that became *The Pilgrim's Progress*. His mind 'suddenly' became crowded with

> more than twenty things, which I set down;
> This done, I twenty more had in my crown,
> And they again began to multiply,
> Like sparks that from the coals of fire do flie.

Their powers of exponential multiplication were matched by their insistent memorability:

> Art thou forgetful? wouldest thou remember
> From New-years-day to the last of December?
> Then read my fancies, they will stick like burs.[10]

And his Giant Despair and soporific Enchanted Ground did indeed stick in readers' minds, for almost as many centuries after he wrote as the monsters of *Bevis* had lodged since its own composition.[11] Modernist and post-modern literature for adults is marked by a distrust of both story and traditional story elements. Bunyan realized that a good story composed of motifs that are already familiar is the most mind-engaging form that there is, and that romances are the very best such stories. It is no coincidence that the authors who kick-started the modern equivalent of the romance, C. S. Lewis and J. R. R. Tolkien, were two of the leading medieval scholars of the mid-twentieth century.

This book is a study of the memes of romance. Its broad argument is that whilst romance motifs remain superficially the same, sometimes even down to verbal detail, the usage and understanding of them changes over time, rather in the way that a word may change meaning: the book traces an analogous historical semantics of the language of romance conventions. It therefore sets itself a very different task from Vladimir Propp's classic formalist analysis of folktales, or, more recently, Susan Wittig's linguistics-based study of romances, both of which seek to identify motifs in tales or romances independent of either the broad culture or the specific circumstances that produced them and in which they were read;[12] or from comparable synchronic surveys of variants on a single motif, such as Margaret Schlauch's study of accused queens.[13] Other fine studies of a single motif—the king in disguise on the Elizabethan stage, the Renaissance boat of adventures—do not aim for chronological or historical depth.[14] 'New readers make new texts'; every generation brings different cultural expectations to works of the past and so finds new meanings and new things to respond to.[15] Even successive recopyings of a single text record a process of shifting interpretations and significances, and those shifts become more marked as traditional elements are re-used in new stories and new contexts. Such differences are intensified as stories and motifs move across authors, periods, readership groups, and changing political and linguistic conditions.

The 'far away and long ago' that is almost a defining feature of the genre, the freeing of romances from familiar place or chronology, makes it especially easy for them to be appropriated for interpretations that fit the immediate historical or cultural moment of subsequent new readers. The half millennium during which romances were the dominant form of secular literature was a period of massive change. When they first began to be composed, England was a multilingual culture, and part of a composite realm that extended over much of the territory of modern-day France; by the time of Elizabeth, England was a fiercely nationalist entity, proudly distinct in language, which regarded the English Channel as its providential bulwark against foreign encroachment. Manuscript culture, with its primary appeal to a rich and leisured or educated élite and to the upwardly mobile, gave way to print, with its potential for mass circulation. Roman Catholic ideology, which emphasized the public outward expressions of ideals and beliefs (from miracles and pilgrimages to virginity), was replaced by the Protestant stress on the inward and individual. It is no accident that the great age of romance was also the great age of faith. The doctrine of salvation, in which the terrible events of the Passion and Crucifixion were made the means by which fallen mankind was restored and the bliss of Heaven once more became possible, received its full theological formulation in the eleventh and twelfth centuries. Romance, with its typical pattern of an opening disruption of a state of order, followed by a period of trial and suffering, even an encounter with death, yet with a final symbolic resurrection and better restoration, offers a secular equivalent to that divine order: a 'secular scripture', in Northrop Frye's phrase.[16] Yet by the late sixteenth century, that providential model of human and divine action existed in uneasy truce, on one side with a sharp awareness that human affairs did not always show evidence of either a benign or a just providence, and on the other with the Calvinist theology of an unappeasable God who predestined every human being to salvation or damnation. Both those were hurdles that romance had to negotiate if it were to survive.

Despite those changes, the continuities between medieval and Renaissance culture in England are exceptionally strong by comparison with France and Italy, but they have been remarkably little studied. Until a few decades ago, scholars of Renaissance literature concentrated almost entirely on humanism and the rediscovery of the Classics; now, the period has been renamed 'early modern', and the emphasis of research has followed suit, to stress the forward-looking, the things that anticipate the modern or the post-modern—an emphasis entrenched by the periodization of both literature and history in universities. Both approaches require 'the medieval' to be dismissed as a category in order for the neo-Classical or proto-modern model to be constructed. Romance, and medieval romance in particular, has accordingly been belittled, as being neither classical epic nor modern novel; yet the history of the genre in the Elizabethan and Jacobean periods constitutes 'one of the strangest success stories in English literature',[17] a story that is a romance in itself. Humanism was a development added on to strong and deeply embedded native cultural and literary traditions, and it was very often that embedded culture that inspired the greatest literary achievements of

Renaissance England and set the model for future change and develop-
ment. Romance was one of the most strongly rooted of all those tradi-
tions. Any classical air about it was rarely more than a surface gloss, for a
humanist author to show off his fashionability.[18] The abiding appeal of
romance resulted partly from its familiarity and its infinite adaptability;
partly also (despite the Catholic associations of the form) from its use-
fulness in the various nationalist agendas for the 'writing of England',
since many of the romances were native stories that asserted the value
and vitality of English originary legends and narrative traditions. The
appendix to this book shows both how extensive was the transmission of
medieval romance to the sixteenth century and beyond, and also how
selective it was: Alexander and Charlemagne barely make the transition
at all, whereas the stories of Arthur, Guy of Warwick, Bevis of
Southampton, and an abundance of other heroes who may not have been
English but whose romances had become thoroughly naturalized are
ubiquitous in the culture. Gawain, Arthur's right-hand man since at least
the early twelfth century, remains the favourite knight of the Round
Table in the sixteenth; Lancelot, a late French import, comes a long way
back in the popularity stakes.

Elizabethan romance could not have possessed its cultural centrality
without those medieval roots. Medieval literature shares with earlier
writing from the Hebrew Bible to *Beowulf* the function of recording the
ideology of an entire community, the values by which it represents itself
to itself. Romance, as the dominant secular literary genre of the period,
was at the heart of such self-representation, a means by which cultural
values and ideals were recorded and maintained and promulgated. The
community of Tudor England similarly looked to romance as the site
where its values could be questioned and tested but ultimately re-
affirmed. That is why it was all but inevitable that Spenser's great poem
on the state of England should take the form of romance. For all the stric-
tures of the preachers against secular fictions, romances in the Middle
Ages were widely regarded as educational. They offered models of
courage and faithfulness; they doubled as courtesy books, or as advice to
princes—a means of training the individual in the ethics and behaviour
required in order for society, one's own immediate community or the
whole body politic, to function at its best. Often they contained discur-
sive passages of instruction: parents or guardians will expound the duties
of a good knight, as the Lady of the Lake does at great length to the young
Lancelot in the French prose *Lancelot*, and wise counsellors will describe
what constitutes good government, as happens to Arthur in the same text

at even greater length.[19] Spenser would not have been telling Sir Walter Ralegh anything unexpected in his declaration in his letter prefacing *The Faerie Queene* that his work offered a means of fashioning a gentleman or noble person in virtuous and gentle discipline; and it was equally expected that this fashioning should be not in the cause of personal fulfilment but in the service of the Church and state. Romance was at the heart of the whole culture, or cultures, of the five centuries of its existence. So far as Elizabethan England was concerned, there were good reasons why romance, like the culture it served, should be English.

Our well-entrenched habits of looking for the grounding of Renaissance literature in the great classical authors (in particular Ovid and Virgil), or in contemporary European works (Ariosto, or the Italian *novelle* that were endlessly pillaged for the plots of plays), are therefore misleading: not because they are wrong, but because they are not enough. Alongside those works, which were accessible only by the intellectual élite unless or until they were printed in English translations, was a mass of stories available to everyone who could read English or hear it read to them, and which indeed were likely to have circulated in oral form as evening entertainment or, just as stories are retold now, as tales for children. These were the stories that the Elizabethans grew up with: which they did not need to learn, because they were so deep a part of their culture. It is that very familiarity, the lack of *need* of any extensive record or concern with preservation, that has made them largely disappear from sight. Yet they remained not just a field of reference but a way of thinking; and for the highly self-conscious writers of the Elizabethan age, they were a way of thinking, not just about spinning new plots for the endlessly voracious appetites of playgoers and readers, but about what it meant to be created human in an age that had abandoned the established schemes of Roman Catholic doctrine; about what England and being English meant in an age of fierce nationalism; and about the dynastic future of the country under a queen increasingly represented as a romance heroine but who had failed to fulfil the dynastic requirement of producing an heir, not so much as one carried off at birth by a bear.

RECOGNIZING ROMANCE

I have so far used the word 'romance' as if its meaning were obvious, and that is not an oversight—not because its taxonomy can be drawn up with the precision that separates biological genera, six-legged insects from eight-legged spiders, but because a shared understanding between author and reader is the crucial feature of generic definition: what Hans-Robert Jauss called a 'horizon of expectation'.[20] Such an understanding—a common perception of a horizon—does, I believe, exist, now as in the Middle Ages, so long as its narrow modern association with Mills and Boon is broadened to include magic realism, a good many historical novels, and much fantasy and science fiction. Those last two are not terms that can easily be extended backwards: early romance insisted on its social relevance, and it was always rooted in a recognizable this-worldly society, even if voyages to exotic lands or the Otherworld were allowed. The memes of romance are none the less largely the same ones as have been made familiar through works such as the Narnia series and *The Lord of the Rings*, and their many derivatives, including Harry Potter and Philip Pullman's *His Dark Materials* trilogy (a serious treatment of adult love being the main absentee; but Pullman does include bears who make their own armoured bearsuits). The clash of good against evil, quests, protagonists of mysterious birth, monsters, the supernatural are more extensive a part of culture now than they have been since the seventeenth century. This has happened despite, rather than because of, the numerous theoretical attempts to draw up defining parameters for romance.[21] There is very little theoretical discussion of vernacular genres in the Middle Ages, as scholastic theoreticians confined themselves to writing about classical forms. The word *romanz* itself initially meant the vernacular languages (especially French) as distinct from Latin: a meaning that effectively removed the whole topic outside latinate scholarly discourse. What discussion of romance there is comes in the form of comments from vernacular authors within their own works, and those make it clear that they, as both readers of earlier romances and writers of new ones, were fully aware of the tradition in which they were writing.[22] The romance genre—any genre, indeed—is best thought of as a lineage or a family of texts rather than as a series of incarnations or clones of a single Platonic Idea. A family changes over time as its individual members change,[23] but equally, those individuals can be recognized through their 'family resemblance': a resemblance such as might lie in a certain shape of nose or mouth, or colour of hair, or laughing in a particular way at a particular kind of joke, or manner of twitching one's eyebrows, even though no one of those is essential for the resemblance to register, and even though individual features (hair colour, eyebrow habits) may contradict the model.[24] The principle of selective resemblance was recognized in the Middle

Ages, as in a quatrain defining the set of qualities required to recognize *gentilesse*, the virtues taken to define high social class:

> In whom is trauthe, pettee, fredome, and hardynesse,
> He is a man inheryte to gentylmene.
> Off thisse virtues four who lakketh three,
> He aught never gentylmane called to be[25]

[Any man who possesses integrity, compassion, generosity, and courage carries a title to gentility. Whoever lacks three of these four virtues ought never to be called a gentleman]

or, to put it another way, any two of the defining virtues would just about be enough, regardless of which two were missing. Similarly with romance, *any* of the features that might be taken as definitive for the genre may be absent in any particular case without damaging that sense of family resemblance, though the dissimilarity increases, ultimately beyond the point of recognition, in proportion as the various elements are missing—or, alternatively, as an atypical element is given prominence. Even the characteristic most widely considered definitive for the genre, the happy ending, can be absent without destroying the sense that one is dealing with a romance.[26] The *Tristan* remains a romance despite the tragic deaths of the lovers, and so, more surprisingly, does the prose *Valentine and Orson*, in the teeth of the unprecedented disaster near its close when Valentine unintentionally kills his father. Intensify the unhappy ending still further, however, as in the case of the terrible final scene and the build-up to it that Shakespeare invented for *King Lear*, and the work moves out of the romance orbit, for all its love-tests and virtuous youngest daughter of three, elements familiar from its earlier romance treatments and from happily ending folktales.

Drawing up a list of the common features that cumulatively indicate family resemblance, generic identity, for romances presents few problems so long as one bears that caveat in mind: that no single one is essential for definition or recognition taken individually. Equally, related genres will share some features even though other unshared elements signal generic difference. Various observers may come to varying conclusions with regard to texts that keep the characteristics of different genres in balance, but that is as inevitable as differences of opinion as to whether someone more resembles a cousin on their mother's side or their father's side. The outward form of romances—that they are predominantly fictional narratives of some amplitude about particular individuals (whether those individuals are named or not)—is one that they share with many other genres, though spelling it out is necessary in order to register the difference between romance and (non-fictional) history, or romance and (the more concise) ballad, or romance and allegory (which replaces the particular with the generalizing), though the borders between romance and all three other genres are highly permeable. The *Faerie Queene* manages to be both full-scale romance and full-scale allegory. Other Elizabethan romances transgress even the boundary of narrative, to take the form of drama, though the playwrights themselves, Shakespeare included, never use 'romance' as a generic term to describe their own writings.[27] Romances are further characterized by exotic settings, distant in time or place, or both; subject-matter concerning love or chivalry, or both; and high-ranking characters—all qualities that separate the dramatic romance from the earlier more quotidian emphases of classical comedy, and the narrative romance from the later more quotidian emphases of the novel. Equally important elements in recognizability are a series of features that serve to distinguish romance from the Old French epic, the *chanson de geste*. These include the shaking loose of the narrative from precise time and space; quests; magic and the supernatural; a concern less with the communal good than with the individual hero's inward thoughts, feelings, and aspirations, and, frequently, those of the heroine too; and a happy ending as normative, that ending often incorporating a return from an encounter with death—a symbolic resurrection. Typical of the treatment of all these elements in romance is a concern with ideals, especially secular ideals, and with human perfectibility within a social context: characteristics that further distinguish romances from another contiguous genre, the saint's life, where the ideals and the perfectibility function in almost complete separation from the practicalities of life in this world.[28] Even if perfection is not achieved, even if the hero in some way fails or the ending is not happy, the ideals themselves are not therefore treated with cynicism.

Those defining features might seem as if they would operate independently of the derivation of the term 'romance' mentioned earlier, as meaning simply a work in the (French) vernacular as against Latin. The two do, however, belong closely together. Latin was the academic and clerical language, the language of ecclesiastical, theological, and philosophical discourse; a language and a series of discourses that were the prerogative of that small percentage of the male population who possessed full Latin literacy. The number of women readers of Latin was tiny, and women writers in Latin need to be individually named rather than thought of as any kind of group. The massive dominance of surviving medieval Latin over vernacular writings is in inverse proportion to those who could understand them: a fact that implies a far greater dissemination for vernacular texts than is suggested by the rates of their survival, unprotected as they were by monastic or cathedral libraries. The vernaculars were equally available to lay and clerical, women and men, and indeed children. They were the languages of the secular world: of the family and its perpetuation through marriage, reproduction, and the transfer of power and property, and therefore also of practical politics up to the highest levels of imperial rule; the languages of entertainment, not least after sundown when most work became impossible, or in any context where leisure-reading, or television, or a trip to the cinema might now be appropriate. The shift from one meaning of *romanz* to the other, from vernacular to story type, is particularly well illustrated around 1190 in the Anglo-Norman *Ipomedon* of 'Hue de Rotelande', Hugh (or perhaps Huw) of Rhuddlan, in North Wales. At the opening he welcomes his readers or listeners with an assurance that he is translating from Latin (a common claim, and by no means necessarily true), since no one will understand the story unless he puts it 'en romanz'; by the end, the phrase 'en cest romanz' carries a full generic significance:

> Ipomedon a tuz amanz
> Mande saluz en cest romanz
> Par cest Hue de Rotelande.[29]

[Ipomedon sends greetings to all lovers in this romance through Hugh of Rhuddlan.]

The audience Hue constructs here is a courtly one, since such a self-conscious concern with loving was strongly associated with the secular and the high-born.[30] When writers in English make comparable remarks about the need to translate from French into English, there is more explicit marking of social class about the statements: the first translator of the French prose *Merlin*, for instance, writing around 1300, notes that English is the universal language across all classes, whereas French is confined to the gentry:

> Freynsche use this gentil man
> Ac euerich Inglische Inglische can.[31]

[The gentry may speak French, but every English person knows English.]

A shift from Latin to French may extend the readership from those with formal education to potentially everyone in France, but to a much more restricted group in England; what is known of the ownership of French romances in England throughout the Middle Ages indicates a strong bias towards the aristocracy.[32] The further shift into English made possible a much wider dissemination for the stories, and ultimately the explosion of readership when cheap prints became available.

The use of the vernacular separated romances from academic discourse. They did not require the strenuous exercise of the intellect; they were immediately accessible by virtue of their exciting narratives as much as by their choice of language, and were therefore ideally suited to being heard rather than read on the page. Most often this would mean that one person in a group (sometimes no doubt the only one with adequate reading skills) would read them to the rest, as a form of communal entertainment in an age before silent reading or cheap multiple copies. The romances were composed in written form and largely disseminated through manuscripts, but some degree of oral transmission, at least of the shorter romances, is also likely.[33] This does not mean that they were designed for the unintelligent. It is easy to assume, in a culture of universal education, that those who cannot read or write are stupid; but stupidity no more follows than it does for the managing director who dictates a letter rather than writing it himself, or for the mathematician who has never mastered the mechanical art of touch-typing. Romances, like novels, can appeal to readers of every level of intelligence, although (unlike the most intellectually demanding, and therefore élitist, novels) they always do their audience the kindness of placing a primacy on telling good stories. Their appeal is not however limited to that basic attraction of narrative excitement. Chrétien de Troyes, one of the earliest and best of the French writers of romance, insists that his romances are different from the mere tales of those who tell stories for a living; in addition to their subject-matter, their *matière*, they have an inner meaning, a *sens*. The terminology was commonplace enough for Chaucer to use the English equivalents, *matter* and *sentence*, without feeling any need to explain them.[34] This emphasis on meaning alongside story, the invitation to readers to think beyond the story, allowed many romances to be designed not just for reading but for discussion. There was a long fashion for debating formal love-questions, *demandes d'amour*, which often took a romance-type story as their point of departure, and free-standing romances sometimes explicitly invite such debate. Chaucer's Knight invites his audience to consider which is the better off, the lover exiled from the sight of his lady or the lover in prison who can see her; but the question is directed less by the Knight to the fictional pilgrims than by

Chaucer to his own real-life audience.[35] It is likely that romances that do not make such an explicit appeal for discussion were still used as material for conversation and argument. It is indeed hard to imagine that the author of a work such as *Sir Gawain and the Green Knight* would not have sought, and elicited, such a response. Debate lay at the heart of much medieval culture, across most of the civil institutions invented in the Middle Ages: in the law courts, in the king's council, in Parliament, in the universities.[36] Romances could provide a secular forum analogous to academic debate. Their audiences expected to respond actively to them, and the writers encouraged such a response.

It is this kind of engaged reception of romances—by audiences who could and did *think* about what they were reading, and who could recognize the resonances of the story across the whole genre—that helped to make plot motifs become memes, with their ability to replicate and adapt. The organisms through which genes replicate require a particular ecological niche in which their life-form can operate; and the texts that contain these gene-like ideas similarly have their particular generic niche specified at the start, to establish the conditions in which their memes can generate. Readers' expectations are typically set in the opening lines, and recognizability can be enforced by direct repetition from one text to another. No fewer than three romances insist in the course of their first stanza in almost identical words that there is a chivalric story to follow, which

> will telle you of a Knight
> that was both hardye and wight

—that particular spelling of the lines being from the version of *Sir Eglamour* recorded c.1648, though they go back to its original composition around 1350.[37] Most romances similarly signal their generic allegiance within the first verse, or even, like *The Faerie Queene*, the first line:

> A Gentle Knight was pricking on the plaine . . .

And it could be done not only in narrative but in the new Renaissance extension of romance into drama, and not only with reference to chivalry but to the whole history of courtly storytelling and its alternative popular contexts. Shakespeare's *Pericles*, the most faithful to its romance source of any play that he wrote (and indeed the most faithful to its source of any outside his Plutarch-derived plays), opens with Gower as Chorus promising 'to sing a song that old was sung', one that

> hath been sung at festivals,
> On ember-eves and holy-ales,
> And lords and ladies in their lives
> Have read it for restoratives.[38]

The difference of the lines from those just quoted from the metrical romances and Spenser is, however, instructive. By this date (*c.*1608), to write a romance can be, not a natural act within a living tradition, but an act of conscious medievalism, a revival of the past. The high courtly past of the romance, the 'lords and ladies', recedes ever further into the distance, with folk-style oral retellings moving to the fore. *Pericles* insists on that quality of telling a story not only by what it says but by how it says it: the lines are spoken by the storyteller Gower himself, and the play enacts his retelling. By the time the play was written, the primary context for the continuing life of medieval romances was through the chapbooks and ballads sold by peddlers and at fairs—and through playwrights hungry for material for the popular theatres.[39] It is not surprising therefore that this most romance-like of Shakespeare's plays was also one of his most popular in its time.[40] His works can be more or less divided into those that make their generic affiliation clear from the start, and therefore invoke a set of audience expectations, and those that keep the audience uncertain, sometimes to the very end. For all the absence of the term 'romance' from Shakespeare, he was thoroughly familiar with the family resemblances and expectations of the form, and it is his most traditional romance that announces its genre most explicitly.

It is the generic awareness shared by author and audience, their common knowledge of how romances work and what they can do, that makes possible the subtlety with which writers can handle the building-blocks of the form, its motifs and conventions. 'Conventional' has become a pejorative word; yet etymologically it derives from the idea of coming together, agreement, a shared understanding. The criticism of modern forms of fiction, more downmarket than medieval romances, that similarly rely heavily on conventions or formulas—adventure stories, the Mills and Boon type of romances—has developed a considerable respect for the power of the formulaic, and in particular for the skill of individual writers in giving 'new vitality to stereotypes' to the point where a new archetype, a new model for imitation, can be created and in turn generate its own posterity. Furthermore, whereas the quality of *universality* has been widely regarded, ever since Aristotle, as what marks out great literature, what distinguishes the best within formulaic literature is the unique: the ability to give the sharpness of the individual to a variation on a known and recognized theme.[41]

EXPLOITING THE FAMILIAR

This ability to vary the pattern, to make a conventional, shared motif new and surprising, pervades early romance. The very familiarity of the pattern of the motif, the meme, alerts the reader to certain kinds of shaping and significance, and sets up expectations that the author can fulfil or frustrate. The same motif will not always mean the same thing, or in the same ways: on the contrary, what matters most is the variations on the ways it is used. Familiarity with the model is used precisely to highlight difference. The infinite adaptation of narrative material becomes a kind of shorthand for meaning, since it draws on what an audience already knows but reconfigures it in different ways. Conventions of this kind are the opposite of clichés, which replicate the familiar without change and are therefore inert. Conventions are what make literature work: they initiate active participation from the audience in the creation of meaning, through resonances with what is currently known and therefore living. Moreover, they only become conventional if they are in some way true to experience.

One of the most familiar conventions, the beautiful heroine, will illustrate how the process works. It makes a good preliminary example because the range of its uses stays largely stable over time, without the complicating factors incurred by cultural change. Its truth to experience comes from the principles of sexual selection: men find beautiful women more attractive, for biological as well as aesthetic reasons. Literature and art in all media have followed suit, throughout the centuries: perhaps the first requirement for any woman appearing in a visual medium now (film, television, advertisements) is a certain Helen of Troy quality, even if it is irrelevant to the job in hand. Works that claim a greater realism by insisting that their heroine is plain—*Jane Eyre*, for instance—will still insist that she has beautiful eyes: there is a minimum of beauty below which a heroine cannot fall. It is similarly the first requirement for romance heroines, and generally, as for film stars, without qualification. It can still, however, take many forms—perhaps more in the Middle Ages and Renaissance than now, since the recognition of the requirement was so overt; there was never any pretence that the beautiful was the norm. The plain fact of beauty, however, is uninteresting; it is the many things that can be done with it that give it power.

An insistence on the fact of beauty is none the less the first and basic form of the convention. Herodis, for instance, the heroine of *Sir Orfeo*, is introduced as 'the fairest leuedi for the nones',

> Ful of love and godenisse,
> Ac no man may telle hir fairnisse.[42]   [but

This is a bare statement of her qualifications for her role as the leading lady: virtue and beauty—and interestingly (not least by contrast with modern culture), in that order. Also interesting, however, is the fact that the phrasing actually avoids description, by leaving almost everything to the imagination: 'no man may tell' precisely puts her beyond what can be said. Those romances (especially French ones) that spell out the heroine's beauty over dozens of lines run greater risks. One risk—which is indeed sometimes incurred deliberately—is that the account invites an intrusive or voyeuristic male gaze, of a kind blocked by the formulation for Herodis.[43] Another, hard to avoid in longer descriptions, is bathos: the heroine's nose will be neither too long nor too short, her chin the model of perfection, and so on for some time. A further danger run by descriptions of any length is a collapse into the inertia of cliché. This is not so common as one might expect from the familiarity of the topos, since beauty is so important: exceptional beauty is precisely what distinguishes the heroine, so the audience is required to be alert to it. There are, however, a few romances where every lady who appears is of outstanding beauty, and the effect, not least as regards the heroine herself, begins to pall. The challenge for an author is to make the beauty of his lady resonant: to bring in to his readers' minds every other beautiful heroine, and every response they have invoked, so as to make the effect of this particular instance of beauty stronger than if it were in actual fact unique. Chaucer offers a remarkable example of such resonance in his description of Emily in the *Knight's Tale*. Over the space of twenty lines, we are told almost nothing factual about her looks except that she has yellow hair; all the rest works by association, simile and suggestion.

> It fil ones, in a morwe of May,
> That Emelye, that fairer was to sene
> Than is the lylie upon his stalke grene,
> And fressher than the May with floures newe—
> For with the rose colour stroof hire hewe,
> I noot which was the fyner of hem two—   [do not know
> Er it were day, as was hir wone to do,   [custom

> She was arisen and al redy dight,   [dressed
> For May wole have no slogardie anyght . . .
> Hir yelow heer was broyded in a tresse
> Bihynde hire bak, a yerde long, I gesse.
> And in the gardyn, at the sonne upriste,   [sunrise
> She walketh up and doun, and as hire liste
> She gadereth floures, party white and rede,
> To make a subtil gerland for hire hede;
> And as an aungel hevenysshly she soong.

CT, I.1034–42, 1049–55

The male gaze here is literal: this is what the knights see as they look through their prison window, as mediated through the narrator's own focus. What they see, however, goes far beyond (or falls far short of) the voyeuristic. Emily is mentioned alternately throughout the passage with May, the month most deeply associated with love, not least in that great allegory of the psychology of falling in love, the *Romance of the Rose*, the action of which is similarly set in a garden. The rose and lily to which she is compared are, respectively, the flowers of eroticism, for the passion she inspires, and of purity, for the chastity she possesses—but chastity itself is a condition that immediately invites male attention. She is not, however, accessible: not only are the two men who are looking at her locked away in prison, but the imagery surrounding her puts her almost on a different plane from them. She and the sun rise together;[44] she sings like an angel. She is described, moreover, entirely in terms of the most spiritual senses, sight and hearing. The knights' instant love for her carries an unmistakable sexual element, but it also suggests an infinity of desire for the unattainable: she is their equivalent of the holy grail, to borrow an image from a different area of romance. Her function in the narrative is to be the undesiring object of male desire, and her introduction is designed to show how fully she justifies such desire by making every reader recognize that response.

Such a straight use of the description of beauty, to identify and define the heroine, is much the most widespread, and it is generically central to the family resemblance between romance heroines; but it is not the only way to handle the convention. Closely related to it is its use for emphasis, to point up a contrast, as for instance when the heroine is surrounded by the less than beautiful. This is commonly the situation of dispossessed heiresses who find themselves among country bumpkins: Spenser's Pastorella, for instance, or Shakespeare's Perdita. The comparative plainness of the other shepherdesses may only be implied, but it is implied by a stress on the heroine's own beauty. Polixenes, cast at this point of *The Winter's Tale* as Perdita's enemy, moves within four lines from noting that she is 'the prettiest low-born lass' to the suggestion that she is 'too noble for this place';[45] and he is, of course, right.

A third use is for poignancy, most apparent when beauty is lost, through hardship or age or grief. There is a particularly moving example of the last of those in Chaucer's *Troilus and Criseyde*, when the heroine has heard that she is to be traded to the Greeks in exchange for a captured knight, and so be separated from her lover. Chaucer accordingly describes her not as looking positively ugly or unattractive but in terms of the beauty and vibrancy she has lost:

> Hire face, lik of Paradys the ymage,
> Was al ychaunged in another kynde;
> The pleye, the laughter, men was wont to fynde
> In hire, and eek hire joyes everichone
> Ben fled, and thus lith now Criseyde allone.
>
> *Troilus*, IV.864–8

Again, the description is very unspecific: it works by association and resonance (the joy of Paradise) more than by statement, appealing to the readers' imagination more than to their list-making faculties. Her abandonment, that she is left 'allone', even if in the syntax only by those scarcely personified joys, stirs pity for her state both now in her desolation and proleptically for the future in her isolation in the Greek camp.

Descriptions of beauty are usually positive, designed to enhance the reader's response to the lady's attractiveness; but not always. The virtue that the author of *Sir Orfeo* mentions before his heroine's good looks is the conventional, expected, accompaniment to beauty: inward virtue is what outward beauty should represent. When that inner beauty is missing, the shock to one's expectations is all the greater. Beauty can function as a rather sinister kind of dramatic irony, to set up assumptions about the matching of inward and outward form in the minds of other characters or indeed of the readers, and then to betray them. There is a whole spectrum of beautiful villainesses in romances, from the diabolic (Perceval's lovely temptress on the Grail Quest is Lucifer himself in drag), through wicked enchantresses (such as Duessa in the *Faerie Queene*), to women who may or not be wicked or enchantresses (most famously, the lady in *Sir Gawain and the Green Knight*), and finally to the women who turn out not to be romance heroines after all but rather the cheap and sexually available female leads of a fabliau (such as May in the *Merchant's Tale*—'fresshe May', a parody of the beautiful Emily, but one who will go to great lengths to ensure male access to her garden). An altogether gentler kind of inappropriateness is found in Chaucer's description of the Prioress, with her unaffected ('simple') smile, soft red mouth, and fashionable grey eyes. That she is attractive is not in question; the question rather is whether she should be displaying it so generously to an almost-all-male company, or whether attractiveness ought to be the most striking attribute of a religious woman.

Beauty is generally thought of, now as in the Middle Ages, as an attribute of women, but another variation on the description of attractiveness is to reverse the gender roles. Not only is the hero handsome: very often, he will be seen as handsome through the eyes of a lady. Criseyde looks out of her window at Troilus and implicitly acknowledges his physical perfection, the glamour of the warrior—'so fressh, so yong, so weldy semed he' (*Troilus*, II.636). More striking still is *Ipomedon*, where Hue describes how first the disdainful heroine, and then a sequence of other women, *look* at the hero, then what they see (his handsomeness and fine body), then how they are attracted to him. Women are not cast merely as sex objects in romances, and especially not in those composed in England. They are frequently given their own thoughts and responses, expressed in soliloquies of self-analysis as they awaken to love, which endow them with the kind of subjective, interior, life that has often been claimed to be exclusively both a male and a modern phenomenon. If it is recognized as pre-modern, it is usually in terms of Petrarchism; but a 'Petrarchan' process of gazing at the object of desire, of falling irremediably in love, and responding in affective monologue, is first developed for the heroines of the very earliest generation of romance as they first see the men on whom they set their hearts, and it remains a forceful convention within Anglo-Norman and English romance through to Britomart and Juliet.[46]

A further variation on the theme of beauty is comic parody. For parody to work, its serious origins must be familiar; so it is interesting that Chaucer parodies the blazon of male beauty in *Sir Thopas*, his mock-romance in which the hero is the object of all-too-many female gazes ('ful many a mayde' sighs for him when they would do better to be asleep). Chaucer's literary self-consciousness and his readiness to encompass every possible variation on convention make him a master in this field: they show again in his description of the hen Pertelote, the favourite of Chauntecleer's seven wives (or more properly his 'paramours': they have not been through any wedding ceremony), which does its best to set up the Nun's Priest's tale as a courtly romance. The language describing Pertelote is Anglo-French, and therefore courtly: she is a 'damoysele', courteous, 'debonaire', and 'compaignable'. Also, rather like Emily, she is 'the faireste hewed', though the colours turn out to be those of her throat feathers. The warning implicit in that mention of her throat, that she may not be everything the reader expects from a courtly heroine, acquires full force only when Chauntecleer thanks God for her beauty three hundred lines later, when her full henliness emerges.

> For whan I se the beautee of youre face,
> Ye been so scarlet reed aboute youre yen,   [eyes
> It maketh al my drede for to dyen.[47]   [allays all my fear

The shape of the formulation is indistinguishable from courtly romance or lyric, but we are not allowed to forget that this all takes place, after all, not in a court but in a chicken-run.

That example also serves to illustrate another way in which the topos of female beauty can be exploited: by verbal variation, by substituting the wrong phrase or detail in a description that would otherwise appear to be set up seriously. Pertelote has red rings around her eyes; Alison, in the *Miller's Tale*, sings not like an angel but like a swallow (high-pitched and unmusical); Sir Thopas's complexion is as white not as a lily but as bread. Sometimes items can be interchanged: Hoccleve rearranges all his lady's attributes to draw a portrait of a freak, just as Sir Philip Sidney later writes a poem in which his mistress's eyes, not teeth, are like pearl, and her skin, not her hair, like gold. Donne similarly describes the 'anagram of a good face' in which all the desirable similes are misapplied.[48] All these examples are parodic and comic; but the idea can also be used with a serious point, as it is most famously by Shakespeare in his sonnet on the less than Petrarchan looks of his mistress, 'My mistress' eyes are nothing like the sun' (Sonnet 130), where he insists that a less than perfect reality is better than 'false compare', inaccurate or impossible comparisons. If a woman's looks are to be a measure of her sexual attractiveness, there is far more *phwoor* quality in a gypsy than in an alabaster statue.

One could map all the other conventions of the romance in similar ways: they can be used straight, for emphasis, poignantly, and in all kinds of variations, including absence. Some of these variations may finally become so anarchic or disruptive as to break the bounds of the genre altogether. Those disruptions need not be comic: some indeed are intensely serious and powerful, especially the denial of the expected happy ending. Some can be pure fun, as in *Sir Thopas*, or, for a modern example, *Monty Python and the Holy Grail*, a film that is a useful reminder of how many medieval romance conventions are still current: how else would one recognize the ludicrousness of its being a young man, not a damsel, who is in distress? Perceval, in Chrétien's famous *Conte du Graal*, fails on his quest by neglecting to ask a question; the Monty Python knights have to answer one, whether the dangerously innocuous 'What is your favourite colour?' or the altogether more demanding, but no less inappropriate, 'What is the capital of Abyssinia?' Some romances work in a single mode, of taking all their conventions straight: those written earliest, when the conventions were still being established, are most likely to do so, since there was as yet no set of expectations on which the authors could play variations. A few late ones, whether fourteenth- or twentieth-century, take all their conventions as parody. Most, however, will mix modes, operate enough conventions straight to lull their audiences into a sense of familiarity, then shock them, for amusement or for disaster, by withholding or perverting what is expected. *Star Wars* has its quest, its princess, its Jedi knights, and its giant hairy monster, but he has to have his hand held when the going gets tough. *Sir Gawain and the Green Knight* uses social comedy to disguise a serious, and potentially fatal, test of chivalric perfection, in which Gawain fails. *As You Like It*, a play with an impeccable romance ancestry, laughs at all the ideals it ultimately supports: love and desire; the preference for an ethically good rather than a luxurious life; idealism itself. Chaucer's *Troilus* is set up as a love story—aristocratic, far away, and long ago, centrally concerned with ideals despite, or because of, its warrior hero's prostration by love— but the failure of its ideals, and the painfulness of its ending, finally take it over the boundaries of what most readers would regard as romance.

All those qualities and responses are made possible, and made powerful, by means of convention: by audience recognition. The familiarity of the memes of romance, its standard episodes and motifs and phrasing, make possible a much greater and more concise subtlety of response than could be achieved by invention from scratch. The originality lies in an author's handling of his materials, his (on very rare occasions, her) ability to disrupt, to startle, to shock. The shock may come from upset expectations, but it may also come from the recognition of something long known but in circumstances that defamiliarize it, that make you recognize it as if for the first time. Such defamiliarization can come even from an unchanged text if it is read in new conditions: an out-of-time romance can intersect with the historical moment of its reading or rereading in new and unexpected ways. The colonels who overthrew democracy in Greece banned a performance of Sophocles' *Electra* in the 1960s for precisely those reasons: its story of principled resistance to tyrannical power in the hope of its overthrow was not a message they wanted to have declared, just as the group that planned to perform the play was well aware that a text over two thousand years old contained an explosive contemporary message. Romances and their motifs had a similar capacity for acquiring new meanings. That is why the fairy queen, bestower of favour and riches, the ultimate mistress both sexually and in terms of power, can become so potent a figure for Elizabeth I; or why Arthur can acquire a second meaning alongside his identity as the greatest British hero, as the embodiment of personal and political misrule that destroys his own kingdom, and so step outside the bounds of romance altogether.[49] Variations on conventions happen not only synchronically, within time, as authors choose the particular angle on a motif that suits them, but diachronically, across time, as cultural, historical, and political change alter beliefs and expectations.

Romance writers developed a remarkable refinement and precision of use of their language of motifs. The rest of this book is concerned with how that language worked, in order to transmit to a new generation of readers the literary competence that Chrétien or the *Gawain*-poet, or Chaucer, or Spenser, or Shakespeare, or dozens of anonymous writers could take for granted in their own audiences.

ROMANCE IN ENGLAND: A SUMMARY HISTORY

This book is concerned specifically with romance written or current in England. The genre developed there in distinctive ways that make its history unique in Europe. In the mid-twelfth century, when the expectations and conventions of romance were being established, England and France largely formed a single cultural unit: they were linked both linguistically (through the aristocratic language of Anglo-Norman, gradually beginning to separate itself from the western dialects of French) and politically (through Henry II's holding of both England and large areas of modern-day France in a single Angevin empire). By the end of the twelfth century, however, French romance was developing a trajectory distinct from Anglo-Norman and its English-language descendants in the genre. Many of the motifs still current in Elizabethan romance have their origins in these earliest Angevin texts; the memes, and indeed a number of the texts themselves, showed remarkable adaptative powers and survival mechanisms over many centuries.[50] The opening date for this book, 1138, is the likely year of composition of the work that set many of the stories of romance on their way: Geoffrey of Monmouth's *History of the Kings of Britain*. The early seventeenth century forms the logical stopping-point, since the generation into which Spenser and Shakespeare were born was the last to be brought up on an extended range of medieval romances in more or less their original forms, and which therefore had access to the full range of their generic codings and intertextualities. A number of the stories continued to be widely disseminated into the nineteenth century through the medium of broadside ballads and chapbooks, but they largely ceased to fertilize the active production of new imaginative literature. Their modern incarnations, from Victorian Arthuriana forward, are more a matter of revival than survival. Romance itself remained important for a few more decades after Shakespeare's death, but in forms that had largely lost touch with the roots of the genre, not least its roots in England. His own last plays are almost the final works to profit from the power of those endlessly transforming traditions.

As a context for the rest of the book, and to demonstrate the continuity of the subject-matter of romance through the Middle Ages and Renaissance, a short summary of the history of the genre in England may be helpful, with a wider glance out at its interrelations with continental romance of various kinds. Much of this will be familiar to readers with particular specialities; but the periodization of literary studies means that not everyone will be aware of (for instance) the dozen centuries that separate Greek romance from Spanish romance, or the sheer longevity of many of the English traditions. A preliminary history will also rescue the stories of individual memes told in the rest of the book from being overwhelmed by too much on-the-spot contextualization. It is necessary too because the history of medieval romance is customarily written from a French perspective, and that is misleading in some crucial respects when it is applied to insular traditions.[51] The two traditions none the less remained interlinked; the examples taken from French romance later in the book are largely from works known to have circulated in England, and which therefore had the capacity for influencing the insular development of the genre.

The larger story of romance begins with Geoffrey of Monmouth, and never quite leaves him behind. *The History of the Kings of Britain* is not itself a romance. It was written in Latin, not vernacular 'romanz'; its scope is that of epic history, covering almost two millennia. Geoffrey's endlessly inventive spawning of legends, however, provided the kind of quasi-historical material that allowed for constant reinvention in alternative, more overtly fictionalized forms down through the sixteenth century and beyond. His account of the foundation of Britain by Brutus, grandson of Aeneas, formed a powerful myth of origin that was rapidly given romance treatment in French and Anglo-Norman, and which four centuries later acquired a new force from the nationalist agendas of the Elizabethans.[52] Holinshed still repeats it as fact in his great *History of England*; Londoners were proud to promote the legend of their city as Troynovaunt, New Troy; and Elizabeth's own reign, attended by none of the disasters of Priam's, could be given mythopoeic treatment by direct contrast with its famous, but doomed, predecessor. Brutus accordingly reappears in the chronicles of the history of Britain, 'Briton moniments', in the *Faerie Queene*, along with another of Geoffrey's protagonists destined for future fame, King Leir.[53] Leir's story as given by Geoffrey, and indeed in all versions except Shakespeare's own, has a happy ending, with his restoration to his throne. It was retold in this form not just in every chronicle history, but in the influential French romance of *Perceforest*, and presumably also in an Anglo-Norman romance of King Leir of Leicester recorded in the thirteenth century, the text of which no longer survives.[54] Geoffrey's most famous and successful invention, however, was the rescuing of a shadowy Celtic hero named Arthur from the hinterlands of oral legend to the full light of a biography of conquest carried to the very walls of Rome, so establishing a legendary imperial past for Britain that reversed the direction of Brutus's westward retreat. Some seventeen years after Geoffrey, his translator Wace, writing his *Brut* in the *romanz* language of Anglo-Norman, added to the story of Arthur an account of the Round Table and its fellowship of knights; and in doing so he created the narrative space for the infinite generation of further stories—further romances—from Geoffrey's time-bound and linear model of conquest and downfall.[55] From these beginnings there eventually emerged such works as Sir Thomas Malory's *Morte Darthur*, with all its derivative Arthuriana in the modern world (including a fast-food restaurant in Tintagel called Excaliburgers), and the *Faerie Queene* itself.

The earliest works that are recognizable as romances—the first texts, that is, to use consistently and purposefully the motifs that became the accepted conventions of the new genre—were probably written, like the *Brut*, in the 1150s, within a couple of decades of Geoffrey of Monmouth's *History*, and look back either to classical epic or to Geoffrey's own additions to Trojan legend. Their difference from their epic antecedents lies partly in their choice of language—*romanz*, this time French, rather than the Latin of their originals—and partly in their shift of emphasis, from the founding of nations to the thoughts and feelings and aspirations of their protagonists. The inwardness of many romances itself reflects a larger cultural movement, from a shame culture, the belief that honour and shame and the acts that incur them constitute virtue and vice, to a guilt culture, the belief that virtue is finally a matter between yourself and the judgement of God.[56] Romance embraces both, sometimes without contradiction, but sometimes in a tension that makes any satisfying ending impossible. There is no such problem with works that are primarily the products of a shame culture, epics and *chansons de geste* such as *The Battle of Maldon* and *The Song of Roland*, where what impels heroism of action is the knowledge that it will be spoken of. Honour remains crucially important in romance, but it can strain other value systems beyond breaking-point. Love, and especially illicit love, was problematic from the earliest development of romance, in the Tristan legend. The hermits of the thirteenth-century *Quest of the Holy Grail* define the problem out of existence by classifying all desire for earthly glory as pride, the worst of the seven deadly sins, and all sexual love as lust, but it was not a solution that could satisfy a genre that founded itself on the principles important to secular society but denied by the Church's downgrading of the world and all its values. The earliest generation of romances bypassed the issue by locating their action outside Christian society altogether, in the classical pagan world. The clash between the rival cultures came later, as romance struggled to incorporate Christianity, and the Church attempted to colonize or suppress the new genre.

These classicizing romances, known generically as *romans antiques*, were therefore free to concentrate on the gap between inward and outward behaviour rather than on the gap between ethical systems. They set in tension the gender-inclusive intensity of private emotion and the male public world of military ambition and engagement. There are three major early romances of this kind: the *Roman de Thèbes*, which tells the story of the 'seven against Thebes' best known from Statius; the *Roman de Troie*, by Benoit de Saint-Maure, a retelling of the story of the siege of Troy that first introduces the love affair of Troilus and Cressida into literature; and the *Roman d'Eneas*, a version of Virgil's *Aeneid* in which Lavinia, the woman whom Aeneas eventually marries, moves centre stage. But however much their narratives may have been concerned with private passion, the texts themselves had higher political concerns. All three were associated with the Angevin court of Henry II and Eleanor of

Aquitaine, and are likely to have circulated on both sides of the Channel. In conjunction with Wace's *Brut*, the last two in particular may have been intended, or regarded, as offering an ancestral history of Angevin sovereignty. The western European kingdoms, France as well as Britain, were believed to have been founded by the progressive journeyings of Aeneas and his descendants, fugitives from Troy, in the movement designated the *translatio imperii*, the westward shift of imperial power that included not only Aeneas' founding of a new Trojan empire in Italy but ultimately the establishment of the papacy at Rome. Once Aeneas was incorporated into the ancestral history of Britain and the Angevins, then the rest of Trojan history followed too.

The chivalric elements of romance figure in the *romans antiques*, but they received their greatest boost from the entry of the Round Table into literature in Wace. Geoffrey's Arthur had been a great conqueror, but the Round Table allowed for the creation of new stories of individual knights, and therefore of the quest romance, of the knight who rides out from court to seek adventure. The great figure here is Chrétien de Troyes, who wrote between the 1160s and 1180s for a number of aristocratic patrons, including Marie de Champagne, daughter of Eleanor of Aquitaine. Chrétien is generally regarded, and with good reason, as the greatest of the romance writers, and his works dominate the criticism of French romance. They were at least partially known in England (*Ywain and Gawain* is a translation of his *Yvain*; *Percyvell of Galles* takes his *Conte du Graal* as its starting-point), but his influence was not paramount for the development of English romance to the degree that it was for French. By far his most influential work, *Le Chevalier de la Charrette*, 'The Knight of the Cart', did for Lancelot and Guinevere what Geoffrey had done for Arthur, that is, invent an enduring story from negligible antecedents, and, in the eyes of many cultural historians, invent courtly love as well;[57] but the story is rarely mentioned in English before Malory in the late fifteenth century, and most definitions of courtly love are simply irrelevant to insular romance. Chrétien's Arthur was, however, taken as part of that great ancestral schema stretching back to Troy: three of the six surviving manuscripts that contain his romances locate them in a chronological sequence that includes a selection of the *romans antiques* and Wace's *Brut*.[58]

The direction of influence in romance is often taken as being westwards, like the *translatio imperii* and its intellectual equivalent the *translatio studii*, in this case from France to Britain; but it was by no means all a one-way movement, as the French adoption of Arthur from Geoffrey of

Monmouth indicates. Geoffrey was probably living in Oxford when he wrote his *History*, and his own origins lie further west still, in the borders of Wales. He and Chrétien both show abundant signs of using Celtic material, from the outer fringes of Britain and mainland Europe—Ireland, Wales, and, for writers in French, Brittany. Legends about Arthur had been circulating in the Celtic areas of Britain for some time before Geoffrey developed them into a full biography; and some of the tales in the Welsh *Mabinogion* show close links with Chrétien, not all necessarily or entirely by derivation from him.

There is one variety of romance that is defined by the pride with which it proclaims its Celtic origins: the Breton lai, as practised by Marie de France and her imitators from the 1170s forwards. The Breton lais are shorter than most full-scale romances; they generally emphasize emotions more than actions; and they announce in their prologues their origins in the stories and songs circulating through Breton minstrels—so making the works that comprise the genre immediately recognizable while leaving the question of formal definition largely opaque. Despite her cognomen, Marie has strong connections with England: she probably lived and wrote there, and she knew its language and at least some of its literary traditions.[59] English developed its own tradition of Breton lais in the fourteenth century, including one by Chaucer (the *Franklin's Tale*), whose claim of Breton antecedents for the work is distinctly cheeky; the few English Breton lais that reached print, however, were assimilated back into the broader genre of romance.

Celtic material was associated not only with particular varieties of romance, or particular heroes, but with certain areas of subject-matter, especially magic and the supernatural. The story of Tristan combines a Celtic hero and setting (Cornwall, Ireland, Brittany) with a magic love-potion as the engine of its plot. The earliest *romanz* version, whether continental French or Anglo-Norman, is lost, but it gave rise to a rush of derivative texts from around 1170 onwards. Chrétien wrote a romance on the subject, also now lost; but it was an Anglo-Norman poet named Thomas who turned Tristan into one of the central figures of the whole romance genre in almost every European language. His own text survives only in fragments, but those can be supplemented by early translations and adaptations into Old Norse, Middle High German (in the famous version by Gottfried von Strassburg), Middle English, and various other languages too.[60] His skill is evident in the subtlety of his treatment of the magic, in which what it *means* is much more important than its quality as mere marvel, what it *does*. The story's power came from its central theme of a love so strong as to override all social and political taboos, since it linked a man with the wife of his uncle and overlord in a love at once adulterous and traitorous. Adultery no more became the norm of later romance than did treason—almost all romances are narratives either of courtship leading to marriage, or of the trials that part a loving married couple;[61] but it was Thomas's handling of the Tristan story that made the revolutionary move of presenting a fully sexual love independent of marriage as both overwhelming and self-justifying. The influence of that move made itself felt almost immediately, in Chrétien's shaping of the similarly traitorous love of Lancelot and Guinevere in *Le Chevalier de la Charrette*. Even as penitential manuals were warning that all sexual desire, even within marriage, was in some degree sinful, and the papacy was concluding its fight to impose celibacy on all priests as a non-negotiable standard of perfection (and as a prophylactic against inheritance claims), the *Tristan* offered a model in which sexual love offers its own challenging, and equally non-negotiable, standard of a secular absolute, irresistible even when it opposes all moral and feudal norms. The consequences of that move have affected attitudes down to the present day. Thomas did not, of course, invent lifelong heterosexual love single-handed, but he gave it a visibility and a language to describe it that it had never had before. That language is still evident in the many love-romances that reject the illicit elements in his formulation of love (England was particularly resistant to those, despite Thomas's Anglo-Norman origins); but erotic rhetoric and the illicit exuberantly ran side by side in many of the mainland European romances, not least those bestselling blockbusters of the early sixteenth century, *Orlando Furioso* and *Amadis de Gaule*.

Love is a feature of both the classical and the Breton material, but the first vernacular European work to ground its whole plot and motivation solely in love, *Floire et Blancheflor*, probably came from a different cultural source, Arabic Spain: the same culture that may have inspired some elements in the Provençal tradition of love-poetry.[62] Its even-handed treatment of its Christian and Saracen characters, even the Emir of Babylon (from whose harem the young Floris has to recover his beloved Blancheflour), may be grounded in such origins, in contrast to the near-universal casting of Saracens as the opponents of Christendom elsewhere in romance. *Floire* was first composed around 1160 in French; it spread rapidly across Europe, with versions appearing in languages from Old Norse to Yiddish and Spanish. As *Floris and Blancheflour*, it was one of the very first romances to be composed in Middle English, in the mid-thirteenth century.[63]

As the instance of Thomas of England demonstrates, it was Anglo-Norman as much as French that set the pace for the twelfth-century development of romance. Not all of this activity was focused on the Angevin court; the genre could flourish wherever there were Anglo-Norman-speaking gentry and patrons, including, for instance, the Welsh Marches that were the adult home of Hue de Rotelande, Hugh of Rhuddlan, the author of *Ipomedon*. The influence of insular material showed itself not only in the dissemination of such works in France and beyond, nor in the French use of British and Celtic legends, but in the retelling of English legends (that is, legends about England after the Anglo-Saxon invasions that gave the country its modern name, and therefore after the end-point of Geoffrey's *History*) in the new form of romance, and the new languages of *romanz*. This 'matter of England'—a new subject-area to set beside the traditional 'matters' of Rome (Troy), Britain (Arthur), and France (Charlemagne)[64]—was especially likely to remain current in England in the sixteenth century, though its origins are sometimes well disguised. Its earliest texts were most often composed in Anglo-Norman, though some of those may have English-language antecedents. The earliest extant version of the romance of Horn, for instance, is Anglo-Norman, but since the story requires some punning on the name 'Horn', which fails to work properly in any language other than English, that Anglo-Norman form is likely to have been based on a story already current in English. What that may have been like may be indicated by the later Middle English *King Horn*, recorded around the mid-thirteenth century. The story has a long history, with a second Middle English redaction in the fourteenth century that itself gave rise to a traditional ballad;[65] the Anglo-Norman was freely rewritten in French prose in the fourteenth century, losing its English connections in the process, and that version was in turn translated into English (twice) under the title of *King Ponthus and the Fair Sidone*, and went through several printed editions under the Tudors.[66] Another 'matter of England' legend, that of Havelok, first appears in Anglo-Norman in the continuation to Geoffrey's *History* written by Gaimar; in due course that too was rewritten as an autonomous romance, both in Anglo-Norman and Middle English.[67] This story also makes a late reappearance, in William Warner's *Albions England* of 1586, from where it jumps into the work of Lodge and Shakespeare. Warner himself turns it into a prefiguration of the story of Elizabeth.[68]

English-language romances did not become common until the fourteenth century. There was a flurry of them, all with French or

Anglo-Norman antecedents, composed around 1300, and the numbers steadily increased over the next three hundred years. Many now survive as part of larger manuscript anthologies, though that format may indicate not so much that they were most often copied in collections as that individual copies were much more likely to disintegrate or be thrown away. Most of these anthologies date from the fifteenth century. The earliest to survive, which in its present damaged form contains sixteen romances along with pious and other works, dates from not long after 1330: the famous Auchinleck manuscript.[69] The latest, yet more imperfect since a number of its leaves were used for firelighting in the eighteenth century but which still contains twelve romances in more or less their original medieval form, is the Percy Folio manuscript, an assemblage of verse narratives, ballads, and lyrics composed at various dates from the early fourteenth century to the time of their collection in the 1640s.[70] Although many of these romances have French antecedents, they take a characteristically different angle on their material. They are generally more compatible with orthodox Christian morality (adultery is out; pre-marital sex is just that, pre-marital, and even that is rare); quite a number are overtly pious, stressing the Job-like endurance of God-given trials before restoration and a Providence-assisted happy ending. They tend to indicate emotion more by action or statement than by soliloquy or formal analysis. They avoid the more extreme flights of fantasy of continental European romance. They tend, in fact, to show many of the qualities often described as being associated with the rise of the bourgeois novel: a parallel that may be connected with their choice of the English language, and therefore with their downward social penetration from the French-reading aristocracy to the gentry and to townsmen.

Once composed, romances showed a remarkable longevity. The great majority of the English romances written before 1350 survive in multiple copies, most of them made in the fifteenth century, and at least eight were put into print by early Tudor publishers, notably Wynkyn de Worde and Copeland. Those eight are *Bevis of Hamtoun*, *Guy of Warwick*, *Richard Cœur de Lyon*, *Of Arthour and of Merlin*, *Sir Isumbras*, *Sir Degaré*, *Sir Eglamour*, and *Octavian*. Translations made after 1350 of a number of other earlier Anglo-Norman romances also reached print, among them being Marie's *Lanval* and Hue's *Ipomedon*.[71] Texts from this corpus still figure prominently three hundred years after their composition in the Percy Folio manuscript.[72] Fifteenth-century romances provided abundantly more printing copy. Most of the printed English romances were written in tetrameter couplets; the other widespread early form, tail-rhyme, had passed its peak of popularity by the end of the fourteenth century, though tail-rhyme romances continued to be composed for a further hundred years. A few of the later romances used more elaborate verse forms, such as the Chaucerian invention of rhyme royal. There were just a few composed in alliterative verse, sometimes with rhyme added, in the late fourteenth and early fifteenth centuries, but these did not have the wide geographical appeal of the metrical romances, and none reached print.

Both the popularity and the longevity of metrical romance are exemplified by two 'matter of England' romances that were universally known throughout the sixteenth century: *Bevis of Hamtoun*, and *Guy of Warwick*. They were first composed in Anglo-Norman in the thirteenth century, probably to celebrate, or to create, founding English heroes for two of the great medieval aristocratic dynasties, those of the Albini family of Arundel and of the earls of Warwick.[73] They were first translated into English around 1300, and in various versions enjoyed a wide popularity, massively increased when they were put into print by Wynkyn de Worde and a succession of later publishers. In contrast to the many medieval romance texts that ceased to be printed after the earlier decades of the Tudor age, these went through numerous new editions throughout the sixteenth century, and in the case of *Bevis* into the eighteenth.[74] Bevis's dragon-fight is replicated in Redcrosse's fight with his own dragon in Book I of the *Faerie Queene*, with a detail that indicates that Spenser's readers were intended to recognize and to respond to its echoes of the previous work;[75] and the hero of Spenser's Book II, Guyon, takes his name, his association with the palmer, and his political resonance from *Guy of Warwick*, whose hero is regularly named as Guyon whenever the metre or rhyme requires it.[76] The stories get a handful of mentions each in the broad corpus of Shakespeare's work, with a casualness that again shows how universal a knowledge of the works could be assumed at every social level of his characters and his audience.[77] The most interesting of these is the quotation that Edgar offers in his disguise as Poor Tom, where the couplet on Bevis's hardships in prison,

> Rattes and myse and suche small dere   [animals
> Was his meate that seven yere

becomes Tom's

> Mice and rats and such small deer
> Hath been Tom's food for seven long year.[78]

Shakespeare seems to be right on the mark here in positing both a noble Edgar who knows his *Bevis*, and an association of such knowledge with the commonest of commoners. This universality, however, implied a populism that led to increasing scorn from the educated, a scorn partly justified in the case of *Bevis* by the desperation of the attempts to preserve rhyme while making the antiquated Middle English comprehensible.[79] Despite that, it still offered enough of a grip on the imagination for John Bunyan to rework his youthful reading of it as the giants and monsters of *The Pilgrim's Progress*; and even after it had ceased to be printed in its medieval shape, it continued a lively existence as a prose chapbook.

Guy of Warwick enjoyed a similar longevity in various forms. Much of its power came from its being the prime story of the chivalric knight who finds that chivalry is not enough. Guy renounces his hard-won wife, Felice (the name is cognate with 'felicity'; Renaissance classicizing habits turned her into the commonplace Phillis), to seek a greater felicity, becoming a palmer and eventually a hermit. The story was sufficiently compelling to be disseminated not only in England but in continental Europe too: literature composed in England was by no means just a receiver of literary influence. The original Anglo-Norman text was rewritten in French prose in the fifteenth century, and had an extensive influence on the Spanish *Tirant lo Blanc* of Joanot Martorell and Martì Joan de Galba. The English text of *Guy* made a final appearance in its medieval shape in the Percy Folio manuscript, but from around 1600 the story was disseminated in a variety of rewritten versions. It was dramatized at least twice for the Elizabethan and Jacobean stage, possibly as many as four times, and one of these plays was put into print after the Restoration.[80] From the 1590s onwards, the story of Guy was a favourite broadside ballad, though the legend moved upmarket as well as down. John Lane, a friend of Milton's father and keen nationalist where literature was concerned (he wrote a twelve-canto completion of the *Squire's Tale*), turned the Guy legend into a poem of even more epic proportions, though it never found a publisher. Samuel Rowlands was much more successful with his markedly Spenserian twelve-canto version of 1607. With the shift of literary fashion towards prose, this was revised to remove the line endings and most of the rhymes, leaving it as a kind of historical novel with the skeleton of the iambic pentameters sticking through the prose, and it was still being published in this form until the late nineteenth century.[81] This, or perhaps one of the many smaller and cheaper chapbooks on Guy, would have been the source by which Samuel Richardson and his readers knew of Guy's greatest exploit, his defeat of

Colbrand, the giant champion of the pagan Danes: an episode still famil-
iar enough in 1740 for the same name to be given to the villain of *Pamela*,
'a giant of a man' whose foot was 'near as long' as his heroine's arm.[82]
Both *Guy* and *Bevis* were as familiar as the legends of Robin Hood or King
Arthur (or indeed of Valentine and Orson) until the start of the twenti-
eth century.

Prose romance reached England late. The first shift of the genre into
prose had taken place in France in the early years of the thirteenth cen-
tury, with the composition of the huge *Lancelot-Grail*, the 'Vulgate cycle'
of Arthurian romances. Its authors are unknown, though it claims to
have been written by Walter Map, the clerical satirist and collector of
unconsidered trifles who lived in the reign of Henry II. The claim is not
sustainable, but it is interesting as demonstrating the dominance of
Anglo-Norman in early romance: if you wanted to advertise the glories of
your romance, you did so by claiming English authorship for it—or, to
be more precise, since Walter was even more Welsh than the Norman-
Welsh Geoffrey of Monmouth, British authorship, though it is not clear
whether early French readers would have registered the difference in his
case. For well over a century, the new form of prose remained limited
even in France to works that modelled themselves directly on the
Lancelot-Grail: the only slightly less huge prose redaction of the *Tristan*,
a free imitation of the *Lancelot* that intertwined the stories of the two
heroes; and the mammoth early fourteenth-century *Perceforest*, which
linked the prehistory of Arthur to Alexander the Great (and which was
one of the influences behind the founding of the Order of the Garter).[83]
It was not until the very end of the fourteenth century that prose became
the medium of choice for French romance. The innovations of the
Lancelot-Grail did not have an immediate effect on romance in England,
though the scanty records of book ownership indicate that copies of the
individual romances it comprised were widely disseminated in aristo-
cratic families in the fourteenth and fifteenth centuries.[84] The first
English translation from Vulgate material, *Of Arthour and of Merlin*,
selects from the French *Merlin* primarily the quasi-historical material
already covered by Geoffrey of Monmouth. It also translates it into verse.
Verse remained the medium for romance in England until the full *Merlin*
was translated into prose in the mid-fifteenth century, and the equation
of the genre with verse was decisively broken only by Sir Thomas Malory
at the end of the 1460s. The most surprising thing about the Vulgate
material, however, is how separate it remained from English-language
romances of Arthur. Occasional writers, notably the *Gawain*-poet, show

signs of knowing it; but its decisive differences from Geoffrey's account of Arthur get only obscure mention in English before 1400, and very little before Malory. These are, first, the pre-eminence of Lancelot, a character who postdates Geoffrey's *History*, and his affair with Guinevere; and second, that Mordred was not simply Arthur's nephew, who rebelled against him while he was away on his career of conquest, but that Mordred was also his incestuous son, whose treachery was made possible by the king's war against Lancelot over his queen.[85] In the English tradition, Gawain remains the top knight of the Round Table; Lancelot is a peripheral French invention, and his affair with Guinevere, if it registered at all, seems to have been dismissed as a French slander on the great British hero.

The greatest influence of the French Arthurian prose romances on later romance was in terms of structure more than of material. The earlier verse romances had traced the adventures of a single hero (or at most two protagonists, or a hero and heroine); the prose romances decisively broke with that model. The *Lancelot-Grail* cycle, the Prose *Tristan*, and the *Perceforest* substituted a structure in which a large number of stories could be pursued in parallel. The model has come down to us in the form of Dickens's advancing a series of plot lines in a sequence of instalments for serial publication, or, in a visual rather than textual medium, in television soap operas. Interlacing enabled expansion, the potentially endless extension of the pleasure of story. The Vulgate romances themselves became especially popular in southern Europe (Dante's Paolo and Francesca famously start their affair through reading the Prose *Lancelot* together), and further prose versions of them were produced in both Italy and Spain.[86] Their interlaced structure was inherited by Boiardo, Ariosto, and Tasso, and in due course by Spenser for the *Faerie Queene*. Sidney's format in his revised *Arcadia* of flashback and digression is a parallel development from the structural experimentation of the *Lancelot-Grail*, mediated in his case more through Spanish romance than Italian.

The second round of French fashion for prose romance, in the fifteenth century, was at its height when Caxton set up his press at Westminster. He had spent much of his career in Burgundy, where some of the most famous of these romances had been composed, and, although he avoided the traditional English metrical romances, he translated and printed a number of these fashionable and wildly successful continental works.[87] His successors in the printing business added more, including *Valentine and Orson* some time in the first decade of the sixteenth century. Their continuing fashionability is indicated by the translations of *Huon of Bordeaux* and *Arthur of Little Britain* made in the reign of Henry VIII by John Bourchier, Lord Berners, both of which remained popular to the end of the century. The prose romances flourished alongside the metrical in the first half of the sixteenth century, but largely outlasted them: a much higher proportion were still going through new editions in the 1590s and later. Spenser made an unusual choice at this date in following Chaucer and Ariosto in his selection of a long stanza rather than prose for his near-epic romance: prose was to be the preferred choice of future generations of serious readers. Verse narrative was increasingly associated with the broadside ballad, or with tales for children; a measure of its separation from narrative fiction is indicated by the difficulty of imagining a rhyming novel.

The rise of prose helped to speed the demise of the metrical romances. The fashionable fiction of the later decades of the sixteenth century consisted of collections of *novelle*, largely Italian in origin; translations of the huge Spanish prose romances, such as *Amadis de Gaule* and *Primaleon* for chivalric romance and Montemayor's *Diana* for the more self-consciously humanist variety; and the occasional Greek romance, the perfervid form of adventure and sexual fantasy that had flourished under the Roman Empire, such as Heliodorus's *Ethiopica* in Underdowne's translation, or Longus' *Daphnis and Chloe* as reworked by Angel Day. One other Greek romance, *Apollonius of Tyre*, had already been translated into English four times before becoming newly fashionable in the Elizabethan era.[88] This long history, and its rather more restrained subject-matter, had naturalized it as English: it is as an old native story, told by Gower, that Shakespeare dramatized it in *Pericles*, and its earlier English versions drop out of sight in the seventeenth century along with many other of the native romances. What is known of the printing history of the metrical romances suggests that new editions were becoming fitful from the time that Henry VIII imposed increasingly draconian state control over publication as the Reformation took hold, and, after a recrudescence in the 1550s under Mary, they became increasingly sparse after Elizabeth came to the throne. It is hard to be sure just how sparse, since almost the entire corpus of printed metrical romance has disappeared: abundant contemporary references to the end of the century indicate that the texts were still widely known, but the younger generation may have read them largely in increasingly tattered copies acquired by parents or even grandparents. Although it is possible to trace a continuous printing history of a medieval metrical text into the seventeenth century and beyond only for *Bevis of Hamtoun*, it is unlikely to have been the only one to be reprinted across the 1600 divide. There is, for instance, a record (but no copy) of a 1577 print of *Eger and Grime*, mentioned as popular in the fifteenth century, but surviving only in the Percy Folio manuscript and later prints from 1669 to 1711;[89] and a comparable printing history is likely for *Roswall and Lillian*, a romance whose form, phraseology, and language show it to have been composed in the fifteenth century, yet which survives only in a series of northern and Scottish prints running from 1663 to 1786 (Sir Walter Scott noted that it was still being sung on the streets of Edinburgh at the end of the eighteenth century).[90] Many other stories survived, but, like *Guy of Warwick*, only in different incarnations. A few were rewritten in prose, at various levels of respectability: Lodge wrote prose versions of both *Gamelyn* and *Robert the Devil*; and the seventeenth-century prose *Guy* based on Rowlands's poem continued a healthy life well into the nineteenth century. It was equalled in the popularity stakes by the prose *Valentine and Orson*, which appeared in prints of every length from chapbooks of single folded sheets to substantial quarto volumes, and inspired a Victorian pantomime or two along the way.

What is abundantly clear is that the native romances retained a popularity out of all proportion to the evidence of the printed record alone. It is as misleading to see the absence of new editions as indicating a lack of knowledge of them as it is to measure their popularity earlier in the century by the number of copies surviving. The evidence lies both in later survivals, and in the vituperation of moralists throughout the sixteenth century about their continued universal popularity: you don't waste your breath, or your ink, condemning a decades-old corpse. The Percy Folio manuscript is a rare witness to this continuing unofficial life: it attests to a massive survival of native romance into the seventeenth century such as has left almost no traces elsewhere in the written record. It preserves a mixture of romances that had appeared in print, either copied direct or quite possibly orally transmitted; romances not known to have been printed, though entire editions may have been lost; and others in the newly fashionable form of the broadside ballad. Further north, in the country of the traditional ballad, other romances were passing into oral form, apparently bypassing the medium of print: *Horn*, *Sir Orfeo*, the romance section of *Thomas of Erceldoune* that tells of the protagonist's sojourn in elfland.

Further evidence from contemporary preachers, moralists, and cultural commentators throughout the half millennium of the dominance of romance gives us not only lists of the most popular romances, but also an indication of how the genre veered from disapproval to approval and back again, as historical, and in particular religious, circumstances changed. Secular fiction had been condemned by Christian writers ever since Augustine deplored his greater readiness to weep over Dido's sufferings than over Christ's.[91] Comparable castigations in the Middle Ages and Renaissance provide a useful index to fashions in romance. Fourteenth-century moralists cited Guy of Warwick's lion, killed defending its master, as a tear-jerker equivalent to Dido; they condemned Bevis, Guy, Octavian, and Isumbras, despite the exemplary Christian penitence shown by most of them; or they set out to replace with Biblical stories a long list of romances including those of Alexander, Troy, Brutus, Arthur and his knights, Charlemagne and Roland, and Tristan and Isolt—all of which were still flourishing, in their original versions or later retellings, in the sixteenth century.[92] The start of the fifteenth century saw a sharp reversal in approved reading-matter, however, as the new Wycliffite translation of the Bible into English suddenly put Holy Scripture, and with it heresy, within reach of those without clerical training. Romances, with their promotion of traditional stable ideologies including the defence of the Church, suddenly appeared a much more desirable area of reading-matter than the English Scriptures, with their innovatory revolutionary potential. Hoccleve accordingly urged knights, in the exemplary figure of the heretic Sir John Oldcastle, to stick with the chivalric reading proper to their station:

> Bewar, Oldcastel, and for Crystes sake
> Clymbe no more in holy writ so hie.
> Rede the storie of Lancelot de lake,
> Or Vegece of the aart of Chivalrie,
> The seege of Troie, or Thebes; thee applie
> To thyng that may to th'ordre of knyght longe![93]

By 1529, when Richard Hyrd was translating Vives' *Instruction of a Christen Woman* for Katherine of Aragon, the conventional moral line had reasserted itself: condemning the usual reading of 'idel men and women', he provides a list of popular English romances alongside the titles already listed by Vives:

those ungratious bokes, suche as be in my countre in Spayne: Amadise, Florisande, Tirante, Tristane, and Celestina the baude mother of naughtynes. In Fraunce: Lancelot du Lake, Paris and Vienna, Ponthus and Sidonia, and Melucyne. In Flaunders: Flory and White flowre, Leonell and Canamour, Curias and Floret, Pyramus and Thisbe. In England: Parthenope, Genarides, Hippomadon, Wyllyam and Miliour, Libius, and Arthur, Guye, Bevis, and many other.[94]

Many of the texts cited here as popular on the continent already also existed in English versions, or were translated later in the century: *Amadis de Gaule*, *Tristan* (in Malory's *Morte Darthur*, along with *Lancelot*), *Celestina*, *Paris and Vienne*, *King Ponthus*, *Melusine*. *Floris and Blancheflour* is less likely to have been known by this date, though the existence of a distantly-related ballad may argue for a continuing oral life.[95] Ovid's story of Pyramus and Thisbe was available in various vernacular versions. And the English titles give a cross-section of the range of romance-reading of the period: fourteenth-century metrical romances now available in print, in *Ipomydon*, *Libius Desconus*, *Guy* and *Bevis*; fifteenth-century verse redactions of earlier French romances, in *Partonope of Blois* and *Generides*; a prose version of a romance already translated once into Middle English verse (in this case, alliterative verse), in *William of Palerne* (the *William and Melior* of the list);[96] and Arthur, by which Hyrd may have meant Malory, or possibly any and every romance that contained Arthurian material.

The Reformation added a new danger to the reading of the traditional romances, for they had been written, as Ascham noted, 'when Papistrie, as a standyng poole, covered and overflowed all England'.[97] Hoccleve, by this interpretation, was right: the texts promoted a Catholic ideology, but that in turn had now become socially dangerous. The romances were condemned for not conforming to the new theology, to the new requirements for pious and Protestant reading, or (in the eyes of cultural critics such as Thomas Nashe, perhaps their worst failure) to the new humanist standards of rhetorical excellence. It became fashionable to sneer at them: they were condemned as having been written by those all-purpose Reformation villains, monks ('abbey-lubbers', in Nashe's contemptuous phrase).[98] But none of this stopped their being read, and, despite the cessation of the printing of many of the texts, remaining thoroughly familiar. There is some evidence that they may have held a particular attraction for recusants—one known enthusiast with strongly Catholic sympathies, Edward Banyster, went so far as to copy out five printed romances to convert them back into manuscript form, complete with illustrations—but such evidence needs to be read against their universal appeal.[99] It is perhaps not so surprising that Captain Cox's library, as recorded in 1575, should have included eight of the medieval metrical romances in addition to an abundance of prose romances, ballads, jest-books, plays, and other works;[100] it is more surprising to find people born in that same decade still growing up to be familiar with a comparable range of stories, as if a whole generation of parents kept a Captain-Cox-style collection of old stories for their children to read. Schoolmasters had to compete for their pupils' interest against quartos of *Bevis, Guy, Valentine and Orson, The Four Sons of Aymon,* King Arthur, and assorted stories of monsters, all damned together as the product of lazy monks.[101] The dangerous papistry of such works was, however, offset by a compen-sating virtue: these were home-grown romances, any continental origins long forgotten. In the great Elizabethan creation of a distinctively national culture and literature, and even a national religion, the native romances could play a central part that Virgil and Ariosto and Heliodorus could not.

It was not humanism nor Protestantism that finally drove such works out of high cultural visibility, but satire. A number of mass-market pot-boilers of the 1590s, which piled on the native romance memes at a rate of several per page, seem poised to invite very different reactions from sophisticated and from less-educated readers—works such as Richard Johnson's *Seven Champions of Christendom,* which provides a full romance set of adventures including lady-loves and children for seven leading saints, and *Tom a Lincoln,* the life story of an illegitimate son of King Arthur that incorporates an affair with a self-styled fairy queen; or Christopher Middleton's *Chinon of England,* in which Sir Lancelot pur-sues and marries a lady with the impeccably Petrarchan name of Laura.[102] The enthusiasm for translations of the long and fantastic Spanish romances, including Cervantes's favourite *Amadis de Gaule,* put English readers in a good position to appreciate *Don Quixote* when it was first translated into English, by Thomas Shelton in 1612–20; and, at the same time, Samuel Rowlands was composing his *Melancholie Knight,* which did for the native tradition of romance what *Don Quixote* had done for the Spanish. His knight is melancholy because he is poor, but he is not in the least virtuous. He has read all the right stories, of Sir Lancelot, Sir Triamour, Sir Bevis, Sir Guy, *The Four Sons of Aymon,* King Arthur, 'the Monster slayers, and the Gyant killers'; and he is himself quite prepared to fight dragons, so long as they are tied up. To demon-strate his learning in 'worthy workes', he tells a sample romance, of the perennial favourite Sir Eglamour, its tetrameters now intensified into nursery rhyme.

> Sir Eglamour, that worthy knight,
> He tooke his sword and went to fight.
> And as he rode both hill and dale
> Armed upon his shirt of male,
> A Dragon came out of his den
> Had slaine, God knowes how many men.

The dragon-fight of *Bevis of Hamtoun* had supplied Spenser with his model for the Redcrosse Knight's long-drawn-out combat against a dragon at once apocalyptic and papal, and Chinon of England first tests his chivalry against a fire-breathing monster; Rowlands, despite, or because of, his fondness for traditional romance, deals with Eglamour's dragon-fight more briskly.

> The Dragon had a plaguy hide,
> And could the sharpest steele abide,
> No sword will enter him with cuts
> Which vext the Knight unto the guts;
> But as in choller he did burne
> He watch'd the Dragon a good turne,
> And as a yawning he did fall,
> He thrust his sword in, hilts and all.[103]

Unfortunately, he loses his sword in the process, but decides it is not worth the trouble of recovering: a decision with which his melancholy narrator fully concurs.

A knight without a sword has lost his chivalric function in life as in literature. A few decades later, Sir Hudibras made the happy discovery that the questing knight needs only one spur, since if one side of his horse goes faster the other is likely to keep up:[104] the effort of winning your spurs can be halved in economic terms without operational penalty. The halving of expense does, however, incur a total loss of cultural capital. Romance had ceased to have a living meaning, its powering ideas rendered obsolete by social change, market economics, and the scepticism towards ideals and towards wonder attendant on the growth of experimental science and literary realism. From being the reading-matter of kings, the stories became the amusement of the semi-literate, the provincial, and children: they were re-absorbed into the popular culture from which the early romance writers had been so keen to distinguish themselves.

CODA: THE RISE AND FALL OF THE KNIGHT

Throughout the first four centuries of romance, until the mid-sixteenth century, romance is inseparable from ideas of chivalry, and from the primary exponent of chivalry, the knight. If the protagonist is not already a knight when his story opens, it will be concerned with his education in prowess, love, and just action that constitute his winning of his spurs. The nature of those chivalric ideals was set out in the ceremonies of knighthood, and in the treatises on chivalry composed down into the seventeenth century. The historical record bears sad witness to how far the ideal was from being normative; but that was, in a sense, the point. The chivalric virtues were not easy of attainment, and the aspiration towards achieving them in itself constituted an ethical quest. The adventures of the hero, his striving towards something beyond him, show the chivalric virtues in action, and show them as difficult—but all the more necessary to strive for on account of that difficulty. The processes of history complicated matters further, as the traditional ideals of knighthood became increasingly anachronistic. By the time Spenser was writing the *Faerie Queene*, the squaring of those ideal simplicities with the complexities of his own political and economic world adds an extra layer of difficulty, beyond the struggle for personal or personified achievement. He was writing, moreover, in a society where knighthood was no longer synonymous with physical and moral excellence, either in aspiration or in practice, and the idea that it might be was beginning to seem quaintly old-fashioned.

In the tripartite division of society devised in the early Middle Ages into those who fight, those who pray, and those who labour, it was the knight who represented the fighting man: that was his function in the Christian community. Aggression, however, is inherently anti-social, and chivalry and the whole chivalric romance ethic were aimed at channelling such aggression into socially useful roles: the support of the weak, the support of the king, the support of God and the Church. As with speed limits, the rules were not always observed, but they none the less influenced behaviour. In the twelfth century, the desire to fight and to acquire an income through fighting, felt especially by landless younger sons, was catered for by tournaments; these offered an outlet for aggression and a way of exercising the physical prowess required of the fighting man, as well as providing economic rewards for the successful.[105] The abundance of tournaments in early romance reflects social fact, and they became embedded as part of the expectations of the genre even after the violent mass *melée* had given way to the more decorous display of the individual joust (the *Arcadia* and *Pericles* are unusual in the degree to which they update their tournaments into the emblem-heavy aristocratic showpieces of the Renaissance).[106] Authors found mass tournaments useful since they provided a locus where their protagonists, even if engaged on a solitary quest, could meet and compete with other knights, demonstrating the superiority appropriate to the story's hero in the process. Tournaments in practice offered substantial economic rewards to the successful, and romances do not altogether overlook those; but they represent fighting more as an ideal of prowess, and extend that from the physical to the social and ethical. Bodily strength divorced from social responsibility is always reprehended. Fighting in accordance with the ideals of chivalry requires that a tournament must be fought without a desire to injure, and real combat demands a cause for which the knight will justly risk his life.

The origins of knighthood are obscure. The term found in historical documents, *miles*, only gradually distinguishes itself from its basic meaning of 'soldier', though the shift from a professional to a social usage seems to have been under way by 1100. The knight's distinctive method of fighting, the horseback charge with a heavy lance supported under the right arm, develops around the same time.[107] It is also in this period that the ceremonial of creating a knight first appears: ceremonies that distinguish knighthood from warrior cavalry in their widespread requirement for a night's vigil, and in their injunctions or vows to protect the Church and the weak (especially women), to keep faith and uphold justice. (Sir William Segar, writing a magisterial account of chivalry around 1600, substitutes the uncontentious loving of God for the defence of the Church.)[108] Symbolic meanings for the various items of the knight's armour and weaponry—that the two edges of the sword represent loyalty and justice, the spurs diligence, or that the hauberk signifies his defence of Holy Church—follow by the thirteenth century. One of the most comprehensive of these symbolic series appears in the course of a manual of chivalry written by the great Spanish ecclesiastic Ramón Lull, in a book eventually translated into both English and Scots; one of the most solidly religious sets appeared, oddly enough, in the Prose *Lancelot*.[109] The First Crusade helped to integrate emerging ideas of knighthood with piety and the defence of the Church. The cult of that most martial of Christian saints, St George, was given a sharp boost in western Europe as a consequence of his reported appearance to the crusaders at Antioch and Jerusalem in 1098. Fighting was compatible with the highest religious devotion, whether in pitched battle against the enemies of God or in single combat against a monster.

The emphasis on knighthood that characterizes the early quest romances, notably those of Chrétien de Troyes, therefore celebrates a comparatively recent phenomenon, though one to which the Arthurian settings of his stories ascribe a long and authoritative pedigree. The *romans antiques* and his own narratives between them write the ancestral romance of chivalry itself. Later writers were equally anxious to locate the origin of knighthood in the distant past: Segar places its roots first in the Roman 'order'of *equites,* cavalry, and then further back still in Aristotle's advice to Alexander to give chains and other badges to warriors of 'notable merit'.[110] He describes virtue as being the primary requirement of a knight, but there is an assumption throughout his work, and increasingly as he moves towards the present, that the knight will be a 'person of honour' in the social rather than just the ethical sense (p. 60). Knighthood was in practice expensive to maintain, and although some medieval lords were prepared to endow less-wealthy men with lands along with knighthood to enable them to fulfil their new role, wealth remained, despite the high ideals, the leading qualification for dubbing after social rank (none of the fair unknowns who seek knighthood in the romances is other than nobly born, even if illegitimately so). Chivalric prowess in practice came a very poor third, though Sir Philip Sidney could still bitterly regret that he received his knighthood at court for diplomatic reasons rather than on the field of battle, and his regret was still fully comprehensible within Elizabethan culture—Gloriana's culture. The images and traditions of knight-errantry preserved in chivalric romances still, as Arthur Ferguson has noted, carried a mystique that elicited 'a special and deeply felt emotional response', but a gentleman who wished to serve the common weal would do so through public or government service, not through the pursuit of private honour.[111] And the person who took such a route, who held such principles of behaviour, now identified himself as a gentleman rather than a knight. Birth was still of key importance, but the dubbing ceremony and its accompanying vows received far less emphasis. The change is epitomized in the titles of Olivier de La Marche's fifteenth-century allegorical quest romance *Le Chevalier deliberé,* translated into Spanish as *El Caballero determinado,* but from Spanish into English in 1594 by Lewes Lewkenor as *The Resolved Gentleman.* Segar himself brings his work up to date by giving advice on ideal behaviour to 'every Knight and Gentleman' without distinction.[112] When James I required everyone worth £40 a year or more to become a knight, the chivalric ideal of knighthood received its deathblow.[113] The 'Fayry Champion' of a parody romance of 1613 is thrilled to discover that 'there were more wayes than one to attaine to a knightship . . . for in the Fayry land they only have it by desert'.[114] Spenser achieved the magnificent feat of harnessing the idealism of romance knight-errantry to practical public service, but his work was becoming outdated even while it was being written. By the time Shakespeare died, to behave like a knight was an anachronism, a reversion to romance rather than a living ideal.

CHAPTER ONE

Quest and pilgrimage: 'The adventure that God shall send me'

> I cannot praise a fugitive and cloistered virtue, unex-
> ercised and unbreathed, that never sallies out and
> sees her adversary, but slinks out of the race, where
> that immortal garland is to be run for, not without
> dust and heat. Assuredly we bring not innocence
> into the world, we bring impurity rather: that which
> purifies us is trial, and trial is by what is contrary.[1]

Milton was moved to write that account of how the 'true wayfaring
Christian' strives after the good life through reading Book II of the *Faerie
Queene*, the book of Guyon, the hero who shares his name with Guy, or
Guyon, of Warwick.[2] It is thus also an account of the practice of the good
life conceived, as Spenser conceived it, as romance quest. At one stage,
Milton was considering Arthur as the subject of the great epic poem he
wished to write, and this passage from the *Areopagitica* gives an insight
into what it might have been like, what appeal he might have found in
chivalric romance. The surface imagery of the quotation may be that of a
Classical athlete competing in a race, but chivalric quest forms its under-
lying metaphor, a substructure that seems almost instinctive rather than
learned. Milton's 'adversaries' are not fellow competitors, but enemies. It
is knights errant, not athletes, who win through the exercise of virtue, and
who are purified by trial against their own or their adversaries' impurity.
'Unbreathed', lacking physical fitness, is the negative form of the
romance term for the stamina of the combatant: Malory uses 'well
breathed' as a complimentary phrase for the physical prowess of his best
knights.[3] By the time the second sentence ends, the ancient Olympic set-
ting has been forgotten, to be replaced by the postlapsarian world and its

unceasing testing of the individual in the combat of good against evil. The passage belongs conceptually where it belongs in time: between the *Faerie Queene* and the *Pilgrim's Progress*, the latter work modelled on Bunyan's adolescent reading in *Bevis of Hamtoun* and the chapbook descendants of romance. Bunyan's narrative supplies the 'wayfaring Christian' with a full chivalric biography, complete with encounters with giants and monsters. What Milton glosses as a race—the dusty and sweaty journey from inexperience to knowledge, even from the fallen world to a triumphant ending in the immortality of heaven—is what allegory shapes as chivalric pilgrimage, and the romance as quest.

The quest provides both the subject of a work and its shape, and to discuss quests is to discuss the point where form and content meet. It is therefore much baggier than the other motifs of romance discussed in this book, even though the underlying meme, the idea with its powerful capacity for replication, is immediately recognizable, whether in the story of the Grail, or Britomart, or *The Lord of the Rings*, or *Star Wars*. Not every romance takes the form of a quest, but it is the model most centrally associated with the genre. To most people, 'medieval romance' probably conjures up first of all the image of a knight-errant riding on horseback through a forest, perhaps with a dragon lurking in the background, and perhaps, as in the legend of St George, a damsel in distress; that is what it conjured up to Spenser, and things have probably not changed very much since. (It is worth remembering, however, that Spenser's St George has to be rescued from distress rather more often than his damsel, and she often helps in the rescue; English romance heroines are notably feisty.) But the quest implies a great deal about the structuring actions of its encompassing work beyond such static visual images. A quest romance is essentially linear, following the line taken by the protagonist's journeyings. The 'plot' will consist largely of a series of adventures encountered along the way: adventures that are usually in some way related to the final object of the quest itself. A journey, however, allows for the easy addition of further adventures, for extra stopovers or digressions or diversions, and later redactors were fully alert to the possibilities of adding extra episodes to a popular original. Chrétien de Troyes' unfinished Grail romance, the *Conte du Graal*, invited potentially infinite expansion in a series of continuations that did not see it as being in their larger interests to bring the story to a close. In the longer romances, and especially in interlaced romances that follow the adventures of more than one protagonist, the deferral of ending becomes part of the point, as in a soap opera: delay is in itself a promise of continuing pleasure.[4] English romance favoured conciseness much more than French or Italian or Spanish, but the combined influences from all those traditions make themselves evident in the middle books of the *Faerie Queene* and in Sidney's digressive and dilating revisions of the *Arcadia*. None the less, few romances are merely picaresque. The aim of the quest, its poetic as well as geographical end, is integral: that is, it defines what the entire story is about and ensures that the journey is something more than random, even though it may start haphazardly, 'by adventure', and proceed with adventures that appear equally adventitious. The achievement of the quest, or even a failure to achieve it, will be not just another episode but the informing principle of the whole romance. The start and finish of most such works are therefore locked together, and the episodes that link the two, although they may appear random, are likely to follow some pattern of interconnection or symmetry unique to that particular quest.

The lucidity that the idea of the quest appears to possess is disturbed on many occasions by the protagonist's not quite knowing until the end of the story what the object of his quest actually is. Further complexity comes from the fact that texts that focus on the ending of their quest may in fact be exercising a 'duplicitous teleology', Monica Fludernik's term for the gap between 'the characters' plotting on the level of the fictional world and the narrative's overall counter-plotting'.[5] *Sir Gawain and the Green Knight* is a clear example of such an opposition, where Gawain's quest for the Green Knight who will deliver the return blow turns out retrospectively to have been more like the Green Knight's pursuit of him; the final encounter between the two, when Gawain believes his quest is complete, is more a revelation of a climax already passed than the moment of narrative crisis. The degree of duplicity here, the gap between what Gawain intends and what the story delivers, makes the work exceptional among romances—indeed, among most literature written before the eighteenth century—in that it changes almost completely between a first and second reading. Usually, the very familiarity of romance conventions ensures that the reader has a fair idea of what is to happen, even if the author does not outline the plot in advance, and even if the hero has different ideas. The reader will always know more than the protagonists (that they will survive their adventures, marry their beloved, win back their kingdom), but that knowledge is a shared assumption between author and audience that bypasses the characters themselves. In the case of *Sir Gawain*, the audience knows one thing more than Gawain, since he expects to be killed, and every reader knows that he lives to fight another day in all those other romances of which he is the hero; but in every other respect, the reader shares Gawain's ignorance rather than a common horizon of expectation with the author.

The quest as motif is further complicated by the fact that it can provide the structure or impulse behind many romances that do not contain any physical journey. The works of Chaucer's that might be considered his greatest romances (in so far as they offer themselves for recognition as such at all), the stories of compelling passion that make up *Troilus* and the *Knight's Tale*, avoid anything resembling a literal quest. Neither has a romance source, being drawn directly from works of Boccaccio's that have rather different generic agendas; but both still contain a sense of seeking, of strenuous mental and emotional aspiration, such as offers a parallel to the journeyings of the knight-errant. The romance quest is closely related to the discourse of desire, since the seeking, the aspiration that constitutes the quest, requires a goal somewhere ahead of you: potentially always somewhere ahead of you, like desire itself. There are clear generic dangers in such material: that great literary critic Sigmund Freud linked desire with the death-wish in ways foreshadowed by Chaucer and in the Tristan romances, and part of the *frisson* of the genre comes from the sense of risk in such illimitable desire.[6] The duplicitous teleology of *Troilus* and the *Knight's Tale* lies in putting that risk into practice, rewarding desire with death in a violent transgression of the bounds of generic expectation. The 'family resemblance' of romance requires rather that a quest must set limits to itself, even if those limits are not quite what the knight-errant (or the reader) expects. Romances at the centre of the genre assume that desire can and should be fulfilled, that there will be a point where it comes to rest.

Those romances of Chaucer's that send their protagonists off on an actual physical journey with a definable end are less problematic. He wrote two of those, and both are deeply embedded in native romance material: the *Wife of Bath's Tale*,[7] and the tail-rhyme *Sir Thopas*. *Sir Thopas* is accurate enough as parody to make what goes wrong, and therefore what ought to go right, immediately visible. His travelling is just that: covering ground. He spurs his horse until it is so bloody that it needs wringing out, but the only result is to tire himself out sufficiently to need a snooze on the grass. He does then dream of an elf-queen and set off on another journey to find her, but less because of desire than because no mere mortal woman is classy enough for him, 'worthy to be my make' (*CT*, VII.792). His quest proves exceptionally brief since he discovers, on meeting a giant guarding the border of her land, that he doesn't have his armour with him; desire falls at the first hurdle. Even now, journeying is deeply integrated with an idea of self-development (that 'travel broadens the mind'). Anyone who goes to Paris and heads for a McDonald's is, we feel, missing the point. But Sir Thopas learns nothing, and neither do his readers. The tale is all *matter* and no *sentence*, subject-matter without any informing meaning, quest as mere narrative that has nothing to say and nowhere to go. The rapist knight of the Wife's tale, by contrast, who is sent off for a year and a day to discover what women most desire, finds that his journey, although successful, is the least important thing about his quest. Finding out the answer is only a step along the way. He has to do all his mental travelling, to distance himself from his former violent and misogynist self, after he is back home at court—specifically, after he is in bed with his loathly bride—before he finds what he did not even know he was looking for: a virtue derived from Christ that is independent both of class and gender. In addition, and not altogether incidentally, he finds that he has in the process acquired a wife who is both beautiful and faithful, in the shape—the altered shape—of the woman who has lectured him at such great length on how he ought to think and act. He gets what he did not know he wanted; she gets exactly what she most desires.

The quest of the *Wife of Bath's Tale* is therefore not primarily a matter of the knight's year-and-a-day travelling nor his search for the answer to a question. It is primarily about what happens inside him. Caroline Walker Bynum has called attention to the shift in the understanding of *change* in the mid-twelfth century, from alteration from one thing into another to the development of a mode of being, as self-becoming: 'The "end" or goal of development . . . was to achieve the ideal version of that type of self . . . to fulfil a given social role and become better versions of virtuous selves. . . . The hero or heroine of secular literature grows into or unfolds rather than replaces a self.'[8] The equation between romance quest, seeking, and that process of self-becoming drives both the narrative, the subject-matter, of the romance (since 'metamorphosis is about process, *mutatio*, story'), and its *sentence*. Quest therefore opens out particularly easily into metaphor, into what is commonly thought of as a quest for identity. The phrase is however confusing, since 'identity' has no exact semantic equivalent in any medieval language and collapses several different ideas into one. A quest for family or social identity, your parentage or rank, is one of those. 'Knowing yourself' in a more ethical sense is another, summed up since classical times in the Latin tag 'Nosce teipsum'. R. R. Bezzola memorably reformulated it for romance as 'le chevalier à la recherche de lui-même'.[9]

Such self-knowledge is most likely, in romance, to mean discovering new capacities that enable you to reach that 'ideal version' of the self. In the paradigmatic Book I of the *Faerie Queene*, that moment is allegorized in the betrothal of the struggling and error-prone human form of holiness, the Redcrosse Knight, to the ideal form of the virtue, Una or Truth. Not every romance quest ends in such achievement, however. For Gawain in his confrontation with the Green Knight, the search for self-knowledge means the impossibility of ever reaching such an ideal, the discovery of limitation or fallibility: a confrontation, in the event, with himself. The discovery of limits can have a less dangerous meaning when the knight is set in competition with his fellows rather than against adversaries. A search for identity can thus offer a range of possible placings for the self in a genealogical or ethical or homosocial topography, being the 'best knight' in terms of lineage or virtue or competitive prowess. The idea of change as development implies a movement within those topographies: a journey in a symbolic landscape.

SOCIETY AND THE SOLITARY KNIGHT

The quest places the focus of a story squarely on the knight as an individual. Just as the vows taken by the newly made knight impose duties and responsibilities on himself alone, most romances—especially the twelfth-century romances, and the insular romances in both Anglo-Norman and Middle English that follow the patterns laid down then—are concerned with the model of knighthood shown by a single protagonist. Gawain alone steps forward in response to the Green Knight's challenge, and his adventures are his and no one else's. Chrétien's Yvain and his English avatar Ywain may hurry to a magic spring to take up an adventure on which another knight has failed, before Arthur and his entire court can get there; but that it is his alone is shown not just by his immediate success but by the whole pattern of love, marriage, and further failure and recovery that follows. Later romances with larger cast-lists still preserve the principle of the uniqueness of each individual quest. The first two books of the *Faerie Queene* each focus on a single knight, and the impossibility of the heroes' being interchangeable is what makes the allegory possible at all. 'The Legend of Holiness' cannot be the legend of anyone else, or of any other virtue; and once that defining virtue is selected, then its particular embodiment follows with what seems like inevitability.

These examples, however, demonstrate how impossible it is to separate the knight's actions from society at large, whether his own community or the community of readers. Gawain acts as a representative of Arthur's court, however unique he may be within it; both he and Ywain serve to define what the best chivalric and courtly standards should be. Redcrosse's uniqueness within the narrative is partly constructed out of connections beyond it, in the world of history or legendary history. He wears battered armour, of which he is evidently not the first bearer, and which is further identified in the Letter to Ralegh as the whole armour of God of St Paul's Epistle to the Ephesians. He carries a silver shield with a red cross, a design first drawn with the blood of Joseph of Arimathea, legendary founder of the first English church, at Glastonbury. This is also the coat of arms of St George, and therefore in the *Faerie Queene* also that carried by the figure identified with him;[10] Holiness is the knight of the Red Cross and all the associations that that carries with it, associations far more extensive than those that define Gawain as the knight of the pentangle. St George, the saint who hallowed Christian battle, had been the patron saint of both the royal Order of the Garter and of England since the fourteenth century; the chapel of St George's, Windsor, claimed to have his heart, and Henry VII a leg.[11] Richard Johnson, in his bestseller *The Seven Champions of Christendom* (*c*.1596), naturalizes him still further by having him born in Coventry; later editions have him father Guy of Warwick. Spenser rewrites his legend so far as to have him 'sprong out from English race', but his main innovation is to make him the patron saint of England's unique religious settlement, the Anglican Church.[12]

The Redcrosse Knight may discover that his future destiny is to be that saint, but he is young and untested, just as the Gawain of *Sir Gawain and the Green Knight* is young and untested. Each of them embarks on a quest of dust and sweat, a process of learning better and emerging the stronger for his failures along the way. Virtue, as Milton insists in the *Areopagitica*, is acquired only with difficulty. It is not the same as innocence. Stephen Hawes's early Tudor chivalric allegory *The Example of Vertue* makes the difference explicit: its hero, initially identified as Youth, is renamed as Virtue only after he has progressed through a dangerous landscape and overcome the three-headed dragon of the World, the Flesh, and the Devil.[13] Both Book I of the *Faerie Queene*, which may draw on Hawes,[14] and *Sir Gawain* are grounded on a similar progression. The young, untried Arthurian court of the opening of *Sir Gawain*, in its 'first age' with its boyish king[15] and idealistic leading knight, gives way to the sadder and wiser Gawain who returns to the court at the end. Gawain's journey measures the distance between them, geographical space stand-ing for mental experience. The pentangle he bears as his coat of arms when he sets out proclaims his naïve belief in the possibility of ideal knighthood; he comes back wearing the girdle as well, symbol of his acknowledged failure to live up to those ideals. Even so, when the other members of the court immediately take it up as their own symbol to des-ignate a new order of knighthood, they are not wrong—or perhaps, if one wants to analyse their psychology beyond the text, they are more right than they know. What Gawain has acquired is a tested virtue, acquired with dust and sweat; without the spotlessness of innocence, and not look-ing very virtuous to himself at all, but with a genuine humility that makes his opening claims of worthlessness appear false, and with a knowledge of what it takes to sustain the ideals of knighthood such as the emblematic pentangle had never taught him. Redcrosse goes through numerous fail-ures in the course of his own quest, but finally justifies his bearing of his coat of arms. Gawain's pentangle stands for an ideal that is finally beyond achievement in a fallen world; but that does not mean that it need not be striven for. An early reader of *Gawain and the Green Knight* added the motto of the Order of the Garter at the end of the poem in the sole surviving manuscript, as if to bring home the relevance of his quest to those knights selected for outstanding chivalry. Whether or not the work was composed for a Garter knight, its connection with the attempts to revivify chivalry through such orders was well recognized in the late fifteenth century, when its tail-rhyme redaction, *The Grene Knight*, turned the story into a foundation legend for the Order of the Bath and for its initiate knights' badge of a white lace. The lace imposed a require-ment for chivalric action, and helped to land Lord Herbert of Cherbury in trouble in the seventeenth century.[16]

   Despite the uniqueness of the hero within each romance, the kind of learning process that both Gawain and Redcrosse undergo is designed to be exemplary so far as the reader is concerned, to offer a model of how to act and how not to act. Foremost among the principles of behaviour pre-sented for imitation is the active readiness to engage with whatever comes, or even to seek it out. According to the Letter to Ralegh, the 'tall clownishe younge man' who comes to be known as the Redcrosse Knight asks the Faerie Queen to be given a boon at her annual feast, in the form of 'the atchievement of any adventure, which during that feaste should happen', so enabling him to claim Una's quest for himself.[17] Knights do not find themselves questing by accident. They may not know quite what to expect, but they seize the initiative, choose to act rather than let themselves be acted upon: they will 'take the adventure that shall fall to them', or 'the adventure that God will send them'. That willed acceptance is one of the driving forces of romance. The questing knight is the one who is prepared to accept the romance imperative, however foolish it may look to everyone else; as Gawain asks in his rejection of his companions' urgings that he should stay at court and not get himself beheaded:

> Of destinés derf and dere   [grievous; costly
> What may mon do bot fonde? [but attempt (them)
> 564–5

The 'mon' in that question is, however, gender-specific, as romances draw a marked distinction between men's journeyings and women's. The outside world is masculine space, where few women venture willingly. Viola, finding herself shipwrecked in a strange country, disguises herself as a young man, but she still seeks shelter within a household, while her twin brother puts up at an inn and walks around the city meeting people at random. Apart from a few women warriors—Grisandol in the prose *Merlin*, the eponymous Silence, Yde in *Huon of Bordeaux*, Ariosto's Bradamante and Spenser's Britomart—women who find themselves in a situation analogous to the hero's quest in romance are most often victims rather than agents, compelled to leave the safety of their own homes and at other people's mercy. The lone woman at large in romance is more likely to be cast adrift in a rudderless boat than to choose to follow the call of adventure: a situation that is considered in more detail in the next chapter.

The readiness of the individual knight to step forward from his larger community puts the quest romance in tension with its larger social purposes. The problem is not resolved by representing knights as companions on a quest, since what happens to each of them is peculiar to himself. In part, this is the result of the romance insistence on meaning as well as event. The more a text is weighted towards meaning and the closer it comes to allegory, the less possible it is for any quest to be shared. Since Galahad is so obviously the knight destined to fulfil the Grail quest, the obvious thing for all the other knights to do would be to follow him; but that is precisely what the logic of the *sentence* forbids them from doing. Each one must go off to his own kind of failure. Lancelot accompanies Galahad for some time, but they are largely defined in opposition to each other. Even the three knights who form the company of the Grail, Galahad, Perceval, and Bors, finally separate to find different destinies. The knights who travel together in the interlaced romances form a

pattern of constantly shifting companionships and alliances, each man
having his own quest to follow or object to pursue that gives his adven-
tures a different shape and meaning from those of his fellows. That stress
on the individual over the group is one of the motifs that most clearly
separates romance from epic or *chanson de geste*. Hector and Achilles are
scarcely imaginable without Troy and the Greek army behind them; *The
Battle of Maldon* names its heroes and its villains only belatedly, to record
the honour or shame they have won in the desperate Saxon resistance to
the invading Vikings. In the *Song of Roland*, Roland may be the hero and
Oliver run him a close second, but it is the great conflict between
Christian Europe led by Charlemagne and the Saracen advance through
Spain that matters. In the *Orlando Furioso*, by contrast, Charlemagne's
defence of Paris against the Saracens largely happens in the background
while the protagonists travel the known and unknown world and beyond
in search of love and adventure, and even when the siege becomes the
scene of the action, individual deeds of prowess take centre stage.

In the long perspective of history, such a shift of emphasis from the
political or communal to the individual seems odd; but throughout the
great age of romance it was overwhelming. In the perspective of literary
history, the shift can appear as an inevitable middle point in the trans-
ition from the archaic to the modern, or the epic to the novel. Spenser,
however, was emphatically not writing a novel; he is centrally concerned
with the political and communal, and the insistent emphasis of romance
form on the individual is one of the basic problems he encounters in writ-
ing his epic of England. The conventions to which he commits himself,
and which are too dominant in sixteenth-century culture for him to
bypass at all easily, focus on the knight, not the society. This has the
advantage of shaping the poem to express an ethic of individual obliga-
tion—the 'gentleman or noble person' that Spenser envisages as his ideal
reader cannot sit back and believe that it is the responsibility of the state
or its institutions to change the world for good—but it does not help him
in shaping his own quest for a vision of what England might be. He uses
Arthur to embody a kind of manifest destiny for the country, but
Arthurian history was not on his side, and Arthur himself within the nar-
rative is another individual with his own unique road to follow.

The romance focus on the individual is given physical expression in
the quest itself. The questing knight rides out from the court, from his
own society, leaving behind everyone and everything that would give him
support and comfort. 'Fer floten fro his frendez fremedly he rydez', as
the *Gawain*-poet phrases it (714)—his hero is far separated from his

comrades, riding in potentially hostile territory. He has to rely on his own strength, his own moral and physical courage, in isolation. Beowulf's followers stay around the mere, hoping for their leader's return from his combat with Grendel's dam, after the Danes have given up and gone home; Roland knows that Charlemagne would come to assist him and will avenge him, and he dies thinking of him; but Gawain is on his own, and Gloriana never sends a rescue party out after any of her knights. Even so, it still matters very much that the knight does belong to some community. He may be alone, but he is not a loner. He will be the scion of a noble family or the vassal of King Arthur, a member of the Order of the Round Table or of Maidenhead. The knight without any such role is immediately suspect: Malory's Sir Tarquin or Sir Breunis sans Pité, or Spenser's many knights who appear from nowhere and exist without a social context, tend to be thugs or wreckers. The principle is confirmed even by an apparent exception such as the 'fair unknown', *le beau desconnu*, the type that gives its name to the popular and long-enduring romance of *Lybeaus Desconus* and its hero.[18] The young Arthur himself, from Geoffrey of Monmouth forwards, is just such a 'fair unknown', brought up in ignorance of his parentage, and he is still in such a state in the *Faerie Queene*, 'both the lignage and the certain Sire | From which I sprong' being hidden from him (I. ix. 3). Such heroes are brought up outside the court and only find their place within it in the course of the romance, but they have a claim to such belonging before they know it themselves, and their recognition by, and integration into, the court marks a key moment in their quest, even its culmination. Spenser's Prince Arthur, who has as yet no such community but who acts as an independent support system for the knights of Maidenhead when they get into difficulties, has as his implied ending within the poem both the discovery of his place in the line of British kings and an acceptance into the faerie court.

It follows from this emphasis on social placing that the questing knight not only rides out from his community, but returns to it at the end. The Lone Ranger may appear from over the horizon to sort out a problem in town, and ride off over the horizon again when he has done so, but the knight-errant does the precise opposite. He sets out from the court into the unknown and returns, bringing with him whatever he has learned in the process. Spenser's Letter to Ralegh declares that the twelfth book of his work will describe the annual feast of the Faerie Queen at which the various knights were sent off on their quests, and gives the details for Redcrosse; but presumably the description of that originating feast would have been given in flashback alongside an account of a further feast at which, like the knights in the *Morte Darthur* from which Spenser draws his model, they would return to report on their degree of success. The overarching story of Arthur's quest for Gloriana must also have been set to reach its climax in the twelfth book, not just by his discovery of his identity and his incorporation into her court, but also by his marriage and coronation. The Arthur of Spenser's poem has not yet entered into his kingdom, and when he does, within this text, it promises to be Gloriana's kingdom: a Britain at once historical, mythopoeic, and contemporary. Such an ending, together with the integration of the tried and tested virtues into a sixteenth-century England, might have turned out to be unwritable, and indeed that may be one reason why Spenser seems to have broken off his composition of the work some years before he died; but the whole weight of the romance tradition he invokes requires such an ending.

The social object of questing is made particularly clear in those romances where the hero assumes the kingship at the end. When the ardent young Floris of *Floris and Blancheflour* discovers that he has inherited the throne while he was on his quest to recover his sweetheart, or Chrétien's Erec is crowned as the final action after his various quests, or a foundling progresses from having nothing (no family, no possessions or obligations or role) to the greatest territorial power and the highest of responsibilities, what is represented is more than just the imposition of the happiest conceivable fairytale ending. Their quests have been a preparation for the rule of others by their own disciplining of themselves. They do not set out with that particular aim in mind, but the shaping of the romance recognizes the connection of the two: the good ruler is the one who has learned the good ordering of himself; and the teleology of the narrative recognizes that even while the characters have their minds on other things. There is of course a strong ideological bias in this, quite apart from the assumption that monarchy is the only right form of government (an assumption that it would be anachronistic to expect to find questioned), but there is also a strong regiminal element, of advice to rulers. These heroes serve as an exemplary model to those who hold power, by reminding them that such power must be justified by the ethical as well as the genealogical superiority of its holder. Kings who fall below that standard (as even traditional heroes such as Charlemagne are shown to do) are forcefully criticized; when Arthur goes wrong in the prose *Lancelot*, he is set right by a lengthy passage of wise advice that struck enough of a chord for it to be made the centre of the late fifteenth-century Scots *Lancelot of the Laik*. The exclusivity of the characters of romance, the concern of the genre solely with the high-born, fuses easily with this active concern with the nature of the good king and good rule. Floris may seem a bad example for this, since his exploits are so consistently focused on the recovery of his beloved, and show nothing of political or martial skills; but his single-minded faithfulness and his readiness to lay down his life for his love demonstrate an integrity that bodes well for his kingship. The parallel may appear like a romance fantasy, but the equation between sexual and political integrity, or marital faithfulness and good rule, is not just a medieval or a romance phenomenon, as the recent history of press comment on politicians' sexual scandals and on the omens for the future of the British monarchy demonstrate.[19] The very point of romances' educative function, in showing how one should ideally act, assumes that most of the time most people do not do so.

MYTHIC SYMMETRIES

This pattern of a return to one's own society, whether that is the Arthurian court, an inherited kingdom, or the family one had lost as an infant, modifies the straight-line structure implied by the quest. The quest romance may appear linear when it is read, but what seems like a straight line ends by doubling back on itself, or completing a circle, back where it began, in a symmetrical process that starts and ends in equilibrium, but which between those points progresses through various ordeals, even to the point of apparent death. 'Symmetry, in any narrative,' wrote Northrop Frye, 'always means that historical context is being subordinated to mythical demands of design and form.'[20] The best-known of such mythical patterns throughout the Middle Ages and Renaissance was that of Christianity itself, in the doctrine of the Atonement fully developed in the eleventh century: the design by which humankind fell from bliss in the earthly Paradise to death, but was restored to bliss in Heaven through the Passion and Crucifixion. Text after text insisted on the symmetries at the heart of God's purposes underlying salvation history. 'For since by man came death,' wrote St Paul, 'by man came also the resurrection of the dead. For as in Adam all dye, even so in Christ shal all be made alive.'[21] Catholic doctrine extended the parallels through exegetic prefiguration, which crucially included Eve and Mary, the Tree of Knowledge and the Cross:

> Reson wyll that ther be thre—
> A man, a madyn, and a tre.
> Man for man, tre for tre,
> Madyn for madyn; thus shal it be.[22]

Only a handful of romances draw an explicit parallel between their own symmetries of structure and God's, and it is rare for there to be even any identifiable sense of analogy; but authors writing within a culture whose deepest beliefs were grounded on such a patterning had an alertness to these mythic forms of narrative design that the modern emphasis on the separation of myth from history has lost. Within romance, that alertness was fostered by the frequency with which the central character passes through some form of confrontation with death to resurrection.

The quest offered a narrative form that accommodated symmetry with particular ease. The mirror symmetry of the outward-and-return journey is one of the most striking expressions of such subordination of historical conception to the mythic, but it is not the only way in which linear quest is restructured in the direction of myth. Symmetry can take the form of repetition, as in the stories of women cast adrift twice (a type of romance discussed in the next chapter): the sense of passing through a symbolic death to providential new life is especially clear in these works. Far from being redundant, the repetition is incremental, a term associated with the repeating of lines within a ballad; the increment lies precisely in bringing that latent sense of myth into consciousness. Repetition also provides an opportunity to re-interpret earlier episodes as they recur, in a process that has something in common with the structuring of many pre-modern academic works as text and commentary—not least glossed Bibles, in which the commentary calls attention to prefiguration and its fulfilment. In the romances that bring the knight back, the narrative may likewise go back through the stages it has come through, in reverse order; but that reversal is not just a revisiting of the same places, but a *re-visioning* of analogous experiences. The outward journey tells a story; the return not only completes the story but comments on that first half.

Other kinds of symmetry have less in common with the patterning of Catholic doctrine, but still function to comment on each other. The two halves of a romance may follow the same adventure pursued by two different knights, as happens in *Eger and Grime*, with a comparable effect of the second half correcting or supplementing our understanding of the first. Alternatively, or in addition, the heroes may effectively be doubles of each other: each of the friends Amis and Amiloun, Palamon and

Arcite, and Mucedorus and Pyrocles pursues a course that offers a series of interlocking variations on the other's. In romances that intercut their narratives with recounted stories from the past, or with visions and their interpretations, those interpolations serve as analogous reflections of the main events.

Such symmetrical structuring, and mirror symmetry in particular, imposes a discipline on many romance authors that the linear quest alone does not, and gives both unity and depth to their texts. *Sir Gawain and the Green Knight* is an outstanding example of such structural and thematic coherence, but it is outstanding more by degree than conception. On a first reading, it appears to describe a succession of events; only with hindsight, or on a rereading, does its true structure of mirror symmetry emerge. It opens by tracking British history from the time when 'the siege and the assault was ceased at Troy', through the arrival of Brutus, to Arthur; it closes in the same way, by pulling back from Arthur to Brutus to the moment when 'the siege and the assault was ceased at Troy'. Within those long shots come the scenes at Arthur's court, the first that assigns Gawain his quest and the last when he returns from it. Integrated within the first court scene and preceding the second come the blow and the return blow; and inside those in this reflecting structure come Gawain's arming with his coat-of-arms of the pentangle and his journey to what seems like the haven of Hautdesert, and his donning both his coat-of-arms and the green girdle before he journeys to the supposed site of his testing to death at the Green Chapel. At the centre of the structure are the scenes in the bedroom, those episodes of apparent social comedy that decide his fate (in effect, whether or not he is to die at the Green Knight's hands), and their counterpart in the lord's hunting and killing of his prey. Bertilak has 'forfaren [destroyed] this fox that he folwed longe' (1895), as the poet announces after Gawain has finally committed himself to breaking his *trouthe*, in the form of his agreement to hand over his winnings. All the significant details of the poem acquire extra resonance from their placing in this pattern. Between the opening description of the court and his striking the first blow, Gawain declares that the only good thing about him is that Arthur is his uncle and he has his blood in his body; after receiving the return stroke and just before he returns to the court, he makes the painful discovery that the old hag at Hautdesert is his own aunt, Morgan le Fay, and therefore that he has as much of her blood in him as he has of Arthur's. He had set out from court showing to the world the symbol of the pentangle, the endless knot, its five points together adding up to a 'syngne . . . in bytoknyng of trawthe'; he returns displaying the girdle, as easily unknotted as knotted, as 'the token of untrawthe that I am tan [taken] inne'.[23] The structure of the quest stands in paradoxical relationship to its central symbol: the progression of plot that at first seems linear turns out to be intricately knotted, its beginning and its ending the same point, the same line; whilst the endless inter-linking of the pentangle gives way to something no more intricate or con-nected than a piece of string.

Gawain and the Green Knight is unusual in the perfection of its struc-ture, but it is by no means unique in its method of knotting and unknot-ting its plot in mirror-image stages. *Dénouement*, unknotting, was not around as a literary term in the Middle Ages or Renaissance, but many authors put into practice the principle implied by the word, not just as a final plot resolution but as an extended reciprocation of the opening complications of structure. The practice is especially well developed in English romance, and shows most clearly in adaptations from French that alter an original, more episodic, plot into a symmetrical one. The deliberateness of such a scheme is evident from the extensive reworking of Chrétien's *Conte du Graal* in the Middle English *Sir Percyvell of Galles*, which eliminates the Grail from the life of its hero in order to shape his whole story into an outward-and-return symmetry of a kind impossible in its unfinished and expansive original.[24] The English author largely follows Chrétien for his initial knotting of his plot, as far as his determ-ination to find his mother; but instead of pursuing his source through the appearance of the Grail at the Fisher King's castle and an extended sec-ond story line about Gawain, the poet revisits each of his plot episodes in turn. Both Chrétien's Perceval and Percyvell start out in the forest, where their mother has taken them to preserve them from the dangers of the chivalric life; Percyvell concludes his knightly adventures by returning to find her, reclothing himself in goatskins such as he had worn as a boy to reassure her as to who he is, and restoring her to health just as she had borne and preserved him. Neither hero knows his name: Perceval intuits his after he has failed to ask the question at the Grail castle, in a scene in which he also discovers that his mother is dead; Percyvell is given his at the centre of the romance, when he is knighted by Arthur. Gawain plays an important role in both romances, but in Chrétien his adventures lead away from Perceval's; the English by contrast makes Percyvell into another nephew of Arthur's, so constructing a parallel between the older cousin who instructs the younger in chivalry, and the younger who must grow beyond that instruction. The return half of *Sir Percyvell* starts with his remembering his mother—at Christmas, the point of the year when

time itself is about to complete one cycle and start again—and setting off
to find her. The romance ends in a family reunion, in which the mother
is integrated into the new household of Percyvell and his wife, her son
having made the full transition to autonomous adulthood. Essentially,
the story of this romance is one of 'self-becoming', in a quest that takes
its hero back to where he started so that he can recognize it for the first
time.

Sir Percyvell demands attention, not only because its radical alteration
of its source shows the deliberateness of its symmetrical structuring with
particular clarity, but because it also shows the very different priorities
obtaining between French and English quest romance in the Middle
Ages. It might not seem a good example to take, in that it is commonly
regarded as an example of the inferiority of Middle English romance; and
indeed Chaucer has it on his hit-list in *Sir Thopas*, not only naming Sir
Percyvell but lifting the rhyme of his name with 'water of the well'.[25] The
Percyvell-poet has, however, gone halfway to meet Chaucer, since
the story of an innocent abroad already has comedy built into it, and the
romance is pervaded by gentle amusement at the gaucheness of its hero.
Neither Chrétien's Perceval nor Percyvell knows how to get the armour
off a dead knight, but only Percyvell thinks that all horses are mares. Its
author none the less resists turning it either into parody, like *Sir Thopas*
itself, or into satire, like *A Connecticut Yankee at King Arthur's Court*—
though he does have a Mark-Twain-like eye for the ludicrous in romance
(as when the Saracens' heads, cut off by Percyvell, hop on the grass as
thick as hailstones, 1190–2). He may mock his hero's inadequacies, but
never the impulses behind his aspirations or the underlying structure of
his story, even though the ideals that inform it are very different from
those of the *Conte du Graal*. The author will have nothing to do with the
increasing mysteriousness of the French Perceval's quest, or with the
impracticality of the notion that success is dependent on asking the right
question at the crucial moment. If he knew, or knew of, the prose ver-
sions of the Grail, he likewise wanted nothing to do with the substitution
of pious fantasy for practical living, or of theological values for secular
ones. Chrétien's Perceval quests for an undefined and undefinable end,
indefinitely postponed; the Perceval of the prose *Quest of the Holy Grail*,
whose qualification for success lies primarily in his virginity, ends in a
hermitage, withdrawing from the world. Percyvell by contrast embarks
on a succession of quests that lead to social integration, marriage, king-
ship, and a reaffirmation of the family. He makes the transition from
adolescence to manhood, the wild boy growing into prowess, love, and

responsibility for his actions, his recognition of his need to make up for his own past errors.

Sir Percyvell opens with the story of his parents, and of the death of his father at the hands of the Red Knight—the man who is the victim of the wild boy's first chivalric adventure. The Red Knight in the *Conte du Graal* is a supplementary character with no prehistory, but the English author integrates his main story with those events from the past in a way that replays the downfall of the father in the success of the son. Such an integration of the past with the present is another recurrent way of expressing the mythic symmetries of romance. The relationship between them is especially strong when the narrative present is interwoven with the past through the retelling of earlier events in inset stories: stories that parallel the main narrative but which also alter the readers' and characters' understanding of the present. Aeneas' recounting of the fall of Troy in Book II of the *Aeneid* is the famous example of the narrative device of flashback cited by the rhetoricians, but romances are sometimes prepared to spend a substantial proportion of their length on earlier events that define their present moment in ways that go beyond narrative alone. The prose *Quest of the Holy Grail* pioneered this technique as a meaning-rich second line of plot running in deep parallel with the dominant quest, in its provision of a sequence of hermits and the occasional virgin to provide lengthy expositions of the prehistory of the Grail or the various items of Galahad's armour (including the silver shield with the red cross borne later by the Redcrosse Knight). The princes' accounts of their earlier adventures that constitute most of the additions to Sidney's revised *Arcadia* are ultimately descended from this model as much as from Virgil, though the *Quest*'s Biblical connotations have been decisively lost by this stage. The stories told by Pyrocles and Mucedorus recount the journeyings that have brought them to their current place of stasis in Basilius' retreat, where their seeking the love of the princesses, quest as aspiration, supersedes their earlier travels.

Sidney gives the *Arcadia* two heroes and two heroines, whose attributes complement each other and whose adventures interlock. A more complex kind of symmetry of structure can emerge in the romances that recount the quests of several knights in parallel—or more properly in interlace, since those adventures will typically coincide, digress, converge, overlap, and part company again. This is a way of telling sequentially a number of stories that happen at the same time, but it is more than just a device for doing that; when the author picks up the thread of a previous story, he does not return to it at quite the same point where he left off, even if the narrative appears continuous when the ends are stuck together. In Rosemond Tuve's words, 'We digress, or seem to, and then come back, not to precisely what we left but to something we understand differently because of what we have since seen.'[26] Retold events from the past make such a shift in understanding explicit; interlace works more subtly, rather in the way of subplots in Renaissance plays, but without the subordination of one element to another inscribed in the 'sub-' prefix. The *Quest of the Holy Grail* in both its French prose form and Malory's redaction uses both techniques, of telling histories and of interlace. The *Faerie Queene* makes a sparer (but still important) use of retellings of the past, but it uses interlace in abundance, most obviously in the central books. Our understanding of the quests of the various model lovers in Book III is perpetually being reshaped by the intervening models of other kinds of love or lust, and the reappearance of a character can just as easily follow the logic of someone else's story as of their own. Spenser's ethical biography of Arthur works in a similar way. The story requires him to be in his youth, but he never has the naïveté of Redcrosse; his established virtue is the accumulation of all the experience acquired by the other protagonists, and so is much greater than his interventions in the narrative alone suggest. Arthur as 'perfection' of the virtues, as the Letter to Ralegh puts it, therefore requires a large cast of supporting, and supported, knights.

Numerous characters are, however, not a prerequisite for interlace structuring; two or three are all that is necessary. Una has her own adventures when she has been separated from the Redcrosse Knight, and her unswerving faithfulness serves to distinguish Truth from the imperfections, confusions, and failures of a struggling human Holiness. We understand Una differently again by seeing Redcrosse's interaction with a third character, Duessa—her antitype, her false mirror image. Allegorical romance, with its cast of characters selected and shaped for meaning, shows particularly clearly how not just plots but *significances* can be interlaced, but romances that set out primarily to tell stories do the same. The fourteenth-century *Sir Orfeo* is a clear and very simple example: after his wife is abducted by the fairies to something like a land of the dead, Orfeo places his kingdom in the hands of his steward, and spends many years in the wilderness before he finds a means to follow the fairy hunt and win her back through his harping, calling in the fairy king's promise to let him choose his reward. He then returns to his kingdom in disguise, and finds that his steward has remained faithful: a fidelity that follows from and reflects both Orfeo's own faithfulness to his wife, and the fairy king's in keeping his word. We have heard nothing about the steward in the interim, but the models of faith in both the human husband and the king of the Otherworld function to guarantee this further example of patient integrity. The hunts and the bedroom scenes in *Sir Gawain and the Green Knight* are yet another example: the alternation between the lady's successive attempts at seduction and the lord's hunting, the changeovers occurring in mid-stanza, conveys almost subliminally the sense that Gawain is likewise a quarry. The parallel sets of scenes appear to have nothing to do with each other except to get the husband out of the way, but their patterning triggers a shift in audience response such as reflects what is happening in the larger plot even before we know it.

Such a strong sense of the potential for symmetry in romance is found in vernaculars other than English, but rarely so persistently or extensively. The Middle English *Havelok* structures its narrative on parallelism rather than a mirror symmetry, creating equivalent biographies for its hero and heroine not found in the Anglo-Norman versions.[27] The Elizabethan romance drama of *Clyomon and Clamydes*, based on episodes from the quite exceptionally long and complicated fourteenth-century French *Perceforest*, similarly creates parallel biographies for its two heroes, both kings' sons, one of whom carries a silver shield and one a golden.[28] Chaucer's *Knight's Tale* offers both parallelism of characters (not only between Palamon and Arcite, but between its human characters and its gods) and mirror-symmetry of plotting, the latter largely absent from its source, but it uses those symmetries to provide a grim irony in the different endings—violent death, marriage—met by its near-identical heroes. This is the work of Chaucer's that Shakespeare (with Fletcher) adapted most closely for the stage, as *The Two Noble Kinsmen*, and the tight ironies of its plotting seem likely to have been one of its attractions.[29] The dramatization of longer romances made it especially important to solve the management of episodic structure, and it was often done through such processes of parallelism and symmetry rather than through the kind of organic unity privileged by nineteenth-century critics. Attention to plot structure in such plays can often therefore be more revealing than characterization or plausibility of action.

Pericles, which is guilty of all the charges of improbability brought by contemporaries against romance drama (the many years covered by its action; its settings widely scattered across the Mediterranean), is a case in point. It shows very clearly the difficulty of staging travel; or rather, it shows the insouciance with which early modern theatre, like the medieval, staged the unstageable—sea-journeys are trivial to playwrights and theatregoers accustomed to watching Lucifer's fall from Heaven to Hell.[30] *Pericles* is concerned with its protagonist's successive quests for a bride, for asylum, for love, for his wife and daughter, though it is unusual as a quest romance in that the journeys that lead him to the things that matter most are not undertaken with the purpose of seeking them out. His initial journey to Antioch is cast as chivalric quest—he describes himself as taking the adventure like a champion in the lists; Antiochus compares the test to fighting a dragon—but his intention of finding a wife by whom he might propagate offspring is fulfilled only later, and then at the instigation more of his future wife than himself.[31] His journey to Tharsus to recover his daughter brings him only to her tomb, and he finds her somewhere else altogether; and his final journey to Ephesus is undertaken at the bidding of Diana without his knowing that he will find there what he most desires. This sprawl of place and time and the irrelevance of human intention is offset by the precision of its symmetries of structure. The play heightens what is already found in the *Apollonius* and Gower as a pattern of repetitions in which each recurrence recasts our understanding of what has gone before. Its outermost form is that of the exile-and-return romance, in which Pericles abandons and resumes his kingship. The relationships of father and daughter, husband and wife, are more central in every sense, from the incest with which the play opens, through the 'good' wooing of Thaisa that concludes with the report of the deaths of Antiochus and his daughter, to the reunion of the family at the end, when marital and paternal and filial love are separated out and celebrated with an intensity greater than the condemnation of the abhorrent affinities of the opening. This is not just plot progression, but a process of commentary, or rather overwriting: aberration, deviance, is replaced by what is good in both human and divine terms. The original romance stressed the parallelism by having its Marina figure draw her unrecognized father out of his grief by asking him riddles, just as he had been faced with a riddle over interpreting the incest; the play uses music at comparable points of the plot, culminating in the music of the spheres (probably actually performed rather than left to audience imagination) that Pericles hears after he realizes who she is. At the centre of the play come both its first climax of joy, in his marriage to Thaisa, and its worst moment, in her apparent death—a death from which the mythic structure of romance pulls her back, to affirm that it is the love, not the death, that matters. The play offers perhaps the fullest experience of grief of any of Shakespeare's happily ending plays. The audience knows, however, as

Pericles does not, that his wife and child are alive, and therefore that at the end of his journeyings he will find them; and even that dramatic irony becomes a kind of structural parallelism within the play, as audience expectations implicitly provide a running commentary on his own tragic text, rewriting and correcting it for good.

The principle of controlling the structure of dramatic romance through patterns of symmetry holds good even where adaptation is not an issue. *The Tempest* acquires its tightness of action, not through its near-conformity to the dramatic unities, but through the various symmetries with which its action is structured, and by means of which it develops its ideas of legitimate and illegitimate power, of love, wonder, and the nature of social living. It works both through the reciprocity of the action of the first and second halves of the play, and through the effect of interlace in the shifts between different groups of characters (not least between the aristocratic usurpers and the rebels of the subplot, Caliban and Stephano and Trinculo). It is designed with a mirror symmetry in which each reciprocal action comments, as in *Gawain*, on its earlier equivalent. Scenes of the separation of families, Prospero as magician, falling in love, and rebellion are resolved in the second half, in scenes of repentance, the masque that celebrates the young lovers' potential fertility, Prospero's decision for virtue over vengeance[32] and his divesting himself of his magic power, and the final scene of reconciliation and recovery. At the centre of the structure, Ferdinand and Miranda pledge themselves to each other, a pledge expressed in terms of a willing servitude to and for each other, a mutual abrogation of power. The whole play is enclosed within two offstage journeys. The first is the casting adrift of Prospero that brings him to the island represented by the stage.[33] The second is not just the return voyage to Milan, but the Epilogue, in which the actor playing Prospero pleads for favourable winds, the spectators' breath that will release him from the island and from the stage. It is a way of returning both actor and audience to the real everyday world that encloses the acting of the play, a return on which they will take with them something of that changed perception of the ordinary.

The travel, in this romance, happens outside the drama: in the casting adrift of Prospero, the voyage to Tunis for the marriage of Claribel, the homeward voyage before its irruption onto the stage in the shipwreck, the return to Milan at the end, the Epilogue. The island setting, the stasis of the action in terms of its location, refocuses those voyages as inward quest, self-becoming. *The Tempest* is a romance of journeyings that all happen offstage; the dramatized narrative gives us only the climax, the central moment around which everything else falls into place. Those symmetries also serve to construct the play as romance. The return to Italy signals repentance, forgiveness, the return of the exile, and young love and its promise of the uniting of the dynasties of Naples and Milan. Less conventionally, the structural patterning finally rejects both magic and colonialist appropriation, and refuses to claim any fantasy perfection. The island is left to the spirits who were its original inhabitants, Sebastian and Antonio notoriously resist incorporation into the harmony of the new body politic, and Prospero does not take his powers as enchanter back with him.[34] Desire here becomes a desire for the familiar world of home, and with that comes a renunciation of romance and its marvels, just as the Epilogue renounces the illusory magical world of the play.

A summary of the journeys that result in the action of *The Tempest* is also a summary of its colonialist, psychological, and ethical concerns; and finally of its religious concerns, too. No romance quest outside *Sir Thopas* is there merely for the story. The word 'quest' itself means seeking, not finding; and that placing of the emphasis, on the process rather than the end, makes some degree of inner meaning almost inevitable. In the case of the Epilogue to *The Tempest*, that inner meaning finally turns outwards, extending into the life of the actors and audience. The judgement the audience give in their favourable breath, or in their withholding of it, is a foreshadowing of their own journey towards the Last Judgement, and the pardon that they themselves may or may not receive:

> As you from crimes would pardoned be,
> Let your indulgence set me free.

> Epilogue 19–20

The deferral of ending so characteristic of narrative romance, and so alien to dramatic form, here opens out into the journey of life, the path of the wayfaring Christian. The final voyage in this play is one that remains in the future for every actor or spectator or reader, the moment when they will cross from this world to God's.

QUESTS WITHOUT MAPS

Since the root meaning of 'quest' is 'search', it follows that even if you know what you are looking for, you do not know where to find it: a quest is a journey to an unknown destination. Neither do you know the roads by which you have to travel, or the landscapes through which they run. Such unfamiliar topography takes to an extreme the practical difficulties of travel in the Middle Ages. Those Englishmen whose professional functions required them to travel—merchants, messengers, friars, the king himself, and all levels of his household from the cooks to the highest barons—were familiar with some of the main roads of England, and perhaps a few of those of mainland Europe. Such people were far outnumbered, however, by those whose horizons were limited by the nearest market town, or by the literal horizon seen from their own village. Maps were rare, and generally not designed to be of practical use;[35] before the mapping of England in the sixteenth century it must have been impossible to have any accurate idea of the layout of the whole country, the relative positions of hills and villages and rivers and monasteries that lay more than a day's journey from each other. A phrase such as 'a day's journey' is in fact tautologous, since 'journey' derives from *journée*, how far can be covered in a day. Distance itself was hard to measure, and the conversion of space into time provided a functional and accessible approximation. The ease of the conversion is itself an indication of how one-dimensional travel appeared, like time itself. The conversion worked in the other direction too, to represent time as space. Dante famously claimed to have had his vision of Hell, Purgatory, and Heaven *nel mezzo del camin di nostra vita*, mid-way along the pathway of his life, in the thirty-fifth year of his allotted seventy. The pathway of life is also the journey of life; life as quest.

One-dimensionality breaks down as a model in so far as it suggests that you can't get lost. The only straight highways in Europe were those built by the Romans, and they were far outnumbered by branching roads and crooked byways. Bunyan was exceptional in providing his wayfaring Christian with a straight and narrow path that would take him exactly where he wanted to go, to the fulfilment of his quest for Heaven; but that path cuts through a landscape that provides an abundance of diversions and wrong routes. Before cartography, and still for Bunyan's Christian, instructions for travellers took the form of itineraries, a sequence of places through which you had to pass to get to where you wanted to go. Topography was linear, familiar in so far as it formed the line of travel, but whatever lay to the side remaining largely unknown.[36] Without the assistance of a single defined highway, journeying beyond an area personally known to you required a guide who had equivalent personal knowledge of the new area, since there was no means of storing or taking with you geographical information beyond the most basic instructions.

Even now, people trying to find a route or an address, a bed-and-breakfast or an ironmonger, will ask a local passer-by for directions; knights-errant take such a need as a matter of course—where can they find lodging, or adventure, or the Green Knight? Once a destination is known, a guide might well still be a necessity if anything more complicated is involved than taking a right turn (*the* right turn, as Auerbach famously pointed out);[37] hence Gawain is given a guide to take him to the Green Chapel even though it is only a short ride from Hautdesert. Guides are not necessarily mere transmitters of information, however, and can lead you astray in more than just the literal sense. Gawain's can direct him to his geographical destination, but his main function is to encourage him to give it a miss, to divert him from his moral destination. The quests of Malory's knights proceed by a process of enquiry, many episodes being triggered not by the dominant quest nor hazards randomly encountered but by successive changes of direction impelled by local report or advice. That, too, had its real-life counterpart. The problems of travel were compounded if the object of a journey were on the move. A messenger or an envoy sent to the leader of an army, or to a journeying king or prelate, would have only an approximate idea of direction, not a known destination. It must have been a commonplace experience to pursue the king from Westminster to Nottingham, and on to Chester, to Shrewsbury, and eventually to catch up with him back at Westminster. You may find the person you were looking for back where you started.

Travel by sea involved further hazards, since the open seas were uncharted, and navigation instruments of limited reliability. The reliance of ships on favourable winds meant that they were easily blown off course and forced to come to land somewhere unintended or even unrecognized. Travellers' tales spoke of hazards beyond the normal terrors of tidal rips and exposed coasts, such as the magnetic island, described by Sir John Mandeville and others, that drew iron-nailed ships to itself. Huon of Bordeaux lands on it despite the best efforts of his steersman, and finds its harbour full of rotting vessels that have never been able to get away, manned by the skeletons of sailors dead from starvation; Spenser turns it into his Rock of Vile Reproach, a place filled with 'carkasses exanimate'.[38] Experienced seamen acquired a lifetime of knowledge of different coasts and harbours, but even the best-travelled could not know the entire coasts of western Europe or the Mediterranean. The problems of topography were compounded by the lack of modern means of communication. Travellers, or whole armies, on ships that set out together but were separated by the weather had no sure way of making contact with their fellows at sea or after they came to land; they might well not know whether they should be searching north or south to try to find them. If someone were abducted in a city or on the road, anyone looking for them would have some idea of where to start; but someone seized and taken away by sea, or abducted by enemy ships or pirates or hostile merchantment, could be taken almost anywhere. Seeking even a known object, a place or a companion, could therefore involve difficulties that modern travellers would think of as insurmountable. Add in the frequently ill-defined nature of the aim of a quest (what do women most desire? how can one win the most glory?), and the 'errancy', the wanderings, that characterize the questing knight become inevitable.

That travel was experienced as linear, however wandering a line it might follow, makes sense of a great deal of what at first appears strange about the journeyings of a questing knight. The story, like an itinerary, focuses on specific loci along the line of travel: the narrative settings are those places where things happen (a spring, a hermitage, a ford, a castle), and they are recognized by their characteristics, not by their spatial co-ordinates. What lies out of sight—and if you are travelling through a forest, you can't see very far at all—is either irrelevant, or potentially threatening. The philosophers of the twelfth-century school of Chartres adopted the word *silva*, forest, as their term for chaos, matter that had not yet been given created form; and it may not be coincidence that the quest romance was developing its own characteristic landscape of forest at the same time. The romance forest is the place that conceals brigands and monsters, where the knight's claims to chivalry are tested, his values and his sense of self challenged.[39]

It rarely matters just where the forest is. A few are named (Broceliande, Ardennes), but the point of any forest, named or not, is that you can get lost in it. The starting-point of Dante's journey through the three realms beyond this world is in a *selva oscura*, a wood of darkness and indirection, from which he needs the help of a guide to escape. *Errare*, to wander, feeds into both the knight-errant, questing with no fixed goal, and errancy, the moral equivalent of physically going astray. Step off the road, and any woodland becomes a Wood of Error: it is not accidental that the first landscape to be described in the *Faerie Queene*, after the undistinguished 'plain' of the opening line, is the 'wandring wood . . . Errours den' (I. i. 13). Features of the landscape are more or less geographically interchangeable if your experience is confined to what you can see of them: a spring may be near Edinburgh or Toulouse, but the fact that it is somewhere where you can drink matters more than its location, and the idea that fairies haunt such places may matter more still. In quest romances (romances of origins operate differently) real places are likely to be named only if they have some symbolic function: a spring near Jerusalem will have meanings that one near London will not. Romances, furthermore, aim for the exotic, the distant. English audiences would be too familiar with springs near London to find them interesting; those occur in romances such as *Amadis de Gaule,* originally composed in Spain and therefore able to regard England as an exotic country. The wetness of England, its abundance of rivers and streams, was for a Spanish audience a signifier of wealth.[40] Locations close to home have to have some weighty reason for being chosen. Imogen in *Cymbeline* sets out on a journey to Milford Haven, a place whose specificity seems anomalous (especially in view of its modern reputation as an oil refinery), but in the sixteenth century it resonated with the landing there of that saviour of war-torn England, Henry Tudor. The romances most likely to name familiar places are those that serve a genealogical function, where the point of the text is to provide a founding legend for a known baronial seat; but the fixed location of a magnate's home territory means that such texts are less likely to take the form of quests. The spring of *Melusine* is near the future city and castle of Lusignan, since the eponymous fairy will be the founding mother of the Lusignan line, but it is her sons, not herself or her chosen husband, who set out from there to journey.

The characteristic setting for a quest romance is most simply described as *somewhere else.* Even if it is given a location, it is in a form its real-world inhabitants might not recognize: water apart, Amadis's England is a legendary land in which marvels can and do happen on a regular basis. Malory is unusual in mapping the fantasy Britain of French Arthurian romance onto the country he knows, identifying Camelot as Winchester and Joyous Gard as Bamburgh in a programme of turning the more implausible stories into a legendary history of the land that he and his readers inhabit. What matters for Malory is that the traces of Britain's heroic past are 'still there', that the countryside preserves the evidence of its originary moment.[41] Caxton takes a similar approach, arguing for the historicity of Arthur on the basis of the physical remains at Caerleon. Yet even in Malory, once his knights have left those named locations, the landscape loses its familiarity and its geographical precision. Quest requires a landscape that follows the co-ordinates of adventure rather than mappable space—which is why attempts to map the *Faerie Queene* are doomed to failure.

The uniqueness of romance geography is apparent by contrast with many of its contiguous genres. Epics and *chansons de geste* are likely to use known settings, and so does that other genre of the happy ending, comedy—or at least, Roman comedy, the model best known in the Renaissance. Terence and Plautus set their plays in familiar cities (most often Athens), and the classicizing satirical comedy of the Renaissance followed suit, as Jonson's London plays testify. The distance of Shakespeare's comedies from that model, and their closeness to romance, is evident in the exoticism of their settings, just as in their patterns of love, loss, searching, and discovery. 'This is Illyria, lady'; but no spectator in their right mind is going to try to identify the modern equivalent of Illyria on a map in the hope of illuminating the play. For all practical dramatic purposes, Bohemia does have a seacoast. One result can be what Northrop Frye has called 'spatial anachronism', where geographical and thematic co-ordinates are at odds.[42] The forest of Arden in *As You Like It* is in some respects a Warwickshire version of the vast and mysterious forest of the Ardennes, but it still contains a lioness, a serpent, and a shepherd and shepherdess named Sylvius and Phoebe. The island of the *Tempest* is reached in one direction from Naples and in the other from Tunis, known places that locate it firmly in the middle of the Mediterranean (Virgil's or Aeneas's Mediterranean); but Shakespeare famously borrows some of its properties from the New World, from accounts of the Bermudas and Montaigne's essay on cannibals.[43] The westward voyages of exploration posed new challenges not just to the explorers themselves but to the imaginative conception of the unmapped; but that was a challenge that romance was well adapted to take up.

QUESTING WESTWARD

The great age of romance began and ended with westward questing. The *Roman d'Eneas* told of Aeneas' travels from Troy to Italy in his search for a new home territory, of land to colonize, and the work's emphasis on Lavine over Dido gave priority to his founding of a dynasty over his adventures on the way.[44] It told of the *translatio imperii*, the westward movement of the centre of power from Trojan Asia Minor across the Mediterranean: a movement that his descendants were to take still further, to the Atlantic edge of Europe. As the *Gawain*-poet put it,

Hit was Ennias the athel, and his highe kynde,
That sithen depreced provinces, and patrounes bicome
Welneghe of al the wele in the west iles . . .
Tirius to Tuskan and teldes bigynnes,
Langaberde in Lumbardie lyftes up homes,
And fer over the French flod Felix Brutus
On mony bonkkes ful brode Bretayn he settez
　　　　　wyth wynne.

5–7, 11–15

[It was noble Aeneas and his princely descendants who afterwards subdued terri-
tories, and became lords of almost all the wealth of the western isles. . . . Tirius
went to Tuscany and founded dwellings, Langobard settled in Lombardy, and far
over the English Channel Brutus the Blessed established Britain in joy across its
wide hills.]

This process of colonizing and enfolding 'almost all the wealth of the
western isles' was recognized as appropriation but not usually as sup-
pression: as the vocabulary of *beginning* in this passage suggests, the
legends presented much of this colonization by Aeneas' descendants as
being of empty lands, or at least of lands that were inhabited only by
creatures such as giants (as Britain was) or who knew little of the arts of
civilization, and so could be represented as properly overcome. The com-
parison with the rhetoric of later exploration is instructive, but the early
legends had the advantage of not having a knowledge of any contradic-
tory fact to contend with. Chrétien de Troyes is typical in describing this
westward movement as encompassing not only territorial expansion but
the ideals of chivalry and learning (the *translatio studii*, learning as car-
ried initially from the Greek- to the Latin-speaking world and then on
westwards):

Ce nos ont nostre livre apris
Qu'an Grece ot de chevalerie
Le premier los et de clergie.
Puis vint chevalerie a Rome
Et de la clergie la some,
Qui or est an France venue.[45]

[Our books have taught us that chivalry and learning acquired their first distinc-
tion in Greece. Then chivalry passed to Rome, as did the greatest learning; and
now they have come to France.]

The identification of the origins of the various realms of western Europe in this process of westward questing remained a point of national pride into the sixteenth century and beyond,[46] and provided a context for exploration still further westwards.

Europe, to its inhabitants and its writers, effectively constituted the known world. In the Middle Ages, it was the East that most exercised the imagination; whatever might lie to the west was largely so unknowable as to be unimaginable—and in any case, since the world was known to be round but the existence of the Americas unknown, imagining the West was indistinguishable from imagining the East. Before the discovery of the New World, romance writers therefore located their most exotic romance landscapes eastwards, in Babylon or India. Even Eden had a geographical location, being shown on medieval world maps at the furthest point eastwards.[47] As Sir John Mandeville noted, it was hard of access. He did not reach it himself ('Of paradys ne can I not speken proprly for I was not there; it is fer beyonde, and that forthinketh me'),[48] but Alexander the Great, in some romance versions of his life, was supposed to have reached its encircling walls.[49] No lands to the west could offer such tantalizing possibilities, but people's imagination had already been stirred by what might lie in that waste of sea beyond Europe. Maps down to the eighteenth century filled the Atlantic not only with newly discovered islands (such as the Azores), but with islands that had a mythical as well as a real existence, and with others that were solely the product of legend.[50] The Canaries were identified with the Fortunate Isles, known to the Greeks as the Islands of the Blest; Geoffrey of Monmouth gives them the alternative name of the Island of Apples, Avalon, and makes them the home of Morgen, the future Morgan le Fay, to which the dying Arthur is taken.[51] The most mythical islands included a number from Irish legend, such as another isle of the Blest, Hy-Brasil.

Legend and fact fed on each other, and cannot always be separated. The story of the voyage to the land promised to the saints undertaken by the sixth-century Irish St Brendan probably records not only an actual journey but one which may have succeeded in crossing the Atlantic.[52] The legend was widely disseminated throughout medieval Europe in the age of romance, in Latin and many vernaculars including Anglo-Norman and Middle English; it not only influenced a number of romances (the most recent, and one of the most faithful, being C. S. Lewis's *Voyage of the Dawn Treader*), but remained as an inspiration in the age of exploration. The object of Brendan's journey was not imperialist expansion, but to see God's wonders in the deep: exploration without appropriation, quest as wonder.[53] Brendan himself had stayed just a few days in his land of promise before being commanded to set out on his return voyage, but the prospect it offered of the fulfilment of desire fuelled further voyages of exploration into the eighteenth century. There seems none the less to have been no notable rush to incorporate the Americas into romance geography, perhaps because the genre was so tradition-dependent. The New World was rarely associated with the kind of wild and fearsome landscapes believed to exist in the East: writers were more likely to use the West as the setting for utopias rather than quest[54]—a land of promise, like Brendan's, rather than threat. Camoens's imperialist epic of the southern encompassing of Africa by the Portuguese, the *Lusiads*, did not spawn offspring with an American setting. Ariosto and Tasso, however, writing up-to-the-minute romances in the decades when the Americas were being opened up,[55] both put prophecies of its discovery into the mouths of damsels guiding their heroes in magic boats in the further reaches of the world, for all that their notional subjects were Charlemagne and the First Crusade. Ariosto presents the American conquests as a continuation of the *translatio imperii*, though here it is the expansion of Charles V's empire, not the movement of his power base, that is at issue. Charles himself took as his emblem a representation of the Pillars of Hercules, entwined with labels reading 'Plus Ultra', 'yet further'—a badge that effectively represented the object of his rule as a westward quest beyond the Straits of Gibraltar. His office as Holy Roman Emperor enabled Ariosto to regard the voyages of exploration as a process of glorious conquest by both state and the church, in accordance with Christ's prophecy in John 10:16, 'There will be one sheepfold, and one shepherd.' In his English translation of 1591, John Harington, not surprisingly, downgraded this prediction of world dominion into a dismissive marginal note.[56] Tasso largely deletes conquest from the surface of his account, but he does stress the more comfortable justifications for the whole colonial enterprise, conversion of the heathen and the need to introduce decent agricultural practices. When Edward Fairfax came to translate this passage in 1600, he altered Tasso's phrasing to associate exploration more with the knight-errant's quest or Brendan's seeking out of wonders than with political or cultural expansion. Columbus accordingly becomes a 'knight' possessed of 'the hardiment | Upon this wondrous voyage first to wend'[57]—an altogether less contentious message for English readers. Both Ariosto and Tasso also set scenes of magic and enchantment, for which their semi-historical worlds of Carolingian or Crusader Europe are inadequate, west of the Straits of Gibraltar. Ariosto

sends Ruggiero on a round-the-world trip by hippogriff, with a set of fan-
tastic adventures on the way in Alcina's island, a seductive paradise that
might be in the West or the East Indies.[58] Tasso's journeying knights find
Armida's 'paradise',[59] modelled on Alcina's island and the forerunner of
Acrasia's bower, at the top of a mountain in the Fortunate Isles, with their
associations with Morgan le Fay.[60]

So far as the New World was concerned, the imitation of life by art
was less important than the imitation of art by life. Until it invented its
own pioneering mythologies, America did not carry the kind of sym-
bolic capital that could readily be integrated into the romance mode.
The most powerful influences were in the opposite direction, from
romance to exploration. The quest, and the possibilities of wealth and
power awaiting in a land of promise at the end of the quest, offered a
conceptual framework for the early voyages. The *conquistadores* took
their idea of marvellous journeys from printed texts of fifteenth-century
French, Spanish, and Italian romances, carried copies with them on
their travels, and on occasion gave romance names (such as California,
originally an island of Amazon women in *Esplandian*) to the places they
discovered; Ponce de Léon famously discovered Florida in the course of
a search for a fountain of eternal youth, and Cortes modelled his reports
on a prose romance of Charlemagne's twelve peers.[61] Romances were so
popular in the early days of the Spanish colonies that there were recur-
rent attempts to ban them. The Americas appeared at first as a land of
marvels, a romance landscape come true. Berners' translation of *Huon
of Bordeaux*, with its particularly far-flung and exotic voyages (including
an island of apples of youth), may be a response to the intense interest
in such discoveries in the early decades of the sixteenth century. Segar
compared Cortes and Pisarro to Ulysses, Aeneas, the journeying knights
of Ariosto and Tasso, and King Arthur; the English explorers are latter-
day Sir John Mandevilles.[62] Spenser justified his invention of Faerie
Land by an appeal to the new discoveries; Ralegh imagined Guiana as
potentially contiguous with the land of the Amazon women, and
Elizabeth as fulfilling her destiny by becoming the sovereign of such a
land.[63] Even as the Old World was mapped with increasing precision,
unknown landscapes of the kind familiar from romance journeyings
opened up in the New. Exploration seemed to offer the prospect in the
real world of fulfilling the aspirations romances had channelled into the
quest: as the father of the Elizabethan captain Sir Richard Grenville
phrased it:

> Who seeks the way to win renown,
> Or flies with wings of high desire;
> Who seeks to wear the laurel crown,
> Or hath the mind that would aspire:
> Tell him his native soil eschew,
> Tell him go range and seek anew.[64]

As in Fairfax's description of Columbus, the language of romance quest and the language of exploration here become interchangeable. But the exercise of such aspirations rarely resulted in the fulfilment of desire. As Ralegh and many others found, the New World was all too often a topography of despair and death, not least in the barren questing for El Dorado, the land of infinite riches.[65]

The Tempest places itself somewhat equivocally within this nexus of competing ideas. It calls attention to its intertextuality with Aeneas' voyagings in the *Aeneid* by its insistence that Tunis is the same as Carthage, by its naming of Dido, and by its close replaying of Aeneas' meeting with Venus in Ferdinand's meeting with Miranda. The play's magical island, which is home to an enchanter, his beautiful daughter, a witch's son, and a spirit, is pure fantasy. Shakespeare's New World source, Strachey's as yet unprinted Bermudas letter, must have been largely unrecognized by its audience, but the play's discourses of occupation and 'plantation' (2.1.149) are explicit—though it is important to remember that it is Ariel who is native to the island, not Caliban, son of the tyrannizing incomer, Sycorax. The internal contradictions in the idea of beneficent rule of the innocent by the experienced are brought to the surface by Sebastian and Antonio's mocking comments on Gonzalo's schemes of perfect government. Gonzalo would like to 'excel the golden age', reinstate the time when desire and fulfilment were one; but the Golden Age, in the paralleling of classical myth and Biblical history, was a reminiscence of Eden, and there can be no going back. Shakespeare will not subscribe to a myth of an unfallen world, whether in a fantasy island in the Mediterranean or in the Americas. Alexander the Great himself could not enter the Earthly Paradise.

LANDSCAPES OF DESIRE AND FEAR

As Milton recognized in the *Areopagitica*, the whole idea of quest assumes the Fall. Quest distinguishes itself from travel partly by its ethical dimension, its concern to distinguish between good and evil and to strive for greater virtue at the necessary expense of innocence. The landscapes of the quest therefore take the form of a series of locations that carry some weight of meaning, and those meanings are most likely to do with the particular form that the quest takes, the individual trials that the knight must undergo and the state of mind he is in. The questing knight is drawn forward by his desire for some aim or object, adventure or glory or a lady or the Grail; the obstacles he must overcome are those that require courage and prowess beyond the ordinary, and therefore that require the overcoming of fear. Bunyan's Christian has to follow just such a route, a 'dangerous journey' of forests, dark mountains, lions, giants, and hobgoblins, an 'inchanted ground' that threatens travellers across it with sleep, and a river with no bridge, before he reaches the country for which he has fallen sick with desire.[66] Many of the landscapes of romance offer themselves for understanding in those terms. There is, however, a large potential for mismatch between a psychological and an ethical landscape. Desire will not always be for the good, nor fear mark the evil that has to be conquered.

Of all varieties of desire, sex is the most potent, and the most ethically and psychologically ambivalent. Romance is the genre of love and the continuation of the family, but it exists in uneasy and often explicit relationship with the misogyny deeply embedded in both medieval and Renaissance culture.[67] Furthermore, in the symbolic progression of the quest with its male hero, the dangers of sexuality will inevitably take the form of a female adversary, whether the point at issue is ultimately about the danger of women, the danger of his own unbridled sexuality, or (as in *Gawain and the Green Knight*) the danger of temptation at large. Any sexually inviting woman in the prose *Quest of the Holy Grail*, with its theology of virginity, is evil personified—evil feminized: such characters are not women at all, but devils. Sexual desire, moreover, comes embedded in a spurious ease, just as Gawain is tempted literally in his bed, in the comfort that lowers his defences after the hardship he has endured in the winter landscape outdoors. The Grail quest's Perceval, narrowly escaped from a demonic horse that self-destructs in a 'a rowghe watir whych rored', finds himself 'in a wylde mounteyne whych was closed with the se nyghe all about, that he myght se no londe aboute hym whych myghte releve hym, but wylde bestes'.[68] Rendered increasingly feeble by hunger and lack of shelter, he is offered shade, food, and rest in a luxurious pavilion by a lady who arrives in a ship, and only the sight of the crucifix set into the pommel of his sword, which leads him to cross himself, saves him from destruction by the devil in person. But even pavilioned luxury with half-naked women is not necessarily evil: for Sir Launfal (or Lanval, or Lambewell, in his Middle English, Anglo-Norman, and seventeenth-century incarnations), it is the fulfilment of a desire he had not even known he might feel—though it is also the beginning, rather than the end, of his quest.

Launfal is unusual, however. For the knight-errant, as Gawain finds at Hautdesert, luxury (etymologically identical with *luxuria*, lust) is almost always a temptation away from the dust and sweat of the way of hardship. Fairfax makes the point explicit, fifty years before Milton, in his translation of Tasso's *Gerusalemme Liberata*, when his knights encounter Armida's land of eternal spring with the satisfaction of all the appetites on offer, 'all daintie food' and the promises made by a pair of naked virgins bathing in a pool:

> 'The fields of combat here are beds of downe,
> Or heaped lillies under shadie brakes;
> But come and see our queene with golden crowne,
> That all her servants blest and happie makes,
> She will admit you gently for her owne,
> Numbred with those that of her joy partakes:
> But first within this lake your dust and sweat
> Wash off, and at that table sit and eat.'
>
> XV.64

Desire here is for the life without dust and sweat, and despite—because of—the echoes of Revelation in that passage, of the blessed as those who are numbered in the joys of the Lamb and who hunger and thirst no more, such desire must be resisted. The setting, a temperate paradise on top of a high mountain, is a parody of the earthly Paradise itself, in which the Fall may be re-enacted. Tasso's original of the passage gave Spenser precisely what he wanted for his descriptions of Phaedria's island and Acrasia's bower (II. vi, xii): in the *Faerie Queene*, comfort and luxury almost always signal danger. The most threatening landscapes of Book I were landscapes of fear, such as the Cave of Despair:

> Darke, dolefull, drearie, like a greedie grave,
> That still for carrion carcases doth crave;
>
> I. ix. 33

but even in that book, the 'wandring wood' first leads Redcrosse and Una astray towards the den of Error by means of its delightful trees and birdsong. The temperate luxuriance of the Bower of Bliss is not quite a new phenomenon, though the intensity of its wish-fulfilment (desire-fulfilment) qualities is unprecedented in the poem. Acrasia herself lodges at the point from which the 'one harmonee' of birdsong, vocal and instrumental music, and the natural music of winds and waters all emanate:

> Such as attonce might not on living ground,
> Save in this Paradise, be heard elswhere.

II. xii. 70

But this Paradise must not be taken as the fulfilment of desire; its bliss is a state that must be destroyed. Those who seek it for its own sake lose their masculinity 'in lewd loves, and wastfull luxuree' (80), ultimately losing even their humanity and turning into beasts. That a landscape of desire should be dangerous is nothing new in romance; that the desire that draws the knight onwards towards the goal of his quest should be inseparable from the destruction of everything that is desirable, is an unfamiliar paradox that is hard to assimilate into the conceptual framework of romance expectations. Tasso deals with a potentially similar problem by having Armida's paradise described in terms of danger before it is seen (XIV.68–76), so that the reader sees through its beauties when they are encountered; and he also has Armida herself call up devils to destroy it after the hero has been rescued from it by his companions. The bewilderment that readers commonly feel in Book II of the *Faerie Queene* is due not solely to the fact that the cuing is misleading—harmony, for instance, here demands to be read as bad—but to a feeling that the quest has no aim other than destruction, that the compulsion towards its completion is also a compulsion towards annihilation.

   That the goal of a quest should include destruction is not in itself either puzzling or unfamiliar. There is a sense in which every knight who kills a dragon has destruction as his aim, though it is usually a means to an end: for the Redcrosse Knight, to freeing Una's parents, and as a preliminary to their marriage. Gawain believes that the end of his own quest will be his death at the hands of the Green Knight, and the final landscape through which he passes—icebound, misty, closed in by crags, to a Green Chapel where the devil himself might worship (2187–8)—looks as if it is leading him to the destruction he expects. The text's most noted editor, J. R. R. Tolkien, makes destruction the aim and object of the quest in *The Lord of the Rings*: it is because the One Ring is the focus of such an intensity of desire that it must be disposed of. Frodo, like every questing knight, takes on the quest voluntarily, but also with a deep reluctance, a resistance to desire that is his main qualification for success. He does not want to be the ring-bearer. The final landscape that he has to cross before he reaches Mount Doom (so allegorical a name as to require a less heavy-handed alternative) is a waste of desolation that overgoes any medieval Waste Land, a fusion of setting and quest that is both ethical, in its representation of evil, and psychological, in its reflection of the draining away of Frodo's vital energies. Tolkien learned his memes from his wide knowledge of medieval texts, and he learned too how to exploit them. The bleakness of the ending might seem to be distinctively modern, but despite the pull of romance towards concluding happiness, the Middle Ages too can produce landscapes that lead inexorably towards disaster. The quest can finish on a one-way road to death. The landscape that Malory creates for the final act of Balin's quest—a setting compacted from a much looser-knit original—sets his hero on a path from which he knows return is impossible:

And so he rode forth. And within thre dayes he cam by a crosse; and theron were letters of gold wryten that said: 'it is not for no knyght alone to ryde toward this castel.' Thenne sawe he an old hore gentylman comyng toward hym that sayd,

'Balin le Saveage, thow passyst thy bandes to come this waye, thefore torne ageyne and it will availle the,' and he vanysshed awey anone.

And soo he herd an horne blow as it had ben the dethe of a best. 'That blast,' said Balin, 'is blowen for me, for I am the pryse [quarry], and yet am I not dede ... Though my hors be wery my hert is not wery. I wold be fayne there my deth shold be.'[69]

And he does indeed die, in a combat against his own brother in which each kills the other.

Much of the power of that passage comes from what is left unexplained: why the cross carries the warning it does; who the old gentleman is; how he knows Balin's name; how he can vanish; who blows the horn and for what purpose; why the road is so well-marked a route to death. It is no more possible to give ethical or allegorical answers to such questions than to give narrative ones. Unlike the grisliness and the corpses of Spenser's Cave of Despair, there is nothing here that is translatable to another level of meaning, and nothing either that is inherently strange. Roadside crosses and wayfarers were commonplace, the sounding of horns nothing unusual. A horn-note could indeed be intended as assistance for travellers, being sounded at nightfall in some wild or forested districts to guide travellers to shelter. Balin's landscape is the familiar gone wrong: that liminal, unexplained, state that we know as the uncanny, a state which, as Freud pointed out, exists in symbiosis with the homely.[70]

There is one romance that exploits this quality of the uncanny to the full: *Eger and Grime*, well known in the fifteenth century though surviving only in the Percy Folio manuscript and later seventeenth-century prints.[71] It tells the story of Eger's despair of winning the love of an earl's disdainful daughter after he has been beaten in combat by a dangerous knight named Graysteel. Eger is left for dead on the field of battle, and on recovering consciousness finds that his right little finger has been cut off and his glove replaced on his mutilated hand—this being Graysteel's trademark of victory. To recover his lady's love, Eger's sworn brother, Grime, impersonates him in a return combat and defeats Graysteel, cutting off his whole hand, in its glove, to prove his success. Structurally the romance works through a symmetry of repetition, the second half both re-enacting and commenting on the first. In the first part, Eger tells Grime of his defeat; in the second Grime follows the same route and finds the same adversary but fights to a different outcome. Graysteel lives in a forbidden country, described by Grime as 'the land of doubt', of fear.[72] The route there seems at first neither special nor distinctive: each knight has to follow a river for two days and cross the wilderness of a forest for a further day. What is strange is that the stages of the journey will last that long no matter how fast each rides: something has gone wrong with the interchangeability of time and space.[73] The doublings and repetitions confuse as much as they clarify, in ways reminiscent of nightmare. Despite the imperfection of the surviving texts, the romance is one of the most unnerving there is—much more so than those involving combats against giants or dragons; and the missing finger (in Freudian terms, a symbolic castration) catches the imagination far more than if an adversary is cut to pieces. Nothing in the basic story is utterly marvellous (there are a couple of magic objects as extra properties), but nothing is quite right either, and the lack of explanation for the phenomena the heroes are up against prevents any emotional response from being anchored by rationality. Although everything more or less works out in the end (more in the Percy Folio, less in the printed versions), it reaches that conclusion by playing on audience anxiety much more than their propensity for wish-fulfilment.

Fear and desire are the features of a psychological landscape most easily recognized by modern readers, and *Eger and Grime* deploys them in abundance. The sense of modernity perhaps stems partly from the separation of such emotions from conventional morality. Psychology in the Middle Ages and Renaissance was largely deployed in the service of ethics, of virtue and its adversaries, and fear and desire most often figure within ethical topographies. The conscience, the capacity to know good from evil, was regarded not as a repressive Freudian censor but as the most important of all mental faculties, since how you thought and acted, your motives and your attitudes, were ultimately to be judged by God. Within romance, however, the complement of seeking to live a life in accordance with Christian ethics is not inner neurosis, but the outer world of reputation. Christian morality is an expression of a guilt culture, but romance also comprehensively embraces a belief in honour and renown, the public judgement characteristic of a shame culture. The two systems may coincide, but they need not, and romance, the genre poised between the two, sometimes sets them at odds. *Gawain and the Green Knight* recognizes the tension between the two, in Gawain's proclamation of his ideals to the world in the pentangle, and his refusal to claim honour at the expense of conscience: he resists the guide's temptation to avoid the final encounter even though no one would know, and he will not keep the shame of his failure secret. Malory's world operates mostly on shame culture principles, in his knight's desire for 'worship', worthship, the point where renown and the qualities that justify it combine; but the hermits of the Grail quest classify all such desire as pride, and all love as lust. Lancelot's pursuit of the Grail accordingly shifts from being a test of prowess to a test of humility, and his quest from a seeking of worship to an externalized penance.

The shift from shame to guilt, renown to conscience, presents problems for a genre that is so dedicated to the telling of stories, the recording of outward events. Storytelling is itself an agent of renown, Old French *renommée*, the renaming of the hero to maintain the fame he has acquired through action (and it is a fiction of all romances that they serve to maintain, not invent, such glory). Church doctrine, however, increasingly located virtue inwards, where it was not visible to anyone but God and the self. The practice of confession was enjoined on the faithful at the Fourth Lateran Council of 1215, at just the same time as the new genre of romance was being consolidated. Oral confession was necessary because no one could know, unless the sinner told them, what sins he or she had committed; and sins could as well consist of thoughts as actions. The concern of romance with ideal Christian knighthood required some way to encompass this inward sphere of action within its narrative of outward event. Allegory was one solution, with its methodology of giving physical form to psychological and religious experience, to all those things that cannot be directly imitated since they are 'hidden and inward', as Tasso put it in his explanation of the allegory of the *Gerusalemme Liberata*.[74] The romance model was easily adaptable to such representations of the inner life since evil was commonly represented as temptation by the devil. The trial that the questing knight must undergo may set him against a fully diabolic adversary; alternatively, the 'wayfaring Christian' may be cast as a questing knight to allegorize his combat with the devil. The Burgundian chronicler Jean Molinet described chivalry as existing in three forms: the heavenly chivalry exercised by the archangels in the defeat of Lucifer; the spiritual struggle of human champions against temptation; and the prowess performed on the field of battle.[75] The motif of the quest could therefore be taken over by religious writers as well as in romances. The author of the *Ancrene Wisse*, close in date to the Lateran Council, describes the life of the anchoress in just such terms, as a journey through a wilderness in which she is assailed by wild beasts whom she must fight off, using the cross as both weapon and shield.[76] Any concern over the paradox that the anchoress is incapable of physical movement, since she is symbolically immured within her anchor-hold, misses the point: this testing of courage and prowess is spiritual, the quest entirely within the mind and soul. For the enclosed religious, quest and pilgrimage alike could take place without any movement of the body. Not coincidentally, there is one manuscript that contains both the *Conte du Graal* and the Life of St Mary of Egypt: religious search as romance quest juxtaposed with religious search as *peregrinatio in stabilitate*, pilgrimage without movement.[77]

Fear is a state of mind, and some romance terrors are as much inward as outward. They appear to have a physical existence, but disappear when faced up to. Lancelot suffers a rare moment of fear—'he dredde hym sore'—at the Chapel Perilous, when he finds himself facing 'thirty grete knyghtes, more by a yerde than any man that ever he had sene', all in black armour, 'and all they grenned and gnasted at sir Launcelot'; but they scatter when he walks through them, and seem to have no power to hurt him.[78] Lancelot has a particular affinity with such episodes, though his adversaries most often take the shape of lions. There is a move towards such an interior *sentence* in Chrétien's *Chevalier de la Charrette*, in which he has to cross a sword-bridge, the further end of which is guarded by two lions; he crosses the bridge, but finds that they have vanished. As he is wearing a ring that guards against enchantment, he looks at it, but the lions remain vanished: they are, in other words, genuinely not there, rather than being invisible. The passage seems to have puzzled its prose redactor, who has Lancelot fight the lions without being able to hurt them, but when he looks at his ring they disappear. Another editor or scribe, still more puzzled, eliminates them altogether.[79] The invulnerable lions of the prose are clearly a phantom produced by magic; Chrétien's beasts cannot be strictly zoological, since they do disappear, but the impossibility of giving them a precise metaphysical status opens the way to reading them as terrors of the imagination.

Such creatures might sound as if they would lend themselves well to allegory, but they are in fact almost impossible to use, since allegory functions by treating the conceptual as real: psychological lions take the form of real ones within an allegorical narrative. The doubling of literal event and retrospective interpretation in the prose Grail quest, both in French and in Malory, enables a rare combination of the two. Faced with (yet another) pair of lions guarding the entrance to Corbenic, the Grail castle, Lancelot draws his sword to enable him to pass them, only to have it struck out of his hand and a voice condemn him for trusting more to his weapons than to God.

> Than toke he hys swerde agayne and put hit up in hys sheethe, and made a crosse in hys forehede, and cam to the lyons. And they made sembelaunte to do hym harme. Natwithstondynge he passed by them withoute hurte.[80]

Bunyan manages to give a close equivalent in the lions that guard the entrance to the Palace Beautiful. They are chained, but Christian cannot see the chains, and so his walking past them becomes a test of his faith that they will not be able to attack him.[81] For Christian as for Lancelot, facing the things of God can be as terrifying as facing the things of the devil.

The *Quest of the Holy Grail* aimed to get the best of the physical and the spiritual worlds at once, to occupy both the high devotional ground (a taste for secular romances was already calling forth condemnations by preachers) and the peaks of adventure. It may have been written by a Cistercian, or so its frequent references to white monks suggest, but he was clearly an author who, like Bunyan four and a half centuries later, was thoroughly captivated by the genre he distrusted. That the *Quest* forms part of the *Lancelot–Grail* cycle of Arthurian romance, and in due course of Malory's *Morte Darthur*, demonstrates its commitment to romance methods: it may not follow all the generic norms, but it never falls outside the parameters of recognizability. The knights within the story, however, and the readers with them, can find such recognizability misleading.

When Lancelot does the correct chivalric thing and supports the weaker party in a tournament, he is, for once in his life, defeated, since these knights turn out to be the vices in combat with the virtues.[82] What has looked like chivalric quest turns out to operate by a different set of rules: the topography has turned allegorical. The narrative proceeds—or is held up—by frequent obscure dreams and their consequent expositions by hermits, or, on occasion, by false expositions designed to draw the knights astray. The hermits, as that image of 'drawing astray' suggests, take on the function of the guide or the giver of directions, only now those directions are to do with spiritual advance. Those knights who are not chosen to achieve the Grail find at worst death, or at best nothing at all; from time to time they meet up and complain about the lack of adventures. Gawain is the key figure here. He was the first to swear that he would seek the Grail, so instituting the whole quest; but he refuses to take the spiritual steps that would bring him closer to it. After one such episode of exposition, a hermit urges him to do penance for his sin:

'Sir, what penaunce shall I do?'
'Such as I woll gyff the,' seyde the good man.
'Nay,' seyd sir Gawayne, 'I may do no penaunce, for we knyghtes adventures many tymes suffir grete woo and payne.'
'Well,' seyde the good man, and then he hylde hys pece.[83]

No medieval reader would have had difficulty in filling in that laconic monosyllable. Gawain will not embark on the only form of quest that matters here, the quest against the Adversary within him. He eventually comes back to the court, with nothing achieved: his quest has led nowhere. Yet Galahad, the chosen knight whose success is never in doubt, is the least interesting of all the characters, and has nothing resembling an interior life. Bors and Perceval both encounter devils in physical form, and resist them. It is the knight whose conflict against evil takes place within his own mind and who undertakes the most severe penance, Lancelot, who comes to dominate the narrative interest. His success may only be partial, but it is the hardest won, and his struggle towards that engages the imagination far more than Galahad's teflon perfection.

SEEKING FORGIVENESS

Romances are keenly interested in perfectibility, but they are not about perfection. A story about Galahad alone would be an impossibility

('Knight seeks Holy Grail. Succeeds. The end'). Milton continues his discussion of virtue in the *Areopagitica* by imagining untested goodness as having an 'excremental whiteness', like a leprous growth. Achieved virtue, by contrast, the kind that has faced its adversaries, will be dusty and sweaty and not very white at all. Nor, in a fallen world, does one start out in a state of innocence. 'We bring impurity much rather'; what may look like innocence is simply lack of experience, and experience means in the first instance a replay of Original Sin. One of the most widespread forms of romance is the romance of atonement: of failure, penance, and a final forgiveness offered by the story in the restoration of order, harmony, and the unity of the family. Its most familiar exemplar now would be *The Winter's Tale*, with Leontes apparently causing the death of his wife and loss of his heirs through ungrounded jealousy, yet after sixteen years of repentance recovering both his wife and daughter. The structuring of the play as atonement is especially marked by contrast with its source, Greene's *Pandosto*, which ends with the suicide of its Leontes figure.

Such a structure, of initial equilibrium disrupted through sin but with a return to a similar or better order at the end, closely reflects the outward-and-return model of quest romance, and potentially its mirror symmetry. Chrétien's *Yvain*, familiar in Middle English as *Ywain and Gawain*, was the first to make it the scaffolding of a whole romance, though it does so in consistently secular terms. Yvain wins his wife by questing for a particular adventure at a magic spring; she allows him leave to maintain his chivalric reputation in the larger world for a year and a day (that period of time that itself implies circularity), but he is to lose her if he fails to return. He does indeed fail, since he allows his preoccupation with chivalry to drive the time limit from his mind. The rest of the romance sees him clawing his way back from madness and anonymity, first to sanity, then to a different, more socially responsible, kind of questing, and finally to winning both her forgiveness and the right to carry his own name. His lady finally accepts back a hero who is decidedly dusty and sweaty, but who has that experienced virtue, a knowledge of good and evil and therefore also the self-knowledge of his own capacity for both, that is more praiseworthy—more worthy of honour—than mere innocence, or any youthful eagerness for adventure.

Yvain is not written with any coding for religious symbolism, but its potential for development in that direction is evident. The inseparability of romance from its nurturing context in Roman Catholic doctrines is most evident in those texts that allow their sinning heroes the space to make up for their failings and failures. The doctrine of humankind's creation in innocence, the Fall with its introduction of death into the world, and the potential for salvation through God's grace, offers just such an imposition of a happy ending on a process that looks catastrophic. 'Imposition' is indeed the wrong word, since the providential scheme underlying salvation insists that that is the *primary* model, and that an ending in disaster is the perversion, not the norm. The doctrine of the Redemption gave humankind a second chance. It does not guarantee salvation, but it offers the possibility of grace for 'those who truly repent', as the Anglican Prayer Book still has it. The romances shifted such a pattern into the secular world. The knights who have to atone for past failings most often do so within an overtly Christian framework, but they do so by their own efforts or by patient suffering, and are allowed that second chance without the necessity of direct divine intervention (though miracle is by no means ruled out). Tragedy is the genre in which consequences far outweigh initial errors; romance is the genre in which such grim consequences are not the final word, but can be followed by bliss within this world. The romances of atonement offer a this-worldly equivalent to the Church's stress on the forgiveness of sin. Penance was one of the seven sacraments, an outward and visible sign of an inward invisible grace.[84] The high value set on repentance allowed for the transformation of guilt and its associated shame into something more admirable. The achievement of the romances of atonement was to make repentance heroic.

Despite the happy endings of most such works, there is no pretence that the process itself is easy. The bulk of every romance consists of pain, trial, and endurance—that indeed is what gives the concluding happiness its weight. The penitential quest is one of the hardest that there is, and the hardship is emphasized by its romance qualities of excess. A work such as *Sir Isumbras*—one of the most popular and most pious of the romances, surviving in nine manuscripts and in fragments of five printed editions—ensured that the model was thoroughly familiar from the early fourteenth century to the late sixteenth.[85] The work builds a quest structure onto a Job-like model of testing, which incorporates an unusually high proportion of miracle. Isumbras himself, blessed with a wife and three sons, forgets his duty to God; a divine intermediary offers him the choice between suffering in youth or in age, and he chooses youth. Immediately, he loses all his property, and he and his family set off on pilgrimage, only for his sons to be carried off by wild animals (a lion, a leopard, and a unicorn) and his wife by Saracens. He spends seven years as a smith, and then, fighting in armour he has made himself, he defeats a Saracen army in a three-day battle (reminiscent of Christ's descent into Hell, and fore-shadowing Redcrosse's three-day battle against the dragon). He spends seven further years as a palmer, until, near Bethlehem, an angel tells him that his sins are forgiven. He is eventually reunited with his wife, who has aided him initially without recognizing him; together they take on a fur-ther army of Saracens, and are given help by three young men who arrive riding on a lion, a leopard, and a unicorn, and who are, of course, their sons.

The sense of replaying events, of everything happening twice, once for loss and once for restoration, is very clear here. So is the sense of a *felix culpa*, of an initial sin on the model of the Fall, that works out finally for the better. In *Sir Isumbras*, it results not only in the restoration of the family, but in the preservation of Christianity against the Muslim advance: the function of knights is to fight, and the highest fighting is against those regarded as the enemies of God. The processes of penance may be recognizable in terms of chivalric romance, as with Yvain's series of restorative adventures, or they may involve putting chivalry into abeyance, as with Isumbras's years as a smith. One extreme form of penance requires the sinner to act the part of a mute fool at court and to eat only what he can seize from the dogs. Such exemplary expressions of contrition are required of Robert the Devil, who was born under the patronage of the devil, and Sir Gowther, who was fathered by one, and who both display their origins to abundance in early careers of murder and rape.[86] The over-mighty monarch Robert of Sicily (as much a homiletic exemplar as a romance hero, as the appearance of the story in devotional manuscripts testifies) has to endure similar privations after he is displaced as king by an angel, and has to live as a destitute fool beneath the stairs of his own palace. That particular model of holy living was ulti-mately drawn from a saint's life, that of St Alexis, who left his wife on their wedding night and returned as a beggar to his own home, being recognized only at his death.[87] All three secular heroes are allowed for-giveness, and Robert the Devil (in most versions) and Sir Gowther marry emperors' daughters too; but other heroes follow the model of Alexis fur-ther, to turn away from the aristocratic or chivalric life altogether. Guy of Warwick lives his final years unrecognized as a hermit close to his own castle. Valentine ends his days dumb and unrecognized as a holy man within the imperial palace he had once ruled. Renaud of Montaubon, hero of an Old French *chanson de geste* and its English prose descendant *The Four Sons of Aymon*, abandons the chivalric life to become a labourer on Cologne cathedral, and ultimately, after his martyrdom by fellow labourers who do not appreciate his extraordinary capacity for heavy work, a saint.

It might be expected that such fusions of romance with saint's life would be approved in the Middle Ages but condemned at the Reformation, but their reception history is both more complex and more unexpected than that. The medieval Church was not won over by such highly fictionalized displays of piety. Even the most ascetic of them, *Guy of Warwick*, was regularly condemned by preachers and moralists as a distraction from true devotion.[88] The lack of Romish approval finds a strange counterpart in the continuing popularity of such stories across the Reformation. *The Four Sons of Aymon* is frequently cited in sixteenth-century lists of romances, whether as attractive reading-matter (in Captain Cox's list of books or *The Complaynt of Scotland*) or for humanist condemnation (by Nashe, Francis Meres, and others), and a dramatized version was still being acted in the seventeenth century.[89] *Robert the Devil* was rewritten by Thomas Lodge, who livens up his hero's penitential career with an episode of temptation by a promiscuous hamadryad in a wild forest, an episode apparently based on Perceval's temptation by the devil in the guise of a beautiful lady in the course of the Grail quest.[90]

Lodge finished his days as a Roman Catholic, but the appeal of such stories cut across all theological divisions—as did their condemnation. The replicability of romance memes, their capacity to stick in the mind like burrs and multiply, took priority over both the theological resonances attaching to them and recurrent moral disapproval. The one time when preachers paused in their condemnation of romances was in the early fifteenth century, when the threat of Lollardy, England's one home-grown heresy, was associated with the reading of vernacular religious works, and romances suddenly seemed a preferable option—even those, or especially those, with minimal devotional content.[91] Strict Protestants in the following century reversed the order of priorities, to condemn frivolous worldly reading and approve Holy Writ. Nothing made any difference to the continuing popularity of the romances themselves, however, and it was left to John Bunyan to combine the two forms, to offer 'truth within a fable'[92] from the happy conjunction of the Bible and *Bevis of Hamptoun*. Christian's chivalric quest and his life of penance, undertaken as a search for salvation, are one and the same. The stereoscopic focus, the merging of two compelling images into one of greater power, ensured that *Pilgrim's Progress* remained as central within English-speaking culture for the next three and a half centuries as *Bevis* had been for the previous four. Bevis had demonstrated his piety in opposition to the Saracen enemies of Christendom; Christian exemplifies a Calvinism strictly defined by its difference from other forms of Christianity. Even so, Bunyan does not shrink from using motifs characteristic of Roman Catholicism, whether devotional practices such as pilgrimage, or literary motifs such as the seductive woman of the Grail Quest and Lodge's *Robert the Devil.* Bunyan's equivalent is the witch who has charmed the Enchanted Ground, and who tells Mr Standfast, 'I am the Mistriss of the World, and men are made happy by me.'[93] The devil in various forms is the most fearsome adversary, but wrong doctrine comes a close second. Bunyan's characters are as rigorously selected for success in their quest for salvation as are the knights of the Grail. However exemplary he may be for the reader, Bunyan's Christian is not Everyman. His fellow travellers may on occasion precede him to heaven, but many more never make it. In the last two sentences of the work, the Anglican of the cast-list, named Ignorance, is ejected into Hell through a trapdoor at the very gates of Heaven. The idea that the quest is in some sense unique to the individual knight, the one who has the courage and the will to take the adventure that God will send him, translates here into predestination, into God's own election of the man who is to succeed on the quest. The doctrinal divisions that emerged within Protestantism are by this time much more insidious dangers than the advance of the Saracens that occupied earlier romance heroes, and even Reformation fears of the recovery of Catholicism can be presented as being as safely in the past as the classical gods:

I espied a little before me a cave, where two giants, Pope and Pagan, dwelt in old time, by whose power and tyranny the men whose bones, blood, ashes, etc. lay there, were cruelly put to death. But by this place Christian went without much danger, whereat I somewhat wondered; but I have learnt since, that Pagan has been dead many a day; and as for the other, though he be yet alive, he is by reason of age, and also of the many shrewd brushes that he met with in his younger dayes, grown so crazy and stiff in his joynts, that he can now do little more than sit in his caves mouth, grinning at Pilgrims as they go by, and biting his nails, because he cannot come at them. (p. 192)

As the crisis over James II was to indicate just a few years later, Pope was in practice by no means as moribund as Bunyan claims; but his very mockery serves to cut the giant down to size, to make him appear not worth following.

Early Reformation England was not so particular about precise theological justification for its reading. *Guy of Warwick*, which has Romish practices too deeply embedded in its narrative to remove, was also one of the most popular. It combined the attractions of dragon- and giant-killing with penance, sexual renunciation, pilgrimage, and withdrawal to a hermitage, and finally rejected a conventional happy ending in this world. Despite that—perhaps because of it, since it offered the familiarity of both romance and traditional devotional narrative models such as were increasingly disapproved elsewhere—it enjoyed a quite remarkable popularity over many centuries, gradually disappearing from sight only a century or so ago. Like so many penitential romances, it is structured as a diptych, and makes the parallelism of the two parts unusually explicit. In the first half, Guy quests across Europe in search of a reputation as the 'best knight', that being the price that the lady he loves, Felice, daughter of the earl of Warwick, has demanded for her hand in marriage. Her name may associate her with felicity, with bliss, but the bliss of earthly love here is not enough. Within a few weeks of their marriage, he realizes, looking up at the stars from that same tower at which he had earlier gazed at his beloved,[94] that all his prowess has been devoted to her service and not to God's, and he leaves her, pregnant with the son who is to continue the line of Warwick earls. He takes a vow of celibacy, and sets out to replay his earlier conquests, but now against God's enemies rather than chivalric opponents. He becomes a palmer, goes on pilgrimage to the Holy Land, and eventually returns to England, where Athelstan is inspired by a vision to select him as the English champion to fight the giant Colbrand, champion of the pagan Danes. After overcoming him, he returns unrecognized to Warwick; receives alms at his own castle gate from the hands of his wife; and eventually dies as a hermit in a nearby cave, having revealed himself to Felice moments earlier after an angel had warned him of his impending death. The romance, in other words, replays the chivalric quest of its first half as penitential pilgrimage in its second half, overwriting secular adventures undertaken for honour and one's lady with spiritual seeking and with deeds of prowess performed anonymously and for the sake of God.

With his conversion of quest into pilgrimage, his renunciation of sex even within marriage, and his angelically-announced death as a hermit, Guy is a hero who has no right to survive the Reformation, but the theological upheavals did not dent his popularity. The medieval romance, in a version of some 8,000 lines, was frequently reprinted until about 1570. His preservation may have been helped by the fact that he was regarded as the ancestral hero of the house of Warwick; Robert Dudley, earl of Leicester and younger brother of the Elizabethan earl of Warwick, had an expensive genealogy made to show his descent from his famous forebear.[95] In 1584 Richard Lloyd recruited him to the ranks of the Nine Worthies (in place of the usual Godfrey of Bulloigne, thus enabling the British/English to outnumber the French two to one among the three Christians of the set), but added a Protestant coda deploring the lack of knowledge of the Bible shown by his hero in his opting to go on pilgrimage to Jerusalem 'to obtaine remission for his sinfull life',

> With punishing his bodie so, as then it was the wonted use,
> Which of repentance plain doth sho a token, thogh through
>   great abuse,
> For want of knowledge of the truth, of holie scriptures:
>   the more ruth.[96]

By 1600 Lloyd's biography of Guy (without this moralizing coda) had become a bestseller as a broadside ballad, and remained so for well over a century. By 1607, Samuel Rowlands felt no need to be apologetic about his hero's Catholicism in his twelve-canto version, noting merely that his withdrawal from the world was typical of the 'devotion of that age'.[97] His one concession to changing theological principles, or changing popular taste, was to fit into his final canto Guy's greatest exploit, the combat with Colbrand, as well as his retreat to a hermitage and sanctified death, so that the culmination of the story is as much chivalric as pious. As the decades and centuries passed, palmers and hermits were losing their edge of political danger and becoming merely quaint.

The ecclesiastical incorrectness of the story makes it especially surprising to find as a favourite subject for the Renaissance stage, despite its potential for irritating the puritan opposition. It was dramatized perhaps as many as four times between 1580 and 1620. Only one text survives, entitled *The Tragical History of Guy Earle of Warwick*, composed in strongly Marlovian verse. It may date from *c*.1593, if an apparent allusion in it to Shakespeare as the newly-published poet of *Venus and Adonis* is to be trusted.[98] The play is notable too for the way it seizes the initiative on Guy's piety, adding in some satirical remarks about the puritan resistance to Archbishop Whitgift's attempts to impose uniformity of clerical vestments in the Church of England.[99] It treats a hermit Guy meets as a respected holy man, not an impostor, and never questions the virtue attaching to Guy's twenty-seven-year 'long pilgrimage'. Just before his death, Guy is given a long statement of his creed, which he speaks in a

tone of affective piety much more reminiscent of the Catholic wing of the
Church than of Calvinist rigour. God, he declares, made man as the only
element of Creation to contain 'the breath of heaven':

> Yet he that late was fram'd of mire and filth,
> Plac'd in a glorious state of innocence,
> Was not content, but striv'd to be as good
> As his great Maker, who could with one word,
> Throw him down headlong to the deepest Hell;
> Yet he in Mercy, Love, and meer good will,
> Did grant him pardon for his foul offence;
> And seeing him unable to perform
> His blessed will, did send his own dear Son
> To pay his ransome with his precious blood,
> And to redeem that soul which sinful man,
> Had forfeited to Satan, Death and Hell;
> And for a death dam'd cursed and unpure,
> He gave him life eternal to indure;
> Which life eternal, grant sweet Christ to me,
> That in Heavens joyes I may thy glory see.[100]

Guy's life and death fuse romance structure with the whole of salvation
history, from his initial untestedness, through his reckless desire for glory,
to the new virtue derived from repentance that enables his entry to
Heaven. The designation of 'tragical history' for the play gives it a secular
emphasis at odds with the piety of its ending. It probably means no more
than that it ends with the death of the hero; but it calls attention to the dif-
ference of this story from the other romances of atonement that allow the
hero the restoration of his earthly happiness before his pious death. The
centre of heroism in *Guy* shifts from earthly chivalry undertaken for love
of one's lady, through prowess performed for God, to the final journey that
takes Guy beyond this world: 'for life and pilgrimage must end together'.

Guy's penitence is modelled particularly closely on the life of St Alexis,
who embarked on his life of penance on his wedding night; Guy does,
however, wait before he leaves his wife until he has begotten the Warwick
heir, rather than before losing his virginity.[101] That dynastic emphasis
puts the story at odds with the transcendent concerns of a saint's life, and
so does the further nationalistic turn that the story acquired in the
account of Guy's combat with Colbrand. On the strength of that, he
entered chronicle history as part of Athelstan's resistance to the Danes.[102]
The combat typically figures as an *exemplum* of God's support of the

English against pagan invaders, an altogether safer message for the story to carry through the Reformation than his rejection of the world. Rowlands hails Guy as 'our famous Countryman', and addresses a dedicatory epistle to 'the noble English nation'. Sober Renaissance historians were however becoming increasingly sceptical. Holinshed allots him a single heavily qualified sentence,[103] and John Selden refrains from any comment at all in his notes to Drayton's enthusiastic account of the combat in *Poly-Olbion*. Drayton has it please 'all-powerfull heaven' that Guy should arrive at Winchester to meet up with Athelstan's vision-inspired search for a champion for the English, and the penitential nature of his pilgrimage is somewhat mitigated by the fact that his palmer's staff is actually a swordstick.[104] The persistent popularity of the story in narrative, ballad, and drama does however show the continuing acceptance of ideas of sexual renunciation, pilgrimage, and the penitent's outward 'punishing his bodie' long after they had been rejected by the established Church, though by the late sixteenth century few people seem to have thought of the legend as containing any reproducible model of the religious life.

The ubiquity of *Guy of Warwick* in its various forms makes Spenser's use of the legend in Book II of the *Faerie Queene* particularly interesting: name your hero Guyon, the standard variant on Guy, and you are inviting an intertextual reading not just from the educated but from every possible reader. Guy's Romish renunciation of the world is accordingly rewritten as Protestant temperance. Guyon too has an ambivalent relationship with chivalry, though in his case not by choice: his horse, the *cheval* of chivalry that gives the knight his literal high visibility,[105] is stolen from him by Braggadocchio, the braggart who is all show and no substance. Guyon, as the knight of Temperance, is all substance and no show—temperance, as C. S. Lewis noted, being a thoroughly pedestrian virtue.[106] Guy similarly abandoned the outward trappings of chivalry to travel on foot as a palmer, though he abandoned his armour too, whereas Guyon's armour stands for the protection offered by the virtue itself, and so cannot be set aside. Guyon's palmer comes not as his alternative self but as his accompanying attribute, the Reason associated with Temperance by virtue of its opposition to passion. The prospect of future marriage is not forbidden to Guyon—and given the emphasis of the poem on proper heterosexual love within marriage, it scarcely could be— but the only lady he serves is his feudal mistress. Arthur, according to Geoffrey of Monmouth, bore the image of the Virgin on his shield, and the Gawain of *Gawain and the Green Knight* carries her image on the inside of his (648–50). Guyon looks as if he shares their piety, but his is both less Catholic and more secular: the 'faire image of that heavenly Mayd' on his shield (II. i. 28) is Gloriana. She is 'my liefe, my liege, my Soveraigne, my deare' (II. ix. 4), an intermingling that casts Guyon as suitor or lover as well as vassal. He assumes that Arthur's highest ambition is to become one of her knights (II. ix. 6), and Arthur tactfully avoids disabusing him. That last detail is a measure of how fully Spenser imagines his narrative; but there is an allegorical agenda behind Guyon's association with Gloriana just as there is behind his association with the palmer. Of all the virtue knights, he is the one who serves her most closely; or, to put it another way, temperance is the virtue most closely integrated with her person. Gloriana may be heading towards marriage with Arthur within the narrative, but, outside it, Elizabeth can share Guyon's distance from sexuality as the practice of a Protestant virtue.

The refiguring of Guy as Guyon bends the line of penitential romance back towards a celebration of the political and the secular. Guyon is unusual among Spenser's male protagonists in that he does not need to undergo penance for deeds misdone. He is tempted, but, unlike Redcrosse or Arthegall (though like the ideal Elizabeth), he does not fall. The closest Spenser comes to the romance of atonement is not in Book II, where Guyon scarcely puts a foot wrong (and must not: for some of the time, he has a fiend stalking behind him waiting for the slightest misstep, II. vii. 26–7), but in Book I, where Redcrosse has to pull himself back from a series of failures in faith, hope, and chivalry before he is allowed a distant glimpse of the New Jerusalem. Holiness has a particularly hard time in this Protestant epic, since the temptations that traditionally beset attempts at living a holy life are compounded by the pull of different theologies. The richest and most resonant religious symbolism was Catholic, but Spenser, like Bunyan, was happy to exploit such symbolism so long as it was allegorical. The Reformation had rejected practices such as withdrawal from the world, the mortification of the flesh, and pilgrimage, and outside Elizabethan England iconic virginity too, though the queen was treated as unique in such matters. Both Spenser's characters and his readers can therefore never be quite sure whether a traditional religious image is going to turn out to be inward and spiritual or outward and papist. Hermits may be either Catholic and therefore bad (Archimago, the archhypocrite, first appears in that form), or with mystical insight and therefore good (as is Contemplation). Despair had long been recognized as one of the major threats to the mental stability of those who would be holy, and Spenser carries that through from a Catholic to a Protestant context; but the seductive Duessa, who temporarily turns Redcrosse aside from his quest, is now not just a Catholic allegory for the devil but Catholicism itself. Dragons had symbolized the devil from the Bible forwards, and the beast that Redcrosse finally overcomes to rescue Una's parents is out of that stable; but the first monster he encounters, Error, with its vomit of books and papers, is a creature of theological controversy. After the batterings he receives from Error and various pagan champions, his abandonment of his damsel, his imprisonment by the giant Orgoglio, and his temptation to despair, he is more than ready for the recuperation offered in the House of Holiness; but that recuperation itself takes the Catholic form of ashes, sackcloth, fasting, and scourgings (I. x. 26–7).

Redcrosse's doctor throughout this process is Patience. Spenser presumably thought of the intense mortification of the flesh as a symbolic rather than a literal requirement, but patience *is* required, though its embodiment must come in the sinner himself. The penances endured by Isumbras and Guy, Robert the Devil and Robert of Sicily, similarly require a long and patient acceptance of suffering. Rosemond Tuve, in an essay linking Redcrosse to the medieval devil-begotten penitents, makes the further point that it is crucial that he is mortal, not fairy: only those of human origin, or with at least one human parent, can achieve salvation, and the patient endurance of suffering attendant on penitence only has meaning within the framework of mortality.[107] When Shakespeare turned to similar models in his last plays, the form of patient penitence was deeply familiar, though—whether because of stage censorship or a deliberate humanism—he substitutes classical gods for explicit Christian doctrine. Conspicuous outward forms of penance do not seem to have interested him; but patience dominates the penitence of Leontes, and Pericles' long years of grief. Pericles' sufferings are imposed by the evil of others or by chance rather than in recompense for any offences against the gods, but his restoration takes place under the aegis of Diana. *The Winter's Tale* is similarly pagan in its theophany, but its conclusion, when Leontes' years of penitence are rewarded by the resurrection of Hermione, is conducted in insistently Christian language:

> Bequeath to death your numbness, for from him
> Dear life redeems you.

> 5.3.102–3

Leontes and Hermione enjoy a redemption that is predicated as fully human, fully secular, a happiness within this world. Pericles' intensity of joy enables him to hear the music of the spheres, that harmony normally inaudible to mortals. *Cymbeline* similarly offers forgiveness and restoration in the eyes of both the gods and human characters to Posthumus after his grievous crimes against his wife. These are the endings that come closest to a representation of that hardest of all states to make plausible, bliss; and they come not after aspiration and achievement, but as atonement after failure.

THE JOURNEY OF THE SOUL

The reunited Sir Isumbras and his family live in such a state of happiness, but not for ever after. In due course, we are told, they die, and find eternal bliss in Heaven. The interchangeability of time and space may allow for the representation of life as a journey, but, for all the resurrections that romances contain, the journey of life is finally one-way. Life as quest does not allow of return, and even King Arthur does not come back. The closer quest comes to pilgrimage, the more likely it is to pass out of this world altogether. The point of the journey undertaken by Bunyan's Christian is *not to come back*: the City of Destruction must be left behind for ever if the Celestial City is to be achieved. Guy may come back to Warwick twice, but only on the first occasion, when his reputation as best knight in the world enables him to marry the earl's daughter, does he bring his new capacities to the service of his own society. The object of his second return, as an unrecognized hermit, is to resist assimilation. He is within reach of his wife and his castle, but he is in exile for as long as he lives within the world, and the felicity he looks for is no longer Felice.

Guy of Warwick and *The Pilgrim's Progress* both merge quest with pilgrimage: *Guy* sequentially; Bunyan by fusing the two. Both kinds of journey suggest both geographical and mental travelling, but pilgrimage distinguishes itself from quest in three significant ways. First, a pilgrimage is almost always made to a known destination—Canterbury, or Compostela, or Jerusalem. Even the most spiritual of pilgrimages has its goal, what Chaucer's Parson describes as 'Jerusalem celestial'. Second, while quests are the prerogative of knights-errant, pilgrimages are open to every wayfaring Christian. The Reformation may have condemned the geographical pilgrimage, but the spiritual kind, as Bunyan demonstrates, retained a remarkably comprehensive hold over the imagination. The quest as pilgrimage is quest democratized. (The outward symbol of that inclusiveness is that pilgrims travelled—or were supposed to travel—on foot: the horse, which raises the knight literally and figuratively above the common people, is replaced by humble 'sandal shoon'.) Third, although most pilgrims expected to return home, that was not the object. Every pilgrimage was a potential allegory of that one-way journey to 'Jerusalem celestial'. A pilgrimage was a penitential act, and dying in the course of it was often taken as equivalent to dying in a state of grace, a direct transition from the physical journey to its spiritual goal.

Crusading linked the two forms, quest and pilgrimage. A crusade was a military expedition to exotic lands, and required all the prowess, stamina, and chivalric equipment of the well-exercised knight. It was also a journey for God; and the early crusades to recover the Holy Land were chivalric journeys to the greatest of all the Christian shrines, where Christ Himself had lived and died and risen. For the participants in the First Crusade, fighting for God may have appeared a natural extension to fighting for a feudal lord, but a journey to Jerusalem was far more than just a journey over physical distance. As the *mappae mundi* showed, Jerusalem was at the centre of a world represented in two dimensions, and for immediate practical purposes its third dimension was most likely to be thought of as spiritual. Sir John Mandeville's travel book served both as a semi-reliable guide to the Holy Land and its surroundings, and as a guide to a spiritual journey. Succumb to the temptation of picking up the gold scattered around in his Vale Perilous, and the devils will carry you off through the entrance to Hell that debouches there.[108] Direct knowledge of the Holy Land, a country of real lions and real Saracens, fuelled the marvels of romance more than it tamed them. Some crusaders settled in the land beyond the sea, 'Outremer'; many others returned home, with tales that sounded every bit as exotic as romances and that no doubt lost nothing in the telling. But returning from a crusade, as from a pilgrimage, was not the point. 'What man of spirit,' Gerald of Wales records one volunteer for the Third Crusade as saying, 'can hesitate for a moment to undertake this journey when, among the many hazards, none could be more unfortunate, none could cause greater distress, than the prospect of coming back alive?'[109]

Since allegory is concerned with inward matters, and therefore most often with the soul rather than the body, allegorical quests are the most likely to take one-way form. The shock of Balin's statement as he rides down the path marked for his destruction, 'I wold be fayne there my deth shold be', comes from its contradiction of expectation within chivalric romance. Christian's near-identical statement by contrast falls naturally within his spiritual questing: 'I would fain be where I shall die no more.'[110] The similarity of expression does, however, conceal a radical difference of desire: one for death; the other for the bliss of eternal life. Galahad, the perfect Grail knight whose quest culminates in death, initially inherits Balin's sword: it has inflicted the Dolorous Stroke that he must heal, but it is also a symbol of the path that does not allow of any return.[111] It had always been difficult to find an object of desire that could live up to the imaginative power exercised by the quest, and if not death itself, then something beyond this world, such as the Grail came to signify, was the ultimate such object. Chrétien seems not yet to have worked out what his Grail might stand for, and death for his hero is not apparently among the options. What does seem clear is that his Perceval, like Wolfram von Eschenbach's Parzival, is set for a return to happiness with his beloved within this world after completing his own romance of atonement, making up for his failure to ask the question at the castle of the Fisher King. Robert de Boron and the redactors of the prose *History* and *Quest of the Holy Grail* had other ideas. By turning the Grail into the vessel of the Last Supper, they made it a figure for transubstantiation itself, the moment when physical substance becomes spiritual: a moment made visible in the *Quest*'s representations of the Mass.[112] Appearing shortly after the Fourth Lateran Council had spelled out the doctrine of transubstantiation, these texts are deeply imbricated in their particular historical moment, in endorsing and disseminating the new dogmatic formulation; Malory's redaction 250 years later similarly acquires a new historical specificity, in the wake of the Lollard attack on the same doctrine. The claim made by the prose quest for the Grail is that it is a moment of contact of time and eternity, an act of transcendence of the earthly. It would be a betrayal of everything this Grail is about if Galahad were to return. Instead, he leaves this world in an ecstasy of fulfilled desire, in the course of a Mass conducted by the son of Joseph of Arimathea.

And so he cam to the sakerynge [consecration of the host], and anone made an ende. He called sir Galahad unto hym and seyde, 'Com forthe, the servaunte of Jesu Cryste, and thou shalt se that thou hast much desired to se.'

And than he began to tremble ryght harde when the dedly fleysh began to beholde the spirituall thynges. Than he hylde up his hondis towarde hevyn and seyde, 'Lorde, I thanke The, for now I se that that hath be my desire many a day. Now, my Blyssed Lorde, I wold nat lyve in this wrecched worlde no lenger, if it myght please The, Lorde.'

He receives the Host and says farewell to his companions, 'and so suddeynly departed hys soule to Jesu Cryste, and a grete multitude of angels bare hit up to hevyn evyn in the syght of hys two felowis'.[113]

The Grail quest achieves the difficult feat of treating *sentence* as *matter*, inward meaning as literal narrative. The claim it makes is that the adventures of the quest are as much part of Arthurian history as the sword in the stone, or Lancelot's affair with Guinevere. Those who try to act as if it were a chivalric quest, however, go badly wrong. Mention has already been made of Lancelot's support of the weaker party of knights who turn out to represent the sins, and of his misapprehension in drawing his sword on the lions who guard the castle of the Grail. The 'right' way is on occasion signposted—or, to be precise, an inscription warns against the left-hand way.[114] The chosen knights frequently have to abandon their horses to embark on rudderless boats, so handing over their will to prowess to the will of God; and those boats and the cargo they carry may themselves come with inscriptions that insist that they are something more, or other, than material objects. 'Thou man whych shalt entir into thys shippe,' reads one such inscription, 'beware that thou be in stede-faste beleve, for I am Faythe. And therefore beware how thou entirst but if thou be stedfaste, for and thou fayle thereof I shall nat helpe the.'[115] The sword and scabbard the companions find on board bear similar threats. Such things constitute not so much adventures or tests as proofs: they confirm what the reader already knows, that Galahad and his companions are uniquely chosen for the roles they play. The ship Faith is itself an earthly construction, designed by Solomon's wife, and containing wood from the tree planted by Eve and under which Abel was slain, but those antecedents distinguish it from any other material vessel. Unlike other ships, it does not take the knights anywhere, or provide the means of travelling between two places. Its role is rather to be a means of access in itself between the physical and spiritual worlds. Such access is more often provided by visions, which are interwoven with the more obviously chivalric adventures and to an extent constitute those adventures. The Grail quest is unique in the amount of time its chosen knights spend asleep, and without that sleep representing a slothful abandonment of the quest. 'And so he leyde hym downe and slepte', we are told of Lancelot, 'and toke the aventure that God wolde sende hym', sleep now being an adventure in itself.[116] Associated visions often take emblematic form: a woman riding on a serpent, a lily ripe for corruption, voices speaking enigmatic metaphors about barren fig-trees.

Allegory and dream are closely related, in that both offer non-material narratives (Holiness is a personification, not a person; the figments of your dreams do not have any physical existence outside the structures of your brain), and both require interpretation. Texts that set out to represent the journey of life or the soul therefore often take the form of allegorical dream visions, with that journey itself represented as quest or pilgrimage, or often as a combination of the two. Bunyan's work is a latecomer in a very long tradition of such works. Most of them are religious in orientation, but not all: one of the most famous, the thirteenth-century French *Romance of the Rose*, is an allegory not of the whole of life but of the lover's quest for his lady, or rather, in Jean de Meun's continuation of the work, for his lady's virginity. The poem ends with a cheerfully blasphemous pilgrimage image, in which the lover enters her shrine with his pilgrim's staff, in a thoroughly secular satisfaction of desire.[117] Something of the same suggestion, in a non-allegorical narrative, lurks behind the welcome to two of Tasso's Christian knights as 'fortunati peregrin', happy pilgrims, as they approach Armida's paradise of lust.[118]

Most visionary quests take themselves rather more seriously, even when their focus is this-worldly. There was quite a fashion for these in the hundred and fifty years up to 1600. One that claims to derive its inspiration from the unlikely mixture of the Grail quest and Jean de Meun is René of Anjou's *Livre du Cuers d'amours espris*, 'the book of the love-smitten Heart', which tells of the quest of the dreamer's heart, accompanied by Desire, to free Sweet Mercy from Shame and Fear.[119] The narrative proceeds with a sequence of adventures of a kind familiar from earlier chivalric texts (the spilling of water from a basin causing a storm, as in *Yvain*; the Heart's falling through a trapdoor into a prison, as happens to Lancelot from the *Chevalier de la Charrette* to Malory) intermingled with emblematic set-pieces, such as the Heart's arming with allegorical armour, or an account of tapestries showing various aspects of passion. This method, of alternating active adventures, usually taking place outdoors, with static emblems typically displayed on or inside buildings, remains the norm for allegorical quests down to and including Spenser—and indeed Bunyan, whose Interpreter's House collects up just such an emblematic series.

Neither author will have known René's work, but there are other more devotional allegories that operate on similar principles and which may well have influenced Spenser. One of these is the first fully chivalric allegory in English, Stephen Hawes's *Example of Vertue*, which went through at least three editions before 1530. This looks as if it is going to be a love-quest, since its protagonist, Youth (the Youth who later earns the new name of Virtue), is introduced walking in a 'medow amerous', and undergoes his various perilous adventures, including overcoming a three-headed dragon, in order to win the hand of the daughter of the God of Love. This is explicitly not a worldly quest, however. In cutting off the first two of the dragon's three heads, representing the World and the Flesh, the knight is conquering 'flesshly desyre' (1458). The third head, representing the devil, contains no flesh or bone and so cannot be killed, rather as some of Spenser's antagonists cannot be overcome; the most the knight can do is to drive him down to 'his derke regyon | Of infernall payne' (1480–2). The lady herself is named Cleanness (purity), and Virtue is eventually married to her by that master polemicist of the virtues of virginity over marriage, St Jerome.[120] By the time their wedding feast finishes, Virtue is 60 years old; and the kingdom his bride brings him, or brings him to, is Heaven, which he proceeds to see in an inset vision after a parallel tour of Hell. The narrative section of the poem ends by dispatching the pair to 'Joye eternall' (2040)—an ending to the quest from which Virtue can no more return than he can recover his former incarnation as Youth. The strangest thing about the text is the difficulty of discovering whether it is in favour of literal sexuality (the God of Love's half-naked state is described as representing the desire that 'true love' feels for the 'very persone and eke body | That he so well and fervently loveth', 1324–7), or whether it is denouncing it. If Spenser did know the work, as seems likely, he found his own Anglican solution to the Catholic equation of the highest virtue with total celibacy. In Carol Kaske's formulation, 'part of his delight in allegory sprang from the fact that *eros* could be made to symbolize *agape*',[121] and as a Protestant he did not need to make any literal rejection of the one before it could symbolize the other.

Part of the attraction of allegorical texts of this kind lies in the illustrations that accompany them. The most famous manuscript of René's work, illuminated under his own direction, contains many of the finest visual representations of the questing knight in existence. *The Example of Vertue* is illustrated by a series of woodcuts closely similar in content and style to those used for early printed romances. They do not insist on their inner meanings: the picture of Pride riding on an elephant might have stepped across from a travel account of oriental wonders, and Youth's combat with the dragon is distinguishable from Bevis's or Eglamour's only by the interlocking symbol of the Trinity on his shield, looking rather like a triple equivalent of Gawain's fivefold pentangle.[122] Spenser's detailed visual imagination converts such emblematic figures into vivid verbal icons. Anne Lake Prescott has argued for Spenser's knowledge of a further allegorical text, Stephen Bateman's *The Travayled Pilgrim* (1569), largely on the basis of its illustrations, which spell out their figurative meanings—the arming of the knight with allegorical armour, the virtues in the House of Reason, and so on—in captions accompanying the pictures.[123] Bateman's title disguises the fact that not only is this a chivalric allegory—his protagonist sets out as a knight in quest of adventure—but also a translation of the *Chevalier délibéré* of Olivier de La Marche, the same text as was translated again twenty-five years later by Lewes Lewkenor as *The Resolved Gentleman*.[124] Both English titles indicate their authors' sense that knighthood no longer carried conviction as a living ideal, but where Lewkenor goes for a social equivalent, Bateman emphasizes the allegorical pilgrimage lying beneath the allegorical quest. For this too is a one-way journey of life, in which the adversary that the hero must face is the invincible Death.

The *Faerie Queene* would not have appeared unfamiliar to its sixteenth-century readers. Not only its giants, and dragons, and fairy queen, but its great emblematic set pieces, its exemplary protagonists, the allegorical nature of the quests they undergo, and the landscapes they inhabit were all part of the culture into which Spenser and his readers were born and educated. None of his methods would have presented any of the difficulties found in them by modern readers brought up on realist fiction. This does not mean that every detail of his allegorical meanings teased out by recent scholars would have been apparent to them, but his methods would have been much more open, and therefore all such meanings more easily accessible, not just because the topical and historical were matters of immediate import but because the structures of thought were equally of immediate import. Even the two devices used by many of the earlier allegorists but not by Spenser can be of help in reading his work: dream, and the conflation of quest with pilgrimage. Dream allows for the elimination of everything not directly significant. Characters do not need to cover ground to get one from locus of adventure to the next, since the significance itself makes the transition. Settings, when they are mentioned at all, are psychological, not localized. In dreams as in allegories, 'then' stands for 'therefore': cause and effect are figured as chronological sequence. Interpretation, furthermore, is separate from action. Spenser does not generally supply any equivalent to the hermits of the Grail quest who interpret visions and actions retrospectively, but he does *name* retrospectively. New characters or places are encountered, their qualities demonstrated in action and learned through experience, but only then is the name attached to them, in a process analogous to the waking from and rational analysis of dream.

Spenser does not obviously turn his quests into journeys to heaven, for all his familiarity with *Guy of Warwick* and probably Hawes and Bateman. The figuring of life as pilgrimage is none the less a powerful subtext in Book I in particular, the book that gives its protagonist a glimpse of 'the new Hierusalem' and sets him in apocalyptic opposition to the Dragon. Its slaughter is not the end of Redcrosse's chivalric career, however. Archimago and Duessa make a final attempt to prevent the union of Holiness and Truth; and when Una's father invites him to enjoy 'everlasting rest' (I. xii. 17), he refuses. He has promised to go back, to aid the Faerie Queene for six more years in her war against 'that proud Paynim king'. Spenser allows a joyous celebration of the betrothal of Redcrosse and Una, but he postpones their marriage beyond the end of the book, and the poem.[125] Spenser's concern with this world rules out an ending in Heaven. His poem is about the continuing struggle of life in the world, the struggle in which both his characters and his readers are continuously engaged. It is only in the very last words of the *Mutabilitie Cantos* that he allows himself to look beyond that, in his prayer for the time when

> all shall rest eternally
> With him that is the God of Sabaoth hight.
>
> VII. viii. 2

'All' are embarked on that one-way journey; but his poem is a narrative of quest, not of pilgrimage. The roads may overlap, but Spenser's concern, even in his Legend of Holiness, is not with transcendence but with the action of his virtues in the world of Elizabethan England.

CHAPTER TWO

Providence and the sea:
'No tackle, sail, nor mast'

> You have none now, that coming . . . [to] a barren
> and desart shore of the sea, most commonly stormy
> and unquiet; and finding at the brinke of it some lit-
> tle cock-boat, without oares, saile, mast, or any kinde
> of tackling, casts himselfe into it with undaunted
> courage, yeelds himselfe to the implacable waves of
> the deepe maine, that now tosse him as high as
> heaven, and then cast him as low as hell.[1]

Don Quixote's conviction that a boat carrying no equipment for steering
or propulsion was a guarantee of providential adventure was based on a
couple of millennia of literary experience. Romance was a comparative
latecomer in adopting the motif, though as Cervantes illustrates, it had
done so wholeheartedly. Over the centuries it had acquired a large and
often contradictory-seeming set of associations—with guilt and pollu-
tion, with sanctity, with political threat and its removal, with chivalric
election, with women—but the meme at the core of all these remained
exceptionally coherent, exceptionally faithful in its replication, not least
by comparison with the sprawling variations on the quest. The coherence
lies in the phrasing and cadences that describe the rudderless boat, and
which remain essentially the same across many centuries and languages:
a boat without oars, sail, mast, or any kind of tackling; with neither sail
nor oar; no rudder, oar, nor helmsman; neither sails nor oars, rudder nor
rigging; no tackle, sail, nor mast. The identifying phrases stand out from
texts in Latin and Old Norse, Anglo-Norman and Middle High German;
they are as recognizable in *Sir Eglamour* or the *Quest of the Holy Grail* as
they are in Greene's *Pandosto*, or *The Tempest*, or *Don Quixote* itself. They
remain the same whether the vessels are tiny, just big enough to take a
baby, or full seagoing ships; whether the journey is readily undertaken as

an act of chivalric adventure, as Don Quixote envisages, or against the will of the boat's occupant.

The phrases announce a story motif, a narrative building-block of strong imaginative power. They also indicate that the story will have some inherent meaning. Such a voyage is never accidental, however unwilled or unintended it may be by the boat's occupant. The range of possible meanings is, however, huge by comparison with the brevity of the identifying phrases, even though these boats are not allegorical. They are real vessels, not ships of Fortune, or fools, or the state, or Love, or the Church.[2] Much more predictable than the meaning of such stories is their outcome. The very danger of being adrift in a rudderless boat was so extreme as to make death likely, and survival therefore almost the only worthwhile narrative option: the only one that will carry suspense, no matter how much the reader may predict it.

A journey in such a vessel was normally a terrifying business, as Don Quixote's description acknowledges. That is half the delight of his own experience in 'a little boat, without oares or any other kinde of tackling' in which he embarks a few chapters later.[3] His insouciance at under-taking the adventure is helped by the fact that he is merely floating down a river (though the boat comes to grief in a mill-race a few yards down-stream, shortly after he has required Sancho Panza to carry out the 'louse test' to discover whether they have yet crossed the equator, it being well known that lice cannot survive equatorial heat). The kind of voyage he envisages casts the boat as a *barca aventurosa*, in the phrasing of Italian chivalric romance, a magic vessel dedicated to adventure.[4] But much the greatest number of voyagers in rudderless boats are victims rather than agents, cast adrift at sea because their society wishes to dispose of them. Both historically and in story, it was a way of getting rid of the transgres-sive (certain types of criminals), the polluted (such as the children of incest), or the dangerous (rival claimants to power). The knight-errant rides out from his society, or on occasion is carried away by his magic boat, and returns; most travellers in unsteerable vessels are ejected by their community by a means that makes it as sure as possible that they will not come back.

Heroic prowess, or indeed any kind of deliberate action, is largely eliminated from such stories. The voyagers' helplessness is reflected in a shift away from the knight as protagonist. The central characters are more likely to be women or children than grown men—a marked differ-ence not only from most romances but from almost all other stories about seafaring, where a homosocial grouping is all but universal. The armour worn by the knight on horseback would be not only useless but a positive disadvantage in an open boat, as Don Quixote discovers when his own capsizes. Masculinity and its associated physical strength are equally useless. Such voyagers, moreover, again in strong contrast to knights-errant, rarely initiate their own exposure. A knight on the more conventional kinds of quest volunteers to ride out from his own society in order to take the adventure that God will send him. The person in the unsteerable boat is outside society in altogether more drastic ways, and is completely at the mercy of the seas and winds, or fortune, the gods, or God. It is an adventure that you are unlikely to take on willingly, though it cannot be other than what God will send you, since your own will can have no effect whatsoever. This is one reason why the victims are so often those who have least agency in a pre-modern, or in any, society. If it is a man who is in the vessel, he is just as helpless as if he were a woman or a child; he may even be asleep, and it makes little difference whether he is or not. At the extreme of this lack of agency, the occupant of the boat is a corpse.

The motif of the rudderless boat goes back beyond legend into myth, though the stories often reflect the actual practice of casting adrift or exposure on water. There is a vast geographical spread of such accounts along seacoasts or major rivers, but there is a particular concentration of them in the territory with the highest ratio of coastline to land: the British Isles, and Ireland in particular. In early societies in which traditional forms of law prevailed, malefactors and the unwanted—social outcasts— were often not put to death by the deliberate act of a central authority, but rather, quite literally, cast out from, and by, their community. Execution would incur blood-guilt, and exile would leave them as a potential threat; exposure at sea puts their fate in the hands of the gods, or of God. The 'adventure that God shall send you' takes on a new order of meaning in such circumstances. Some of the earliest of these legends come from the Middle East and around the Mediterranean, often in accounts of the birth of a hero in which the gods take a particular interest.[5] Many of these early victims are infants who must be disposed of because they constitute a political threat—Perseus (son of Zeus) in the Peloponnese, Romulus and Remus (supposed sons of Mars) for Rome, and (at least in medieval interpretations) Moses in Egypt. Sometimes the very point of the unsteered craft is to keep the child's origin mysterious, as with the legend of Scyld recorded at the opening of *Beowulf*. Although the setting of the voyage is in the Baltic, Scyld's arrival over the water is a distinctively English tradition.[6]

Ireland generated accounts of rudderless boats in the greatest abundance, and the historical practices that underlay them are particularly well documented there. The language itself made a distinction between voluntary voyaging for adventure, the *imramh*, most often conducted with tiller and oars but sometimes without, and the compelled journey, the *longeas*.[7] The Irish Laws prescribed exposure at sea for certain classes of wrongdoers, foremost among them being women and kin-slayers. The victims were cast out to sea with an offshore wind in a curragh (a leather-covered coracle) made from a single hide, and provided with food and water for twenty-four hours. They were also given a single oar—which would give limited steering power to an almost-round coracle, but minimal propulsion—and, if a passage of doubtful interpretation in the Laws is to be believed, a sledgehammer for fighting off seamonsters.[8] The provision of an oar and some food makes it clear that the object here is not simply to cause the death of the malefactors, but to give them a fighting chance of survival. If they come ashore, it will at least be somewhere else; and it will be because God has willed it.

The Laws also make provision for children polluted by the circumstances of their birth. They were to be put into a leather box that was taken out to sea and thrown into the water as far out as a white shield on the shore was on the edge of visibility: far enough, in other words, for the box not to be washed back ashore at the next high tide. The law was recorded in the sixteenth century, but the practice is much older: the earliest known instance is described five hundred years before that.[9] The simpler practice of floating an unwanted baby down a river or away on an offshore tide, whether to be lost or committed to the 'kindness of strangers', was a form of exposure used in many societies over many centuries. Where such practices could result in charges of infanticide, exposure had to be secret and therefore unrecorded, so it is hard to get any idea of its frequency. The ballad of *Mary Hamilton*, popularized by Joan Baez, tells a story originating in the sixteenth century but which probably for long needed little historical imagination from its audiences: the Scottish queen's maid-in-waiting is hanged after she admits to having put her new-born bastard son

> in a little boat
> And cast him out to sea;
> And he may sink, or he may swim,
> But he'll never come back to me.

The practice continued until surprisingly recently, often motivated by sheer poverty rather than illegitimacy. One baby too many from a poor

Welsh home was about to be floated down the Teifi into Cardigan Bay at the start of the twentieth century, only for her mother to decide that she was so beautiful she could not bear to part with her; the child grew up to be the great-aunt Martha of one of my own students.

The motif flourished in a series of different literary niches before it found particularly fertile ground in romance. Romance seems at first glance to be an unlikely home for it. There is no immediate reason why being adrift on the seas should be linked with chivalry, or love, or high birth; it is a scenario that gives minimal opportunity for any kind of active heroism or prowess; and the chances that such an event will have a happy ending are remote. That very remoteness, however, makes a romance shaping almost inevitable if the victim does survive. The happy ending of romance is one achieved *against the odds*, and the odds in this case are very high indeed. Survival for an infant marks him (or occasionally her) as special, favoured by God or the gods: hence the association of the motif with the birth of the hero, in early modern literature as in archaic. Finding herself pregnant in a society that prescribes death for unchaste women, the mother of the hero in that Renaissance favourite *Amadis de Gaule* has her baby cast away in a little chest, which, 'by the will of the highest (who makes impossibilities easy)', is found by a passing ship. Ignorant of his birth, Amadis is known when he grows to manhood as 'the Gentleman of the Sea'. The primacy attaching to the motif is indicated by the title page woodcut of the 1619 edition of Antony Munday's translation of the work, which shows the chest being fished out of the water.[10] Christian Providence is seen to intervene most directly in the case of saints and penitents rather than heroes, but its workings are stressed in romance when they operate to preserve the innocent or the true ruler. Exposure at sea constitutes a *iudicium Dei*, a judgement made not by men but by God; it is a marine equivalent of the testing of right in chivalric combat. The history of the motif from the Middle Ages across the Reformation sees a gradual shift from its lying on the border with saint's life to a greater concern with politics and the rightful heir. Prospero is far from being a saint, but he and his daughter are saved by 'providence divine' (1.2.159) when they are set adrift on the high seas after his depositon. The element of overt miracle is downplayed in the more political texts, but God's intervention in the working of the physical world is evident in both kinds of story. As with the magic of the *barca adventurosa*, this is one meme in which naturalism is not enough.

The outcome of such narratives correlates closely with the point of view from which it is told. If, as occasionally happens, a casting adrift is focalized through those left on shore, watching the unsteerable boat float away, then it is a safe conclusion that the near-inevitable happens and the victim is never heard of again. In 1509, a group of early Spanish explorers in central America disposed of an unpopular governor, Diego de Nicuesa, by just such a means: they put him in a rotten boat with no tackle and set him adrift, jeering at him that he should report back his grievances to the king in Castille.[11] Tyrannical authority figures in fiction, notably fathers, are sometimes given equally summary dispatch: in that compendium of every available romance motif, Richard Johnson's *Tom a Lincoln*, one such is 'put into a boat alone, and so sent to the sea to seeke his fortune'.[12] If the narrative accompanies the victim, by contrast, then a happy ending is guaranteed. A few stories in effect start with the happy ending, by taking the point of view of the people on a different shore who find such a vessel arriving. In this last case, the origin of the boat will be unknown, so ensuring some degree of romance-like strangeness about the episode beyond the sheer improbability of survival for the voyager. That very improbability, however, indicates that the survivor will be in some sense extraordinary. These shifts in focalization—from the perpetrators to the victim, from the victim to those who find the boat on its arrival—also measure how the geographical perception of such voyages is turned inside out. The point of exposure at sea is to expel the victims, to dispose of them beyond the margins of the society that wants to get rid of them. A narrative that travels with them, or that recounts the discovery of the boat on a new shore, turns the periphery into a new centre. The sea represents a threshold to be crossed, a gateway to a new society. It is Prospero's island, not Milan or Naples, that occupies the stage in *The Tempest*.

Journeys in romance are usually intimately related to questing, to the knight in pursuit of chivalric prowess: the very etymology of 'chivalry', courtly French for horsemanship, would seem to preclude ship travel except as a means of getting to or from an island, or travelling between widely separated lands—a blank space between adventures, which the knight will encounter only when he comes ashore. The landscape of his journey is most often unknown, and he has no kind of map, topographical or moral, by which to find the object of his quest. He moves off charted territory into those blank areas supposedly marked by cartographers only with 'Here be dragons', and dragons and other chivalric tests will duly confront him in abundance. The occupant of a rudderless boat moves off the map yet more decisively. The open seas constituted a landscape more desolate and uncharted than the most hostile and unknown of forests or wastelands. The knight may not know where his horse should go, but he can, most of the time, steer it; there is often a friendly hermit not too far away to help out with lodging and sustenance, or at the least there will be a tree for shelter and some minimal supply of drinking water. Exposure in an open boat is a grimmer business altogether.[13] The 'no oar nor rudder' often carries as a rider that there is no food or water either, or only minimal provision. At least one historical victim, Edwin, the half-brother of the tenth-century King Athelstan, seems to have drowned himself in preference to waiting for death after he had been set adrift 'in an old rotten vessel without rower or mariner', as Holinshed phrased it.[14] Such despair was widely recognized as a more immediate danger than capsize or starvation. A character in Lady Mary Wroth's *Urania* is cast adrift by pirates 'without oar, sail or hope'.[15] Shakespeare, whose reading on rudderless boats is likely to have included Holinshed's account of Edwin, has Prospero describe himself as being preserved in a decrepit and rudderless vessel only by his baby's angelic 'fortitude from heaven', fortitude being the remedial virtue for despair.[16]

There were two possible ways of setting adrift: to push the victims out to sea on a falling tide and with an offshore wind; or to cast them off from a larger ship well away from shore. In a play misascribed to John Webster entitled *The Thracian Wonder*, the father of the heroine condemns his pregnant daughter and her lover to the two forms of exposure: they are to be cast adrift on different tides and with contrary winds so that there is no possibility of their vessels meeting:

> She in a small boat, without man or oar,
> Shall to the mercy of the waves be left;
> He in a pinnace, without sail or pilot,
> Shall be dragg'd forth some five leagues from the shore,
> And there be drench'd in the vast ocean.[17]

Prospero, with the infant Miranda, suffers the second kind of fate, and 'fate' becomes even more compelling a term since the craft in which they are put is unseaworthy.

> They hurried us aboard a barque,
> Bore us some leagues to sea, where they prepared
> A rotten carcass of a butt, not rigged,
> Nor tackle, sail, nor mast—the very rats
> Instinctively have quit it. There they hoist us,
> To cry to th' sea that roared to us, to sigh
> To th' winds.   *The Tempest*, 1. 2. 144–50

The lines represent a defining moment for *The Tempest*. The 'rotten carcass of a butt' is not the only boat of the play—it is not even the first: the whole play opens in mid-shipwreck with a crack of thunder. In that first scene, the tackle, sail, and mast of an altogether finer ship than Prospero's worn-out craft are useless against the violence of the sea, and the mariners are doing their best to get rid of them. At the end, the ship turns out to be undamaged, and waiting offstage to take the various castaways back to Naples, helped along by the 'calm seas, auspicious gales' that the mage Prospero will ensure as his final act of enchantment. But it is the rotting dinghy in which he was abandoned, 'nor tackle, sail, nor mast', that alerted the original audiences to a set of resonances and traditions of particular richness. They connect the exiled duke and his daughter to a line that includes great saints and great sinners; infant heroes, and children whose birth is deeply tainted; politically dangerous men, and falsely accused women; both women and men with powers beyond the ordinary; and the whole programme of colonial expansion.

POLLUTION, GUILT, AND THE STATE

The meme of the rudderless boat links meanings or conditions that at first glance appear widely diverse: pollution, guilt, and the fate of nations among them. There is an evident parallel between guilt, attaching to sin or crime (including illicit sex), and pollution, the stigma attaching to those who involuntarily transgress some taboo within their culture (such as the offspring of such sins); but considerations of state would seem separate. The link lies in the threat inhering in procreation in patrilinear societies, such as can turn blood relationship, small babies, or pregnant women into a political danger. Victims of casting adrift who are regarded as a threat to the state are sometimes the subject of a prophecy that they will cause the death of the king; or they may simply have *too much legitimacy*. A linear claim, like ritual pollution, inheres in the potential heir: if you have a right to the throne, or have a certain future predicted for you, there is no more you can do to free yourself from that right or that prophecy than you can free yourself from bastardy or incest. From the ruler's point of view, such figures are also potential traitors, threatening deposition or assassination. Casting adrift is a way both of sidestepping direct action against them, and of avoiding treason to come.

Exposure by water was the perfect way of disposing of a political enemy beyond the reach of rescue or restoration but without incurring

blood-guilt in the process. This is likely to have been behind the muti-
neers' choice of fate for Diego de Nicuesa, the man set in authority over
them by the king and, by implication, God. It was an especially attractive
option if the victim were someone such as a close relative or a baby,
whose assassination would transgress stronger taboos than would the
killing of a stranger. It was also attractive if the execution or murder of
the victim would be likely to result in an upsurge of popular support, a
rebellion against the ruler who ordered it. This seems to have been the
reason why Athelstan chose to cast his brother adrift after he was accused
of conspiring against him: Edwin was too dangerous to keep alive, but
putting his fate into the hands of God transferred the question of his
death or survival to powers other than the king's. Prospero suggests that
he owes his own survival to similar motives after Antonio had deposed
him. When Miranda asks him why they were not both put to death, he
replies,

> They durst not,
> So dear the love my people bore me; nor set
> A mark so bloody on the business.

> *Tempest* 1. 2. 140–2

Alonso and Sebastian are thinking primarily in terms of pragmatic poli-
tics, but perhaps also of the judgement of God on them. That God might
have views on Prospero as well does not seem to occur to them: they
assume that casting adrift is equivalent to a bloodless assassination.

But, of course, in romance and comparable legends it does not work
out like that. Perseus was thrown into the sea as a baby along with his
mother Danaë, as a consequence of a prediction that he would kill his
grandfather, but that did not prevent the fulfilment of the prophecy.
Aeneas may have founded a state in Italy after a voyage from Troy in a
properly-equipped boat, but Rome itself owed its foundation to twin
babies who were exposed on the water in a little basket. Romulus and
Remus were marked for destruction twice over: they were the grandchil-
dren, and the only male descendants, of Numitor, who had been deposed
by his younger brother, Amulius; and the usurper had compelled their
mother to become a Vestal Virgin, with the intention of preventing the
birth of such descendants, or at least of attaching the stigma of pollution
to any children she bore. Amulius accordingly had the babies 'committed
to the flowing river' in an attempt to dispose of them. The little vessel in
which they floated was left stranded by the retreat of the flooded Tiber,
so allowing them to be found and suckled by a she-wolf. The twins grew

up to kill the usurper, restore their grandfather, and in due course to build the new city of Rome.[18] The point of this story lies in the fact that they *come back*: what is supposed to be a one-way journey goes badly wrong for the wicked great-uncle. For those victims who survive such an ordeal, their return is likely to be as dangerous for those who set them adrift in the first place as exposure was for the victim.

The founding of monarchies could rest on guilt rather than pollution, with the rudderless vessel operating as a means to convey its passengers between states of being as much as nation-states. Brut came to Britain, by ordinary boat, after accidentally killing his father; he found a land inhabited by giants, descendants of the first colonizers of the country, the forty-nine daughters of a Greek king, who had cohabited after their arrival with incubi. Those daughters had all been married on the same day and plotted to kill their husbands on their wedding night, but the fiftieth sister revealed the conspiracy. Their father, or in some versions her husband, is reluctant to put them to death, on account of both their high birth and their close kinship to him; so instead, as Holinshed puts it, he

commanded them to be thrust into a ship, without maister, mate or mariner, and so to be turned into the maine ocean sea, and to take and abide such fortune as should chance unto them.[19]

Anglo-Norman and Middle English accounts add further detail about the condition of the ship: according to the *Anonymous Metrical Chronicle*, it was 'withouten seyl, withouten ore', and without a rudder; in its Anglo-Norman and Latin versions, it was without food, too.[20] Nevertheless, the sisters survive, drifting to the coast of the as yet unnamed Britain—the unlikelihood of navigating the Straits of Gibraltar is never an issue in the many stories that take these unsteerable boats from the Mediterranean to the English Channel. At the suggestion of the eldest, Albina, the new country is named Albion. There is no question here of any return to their homeland; the land to which they come is effectively empty, awaiting colonization and (under Brut's sovereignty) civilization. The disparity between the normal expectations of the meme and the meaning given it in the legend proved troublesome to some of the historians. The author of the anonymous *Chronicle*, worried by the incongruity of the women's eventual fate in contrast with their guilt, suggested as an afterthought that perhaps the youngest daughter's accusation was in fact slanderous (l. 305). Holinshed doubts the truth of the story, but partly on the grounds that other sources that list the daughters of Danaus, as he names their father, do not mention any called Albina.

The original inspiration behind the story of Albina is not known, but it offers a parallel to accounts of the exposure of heroes, as if a great nation, like a great man, needs some kind of mysterious origin from which to emerge, some element of magic or miracle or providential care that makes its founding a matter of something other than chance. The narratives of the exiled sisters accompany them on their voyage, and are recounted from the perspective of an English author—the perspective of the land to which they come. The interest lies not in their original home-land, but in Britain: the land on the edge of the known world that has become the new centre, the society of the chroniclers and their listeners or readers, and which down to the sixteenth century finds legitimation in a legend of origin in the form of an unsteered boat arriving from over the sea.

Most English stories of women in open boats have them cast adrift as a consequence not of intended husband-murder but of real or supposed sexual misdemeanours, along with the baby born as a result of those. As in the case of Albina, the motif is strong enough to override all geo-graphical plausibility, or indeed to recast geography altogether. The Constance of Chaucer's *Man of Law's Tale* and its sources drifts from Syria to Northumberland and back to Rome, her own city of origin. Eglamour sleeps with his betrothed lady Cristabelle, daughter of the earl of Artois, after success in the trials her father has set him, but he leaves to take on an extra dragon before they are formally married; her father sets her adrift along with the baby he charges with bastardy, in a boat with 'nothere mast ne rothere'.[21] When the boat comes briefly to land, some-where in the Mediterranean, her son is carried off by a griffin to Israel, and the rest of the story takes place around Egypt and the Holy Land. Desonelle, the beloved of Torrent of Portingale (Portugal), undergoes a similar, and similarly located, ordeal, with twins, though she does at least start out from nearer the Mediterranean. Both romances, *Eglamour* in particular, remained favourites in the sixteenth century. Against such a background, it seems less surprising that the Bohemia of Greene's *Pandosto* and *The Winter's Tale* should have a seacoast; for although Perdita herself, accused of being the offspring of adultery, is brought there by ordinary ship to be exposed on the land, her literary predeces-sor, Greene's Fawnia, is cast adrift in her own little vessel, 'having neither saile nor rudder to guid it', and left 'to the mercie of the seas, and the des-tinies'.[22] In all these cases, the destinies do, of course, live up to romance expectations, and save the voyagers. The result is the preservation of the true line of descent that male cruelty or suspicions have threatened to destroy. Constance's son Maurice inherits the empire of Rome from her father, despite the slander told to her husband that the child was monstrous. Cristabelle and Desonelle, both heiresses, pass on their fathers' lands to their recovered children. And Fawnia, like Perdita, returns from over the sea as the lost heir.

The return of the victims in these stories amounts to a guarantee that the true line of descent does indeed run through the children, whatever the suspicions of the reigning monarch. Their recovery is a mark that the succession is ensured by God Himself; that bastardy does not inhere in the infants, that they are indeed true born. Other stories, occurring throughout the Middle Ages and Renaissance, never question the legitimacy of the heir—that is indeed why they need to be disposed of—but show God's defence of the true line of succession against invaders or usurpers. A late example comes from the *Orlando Furioso*, where Ruggiero, founding father of the house of Este, and his twin Marfisa are preserved after their uncles kill their father and expose their mother at sea to die.[23] *The Tempest* is almost unique among these stories in that it is a father and daughter, not a mother and son, who are set adrift. The change serves to emphasize that it is legitimacy, not illegitimacy, that is at issue.[24] Still more, the change calls attention to the distinctiveness of Shakespeare's own insistent interest in his last plays on fathers and heiresses.

The successive reworkings of the story of Horn show how much individual authors can vary the motif of casting adrift within what is essentially the same narrative. The story forms part of the 'matter of England', English originary romance; the earliest surviving text is Anglo-Norman, though that is itself probably based on an English version.[25] The king, Horn's father, is killed by invading Saracens (a twelfth-century updating of the pagan Vikings: the various proper names of the text are Scandinavian or Germanic in origin). They consider murdering the boy, but (as in the case of the Welsh baby Martha) they are moved to pity by his beauty, and instead they cast him adrift with a group of companions. In the oldest Middle English version, the youngsters are provided with oars; but in Thomas's Anglo-Norman *Romance of Horn*, they are towed out to sea in a rotten boat with 'no mast nor oar, rudder nor steersman' and set adrift, with the intention that they will never be heard of again. In the event, God acts as their steersman and brings them to shore, where the boat breaks up in the surf but the children reach land safely.[26] The Anglo-Norman version was in due course recast in French prose with its hero renamed, and that in turn was translated at least once, probably twice, into Middle English, under the title *King Ponthus*. Printed early in the sixteenth century and still of commercial interest in the 1580s, it was one of a number of romances that preserved for the Renaissance the motif of the casting adrift of a political rival.[27] *King Ponthus* varies the story to lessen the sense of miracle while still preserving the motif. Ponthus's father, like Horn's, is killed by invading Saracens, and the child and his companions are handed over to a knight named Patryke to be disposed of. Patryke provides them with a ship, a month's supply of food, and a mariner, and sends them off with good hope of their safety. When he reports back to the Saracen king, however, he tells a different story:

Syr, seyde the knight, ye shall never see them; for I have set them in an olde shyppe without ony maner of lyvynge of the worlde. And within have I made two or three holes, and let draw the sail up to the top which bare them into the sea, that never shall ye hear tidings of them.[28]

Patryke's role foreshadows that of Gonzalo in *The Tempest*. Gonzalo does carry out his orders faithfully, but he also provides the food and water that preserve the dispossessed duke and his child, and the clothing and the books that will provide them with all they need on the island. Both Horn and Ponthus, like Prospero, do of course live to reassert their rights, the early heroes to take vengeance on the usurpers, Prospero to forgive them.

In telling the story of the setting adrift of his dispossessed hero, the Anglo-Norman Thomas sought for an analogy of God's providential care for those exposed on the water in the account of the infant Moses in the bulrushes: 'Now may He preserve them who saved Moses, when he was thrown as a child into the river in the ravine.'[29] In this story too, the issue is a threat to the ruler's security, when Pharaoh is alarmed by the danger posed by the Israelites' fertility. His first intention is to have the male children killed at birth, but when the midwives avoid co-operation, he comes up with a different idea:

Pharaoh therefore charged all his people, saying: Whatsoever shall be born of the male sex, ye shall cast into the river. (Exodus 1:22)

Thomas evidently took this to mean that the children were thrown into the river in little vessels. Given the widespread reluctance, evidenced in the story by the midwives, to murder babies outright lest it transgress divine sanction, this may well be the right interpretation. Unusually for such legends, though in ways not dissimilar to Patryke or Gonzalo, providential care in the case of the infant Moses is effected through human ingenuity. His mother and sister lodge the waterproofed basket that carries him in the reeds, to make it look as if his little craft, like Romulus and Remus', has grounded of its own accord, ready for Pharaoh's daughter to find the baby and foster him. The rest of that story, too, is a kind of history, only one that adds the purposes of God to an account of dominion, as the adult Moses leads God's people out of slavery to the Promised Land.

'GOD IS OUR PILOT'

Such human interventions to jog the likelihood of a happy ending remain exceptional: the sheer helplessness of the victim exposed on the water normally makes survival uniquely dependent on God. That these victims are under His direct protection is emphasized by the recurrent analogy drawn in text after text with Jonah.

> Who kepte hire fro the drenchyng in the see?
> Who kepte Jonas in the fisshes mawe
> Til he was spouted up at Nynyvee?[30]

A whale may not appear much like a rudderless boat, but they do have a lot in common, most particularly in the helplessness of the person inside them to direct where they are going. Like the boats, too, the whale carries Jonah to the *right* place—the place chosen by God. The story of Jonah, moreover, follows the outline of the romances of atonement: his penitence in the belly of the whale is accepted, and his deliverance follows. The story was interpreted in the Middle Ages as a prefiguration of Christ's descent into Hell, and Jonah's emergence as a figure for the Harrowing, when Christ led out God's faithful to eternal bliss in Heaven. Besides being an analogy for God's providential care for His chosen ones, therefore, the story offers a larger analogy to the patterning of romance on the model of the Fall and Redemption, a patterning made explicit in some of the romances of casting adrift.

The same idea underlies a second analogy developed in the Middle Ages, the story of Noah. There is no point in steering the ark when there is no dry land left to which to journey, and God's detailed instructions for building it (Genesis 6:14–16) accordingly make no mention of mast, sails, or rudder. That silence in the originary text becomes a positive absence in the Middle English *Cleanness*, which spends four alliterative lines describing its lack of mast and mast-step, bowline, cable and capstan, anchor, rudder, helm, and sails.[31] Orthodox exegesis interpreted the ark as an allegory of the Church in which the faithful are preserved, but the letter of the story suggested a different reading, in which the vessel serves as a point of both generic and genealogical transition. All living things, human and animal, contained in the ark are uniquely in the hands of God; the story tells of their survival, their rebirth after threatened death. Noah accordingly becomes the re-founder of the entire human dynasty. The myth of Adam and Eve ends in disaster, God's condemnation of humankind; the myth of Noah ends with His promise never to destroy the earth again. Every medieval and Renaissance genealogy incorporates one of Noah's sons into its line of descent. The Bible has often been regarded as a compendium of genres, and the story of the ark is the ultimate ancestral romance.

Such explicit theological links are reflected in the abundant appearance of boats without sail or oar in devotional rather than secular literature, not least in saints' legends. The sixth century, the Irish Age of Saints, generated a large number of such stories, many of which have their grounding in actual practices. Hard fact is, however, difficult to be sure of, both because the stories were not recorded until some centuries after the events they purport to describe, and because hagiography is not noted for its historical accuracy. In the Irish stories that claim to be factual, survival in itself seems to have become a marker for sanctity, for God's especial favour to the victim. Such stories occasionally tell of the preservation of children who grow up to be saints; some concern sinners undergoing an especially harsh penance, and whose repentance, like that of the sinful knights in the romances of atonement, is accepted by God. Some record voyages undertaken voluntarily, where the travellers put themselves into God's hands as an act of willing faith.

Death for a saint cast adrift in an open boat would be a kind of martyrdom, an ending that ensures bliss in the next world by way of suffering in this: the classic form of hagiography. God's providential care, however, ensures survival in this life, a marker for romance; and so such saints' legends tend to lie on the border between the two genres. Three such stories from across Europe—one about a woman, two about babies—set their protagonists adrift in especially romance-like ways.

The woman is Mary Magdalene, who, according to legend, served as the apostle to the French. She is set adrift from the Holy Land with her brother Lazarus and a number of companions, in

> Ane olde schip withouten mast,
> Withouten are, anker or any gude   [oar; provision
> That suld fend agayns the flode,   [might preserve (them)

and with no food or water either.[32] Although they come close to starvation while they drift around the Mediterranean, Providence eventually brings them ashore at Marseilles. Mary's cult was widespread in the Middle Ages, and she was the patron of many English churches; the legends were therefore well placed to survive the Reformation, a process no doubt helped by surviving copies of Caxton's version of the same story in his translation of the *Golden Legend*, an account complete with a ship 'without any tackle or rudder'.[33] Later parts of her legend include the abandonment on an uninhabited island of the wife and child of one of her converts, apparently dead in childbirth; they are in due course rediscovered alive and well, through the intercession of the saint. The story offers a Christian analogue of the apparent death in childbirth of the wife of Apollonius of Tyre, and her surviving her committal to the sea in her own vessel without sail or oars, a coffin: the story familiar from *Pericles*.

Of the future saints who are cast adrift as babies, one, St Kentigern, is preserved in circumstances rather like the children of Cristabelle and Desonelle. On being found to be pregnant under unexplained circumstances, his mother, an early British Christian, was first thrown from a cliff, and, when that proved ineffectual, she was cast adrift in a leather coracle 'made after the manner of the Irish, without any oar'. Like the Spanish mutineers in Central America, or the onlookers at the Crucifixion, the perpetrators jeer at her as she embarks on her ordeal: 'She trusts in Christ; let him deliver her if he can from the hand of death, and the peril of the sea!'[34] So far as the narrative focus is concerned, it is the onlookers who are left behind; and Christ does indeed, of course, save her.

The suspicion of illegitimacy about Kentigern becomes full incest in the case of St Gregory. He is the protagonist of a story-type invented in the Middle Ages, of double incest: stories in which the son of an incestuous affair between a brother and sister comes back as an adult stranger and unknowingly marries his mother. Between the two episodes, as the event that prevents recognition, is a casting adrift: an attempt to dispose of the child without adding the sin of murder to the sin of incest, and a way of committing his fate to God. So the mother of the infant Gregory 'bitaught him God and the salt see', having him thrown into the water in a little tun so that Christ could save him if it were not 'agen his will'.[35]

That Christ does indeed intervene to save him makes his return and eventual marriage to his mother altogether more ironic than in the other cases where castaways are preserved by divine Providence. Providence does however continue to aid him in the penance he inflicts on himself after his discovery of their relationship, keeping him alive for seventeen years on a rock in the sea to which he chains himself, and restoring the key of the fetters in the belly of a fish just as emissaries from Rome arrive to seek out a man named Gregory chosen by God to be pope. Like a romance, the work ends with a further reconciliation, when his mother and wife comes to Rome to seek further penance for herself, and meets again with joy her son and her husband.

The legends about children of incest mark them out either for great sanctity or for great evil: they are marked for good or ill from the moment of their conception. Bringing the Christian God into such stories is commonplace but theologically difficult, as the protagonists are evidently polluted in the circumstances of their birth and, in the case of double incest stories, sinners in their marriages, but without any intention to sin on their part. Gregory is attempting to do the right thing in God's eyes and redeem himself from the curse of his origin when he marries: an attempt at a righteous life that goes horribly wrong, yet which incurs its own extreme penance. Making a man with such a biography into a saint is counter-intuitive, and indeed the point of these stories seems to have lain in the idea that God can forgive even the most extreme sins;[36] incest incurs abhorrence even when it is unwitting. God's purposes become even more inscrutable, though the trajectory of destiny more darkly logical, in the case of the wicked, traitors to the king or to God. The Middle Ages produced two such counter-examples to the providential saving of the innocent, in Judas and Mordred. Both are cast adrift in an attempt to avoid prophecies of disaster, and both are preserved to make their great betrayal; their stories are discussed more extensively in the final chapter.

Casting adrift can itself be a test of guilt, or of hope following from repentance. Most such narratives offer a close parallel to the penitential romances, in which sinners are allowed to make up for past misdeeds. Three Irish brothers who had been born, like Robert the Devil, after their mother had prayed to the devil, undertake such an ordeal on the ocean as penance after a similar career of church-wrecking.[37] When St Patrick discovered that a bandit named Maccuill had planned to kill him but repented, he committed judgement on him to God, ordering his would-be assassin to go unarmed into a one-hide coracle with no rudder or oar, food or water; his feet were to be fettered, and the key thrown into the sea. The man's penitence was accepted by God: the boat was blown to the Isle of Man, where Maccuill was rescued by the bishop, and in due course succeeded him to the office.[38] His elevation may be ecclesiastical rather than secular, but the pattern it follows is very close to God's preservation of the penitent or righteous for reward within this world.

The workings of Providence are evident in the story of Maccuill, but to the eye of faith, there was no need for God to be prompted into action as a response to punishment. The most intrepid group of such seafarers chose exposure in a rudderless boat of their own volition, precisely in order to put themselves into the hands of God: to take the adventure that God would send them in the most literal of ways, and, to anyone without such faith, the most terrifying. They were again most often Irish, and their adventures are frequently preserved in saints' lives—or indeed *as* saints' lives, since such an expression of trust in Providence constitutes faith of a heroic order. The idea seems to have come, at least in part, from the analogous judicial practice. When sixty couples of the men of Ross were cast adrift as a punishment, so that 'God would pass His judgement upon them', two of the spectators, named Snedgus and MacRiagla, decided that they should themselves go 'with their own consent'— unforced by any authority other than their own or God's—not as a punishment but 'into the outer ocean on a pilgrimage'. Initially, they use oars; but after a while they ship them so as to entrust their journey entirely to God.[39] This most extreme form of pilgrimage is attested by record as well as by story. There is a famous entry in the *Anglo-Saxon Chronicle* for the year 891, which recounts how three Irishmen came ashore in Cornwall in a coracle 'without any oars'. They spent a few days recovering, but insisted on putting to sea again, since their object was to seek exile from men for the sake of God.[40] The presence of Irish hermits in Iceland, which was otherwise uninhabited when the early Norse settlers arrived, further attests to the practice of pilgrimage on the open seas. They may or may not have used oars for their journey, but it might not have made much difference to their chances of striking land before they died of exposure or thirst. Since they probably did not know of the existence of Iceland when they set out, and had no means of pinpointing its whereabouts at all precisely if they did, they would have had a fairly equal chance of reaching it whether they could propel or steer their boats or not, given assistance from the prevailing winds blowing northwards through the Atlantic. They did not, so far as we know, set out with any intended destination in mind: they put entirely into the hands of God where, or whether, they would reach land. If they were lucky, they would touch Iceland; if they were even luckier, they would touch the face of God. The primitive nature of the marine technology used by these pilgrims of the sea would have made it harder for them to make the return journey against the prevailing winds, and, in any case, return was not an issue. It was not the point of these journeys that you should come back to your own society. The object of a pilgrimage on land, a shrine or holy place, 'represents a "threshold", a place and moment "in and out of time"', and the pilgrim 'hopes to have there direct experience of the sacred, invisible, or supernatural order'.[41] Pilgrimage at sea, its destination unknowable even as to whether it would be in this world or the next, represents the crossing of a threshold out of human time to the sacred in the most direct and challenging of ways.

The most famous of these Irish voyagers is none the less one who did return: St Brendan. If he and his followers had acted like the other pilgrims of the sea and set up hermitages or a monastic community in their newly discovered land, there would be no legend. The fact that the story exists at all predicts that they will return to tell their tale—that they have returned, in order for their adventures to be recorded, rather as Malory's knights have their deeds chronicled back at court. The legend indeed starts with the telling of a story by a kinsman of Brendan's named Barinthus about his own voyage to see the wonders of God in the deep; and it is this that inspires Brendan to do likewise, rather as Yvain's initial adventure at the spring is inspired by the tale told about it by one of his fellow knights. The eventual return of Brendan and his companions is a further reason why the legend reads almost as much like romance as hagiography. Other similarities lie in the extensive and unlocalized space of their travels, and in the marvels they encounter in the seven years they spend on their voyage. The appeal of his legend to secular audiences is evident from the number of vernaculars into which it was translated, including an early and influential Anglo-Norman version. It might be objected that his ship was well equipped—tackle, sail, mast, and rudder, as with Tim Severin's reconstruction of both his boat and his voyage—but the difference between his craft and those with no means of control is one that the legend is keen to minimize. At key moments, Brendan instructs his fellow seamen to commit themselves entirely to God:

'God is our help, our pilot and helmsman who will steer us. Ship all the oars and the rudder, likewise furl the sail, and let God do what He wills with his servants and his boat.'[42]

A piously motivated voyage of exploration will be guided at least as well without equipment as with it, as the absence of oar and rudder is reformulated as the promise that Christ will be their pilot and helmsman.

The Atlantic across which Brendan and his companions journey is as full of marvels as any knight-errant's forest or Orient: their uncharted waters would amply fulfil any promise of 'Here be sea-monsters'. There is, however, an interesting difference between the knight's linear progress and their own mode of advance, since in each of their seven years at sea they spend the periods around Easter and Christmas in the same series of places, mostly islands, though Easter morning is always spent on the back of a helpful whale, named Jasconius. Those liturgical feasts serve as the only temporal and spatial co-ordinates of their voyage. They are, in other words—in modern words—going round and round in circles, though it never seems to have occurred either to Brendan or to the compilers or readers of the legend to interpret their travels in such a way. Their recurrent visits to the same places mark the cyclical time of the liturgical year, time measured as space, the unmeasured wastes of the Atlantic mapped like the calendar. Their continued journeyings are therefore translated from representing geographical movement to spiritual progression, as if the length of their ordeal served for inward purification. In due course they do indeed reach the Land of Promise, or perhaps it was America. They are not allowed to stay there, however: a divine-seeming young man appears and bids them return, first loading their boat with fruit and precious stones (that too being picked up by later romance: Huon of Bordeaux loads magic fruit and powerful gems onto his own self-guiding ship, to which he is directed by an angel).[43] He warns Brendan too to prepare for the ending of his pilgrimage, his *peregrinatio*, not this time at sea but on earth.

The mapping of a voyage in an unrigged boat onto the liturgical calendar was not confined to hagiography. The same happens in the thirteenth-century *Roman de la Manekine*, whose author, Philippe de Rémi, was a continental French writer with particular interests in England.[44] *Manekine* is partly set in the British Isles, but it starts in Hungary, which, like Shakespeare's Bohemia, has a seacoast. After the death of his wife, the king seeks to marry his own daughter, a girl named Joïe. To prevent the marriage, she cuts off her hand. Her father condemns her to be burned, but his seneschal takes pity on her—comparative pity—and instead casts her adrift with no mast, oars, or rudder.[45] After making a prayer that contains an outline of Redemption history—the Harrowing of Hell, the Resurrection, the Ascension—she eventually comes ashore at Berwick, on the first Sunday in Lent. She refuses to reveal her name, but the Scottish king nicknames her Manekine. He falls in love with her, and marries her at Pentecost; by the following Easter, she is pregnant. While he is away practising chivalry, she gives birth to a son; her mother-in-law substitutes letters saying she has borne a monster in place of those announcing its birth, and others demanding Manekine's burning to death in place of the king's more temperate reply. Once again, she is saved by being set adrift with her baby, in the same boat, without mast or sail, rudder or oar, in which she had arrived. In due course she comes ashore at Rome, and is given shelter there. For seven years, the king seeks her, in a ship whose full complement of tackling is emphasized as much as is its absence from his wife's boat, and one Palm Sunday he too arrives at Rome. He takes lodgings in the same house as his wife and son, and discovers their existence through a ring with which the child is playing. In that same Holy Week, the king of Hungary arrives in Rome to do penance for his past sins, and he too is reunited and reconciled with Manekine. Her happiness is completed by the miraculous rediscovery and restoration of her hand, which has been preserved in the belly of a sturgeon, in a glove-shaped place like a reliquary (so overgoing the miraculous return of the key to Gregory's fetters; the fish, somewhat ungratefully—though perhaps not impiously, given the associations with Easter week—is eaten). The family attends all the Easter services, and on the night of Easter Sunday, when the penitential season of Lent is over, Manekine, now with her name of Joïe restored to her, shares a bed with her husband again. They return to Scotland the following Easter Day, to public celebrations. They have more children, all of whom in due course become kings and queens; and Philippe ends by insisting that God can restore all losses and injuries to those who remain faithful.[46] The steady insistence on the events of the Passion and their replaying in the liturgical calendar makes explicit what in many romances remains latent: the parallel between the shaping of romance and the *felix culpa*, the loss of happiness that yet results in greater joy through direct divine intervention. The same point is made by the choice of proper name for Manekine, Joïe, and its restoration to her.

Le Roman de la Manekine is one of a number of closely related romances that probably have folktale origins.[47] The analogous stories composed in England keep the malevolent mothers-in-law and the rudderless boats, but delete the amputation and the miraculous fish. In *Emaré*, of *c.*1400, the boat in which the heroine is twice cast adrift is not only without 'anker or ore', but without food or water, and she is almost crazed by hunger and thirst as well as terror by the time she reaches land.[48] Although Emaré's own piety is stressed, the emphasis of the romance falls on marvel more than miracle. Throughout her successive ordeals, she wears a dazzling robe made by a pagan emir's daughter, which has a pair of famous lovers embroidered in each corner. Although her Christian goodness is made evident, the cloth serves to shift attention from Providence to herself, in a quasi-magical projection of her unchanging beauty and goodness. The other *Manekine*-type story moves in the other direction, towards hagiography, since it stresses the role of its heroine, Constance, daughter of the emperor of Rome, as a Christian evangelist in each new destination to which she travels. The new emphasis (not to mention the deletion of the incest motif) may have been thought especially appropriate for convent reading, as Nicholas Trevet, in whose Anglo-Norman *Chronicles* the story first appears, was writing for a daughter of Edward I who had become a nun at Amesbury. By pleasing coincidence, he gives the story a sixth-century dating that would make Constance's second voyage exactly contemporary with St Brendan's.[49] The story was picked up both by Gower in the *Confessio amantis* and by Chaucer as *The Man of Law's Tale*, each retelling treading the border with saint's life. Constance's name is not in the first place allegorical—her father is named Constantine, and Chaucer calls her Custance, possibly to increase the sense of her as a person rather than a personification—but the name none the less insists on her capacity for the Christian virtue of faithful endurance. Her first casting adrift is a consequence of her marriage to the sultan of Syria, who is prepared to accept conversion to Christianity in order to win her hand. His mother, however, slaughters him and the whole Christian party at the wedding feast, Constance alone being saved from immediate death for exposure in a ship (without sail or oar in Trevet, 'al steerelees' in Chaucer), so that, in the jeers of the perpetrators, she can learn to sail home to Italy.[50] After a voyage of many years, she eventually arrives in Northumberland, pagan since the flight of the Roman Christians, and in due course converts many of its people and marries its king, Alla. After an accusation, like Manekine's and Emaré's, of bearing a monstrous child, she and her son are again cast adrift. Christ, however—or perhaps in this case the Virgin—acts as her sail and rudder (*CT*, II. 833) and guides her boat to Rome, where she is eventually reunited with both her father and her husband. Her son in due course inherits the empire, and becomes a devoted supporter of the Church: this is not only a story of miraculous preservation of a virtuous woman, but of the recovery of a lost heir.

The story has the capacity to be a full romance, but its ending remains oddly muted, not least by comparison with *La Manekine*, or even the legend of Gregory. This is readily explicable in Trevet's version, since the forward drive of chronicle towards the next ruler eliminates any possibility of pausing on a happy ending, but it is more surprising that the independent treatments do not make more of the romance elements of the story. There is no equivalent to the joyful sexuality of Manekine and her husband; Chaucer's version indeed goes out of its way to say that his Custance did no more than put up with her husband's attentions (709–14). The emphasis at the ending falls less on the 'joye and blisse' of family reunion (1119) than on its brevity, cut short as it is by Alla's death. It may have been that capacity to shift from hagiographic romance to the mortality of history that attracted not only new readers but new writers in the sixteenth century. It was made the subject of the first modernizing of Chaucer, around 1520, by one Thomas Alsop, in a version called *Fair Custance*—a version which, despite its pre-Reformation date, describes the tale in its colophon as a 'tragycall hystorie'.[51] In 1600, the story was dramatized by Thomas Dekker and others as *Fair Constance of Rome*, now lost.[52] Shakespeare never dramatized the story or echoed its text; but the patient suffering of the women in his own late plays often resonates with that of Constance, not least in their treading of the border with tragedy and the recurrent presence of the sundering and restoring sea. The pagan providence of his own romances none the less produces a surge of intense happiness at the end such as the Christian story of Constance never elicits.

FROM MIRACLE TO MAGIC

Not every unsteered boat is potentially fatal. There is also a large group of vessels, often full seagoing ships, that represent something more like the ultimate in luxury travel than extreme privation in rotten skiffs. They may therefore be fully equipped with sails and rudder, or the presence or absence of tackle may not even be thought worth a mention. None the less, they touch on the meme of the rudderless boat at so many points that the two kinds of vessel cannot finally be separated from each other. The recurrent feature of these ships is less consistently an absence of tackling than an absence of crew: they sail with no one to operate them. None the less, these, even more reliably than the boats without sail or oar, take their passengers to the *right* place, to an adventure that awaits them. They travel without helmsman or sailors, by magic and usually at great speed, to wherever the voyager wishes to go, or, more often, to wherever the boat or the person who has devised it wishes to take them. And most often, that person is a woman.

It is evident why women should so often serve as the protagonists in stories of casting adrift: God's power is made most apparent by contrast with the weakness of the victim. It is much less clear why women should be recurrently associated with boats of the *barca aventurosa* variety, not now as voyagers, but as their creators or controllers, in the role elsewhere taken by Providence itself. From casting women as the most helpless of romance characters, the ship with no apparent means of guidance can also cast them as some of the most powerful, in the sense of commanding supernatural powers.

The origins of the association of such boats with powerful women are obscure, though some of the earliest examples, like some of the earliest hagiographic legends of casting adrift, are likely to have Celtic origins. They are also often deeply enigmatic. Geoffrey of Monmouth first invents, or records, the legend of the dying Arthur's departure to the 'Island of Apples' in a boat under the aegis of the benevolent fairy Morgen, in his *Vita Merlini*. This vessel has a helmsman, but Geoffrey names him as Barinthus, Brendan's precursor in his wanderings over the ocean, 'because of his knowledge of the seas and the stars of heaven',[53] and presumably also because his voyage likewise took place on the threshold of the geographical and the supernatural. There is a different kind of threshold to be crossed in those early versions of the *Tristan* story that have the hero set adrift in an unsteered boat when he finds that the wound he received from Marhalt's sword cannot be cured; the voyage takes him between plausible geographical settings, Cornwall and Ireland, yet it also constitutes a transition from Mark to Isolt, social conformity to transgressive passion. Its destination appears fortuitous, but there is too strong a sense of both destiny and powerful women about the voyage (Isolt's mother is the only person capable of curing him) for chance to be sufficient.[54] The core narrative of Marie de France's *Guigemar* is similarly Celtic: it begins in Brittany, in the Léonnais, where the hero is wounded while hunting a talking hind, but he is carried by an unmanned ship to a city which is never named and has no place on a map. The hind tells him that he can be cured only by a woman who is prepared to suffer as much for love of him as ever woman suffered; finding the ship empty by the shore, he enters it and falls asleep, and it transports him to the unknown lady. They duly fall in love; but when they are discovered by her jealous husband, the boat reappears to fetch him away, and then returns again to take the lady after him. The source of its magic powers is never specified, and the lady herself is as mystified by it as is Guigemar; yet some connection between boat and woman is clearly implied. Reading the *lai* is rather like coming in on a conversation that is already half over, as if all the explaining required by the narrative has happened somewhere else. The very mysteriousness of the boat, however, makes it grip the imagination in ways that explanation can only spoil.

The hazards of rationalization are illustrated in the near-contemporary French *Partonopeus de Blois*, which was translated into English in the fifteenth century. Its hero, lost in the forest while hunting, likewise boards an unmanned ship that he finds by the seashore; the sails are spread without any visible human aid, and it transports him to a city that likewise appears uninhabited except for its young queen, Melior, with whom he falls in love, but whom he is forbidden to see. It transpires that she has devised this means of bringing him to her by rendering both the crew of the ship and the inhabitants of the country invisible to him, thanks to her education in magic.[55] As explanations go, this is still on the fantastic side of the rational; but it none the less reduces the intensity of fear and wonder evoked by Partonope's initial mysterious voyage. The boats of both the *lai* and the romance do, however, function in comparable ways as a test of love, a secular equivalent to the *iudicium Dei*. Guigemar's vessel takes him to the one woman who will love him enough to make his cure possible, and restores her to him. Partonope destroys the magic of Melior's vessel by his failure in trust when he insists on looking at her, and, like the knights of the romances of atonement, he has to struggle back to her acceptance.

Despite these examples, the Anglo-Norman and English tradition of romance treated the motif of the magic ship devised by a powerful woman with rather more caution than did the French and its southerly derivatives. Such vessels appear in a few translated or adapted texts, including the Grail section of the *Morte Darthur* (on which more below), but England created few new ones of its own. The main reason for this seems to have been the greater insistence in English romance on some degree of plausibility, both for its boats and its women. Preservation in an open boat is unlikely but possible, especially in an age of faith. The self-steering magic ship is pure fantasy, such as is typically an element of French or Italian romance. The difference can be seen even in different versions of the same story. In Malory, the corpse of Elaine of Ascolat is laid, richly dressed, in a little boat covered with black samite, which is steered by a single boatman down the Thames to Arthur's court. In the version told in the late thirteenth-century Italian story-collection *Il Novellino* she is placed alone, with a crown on her head as well as rich clothing, in a small ship adorned with scarlet samite and precious stones, but with no sail, oars, or living help, to be guided to Camelot by the sea itself.[56] Malory's Elaine is naturalistic and psychologically plausible; the Italian Elaine, like most of these women who are able to exercise control over unsteered boats, has powers that make her both inimitable as a role model, and impossible to empathize with.

If either the corpse or the living woman is a saint, however, then Celtic and English traditions are more hospitable. Magic and miracle can interlock, and there is not always an easy distinction to be made between the two. Early saints' legends bristle with accounts of saints, both male and female, who are transported upstream or across the sea by self-steering boats, or whose remains are taken by similar means to their divinely appointed shrines (so explaining, lest the sceptical ask questions, why their relics should be available for veneration in some place other than where they died).[57] English pragmatism or sophistication led away from such representations in its secular fiction, however, whereas southern European fantasy found ways to accommodate them. In its Italian composition, its setting in North Africa, and its all-male cast, the episode in the *Orlando Furioso* when Astolfo provides himself with an entire fleet of ships, complete with oars, sails, rigging, and indeed sailors, would seem as far distant as possible from a Celtic woman saint's minimal means of sea-travel; but he obtains his ships by miracle, by casting leaves on the sea to be transformed into galleons, in a piece of providential magic identical except for the upgrading in scale to the voyage from Ireland to Cornwall made by the virgin Hya, on a leaf enlarged by a touch with her staff.[58]

The urbane Renaissance Ariosto can hardly have expected his audience to give any credit to his story, set as it is within a fiction that includes travel to the moon by hippogriff, and indeed one wonders how many of the pious would have given literal belief to the story of Hya; but miraculous means of sea-transport in the prose versions of the Grail, composed within the overtly fictional framework of romance, sometimes reappear in chronicle accounts, as if piety could cover all gaps in plausibility even in historiography of the high Middle Ages. John of Glastonbury, in his *Chronicle of Glastonbury Abbey*, recounts the legend of how the son of Joseph of Arimathea and his most pious followers crossed the English Channel on his miraculously lengthened shirt, correctly citing the book 'qui Sanctum Graal appellatur', the French prose *History of the Holy Grail*, as his source. This was not just a boat without sail or rudder; it was a sea-crossing 'without a ship and without oars'.[59] Those of his followers who had less faith were allowed to make the crossing by a more orthodox kind of boat, except that it had been made by Solomon. In the sequel to the *History*, the *Quest of the Holy Grail*, supernatural vessels do at least take the form of boats, but they are associated with a sequence of women—or at least apparent women. The first is the beautiful damsel who attempts to seduce Perceval and who turns out to be Lucifer in female disguise; another is saintly in all respects except canonization, Perceval's virgin sister; the third is Solomon's wife, cast as a wicked woman in accordance with Solomon's strictures on the whole sex,[60] yet who masterminds the building of a literal Ship of Faith.

Despite their apparent differences both from each other and from other stories of unmanned or rudderless boats, each of the ships of the Grail quest has some function as a *iudicium Dei*, a means of making visible the judgement of God. Perceval has to undergo a testing that refashions chivalric *épreuve* as the temptation of the saint, in his resistance to the seductive fiend who visits the waste island where he is marooned, in a ship that sails as fast as if 'all the wynde of the worlde had dryven it'.[61] By contrast, the companions of the Grail enter the ship that will carry them further on their quest by divine invitation, Galahad being brought by the woman who later identifies herself as Perceval's sister; their presence on the ship confirms their status as elect. This ship is guided by God alone, without any action or direction from its passengers. It is the maiden, however, who acts as their guide and informant on the further vessel to which it takes them, the one made by Solomon's wife. This has sailed unmanned since its construction in the Holy Land, its journeyings taking in Ireland.[62] It bears the warning inscription,

Thou man which shalt entir into thys shippe, beware that thou be in stedefaste beleve, for I am Faythe

—indeed, as the virgin informs them, if they have anything less than perfect faith, they will die on entering it.[63] She confirms its dangers by telling them how the Maimed King, despite being a man 'ryght perfite of lyff', received his still unhealed wound from the sword he found after boarding the vessel, and which is intended for Galahad alone. The knights' response is to go on board, precisely because if they are 'a myssecreature other an untrew knyght', they will perish, just as Providence will execute its judgement on the guilty on the open seas.

The last of the *Quest*'s series of boats seems at first sight the most commonplace. In contrast to the marvels of the ship devised by Solomon's wife, there is nothing inherently distinctive about it, except for that mark of lack of distinction, that it is 'withoute sayle other ore'.[64] It functions in the same way as the other unequipped boats that carry saints across seas or rivers, or which transport their relics to new shrines: it constitutes less a test of the virgin's holiness than a demonstration of it. The virgin has no doubt as to its powers—or hers, or God's:

As sone as I am dede putte me in a boote at the next haven, and lat me go as aventures woll lede me. And as sone as ye three com to the cité of Sarras, there to enchyve the Holy Grayle, ye shall fynde me undir a towre aryved.[65]

They obey her instructions, and the wind carries the boat out of sight, and into God's hands. There is nothing random about her journey, and her certainty of her destination marks her as retaining her qualities as guide or pilot, not by means of helm or tiller, but by privileged spiritual knowledge.

The disappearance of the boat from the companions' gaze does not mark its disappearance from the narrative, however, even before it reaches its promised destination. In due course, first Lancelot, then Galahad, are directed to enter it. As with the knights on any quest, their travelling together is only temporary, and the destinies of the boat's passengers are very different. Galahad, like those Irish saints, is on a one-way journey, which will take him ultimately to God. It looks as if Lancelot is likewise travelling towards such singularity, a singularity figured by the holy corpse that he accompanies; but finally his heart retains its centre in the society, and the queen, to which he will return. The maiden herself completes the journey she has prophesied, to Sarras, where the companions of the Grail bury her.

In the course of its journey, this boat takes Lancelot and Galahad around 'yles ferre from folke, where there repayred none but wylde beestes, and ther they founde many straunge adventures and peryllous'.[66] It thus doubles as a *barca aventurosa*, the kind of vessel recognized so immediately by Don Quixote. Tasso, who coined the term in his *Rinaldo*, makes a parallel connection with a chaste woman of exceptional powers, though hers are magic rather than divine. She is a queen named Alba, and it is she who devised for Rinaldo (in John Hoole's eighteenth-century translation)

A wondrous bark of magic texture fram'd,
And this the queen the BARK ADVENTUROUS nam'd;
For every warrior that in this confides,
The vessel swift to some adventure guides.
Without a pilot's aid, by spelful force,
Through billowy seas she holds her certain course.[67]

Tasso elaborates on the motif in the *Gerusalemme Liberata*, for which he supplies two such boats, one bad and one good. A less-innocent Rinaldo is trapped by the enchantress Armida by means of the bad one: she leaves a 'little frigot' by a river-bank, bearing an inscription that seems to promise just such chivalric exploits, on the safe assumption that he will immediately accept the adventure it offers.[68] Its good counterpart carries two of his Christian fellow knights to the Fortunate Islands on a mission to rescue him from her clutches. This is piloted by another lady of more than natural powers, 'in looke a saint, and angell bright in shew', who is virtuous in substance as well as appearance. Her 'little barke', like those of other enchantresses or indeed Perceval's Lucifer, travels at remarkable speed: it 'scant toucht the troubled maine', like a pre-modern hydrofoil. Although she can steer it, she does so by magical knowledge, 'withouten needle, map or card', not by the technological instruments of navigation.[69] It is this female pilot who prophesies to her passenger knights about the Renaissance voyages of discovery of the New World in ways that make their own voyage a prototype for those, turning romance into a figure for history.[70]

The motif of the ship sailing at the bidding of a powerful woman might seem to be ideally formulated for the Elizabethan explorers to take up, but it did not happen. It may not have been sufficiently embedded in English tradition; it may have been associated too much with women who did not make obvious subjects of panegyric—the later and more sinister Morgan le Fay, for instance, is something of a specialist in such vessels.[71] Or it may have been due to a conviction that it is hard work, not magic, that produces results. Such a belief is clearly at work when Spenser turns his attention to the marine section of the *Gerusalemme Liberata* in Book II of the *Faerie Queene*. Here, he cross-fertilizes the meme of the boat controlled by a woman with that of the boat without sail or oar, and imitates Tasso's allegory as much as his narrative. Rinaldo, according to Tasso's own allegorical interpretation, represents the ireful capacity of the soul in conflict with reason, which is represented by Godfrey; Armida, in Fairfax's phrasing, 'is that temptation which laieth siege to the power of our desires'.[72] In just the same way, the passionate Cymochles is attracted to the 'little Gondelay' carrying Phaedria (who is glossed in the verse summary to II. vi as 'immodest mirth'): a boat that travels over the sluggish waves of the Idle Lake

> Withouten oare or pilot it to guide,
> Or winged canvas with the wind to flie.

> II. vi. 5

She can steer it by turning a pin, but since the boat chooses its own way, she does not usually bother. She takes Guyon too over the water to her island when he is looking for a ferry over the lake, but he has to leave behind his palmer, his own representative of reason. Once he has escaped from Phaedria, Spenser describes him resuming the proper course of his quest like 'a pilot well expert in perilous wave', who keeps his eye on 'his card and compas' and his hand on the tiller (II. vii. 1). The metaphor becomes literal in the final voyage Guyon makes with the palmer to Acrasia's country, where the palmer himself steers their 'well rigged boate', and where, when danger threatens, the response is not to ship their oars but to drive them all the harder. Their effort is all the more noticeable by contrast with their further encounter with Phaedria, whose 'boate withouten ore' travels with none of the labour that their own demands.[73] Catholic miracle had demonstrated divine approval of the saintly through the removal of effort, in a figuring of a prelapsarian or a heavenly state without labour; a Protestant work ethic requires that the virtuous must demonstrate their status as elect by strenuous exertion.[74]

'A shippe without sayle other ore' takes you out of your familiar community in more than one sense, and more decisively than any other kind of quest. To survive such an ordeal you must be in effect elect: specially favoured, perhaps by a lady, most often by God, whether you are an innocent victim, or a penitent, or a saint, or a knight. The corollary of that is that your own society is in some sense a failure: unsatisfying, unjust, or of insufficient faith. The transition to the ship from the chivalric quest, the quest on horseback, marks a transition to a new level of experience altogether: one in which the journey constitutes the adventure in itself. On a horseback quest, you journey from the centre of your society to the periphery, and return to the centre to strengthen it. A rudderless boat impels you to the periphery; the centre rejects you, or you turn your back on it. What you find, however, is that what had seemed to be an edge is in fact a new and truer centre. That turning of ethical geography inside out may be another reason why Spenser finds the motif unusable. Book

II opens with a comparison between the still undiscovered world of
Faerieland and the newly discovered world of Peru, the Amazon, and
Virginia (II Proem 2). The object of exploration is to come back, to bring
back the spoils of discovery and colonization to the home country. The
object of his creation of Faerieland is to create a figure for Elizabeth's
'owne realmes' (4). So far as Spenser is concerned, the very point of his
poem is that England is the centre to which all else relates.

CHAPTER THREE

Magic that doesn't work

Romance promises a world of dragons and giants, magic weapons and protective rings, flying horses and self-steering boats. Magic and the supernatural rank high among the distinguishing features of the genre, the most recognizable elements of family resemblance. The association of romance with the marvellous was as high in the sixteenth century as in the Middle Ages: hence the monsters and enchantments that Spenser assembles in the *Faerie Queene*, or the brown-paper dragons and stage giants that inhabited Elizabethan drama before Marlowe and Kyd changed the fashions.[1] It is none the less rare for any romance not to leave a sense of disappointment about its marvels. 'Marvel', by derivation, means what is to be wondered at—from the French *merveiller*, semantically overlapping both with the English *wonder* and with the Latin *admirare*; but all too often romance marvels are neither very wonderful nor very admirable. The dragon is always destined for the chop; a 14-foot giant is bathetic when the gold standard for giants has been set at 16 feet;[2] an oracle carries as much plot intrigue as a detective story where the clues are explained in advance. Still worse, the best chances of creating a sense of wonder or fear are frequently thrown away, as if the authors, having once introduced the requisite supernatural elements, did not know what to do with them. Far from being the most exciting features of a plot, they have the potential for being among the most boring. Peele's *Old Wives Tale*—as its title indicates, a compendium of everyone's favourite motifs from popular romance and folktale—promises a were-bear, a man transformed every night into 'the White Bear of England's wood'; but we only get to see him in the daytime, in ordinary human form.[3] The text as we have it may have been cut, but there still seems to be the implication that a reference to the bearsuit in the property cupboard carries as much, or as little, excitement as putting it on stage. The more that enchantments or fairies or magic potions are expected, the less enthralling they become.

Magic is above all a narrative issue: a way of telling a story; or a problem that gets in the way of telling a story well. The very replicability of magic, the ease with which it can be incorporated into a story, threatens to make it not just a set of memes but a set of clichés. This chapter is exceptional in this book in that it is not about a meme, but about ways of tackling a meme that got out of hand. There is no simple formula for such a process, no equivalent to the rudderless boat, so it was never easily replicable. Yet whether by selective imitation or by a recurrent process of reinvention, one particular way of making magic central to romance appears again and again in the work of the most skilled craftsmen of the genre, and that, paradoxically, is by sidelining it, diverting its wonder elsewhere.

There are all too many examples of why a solution was needed. The collapse of wonder at the marvellous was evident enough to invite parody in *Sir Thopas*: a giant should at least be a safe test of the hero's strength, but Sir Thopas's giant has to be supplied with three heads shortly after his first appearance in an attempt to keep up the interest. The supernatural, in the form of the fairy realm, can on occasion be almost indistinguishable from the human, hence Richard Johnson's fairy queen in *The History of Tom a Lincoln* who *is* indistinguishable from the human. The problem of frustration is intensified in the case of magic objects and amulets, where the reader's expectations are often baffled in ways that can seem quite perverse. There is frequently—indeed, normally—a lack of excitement in the treatment of such talismans, which is reinforced by the minimal part that they play in the plot. Chaucer himself assembles a fine collection of magic objects in the *Squire's Tale*, and then stops short, as if, having once gathered all these marvels together for display, he was not really interested in developing a plot from them. It is quite common for the hero to be given a magic ring—Richard Cœur de Lion gets two, one to protect him against water, one against fire—which is never mentioned again.[4] Of all the magic objects in the *Morte Darthur*, one whose magic power is among the most highly praised is the scabbard of Excalibur, which prevents its wearer from losing blood; but Arthur himself never has the opportunity of using it, and it is thrown away irrecoverably into a lake after it has had only one chance to show its virtue, and then on another man's behalf.[5] Malory leads us to expect that the scabbard will play an important part in the romance, but it is lost forever, without so much as a samite-clad arm in the water to receive it back. Even more baffling than such instances where our expectations are frustrated in one way or another, is a large group of magic objects, distinctive of many of the greatest romances, which are introduced with all the emphasis appropriate to them, and then, when the critical moment arrives, their magic fails to work.

The particular oddity of this lies in the fact that the existence of magic, like God's intervention through miracle, can be demonstrated only by the fact that it does work. A cloak that fails to turn its wearer invisible is likely to be a fraud; and so are recipes for making the philosopher's stone, even though they may incorporate correct chemistry along the way. As the case of alchemy indicates, there is a shifting borderline between magic and science that complicates the issues, since science, like magic, demonstrates its truth by working. It was widely believed that there were special virtues inherent in particular stones, and sometimes there are: magnets *do* attract iron, for reasons that looked like just such a marvellous power until the underlying physical principles were explained. The possible existence of a magnetic rock so powerful that it draws all ships to it and lets none escape, of the kind that keeps Huon of Bordeaux trapped for months and provides Spenser with his Rock of Vile Reproach, was a marvellous extrapolation from an observable fact.[6] And since magnets also have an inherent power to point towards the north, it was not so far-fetched to believe that (for instance) an amethyst would protect its wearer from drunkenness. One might expect that experience would rapidly falsify such a belief, but there is something of a catch-22 about experience: if you get drunk, clearly what you are wearing is not a genuine amethyst. Romances offer an array of plants that have implausible powers of healing, but that some plants have medicinal properties was a fact acknowledged in every manor garden and increasingly by modern pharmacology. What is at issue in instances like these is less magic as beyond the order of nature, than a kind of technological marvel operating just beyond the borders of replicable experience, rather as in modern science fiction. The borderline between fact and magic may involve not a category change but simply the crossing of a very narrow line of possibility. Jays and parrots can talk, sparrowhawks should not; chimpanzees can acquire some principles of unvocalized language, a speaking hind comes from the world of the supernatural. A rhinoceros is every bit as implausible as a unicorn to the vast majority of early modern populations who had never seen either; and the occasional washing up of a narwhal horn on a beach, up to 9 feet of breathtaking spiralling ivory, provided strong evidence for the existence of unicorns. 'Real' unicorns, by contrast, in the shape of Sumatran rhinos, may have been 'marvellous' to the European, but they were also a sad disappointment. 'They are very ugly brutes to look at,' lamented Marco Polo, as he described their swine-like heads drooping downward towards the mud-puddles in which they liked to stand. 'They are not at all such as we describe them when we relate that they let themselves be captured by virgins, but clean contrary to our notions.'[7]

As that example indicates, new discoveries, whether geographical or scientific, could unweave the rainbow, remove the marvel from the marvellous. It had long been recognized that much of what incited wonder was simply unexplained nature: in Gervase of Tilbury's formulation, in which he distinguishes miracle, the preternatural workings of God, from the marvellous,

> We call those things marvels [*mirabilia*] which are beyond our comprehension, even though they are natural: in fact the inability to explain why a thing is so constitutes a marvel.[8]

Yet there is no reduction in the literary category of the marvellous over time. As more and more things were explained, the marvellous expanded its frontiers to match, to the point of inventing new worlds when the old one had yielded up its secrets (Ariosto includes space travel, Spenser creates Fairy Land, modern writers invent fantasy worlds that may be accessible from this, as are Narnia and far-flung galaxies, or may be somewhere else altogether, as are the Shire and Mordor). And explanation left magic, an intervention in the course of nature by non-natural means, largely untouched. Magic occupied a distinctly shady area between the natural and the supernatural, the miraculous and the superstitious. Some of the best brains of the sixteenth century devoted their efforts to understanding magic, in the belief that it, like the physical world, could be made subject to explanation, and therefore control. The same mathematical skills and desire for knowledge that impelled the advances in the understanding of the universe also served as an incentive to put hermetic magic on an equally sound mathematical and astronomical footing. Even the simpler magic or marvellous of the romance variety often reflects far more of observation and experiment than we commonly acknowledge. Dragons, giants, and monstrous beasts may have had their origins, or at least received confirmation, in the discovery of huge fossil bones, which evidently once belonged to something not found in the everyday order of nature.[9] Astrology starts from a firmer experiential base. It is obvious, and correct, that the sun and the moon govern the sequence of night and day, associated circadian rhythms, the seasons, and the tides, and it was easy to extrapolate from that to more distant heavenly bodies, and to regard as causes what we would at best regard as correlations (such as the summer ascendancy of the dog star causing the diseases associated with hot weather). The continuing importance of the pagan gods in the medieval world springs very largely from the fact that the planets carry their names: that the goddess Venus influences love is a personification—a deification—of the amorous influence of the planet Venus on humankind. So, in the *Knight's Tale* and *The Two Noble Kinsmen*, the principles of love (Venus) and war (Mars) find themselves at odds; their dispute is resolved by Saturn, malevolent fortune, in the form of Arcite's horse rearing and mortally injuring him—malevolence personified as Saturn in the tale, but no more than an accident with a strong Saturnian colouring in the play.[10] In both, Emily, who prays to Diana/Lucina for perpetual virginity, overlooks the fact that the moon is also the presiding power over change,[11] and, since female fertility correlates with the lunar unit of the month, over childbirth. Aurelius' first idea for drowning the rocks in the *Franklin's Tale* is to pray to Apollo that he and his sister, Lucina, should stay in exact opposition for two years: that is, that the sun and moon should become in effect geostationary satellites, and so hold the tide high. Not just astrology, therefore, but supernatural machinery needs careful reading: there may be more of the ordinary processes of nature in it than first meets the eye.

Such encompassing of marvel and the supernatural within the physical cosmos removes some of the sense of otherness, of some extraordinary intervention in the familiar world, that magic needs if it is to stir a proper sense of wonder. A further problem arises from the devaluing of the preternatural by its very predictability in romance: what is expected is not likely to be exciting. Even with three heads, Sir Thopas's giant is rather *déjà vu*, and his fairy mistress is little better. She is, first, simply preferable to the other women on offer:

> An elf-queene wol I love, ywis,
> For in this world no womman is
> Worthy to be my make
> In towne;

> VII.790–3

and he proceeds to look for her rather as a twitcher would pursue an unusual species of bird:

> Into his sadel he clamb anon,
> And priketh over stile and stoon
> An elf-queene for t'espye.

> 797–9

How do you keep the marvellous wonderful? Many of the most popular romances, such as *Bevis of Hamptoun*, use it to provide a bit of extra thrill or to cover a need in the story that is hard to plot in any other way: giants and dragons make more exciting opponents than ordinary knights, and Bevis's future wife, Josiane, preserves her virginity for him through several years of marriage to a heathen king by means of a different talisman or charm in almost every surviving text—its precise nature does not matter so long as it serves the required end.[12] One way to restore the wonder to such episodes is to intensify the naturalism of the background: to portray a world that looks as if it operates by familiar criteria, and then to disrupt it. That master storyteller J. R. R. Tolkien gets the story of *Farmer Giles of Ham* under way with an account of how Farmer Giles's dog manages to escape from the kitchen one night to go for a walk:

He had a fancy for moonshine, and rabbits. He had no idea, of course, that a giant was also out for a walk.[13]

And the *Gawain*-poet uses exactly the same technique, first drawing the Christmas revels at Arthur's court on the model of those found in fourteenth-century Windsor or Westminster, without even a Round Table to mark the difference, and then having the entry of the huge green man on his green horse silence the revelry. The Green Knight keeps his spookiness by never being explained—and tends to lose it at the end of the poem when explanations are offered. Its Percy Folio retelling, the *Grene Knight*, explains him at the start, and loses the spookiness accordingly.[14] It is as if the supernatural is killed by the rational, but can only be saved by the commonplace.

Even working magic has its problems, for the more one wonders at the marvel, the less admirable is the hero who benefits from it. An invincible sword might just as well be wielded by a coward as a hero, since it makes bravery or physical prowess unnecessary. A protective ring is very nice for the wearer, but its wearer could be anybody. The more special the magic powers, the less special the characters appear who have them at their disposal. Magic and heroism find it very hard to occupy the same text, or the same portion of the text. Ariosto's Ruggiero possesses a magic shield that renders his opponents helpless, but he is careful to avoid what might be thought the fraud of using it, and after he accidentally does so, he is so anxious lest all his prowess be ascribed to magic that he throws it into a well—thereby winning all the greater renown.[15] Gawain is on occasion endowed with strength that increases double or threefold up until noon; but it figures most strongly in the romances in which the protagonist is fighting against Gawain rather than those where he himself holds centre stage. The highest heroism lies in the ability of a mere man to resist such supernatural powers: Malory cites them when our sympathies lie entirely with his opponent, Lancelot.[16] The scabbard of Excalibur is a striking instance of the same phenomenon. In the one episode in which it plays a part, it has been stolen along with Excalibur itself by Morgan le Fay, for her lover Accolon to use in his combat with Arthur. The king has to prove his heroism, not while he is protected by the scabbard and fighting with the sword that draws blood at every stroke, but when his opponent has them; he has to fight against supernatural odds, and yet he wins.

The magic in this instance works, but not in the way that the plot had seemed to promise. The episode elicits a reaction of wonder, not at the magic of the weapons but at Arthur's own prowess. This effect has been named by Caroline Walker Bynum, in her study of wonder, as a 'significance-reaction'.[17] The magic is not important in itself, but for what it reveals: human qualities at their highest can be appreciated to the full only when they are measured against the supernatural, not when they operate in conjunction with it. What we are invited to marvel at is not the magic, but at courage and endurance unaided by magic. Wonder and admiration are transferred from the supernatural to the human.

Romances therefore rarely make magic the driving factor in the plot, or the decisive factor in the hero's or heroine's success. Magic and the supernatural often appear oddly supplementary: decoration rather than substance. *Sir Launfal* and *Huon of Bordeaux*, with their active fairy involvement with the hero throughout the story, are the exceptions, not the norm; they fall in that respect closer to fairytale, a genre that might be thought closely analogous to the romance but which is much more likely to make the supernatural of central importance. The life of the heroine of a fairytale can be changed by a fairy godmother, or preserved by a goblin who can spin straw into gold; the hero can find himself quite unexpectedly in possession of a magic flute or lamp. Even in fairytale, however, magic often gives way to practical possibility and human determination at the end. Once the magic has served to bring Cinderella to the notice of the prince, he searches her out himself. Rumpelstiltskin gives away his own secret and so enables the heroine to release herself from his schemes. One of the slightly disconcerting things about the end of *A Midsummer Night's Dream* is that it fails to restore this emphasis on the human: the fairy magic is needed to sort out the lovers into the right couples; love will not do the work by itself. Such unconditional driving of a plot by magic or the supernatural does, however, move towards the edge of the generic spectrum of romance. The social concerns of the genre may be one reason for this: magic of this kind is not going to be encountered in the real world, nor can it in itself supply any model of behaviour unless it becomes allegorical (hence its extensive use in the *Faerie Queene*). The hero, the heroine, and their processes of self-becoming require more of a human focus. The most striking way for an author to integrate the two, to fulfil the audience's pleasurable expectations of magic while keeping the inner meaning of the story insistently on the central characters, is for the magic not to work—or more accurately, when what works is not any power or virtue within the magic object, but some power or virtue in its bearer.

NON-FUNCTIONING MAGIC

Such a use of magic emerged as the problem of the predictability of marvel became evident. Magic was beginning simply to fail to work, both literally and in audience effect, without any compensating human significance. A single example—fictitious in every detail but based on actual romance situations—will show the range of ways in which these failures manifest themselves. Let us suppose that the lady has presented her knight with a magic flying horse, one like those of the *Squire's Tale*, *Valentine and Orson*, and *Don Quixote*, that is operated by a pin in its ear.[18] She has now been carried off, and is enclosed in a tower in Babylon in dire peril; and if the knight does not arrive by nightfall she will be burned alive, or married, or meet some equally dreadful fate. The hero has at his disposal the horse, and also an airline ticket for a scheduled flight from London Heathrow. (This is important: it is generally only in fairytales, as distinct from romances, that the magic is forced on the hero—that he rubs the lamp and the genie appears, whether he is wanted or not. In romance the hero has the option of refusing the magic.) It might now be expected that the author would next describe the hero's astonishing and extraordinary flight through the air on his magic horse; but this happens surprisingly seldom, even if those romances are included where the equivalent of the journey by flying horse is as routine as the scheduled flight. It is much more likely that the hero will get onto the horse—and nothing will happen. He has to flag down a taxi, rush to the airport, and arrive both there and (after a further delay on the runway) at Babylon after everyone thinks he will be too late. That the author may mention later that the horse was programmed only to fly to Camelot does not enhance its reputation as magic in the reader's eye. Alternatively, the horse may indeed be programmed to fly to Babylon, but on arrival the hero discovers that the lady has been moved to Peking; so he has to take a scheduled plane flight in order to reach his desired destination. Worse, there are occasions when the hero hears the dreadful news, rushes desperately after the taxi, the plane, and so on, arrives safely, and only remembers at that stage that he had the simple option of flying by horse instead. Or the lady may have given it to the hero with stern warnings about what will happen if he carries more than 20 kilos of baggage on it. In the excitement of the moment, he slings his battle-steed behind the saddle of his artificial horse, and loads on a couple of spare suits of armour as well; the magic horse operates as promised, and all that happens afterwards is that the lady tells him he should not have taken the risk. There is also the possibility—perhaps the most frustrating of all— that the poet will state the initial situation, and then, in the next sentence, present his hero safely arrived in Babylon and carrying on with his adventures, but with no mention at all as to which method of transport he used.

Ludicrous as these situations sound, they can all be paralleled many times over from medieval romances. The horse that will not take off because the programming is wrong is represented by Lancelot in the *Chevalier de la Charrette* of Chrétien de Troyes, who finds himself trapped by a portcullis; he accordingly gazes on the ring that will protect him against enchantment. But the trap is quite natural; nothing whatever happens, and Lancelot has to fight his way out by ordinary means.[19] Was the ring really magic? We have to take Chrétien's word for it; but it is perhaps not asking too much of an author that his magic should not only exist but be seen to exist. The need for the plane flight in addition to the horse is the situation of the lady Ydoine in the Anglo-Norman *Amadas et Ydoine*, who is about to be married to an unwanted suitor; so she arranges for three *sorcières* to enter the chamber of her bridegroom-to-be through a tiny hole in the wall, and terrify him with terrible prophecies about what will happen if he goes ahead with the marriage. The sorceresses do their stuff, but what Ydoine has overlooked is that the man is *hardis et corageus*, and decides to marry her anyway. She therefore has to invent an entirely natural set of excuses to prevent his sleeping with her.[20] The hero who overlooks his flying horse is Huon of Bordeaux, who fights a mighty combat to get past the porters defending the entrance to the castle of the Emir of Babylon because he simply forgets that he has acquired a ring from a giant that will take him past them without opposition.[21] Instead, he tells the porters that he is a Saracen, in direct contravention of his oath

to the fairy king Oberon that he would never lie; but the breaking of the
prohibition has none of the dire consequences that had been promised,
nor indeed any consequences at all. A comparable ignoring of the excess
baggage warning occurs in Chrétien's *Yvain*, when a damsel smears the
hero all over with a magic ointment when she has been strictly instructed
only to put a little on his temples; she throws the box away, telling her
mistress she dropped it; the lady expresses bitter regret, and that is the
end of the matter.[22] The audience's expectations are aroused and then let
down, for no apparent reason. As for not knowing what happens,
whether the magic works or not, Yvain is given a ring by his lady that will
protect him against all evil, sickness, and imprisonment; at the end of a
year, when the ring is taken away from him, he is certainly still healthy
and free, but we are never told whether the ring had anything to do with
it.[23] Once again, it may be magic, but it is not seen to be so. The frustra-
tion is the same as in the *Old Wives Tale*, where the actors seem to
promise that the bearsuit will be got out of the property cupboard, but it
never appears on stage; or as if an empty bearsuit did indeed appear, but
with neither a role in the plot nor any actor inside it to make it move.

   Huon of Bordeaux might be accused of having a scattershot effect about
its magic, but the same is not true of *Amadas et Ydoine*, and Chrétien is
generally credited with actually possessing the high level of thought about
how he writes that he claims for himself. These examples would seem to
suggest a certain mindlessness at the level of both narrative and meaning,
matter and *sentence*. The texts read as if a gesturing towards magic were
sufficient to fulfil audience expectations, however badly those expecta-
tions might be let down at the level of plot: as if a token generic require-
ment mattered more than coherence of action. Their narrative
uselessness is matched by their lack of any obvious ethical or emotional
function. But one of these incidents does carry a significance that takes it
beyond bathos, and that is the last—Yvain's protective ring. It certainly
seemed significant enough to the early fourteenth-century English
adapter of the romance for him to follow his source particularly faithfully
at this point in his own version, *Ywain and Gawain*. The lady gives it to
Yvain/Ywain after their marriage, when he requests leave of absence to
maintain his knightly reputation in the chivalric world. She grants this on
condition that he return in a year's time, the penalty being that he will
lose her if he fails. He is horrified by the thought that he might be sick, or
wounded, or in prison, and so lose her against his will; and she gives him
the ring to protect him against all such eventualities. Her speech in
Middle English runs as follows (the italics are mine):

I sal lene to yow my ring,   [shall lend
That es to me a ful dere thing:
In nane anger sal ye be,   [no distress
Whils ye it have and thinkes on me.
I sal tel to yow onane   [at once
The vertu that es in the stane: [stone
It es na preson yow sal halde,
Al if yowre fase be manyfalde;   [even; foes; many
With sekenes sal ye noght be tane,   [taken
Ne of yowre blode ye sal lese nane;   [lose none
In batel tane sal ye noght be,
Whils ye it have and thinkes on me;
And ay, whils ye er trew of love,
Over al sal ye be obove.[24]   [victorious

Ywain will be protected by two things: the ring itself and his love for his lady. The ring's operation is guaranteed only as long as he holds her in his mind—the twice-repeated 'whils ye it have and thinkes on me'. The only thing that will prevent Ywain's return, in other words, is Ywain himself. Every physical barrier has been removed in advance. In the event, he forgets; the ring is taken back, and the knight, faced with his own disloyalty, his breaking of *trouthe*, goes mad—a literal acting out of his loss of any claim to knighthood or integrity.[25] He has to fight his way back to chivalric recognition, and to his wife, under his own strength. The magic of the ring has served no plot function in itself, and we have never seen it in action; but its very existence serves to highlight something in Ywain, to tell us about the nature of his failure and the nature of knighthood. The very lack of wonder attaching to the marvel here transfers to Ywain: not only has he not done anything extraordinary, he has failed to live up to any husband's basic obligation of remembering his wife.

The idea behind all this seems to be that while 'ordinary' magic—magic that works—may be of some use for the plot, it does not add anything of genuine significance. It may be appropriate for ballad or fairytale, but the process of turning tale into high-culture romance requires something more. Magic that does not work, by definition, has little to do with plot; but it can be used in a different way—psychologically rather than magically. It is, in fact, characteristic of the romances that handle the conventions of the genre most thoughtfully that the magic that fails to work should divert its expected quality of marvel to showing what unaided humanity can do—or occasionally, as in Yvain's case, what it fails to do. The earliest generation of romance-writers still seem to have been working their way towards a full understanding of this use of magic: Chrétien does not always make the function of his ineffective magic so clear. He could indeed be charged with not having even this incident of the ring fully worked out: since its magic depends on Yvain's remembering his lady, and since he in fact forgets her, does the magic still operate, or is it rendered useless? Is he saved from sickness and imprisonment by wearing it, even though he does not fulfil the condition of thinking of her? The ring is never put to the test; but it is no more necessary for it to work logically than magically. It fulfils the function required of it—to demonstrate Yvain's natural failing—and that is enough. A demonstration that it did or did not have real magic powers would be no more than a digression: in the economy of the narrative, the ring is necessary, but not its magic. The wonder that you might expect to expend on the magic is transferred to the emotional or ethical meaning it points to; and the frustration of plot, in the talisman that never does anything, is transmuted into a development of its inner significance, *sens* over *matière*, Bynum's 'significance-reaction', that could never be so clearly achieved in any other way.

It follows from this that it is the authors who have the greatest concern with the *sentence*, the inner meaning, of their stories, or with the emotional life of their characters, who will use the motif most fully. Not surprisingly, one of the earliest writers to exploit its potential to structure an entire romance—or at least, a mini-romance such as comprises a Breton *lai*—is Marie de France. The sheer scale of a full-sized romance demands an emphasis on plot and event such as tends to call for a more functional kind of magic, but Marie's *lais* transfer the interest from the external event to the internal, the emotional. Her *lai* of the two lovers, *Les Deux Amants*, can be taken as a defining example of magic that fails to work magically but that does work for the poem. Here, the heroine's father has laid down that no one shall marry his daughter unless he carries her in his arms up a steep mountain: a task that is in human terms impossible. A number of suitors try, and inevitably fail; but finally, a young nobleman falls in love with her, and she with him. In order to enable him to pass the test, she sends him to her aunt, who is skilled in herbs and medicines, to get a potion that will give him the necessary strength: a potion, in other words, that will give him superhuman powers. He obtains the potion, but, on the day of the test, he is so overjoyed to see his lady that he forgets to drink it. As he climbs with her she realizes that his strength is failing and urges him to drink, but he refuses, twice. He completes the climb under his own strength; but, when he reaches the top, he dies. Having tried unsuccessfully to revive him with the potion, she breaks the vessel and spills it. She dies on her lover's body, and they are buried in a single tomb.

A man needs more than human strength to surmount this barrier to love: the drink is provided as the necessary supernatural means, but in fact the superhuman power is to be found in his love itself. The supernatural properties of the potion are transferred to his emotion—they become the means by which the power of love is made manifest. The magic liquid becomes the focus, the measure, and the means of definition of heroic ideals and sublime emotions, and how those ideals and emotions can break the limits of bodily capacity. As magic, it is useless; but magic is not in fact what is at issue here. The drink is used to make a point, not about the nature of the supernatural, but about the nature of love.

Marie's *Lais* have a particular concern with *sens* as well as *matière*, as befits an author writing in the courtly language of French in England. It is more surprising to find a closely comparable use of magic in the very earliest examples of Middle English romance, and it is a salutary reminder, too, that the shift in language does not necessarily signal any major shift in audience sophistication. In *King Horn*, the magic object is a ring, and it is used, or has the potential for being used, in just the same way as the potion in *Les Deux Amants*, as a means of defining the emotional statement that shapes the story. Rimenhild, daughter of the king who has taken in the exiled Horn, falls in love with him and offers herself to him as his wife. He refuses to be acknowledged as her suitor until he has proved himself in battle; and she gives him the ring to assist him.

> Tak nu her this gold ring;
> God him is the dubbing.   [it is finely ornamented
> Ther is upon the ringe
> Igrave 'Rymenhild the yonge';   [engraved
> Ther nis non betere anonder sunne,   [under
> That eny man of telle cunne.   [could tell of
> For my luve thu hit were,   [wear
> And on thi finger thu him bere.
> The stones beoth of such grace   [are of such power
> That thu ne shalt in none place
> Of none duntes beon ofdrad,   [be afraid of any blows
> Ne on bataille beon amad   [lose your nerve
> *Ef thu loke theran*
> *And thenke upon thi lemman.*[26]

As that last couplet shows, the condition of thinking of his lady to make the magic work—the condition that Chrétien fails to follow up in *Yvain*—becomes the focus of the story. In Horn's progress upwards in social and chivalric recognition, which culminates in his winning back his kingdom and consummating his marriage with Rimenhild, whenever he is in battle against heavy odds,

> He lokede on the ringe,
> And thoghte on Rymenhilde,
>
> 617–8; cf. 881–2

and each time he gains the victory. This could hardly be less convincing as magic. If he remembers to look at the ring (and he makes a habit of doing so before fighting), then of course he is thinking of her; and it is a courtly commonplace that a knight who sets his thoughts on his lady in battle fears no blows and emerges victorious.[27] 'Think on me' or 'think on your lemman' indeed becomes a meme in itself, with just such a meaning.[28] There needs no magic ring to tell us this; and, indeed, if it were not for Rimenhild's statement that it is the special 'grace' of the stones that gives him courage, it would never to occur to us that magic was involved at all. In effect, magic is not involved; the ring becomes simply a symbol of their love. *King Horn* is not a poem in which either the poet or the characters spend time analysing what is going on, but the outward statements and actions serve to demonstrate the inner invisible grace that comes from love, not from gemstones of power.

That *King Horn* is not an isolated instance is shown by a comparable use of magic in the romance that appears alongside it in its earliest manuscript, the thirteenth-century *Floris and Blancheflour*. Floris too is given a ring, in his case by his mother, the queen, as he sets out to search for his sweetheart Blancheflour:

> Of hur finger she braide a ring: [took
> 'Have now this ilke ring:
> While it is thine, dought no thing   [fear
> Of fire brenning ne water in the see;   [burning
> Ne iren ne steele shal dere thee.'[29]   [harm

This is a talisman of invulnerability almost without conditions: 'while it is thine' is the only qualification. Floris eventually finds Blancheflour in the tower of the emir of Babylon; the catastrophe is precipitated when the emir finds them in bed together, and they are taken out to be burned.

Florys drough forth that ring
That his moder him gaf at her parting:
'Have this ring, lemman min:
Thou shalt not die while it is thin.'
Blaunchefloure seide tho,
'So ne shall it never go:
That this ring shall help me,
And the deed on thee see.'   [see you killed
Florys that ring hur raught   [gave
And she it him again betaught;   [gave back
Nouther ne will other deed seene:
They lete it falle hem bitwene.
A king com after; a ring he fonde
And brought it forth in his honde.[30]

All the onlookers except the one who matters, the emir himself, are filled with pity. The king who picked up the ring also 'wolde hem save to the lif, | And told how for the ring they gon strif' (1000–1); and he manages to persuade the emir to recall Floris for questioning, twice, so that finally the whole story comes out and everything ends happily, with the emir marrying Claris, Blancheflour's companion, and Floris becoming king. But is it the ring that saves them? Does it, by a special extension of its magic powers, protect them both, even though neither of them is wearing it? The repetition of 'that ilke king *that the ring fonde*' whenever he intervenes to save them suggests that perhaps it does. But the question is irrelevant to the central issue. What saves them is their total faithfulness and courtesy towards each other, and the ring does nothing except epitomize the absoluteness of their love.

It was a brilliant and powerful solution to the problem of magic. It is not, however, one that can become a burr in the mind, that can be lifted whole and transferred to other texts; and even in this story, as its numerous translations and adaptations show, it was found intensely puzzling. Working magic may have the memetic quality of replication, but magic that doesn't work, for all that it is found so widely, is more problematic. In the genetic analogy for the memes of romance, magic that doesn't work behaves more like a recessive gene, or a recurrent mutation—though it is one that is entirely under the control of the authors who activate it.

NON-REPLICATING MAGIC

As a solution to the problem of making magic interesting, magic that does not work magically appears in a wide variety of texts and authors across widely varying historical or political contexts. Many of the most striking examples occur in French, Anglo-Norman, and English, but others occur in further romances across many different languages and centuries. Despite this wide dissemination, it is neither universal nor random. It never seems to have been part of the stock-in-trade of romance conventions; it is produced by writers with the most conscious sense of literary purpose beyond storytelling alone, and lost by those who are most concerned just with telling the story. Its wide diffusion cannot therefore be accounted for by the fact that it is part of the subject-matter of a series of different stories. It is almost of the essence of non-functioning magic that it is not part of the plot, and so not part of the basic outline of a story such as is likely to be preserved in oral tradition or in repeated treatments of the same material. A translation or a close adaptation is likely to preserve it, but the creation of a new text from the same story outline will not. The faithfully replicating memes of working magic belong to the sphere of *matter*, non-functioning magic much more to *sentence*. It is typical of courtly romance; it is almost unheard of in popular romance or ballad or folktale. There, magic either works or else it is forgotten, and in either case its interest generally stops there. The differences in the treatment of magic therefore correlate less with region or historical change than with social level.

In the great romances, the magic that fails to work magically goes in tandem with their concern with ideals of behaviour and human perfectibility. Its appearance depends on the cultural capacities of particular audiences, and on the narrative skills and priorities of individual authors. The meaning inherent in the motif varies only slightly from one culture to another—all the authors who use it seem to be primarily concerned with the production of wonder at human capacities (or the negative of that) rather than with anything more topical—but that comparative lack of sensitivity to historical moment is offset by the social particularity of its use. Whether it figures at all depends primarily on what Jacques le Goff has described as the 'humus sociale', the fertilizing medium of social placing that operates as the key determinant of literary production and meaning.[31] It is constantly re-invented by sophisticated authors writing for the more élite, more thoughtful, or more leisured audiences, who are accustomed to thinking of literature as carrying an inherent cultural capital, as something more important than entertainment and more subtle than direct preaching. Such magic has a high potential for becoming a focus for discussion or debate: it appears most often in works designed for reading in social contexts that would enable such debate, the parlour or chamber rather than the hall or the inn, or by those with sufficient literacy and leisure for personal reading, for whom private thought can take the place of discussion. The way the motif is used can therefore be informative in charting the relationship of various versions of the same story, partly in terms of a stemma of redactions, but more importantly as evidence in establishing the social level of a text. It becomes a marker for the division between high and low culture: not because it is consistently found in high culture, but because it is almost never found in low, and its disappearance between one and the other can be traced with unusual precision. The main exception is in Shakespeare himself, writing for the equally exceptional social inclusiveness of the audiences for Elizabethan drama, from the queen to the apprentice. Even while he was creating new examples of the motif, however, other existing instances were disappearing at an ever-increasing rate as romances slithered down from an élite manuscript culture into bulk prints and then into ballads and chapbooks. What happens to magic can show right in front of our eyes a story's transition into high culture, or the popularizing of narrative for less-sophisticated readers.

Marie de France was writing for a courtly audience, and *Les Deux Amants* was not one of her lais that was given the accolade of rewriting: perhaps the impossibility of making the magic actually drive the story kept it reserved for a cultural élite. The way such magic disappears from the less courtly or less-thoughtful treatments of a story is, however, abundantly demonstrated by the dissemination history of a number of romances, *Horn* being in the forefront of them. The process can be seen in action across its various texts in Anglo-Norman and Middle and regional English. Despite the existence of an Anglo-Norman version from *c.*1170, the earliest surviving English redaction, the thirteenth-century *King Horn*, probably represents the original most closely, and further evidence for that precedence lies in the fact that it is in this version that the ring functions most effectively as symbol and least effectively as magic.[32] The other versions of the romance show what happens when a different poet treats the same story, or when it is popularized—or even just when it is re-copied: one of the manuscripts of *King Horn* cuts out the crucial couplet that Horn must 'think on' Rimenhild,

presumably because it did not register with the scribe as being impor-
tant.[33] The Anglo-Norman *Romance of Horn*, for all its courtliness, loses
much of the symbolic power of the ring by making it more magic. Its
introduction into the poem is weakened by the fact that it is the third
occasion on which Rigmel/Rimenhild has offered Horn a ring: once he
refuses; the second time, after fighting a major battle, he accepts the same,
non-magic, ring as a love-token; and the third time, after a further battle,
Rigmel exchanges this for the magic ring. This second ring will protect
the wearer from death by fire, water, or battle[34]—the first two of these
being irrelevant, and the last seeming rather *de trop* when he has already
fought so much. Any risk that it might detract from his prowess is
avoided by the fact that he has established his chivalric credentials with-
out its assistance; but that in turn means that the ring receives very little
further mention. The one time it is recalled is in the course of Horn's
combat against the pagan who killed his father; and then it is made clear
that it is desire for vengeance more than the love of Rigmel or possession
of the ring that spurs him to victory.[35] The main function of the ring in
this text is to serve as a recognition token when he returns to Rigmel in
disguise, for which its magic powers are irrelevant. Just how irrelevant is
indicated by the prose version made in the fifteenth century, which was
itself twice translated into English and printed over several decades under
the title of *The Noble History of King Ponthus* (the new name for the Horn
character): here, there is just one ring, and it is not magic at all. Ponthus
has the same powers as a fighter as in *King Horn*, but without any assist-
ance apart from the fact of his love: 'It was not I, that dide the aventures
of armes, bot it was ye; wherof I thonke your goode ladyshipp—for the
might and the hardenes that I have, I have itt of you, for of my selfe I
couthe not undretake itt.'[36] The only use made of the ring is, again, as a
recognition token. The same recognition scene occurs in *King Horn*, but
there, where the ring has already acquired its quiet potency as a symbol
of love, the incident becomes much more charged; it is the power of love
signified by the ring as much as the object itself that reveals Horn to
Rimenhild.

There are two other English versions of the story, the romance of *Horn
Childe* from the early fourteenth-century Auchinleck manuscript, and
the ballad *Hind Horn*. In both these, the magic ring is essential to the plot,
in that the stone turns pale if the heroine's love fades.[37] Horn notices its
pallor while he is away from his beloved, and hurries back to prevent her
from being married to another suitor. This looks like a rationalization of
the *King Horn* kind of ring, in that the magic works magically; but the

change loses the point of the original. It even loses its own point, in so far as Rimnild's love for Horn is threatened rather than diminished. These more popular versions have substituted a different folklore motif in what seems to be an effort to make the magic work.[38] The ring fulfils the function that might be taken by an email or a mobile phone in a modern version, as a means of communication over distance, and the essential quality of *fin amor* of the earlier version is lost to a piece of supernatural mechanics. The redactor who produced *Horn Childe* (perhaps on the basis of a version current in oral tradition rather than directly from either the Anglo-Norman or the earlier English text), and the oral transmission that preserved the ballads, lose the point of magic raised to the level of symbol; only the *King Horn* poet invents it or recognizes it from whatever the ultimate source of the story was. The difference between expressing a *sentence* and reproducing subject-matter emerges very clearly from such an array of different versions. Chrétien's careful distinction between himself and 'cil qui de conter vivre vuelent', professional storytellers who spoil and corrupt their stories, acquires a new kind of particularity when it is placed in a context of this kind.[39]

The array of versions and the variations in their treatment of the protective ring is even greater in the case of *Floris and Blancheflour*. The principle that magic that fails to work is characteristic of individual courtly treatments of a story still generally holds good, but the matter is unusually complicated because of the Europe-wide dissemination of the romance and the still unsettled debate as to which versions derive from which others. It was first composed in France, probably around 1160, but it exists in two distinct versions, known (with misleading particularity about readership) as the 'roman aristocratique' and the 'roman populaire'. Even the two-and-a-half surviving manuscripts of the 'roman aristocratique' vary markedly in their treatment of the ring, as if individual scribes were trying to rationalize the material they were copying.[40] Besides its Middle English version, the romance also exists in Middle High German (by Konrad Fleck), Low German, Dutch (by Diederik van Assenede), Norse, Swedish, Italian, Spanish, Greek, and a few other languages and dialects, each deriving ultimately from one or other of the French redactions or their lost common source.[41] One group of versions, including the English, Fleck's, and Diederik's, derives from one particular variant of the 'roman aristocratique' and replicates both its ring and its non-magical operation to save the lovers, as described above. The northern versions have the ring work magically, but alter its powers to endow invincibility: it ensures Floris's victory when he offers to prove their innocence by combat.[42] The 'version populaire' contains no ring at all, but it does give Floris a sword with a hilt containing relics that give victory to the defender of a just cause; he accordingly—or at least, subsequently—saves his beloved from being burned in an episode placed earlier in the romance, when she is the victim of a false accusation before she is carried off to Babylon.[43] A further group, consisting of the Italian *Cantare de Fiorio e Biancifiore*, Boccaccio's *Filocolo*, and the Spanish romance, contains two rings. The first is given to Floris by Blancheflour, and its property is to turn pale if she is in trouble—rather like the ring in *Horn Childe*. It functions, correctly and magically, in the episode of false accusation. The second ring has the same properties as the one in the 'roman aristocratique', but here it works: the lovers each try to give it to the other, then they both hold it, and they are preserved in the midst of the flames.[44] In the *Filocolo*, they also call on the gods for help, and the gods duly step in to save them, though Boccaccio notes that they need not have bothered since the ring would have been sufficient.[45] The goddess most involved in their rescue is Venus: in theory, she could represent the power of love rather than just a piece of Classical machinery, but in practice Boccaccio treats her as an actual goddess, perhaps as an expression of his proto-humanist reading of Ovid and Virgil. She is shown acting supernaturally, just as we are told that the ring acts magically: neither is allowed to function through symbolic power alone. Plot marvels substitute for the wonder of the 'significance-reaction' at a love stronger than death.

The association between magic and wonder is almost a reflex response, and if the narrative treatment of magic promises to be powerful in itself, it takes quite strong action on the part of an individual author to divert the wonder onto the human meaning of the story. On occasion, it is possible to see such a process in action, where a writer takes up a promising motif of magic and disables it in front of our eyes. That the most notable examples of such a process occur in the work of Gottfried von Strassburg and Chaucer is an indication of the degree of literary self-awareness involved in such a move.

The disabling is entirely literal in Gottfried's *Tristan*, and its purpose in displacing wonder from magic to emotion unusually clear. The episode concerns the marvellous dog Petit-creiu.[46] The lovers are undergoing one of their periods of separation, and they are desperately unhappy. Tristan, who has withdrawn to Wales, defeats a giant in order to win the animal, which has two remarkable properties: its fur is of every conceivable colour; and from its collar hangs a bell whose sound banishes all sadness—a magic bell, in fact. Tristan wants the dog not to solace himself but to send to Isolt, who has it carried around with her everywhere. Up to this point, Gottfried is known to be following his source, the Anglo-Norman *Tristan* of Thomas, since the Norse and Middle English versions based on that both contain the incident.[47] But in Gottfried's conclusion, Isolt breaks the bell off its chain, for she has no wish to be happy while Tristan is suffering, and the dog's constant presence increases her grief by reminding her of her lover's absence. The genre's insistence that the use of magic lies in the protagonist's own choice here takes the unusual form of having them actively refuse it, Tristan by giving the marvel away, Isolt by rendering it un-marvellous.[48] The disabling of the bell makes no difference at all to the plot. Once again, the magic that does not work, the happiness-inducing bell that increases sorrow, has nothing to do with the inherited story-line and everything to do with the courtly development of inner meaning. The plot stands still while the episode is acted out, but the pause in the action allows space for a wonder that has nothing to do with the marvellousness of the magic.

Chaucer's analogous episode is strictly an act of elimination of magic from his source rather than its disabling within the narrative: the removal of the rocks from the coast of Brittany in the *Franklin's Tale*. The tale claims at its opening to be a Breton *lai*, but it is not a story with Breton antecedents: if the generic claim means anything, it is perhaps designed to call its audience's attention to a shift in focus from plot to emotion such as is typical of Marie's own work, and perhaps to a greater allowance for magic than Chaucer usually makes. The story itself is a free variation on a tale of Boccaccio's, about how a suitor to a married lady fulfils her impossible condition for loving him, that is, that he should create a blossoming garden in the middle of winter.[49] Boccaccio's lover hires an enchanter to conjure up such a garden, and the lady and her companions walk through it. Chaucer's lady, Dorigen, declares that before she will love the squire who is soliciting her, he must remove the coastal rocks that threaten her husband's homecoming. It is a euphemism for rejection, her synonym for 'never': 'for wel I woot that it shal never betyde' (*CT*, V. 1001). Despite being such a cause of anxiety to her both before and after their disappearance, however, the rocks as physical objects are remarkably unimportant in the story. They are significant because they represent Dorigen's fears for her husband, and therefore for her future happiness; but even when the 'subtil clerk' who effects their disappearance has completed his machinations, the status of the rocks remains equivocal. 'It *semed* that alle the rokkes were aweye' (1296), and whether

an illusorily absent set of rocks might still wreck a ship is by now beside
the point, since the husband has arrived back safely some time before
with any dangers from the rocks unmentioned. It is of no consequence at
all whether they are really still there or not, and nobody in the tale appar-
ently goes to look: wonder at the marvel is entirely absent, even though
their disappearance for 'a wyke or tweye' (1295) makes it quite clear that
merely natural processes, such as high tides, are out of the question.[50] By
the time Chaucer has moved into the consequences of the magic on the
characters, the rocks have sunk well below the threshold of conscious-
ness. The question at issue is not how or whether the magic has worked,
but how this will make everyone behave. The vanishing of the rocks con-
stitutes a trial, a kind of moral *épreuve*, through which each of the men in
the story must pass by releasing his claim in a promise made to him, a
promise itself being a pledging of troth. The husband must respect his
wife's *trouthe*, her word given to the squire, above her marital oath made
to himself; the squire must release the lady from her unintended oath,
and so forgo the sexual pleasure he desires; the clerk must release the
squire from his monetary contract and forgo his payment. Each act of
renunciation encourages the others to follow suit, to enable the tale's
happy ending.

As in the case of *Horn* and *Floris*, such a use of magic did not transmit
through retellings, and it is handled very differently in the early seven-
teenth-century dramatization of the same story by Nathan Field and
John Fletcher, *The Triumph of Honour*. There, the setting is transferred to
the Graeco-Roman world, and the rocks are never mentioned until the
play's tough-minded Dorigen swears by them in her refusal of the propo-
sitions made to her by the general who has just invaded her country and
defeated her husband. Unexpected as the rocks are in the text, a theatri-
cal audience would have been prepared for something of the kind by their
actual presence as stage properties. Their disappearance is represented in
the stage directions by 'Solemn musick. A mist ariseth, the rocks
remove.'[51] However the 'mist' was contrived (presumably by a veil;
smoke would be hard to control with sufficient precision), the magic is
seen to work by the spectators; but any wonder attaching to it is not
reflected in the behaviour of the key men of the play, the general and
Dorigen's conquered husband, which falls far short of the wonderful.
They dishonour themselves comprehensively: the husband by assuming
that his wife is unfaithful; the suitor by intending to go ahead with his
demand for sex with her. Both the casualness of the introduction of the
magic and the misbehaviour of the men (at least until the wife's threat of

a Lucretia-like suicide brings them to their senses) mark a shift of the story over the bounds of romance to something both more schematic and more cynical.

None of these examples of non-functioning magic seriously invites the reader to doubt that the magic would work if it were given the opportunity. Several of the authors are at pains to confirm that it would: Tristan gets the idea of winning Petit-creiu for Isolt because it makes him feel happy himself; the vegetation around Marie's mountain grows extra thickly where the potion is spilt; Floris and Blancheflour are indeed saved; Horn does fight better for looking at the ring; and there is at least the illusion that the rocks have disappeared, which is marvellous enough in itself. The magic is not rationalized into anything *merely* human: it has to keep its inherent wonder in order for the transfer to the hero or heroine to be possible at all. But in *Sir Gawain and the Green Knight*, a romance that rethinks every technique or convention of the genre, the poet anticipates the reader in asking the question himself. He creates a situation that looks identical, with an object that has magic properties ascribed to it, but which does not work in the way the reader expects. In fact, however, he reverses the terms, for the object in question, the green lace that the lady gives to Gawain, is the only instance in romance where readers are encouraged to assume that the magic does not work, even that it is not magic at all, though the lingering question remains as to whether it might have been magic after all. The lady assures Gawain that he will not be killed while he is wearing the girdle, just as Floris's mother assures her son of the property of the ring she gives him, and neither hero is killed; but there must be very few readers who take it that Gawain survives his covenanted beheading by the Green Knight on account of the girdle. The *Gawain*-poet's solution of the problem of how to make a talisman that bestows invulnerability interesting is peculiarly drastic. Even Gawain does not put very much faith in the girdle (he would not be so scared if he thought he could not be harmed), and it turns out to have just the opposite qualities from those he had been promised, so that it becomes not the reason for his survival, but the reason for his injury. That the hero has the option of refusing the talisman becomes the central issue of the romance: presumably, if Gawain had maintained his *trawthe*, his integrity, and had either refused to accept the lace or had handed it over to the lord as he had promised to do with all his winnings, he would not have been wounded at all. So much, at least, the Green Knight implies in his exposition of the plot of which Gawain was the victim;[52] but it is only his word against the lady's, and it is no more possible to prove that Bertilak is speaking the truth than that it is the power of the stones in Horn's ring that gives him strength. The question is much more interesting for being left open. *Sir Gawain* may not end with a question addressed directly to the audience, but it would be an unusual audience that did not want to debate what they had just heard.

That potential for discussion is emphasized again by the fact that the *Gawain*-poet gives his talisman of invulnerability a meaning directly opposite to the normal significance of the magic object. Far from inviting a transference of the wonder from the marvel to the qualities of the hero, the girdle quells any wonder at either. Gawain's chosen badge, the pentangle that he presents to the world on his shield and surcoat, is a symbol of *trawthe*, of interlinked virtues that together encapsulate knightly perfection. When he goes out to meet the Green Knight, he ties the girdle over his surcoat: knotting the ends of the lace over the 'endeles knot'.[53] The girdle symbolizes not Gawain's achievement but his failure, and his failure on that very same issue of whether he could transcend the ordinary. He is not, after all, superhuman, but human, and therefore fallible.

Is the girdle magic? That it is a gift from a lady who has some never-defined connection with Morgan le Fay suggests associations with the darker side of magic. It was, so Bertilak states, woven by his wife herself (2359), and therefore also carries to modern readers suggestions of women's weaving of spells. That particular idiom, however, is not a medieval one; metaphorical weaving might be concerned with plots and deceits in fourteenth-century Middle English,[54] but, despite the broad cultural distrust of women, they were not at this date given the kind of immediate association with dark enchantments that followed from the later witch-hunting frenzy. Witchcraft in the Middle Ages was taken to be an act, not a state, and it was an act that was at least as likely to be performed by men as by women. Merlin is accused of being a witch in the *Morte Darthur*, but not Morgan.[55] She herself starts her career in Geoffrey of Monmouth as a fairy (a career discussed in the next chapter); in the texts that treat her less sympathetically, she is presented as a woman who gets up to bad things rather than as someone inherently diabolic. Skill in enchantment is in any case not necessarily bad. Some women acquire their status as heroine through their possession of such skills: it happens strikingly in *Partonope of Blois*, a thirteenth-century

French romance in origin but which became an early Tudor favourite.[56] Its heroine, Melior, possesses powers of enchantment that Partonope initially believes to be supernatural, but which she eventually reveals (at the moment when those powers are broken) to be the result of learning in the seven liberal arts, plus a little 'nigromancy' on the side.[57] It sounds highly suspect, but it is not treated in the text as a matter for condemnation, and Middle English 'nigromancy' is much less pejorative a term than the modern 'necromancy': it is magic on the edge of acceptability, not magic conducted through the agency of the dead. Although its derivation is equivalent to 'black magic', the word is often used for supernatural powers derived from sources other than God rather than necessarily from the devil. It can thus even appear among a list of attributes of the heroine, as happens in a fifteenth-century account of Jason that takes a generally kindly attitude to Medea: she

> was passing eny other as wel of beute of persone, as of konnyng, nurture, and knowing of al the sciences, nigromancy, magyk, sorcery, and other enchauntementes, that nowe be forbode.[58]

The last phrase strikes a cautionary note, but it seems to allow at least that pagan women had greater freedom in such matters: nigromancy is not inherently evil, just forbidden to Christians. Melior is Christian, as she stresses, and the term most often used in the narrative to describe her ability is accordingly just 'craft': the same word as is used for any area of expertise—shoemaking, or medicine. The nineteenth-century editor of the text, summarizing the story in the margin, paraphrases it on its first occurrence as 'witchcraft',[59] but that is misleading: witches were associated with the devil, and although Partonope's mother suspects that the invisible woman with whom her son is having a passionate affair must be a fiend, she is entirely wrong. Morgan likewise acquires her magic through education. She learns it from Merlin in *Sir Gawain*, or in Malory as a result of having been 'put to scole in a nonnery, and ther she lerned so moche that she was a grete clerke of nygromancye': phraseology that suggests a suspicion of learning in general as well as of magic, so need not be as satirical as it sounds.[60] So, although the hideousness of the old woman in *Sir Gawain* does not foster confidence and we are told that she is out to get Guinevere, it is still dangerous to assume too automatic a connection between the girdle, evil magic, and Morgan: especially dangerous since no such connections are offered in the text. All we *know* is that the lady gives the lace to Gawain with a claim about its magic powers, which may well not be true anyway. Anything beyond that lies in the

suggestive hinterland of audience imagination, and modern imagina-
tions, thoroughly familiar with the later association of women and witch-
craft and with Morgan as an increasingly central character of the
Arthurian legends, may well respond differently from medieval readers.

Women, weaving, and spells do, however, come powerfully together in
a later and much more sinister use of the idea of 'magic in the web', and
one which raises the question of whether magic is actually present with
much more urgency. This occurs, like the phrase itself, in Shakespeare's
Othello: a work that repeatedly invokes the motifs of romance such as
lend a contextual plausibility to Othello's claims about the magic, even
though its ending breaks those generic associations so decisively. The
'web' itself, the woven fabric with its claim of manufacture by a woman
with supernatural associations, is, of course, the handkerchief that Iago
claims that Desdemona has given to Cassio, and which substitutes for the
'ocular proof' of her unfaithfulness that Othello demands. It first appears
not in words but as a stage property. Othello has already moved, in the
course of a single scene, from a cool dismissal of Iago's hints as to
Desdemona's unfaithfulness to blind belief: 'She's gone. I am abused.'[61]
He is already thinking of his cuckold's horns, the 'forkéd plague', when
Desdemona enters and asks him if he is not well; when he claims a
headache, she offers to bind his forehead with her handkerchief, only to
have him knock it out of her hand in a stage direction regularly added
between the lines by editors but left by Shakespeare as an instruction to
the actors implied by the dialogue:

> Your napkin is too little.
> Let it alone. Come, I'll go in with you.[62]

And he takes her off stage, neither of them thinking twice about the fallen
handkerchief, expressive as it is only of her care for him. Yet after Iago has
claimed it to be her love-token for another man, Othello gives it a full
history of its own:

> That handkerchief
> Did an Egyptian to my mother give.
> She was a charmer, and could almost read
> The thoughts of people. She told her, while she kept it
> 'Twould make her amiable, and subdue my father
> Entirely to her love; but if she lost it,
> Or made a gift of it, my father's eye
> Should hold her loathèd, and his spirits should hunt

After new fancies. She, dying, gave it me,
And bid me, when my fate would have me wived,
To give it her. I did so, and take heed on't.
Make it a darling, like your precious eye.
To lose't or give't away were such perdition
As nothing else could match.
DESDEMONA. Is't possible?
OTHELLO.   'Tis true. There's magic in the web of it.
A sybil that had numbered in the world
The sun to course two hundred compasses
In her prophetic fury sewed the work.
The worms were hallowed that did breed the silk,
And it was dyed in mummy, which the skilful
Conserved of maidens' hearts.

3.4.55–75

Is there indeed 'magic in the web'? There is a whole range of possible ways
to read the exchange, and it is not easy to bring out any difference
between them on stage. One is that the handkerchief is indeed magic,
made in the way that Othello describes and containing all those proper-
ties. It would match with the exoticism of the Moor, a companion piece
to his stories of the anthropophagi and men whose heads did grow
beneath their shoulders. Another is that a humanist Shakespeare and the
upper echelons of his audience are much too sophisticated to believe
such magic themselves, but are happy to believe in an Othello who
believes in it: he is telling what he believes to be the truth even though
'we', like the audience that Chaucer's Franklin addresses, know better
than to imagine any such thing could happen, and especially not in an
increasingly scientifically-minded Christian Europe. Another is that
Othello is making it up: telling a fable that contains an accurate moral, a
sentence that he means unequivocally, but where all the apparently
authenticating detail is fictional. The last few lines might be taken as sup-
porting that last view, in that he seems to be protesting on behalf of the
magic rather too much. But the effect of those last few lines is intensify-
ing for Desdemona: they decisively give the death to any hope she might
have of explaining her situation. This is no longer a matter of transfer
between enchantress and mother and son or of love between wife and
husband, but an issue locked into the sympathetic magic of the cosmos.
There have been plenty of other mothers who give talismans: the ring
given to Floris by his mother in some versions confers amiability as well

as invulnerability on its wearer; Isolde's mother gives her the love-potion to share with Mark. The suggestion of cosmic forces woven into the handkerchief—the prophetic sybil, the hallowed worms—are not so far either, at least to Othello's non-expert auditors on or off the stage, from the hermetic magic studied with intense seriousness by academics across Europe, such as the royal astrologer Dr John Dee. The magic is endorsed by both familiar story and by quasi-scientific belief.

But to ask 'is the handkerchief magic?' is as meaningless a question, and as unanswerable, as asking whether the girdle in *Sir Gawain* is magic. Its function is not to work magically, even though its loss brings about precisely the effects that Othello describes. Whether or not the weaving of the handkerchief incarnates Othello's love for his wife, it symbolizes it in the most literal of ways: its loss means the destruction of that love, and 'perdition' for both of them. The fact that he himself made her drop it in the first place, or at least prevented her from picking it up (either or both possibilities are implied by the dialogue coding the stage direction), is remembered by neither of them.

MAGIC ENACTED

There is something sinister about the magic of both the handkerchief and the girdle, whether it is real or not. The magic they claim is not inherent or natural, like the marvellous properties of a magnet, but deliberately induced, so raising questions over its moral or theological status. The transfer of wonder onto the human in magic that fails to work magically has the advantage of bypassing such questions, whereas the active operation of magic tends to highlight them. Chaucer, or his Franklin, starts off by suggesting that the esoteric manipulation of cosmic sympathies is no more than 'magyk natureel'; but by the time the 'magicien' has embarked on the elaborate astrological calculations that will result in the illusion of the rocks' removal, medieval astrophysics has shifted over to being 'supersticious cursednesse'.[63] Working magic was regarded with deep suspicion, and that too is a problem that romance writers had to negotiate.

One way of negotiating it, used increasingly in the sixteenth century, was to allegorize it. Ariosto downgrades a magic ring that enables its wearer to see through enchantment by noting that the ring of Reason would be even better for such a purpose.[64] If a ring of Reason were actually to figure within a narrative, it would be an allegorical ring, and if it were itself presented as magic it would be in order to call attention to the quasi-marvellous workings of its real-life equivalent. Allegory thus particularly favours magic even while the allegorizing process tends to devalue the wonder attaching to the magical, since the point of it will lie in something other than the fact that it is magic. Allegory gives primacy to the inner meaning, the *sens* or *sentence*, in its selection of narrative event: what is marvellous within the human is allegorized as magic, so the wonder at the human that elsewhere drives the 'significance-reaction' is here expressed by having the magic work. The *Faerie Queene* abounds with shields and weapons of invincibility, as with giants and monsters, but Spenser's chosen medium sets a limit on how far he can exploit the qualities of strangeness they might carry: set a story in Faerie Land, and a fairyland moreover where everything carries a specific further meaning, and such properties are both expected and explained. Britomart's magic lance, which represents the irresistible power of good love, must necessarily unhorse every opponent in order to demonstrate that power. Even so, Spenser works a number of variations on this model, some more exciting than others. Arthur is equipped with magic arms made by Merlin, but he keeps his invincible shield covered for much of the time, so enabling him to show his prowess; it proves its continuing powers by accidentally flattening a few friends on occasion.[65] His sword, Morddure, like Excalibur draws blood at every stroke, but it has the further property of refusing to strike its true owner. Spenser, like Malory, has it stolen, for use in a combat against him; but where Malory's Arthur has to demonstrate outstanding prowess to resist Excalibur's onslaught, the only problem for Spenser's Arthur is that he has to fight with just a lance against a sword that will not strike him anyway. The next time we hear of Morddure, it is failing to live up to its promise in a different way, since although it wounds Maleger the injuries have no effect on him, and Arthur is reduced to wrestling instead.[66] It is possible to work out reasons for such passages, but their lack of perspicuousness on the moral level does not altogether redeem the sense of narrative bathos. More compelling, and closer to the romance transference from the magical to the human, is the fact that, despite the belief of his enemies to the contrary, Redcrosse's arms and armour are not magic at all. When things come to the crunch, he has to rely on his own strength: the whole armour of God will function as protection only so long as the individual who wears it has the necessary faith. The cross on his shield can become unreadable in the outflow of his blood; his armour will not glow in the dark, or not very much; and, at particularly awkward moments, he isn't even wearing it.[67]

The man struggling to embody holiness has to rely on 'native vertue', not miraculous intervention.

If magic works magically in the *Faerie Queene*, it is most likely to be in the possession of adversaries. One major difference between the late sixteenth-century understanding of magic and the medieval lies in the closeness of its association with the diabolic. It had always had such a potential, but the same anxieties that fuelled the Renaissance witch-hunts pushed such an interpretation to the fore to a degree that is not characteristic of earlier centuries. Spenser's good characters may carry magic weapons made by others, which represent the power of virtue, but practitioners of magic were regarded with immediate and intense suspicion. The primary enemy in the early books of the *Faerie Queene*, not least of the explicitly Christian hero Holiness, is the arch-magician Archimago. He works with magic books and conjurations: his very first, and therefore defining, action in the poem is to retreat to his study after darkness has fallen to 'seek out mighty charms' to disturb Redcrosse's and Una's sleep.

> Then choosing out few wordes most horrible,
> (Let none them read) thereof did verses frame,
> With which and other spelles like terrible,
> He bad awake blacke Plutoes griesly Dame,
> And cursed heaven, and spake reprochful shame
> Of highest God, the Lord of life and light.
>
> I. i. 37

Merlin within this poem is in some senses his allegorical opposite, the man who uses his occult powers for good, and who seems to do so by inborn knowledge rather than devilish art. The same ideas extend beyond allegorical romance to its narrative counterpart, with magicians and enchanters becoming the diabolic arch-rivals of heroes who are fighting for Christ. Such a one-sided use of magic is clearly unfair to the Christians, but, as in the case of the stolen magic swords, it increases the sense of their courage and resourcefulness. It is almost part of the definition of Guy's Christian prowess in *The Tragical History of Guy of Warwick* that he should number two enchanters among his antagonists. Peele's *Old Wives Tale* has a wicked enchanter as its villain, who can turn himself into a dragon (not shown on stage) as well as other people into bears, eliminate memory, and strike his opponents immobile. Too natural an opposition to such magic can, however, be a drawback in terms of narrative suspense. In an earlier romance, Oliver, one of the heroes of the 'matter of France', finds himself facing a heathen opponent who has the advantage of a couple of bottles of magic balm that cures all wounds hanging from his saddle; Oliver deals with them by cutting them off and throwing them in the river.[68] Saracen princesses are, however, allowed to use magic to good effect, at least before they are christened. That same heathen has a sister named Floripas, who, having fallen in love with one of the peers and run off with them after releasing them from her father's prison, keeps them from starvation through a long siege by means of her magic girdle—a girdle that unequivocally does what it is supposed to.[69] In a Christian context, the practice of magic almost always elicits anxiety, and increasingly so over time. Merlin is the son of an incubus, and, although his devilishness has been overridden by baptism, there is always a sense that his activities border on the realm of the forbidden. One of the most popular of the prose romances through the sixteenth century, *The Four Sons of Aymon*, enables the four sons to survive their horrendous adventures through the help of a cousin, Maugis, who is skilled in magic, but he renounces it at the end to become a hermit. *Valentine and Orson* contains both good and bad enchanters—that is, enchanters who aid the Christians and the Saracens, respectively—but they have been trained in the same school, and the work finishes with a comprehensive and fierce condemnation of the practice of magic by anyone for any purposes.[70]

One way to keep the pleasure of magic in a text while avoiding the suspicion attendant on its practice by ordinary mortals is to have it used by fairies, the subject of the next chapter; they do not fall under the ban attendant on being human, but they were themselves widely regarded with suspicion as too close to devils.[71] More problematic are characters who have something of the fairy about them, but who are none the less mortal: who practise magic through skill rather than through inherent supernatural power. Such figures elicit anxieties of their own that the texts often tackle explicitly, even to the point of making such anxiety central to the plot. This is the driving force of the story in *Partonope of Blois*. The hero is caught up in a succession of supernatural adventures, and his fear that they may be diabolic impels much of the narrative. They begin when, after pursuing a wild boar through the forest of Ardennes, he finds himself lost on the seashore, with no way of escape but by means of a ship riding at anchor there—a ship equipped with tackle and sails, and which is guided to where it should go, but all without anyone visibly operating it. It takes him to a country also devoid of visible inhabitants, and which is lit as if with daylight even though it is night 'uppon the see'.[72] The ship, he thinks, could only be made by human hands through a suspect 'nygromansy', if at all; and the brilliantly jewelled town and castle to which he is taken makes him think

> he was but in fayre,   [fairyland
> And weneth it were the develles werke.
>
> 887–8

The readers at this stage know no more than Partonope himself,[73] and although all the narrative motifs point to the first of these being the right answer—fairy, not the devil—the two were not easily separable. He is served by invisible attendants, brought water for washing, fed sumptuously, and led to a magnificent bed. Once there and the lights removed, he lies in a state of terror, not helped when he becomes aware of someone—as he believes, 'sum evylle thynge' (1190)—crossing the floor and getting into bed beside him. The reader is allowed to know at this stage that it is 'a yonge mayde'

> of grette degre,   [high rank
> That homely to hyr owne bedde come,
>
> 1195–6

that 'homely' being immediately reassuring—though not to Partonope, who is accorded no such inside knowledge. They lie slightly apart, he petrified, she 'for shame' (1213), until slight body contact leads to an exchange of words, in the course of which she twice names the Virgin Mary—so sufficiently reassuring Partonope that she is indeed human for him to take sexual advantage of her. It sounds like a rape; but then it transpires that it is she who is responsible for his being there at all. She is, she tells him, empress of Byzantium, and she has chosen him to be her husband. It was she who arranged for the boar to lead him astray, for the ship to bring him to her, and for him to be led to her own bed. There is, however, a condition on the continuation of their love: although he may enjoy every pleasure except human company by day, and although she will come to him every night in bed, he is never to attempt to see her until two and a half years have passed. If he observes that prohibition, at the end of that time she will tell her lords and parliament whom she has chosen, and they will be openly married. If, however, he sets eyes on her, an act which will itself require 'crafte of nygromancy', he will die, and she will be shamed for ever.

The story would not be worth telling if Partonope did not disobey. After he has returned home, loaded with wealth, he is compelled by his mother to make confession to the bishop of Paris and reveal what has been happening. Convinced that he has been seduced by 'ffendys of ffayre' (5656), they bully him into believing that the only way to ensure his soul's salvation is to betray his lady's trust and break her prohibition. His mother gives him a lantern, made by means of her own enchantments, which cannot be extinguished, and so will reveal to him just who he has been sleeping with. He shines it on his beloved, and so discovers at that same moment that he has lost

> the ffayreste shape creature
> That ever was formed thorowe nature
>
> 5864–5

—'fairy' redefined as an entirely natural fairness. Only then does she reveal to him that she is an ordinary mortal, her magic powers merely learned skills; but those powers are none the less ended by his failure of trust. He is exiled from her country, in the same ship but now with its crew made visible and ordinary, and the journey that had taken a day and a night when he first made it now requires fifteen days. Wonder and its failure once again correlate with the failure of the hero himself—though the lady herself never loses her quality of wondrousness, even when her powers of enchantment cease. She is represented throughout as both lovely and admirable; perhaps *admiranda non imitanda*, to be wondered at rather than imitated, in the phrase used for the more extreme kind of martyrs, but remaining the central focus of Partonope's right desire.

None the less, the narrative gives powerful expression not only to fears about enchantment but to fears about women, and especially learned women. Such fears are taken as the premiss of the story; it could not exist without them, and they serve as the grounding of its plot—a fact that explains the consistency of the treatment of its magic throughout all its versions. The point of the romance, however, is to show such anxieties to be wrong, at the point where they appear most threatening. It is the 'safe' magic exercised by Partonope's mother in conjunction with the bishop, her attempt to undo magic that she believes to be diabolic, that causes disaster. Her fears read like what we would call middle-class morality, and although the class labelling is both anachronistic and inaccurate, the hero has to follow a higher imperative such as is associated with the courtly or chivalric; common sense, as in most romances, is emphatically not enough, whether that takes the form of parental control or priestly meddling. Common sense may say that powers of enchantment must be diabolic, and female form a favourite disguise of the devil; romance can take a different view of both. Yet *Partonope* ends without magic, as the hero, like Ywain, has to demonstrate a continuing faithfulness even when hope seems gone, and win back his beloved by human means alone.

Shakespeare's uses of magic show a considered negotiation of all these problems. Only the fairies of *A Midsummer Night's Dream* are allowed to use magic with the casualness of normal practice, and not to elicit criticism for doing so[74]—they cannot indeed elicit criticism within the play, since none of the human characters (with the equivocal exception of Bottom) knows that they exist at all. Elsewhere, magic is almost always of the kind that does not work magically. In *As You Like It*, we can safely assume that Rosalind's magician uncle, who she promises will give the lovers their sweethearts for the final scene of mass weddings, is a fiction: in fact she fixes everything herself, by entirely natural means. The fiction she chooses none the less has a similar effect on the other characters to 'magic that doesn't work', in transferring the wonder attendant on the happy untangling of the plot onto Rosalind herself. There is also a god present, in the shape of Hymen; but there is no suggestion that Rosalind has the power to invoke spirits, any more than when she 'conjures' the audience in the Epilogue. Shakespeare gives not the slightest hint in the text as to Hymen's status, though a stage production is pushed towards making a decision as to whether to present him as a god (so that the episode becomes a theophany, like the visionary appearances of Jupiter and Diana in *Cymbeline* and *Pericles*), or as a country yokel, or as one of the Duke's servants dressed up. But even on stage, a decision does not *have* to be made, or made apparent. Even if the part were originally played by the singer who acted Amiens, as would have been likely, the change of costume involved, and the habit of doubling parts, would leave it open as to who or what the figure now represented. As so often with the planetary gods, Hymen is more important as the symbolic personification of a principle than as a divinity.

In *The Winter's Tale* and *The Tempest*, magic becomes a more contested issue. Making the dead walk was one of the most terrible activities of necromancers, and in *The Winter's Tale* Paulina is anxious to deny any such association:

> If you can behold it,
> I'll make the statue move indeed, descend,
> And take you by the hand. But then you'll think—
> Which I protest against—I am assisted
> By wicked powers.

5. 3. 87–91

Those that think it is unlawful business
I am about, let them depart.

96–7

But the statue does move, the dead does come back to life, and Leontes
turns Paulina's anxieties around: 'If this be magic, let it be an art I Lawful
as eating' (110–1). He is, of course, not wanting the same freedom that
fairies have to practise magic as a commonplace activity; what he wants
is for this magic not to be magic at all. This magic does not repeat the pri-
mal sin of devouring forbidden knowledge; it belongs to the everyday
processes of nurturing and sustaining life. Even while she is denying that
Hermione's coming back to life is magic, Paulina hints that it is miracle,
dependent on the requirement that the spectators 'awake their faith'; but
it is not miracle either, though the phrase is enough to trigger a recogni-
tion of the providential movement of the play without ever letting the
analogy turn into allegory. What is not disputed is that the coming to life
of the statue is a 'marvel' (100), eliciting wonder; and it is explicitly the
wonder of romance, 'like an old tale' (118). This is not magic that doesn't
work, but magic that was never there in the first place; yet the scene pro-
vides perhaps the most powerful displacement of wonder onto the
human action in the whole corpus of romance.

It was almost, but not quite, Shakespeare's last word on the subject. He
returned to magic again in *The Tempest*, more comprehensively than ever
before. The *Dream* confines its supernatural to the fairies; here, Prospero
is an enchanter skilled in the magic arts. We know how the play ends up,
so we are accustomed to taking on trust that Prospero is a 'good' charac-
ter; but it is far from evident that that was how the first audiences would
have reacted. He is introduced dressed in his 'magic garment', in the very
act of masterminding a shipwreck. He may have freed Ariel from the
punishment inflicted by a witch, but he keeps him as an unfree servant of
his own, and can summon more sprites at will in a way too close to
Archimago for comfort. Archimago uses the sprites he calls up 'to aide his
friends, or fray his enimies' (*FQ*, I. i. 38), and that is precisely the business
in which Prospero employs his. He even strikes his enemies immobile, in
a scene that replicates the actions of the first wicked enchanter in the
Tragical History of Guy.[75] His feared 'ending in despair' of the Epilogue
has something of the damnation of Faust about it as well as the aban-
donment of hope of the man exposed in a rudderless boat—and, of
course, of the actor nervous about unpopularity. He ascribes his decision
for virtue over vengeance to following his 'nobler reason', as if, as with

Ariosto's advocacy of the ring of Reason, virtuous rationality outdoes the exercise of magic.[76] His own renunciation of magic follows immediately. It starts gently enough, with the invocation of the 'elves of hills, brooks, standing lakes and groves' with their 'printless' and so by implication harmless feet, but those members of the audience who knew Golding's translation of Ovid might already have been recognizing traces of Medea behind the language, and the Renaissance Medea was by no means as benevolent as the fifteenth-century one. The speech builds to a climax in full-scale necromancy:

> Graves at my command
> Have waked their sleepers, oped, and let 'em forth
> By my so potent art. But this rough magic
> I here abjure.

5. 1. 48–51

His final act of magic is to draw together the courtly characters of the play within a charmed circle to the accompaniment of 'heavenly music', and then to release them from enchantment. His abjuration of magic recalls that of Valentine and Maugis, but it is significantly different: they renounce the devilish for the religious, Prospero renounces enchantment for the ordinary. His giving up his marvellous powers is presented as climactic, as part of the play's happy ending. The magic provides the most spectacular action, but wonder is explicitly focused on the human: on 'admired Miranda' (her name itself meaning 'to be wondered at'), and on her own wonder at the 'brave new world, that hath such people in it'. Prospero's deflationary response (''Tis new to thee') does not altogether override her excitement: the audience is invited not only to evaluate her naïvety against her father's cynicism but to look at the world as she does, with fresh eyes, and see its potential for being wonderful. There is no doubt at all that Prospero's magic works—we spend the whole play watching it do just that. There is no doubt at all that Shakespeare's magic works—we spend the whole play giving imaginative credence to the creation of a vision made out of a baseless fabric. But finally, as with magic that doesn't work magically, the most wonderful things turn out not to be supernatural at all: the choice of virtue over vengeance; the sheer marvel of ordinary human beings; and the illusion that lasts just a couple of hours of a newly created alternative universe. Romance reconfigures the supernatural as the superhuman; *The Tempest* reconfigures romance as the familiar world.

CHAPTER FOUR

Fairy monarchs, fairy mistresses: 'I am of ane other countree'

Magic may be at its most compelling in a romance when it does not behave magically, but a being from another world—from *the* other world, the world of fairy—who showed no supernatural qualities would be a sad disappointment. It is the fairies' difference from ordinary humanity, or even heroic humanity—their freedom from the pains and limitations of mortality; their ability to break the rules of nature and time and physical space; their capacity to bestow unstinted wealth; their independence of moral conventions; their sheer unpredictability—that gives them their narrative interest. The ultimate fairy queen, both monarch and, potentially, mistress, in whom all those properties are contained, is Spenser's Gloriana: the figure who gives her title to England's national epic.

Just as the ultimate goal of Arthurian quest finally defines itself as the Holy Grail, the object that can never be assimilated into the real world, so the ultimate woman of romance is a fairy mistress, or fairy queen. Like the Grail, she can be accessed—or rather, she can make herself accessible—within chivalric society, but she comes at her own will, not anyone else's. The Grail appears at the moment it chooses, and it is 'achieved' only by those few who are elect, not by all who seek it. Fairy queens, or occasionally fairy kings, similarly choose their own moments of appearance, and they bestow their favours on a similarly elect group. The fiction of the later Grail romances is that the election is done by God; despite not being able to claim the same ultimate status, fairies usually represent the final supernatural arbiter within the works in which they appear. Although they were sometimes given a place in the divinely created order of beings, fairies sit very uneasily with a Christian context, and tend to be made the subject of works whose ideologies are oblique to orthodox piety (Spenser gets away with combining fairies and Anglicanism by making his faery land allegorical). Above all, they are *other* in a fuller sense than almost any of the ways in which the term is now used. Most 'others' are alien because of unfamiliarity, or sexual or cultural difference, or social or geographical distance: unfamiliarity and difference and distance that ultimately offer the possibility of closer knowledge and understanding. Fairies come from the Otherworld, and are unassimilable. It is never going to be possible to bridge the gulf between the two worlds, even though a being from one side may occasionally take up habitation on the other. That sense of separation held good even when fairies were the object of widespread belief; and now, in a world that claims to be rational (that is, which has substituted a widespread belief in abduction by aliens for abduction by fairies), they have retreated beyond the borders of experience or of intellectual analysis to a world defined as fantasy. Even in the pre- or early modern period, the fairies of romance did not require belief, but they probably needed rather less suspension of disbelief. What they do require is a recognition on the part of readers and audiences that the real world cannot be reduced to the rational. Fairies occupy that dangerous borderland that cannot be controlled by human will and is not susceptible to the normal operations of prayer.

Only a handful of the fairies of romance have retained any measure of fame into the modern world. One of these is Gloriana herself, who is introduced (under the name Tanaquill) as early as the second stanza of the Proem to the *Faerie Queene*, as being the ultimate, Grail-like, object of the quest of 'that most noble Briton Prince'.[1] Another is the figure on whom she is partly based, the 'elf-queen' of Chaucer's *Sir Thopas*—the tale which is the pilgrim-poet's personal contribution to the Canterbury storytelling, and a deadly parody of the less-sophisticated kind of contemporary romance. It should by rights have killed the whole motif stone dead, but so far as memes are concerned all publicity is good publicity, and the fairy queen went from strength to strength, reaching her epic apogee in Spenser. And some four or five years after Gloriana had first appeared on the market—a year or so before the second instalment of the poem was published, and around three before Speght's new edition of Chaucer's works—Shakespeare's Titania and Oberon made their appearance on the London stage: the only literary fairies who can still rely on wide reader recognition beyond academia. They have among their sources another Chaucerian fairy pair, the quarrelling fairy king and queen of the *Merchant's Tale*. And behind them all is a supporting group of fairy aristocrats and monarchs—most often queens, occasionally kings—who dispense threats or favours, wealth or death; who act as challengers or benefactors, as moral teachers or prophets, or, in the case of female fairies, as mistresses or as founding mothers.

A further four such otherworld figures, who have largely dropped out of sight since the sixteenth century, carried as wide reader recognition for the Elizabethans as Titania does now. Three of them are female, one male, and each has a function characteristic of fairy characters. Their lack of familiarity in the modern world requires fuller descriptions for each of them.

The first comes close to being the quintessential fairy mistress (much more so than Gloriana, since she makes her sexual favours fully available on her very first appearance in the narrative): the lady who bestows herself and accompanying wealth on the knight successively named as Lanval, Landeval/Launfal, and Lambewell, in his Anglo-Norman, two Middle English, and Renaissance incarnations. She herself is anonymous except in the Middle English *Launfal*, where she is called Dame Tryamour. Only scraps of the printed editions survive, but the full Renaissance text is preserved in the mid-seventeenth-century Percy Folio manuscript.[2]

Second is the elf-queen who gives both the power of prophecy to Thomas of Erceldoune, and also a long series of prophecies for him to utter: hence one of his alternative names, True Thomas. His story accordingly falls into two main parts, the first part constituting a romance that describes his affair with her and his sojourn in her 'other countree'; the second recounting the prophecies. The textual histories of the two parts developed in parallel, but with much interweaving, from the early fourteenth century onwards,[3] though the earliest full text to survive— containing both parts, the story of the love-affair and the prophecies— dates from the 1440s. It was copied several times over the next hundred years, though its first known printed edition dates from 1652. By the early sixteenth century this two-part version existed alongside a more prophecy-heavy text, with an adapted and abbreviated romance intro- duction,[4] and one or both versions apparently influenced Spenser. The romance section alone, without the prophecies, also at some point began a parallel independent existence, passing into oral tradition as the ballad known by its protagonist's third name, *Thomas Rymer*.[5]

Third, and the least well known in England at the popular level, is Melusine, the founding mother of the house of Lusignan. Her romance was given both a prose and verse treatment in French, on each side of 1400, and both were translated into English, as *Melusine* and the *Romance of Partenay*, though only the former is known to have been printed. The few printed fragments surviving of her romance may none the less indi- cate a process of reading to extinction rather than scarcity. She was famous enough for Richard Hyrd to retain Vives' condemnation of her in the early years of the century, and she was listed alongside heroines such as Dido, Lucrece, and Polixena in a poem printed in 1572.[6]

The name of the fourth figure has already been mentioned: Oberon, the fairy king who typically acts as judge or arbiter, though his arbitration may show more of arbitrariness than of justice. He requires a further listing since he was thoroughly familiar as a character before *A Midsummer Night's Dream* was ever written, having made his first appearance some centuries earlier in *Huon of Bordeaux*. Originating as an early thirteenth-century French poem on the borderline between *chanson de geste* and romance, and rewritten in prose in the fifteenth century, the work decisively entered Tudor consciousness with Lord Berners' translation of its prose version. Oberon's wide recognition factor in the late sixteenth century came not only from reprints of the romance itself but from the work's being given its own dramatization.[7] The text of the play is lost, but some idea of it may be gained from the chunk of *Huon* material, Oberon and his fairies included, that constitutes the second act of *The Tragical History of Guy of Warwick* of the early 1590s. The Oberon of the original romance, like Melusine, is the child of a fairy mother and a mortal father (and, for all his longevity, eventually dies), but his later incarnations, in writers such as Greene, Shakespeare, and Jonson, made him fully fairy.

If a fairy king is named in a text, the name chosen is almost always Oberon: the medieval name. Fairy queens have no such generic name until the very end of the sixteenth century, when 'Mab' begins to make its appearance, but there was still a generous possibility for choice. Shakespeare's Titania allows a surface gloss of the classical supernatural: the name is used for a number of figures by various Latin authors (etymologically it means simply a descendant of the Titans), but the best known of them, Ovid, applies it to both Circe and Diana,[8] Diana being the earthly form of the triple goddess Lucina–Diana–Hecate, and Hecate in turn being identified with Proserpina. Both sets of association, Circe and Diana, stress the potential danger of such a figure, as both have the habit of turning mortals into beasts—a power that resonates with Bottom's 'translation', even though it is Puck who manufactures that. The Proserpina connection also, however, takes Titania away from Ovid back to her source in that other fairified goddess, the Proserpine of the *Merchant's Tale*.[9] Her name notwithstanding, both Titania and Oberon remain firmly in the native fairy tradition, with its pucks, its mischief-making, and its household elves who creep out when all the mortals have gone to bed.

Some slippage between the classical and native traditions was common in the sixteenth century. As a knowledge of classical mythology spread across in the Middle Ages from those learned in Latin to vernacular speakers, there had been a tendency to equate the demi-gods with native fairies, not least since both groups were connected with water and woods. Before the word 'nymph' was borrowed into English, the Old English-derived 'elf', or, from the early fourteenth century, the French-derived 'fairy' were the standard terms for such beings. The coupling of classical and native terms becomes more self-conscious as familiarity with the classics increases. *Melusine* uses 'nymph' as an occasional synonym for 'fairy'; Spenser sometimes pairs the words.[10] Golding translated Ovid's gods of the natural world as 'elves of hilles, of brookes, of woods alone, | Of standing lakes', and Shakespeare followed him in *The Tempest* in Prospero's great speech renouncing magic. Prospero may invoke Neptune as a metonym for the sea, but his 'elves of hills, brooks, standing lakes, and groves' have thoroughly fairy habits: they are 'demi-puppets', not demi-gods, who

> By moonshine do the green sour ringlets make
> Whereof the ewe not bites.[11]

No self-respecting nymph ever left the trace of a fairy ring. Even in such an Ovidian context, Shakespeare is affirming native traditions of fairy, just as he does in *A Midsummer Night's Dream* and *The Merry Wives of Windsor*. In the latter, the retributive fairies who pinch Falstaff are fake, and their victim seems to be the only person to believe in their existence—or, at least, the women who arrange it all would presumably not have done so had they thought that 'real' fairies might be cavorting around Herne's Oak at midnight. It is one of the more wonderful effects of the *Dream* that the audience so completely believes in their existence for the purposes of the play, even to the point of swallowing Oberon's 'I am invisible' as a simple statement of fact (2.1.186). Although by this date classicism might add a resonance or a kind of authority to fairies as demi-gods, English romances kept the classical supernatural firmly secondary until Spenser interwove classical machinery into his native epic. The elements he borrows are precisely those that will fit most easily into a fairy land: Diana and her nymphs, not Apollo or Jupiter.[12]

The history of fairies in Britain takes somewhat different forms in folklore and romance. Fairy beliefs at the popular level seem to have been continuous from Celtic times forwards; the more literary kind of fairy was conveyed into French literature by way of parallel Celtic traditions in

Brittany, and from there back across the Channel to England. Direct transmission from Irish or Welsh to English is hard to trace, and seems to have been unimportant by comparison with the Breton and French route.[13] The folklore history of fairies has been the subject of much scholarship and more speculation, but lies beyond the scope of this book. The question here is what kind of generic niche was occupied by the fairy, and the fairy lady in particular, after her arrival on the romance scene, and how she adapted and changed for different purposes and over time—her quality as meme within the corpus of romance. There is probably now a tendency to equate the fairy queen and the fairy mistress, and the equation has a long history; it also gets strong endorsement from that trio of couples, Sir Thopas and his prospective elf 'lemman', Arthur and his visionary, Gloriana, and one man who has no intention of ever seeking a fairy mistress, Bottom, and the besotted Titania. If that were all there were to such a figure, however, if she were no more than the ultimate sexual fantasy, then she would have sunk to the level of cliché long before *Sir Thopas* placed her there, and stayed at that level.

If there is a single defining quality of the fairy monarch, of either sex, it is not sexuality but power: power that may well be exercised in the cause of justice, but which is primarily characterized by its arbitrariness. There was an Irish myth that equated the fairy hag who could turn beautiful, the 'loathly lady' motif, with the territorial dominion of Ireland, in what seems to be a relic of mythology of the goddess Ériu. That she bestowed rule on the man who was prepared to kiss her, however it might be allegorized in terms of the difficulty of obtaining the kingship and its later sweetness, has an arbitrariness about it, a mismatch between ends and means, that fits the fairy world in inverse proportion to its logic in the real world.[14] The mortal partner of a fairy may not have any notable attribute other than an equivalent arbitrariness about his selection: Thomas of Erceldoune (who seems to have been a real historical person leaving normal traces in the records) has no claim to distinction until his otherworld mistress has given him her store of prophecies. God, in romances as in homilies and saints' lives, can be relied on to act providentially, but such generic expectations of goodness, mercy, and due reward are not a necessary predicate of fairies. The Oberon of *A Midsummer Night's Dream* does get the various lovers sorted out into pairs, at the second attempt; but he might just as easily have chosen a less happy ending for them. And just what he thinks he is doing with his wife and Bottom, or with her 'little Indian boy', does not invite, or receive, close scrutiny: for another quality of fairies is that they are inscrutable.

Fairies were an anomaly in the divine order of creation, and romances are rarely interested in defining their precise metaphysical or theological status except in terms of what they are not: it is frequently insisted that they are not diabolic. Intellectual explanations for their existence in the Middle Ages sometimes cast them as angels who had remained neutral in the War in Heaven. They were therefore not damned, as the rebel angels were, but they lost the right to remain in Heaven, and so descended to middle-earth to lead a quasi-material existence in parallel with the physical existence of the human race.[15] Such an explanation was, however, too close to the diabolic to be altogether comfortable, as the recurrent anxiety to stress that fairies are not in fact devils indicates. They themselves are often at pains to make the distinction clear, sometimes by passing a test of true faith such as partaking of the Eucharist, or simply by naming God. One manuscript of *Thomas of Erceldoune* adds in such a reassurance, having its elf-queen remain unfazed when Thomas invokes the Trinity for protection against her.[16] Just occasionally—it happens to the mother of the future Richard Cœur de Lion, in his eponymous romance—a woman who appears mortal will be proved otherwise by her inability to pass such a test: forced to remain present through the sacring of the Mass, she breaks free from the men holding her and flies out through the roof, never to be seen again; but she is something of a rarity.[17] Sometimes figures who appear supernatural will insist outright, even against the plain statement of the narrative, that they are actually human.[18] If they are not devils, neither are they ghosts: the Oberon of *A Midsummer Night's Dream*, hardly the most theological of plays, firmly differentiates fairies from such 'damned spirits' (3. 3. 382–9). The equation of fairies with nymphs and dryads was not entirely straightforward, partly because the pagan gods were often given a Christian definition as devils, partly because the natural history of the two groups (both habits and habitat) did not offer a precise overlap. Having had his pageant of water-nymphs washed out by a storm when Elizabeth visited East Anglia in 1578, Thomas Churchyard hastily recycled them as fairies for her departure, though he had to write a new speech apologizing for their inappropriate costumes and appearance.[19] Popular belief, and the romances with it, most commonly took fairies to be outside theological schemata, a third order alongside the angelic (fallen or not) and the human. The place occupied by the fairies was, therefore, most often defined simply as *somewhere else*: a fifth world to set beside Heaven, Hell, Purgatory, and middle-earth. The lady of *Thomas of Erceldoune* leads him to a place where the roads between those various worlds intersect: one can pass direct to Paradise, or Hell, or Purgatory, or from Purgatory to Heaven; or else finally to a marvellous castle on a hill, unparalleled 'in erthe', in an 'other countree' that is never given a name but which is not a part of any of those recognized worlds.[20] The ballad version simplifies the topography to three roads away from middle-earth, the paths of righteousness ('though after it there's few enquires') and of wickedness, and the 'bonny road' to elfland.[21] The lady of the romance instructs Thomas:

> 'Take thy leve of sone and mone,
> And the lefe that spryngyth on tre;
> This twelve monthes thou most with me gone,
> Midylle erthe thou shalt not see.'[22]

She then leads him in at a hill, into pitch darkness, through water up to his knees, and in constant earshot of the 'swoghynge of the flode' (174)—a three-day journey intensified in one version of the ballad to the fearsome

> For forty days and forty nights
> He wade thro red blood to the knee;
> And he saw neither sun nor moon,
> But heard the roaring of the sea.

Child, A.69–72

Elfland is not, it seems, equidistant from Hell and Heaven. The infernal quality of the journey is endorsed in the romance by the fact that the fiend regularly descends on the lady's country to levy a tribute (289–90). Thomas must be returned to middle-earth, after what seems to him like three days but is in earthly terms three years, lest he be carried off to Hell.

The Otherworld of the *Thomas* texts is 'somewhere else', and at a further remove of distance from the somewhere else of most romance quests. Unusually, it is accessed from a very specific place, from Huntley Banks or Eildon Tree: real locations that serve to lock the prophecies that conclude the romance version into the real world of time and place.[23] Other romances that contain fairies associate them with a direction, often the west, rather than a place. Folklore fairies tended to be denizens of the night, as in *A Midsummer Night's Dream*; in the romances, they are more widely associated with 'undern', when the sun is at its zenith in the south. Sir Thopas heads off in diametrically the wrong direction, 'north and est', in a fashion that indicates how commonplace the motifs must have been.

The midday heat can lead the mortal to invite further trouble by lying down under a tree to rest. It is while Orfeo's queen, Herodis, is taking her midday rest in an orchard that she is abducted by the king of the fairies, first in a dream, then in actuality.[24] Trees and forests are dangerous locations; still more dangerous are liminal settings, alongside wood or water. Sir Lambewell, the Renaissance equivalent of Sir Launfal, sets off

> towards the west,
> betweene the water and a faire fforrest,

and when he wakens from sleep he is greeted by maidens who come out of the forest to summon him to their fairy mistress.[25] The 'fontayne of fayerye' where Melusine first appears to her mortal lover is set between a meadow and a forest.[26] It is 'by a forest side' that the knight of the *Wife of Bath's Tale* comes across twenty-four dancing maidens who disappear when he approaches; Spenser, who imitates the passage when Calidore encounters the disappearing dancers on Mount Acidale, has the knight watch them from under 'the covert of the wood'.[27] Prince Arthur imitates Sir Thopas in the run-up to his vision of his fairy queen by breaking off from 'raunging the forest wide' to rest on the grass.

Fairies are most frequently to be met as a manifestation within this world. The 'Quene of Fairy land', Aureola, who figured in an entertainment at Elvetham in 1591, emerges from her normal abode 'in places under-ground' to welcome Elizabeth, drawn to the real world by her wish 'to doe [her] duety' to the more powerful monarch.[28] It is less usual for the human to gain access to the fairy world, though sometimes the two overlap: the much-feared forest through which the young Huon rides is 'ful of the fayrey and straunge thynges, that such as passe that way are lost'. It is the earthly haunt of Oberon, though his favour towards Huon modifies his dangerousness: the forest becomes a place of recovery for the hero and his men, as the fairy king summons up a feast for the starving company and a magnificent palace in which to serve it, with hangings of silk and beaten gold and jewelled ivory benches.[29] Access by mortals to a fully other world is often through a cave or into a hill: this is the route taken by Thomas of Erceldoune and Orfeo, and by visitants to Celtic fairy worlds. Huon and his wife vary the pattern by making their final journey (a one-way journey, with no return) to Oberon's fairy realm by air. The difference of these countries from the familiar world is most immediately marked by the surpassing splendour of their palaces, castles and towns. Thomas's lady asks him, as they come in sight of her home:

> Seist thou yonder, that fayre castell,
> That standyth hye upon that hyll?
> Of townys and towris it berys the bell;   [is ranked foremost
> On erthe is lyke non other till.[30]   [no other can compare with it

Huon first sets eyes on the fairy capital city of Momure from a distant hilltop, from where he can see its white marble walls and towers shining like crystal, rather as the Redcrosse Knight sees the New Jerusalem from the Hill of Contemplation. Spenser's New Jerusalem is filled with angels going up and down from 'highest heaven'; Momure (in contrast to Thomas's elfland, with its easy access to Hell) is likewise accessible to the angels, who descend in 'a great multytude' to take Oberon's soul into Paradise.[31] The unearthliness of the Otherworld is sometimes made explicit through direct comparison with Paradise. The crystal walls of the castle that Orfeo finds, encompassing dwellings made 'all of precious stones' that shine so brightly that there is never any darkness, recalls the New Jerusalem and foreshadows its description in *Pearl*:

> No man may telle no thenche in thought   [think
> The riche work that ther was wrought.
> By all thing, him think that it is   [it seems to be
> The proude court of paradis.[32]

Spenser, by contrast, first compares his own fairy city, Cleopolis, unfavourably with the heavenly Jerusalem, though he allows its primacy among the less than heavenly: if it is not eschatologically 'the fairest Citie . . . that might be seene' (I. x. 58), and its crystal tower is no more than glass beside the 'Angels towre', it is at least

> for earthly frame
> The fairest peece, that eye beholden can.

> I. x. 59

Just as the fairies occupy an equivocal position between humankind and the angels, so Cleopolis is here marked out as something beyond the normal and yet still 'earthly': perhaps less a statement of the city's metaphysical status than an insistence on Spenser's part that his Faerie Land is not finally of a different order of being from England.

Surpassing beauty is also, and more famously, an attribute of fairies themselves, and not just of their queens: Oberon is likewise the fairest being Huon has ever seen.[33] The lady who becomes mother to Richard Cœur de Lion is the most beautiful in the world, 'bryght as the sunne thorwgh the glas', and is encountered travelling in a ship made of gold and ivory with sails of samite.[34] The story of Launfal, in all its versions, is structured so as to have a kind of beauty contest as its climax, in which the hero's rash boast of the supremacy of his mistress's looks to Guinevere's is shown to be justified by a procession of maidens of ever-increasing beauty, whom the onlookers believe, in turn, must be his mistress, and which culminates in the appearance of

> a damsell by her selfe alone.
> on earth was fairer never none,—
> upon a fresh ambling palfray,—
> much fairer then the summers day.
>
> *Sir Lambewell,* 507–10 (*Percy*)

The people rush to gaze on her as if she were divine:

> and all still uppon her gazinge
> as people that behold the sacring.   [elevation of the Host
>
> 525–6

She carries, in other words, the quasi-divine quality of the Host of the Mass—an interesting simile to find surviving the Reformation by a century.[35] Both Lambewell and Launfal speak of their mistress in terms normally reserved for the Blessed Virgin, as the one who 'me out of baile shall bring', who can redeem the sinner from the sorrow attendant on sin.[36] The processes of textual transmission elsewhere assimilate the otherworldly with the heavenly. Thomas of Erceldoune, in both the romance and the ballad, at first believes that the woman he sees is so beautiful that she must be the Virgin; sixteenth- and seventeenth-century texts of the prophecies actually turn her into the 'Queene of heaven'.[37] There is an increasing tendency in panegyrics of Elizabeth to elide the earthly and heavenly Virgin Queens, but Spenser largely resists the opportunities offered by the mediating form of fairy to push such a substitution.[38] He describes his Gloriana as beyond the earthly:

> So fair a creature yet saw never sunny day
>
> I. ix. 13

but, just as he explicitly avoids turning Cleopolis into Paradise, so he holds back from suggesting that his faerie queen might be an object of worship. Gloriana is defined in opposition to everything that hints of Catholicism. Even so, the Otherworld of faerie allows Spenser a place, normally disallowed by Protestantism, in which the material world and its inhabitants can take on something of a sacramental quality, of spiritual sign.

If the fairy queen can be pushed upwards towards the divine, fairies may also be rationalized, turned into mortal women whose supernatural powers are acquired by more ordinary means. In the text that probably represents the earliest form of the story of Lancelot, Ulrich von Zatzikhoven's *Lanzelet* (which itself had an Anglo-Norman source), the Lady of the Lake who nurtures its hero is a *merfeine*, a water-fairy, who lives in a land of ten thousand maidens (and some mermen).[39] In the prose *Lancelot* she is redefined as a woman with skills in the magic arts:

> Now, according to the story, the damsel who carried Lancelot off into the Lake was a fairy. At that time, the word 'fairy' was used for all women who practised magic, and at that time there were many more of them in Great Britain than in other lands. According to the story in the Breton [British?] chronicles, they knew the powers of words and stones and herbs, which allowed them to retain youth and beauty and enjoy whatever wealth they wished.

This particular woman has learned her magic from Merlin, and the lake in which she lives, in this text, is simply an illusion created by her to conceal her estates from view.[40] She is quasi-fairy, with supernatural powers without being supernatural herself. It was not an altogether satisfying strategy, and most other texts return her to being more fully otherworldly, her habitation in the lake being evidence of that. Malory makes an initial distinction between his supernatural Lady of the Lake, who can walk on water (real, not illusory, water), and her damsel Nenive, who adopts her title later, but who has to learn her magic from Merlin.[41] The push towards rationalizing supernatural women is the inverse of the process of rationalizing magic that doesn't work. That results in increasing the supernatural element, making it work, over the course of retellings. Here, the properties of the magic do not change—these women really do have powers of enchantment—but the source of such powers is demythologized. They may still be marvellous in the sense of being an object of wonder, but they are not inherently supernatural.

Morgan le Fay is the best known and most discussed of such figures. She first enters written literature in Geoffrey of Monmouth's *Life of Merlin*, where she is the most beautiful and the most skilled in healing of the nine sisters who rule over the 'island of apples', an island of eternal spring that combines the qualities of Avalon and the Fortunate Islands, to which the wounded Arthur is brought.[42] Within twenty years of that first appearance, by 1169, in a somewhat satirical section of Etienne of Rouen's political poem *Draco Normannicus*, she is described as Arthur's sister, and as a *nympha perennis*, a long-living fairy.[43] A year or two later, she makes her first vernacular appearance, again as Arthur's sister skilled in healing, in Chrétien's *Erec* (l. 4220). Her first appearance in English is in Layamon's *Brut*, where she carries a different name, Argante, though her function is the same as in the *Life*.[44] The wounded Arthur declares that he will go to Avalon, 'to the fairest of all maidens, to the queen Argante, most beautiful of fairies; and she shall make my wounds fully whole'. A boat arrives bearing two unnamed women, who take the king away; and 'Britons still believe that he is alive, and lives in Avalon with the loveliest of all fairies':

> Bruttes ileveth yete that he bon on live,
> And wunnien in Avalun mid fairest alre alven.[45]

The literary offspring of these early Morgans are queens of magical islands of eternal spring: some wicked or enchantresses or both (such as Ariosto's Alcina and her descendants in Tasso and Spenser), some benevolent. In these early manifestations, by contrast, Morgan is distinguished by her separation from sexuality. That tradition too continued, sufficiently for Bacon to note Elizabeth's manipulation of the concept, controlling her courtiers

much like those accounts we find in romances, of the Queen in the blessed islands and her court and institutions, who allows of amorous admiration but prohibits desire.[46]

One of the models proposed for Spenser's Gloriana, the fairy queen Proserpyne of *Arthur of Little Britain*, is of this kind, though in contrast to Elizabeth her prohibition of desire applied only to herself: indeed she masterminds (or mistress-minds) the love between her protégée, Florence, and Arthur (son of the duke of Brittany, and unconnected with the British hero). She tests this Arthur's faithfulness by appearing to him by moonlight, 'betwene a fayre forest and a grene medow', and making as if to seduce him—a temptation he successfully resists.[47]

Although some late works that decisively broke with even the most legendary kind of history (such as the wildly fantastic *Mervine son of Oger*, of the 1590s) made Morgan fully fairy,[48] her supernatural nature was downplayed in the heyday of Arthurian romance. She was there refigured as Arthur's sister, and therefore as a mortal woman. In the prose *Merlin*, she is given human parentage, as the daughter of Arthur's mother Ygerne by her first husband Gorlois, and 'le Fay' accordingly becomes a courtesy title granted her on account of the exceptional learning that supplies her skill in magic. The title is on occasion upgraded still further into 'goddess', picked up in *Sir Gawain and the Green Knight*:[49] an upgrading that also emphasizes its courtesy quality, since, although fairies might perhaps exist, goddesses, in a Christian world, do not. The human Morgan's use of her learning is, notoriously, rarely for good: she is unusual among this group of fairy-derived mortal women in that in her later and best-known manifestations she is largely malevolent, and her malevolence increases in proportion to her humanity. Only in her action in taking away the wounded Arthur, which continues to associate her with Avalon, does she consistently retain any alternative role. At the end of Malory's narrative, furthermore, despite the acknowledgement of his prophesied return, Arthur does not reach any magic country for healing, but dies and is buried at Glastonbury.[50] His tomb, still containing his corpse, was supposedly discovered there in 1191. There is no medieval narrative of Morgan's death; but, unlike Merlin or Arthur himself, she never figures as one of the undead.

Most of the women who have the appearance of being rationalized fairies are rather more attractive. The heroine of Marie de France's *Guigemar* has more supernatural associations than powers. Guigemar is brought to her by a magic boat which he finds after encountering a talking hind while hunting, but she is not responsible for either the hind or the ship, and their origins remain mysterious. She can, however, tie a knot in his *chemise* that no woman but herself can untie. The author of *Partonope of Blois* presents Melior for the first 6,000 lines of the romance as a mysterious and unknowable figure with fairy powers, including diverting him from hunting to a magic ship, but in its second half she is simply human, with all the vulnerability of a young woman betrayed by her lover. The two stories are found combined in *Generides*, a fifteenth-century romance that was especially popular in print.[51] Its heroine, daughter of the king of Surre (Syria), inhabits a jewelled palace in the forest, to which the hero is destined to find his way when he gets lost while hunting. She declares her love for him, and when he has to leave her, she weeps on his shirt, her tears staining it so that only she can wash out the marks. For all their fairy resonances, all three heroines are presented with the sympathy attached to any young woman in love, whose difficulties in pursuing their love cannot be solved by any easy exercise of supernatural powers. These authors get the best of both worlds, this and the Other.

Such quasi-fairy figures offer another way of thinking about Gloriana. She does not need to be rationalized, since allegory bypasses the question of factual plausibility and provides a bridge between the human and the supernatural. Queen Elizabeth herself, however, certainly had powers of her own, even if they did not stem directly from her learning: powers to grant or withdraw favour, ultimately powers of life or death. In many ways, Elizabeth has more in common with a Melusine or a Melior or the Lady of the Lake than with ordinary (mortal) romance heroines, and figuring her as Gloriana embodies that distinction. Spenser also co-opts a further quality of the supernatural in connecting this latest representative of the house of Tudor with the fairy world, and that is prophecy. This helps to give specificity to his claim of divine endorsement behind his faerie queen; divine endorsement is indeed partly what the poem is about. It is channeled not only through Gloriana and the whole representation of the Elizabethan church settlement as Truth, but through the sense of Providence accompanying the culmination of British history in the Tudor dynasty. The Tudors are presented as the fulfilment of political prophecy; and, so far as humans are concerned, that is less a matter of divine foreknowledge than of second sight—not least the second sight associated with the inhabitants of the Otherworld, but applied within this one.

'SOME UNCOUTH TIDINGS TELL YOU ME'[52]

Prophecy of the present—writings that claim that the events of the moment have been long foretold—requires a past from which the future can be predicted. Renaissance prophecies therefore not only relied heavily and explicitly on their medieval forebears, but could be expanded indefinitely forwards to keep them up to date. Prophecy also requires access to privileged knowledge. Such knowledge may come from God, though God notoriously tends to class His plans for the future as divine secrets, a forbidden area of enquiry. It may come from the devil, and those who foretold the future were accused of diabolism almost as a matter of course. Fairy offered a third way, a medium that neither transgressed God's prohibitions nor invoked the powers of Hell, and it was accordingly a useful channel for prophecy. Holinshed interprets the 'three women in strange and wild apparell, resembling creatures of the elder world,' who accost Macbeth and Banquo to predict their royal destinies, as 'either the weird sisters, that is (as ye would say) the goddesses of destinie, or else some nymphs or feiries'; and that he ascribes such an interpretation to 'common opinion' suggests that the association of fairies with prophecy was commonplace.[53] The Fates and fairies indeed share a common etymology in prophecy, in *fata*, things said, and 'fairy' could on occasion serve as a synonym for 'prophecy'.[54] The higher ranking the fairy, the more authoritative the prediction; and since romances were the natural generic home for such figures, there is a marked overlap between romance and prophecy—an overlap on which Spenser capitalized. That fairies' privileged knowledge was as good as any that might come from God or the devil was stressed in various ways. Melusine, half-fairy foundress of the house of Lusignan, repeatedly assures her chosen lover that her foreknowledge is 'of God', not of the devil, and further insists that she is not a heretic either.[55] Thomas of Erceldoune supposedly received his ability to prophesy twice over: once because on parting from him his elf-queen gave him the gift of telling, or foretelling, the truth—hence his byname of 'True Thomas'; and again because she left him with a substantial store of prophecies spoken by herself. The upgrading of her in the early sixteenth century into the Virgin took the process a large step further: if Mary herself foretells the future, then such revelation must be agreeable to God, even if she has acquired the attribute by literary descent from an elf-queen.

Romance made room in two ways for such supernatural figures with their paranormal powers of knowledge. First, the readiness of the genre to incorporate the magical and the fantastic gave them an easy home. Second, the foundation legends that so often took romance shape are themselves a form of prophecy of the future. Melusine can name Raymondin, her future husband, on their first meeting; she knows of his accidental killing of his uncle, although the action was unwitnessed; and she gives him exact instructions as to how to bring about his future prosperity, including such details as that he must buy a deerhide from a man he will meet by the road. She knows, too, later in the story, of his secret action in breaking the taboo she has laid on him never to see her on a Saturday, when she becomes a serpent from the waist down; and she predicts the terrible consequences for their descendants, in the present of the romance's writers and readers, that will follow from his action.[56] In the case of the parvenu Tudors, prophecy could serve as an insulation from their shaky dynastic claim to the crown. The second sight of the seer could reveal the rightness and necessity of their accession such as were hidden from ordinary mortals. And James VI and I seems to have had the additional advantage that his accession, and the union of the crowns of

England and Scotland, really had been prophesied in advance with the help of Thomas of Erceldoune's supernatural instructress.

The human characters of romance have to work through experience or learning. Raymondin has to see his wife on the forbidden day before he knows her secret; his uncle, who earlier predicts his own death and his nephew's prosperity, gets his knowledge from skill in reading the stars. Those of supernatural origin know of hidden things directly, by a privileged form of consciousness unlike ordinary forms of thought. It follows that they are almost never portrayed from the inside: we are not shown what kind of thought-process produces such knowledge. The workings of Gloriana's mind are never touched by Spenser's narrative; even in Arthur's vision of her, she is apprehended through him, and her private thoughts and motives lie beyond explanation or examination. Melusine's mind is shown only when she is operating with the emotions of a wife or mother— of a woman—not when she speaks in prophetic or privileged mode, as a fairy. Telepathic powers are given a kind of explanation in *Huon*, but only to stress how inexplicable they are: Oberon was given such a gift by one of the fairies who attended his birth, that he should know 'all that ever any man can knowe or thynke, good or yll'.[57] The Fairy Queen Titania, who represents Elizabeth 'in tropicall and shadowed collours' in Dekker's 'dramaticall poem' *The Whore of Babylon*, has a similar power. Alongside her public and political interactions, she has a form of knowledge that comes to her 'strangely', and which gives her insight not shared by her courtiers and advisers: for instance, the intuition, or second sight, to identify a potential assassin when there is no apparent reason for suspicion.[58]

The language of prophecy similarly distinguishes itself from everyday speech, by its form as much as by its predictive content. It includes not just a heavy strain of the enigmatic—and the more the prophecy refers to the future of the reader, to events that have not yet happened, the more obscure the enigmatic coding is likely to be—but often also a kind of moral apocalypticism, most familiar now through the Fool's parodic prediction of one of Merlin's prophecies ('this prophecy Merlin shall make; for I live before his time') in the Folio version of *King Lear*, a parody that 'predicts' a mixture of the standard abuses of the world as it is with a vision of a world so perfect that it will never exist:

> When priests are more in word than matter;
> When brewers mar their malt with water;
> When nobles are their tailors' tutors,
> No heretics burned, but wenches' suitors,

> Then shall the realm of Albion
> Come to great confusion.
>
> When every case in law is right,
> No squire in debt nor no poor knight;
> When slanders do not live in tongues,
> Nor cutpurses come not to throngs . . .[59]

The Fool's immediate model is a six-line prophecy variously ascribed to Merlin and Chaucer, which similarly predicts confusion for Albion 'whan faith fayleth in preestes sawes . . ..'[60] The formal model for such language is set by the earliest Thomas prophecies, recorded around 1340:

> When men desire other men's goods more than their own . . .
> When men make stables of churches . . .
> When pride spurs and peace is laid in prison . . .[61]

Similar prophecies were circulating orally and in manuscript at least from the fifteenth century, and in print in the seventeenth. So it is not surprising that Dekker's Titania should use similar language to predict what will never happen, as a way of rejecting the Catholic monarchs who seek her hand:

> When a court has no parasite,
> When truth speakes false, and falshood right:
> When Conscience goes in cloth of gold,
> When offices are given, not sold . . .
> And lawyers sweare to take no fees,
>
> I. ii. 241–4, 248

only then will she be prepared to listen to suitors. The speech functions within the action as a political statement, but it is presented as a way of keeping at bay the monarchs' 'bewitching charms'; and it endorses the sense that Titania is a figure who might, if she chose, use such language not just as rhetorical elaboration of a 'no' but to mediate second sight.

Those who have no such supernatural powers or origins have to rely on others to do their prophesying for them. The perennial favourite as soothsayer was, as *Lear*'s Fool notes, not a fairy but a man with comparably supernatural origins: Merlin, who owed his power to see hidden things to the fact that he was the son of an incubus. Merlin enjoyed Europe-wide currency, whereas Thomas of Erceldoune, and the fairy queen for whose prophecies he served as the medium, seems not to have been known outside Britain, and had their greatest fame in the North. Geoffrey of Monmouth was responsible for this huge diffusion of Merlin, both by inventing a biography for him in his *History of the Kings of Britain* and his *Life of Merlin*, and through his composition (or perhaps mediation) of the 'Prophecies of Merlin', which were incorporated into the *History* and which also received widespread dissemination as an independent text throughout the Middle Ages and in printed form into the seventeenth century. The prose *Merlin* of the *Lancelot-Grail* cycle added a concluding episode to his biography, with the story of his being buried alive beneath a rock by a woman with whom he had become so besotted that even his knowledge of the outcome could not prevent his revealing to her the secrets she needed to immure him. He is acting as one of the 'undead' in the *Orlando Furioso*, when he reveals to Bradamante the future of her dynasty. Britomart similarly has the line of her descendants described to her by Merlin, though when he is still fully alive within this world;[62] the choice is particularly appropriate for Spenser's prophecy of the Tudors, since Henry VII had made the most of the Welsh prophecies that might be taken to predict his accession, and Merlin continued to carry authority, especially in his homeland of Wales, through the sixteenth century and later. The ancient prophecies of a messianic Welsh saviour, *y mab darogan*, the son of prophecy, were associated with him, and optimistically applied to various historical figures: not just Henry Tudor, but Owen Glendower before him, and Henry's eldest son Arthur.[63] In Malory and his sources, Merlin regularly acts as prophet for King Arthur (though, as in his own case, knowledge of the future does not prevent it from happening). Tudor readers derived their knowledge of Merlin variously from chronicles, from prophecies, from oral traditions, and from romance sources: in particular the *Morte Darthur*, and the print of *The Byrth and Prophecye of Marlyn*, a metrical version of the early part of the prose *Merlin* that largely overlaps with Geoffrey of Monmouth's account of him.[64]

Making a real prophecy about the future, especially if it encompassed the death of the monarch, was an altogether more dangerous matter, and one that called down sharp punishment. There were successive attempts to prohibit the circulation of prophecies throughout the Tudor era, enough to prevent their printing but apparently with no effect on less formal means of dissemination.[65] Ascribe your prophecies to someone safely in the past, however—whether Merlin or Thomas of Erceldoune, or, on occasion, both together—and it was easy to disclaim responsibility, even if the traditional text might look suspiciously updated. A disclaimer of personal invention in the present added authority for what still lay in the future. By the early sixteenth century, in *The Prophisies of Rymour, Beid and Marlyng*, Merlin and Thomas Rymer's elf-queen (now transformed into the Virgin) were sharing a single prophetic text that did project forwards in time. The work apparently dates from some time between 1513 and *c.*1530, and rapidly achieved notoriety.[66] An adapted text was printed in 1603. It is a work that makes a heavy investment in the Tudor dynasty. The man who speaks its predictions (variously citing as his authorities, as its title indicates, 'Arsalldoune', Bede, and Merlin) includes a prophecy of the Wars of the Roses, when 'the sone ageinst the father shalbe' (111),[67] and of the coming of Henry Tudor:

> Then shall entre at Mylford haven
> upon a horse of tree   [i.e. by ship
> A banyshed barone that is borne
> of Brutes blode shalbe,

who will join battle at Bosworth Field (143–6, 149). The work ends with an extended prophecy of a great English king who will reign for fifty-five years, who will defeat the French, be welcomed into Rome by the pope and cardinals, and then proceed to conquer Jerusalem and win the Holy Cross. Alarmed by its potential for stirring political and religious opposition, Henry VIII's council both forcefully attempted to halt its dissemination and encouraged an alternative interpretation by which the Holy Land would be metaphorically reconquered by the overthrow of the pope and the putting of the Scriptures into English.[68] The text continued to be adapted and read into the next century, now with the wider dissemination of print, and notwithstanding the continuing presence of the Blessed Virgin its function within a Reformation agenda remained assured. The deep suspicion with which it continued to be regarded under the Tudors had more to do with its open-endedness, and therefore its potential for being extended in dangerous ways. One man was interrogated as late as 1586 for disseminating the Erceldoune prophecies.[69] The various texts available in scholarly reprints give little idea as to why they might still have been so dangerous; but the version printed in 1652 fills in the gap, and demonstrates why they could incur such suspicion. This is the original romance version (very close, indeed, to its early fifteenth-century text), with the standard prophecies appended; but it includes a coda about the Tudors, accurate up until at least the 1550s, but then culminating with a prediction for the 1590s of Elizabeth's death or removal, followed by national breakdown on an apocalyptic scale.[70]

This kind of evidence for the oral dissemination of the Thomas prophecies in the sixteenth century suggests that they were much more widely known than the manuscript record alone would indicate; their use after Elizabeth's death, discussed below, indeed invites the speculation that they were universally recognized, whether generically or as individual texts. The *Prophisies of Rymour* seems to have been the best known, and it is particularly interesting for the closeness with which it meshes with the opening of the *Faerie Queene*. Its narrator asks a man he meets for news, and is shown a vision of a 'crowned quene' accompanied by angels; like her literary ancestress, the elf-queen of *Thomas of Erceldoune*, she rides on a dapple-grey steed, 'of a ferly kynde' (19–24). He looks again, and sees 'a goodly man as armyde knyght' riding over a 'bent', a plain, and who

> bare a shylde of sylver shene.
> A crosse of gowles therin did be.   [gules, i.e. heraldic red
>
> 52–3

The knight is not identified until a few lines later, when the lady addresses him as 'Seint George'. Here, he is very much an English St George, who is at odds with the Scottish St Andrew, and the lady's function is to appeal to their better nature ('Remember that ye be sayntes in heven', 65) and keep them apart. His appearance, however, is strikingly similar to Spenser's 'gentle knight'

> pricking on the plaine,
> Y cladd in mightie armes and silver shielde,

with both his shield and surcoat bearing a 'bloudie Crosse'.[71] As the iconography makes plain long before he is named, this figure too is St George. As the *Prophisies* records (69), St George commonly bore the epithet 'Our Lady's knight'; in the *Faerie Queene*, Redcrosse has been sent forth by a different lady, 'the greatest Glorious Queene of Faerie lond' (I. i. 3), but she, in so far as she figures the head of the Church in England, has need of her own saintly English knight to serve her.

The existence of the St George of the *Prophisies of Rymour* makes a powerful difference to how the opening of the *Faerie Queene* might be read. Did Spenser know the work, or equivalents to it? If he did, and if he could assume a similar familiarity in some or all his readers, then his epic announces itself forcefully from the start as political prophecy. It is impossible to prove such knowledge—if one is to allegorize England in the person of St George, there is bound to be an overlap of attributes, and the similarities could be mere coincidence. But the existence of the prophecy at the very least reconfigures the cultural context for the reception of the *Faerie Queene*. A Redcross Knight was already an established figure within the febrile atmosphere that always surrounded political prophecy; to open the epic of England with such a figure would have announced more than it does to a modern readership unfamiliar with the tradition. The culminating prediction of the *Prophisies*, about the great English monarch who would enter Rome in triumph and win the Holy Cross, had already been given the lie in its most literal detail by the passage of time; but the ideas of conquering Rome and building God's kingdom had a new dynamism after the Reformation. In retaliation for Roman demands for tribute, King Arthur had supposedly reached the very walls of Rome—according to John Harding and Malory, he had been crowned as emperor.[72] The Prince Arthur who seeks Gloriana still has that in the future; and perhaps that future was one already current in prophecy for the house of Tudor. Spenser seems to hint at a fusion of the two conquests of Rome: Arthur's in the future for the young prince of his poem; and the other in the future for England, in a way that would fit with his knowledge of these prophecies. The apocalypticism of Redcrosse-St George's overcoming of the dragon already had its match in a prediction relating to an English monarch who would subdue the pope and assume imperial power.[73] Both provided powerful counter-models to the prophecy of imminent disaster due to befall England in the 1590s.

Interpreting a prophecy to fit new facts, and a new set of hopes or anxieties or fears, is a well-established and near-universal human characteristic, and later rewritings will make sure the prophecy conforms a little more closely to whatever eventuated. The earliest known print of any form of the *Prophisies of Rymour* is the closely related 'Prophicie of Thomas Rymour', apparently composed in the mid-fifteenth century; it is one of the texts in the anthology of prophecies printed in 1603 as *The Whole Prophesie of Scotland*, probably in London, though it carries an altogether safer Edinburgh imprint on its title page.[74] And this version carries the story forwards, beyond the appearance of the Virgin and the hostile saints George and Andrew and the prophecies that follow, to the union of the crowns of England and Scotland. The culmination of the text comes at the very end, when the narrator asks the thousand-dollar question, and along with the answer is given the name that lends the prophecy its authority:

> When all these ferlies was away   [marvels
> Then sawe I non, but I and he.
> Then to the birne couth I say,   [man
> 'Where dwels thou, or in what countrie?
> Or who shal rule the Ile of Bretaine
> From the North to the South sey?'
> 'A French wife shal beare the Son,
> Shall rule all Bretaine to the sey,
> That of the Bruces blood shall come
> As neere as the nint degree.'
> I franed fast what was his name,   [asked eagerly
> Where that he came from what countrie?
> 'In Erslingtoun, I dwelle at hame,
> Thomas Rymour men calles me.'[75]

It is much easier to write prophecy retrospectively, once one knows what one has to prophesy, but the prophet on this occasion had been writing a little too early. The line of Brut of the Tudor prophecy (the 'baron . . . of Brutes blode' quoted above) has been transformed into the line of the Bruce, to turn it into a prediction of the Stuarts; but the change was originally intended to refer to a child one generation earlier than the man who did eventually inherit both crowns, James VI, since he was of the tenth degree, not the ninth, from Robert the Bruce.[76] Inaccuracy was, however, a trivial price to pay for the additional authority the prophecy acquired from its having actually been current before the event. Both John Colville, in his funeral oration on Elizabeth, and John Spottiswood, archbishop of St Andrews, were happy to point out that James's accession fulfilled Thomas's prophecies—strictly speaking, that is, the prophecies given by the elf-queen for whom Thomas served as spokesman.

The prophecies of . . . Thomas the Rymer, may justly be admired, having foretold so many ages before, the union of the kingdomes of England and Scotland, in the ninth degree of the Bruces blood.[77]

The archbishop does not commit himself on the matter of elf-queens, but the arrivals of both the Tudor and Stuart dynasties were authorized by fairy prophecies. The union of the crowns was still in the future for Spenser, but he could have found it already adumbrated by Thomas of Erceldoune. The elf-queen of the romance had given Thomas his store of prophecies; Elizabeth, in keeping with the inscrutability of the fairy, kept the secrets of the future to herself, and unlocked them only by a single gesture on her deathbed. Even if Spenser did know the prediction, he most certainly could not incorporate it into his poem: his own living Faerie Queene was much too dangerous for him to take such a step, as her fierce prohibition of prophecy demonstrates.

It was a different matter after her death, when Dekker apparently reworked the scene of the hostility of St George and St Andrew for the intended original opening of the 'Magnificent Entertainment' designed to welcome the new King James into the City of London in 1603.

Saint George, Saint Andrew, (the Patrons of both Kingdomes) having a long time lookt upon each other, with countenances rather of meere strangers, then of such neare Neighbours, upon the present aspect of his Majesties approach toward London, were (in his sight) to issue from two severall places on horsebacke, and in compleate Armour, their Brestes and Caparisons suited with the Armes of England and Scotland, (as they are now quartered) to testifie their leagued Combination, and newe sworne Brother-hood.[78]

The knights were to 'ride hand in hand, till they met his Maiestie', where-upon the (female) Genius of the city was to make an appearance to demand of them why they were in armour and conjure them to peace, a peace appropriate for the time when the 'proud buildings' of New Troy 'shew like Fairie-bowers' (87). It is not essential that Dekker and the watching Londoners should have known the prophetic text in order to symbolize the amity of the kingdoms in the persons of their patron saints; but the pageant acquires extra depth and resonance, and the exceptional representation of Genius as a woman on horseback would be explained, if it were written as a sequel to, and completion of, the Rymer prophecy on 'the union of the kingdomes'. The elf-queen who had been transfigured into the Blessed Virgin now becomes a figure for civic pride; Mary's virginity is transmuted into an image of an un-invaded England:

> 'bout whose Virgin-waste,
> Isis is like a Cristall girdle cast.   [i.e., the Thames
>
> 104–5

The reconciled saints together with the fairy bowers and that reminis-cence of Florimell's girdle of chastity refigure London as the place where Thomas's elven prophecies and Spenser's ideal Faerie Land merge and are given material form in the historical world.

The accession of James and its immediate aftermath were as far for-ward as the Thomas prophecies had gone. Their speciality had lain in the troubled history of Anglo-Scottish relations, and the smoothness of James's succession not only appeared to complete that story but gave the lie to the more apocalyptic predictions about the consequences of his inheritance of the crown. So far as Dekker was concerned, his pageant offers an end of history, or at least of prophesied history. It was a history, however, that had by now dispensed with Gloriana.

'I LOVE THEE WELL BY CAUSE OF THE TROUTHE THAT IS IN THEE'

Fairies possess not only the ability to see into the future but also the ability to see into the heart. That is what Dekker's Titania does, when she can identify a likely murderer. Despite the unpredictability that makes any encounter dangerous (and there is still some touch of that in the representations of Elizabeth as fairy queen), fays can act as arbiters of justice when its human forms fail; and they may also act to encourage future virtue in the protagonist as well as to acknowledge it in the present.

Supernatural intervention recognizes both the imperfection of human attempts at justice and the mismatch between the exercise of justice and power. When Malory's Guinevere is accused of poisoning Sir Patrise and attempting to poison Gawain, Lancelot can save her from judicial burning by combat, but it takes the quasi-fairy Damsel of the Lake to identify the true culprit.[79] Two of the most widely known fairy benefactors, Melusine and Oberon, similarly come to the aid of their chosen heroes after they have become criminals to mortal eyes, but when supernatural insight can recognize their guiltlessness. Raymondin accidentally kills his uncle, the earl of Poitiers, in attempting to defend him from a wild boar. Melusine intervenes to prevent Raymondin's part in the death from being known, and gives him the advice that sets him on the path to wealth and greatness. Huon of Bordeaux unwittingly kills Charlemagne's son as the result of a plot on the part of the emperor to ambush and kill him; and despite clearing himself by both oath and combat he is sent off by Charlemagne on a quest that should lead to his death. Oberon gives him instructions and the magic help that will enable him to survive his adventures. Their supernatural aid is not unconditional, however. Raymondin has to love and trust his wife despite her prohibition from his ever setting eyes on her on Saturdays; his trust briefly survives his breaking his deeply sworn oath never to attempt to see her, but not for very long. Oberon declares that he will assist Huon 'by cause of the trouthe that is in thee',[80] but he also insists that Huon should maintain further standards of virtue if his help is to continue, and Huon proves much worse at those. The magic cup he is given will continue to refill itself only if he never lies; he is never to be so rash as to try out the magic help-summoning horn without due need. The consequences of disobeying Oberon are embodied in one of his followers, who has been condemned to have the form of a sea-beast for thirty years. Huon gets off more lightly: he infringes both injunctions, though the narrative suspense as to what will happen next is rather dispersed by Oberon's forgiveness. More dire consequences follow from his breaking the oath Oberon demands from him that he is to remain chaste before his marriage. His forcing of his future bride on the ship that is carrying them back to France results immediately in a ship-wreck, her abduction by pirates, and he himself being bound, blind-folded, tortured, and left to die—though again, Oberon opts to take pity on him and send help.[81] The adventures Huon undergoes and the trials he encounters have almost as much to do with his repeated moral failures to live up to Oberon's commands as with the machinations of his ene-mies, whether at home in France or abroad in various pagan kingdoms.

In the case of Huon, his *trouthe* is a given of the story, and tends to be proved more by Oberon's favouring of him than by any outstanding demonstration of it on his part. There is a strong suggestion, however, that Oberon's education of him does work to make him into something more like an ideal knight, worthy of the final choice of him to succeed to the throne of the fairy kingdom; and such an assumption presumably underlies Spenser's choice of Huon as the being who has knighted his own faery protagonist, Guyon (II. i. 6). Just how readily contemporary readers recognized the role of fairies, and Oberon in particular, in chivalric education is indicated by the perfunctoriness of Christopher Middleton's introduction of him as instructor in his *Chinon of England*, of the 1590s. In the early stages of the romance, Chinon has no intention of pursuing a life of prowess; after his conversion to such a mode of liv-ing, his first adventure takes the form of a combat against a fire-breath-ing monster, which turns out to be the fairy king acting in test mode.[82] Otherworldly support may also be a narrative shorthand for virtue that has to be taken somewhat on trust by the reader. Launfal, in his various incarnations, is not seen exercising any remarkable virtues, though every text makes clear that he deserves more than he gets: in Marie de France's original, he is distinguished for his valour, largesse, and prowess, as well as for good looks; in *Sir Launfal*, it is his largesse alone that is singled out for high praise; in *Sir Lambewell*, that virtue has become a downright liability, as he progresses from spending 'worthi-lye' to 'outragiouslie'.[83] It is when he is overlooked for reward and has to leave the court to avoid the disgrace of evident poverty that a fairy mistress steps in to supply him with the favours that Arthur has failed to provide, and sexual favours too. There seems here to be something of an excess of favour over desert: an excess made evident in the story when Launfal breaks the prohibition on speaking of her and loses everything she has given him, herself included. As in *Huon*, however (or as in *Yvain/Ywain*, or any of the other romances of atonement), there is space for penitence, forgiveness, and recovery, as she finally returns to justify his boasting of her beauty. Just how much forgiveness she shows varies from text to text, though all have a happy ending. In *Sir Launfal*, his fairy squire restores his horse to him so that he can follow her to the Otherworld. In *Lanval* and *Sir Lambewell*, he leaps up behind her onto her own palfrey without asking her leave, the Percy Folio text adding a defiant assertion of his faithfulness:

> 'Madam, with reason and skill
> now goe which way soe-ere you will,
> for when you light downe, I shall stand,
> and when you ryd, all at your hande,
> and whether it be for waile or woe   [weal, i.e., happiness
> I will never depart you froe.'

611–16

He may have transgressed and lost her once, but she does not exercise her magic powers to dismiss him after this insistence on his love and service. He has now, in a way, achieved her love by right of his faithfulness in suffering rather than through her grace alone.

Justice can bring punishment as well as reward, and fairy justice can be extreme in both. The story of Launfal's neglect and reward, disobedience and recovery, encloses a further plot line, in which his rejection of Guinevere's advances results in a formal trial for shaming her, on the grounds that he had propositioned her (a false charge, invented by the queen as revenge) and slandered her (because he had claimed that his mistress's lowest handmaid was more beautiful than the queen; something he had done, but it falls as a charge when the fairy lady and her maidens make their appearance to prove the statement true). The Middle English version is meticulous in setting up the formalities of the trial, with twelve knights being commissioned as the equivalent of a jury and two more acting as bail for him. The delivery of justice at the end of the romance, however, lies not only in their clearing of Launfal, but in the fairy's punishment of Guinevere:

> Dame Tryamour to the Quene geth
> And blew on here swich a breth
> That never eft might she see.

1006–8

The Anglo-Norman and Percy versions instantiate the story's generic happy ending solely in terms of the hero: they have his guiltlessness recognized at law, and allow his repentance as sufficient for reconciliation with his mistress. The Middle English adds to its restoration of moral equilibrium the retribution delivered on the villainess, by a fay who has both the second sight to know the truth, and the power to blind by her breath.

Fairies are not, however, either reliable or predictable, and their capriciousness can produce a kind of justice that does not follow normal mortal rules. If the guilty Guinevere is blinded, that epitome of blind male folly, January, in Chaucer's *Merchant's Tale*, has his physical blindness cured by the 'kyng of Fayerye', here identified with Pluto, in pursuit of his quarrel with his wife, Proserpina. It is, once again, in the heat of the day, and the fairy king and queen are following their usual habit of passing their time beside a well under a tree in January's pleasure-garden.[84] January may be the injured party at the moment when he is given his cure—his young wife May and her sprightly lover have just managed to couple in the pear-tree over January's head—but his persistence in moral blindness marks the limits even of fairy power. May, caught *in flagrante delicto*, is herself given the power of a quick-witted defence by the 'queene of Fayerye' herself, and all women after her. Both husband and wife are in effect rewarded rather than punished for their vice. Chaucer's alterations to his sources none the less represent an advance in tastefulness: the closest analogues to his story cast the supernatural agents as Christ and St Peter.[85] Changing them to fairies taps into the arbitrariness that potentially lurks within otherworldly arbitration: this is the exercise of power without responsibility, carried out more for the fairy gods' self-interest in the progress of their own marital quarrel rather than to serve as a corrective in the mortal world. Yet there is an appropriateness in the outcome that is analogous to justice, in that it intensifies and makes evident what was already there by implication. The wilfulness of January's blindness is highlighted by his refusal to see what is there in front of his eyes; May's reneging on the *trouthe* of her marriage vows is pointed by her outright lie (that she was just struggling with a man in a tree in order to restore her husband's sight), and her quick-wittedness confirms her triumph over the man who had tried to exercise absolute control over her.

Fairies can be arbiters not only in matters of virtue and ill-doing but in matters of love. Shakespeare's Oberon, whose quarrel with his wife has the *Merchant's Tale* in its hinterland, decides somewhat casually to sort out the mortal lovers into appropriate pairs by a process of eye-altering. That this is less justice than caprice is indicated by his other use for the love-juice, to make his wife adore whatever hideous thing she first sees on waking: it is designed as a way of making her give up her foster-child to him, for purposes that seem unlikely to be moral by human standards. He claims that his action is a kind of punishment, but it is much closer to malice than justice: in all their various reasons for quarrelling, Oberon tends to come out as the guiltier party—especially so since fairy wives are not bound by the rules of subjection to their husbands imposed on the daughters of Eve.[86] There can, however, be more satisfying supernatural interventions in matters of love. Nenive (the character in Malory who starts as a damsel of his Lady of the Lake but then takes over her title) takes action to correct the injustice suffered by Pelleas, the passionate devotee of the scornful Ettard; Ettard's mistreatment of him, and her readiness to indulge in an affair with Gawain instead, are repaid when Nenive makes her fall hopelessly in love with Pelleas at precisely the same moment when she makes Pelleas fall out of love with her. He is rewarded, not just by relief from past torment, but by the Lady of the Lake herself, who can appreciate a deep capacity for love when she sees it. When Ettard laments her state, Nenive calmly assures her that what she is suffering is 'the righteous judgement of God'; when Pelleas thanks God, his bene-factress declares simply, 'Thank me.' And the knight and his supernatural rescuer proceed to love happily ever after.[87]

The most compelling instance of the supernatural arbitration of a mortal lover's faithfulness occurs towards the end of the Anglo-Norman *Amadas et Ydoine.* Its imaginative power stems partly from the fact that we are not told outright at any point just what the metaphysical status is of the knight who tests Amadas' trust in his lady: his conformity to the conventions of fairy emerges only gradually, and even when he leaves the text he carries with him as many qualities of the uncanny—the liminal, the unexplained—as of the Otherworld. The romance, moreover, has not made any use of fairies before this point: there is nothing to warn the readers what to expect. The episode occurs after Ydoine has died (as the narrative flatly states), and Amadas is watching over her tomb within a walled cemetery. The lover had already undergone one test of how much he loves his lady, when she had insisted to him, in a desperate attempt to prevent him from killing himself after her own death, that she had had a number of affairs before she fell in love with him and had murdered the resulting offspring, so that it is imperative that he stay alive to pray for her soul. She had at the same time insisted, none the less, that her love for him was deep and faithful. This is what the scene in the graveyard now calls into question. Just before midnight, Amadas sees a huge company of noble people approaching. They bring with them a beautiful milk-white palfrey with bells on its harness, which has no function in the narrative unless perhaps as a sign of fairy.[88] Then their leader, a knight in full armour, leaps the wall on his charger and confronts Amadas, telling him that he is mad and a fool for believing in Ydoine's love: he himself, he declares, was the man she really loved, and to prove it he shows Amadas the ring that he, Amadas, had given her, on his own finger. Although the young man's confidence is briefly shaken, he gazes at her tomb, and just as Percival recalls God in looking at his sword when he is tempted by the devil, so Amadas recovers his faith in his lady from the sight of where her body lies. He and the strange knight fight bitterly, the knight twice pausing to give Amadas the opportunity to deny Ydoine's love. At last Amadas manages to inflict on him a mortal wound—or a wound that should be mortal; but instead, unexpectedly, the knight congratulates Amadas on his courage and loyalty. He assures him that Ydoine is not dead: all the young lover must do is exchange the ring the knight had shown him, which he had stolen from her finger, for an enchanted ring he had substituted for it, and which gives the appearance of death. He also tells him—for this knight, like Dame Tryamour and Melusine, has privileged knowledge of the truth—that all that Ydoine had told him about her past was untrue. He further declares that he himself is of such a nature that weapons cannot kill him. Before day breaks, he has to go to God, 'a Diu' (might he after all, indeed, be an angel rather than a fairy?); and he and his company leave Amadas alone in the graveyard to open the tomb and restore his sweetheart to life.[89]

It is an extraordinary episode. It is almost unique in having the lover assert his faith in his beloved despite having (as he believes) genuine knowledge of her unchastity, from her own mouth. It also sets a clear limit on such male knowledge of a woman's sexual history: some things can be known only to those with second sight; or to those with love so absolute and unconditional that their trust will override rational evidence. In that respect it parallels the motif of magic that doesn't work. The magic here palpably does work—even the audience, as well as the fictional characters, believe Ydoine to be dead; the knight is indeed, it transpires, a supernatural being—but, as with non-functioning magic, it is the surplus over and beyond the everyday but contained in human emotion that matters; not the fairy enchantment, but Amadas' depth of love. Amadas' combat against the supernatural being turns out to be a combat against the temptation to replace his difficult faith in Ydoine with the easy prejudices of entrenched antifeminism. This is, moreover, not a diabolic challenge: the strange knight names God in the course of his first exchange with the mourning lover, as well as on his departure. Amadas' triple insistence before daybreak that he will *not* deny his love, twice when the combat is suspended and implicitly in his victory, invites a contrast with St Peter's lesser loyalty, though the parallel is never spelled out. There is no claim either that the test of Amadas is instigated by God; but the knight's departure to God implies that it carries divine approval, and that the lover's triumph is right by more than human standards.

The strange knight's congratulations to Amadas on passing the test, the discovery for both the lover and the audience that the challenger was, after all, on his side, is echoed in *Sir Gawain and the Green Knight*. The Green Knight never claims to be an otherworldly being, but Gawain, and the audience with him for much of the poem, have a strong suspicion that he might be. Whether he is merely Sir Bertilak turned green is, moreover, something that the poet avoids resolving: such an explanation has barely been given before it is called into question again by the Green Knight's riding off 'whither-so-ever he would', and still green. A solidly human figure might be expected to de-enchant at that point, to turn back into his human form (as indeed happens in two of the later analogues),[90] and return to his castle. He carries with him enough associations of the non-human—the unnatural colour of his skin and hair, his ability to survive decapitation—for his function as moral arbiter to work in similar ways to that of fully fairy figures. Like the knight of *Amadas*, he proves that he is on the side of God, here by the regular performance of Mass in his castle. And the test turns out to be one not of good against evil, but of how good the good really is: a test of Gawain's, as of Amadas', *trouthe*.

The fairy knight and the Green Knight both initially appear to be set on killing the heroes, and only the generic expectations of the romance limit their danger. The challenger in *Amadas* is physically formidable, 'grans et fors' (5653), and the magnificence of that opening image of his charger leaping the cemetery wall casts him as a fearsome opponent. The Green Knight is not only huge, and green, but inclined to terrifying whimsy: cut off my head, and get your own cut off in a year's time. There is obviously a catch in it somewhere, hence the refusal of any knight except Gawain to accept the challenge. It is only at the end that the moral force behind the terms of the challenge, the testing of *trouthe*, is made manifest. Even the most capricious and dangerous of fairies follow a code of conduct of a kind, in which they respond to human goodness and are bound by certain codes of their own—not least by the point on which Gawain is tested, faithfulness to their given word. Such faithfulness from supernatural beings can, as in the case of Launfal's lady or Huon's Oberon, mean trouble when they have promised retribution for the hero if he breaks promises of his own. Gawain likewise receives a small wound on the third descent of the axe for his failure to keep his word to exchange winnings with the lord. Even a fairy who has become fully humanized in the course of a story's transmission, as is taken to be the case with Ywain's Alundine (Laudine in Chrétien's original), retains this power of absolute fulfilment of her warnings—in her case, to reject him if he fails to return to her within a year. The punishment has less of the quality of personal pique about it than of taboo or the Celtic *geis*, an imposed binding condition that operates at a level beyond ordinary human pacts.[91] She, like Dame Tryamour and Oberon, also has the power to relent if the hero has sufficient inward *trouthe* to justify forgiveness, but there is no suggestion that the hero can enforce such forgiveness. The fairy king of *Sir Orfeo* fulfils his threat to carry off Herodis, but he also keeps his word to Orfeo to give him whatever reward he wishes in return for his harping; his only objection is that Herodis is too lovely to be given to the ragged and filthy minstrel who has spent ten years in the forest. Despite this rather surprising sense of what is socially or aesthetically proper, he is meticulous in matching Orfeo's faithfulness with his own *trouthe*—and, unlike in the Greek myth, the reward is unconditional, and Orfeo does indeed lead his wife back, hand in hand, to the world of the living.

Orfeo's faithfulness comes close to setting a standard for the fairy king to follow. There are other occasions, by contrast, when the protagonist has deep moral flaws, and an encounter with a fairy is educative and restorative. This is what happens in Chaucer's *Wife of Bath's Tale*. Unlike in the analogues, the knight who has to find what women most desire must do so in order to prevent his execution for rape. The hag who tells him the answer is not, as in the other versions, a mortal woman under a spell, but, it seems, a fairy.[92] The tale is set in the times when

> The elf-queene, with hir joly compaignye,
> Daunced ful ofte in many a grene mede.

> *CT*, III. 860–1

So one is invited to draw the obvious conclusion when the twenty-four ladies whom the knight sees dancing disappear, leaving only one hideous old woman. That she is indeed supernatural is implied again by the fact that the power to turn beautiful lies with herself, not (as happens in the analogues) in any undoing of someone else's enchantment. She does so, however, only after she has delivered the rapist knight a mighty lecture, occupying a full quarter of the tale, about the nature of true virtue and its derivation from God.

Chaucer does not require any belief on his readers' part in fairies: the moral advice holds good as serious Christian doctrine regardless of who speaks it. The serious moral use of fairies, as giving supernatural endorsement for ideological statement, generally required a less-sceptical attitude towards them. Jean d'Arras, who wrote the French original of the prose *Melusine*, spends a long introduction arguing the case for their existence. When Melusine herself marks Raymondin with her favour, it amounts to a supra-human endorsement of the probity of the male founder of the house of Lusignan, intended to carry a weight beyond mere fantasy. Similarly, when she gives her departing sons long lectures on good and prudent living—like Polonius, holding up the sailing of their ship in order to do so—her fairy origins are designed to endorse the conventional wisdom of the advice, to make it appear not just conventional but right by more absolute standards, deleting any possibility of social or historical relativism. It is not just a mother's or a woman's advice, but that of a fay who is 'of God', and whose instructions therefore carry more weight than would their mortal father's. She accordingly tells them to support Holy Church; protect widows and orphans; keep company with gentlemen; avoid borrowing beyond their means to repay; not to cede any seigneurial privileges in subduing rebellion; to tax reasonably; and to watch out for the small print of treaties. 'Thus, as ye here, chastysed and endoctryned Melusyne her two sones,' and their careers prosper accordingly.[93] A similar desire to have more than human endorsement for chivalric ideology lies behind the most extended instruction in chivalry in the French *Lancelot-Grail*, which is delivered to the young Lancelot by the quasi-supernatural Lady of the Lake. She instructs him in all the duties owed by, and to, the knight: that he must defend Holy Church, as he is defended by his shield and hauberk; that the double edge of his sword signifies that he must be a soldier both of Christ and of the Christian community, executing justice on thieves and murderers; and that he must guide the common people as he guides his horse, and they, in turn, must supply his needs, just as his horse bears him, 'in legitimate subjection'.[94]

It is against such a background that the nature of fairy education in the *Faerie Queene* needs to be set. Arthur has been trained 'in gentle thewes and martiall might' by a 'Faery knight' named Timon (I. ix. 3; the name comes from the Greek for 'honour'), not, as one might expect, a mortal, though Merlin has general oversight of his upbringing. Timon is of sufficient importance to be mentioned as Arthur's tutor in the 'Letter to Ralegh', and there he is juxtaposed with another scheme of education: the fashioning of 'a gentleman or noble person in vertuous and gentle discipline'. The whole context of authoritative instruction from beyond this world gives the moral and political programme of the poem the fiction of endorsement from outside the messy relativities of Spenser's own time and place. This may indeed be one reason why Spenser chose the 'fairy' form for the poem at all.

Arthur and the other virtue knights are characters within the fiction who serve as surrogates for the reader in this process of education. The scene on Mount Acidale operates within a similar context, but extends its idea of authoritative fashioning beyond Calidore, the knight of Courtesy, and the readers, to the poet himself, in the form of his *alter ego*, Colin Clout. 'Nymphes and Faeries'—the Classical and English forms of otherworldly beings—sit by the banks of the river at the foot of the hill, and dance on its flat summit. When Calidore approaches and hears the 'merry sound I Of a shrill pipe' and the thumping of feet, the description strongly invokes fairies; their disappearance when he steps out, 'vanishing away' just as the fairies in the *Wife of Bath's Tale* had done, confirms the identification, even though Spenser goes on to define them more formally as graces in Venus's service. That the three Graces at the centre of the dance bestow 'all the complements of curtesie', and teach the skill of civility,

> how to each degree and kynde
> We should our selves demeane, to low, to hie,
>
> VI. x. 23

resonates with this long background in which ideological instruction is confirmed by its stemming from beyond the world of the everyday. The ultimate model of this teaching within the poem lies in the woman at the very centre, Colin's beloved; and importantly, she partakes both of the fairy, in her vanishing, and of the human, in so far as she is a 'Shepheards lasse' (VI. x. 16). Her attributes are a summary of the virtues of each of the heroines of the books of the *Faerie Queene*—'divine resemblance' for Truth, 'excelling much the meane' for a perfection of temperance, supreme beauty, chastity, and courtesy—in a way that turns her into the 'Idea or fore-conceit', in Sidney's phrase, of the whole work.[95] Not by anything she might say, but by what she *is*, the 'lasse' at the heart of the dance instructs the poet in what his work can be. She is at once fairy, authoritative model and inspiration, and the woman he loves. Oberon had loved Huon for the *trouthe* that is in him. We never see inside the lass's mind, or see enough of Colin's, to know whether such a motive still holds true; but what matters here, is rather that she *is* the *trouthe* that is in him.

The moment when things started to go disastrously wrong in the entertainments that Leicester laid on for Elizabeth at Kenilworth in 1575 occurred while she was still making her way in through the various defences of the castle in the course of her arrival. As she approached the inner gate, she found

the Lady of the Lake (famous in king Arthurz book) with too Nymphes wayting upon her, arrayed all in sylks attending her highnes comming: from the midst of the Pool, whear, upon a moovable Iland, bright blazing with torches, she floting too land, met her Majesty with a wel penned meter and matter after this sorte: First of the auncientee of the Castle, whoo had been ownerz of the same, een till this day, most allweyz in the handes of the Earls of Leyceter, hoow she had kept this Lake syns king Arthurz dayz, and noow understanding of her highnes hither cumming, thought it both offis and duety in humbl wyze too discoover her and her estate: offring up the same, her Lake and poour thearin, with promis of repair unto the Coourt. It pleazed her highnes too thank this lady and too ad withall, we had thought indeed the Lake had been oours, and doo you call it yourz noow?[96]

The entertainment was intended as a compliment, as the handing over of power and territory by a fairy to the queen. The queen would have none of it: the power and the territory were hers, and Leicester was not to forget it.

Power was largely measured in the Middle Ages and the early modern period in terms of territory. Fairy monarchs, and even ladies of the lake, derive much of their power from the fact that they possess such domains; but Elizabeth will not cede any of her own power. In casting her as the Faerie Queene, Spenser is also giving her autonomy as a ruler, a notional freedom from political constraint, and also from male constraint. Fairy queens (like goddesses) are not under the control of fathers or husbands, nor (unlike mortal queens) are they answerable to councillors and subjects. They have absolute sovereignty, of a kind that goes far beyond the human sort at issue in the *Wife of Bath's Tale*: you have to be a fairy or a goddess, not a mortal woman of however high a rank, to have complete freedom. Gloriana is the absolute ruler of her kingdom, and she has the disposition of her self entirely in her own control. There was no fairy queen among the entertainments at Kenilworth, but Elizabeth made sure that she acted an analogous part herself.

Material and territorial power were among the identifying features of fairies, alongside their less tangible power of privileged knowledge and their assumption of the role of moral arbiter, teacher, or judge. More importantly, they can confer material possessions and the power that goes with them. Malory's Lady of the Lake is the patroness who gives Excalibur to Arthur—the sword that comes from the lake, and that must be returned into the water at his death.[97] The sword itself serves as a metonym for Arthur's military strength: power as derived from battle, and the territorial conquests that result. In the *Draco Normannicus*, Etienne of Rouen suggests, not altogether seriously, that after Arthur's revival by Morgan she turned him into a fairy and gave him the Antipodes as his kingdom—the other half of the world, if not exactly the Otherworld—and that that realm serves as his power-base for any prospective return to intervene in human affairs.[98] Melusine does not actually own the land that provides the power-base for the house of Lusignan, but she instructs Raymondin how to obtain it (by cutting a deer-hide into an unbroken thong and claiming the land that it encompasses, a legend traditionally attached to Dido). Oberon inhabits not only the dangerous forest that Huon has to cross, but also his own fairy realm accessible only by supernatural means and from which mortals do not return. These territories may be 'somewhere else', but they can provide a supernatural army whenever necessary to intervene in earthly crises. At the close of the work Huon succeeds Oberon to the throne of the fairy kingdom: a new role that is presented as an upwards career move, not simply as a removal from this world. King Arthur, indeed, is Huon's rival for the throne, the implication being that ruling fairyland would be the culmination of his imperial ambitions. War between the two is avoided only when Oberon threatens to turn Arthur into a werewolf unless he accepts Huon's promotion, a threat that brings about immediate peace.[99] Elizabeth may not have been able to turn Leicester into a werewolf, but she too was dangerous to those who tried to play power politics at her expense. At Kenilworth, what was at stake was not just marriage as personal and erotic fulfilment, as Leicester suggests for his Zabeta in the various masques and entertainments he laid on for her, but the realm itself. Elizabeth as Gloriana, by contrast, chooses her own future husband; if the Arthur of the *Faerie Queene* is to have imperial power, it will be channelled through her. Oberon had cut off the earlier Arthur's imperial ambitions of ruling the fairy realm; Spenser's Arthur, it is implied, may yet make those dreams a reality.

The ability of romance fairies to confer material goods on those they favour has an evident appeal to fantasy. The unlimited wealth enjoyed by Launfal or Partonope until they infringe their lady's injunctions makes a direct appeal to the human desire to have something for nothing, and what happened in romance had its counterpart in real-life frauds. It was not uncommon in the sixteenth century for conmen to attempt to take money from the gullible in return for an introduction to the fairy queen, and even more common for Renaissance playwrights to write plays on the subject. The standard fiction, as in the romances, was that the fairy herself was already seeking out the gull with the desire of bestowing her favours on him: the ultimate fantasy that was just sufficiently plausible to the credulous to be played for real. It was the fabulous wealth to which fairies supposedly had access that was the attraction here, not, as in the romances, love or sexual favour. The fairy queen invented by the fraudsters of Jonson's *Alchemist* has her particular favour explained on the grounds that she is the gull's aunt. The lack of sexual interest meant that the fairy king could, on occasion, be substituted for the fairy queen, with the possibility (as in *Huon*) of the inheritance of the fairy kingdom thrown in as an added attraction.[100]

Within romance, the fairies' conferring of prosperity is less common as a motif than their exercising power over mortals, often at the humans' expense rather than to their advantage. *Sir Orfeo* is one of the grimmer examples, where the invisibility of the fairy king and his host means that they can abduct Herodis despite all the chivalric force the mortal king mounts against them. Fairyland in this text doubles as a land of the dead, or of the living dead—the lack of precise definition for the state of the corpses 'liggeand within the wall' of its king's castle intensifies the alienness of the whole strange experience. He is not, however, infernal, despite his ancestry in Pluto. Dekker makes analogous reference in *The Whore of Babylon* to 'hurtfull Sprites' who spread desolation over the good fairies' country and fill its cities with the dead; but this is less a supernatural act than the annexing of diabolic abilities to the Catholic ravaging of the Netherlands.[101]

The arbitrariness of fairy power often takes the form of some kind of taboo or injunction (the Celtic *geis*) that the mortal must not break. There may or may not be a reason behind it, but the mortal must accept it on its own terms. *Melusine* is structured on three such prohibitions, each laid by a fairy woman on a mortal, and each serving to establish a distance between the three supernatural women whose powers control the story and the men who seek intimacy with them.[102] The story starts with Pressine's forbidding of her mortal husband Elynas, king of Scotland, from seeing her in childbed: after she has borne girl triplets, he simply forgets, and enters her chamber. Reproaching him bitterly, his wife disappears for ever into Avalon, 'that was named the yle lost, bycause that all had a man ben there many tymes, yet shuld not he conne retourne thither hymself alone'.[103] She brings up her daughters there, constantly lamenting her loss: clearly, the taboo was an inherent property in her nature, not a willed exercise of power. Melusine's weekly serpentine transformation is likewise not in her own power but the consequence of her mother's curse, imposed after she and her sisters shut up their father in a mountain in Northumberland to punish him for his act. Her injunction to her husband against seeing her is a way of holding off the worse effects of the curse. Yet there are also strong human reasons why Melusine would not wish Raymondin to see her in her deformed shape, and those seem to predominate when nothing initially happens after he has transgressed her prohibition. It is only when he reproaches her with her shape-changing some time later that she turns fully into a serpent, a shape she must keep until the day of doom. The third prohibition tells of a descendant of her third son, who has succeeded to the throne of Armenia. He decides to attempt the adventure of the Sparrowhawk Castle: if any man can watch the hawk for three days and nights without falling asleep, the beautiful lady who owns it will grant the successful knight any worldly gifts he wishes—castles, lands, wealth—excepting only her self. Those who fail lead the rest of their lives in comparative happiness, but are never allowed to leave her castle; anyone who asks for her body is condemned to misery. The young king manages to stay awake, partly by admiring the pictures in the hall that show the history of Elynas and Pressine. He fails to take warning from them, however, and on completing the test he asks the lady for her hand and body. She turns out to be Melusine's sister, and the young man's request therefore infringes not only the supernatural taboo on a request for sexual favours, but the human taboo on incest. The consequences of his breaking the terms of the prohibition duly work themselves out, with his own descent into decay and the eventual loss of Lusignan sovereignty over Armenia.[104]

Supernatural assistance in acquiring wealth and territory, according to such stories, brings fewer perils with it than sexual access, or attempts at sexual access. The encounter between Elizabeth and Leicester's Lady of the Lake takes on a deeper subtext in the light of such a background. The territorial dispute—who owns the lake—becomes a metonym for the queen's sexuality: threaten one, and the other will demonstrate its independence. Elizabeth's power to disappear may have nothing supernatural about it, but disappear she certainly did, leaving Kenilworth several days before she was due to depart.

Gloriana, like Elizabeth, is a queen regnant. Her realm is inalienable, and her body is in her own disposition.

'AN ELF-QUEEN SHALL MY LEMMAN BE'

One does not set out to find a fairy mistress: Sir Thopas's decision that nothing less will do for him shows, as usual, that he has got his memes in a twist. The statement in the Proem to the *Faerie Queene* that Arthur is seeking 'fairest Tanaquill' throughout the world is later modified by the explanation that his quest is a response to her declaration of her love for him in a dream: it is she who has initiated his search. That the amorous fairy first seeks out her lover, not the other way around, is the rule. The summons to Lanval by the fairy lady's handmaids shows how such things ought to be done: 'Sir Lanval, my lady, who is most noble and wise and lovely, has sent us for you, so come with us!'[105] By the seventeenth century, the invitation is less peremptory but more explicit:

> 'My lady thats bright as blossome or flower,
> thee greets, Sir Lamwell, as her paramoure,
> and prays you for to speake with her
> and if it be your will, faire Sir.'[106]

Her pavilion is only yards away in the forest alongside which he is resting, and the lady declares her love for him the moment he enters:

> 'Sire Lambewell,' shee said, 'my harts sweete,
> for thy love my hart I leete.'   [lose

139–40

Sexual fulfilment follows as the culmination of that first meeting. Gloriana's appearance to Arthur as he sleeps while 'raunging the forest' is made with the same directness, and without intermediaries:

> Me seemed, by my side a royall Mayd
> Her daintie limbes full softly down did lay . . .
>
> Most goodly glee and lovely blandishment
> She to me made, and bad me love her deare,
> For dearely sure her love was to me bent,
> As when just time expired should appeare.

FQ, I. ix. 13–14

Spenser holds back from declaring precisely what happens in the encounter—Arthur's assertion, 'Was never hart so ravisht with delight', is coupled with the further statement that she spent 'all that night' speaking words such as living man had never heard before. This sounds more like the loathly lady's pillow-talk in the *Wife of Bath's Tale*, or the topos of inexpressibility associated with a vision of Heaven, than the sensuality implied by 'blandishment' and 'delight'. Spenser holds back, too, from giving any metaphysical status to the visit. Arthur is asleep, but it is more than a dream: when he wakes, he finds beside him the 'pressed gras, where she had lyen' (15)—phrasing that again suggests a sexual encounter. But the point does not lie in any law-court style evaluation of evidence as to what did or did not take place between them. What has happened is that a woman with the absolute autonomy of the 'Queene of Faeries' (14), and her freedom to dispose of her favour and her love wherever she chooses, has chosen Arthur; and that the encounter sets him off on the quest that would, somewhere beyond the end of the poem as we have it, and some time outside history, lead to their continuing union. Launfal achieves such lasting consummation only after leaving this world for another; Arthur is searching Faerie Land rather than Britain. The 'just time expired' of the quotation keeps the ambiguity of temporal possibility, as in the fulfilment of a prophecy—a prophecy along the lines of an English monarch's being welcomed in to Rome and winning the Holy Cross, for instance. But history was running out on Elizabeth, and the phrase carries strongly apocalyptic resonances too. As after Redcrosse's overcoming of the dragon, when the final unbroken union of Holiness and Truth must be delayed until after his duty to his 'Faerie Queene' has been fulfilled, history has to be completed and time expire before there can be eternal stability.[107]

As with all romance conventions, the variations on the fairy mistress can be as striking as the dominant themes, and even the requirement that the fairy should choose her own lover is not universal. A fairy woman could presumably resist rape by a mortal man (she has all those supernatural powers on call), and a mortal's taking the sexual initiative often turns out to be illusory. Graelent, in the Breton *lai* that bears his name, finds a fairy maiden bathing in a pool, and takes her clothes; he is prepared to return her shift to her, but when she refuses him her sexual favours, he proceeds to make love to her anyway. At that point, however, she informs him that she had come to the fountain for his sake, and that she knew in advance 'ceste aventure', all that would happen.[108] She exercises her power over him only when, like Lanval, he later breaks her taboo on speaking of her. Thomas of Erceldoune is perhaps the most forward of mortal lovers, and risks the most. After establishing that the supernatural lady he has encountered is not the Virgin Mary, he proceeds to proposition her, but it is a dangerous move. She warns him that he will wreck all her beauty, and indeed after making love to her (seven times),

> Thomas stode upe in that stede,
> And he by-helde that lady gaye;
> Hir hare it hange all over hir hede,
> Hir eghne semede owte, that are were graye.   [eyes; before
> And alle the riche clothynge was awaye,
> That he by-fore sawe in that stede;
> Hir a schanke blake, hir other graye,   [one leg
> And all hir body lyke the lede.[109]

The transformation convinces him that she is, like Percival's beautiful temptress, a devil in drag, and therefore that he is damned, but she does not allow him to escape: she carries him off with her, as he desperately prays for deliverance. Only on reaching her homeland, beyond this world, does she recover her beauty.

It is an episode that invites a symbolic or moral reading, but it is not at all clear what it should be. 'Don't make the first advances to fairies' seems too simplistic, though that might have been enough for those in the audience who did believe in their existence—and the widespread credence given to Thomas's prophecies implies belief in the source of his prophecy as well. The mysteriousness of the elf-queen's turning ugly is itself much of the point: we do not even learn whether changing her looks lies in her own power, or, like Melusine's serpent form, in enchantment or a curse; or whether it is an inherent consequence for her of pollution by sexual activity or by congress with a mortal. Despite his initial fear, Thomas is rewarded, not damned, for what may be defined as a sin of lecherousness, or as sexual bullying (she does consent, so it is not a rape, but it is scarcely a freely willed choice on her part), or for consorting with a fairy. It is not even clear if it is sin that is at issue at all: fairies lie outside normal morality, especially where sex is concerned. The episode inverts the pattern of the *Wife of Bath's Tale*, where the hideous old woman with her fairy associations chooses to turn beautiful. That too is only a first step: she gives her husband the choice as to whether she should be ugly and faithful, or beautiful with all its associated risks. Only when he returns the choice to her to make does she assure him she will be both beautiful and faithful. Again, there is no explanation as to whether he has himself unconsciously performed some kind of magic action to enable such an outcome (as happens in the analogues, where it is a matter of breaking an enchantment imposed on a human woman), or whether—as seems to be implied—she makes the decision for herself, as a generous response to his generosity. Symbolic and moral readings are much easier to provide for the *Tale* than for *Thomas*—almost too easy, indeed. The hag's transformation can be read as a shift from a misogynist to a pro-feminist paradigm, in parallel with the knight's progression from his initial rape of a young woman to granting his wife freedom of choice: the hatred and objectification of women expressed in the rape, and his reluctant marriage to his repellent rescuer, indicate his estimate of women as despicable; his conversion to an understanding of gender-inclusive virtue, and of the right of women to autonomy equal with his own, enables him to recognize their human loveliness. A parallel reading could be given from a female point of view, as the recuperation of the raped woman's self-hatred and sense of corruption to the beloved woman's sense of self-worth. By these readings, the magic of the transformation simply gives physical form to the enactment of moral change: the magic does work (unlike in all those nonfunctioning talismans discussed earlier), but it is enabled to work by the moral and emotional state of the mortal at the centre of the story. But plenty of other more sceptical interpretations of the tale are possible, including seeing it as the Wife of Bath's own fantasies about recovering her youth and beauty, or as Chaucer's satire of female fantasies of sovereignty. *Thomas* seems to have more to do with male fantasies than with female ones; but there too the woman's ugliness is associated with the man's use of her as sexual object, and beauty with her recovery of power.

Such a variety of readings is possible for the *Wife of Bath's Tale* partly because the eldritch woman is never explicitly defined as a fairy, so her powers are never linked solely to the supernatural. Her conversion of her husband is done through moral harangue, not enchantment, even if her own metamorphosis helps matters along. A fully certificated elf-queen, by contrast, with her freedom from theological or patriarchal control, is scarcely a topic on which to build morals about normal human relations, and especially not sexual relations.[110] There are almost always dangers attached to a fairy's sexual favours—some kind of ordeal or prohibition or *geis*—but they do not stem from any male owner of her sexuality. They are, therefore, very different from the ordeals imposed by fathers or husbands to keep daughters or wives safe from predatory or adventurous men.[111] The conditions set by fairy mistresses are theirs alone, and are more often concerned with the continuation of their love than the initial winning of it. The punishment for infringement most often appears as an instant and automatic consequence of the lover's disobedience. That punishment, furthermore, generally bears no logical relationship to the terms of the initial condition. It is not evident, for instance, why her husband's seeing Pressine in childbed must result in his losing her (it seems even to be against her own will), whereas it is very obvious why inadequacy in fighting a dragon will have immediate adverse effects. The prohibitions therefore have something of the illogic, the quality of pure trial divorced from rationality, of the forbidden fruit of Genesis. The stories are not allegorical, but the taboo is backed by devastating supernatural consequences.

That the danger involved in the relationship should have no evident physical mechanism within the narrative comes close to defining a woman as supernatural: supernatural at least in origin, even if the existing version of the story redefines her metaphysical status towards the mortal. *Partonope of Blois*, with its heroine on the cusp between supernatural and mortal, is a leading example. The abduction of the hero to an enchanted country at its queen's behest, their ensuing affair, the riches she gives him, and the prohibition on his seeing her until due time has expired all cast her in the role of an elf-queen. Yet, after Partonope has broken the prohibition and her powers together, the focus of the romance shifts largely to her. Its second part is primarily concerned with her anxiety over whom she will be compelled to take as her husband. The inscrutability that is one of the distinguishing features of the fairy is lost, and we see generously inside her mind and her feelings. In its first half, the story makes the most of the mysteriousness, suspense, and danger associated with fairy; in its second, it swaps over to the conventions of the heroine embarking on love, with all the interiority and sensitivity to her inward feelings that characterize the treatment of so many romance heroines—an interiority that is the subject of the next chapter.

Despite Richard Hyrd's testimony to the popularity of *Partonope* in England around 1530, it is hard to trace any continuing reading of it into Elizabeth's reign. The distinction it makes between the heroine as fairy and the heroine as mortal is however one that continued to be understood. It is there in the difference of treatment between Gloriana, who can be described by those who have seen her in vision or in actuality, but whose mind remains completely hidden; and the mortal Britomart, who is given the closest and subtlest psychological exploration in the whole *Faerie Queene.* It is there too in the contrast between Helena and Hermia, with their hopes and fears and confusions, and the enchanted Titania's calm imperiousness as she adopts Bottom as her Most Favoured Being. Just what her relationship with him involves—or indeed her relationship with Oberon or with Theseus—is never fully revealed. The fairy woman retains to herself a reserve of unknowability. So far as Elizabeth I herself was concerned, such a role gave her distinct political advantages, even while—or because—it cast those around her as unable to access her mind or her motives.

There is one further reference to Elizabeth that belongs in this context, though it is one designed to separate her off from every other fairy mistress, Gloriana included. This is Oberon's reference in *A Midsummer Night's Dream* to the 'fair vestal thronèd by the west' whom Cupid's arrow passes by. There could, as critics have noted, be many other fair vestals; but there is only one who holds a throne in the west, and any Elizabethan audience would have taken such a phrase as a reference to the queen.[112] The lines, moreover, serve no dramatic function; their only conceivable purpose is as political panegyric. They define the 'imperial votaress' by her difference from both other mortals and other fairies. Oberon's description of her follows soon after the account of the confusion of the seasons consequent upon his marital quarrel between the fairy monarchs, and, more immediately, from Titania's account of the brimming fertility and the death in childbirth of the mother of the little Indian boy, a 'votaress' of her own order (2. 1. 123–35). This is the world of time and change, which the panegyrics of the 1590s increasingly represented Elizabeth as transcending: far from seasonal alteration, she brought an eternal spring, always the same, *semper eadem.*[113] There seems to be an apotropaic element in such encomia, an attempt to keep at bay the possibility of the queen's death and the risks of civil breakdown attendant on an uncertain succession. The scene in *A Midsummer Night's Dream* sets the unchanging world of the untouched virgin alongside the world of mortality, where women's reproductive powers and death accompany each other. The description of the 'fair vestal' sets Elizabeth outside the play and its concerns with desire and jealousy, whether fairy or human.[114] The flower touched by Cupid's arrow produces a love-juice that affects mortals and fairies equally: it is under its influence that we see Titania acting not as disaffected fairy wife but actively as fairy mistress. It does not touch the cold virgin. Shakespeare's Titania falls victim to magic against her will; Dekker's Titania, a decade or so later, resists her suitors' charms under her own powers. The 'imperial votaress' exists outside the discourses of desire altogether.

CHAPTER FIVE

Desirable desire: 'I am wholly given over unto thee'

The medieval romances 'created a series of female characters who were both passionate and pure, who gave their hearts spontaneously into the keeping of the men they loved and remained true to the bargain in the face of tremendous odds. The women's steadfastness is in direct relation to their aggressiveness . . .' That is not the way we are accustomed to thinking about medieval women; and indeed Germaine Greer wrote the passage, not about early romance but about Shakespeare.[1] The phenomenon she ascribes to his originality was in actuality already endemic as a meme. At issue is not just the matter of claiming originality for Shakespeare where he is drawing directly on the embedded culture of his medieval antecedents, but the risk of missing the powerful resonances that the meme of the 'passionate and pure' woman brings with her—the woman who focuses all her newly awakened sexual desire on the man she chooses to be her husband. Such a heroine is generically central for the romance: that is, while there may be plenty of female characters who do not conform to such a model—who are the variations on the central theme of the actively desiring and faithful woman—the Shakespearean variety of heroine defines a work as romance almost as decisively as does a happy ending, and does so from the very inception of romance in the mid-twelfth century. The presence of such a woman at the centre indeed promises the happy ending, and it is only in a handful of works that deliberately set out to confound such an expectation, to disrupt generic norms, that the two do not go together. Furthermore, as the romances make clear, the happiness is not just a personal matter. The strong and loving heroine is typically an heiress, even the founder of a family or a dynasty: a fact that was already familiar to Elizabethans reading about Britomart, or watching Rosalind or Miranda.

Love, even more than questing or chivalry, is the concept most closely associated now with romance. The Mills and Boon phenomenon, with its billions of sales, indeed reduces romance to a matter of female love, which until very recently excluded overt sex. Its writers and readers, overwhelmingly, are women; by prescription, the stories have a woman as the central character, and follow her actions and (in particular) her feelings. Such a focus on women's emotional inward life is generally regarded as a field of action developed in the novel, with writers of the stature of Jane Austen and George Eliot as its giants. That the Mills and Boon books are known as romances none the less contains an important element of historical truth. They deserve the title, not just because of their compulsory happy endings, nor even because their aim of being accessible to women readers is in keeping with the romances' original emphasis on the vernacular; but because, historically, the concern with women's actions and inward lives first emerges in their direct line of ancestry in the medieval romances. That concern is closely linked with their entry into love, a love that never denies its sexual component. 'In the space of a few centuries,' wrote Foucault, 'a certain inclination has led us to direct the question of what we are, to sex . . . Whenever it is a question of knowing who we are, it is this logic that henceforth serves as our master key.'[2] As with so many statements about the modern world, the Middle Ages is an important forerunner, in this case specifically in romance; and most particularly, since the adventures available to women focus so largely on their transition from maidenhood to marriage, in the heroines of romance. For a young woman of the pre-modern or early modern world, this is what any *bildungsroman* that makes any claim to reflect the real world must focus on. Her growth into sexuality, and the leaving of her father's house for her husband's, were the female equivalent of the hero's leaving home to make his own mark in the world. The men have a much greater range of possibilities for action, which the stories take up in abundance. Love-romances therefore typically cover a far greater range of time, characters, and experience than do their modern analogues; they incorporate many conventions that would now belong to other genres, not least the adventure novel or science fiction; and they have all the resources to hand that only poetry can provide, to offer a mimetic evocation rather than a mere statement of what it feels like to be in love. Their conventions offer a huge capacity for encompassing many of the characteristics of literature most valued in the modern world, not least in their representation of women.

It is in the early romances that a sense of women as 'subjects' in the full modern sense of the term, as unique individuals with a self-conscious awareness of their own place in the scheme of things, first begins to develop. This self-awareness is linked to the awakening of their sexuality;

and women's sexuality is centrally regarded as positive, to the point where it is one of the key factors that enables the restoration of social and providential order. Such an emphasis functions as a strong generic marker—this is what romance is *about*. Female sexuality, moreover, is at its most powerful in working towards such an end when it is directed not by the man who has the social and familial responsibility for its control (normally the father), but by the woman herself. Thaisa, the feisty and desiring young woman who selects Pericles as her husband, is an example that runs across the whole historical range of the Middle Ages and Renaissance.[3] Spontaneous and active female desire, rightly directed, becomes a driving force in the larger providential scheme, the secular scripture, that most strikingly differentiates the romance from contiguous genres such as epic or history. Only one genre shows a comparable emphasis, and that is the life of the female saint, where the active desire is redirected towards Christ.

That last paragraph runs counter to almost every critical and theoretical presupposition of the last century or more. Germaine Greer's remark quoted at the head of this chapter follows from a claim that Shakespeare 'rejected the stereotype of the passive, sexless, unresponsive female and its inevitable concomitant, the misogynist conviction that all women were whores at heart', and such an assumption about the stereotypical image of woman is made by almost every critic of the Middle Ages and early modern period. As is inevitable with such a vast topic as women's sexuality, however—affecting half the human race directly, and the other half by association—things are not simple. This chapter is accordingly concerned not only with the meme of the desiring woman but with the political, social, and theological contexts that encouraged her existence. The romance texts provide overwhelming evidence for a belief in the desirability of active female desire and for the exploration of women's subjectivity. These attitudes to women are most characteristic of insular writings, in both Anglo-Norman and English. The mistaken assumptions about the stereotypical woman tend to be the result of approaching insular writings through French and Latin, which prioritize different models: the more courtly, and the overtly misogynist. English romance-writers were aware of those rival discourses, and their responses to them form the subject of the next chapter; but their own ideas of women's love and sexuality were very different.

The ideological centre of romance—the point where family resemblance is at its strongest—insists finally not on such surrounding complications but on an idealized simplicity, in which the emphasis given to female desire raises it to rank equally with male, in a powerful image of good love as reciprocal and mutual. The idea is perhaps best expressed in a verse of William Blake's, written in a very different historical context, but, like the romances, recording a positive rejoicing in mutual sexuality, independent of ideological constructions of women as dangerous and in need of control:

> What is it men in women do require?
> —The lineaments of Gratified Desire.
> What is it women do in men require?
> —The lineaments of Gratified Desire.[4]

Blake may have been unique even in his own time, but it goes against all human experience to imagine that that particular belief was unique to him, or that it cannot be transhistorical. Love between a woman and a man at its fullest includes 'gratified desire', the body as well as the heart; or, given the unprecedented modern emphasis on sex, perhaps one should say the heart as well as the body. The most widely used medieval term for such love was simply that—love; though to insist on the distinction of love from lust, physical attraction that does not involve the heart, Middle French sometimes used phrases such as *fin amor*, 'refined love', adopted by Chaucer to indicate the highest human love as 'fyn lovynge'.[5] The fineness of *fin amor* precisely indicates the surplus involved in such love: the emotions as well as the body, and, with the emotions, the potential for the infinite linguistic and rhetorical exploration of that surplus that is the special domain of love-poetry. There is, however, a crucial difference between love-lyric, which overwhelmingly presents the man's point of view—his pining for the lady he desires, his unfulfilment providing the space for the poetry; and love-narrative, which, in England in particular, frequently portrays a woman's desire that takes fulfilment as its only end. The aim of love, in these romances, is mutual; its genesis lies in the woman.

THE POLITICS OF WOMEN'S DESIRE

What differentiates the romances most strongly from Blake's formulation is that they build into the model of desire a strongly political element, though one very different from the modern feminist connection of the personal with the political. In the pre-modern world, or more specifically the pre-contraception world, sexual activity and childbirth were inseparable; and procreation was the means by which dynasties and great families maintained their existence. Female sexuality was therefore a matter of direct high economic and political concern: hence the anxiety over male control in a system of patrilineal inheritance, and the high premium on female chastity in the form of virginity before marriage and faithfulness within it. The woman's desire as well as her virtue was, however, crucially important. The most widespread belief about conception was that both partners produced seed at orgasm, and so mutual pleasure, or ideally simultaneous orgasm (the most gratifying gratification of desire), was most likely to result in offspring. Romances frequently mention that the lovers conceive a child on their wedding night. This happens in texts as various in origin as the Apollonius story, in almost all versions including *Pericles*, and *Guy of Warwick*, where it marks Felice's transformation from the disdainful object of desire to the desiring wife. The couples' mutual fulfilment of their sexual longing is itself a guarantee of dynastic continuity.[6] The romances therefore do not offer any revolutionary attack on conventional sexual morals or a patriarchal system of dynastic inheritance, but they do repeatedly show women exerting their freedom within the system, insisting on the precedence of their own desires over any schemes of their fathers', and constructing their new families in accordance with their own fixed and faithful love of both heart and body. The endorsement offered by the genre to the heroine's assertion of personal choice gives it a major claim to being the most compelling element of generic identity in love-romances, the point where 'family resemblance' is at its strongest, and to which other patterns of love and marriage are secondary.

The active and desiring heroine none the less receives varying degrees of recognition both over time and in different social contexts and language areas. Her sudden emergence as the central figure in the twelfth century reflects two elements of social change: first, the insistence by Pope Alexander III that what made a valid marriage was neither parental decision nor a public ceremony, but the consent of the spouses; and second, a shift in patterns of inheritance, especially in England and France, by which the property of a man who died with no sons necessarily passed to his daughter. Such an heiress, moreover, could inherit not only property but the political power that went with it—a power that was then exercised by her husband.[7] The combination of these factors made for some explosive writing, in which women were invested with rights of both erotic and political patronage such as they had never had before. The lady in many of the early romances, including some of the most famous and influential, is accordingly an heiress, with very clear ideas as to whom she is prepared to marry. Her heritable land is embodied in her: she becomes almost a metonymy for the immovable territory, 'immeuble', that she can bring to her husband, but a metonymy with a will, and a body, of its own.[8] In France, whether because the shock of the new faded away, or because new dowry customs reduced the importance of the heiress, the motif of the actively desiring woman lost much of its dominance in the thirteenth century,[9] though it never entirely disappeared. The English tradition was markedly more hospitable. Perhaps fostered by the disruption of lineage and the desire of the Norman newcomers to establish origins for themselves in the wake of the Conquest, Anglo-Norman romance of the twelfth century gave the idea an even higher profile, and carried it through into the next century too;[10] and English-language romance makes the actively desiring heiress its central model throughout the Middle Ages and into the Renaissance. Marriage to an heiress remained one of the most significant means in England by which a man could transform his social and financial prospects, in the fifteenth century as much as in the twelfth.[11] English social customs, deriving from Germanic and Norse models, also seem to have been better adapted for allowing such a convention to continue, in that they appear to have allowed women somewhat more freedom of movement than in France or Italy—even if not in practice the degree of freedom the romance heroines seize for themselves. Erasmus's delighted surprise that the expected greeting between a man and a woman was a kiss on the lips is a measure of the different expectations on the two sides of the English Channel by the end of the Middle Ages.[12]

An heiress's choosing of her own husband, without or against parental authority, was scarcely an approved model in actuality, though it did on occasion happen.[13] Romances generally attempt to square her desire with larger social and parental approval by having her engineer the consent of her father, her other senior male relatives, or her council; sometimes their opposition is overcome by the discovery that the unknown young man is an heir in his own right, but when he is not, or not known to be, the heroine has to put in rather more work. Ydoine, the capable heroine of the widely-known Anglo-Norman *Amadas et Ydoine*, is initially reluctant to return the love of Amadas, who is merely the son of her father's seneschal, but, once she has committed herself to him, she has to show constant resourcefulness in converting her father's plans to fit with her own. The initial marriage he arranges for her, thanks to some strenuous efforts on her part, remains unconsummated; once she has managed to free herself from that, she takes a belt-and-braces approach to the issue by persuading her father to allow her her own choice of husband, but then graciously gives up her newly-won right once she has made sure that he and his advisers will select Amadas for her anyway.[14] It is rare for the younger generation never to receive some kind of blessing from the older, or for a father to remain implacable—or if he does, as is the case with Desonelle's father in *Torrent of Portyngale*, he is asking for trouble: the punishment he had inflicted on her, of being cast adrift in an open boat, is in turn inflicted on him, and the Providence that had preserved the faithful daughter does not save the guilty father.[15]

The romances recognize a further important social and psychological fact in presenting their heroines as active participants in forging their own destinies. Women of any historical period can be just as resourceful at putting their wishes into action as their menfolk—if not more so, since, unlike the men, they rarely have in their own hands either political or physical power as a fallback. Women in both romances and real life may appear to be restricted to their roles as maiden, wife, mother, widow, and very occasionally nun; but with men from the upper levels of society often away in attendance on the king in peace or war, and with merchants often away on business, women's roles easily extended to estates manager, business manager, even to battle leader—the latter being exemplified not just by Edward III's queen Philippa leading an English army against Scottish incursions while her husband was fighting in France, but by the gentry wife Margaret Paston attempting to defend a family property at Gresham against armed assault by a rival claimant.[16] Meek and passive wives had distinct drawbacks. The role played by the long-lost wife of Sir Isumbras alongside her husband and sons in defeating an army of 30,000 Saracens has more to do with fantasy miracle, but it must still reflect some capacity for identification or admiration in the readers; and perhaps it brought with it too some memory of events such as the defence of Tortosa against the Moors by women armed with hatchets, an event commemorated by the count of Barcelona by the founding of a female equestrian religious order, the Order of the Hatchet.[17] Of more immediate practical use might be a partner along the lines of Ydoine: she keeps the whole story on course towards its happy ending while her lover can do no more than languish in agony for years at a time, or even, after he hears about her marriage to someone else, require incarceration with his parents after losing his mind. It is Ydoine who keeps at bay the husband given her by her father, restores Amadas' sanity, finds a way when she herself is about to die to prevent his committing suicide, and finally (after her magic recovery) sets up her marriage to the man she loves. Amadas is given an active role in only one late episode, his enthralling encounter with the fairy knight who tests his belief in her faithfulness to him despite all the evidence to the contrary. Tristan and Isolde may be more famous, but Amadas and Ydoine were celebrated in England as exemplary lovers alongside or even ahead of them.[18]

Romances in part feed their audiences' appetite for fantasy; but that statement invites the question, whose fantasy? Marriage can still be a means of social and economic advancement, as it is in the traditional Mills and Boon novels. In a linear system of inheritance, it is crucial. For the readers of Mills and Boon, the fantasies are obviously and intentionally women's, with the promise of marriage to a rich and handsome man, physically and financially desirable. The configuration of early romance is in some respects the exact opposite, in reversing the gender roles both for characters and for readers. In the typical Mills and Boon plot, the heroine's family is dead or otherwise removed from sight, and the hero is successful, rich, and domineering.[19] The typical medieval romance of love portrays a hero whose family is dead or invisible, and who becomes the object of desire of an heiress who can bestow on him both wealth and rank. The man's own exceptional attractiveness may be delineated through the lady's falling for him despite her being, like the tough modern hero, capricious, or domineering, or reluctant to engage in a relationship: hence names for her bespeaking pride, such as the Fere, La Fière, in *Ipomadon*, or the Orgueilleuse d'Amour, 'the proude lady in love', in *Blanchardyn and Eglantine.*[20] The gender reversals highlight how far the early narratives serve the wishful thinking of male readers, with their recurrent promise of marriage to a beautiful woman who is desirable both physically and in terms of wealth and status (at the extreme of fantasy, a fairy queen). The new customs of primogeniture not only provided a supply of wealthy heiresses in families without male heirs, but a large number of younger sons with no landed inheritance. For such young men, as for those belonging to any class except the very highest, marriage provided the best way to rise in life. The romance model of the strenuous processes involved in winning the lady gave a reassuring colouring to the need for such men to have the competence to manage well the power they acquired through their wives.

The point of view from which the stories are told, however, does not show so simple a pattern of gender reversal. The Mills and Boon stories always identify with the woman, in a stereotyped development from the novels' explorations of female psychology; early romances most often focalize predominantly through the man, but they also spend consider-able time exploring the minds of their women. The potential of these romances to serve male fantasies is therefore constrained by their readi-ness to project the narrative through their heroines. Readers will inevitably show an empathetic attachment to a character whose point of view is represented with any degree of credibility; and finally, 'the ontol-ogy of the text . . . is embodied in the reader',[21] not the author. The romances' readiness to enter the minds of their heroines makes it all but inevitable that women readers or listeners should empathize with them, even project some degree of their own wishful thinking onto the stories, and not only through the regular provision of strong and handsome lovers. As Chaucer knew, the answer to the question 'What do women want?' is 'sovereignty'—not necessarily or primarily in the sense of rule or dominance (though the heiress heroines have some degree of that too), but, as the Wife of Bath's exemplary tale proceeds to demonstrate, the freedom to make their own choices affecting their own lives.[22] The romances are fully conscious of the male power to which their young women owe a duty of obedience, and of the likelihood of their desire to resist it. Such resistant readings are often actively encouraged by the authors: the degree of narrative sympathy accorded to these indepen-dent-minded heroines can hardly be accidental, whether in Anglo-French or medieval or Renaissance English. Silence, the young woman brought up as a boy in the *Roman de Silence* of Heldris of 'Cornuälle' (which may well indicate Cornwall, where Silence finds refuge), makes a deliberate choice to follow nurture rather than nature and continue to live as a man for just such reasons of personal independence, with Reason backing up her decision: she sees no reason to place herself low when she is on top, 'quant sui deseure', especially since continuing to play the role of a man will also enable her to inherit, within a legal system that has for-bidden inheritance through women.[23] The revelation of her true sex incurs respect and love, not horror.

The active heroine who chooses her own husband regardless of her father's intentions is represented in romance as admirable. Romances are usually thought of as serving the ideology of the élite, but in this respect they begin to look almost oppositional—sufficiently indeed to cause occasional anxiety in their authors, who sometimes try to find ways around presenting such independent-minded heroines as role models. One way to avoid the problem was to substitute a figure so exotic as to place her beyond imitation: a passionate fairy, for instance, or a Saracen princess. Saracen women, in blithe authorial ignorance or carelessness of

Islamic *mores*, are allowed to take an especially aggressive approach towards identifying and winning their man. The Sultan's daughter, Floripas, for instance, in the *Sowdone of Babylone*, engineers the release of her father's Christian prisoners by pushing her uncooperative governess out of the window into the sea, and then beating out the gaoler's brains with his bunch of keys (the object of her passion, Guy of Burgundy, is decidedly less enthusiastic, and has to be persuaded by his fellow paladins to accept her love). The social transgression inherent in a young woman's active emotional and sexual choice is much more evident, and potentially troublesome, if she is a Christian, and even more so if she is a Christian heiress, capable of bestowing wealth and rank on her chosen knight. Again, few men would be reluctant to identify with such a hero; but there would seem to be abundant social risks in presenting such role models for women. Famously, in Gayle Rubin's description, women in patriarchal societies function as commodities traded between men.[24] That may be an over-simplification in all kinds of ways, but the Middle Ages were aware of the issue—'we usen here no wommen for to selle', says Chaucer's Hector when the Trojans are asked to trade Criseyde for the captured Antenor, just before they do indeed agree to 'sell' her.[25] The heiress is not only a commodity but a major capital asset, and, through her capacity to bear children, a guarantee of a return on investment for the future. One would not normally expect one's capital assets to have a mind of their own, to choose their possessor, or to determine their own investment in their future; and even less that such a capital asset should be represented as the most desirable kind of all. In the romances, however, that is exactly what happens, on numerous occasions. The heiress who insists on her freedom to love where she will, and who sets out to win the man she has chosen, is not only endorsed but celebrated.

The pattern is set as early as the *Roman d'Eneas*, a text both widely known and radically influential: as one of the very earliest works to be definable as a romance (a fact emphasized by its vernacularization of the Latin Virgil), its practices rapidly became the conventions that made the new genre recognizable. Part of that alteration of genre lies in its change of heroine: not the transgressive Dido, who kills herself after her lover abandons her, but Lavine. Marriage to her gives Eneas territorial dominion within Italy, in the first step of the westward *translatio imperii*, and their descendants found the dynasties of western Europe. The shift of female protagonist helped to establish romance's generic wariness about illicit love (Eneas' as much as Dido's: it is he, as Chaucer emphasized, who is the unfaithful one),[26] but it also helped to establish a pattern by which heiresses converted their latent political power into a direct exercise of sexual patronage. In contrast to her prototype in Virgil, Lavine takes the lead in initiating the love between herself and the man she has chosen (and, although her father favours the match, her own choice is the one that gets the narrative attention). Lavine is not, of course, Christian; but there is no sense, as there is with the Saracen princesses, that she belongs to a society that operates by customs alien to the readers' own. The text counterbalances the intensity of Dido's passion by a still more aggressive passion in the ultimately legitimate Lavine, as if the originary legend for a dynasty required a forceful input from its founding mother as well as its founding father.

The phenomenon of the dominant founding mother is most evident in the legend of Melusine, who has the excuse of being half fairy, but many ancestral romances make their heroines particularly strong characters. Spenser is following widespread romance norms when he makes Britomart look into Merlin's mirror, fall in love with the man she sees there before he even knows of her existence, and set out to find him. She is just one of many maidens who are neither pagans nor fairies and yet make the running in choosing their mate, and marriage is not always the only thing on their minds. Rimenhild, King Aylmar's heiress daughter in *King Horn*, loves the dispossessed Horn passionately despite never having exchanged a word with him; she sends her father's steward to summon him to her 'bower', the female space within the castle or household, but he, for the revealing reason that Horn is altogether too attractive for him to trust her, sends a different man.[27] In the event, when she gets hold of Horn, she expresses her desire for him in terms of an offer of marriage—an offer which he initially rejects, on the grounds that the disparity in rank between them is too great. Both lovers then undergo parallel processes of testing and trial: she by resisting rival suitors; he by demonstrating his merit through a succession of combats that finally win him back his own kingdom. The 'lusty lady Lillian' in *Roswall and Lillian,* a fifteenth-century text now known only through seventeenth- and eighteenth-century prints, chooses the exiled Roswall (apparently poor and of low birth, and going under the name of Dissawar) to be her chamberlain the moment he arrives at her father's court, and then makes her feelings for him very clear—as lover first, and as husband second:

> 'Dissawar, my little flower,
> I wish thou were my paramour.
> God, sen I had thee to be king,
> That I might wed you with a ring.'[28]

Roswall's response is considerably more enthusiastic than Horn's:

> 'I vow, lady, [till] I die,
> To love you again most heartilie.'
> Within his heart he was right glad
> And he did think mair than he said.
>
> 383–6

It is especially likely that the women will do the wooing if they are higher ranking than the men (or appear to be so: both Horn and Roswall are in fact heirs in their own right). This might appear like a forerunner of later royal protocol—Queen Victoria proposed to Prince Albert, on the grounds that no one but a monarch could initiate such a match—but being a reigning queen means that one's father is already dead; and neither Rimenhild nor Lillian is in that position. Their fathers are living kings, with a crucial interest in the descent of their blood line. Lovers accordingly have to take extreme action if the father opposes the match. When the Melior of *William of Palerne,* daughter of the emperor of Rome, falls for the foundling William but finds herself promised in marriage to a Greek prince by her father, the lovers elope in white bearskins, a choice of disguise that fails to camouflage them every bit as much as one would expect: the bears in this case are not the pursuers but the pursued. Here, however, as in a high proportion of such romances, her father is finally won round to approving the match, not least when the foundling turns out to be a long-lost prince. Patrilineal interests finally mesh with male fantasies of marrying a beautiful and desiring heiress, and with female fantasies of unconstrained sexual choice. The order of priorities is none the less transgressive. The fullest happy endings for romances, both medieval and Renaissance, privilege young love over patriarchal direction, and focus on the woman's desire as much as, or more than, the man's.

EROTIC THOUGHT: THE MIDDLE AGES

The heroine's falling in love follows a regular pattern. She sets eyes on the man she is to love and is smitten with desire for him, typically by the arrow of the God of Love piercing through her eye to her heart. She is overwhelmed by the strangeness and paradoxical nature of the feelings that ensue, and engages in a long monologue with herself, usually as she lies in her bed, while she tries to come to terms with what has happened to her. She then devises means to let the man know of her desire. It is a clustering of memes that is thoroughly familiar, but which is now universally thought of as being the courtly or Petrarchan model that gives agency to the man, not to the woman. Petrarchism is the form in which the language of emotion of the later Middle Ages and the Renaissance is now most familiar, and that notoriously presents a male gaze at a woman, or at an idea of a woman. Its metaphors—of burning and freezing, soaring in flight and immobility, being sea-tossed or shipwrecked—suggest an inward self-analysis such as opens up the modern understanding of subjectivity: the feelings are too invisible to anyone else to be spoken of other than in the first person. So the God of Love takes his revenge on the disdainful Troilus by having the sight of Criseyde strike him to the heart's root, in a physiological expansion of the metaphor of Cupid's arrow.[29] As soon as Troilus finds himself alone, Chaucer gives him a soliloquy analysing the strange and unfamiliar emotions of being in love, in the form of the first translation of a Petrarch sonnet into English. He is 'al stereleees withinne a boot . . . amydde the see, bitwixen wyndes two'; he is dying 'for hete of cold, for cold of hete'.[30] Petrarch, and Troilus after him, is however using a language that had to a large extent been developed for young women first awakening to love. There is none the less a key generic difference between such language when it is ascribed to women, within romance narratives, or to men, in sonnets or comparable self-contained lyric forms. The lyric encourages stasis, an analysis of emotion that relies on the woman's unresponsiveness.[31] That 'stereless' vessel, with its associations of female passivity derived from the typical occupants of rudderless boats, is not going to get the lover anywhere, and it is in Petrarch's interests as poet that it should not. Narrative by contrast requires action, and the women of the early romances take their soliloquies as a preliminary to getting their man, to converting their expressions of emotion into practical action.

In these early romances, the woman shows none of the passivity so often cited as a misogynist element in male-focused discourses of love; she is the agent, exercising her own freedom to love where she will and to further that love by whatever means she can—except that that freedom is represented as compulsion or necessity, symbolized by the overwhelming power of the God of Love. That sense of *loss* of agency is inseparable from romance love, for both male and female protagonists; though with almost equal frequency, they declare a willed commitment to loving, even if they put up some resistance first. Love at first sight, irresistible, absolute, and lifelong, is the typical way of falling in love throughout all romantic literature: not because it is conventional, but because the convention itself reflects real experience—it is still a great deal more common in actuality than a cynical modern age likes to believe—and because being so totally overwhelmed carries with it that same heroic quality of excess as killing dragons does for the heroes. The metaphor of the God of Love, however, casts the protagonist in a role more like the dragon's: both are conquered victims, even if the lover remains alive after his encounter with the undefeatable god. The invincibility of love puts the lovers beyond the possibility of resistance, just as the magic of the potion does in *Tristan*. Falling in love also carries with it a whole set of inexpressible feelings, which romance and lyric set about devising a language to express. Although such language is generally assumed to be male-focused, representing male desire for the woman, in many romances the most ardent language of desire is put into the mouth or the mind of the lady, in speeches of private self-analysis. From the twelfth century, romances show a concern with the interiority of their heroines, in a way that takes them beyond representations of women as 'other', or as mere male reflection, to treat them seriously as subjects in their own right. The very fact of their desire for someone outside the bower shakes these young heroines out of their unthinking acceptance of their place within the family or household to a new sense of individuality and autonomy.

The process appears fully developed as early as the *Roman d'Eneas*, foundational for the genre of romance as for the legendary history of western Europe. It is Lavine, not Eneas, who first falls in love, and who compels his response. As she gazes out of her tower window at the Trojans beneath the town walls:

> Amors l'a de son dart ferue;
> ainz qu'el se fust d'iluec meüe,
> i a changié cent foiz colors:
> or est cheoite es laz d'amors,
> voille ou non, amer l'estuet.[32]

[Love struck her with his arrow; before she moved away from there, she changed colour a hundred times. Now she has fallen into love's snare, whether she wishes or not, she has to love.]

She proceeds to make the allegory of the dart of love literal, by having an arrow shot to Eneas' feet with a message declaring her love wrapped around the shaft; only then does Eneas, gazing at the tower to see where it has come from, set eyes on her and find himself similarly smitten. When she had asked her mother shortly beforehand what love is and how she should recognize it, her mother had insisted that only experience can inform her: this is not public knowledge that can be shared, but a recognition that comes from inward feeling (7902–14). Her response to seeing Eneas, like Troilus' to seeing Criseyde, is a soliloquy, in which she uses all the language that Petrarch and Chaucer were to appropriate later: she is at once wounded and healthy; she feels both chilled and feverish; she cannot tell if love is good or evil, bitter or sweet, though she is sure that Love personified or deified is a tyrant; and she feels the truth of her mother's statement that only experience could reveal to her what love is like. Her monologue runs for almost 400 lines (8083–444): a length sufficient in itself to compel reader empathy with her voice and her emotions. The influence of the *Eneas* shows itself in almost all later romance, even after the text itself had disappeared from view.

Lavine's soliloquy constitutes the most extended analysis of love produced in Europe since Ovid. Those works of his that contain monologues spoken by passionate women, both the *Metamorphoses* and the *Heroides*, might be proposed as authorizing forerunners for Lavine; but the model offered in the *Eneas* is radically different. Women's passion in the *Metamorphoses* tends to be transgressive: Myrrha's sexual hunger for her father, for instance. The women of the *Heroides* describe, not their love, but its betrayal, by lovers who have abandoned them. Neither work presents anything comparable to Lavine's passion as the grounding for a dynasty, and therefore of its celebration. Furthermore, the longest stretches of poetry that Ovid puts into women's mouths, the complaints of the *Heroides*, necessarily tell stories, even if in the form of their first-person memories; there is therefore less space for the extensive exploration of their inner feelings than in the romances, where the narrative context provided by the rest of the work allows the love-soliloquies to have more of the quality of lyric. Clerical and humanist reading of Ovid's work fed into writings on love, especially men's love, for the next 500 years after the *Eneas*; but this first romance starts a new tradition that is already affirming its independence from Ovidian roots.

Where Lavine led, other heroines were quick to follow. The early versions of the *Tristan* story were probably composed very shortly after the *Eneas*; and in all the extant versions that cover the protagonists' falling in love, Isolde is given the first and longest soliloquy, in which she attempts to analyse her feelings after drinking the potion. The earliest to survive complete (*c.*1170–90), Eilhart von Oberge's *Tristrant*, goes long and generously inside her mind, in a soliloquy of some 200 lines.[33] The Carlisle fragment of Thomas's text preserves a similar long soliloquy, in which she puns generously on *l'amer*, loving, *la mer*, the sea, and *l'amère*, bitterness: she is deliberately covering her love with an excuse of seasickness and playing on the paradoxical sweetness and bitterness of loving, in a way that has a long history down through the Petrarchan imagery of love as the sea.[34] The passage caught the imagination of contemporaries sufficiently for Gottfried von Strassburg to retain it in his own *Tristan* despite the degree of awkwardness incurred through the change of language. Rather than give his Isolt the sole attention, however, he offers a linguistic and rhythmic imitation of mutuality in a long passage that intertwines the words 'maget', 'man', 'minne': the maiden, the man, and love. He opens with the responses to the potion of the lovers, 'diu maget unde der man, Isot unde Tristan', then focuses on Tristan's finding in his heart nothing but 'Isolt, and Love':

> son was ie niht dar inne
> wan Isot unde Minne,

then on her own reciprocal inability to think of anything but 'Love, and Tristan':

> son was ie diz noch daz dar an
> wan Minne unde Tristan.[35]

The early versions of *Tristan* served as foundational texts, alongside the *Eneas*, for the expressions of female desire in later works. The romances of Chrétien de Troyes are at first sight more focalized through their heroes, but in his anti-*Tristan* story of *Cligés* he follows a similar pattern. The heroine of the first generation, Soredamors, falls in love and reacts in self-interrogating soliloquy before the hero's own feelings are described (450–532). The lovers of the next generation, Fénice and Cligés, fall in love simultaneously and mutually, but it is still her feelings that are given the fullest analysis—here, because her father has arranged a marriage for her with another man, and she is going to have to acknowledge her predicament, her pleasing sickness and distressful desire, to her wise nurse in order for her to find a way out (2941–3124), just as the distressed Britomart does four centuries later. Britomart and Gloriana also have an interesting joint precursor in the Iblis of the originally Anglo-Norman *Lanzelet*, who dreams of the hero and decides that he is the man she will marry the night before she first lays eyes on him.[36]

English-language romance, with its greater emphasis on outward action, was selective in how readily it adopted such displays of fine feeling. It was especially reluctant where the love could not be celebrated or approved.

Thomas's Anglo-Norman *Tristan* loses all its analyses of love, whether nar-ratorial or soliloquy, in its summary Middle English version, *Sir Tristrem*. But the motif remains frequent enough to show that it was well recognized, both available to poets and accessible to readers, and most particularly when the woman is the first to fall in love and the end and aim of that love is marriage. There is no Middle English version of the *Eneas* itself, but it was a text known in the Angevin court of Henry II, and its treatment of love was rapidly transmitted into the English romance tradition through the media-tion of French and Anglo-Norman authors who knew it and whose influence can be directly traced in England. The centrality of its representa-tion of desiring women was passed directly forwards into early printed romances, along with their Petrarch-like language of desire. *William of Palerne* is a particularly generous instance of such transmission. Tudor readers knew it in a prose version made from a mid-fourteenth century alliterative poem that was itself based on a French original written shortly after 1200;[37] its wide dissemination in printed form is evidenced by Hyrd's sixteenth-century castigation of its popularity, though excessive reading has destroyed all the material evidence of its printing except for a single fragment.[38] That, however, is enough to show how closely it followed its original, and there is no doubt that Tudor readers, like their medieval pre-decessors, were treated to the long and touching soliloquy given to the emperor's daughter Melior when she falls for the foundling brought home by her father. Her love, like Lavine's, starts from *looking*, and she alternately blames and absolves of blame her eyes and her heart: the raw materials of love poetry down to Shakespeare's sonnet 'Mine eyes and heart are at a mortal war' and beyond. She concludes, as the Iblis of *Lanzelet* and others had done before her, with a willed commitment to love:

> Theigh I winne with mi werk the worse evermore,
> so gret liking and love I have that lud to bihold,
> that I have lever that love than lac al mi harmes.
> Nou certes, sethe it is so, to seie the trewthe,
> thann have y had gret wrong myn hert so to blame
> for eni werk that he wrought, sethe I wol it hold;
> ne wold I it were non other, al the world to have.[39]

[Even if my actions were to cause me grief for ever after, I have such great pleas-ure and love in looking at that man that I had rather have that love than be with-out all my troubles. Now truly, since it is indeed so, then I have been very wrong to blame my heart for anything it has done, since I want to keep it that way; I would not want it to be otherwise, not for all the world.]

Although the soliloquy does not form part of the surviving printed frag-
ment, the title that Hyrd gives the work, 'Wyllyam and Milior', is a recog-
nition of the leading role she plays alongside the hero—and indeed
indicates that she was regarded as more important than the bewitching
and bewitched character whose name is often joined with William's in
the alternative modern title, 'William and the Werewolf'.

Hue of Rhuddlan, who knew the *Eneas* well, wrote such soliloquies gen-
erously into his Anglo-Norman *Ipomedon*, and they are reflected in all
three Middle English versions, including the 'Hippomadon' castigated by
Hyrd alongside *William of Palerne*. Hyrd presumably knew the printed
couplet version, which is considerably abbreviated from the original;
Hue's soliloquies appear at their greatest length in English in the fuller
fourteenth-century tail-rhyme redaction. These love-monologues are
particularly interesting since no fewer than three women successively fall
in love with the unchivalric-seeming Ipomadon: the Fere (Hue's La
Fière), the proud, stand-offish lady whom he will eventually marry; her
high-ranking handmaid and confidante, Imayne; and the married queen
into whose service he enters on condition that he can be called her sweet-
heart, 'dru la reine', and kiss her every evening. These women regularly
articulate their desire as pillow soliloquies, and the very proliferation of
such loving and recurrently wakeful women here and in other romances
may be behind Chaucer's parody in *Sir Thopas*, in which 'many a maiden'
lies sighing for the hero when they ought to be sleeping. The line is com-
monly taken as being funny because of a gender inversion (this is what
knights do for their ladies); the texts suggest rather that it is funny because
it is accurate. The whole plot of *Ipomadon* is largely driven by the desiring
women, most particularly the Fere, a ruler in her own right, who resists
making a sexual choice and taking a husband. In many respects the
romance is as much her story as Ipomadon's, as she is impelled into reluc-
tant love for the apparently useless squire who comes anonymously to her
court, and has to suffer the emotional revenge of a desire that appears
unrequited. Hue gives his own version a distinctly ironic tone, especially
where the women are concerned, and he occasionally drops overtly
antifeminist remarks into his narration;[40] but the story itself takes its
characters rather more seriously, and by the time it has crossed the lan-
guage barrier into English both the irony and the antifeminism have gone,
to leave a romance that concentrates the experiences of love strongly and
directly on the women. Their sexual response to Ipomadon is presented as
both natural (even proper, so long as they do not act on it outside mar-
riage), and as a code by which the reader recognizes his status as hero, just

as the man's response to a beautiful woman in the Petrarchan tradition marks her out as the heroine. In an interesting inversion of the theory of the male gaze developed in relation to film and applied by modern scholarship to the Petrarchan lover's gaze, these women, the Fere and Imayne in particular, make Ipomadon the object of their own gaze, and a very attractive object he is too.[41] As Lavine and Melior and an abundance of other young women demonstrate, they are far from being alone in the intensity of their reaction to an active process of *looking* at the hero. The strength of the Fere's response embarrasses her into accusing someone else of her own guilt, as she delivers an unprovoked rebuke to her cousin, Jason, for looking too lovingly on Imayne. When it is Imayne's turn to fall for Ipomedon, he is disguised as a fool, in rusty and ill-fitting armour, and she has been playing a role as the damsel scornful of the unknown young man who has been foisted on her in her quest for chivalric help, like Malory's Lynette in his 'Tale of Gareth' (who is indeed likely to be her direct literary descendant). Also like Lynette, she remains stubbornly unimpressed by the combats he undertakes on their journey; and it is only when he disarms and sits beside the fire at a small country inn where they have taken lodging that she looks at him properly for the first time and responds to the sheer physical appeal of his body. After they have gone to their separate beds in the inn's single chamber, she engages in an agonized debate with herself before creeping across to his bed to declare her love and offer him the freedom of her body, with marriage to follow. He responds by seizing her hand and making as if to bite it, in order to convince her of the genuineness of his disguise. He (like Sir Thopas, and in contrast to those romance heroes who have a greater eagerness than their ladies for sex before marriage) is 'chaast and no lechour', and will not respond to any of the women who 'moorne for hym paramour', except, eventually, his own beloved, the Fere. The queen never gives outward expression to her own desire for him, and it is revealed in the text in her unspoken thoughts: in her too, the women are given a more extensive internal life than the men of the story. The author of the tail-rhyme redaction shows his awareness of the inversion of gender roles in all of this when he gives her a version of a proverb most commonly associated with a man's failure to make the most of the availability of a woman: 'he that will not when he may, shall have not when he would'.[42]

The intensity of the women's gazing in all these works raises the possibility, not of the woman as the agent of the look, but of these episodes as male narcissism—as the author's appropriating the woman's gaze merely for the purposes of male self-admiration, as is suggested by the succession of beautiful and high-ranking ladies falling for Ipomedon's handsome body.[43] It would be foolhardy to deny that there is never any element of that in the mix (and for Hue in particular it seems to be an element in his alertness as to what will give his romance maximum appeal to a mixed audience), but the attention paid to the thought-processes of the various women, in which they analyse their own disturbance of emotion almost independently of the object of their attraction, finally keeps the balance tilted towards the female subject. Their soliloquies, however, raise an analogous issue: their occurrence in male-authored works raises the question of how far they should be read as male ventriloquism, as men fashioning women according to their own notions of how they would like them to think and speak, and so finally still denying women any subject-hood.[44] In the texts themselves, there is something of a spectrum from those monologues that invite such a reading to those where it defies cred-ibility: around half of the eight thousand lines of *Amadas et Ydoine*, for instance, are focalized through the heroine, with abundant access into her thoughts. Even if the author were creating his own idea of a woman (as any author does, whether male or female), it is impossible for readers not to empathize with Ydoine as an autonomous character. The impres-sionist response to most of the soliloquies of female desire, however short, is that they should be taken seriously, and there is no obvious rea-son why medieval readers' responses should have been different—not least women readers'. 'This yonge man whome I never saw before,' thinks Huon's daughter Clariette when she first sets eyes on the young Florence, 'maketh me to thynke that I never thought before, so that it maketh my blode and all my mymbres to tremble.'[45] The very refusal of specificity—what she 'never thought before'—both serves as authenticating detail for her brief and forceful response to desire, and invites imaginative comple-tion from the audience.

There is furthermore a useful control on what a female language of desire actually looks like, from women writers both secular and religious. The *Lais* of Marie de France frequently focalize through their women protagonists, and the longest of them, *Eliduc*, allows the space for a series of spoken and unspoken expressions of desire from the maiden Guilliadun for the lover, the *dru*, she selects for herself. She has heard him well spoken of, but it is her first gazing at him that stirs her desire:

> Icele l'ad mult esgardé,
> Sun vis, sun cors e sun semblant;
> Dit en lui n'at mesavenant,

Forment le prise en sun curage.
Amurs i lance sun message,
Que la somunt de lui amer.[46]

[She looked at him closely, his face, his body and his whole appearance; she said to herself that there was nothing unbecoming about him, and prized him highly in her heart. Love directed his message there, which summoned her to love him.]

Marie is unusual as a woman writer of romance, but there were many female mystics who recorded their own feelings of longing for Christ, and whose writings offer a check on reading the male-authored texts as solely masculine in orientation. These women commonly express their desire in more fervent and often more sexually explicit language than the romance heroines use, an explicitness allowed by the transfigured nature of their desire. The thirteenth-century Flemish mystic Hadewijch speaks of how she beheld the Beloved, Christ, in a vision after the Eucharist, and how he

took me entirely in his arms, and pressed me to him; and all my members felt his in full felicity, in accordance with the desire of my heart and my humanity.[47]

The lineaments of gratified desire are precisely what is at issue there: not in the way a secular age would choose to understand Blake's formulation, but carrying immense psychological, spiritual, and physical power within medieval Christian culture. English mystical works, like English romances, tend to be more reticent in their use of erotic language than continental ones, but Margery Kempe, perhaps influenced by works from that continental tradition, is prepared to take a similar approach. She looks at handsome young men eagerly in the hope of seeing Christ's form in them; she has Christ urge her, 'Whan thu art in thi bed, take me to the as for thi weddyd husbond'—a formulation reinforced by the fact that she has already gone through a wedding ceremony with the Father.[48] The mystics are important for an understanding of romance because they so often formulate an autobiographical language of female desire. This does not mean that the secular soliloquies necessarily imitate or parody mystical texts: the chronological sequence suggests that influence runs the other way—that the mystics identified with the language of desire of the romance heroines. Both secular and religious texts respond to the same paradox, that the sense of intimate connection with someone outside your own self jolts you into a full awareness of your own unique subjectivity, of heart and mind and body.

Such a connection reaches its ideal when it is mutual: when the gaze and the embrace is returned, desire gratified. The romances have ways of expressing this too, but in action more than in soliloquy—*soliloquium*, 'speaking alone', would be mere distraction once love is fulfilled. The look of longing can become a mark of mutuality in love, as when Chrétien's Erec and Enide gaze wordlessly at each other's naked bodies at their first entry into the joy of their wedding night, and the syntax runs together into a single action the pleasure shared by the two lovers.[49] Mutuality is often given mimetic expression by the use of the syntactic pattern by which each lover occupies both the subject and the object position of a reflexive verb, found for instance at its simplest in Malory's description of the coming together of Gareth and his lady Lyonesse, 'eythir made grete joy of other'.[50] French romance sometimes expands this pattern generously: it extends over most of a hundred lines in the scenes of the marriage and wedding night in the thirteenth-century *Jehan et Blonde*, where the lovers exchange rings with each other, gaze on each other, embrace each other; or, when one lover is chosen as the subject of a sentence, the other immediately follows, so that both are given an equal share in the language as in the joy.[51] Blonde is the daughter of the earl of Oxford: English lovers are just as capable of such an abundance of mutual joy as French, though English authors are more reticent. Malory writes his most compelling account of such reciprocal intensity at the moment when two of his lovers first set eyes on each other, though once again the woman is the instigator. Fair Alys, 'La Beall Pylgryme', lodges herself alongside the piece of ground that Sir Alysaunder is defending against all comers, and it is she who first both reacts to the sight of her future husband and declares her love. When she sees him joust, she at once 'lepe oute of hir pavylyon and toke sir Alisaundir by the brydyll', and asks to see his face—'Of thy knyghthode, shew me thy vysayge.'

And than he put of his helme, and whan she sawe his vysage she seyde, 'A, swete Fadir Jesu! The I muste love, and never othir.'
    'Than shewe me youre vysage,' seyde he.
    And anone she unwympeled her, and whan he sawe her he seyde, 'A, Lorde Jesu! Here have I founde my love and my lady!'[52]

Each request and action and response reciprocates the other's; and the lovers' invoking of Jesus is a way of sacramentalizing that act of immediate and lifelong commitment, made at sight and mutually.

Desire is not always mutual, however, and some of Malory's most compelling portrayals of women are of those who love without hope of response, in particular the two Elaines who love Lancelot. Elaine of Corbin is predestined to bear Galahad, and, despite the accompanying paraphernalia of prophecy and miracle surrounding the Grail knight's life, and in contradiction of the theology of perfect virginity obtaining on the Grail quest itself, Malory makes her love fully sexual. Even after the excuse of conceiving the Grail knight is passed, Elaine continues to trick Lancelot into her bed whenever the opportunity offers—'for wyte you well, oute of mesure she loved hym'.[53] While Guinevere exists, however, there is nothing she can do to elicit a corresponding love from Lancelot, and she makes a bitter complaint to the queen against her deprivation.[54] Elaine of Ascolat, in the longest speech given to a woman in the whole of the *Morte*, utters a passionate defence of earthly love, and specifically her love for Lancelot. She too has lost her heart to him with no hope of reciprocation, and (unlike the other Elaine) with no assistance from either prophecy or magic. Her brother is equally devoted to him—'she doth as I do, for sythen I saw first my lorde Sir Launcelot I cowde never departe from hym, nother nought I woll, and I may folow hym'[55]—but he can put his love into effect within the accepted practices of male bonding and knightly fellowship. The only possibilities that Elaine will contemplate, since she rejects Lancelot's clumsy offer of a massive dowry and annuity if she marries someone else, are that he should be her husband or her paramour. He, of course, refuses both; in which case, as she tells him, 'I muste dye for youre love,' and she does so. On her deathbed, she defies her confessor who commands her to stop thinking about Lancelot.

Than she seyde, 'Why sholde I leve such thoughtes? Am I nat an erthely woman? And all the whyle the brethe ys in my body I may complayne me, for my belyve ys that I do none offence, though I love an erthely man, unto God, for He fourmed me thereto, and all maner of good love comyth of God. And othir than good love loved I never sir Launcelot du Lake . . . And sitthyn hit ys the sufferaunce of God that I shall dye for so noble a knyght, I beseche The, Hyghe Fadir of Hevyn, have mercy uppon me and my soule. '[56]

When it comes to writing the polemics in favour of virginity in the Grail section of the work, Malory is content to transcribe directly from his French source; here, as when Elaine of Corbin cries out against Guinevere's thwarting of her love for Lancelot, Malory breaks free and writes for himself. Elaine of Ascolat is a 'clene maydyn for hym and for all othir', but she does not link that to any inherent desirability in virginity. It is hard to separate Malory's God from hers: a God who is on the side of the sexual desire inherent in 'good love'.

SANCTIFYING SEXUALITY

Elaine's claim that God is in favour of love between men and women is unusual only in its setting at the moment of her death. It was not only in romance that sexuality was regarded as a ground of delight and approval. There is abundant evidence in early modern culture that shows how familiar such a way of thinking was: romance grounds its discourse of desire in a broader social, intellectual, and even theological context. Such approval, especially of female sexuality, was by no means universal, as any broad reading in medieval texts indicates and as modern scholarship has abundantly documented; it always coexisted with the political, legal, and theological subordination of women, and with the fear of aberrant sexuality inherent both in a secular patrilinear system and in ecclesiastical celibacy. Yet despite all that, the desirability of desire, male and female, was widely acknowledged as a part of God's design for the universe. Although the narratives of romance give it the specificity of individual experience, their discourse of desire is also the discourse of Nature as *vicaria Dei*, 'the vicar of the almighty Lord':[57] a discourse strongly promoted in the late twelfth century, at the same time as the rise of romance, by writers such as Alain de Lille, and often appealed to, explicitly or through imagery, in the romances themselves. Around the same period, marriage was made a sacrament of the Church: an outward and visible sign of an inward invisible grace, comparable with the other sacraments of baptism and ordination and the Eucharist itself. The increasing interest in individuals' inward lives evident in romance, and especially in its treatment of love, had its religious counterpart in an increase in mysticism, and as devotional women such as Hadewijch and Margery Kempe indicate, the discourse of desire could be turned to spiritual as well as earthly ends. The sublime eroticism of the *Song of Songs* was officially allegorized into the love of Christ for his Church (some modern Bibles still give that as a running head to the book), and mystical writers drew abundantly on that too; the Church has never been able to find higher imagery to express the love of God than the imagery of earthly desire.

Sexual desires were acknowledged to be universal; that was why they were so dangerous. Temperance, as Spenser knew, is a life lived in fighting off temptation. They also had their being within the scope of God's purposes, as the means by which the created world maintained its existence. The sexual act is often insistently associated with the language of nature, so bypassing the penitential discourses that associate it with sin. So Chaucer describes the embrace of Troilus and Criseyde,

> As about a tree, with many a twiste,
> Bytrent and writh the swote wodebynde,   [entwines; twists
> Gan ech of hem in armes other wynde.

Troilus III. 1230–2

The impossibility of assigning separate gender roles to the lovers, any more than to the woodbine and the tree, echoes the romances' reciprocal language of consummation; yet the image is a particularly useful one for Chaucer in that it bypasses any questions about the status of the lovers' relationship.[58] Marriage is an institution unique to humans, so there is potentially a faultline between the regenerative activities of the created world and those of the highest element in that creation, humankind. Even so, Chaucer spells out the cosmic and divine extensions of natural love in the proem that introduces Book III, the book of the lovers' consummation, where he describes how God's eternal principle of love is channelled through the astrological influence (the 'vapour') of Venus, which runs through all the temporal cycles, the 'tymes', of the seasons, and through all living creatures:

> Man, brid, best, fissh, herbe, and grene tree
> Thee fele in tymes with vapour eterne.
> God loveth, and to love wol nought werne;   [refuse
> And in this world no lyves creature   [living
> Withouten love is worth, or may endure.

III. 10–14

There, regeneration, procreation, and divine and human love are all set on the same spectrum.

More extended theoretical discussions in the pre-modern world often took the form of allegory: where we would write a monograph or a textbook, medieval and Renaissance thinkers would offer the same kind of generalizing theory through extended metaphor, or through the symbolism of the dream poem. Chaucer and Spenser both offer such extended allegorical studies of the place of sex in the natural order alongside, or within, their romance narratives. Spenser's is the Garden of Adonis, placed in Book III of the *Faerie Queene* so as to provide the theoretical model that the central books on love illustrate in operation. The Garden models itself in part on Chaucer's invocation to Venus quoted above: it is the place where the outward forms are provided for the 'reasonable souls' of humankind, and also for beasts, birds, and fish (III. vi. 35). Venus is the deity who presides over all procreation and regeneration; and at the heart of the garden, as has often been noted, is a landscape designed to model the woman's own generative body (43–4). Venus' activities can scarcely be taken as a social model for humans, but it is still interesting that it is she, and not Adonis, who 'reape[s] sweet pleasure' here from her lover (46). The woman's desire, as so often in the romance background, is also coupled with mutual pleasure, independent of any social or religious constraints:

> Franckly each paramour his leman knowes,
> Each bird his mate, nor any does envie
> Their goodly meriment, and gay felicitie.
>
> III. vi. 41

The parallel implied there between human and avian love picks up from Chaucer's analogous allegory in which he studies the operation of natural desire, the *Parliament of Fowls*. The association of birds and humans is not without reason: the mating patterns of birds—basically monogamous, but with the occasional bit on the side, and with some extreme cases of parental irresponsibility such as cuckoos—offer the closest parallel to human habits within the natural world. It is therefore striking that the action of the *Parliament* concerns the free choice in mating given to a formel (female) eagle: a choice that in this poem she exercises by requesting a year's delay. The poem makes no attempt to present as natural—or to present at all—female choice as being controlled by a dominant male. This is not necessarily quite the whole story, since outside the dream world there may be a set of allusions to the marriage negotiations for Richard II, in which the lady in question would certainly not have had such uncontrolled freedom of choice;[59] but if such a topical reference for the poem is correct, it makes the naturalization of the female's refusal all the more interesting. It may be a way to cover political embarrassment, but it also insists that the God-given order of Nature may make such embarrassment inevitable. Within the world of nature that encompasses the world of politics, female choice is the scenario that holds good. The eagle at the centre of the debate is free to make her own selection of a mate, or indeed to withhold it.

The emphasis on Nature in numerous romances and in major individual works both Latin and vernacular offers an important reminder that the clerical promotion of virginity was always a specialized discourse aimed at initiates, those ordained or under vows. Procreation is natural, normal, and normative: a statement so obvious as not generally to need spelling out, any more than pop lyrics comment on the biological principles of sexual selection. The resulting medieval silence on the normality of heterosexual activity tends to be filled by other, competing, discourses, not least by the penitential stress on the sinfulness of carnal desire (God's purposes having been corrupted by the devil from the Garden of Eden forwards), and by antifeminist diatribes. The discourses of nature do not, however, simply bypass morality. The tenets of natural philosophy—or natural theology—show the same anxiety as the principles of patriarchal family organization to establish limits: a God-given procreative Nature abhors 'unnatural' sexual practices as much as a patrilineal society abhors adultery or illegitimacy. Sexuality in every culture engenders anxiety about the distinction between the right and wrong uses of desire, even though different cultures draw the boundaries in different places: Shakespeare lived in a society that prescribed the death penalty for homosexuality, but which found no problems in a Juliet who had not quite turned 14. Sex as normative tends to be made explicit only when it seems to be threatened, for instance by Alain de Lille in his *Complaint of Nature*, written to combat what he saw as a rise in (nonprocreative) homosexual activity. *Cleanness*, one of the works that shares a manuscript with *Sir Gawain and the Green Knight* and is likely to be by the same author, takes the further step of condemning the evils of Sodom and Gomorrah primarily through a eulogy of heterosexual sex, put into the mouth of God. He Himself, He claims, invented the pleasures of the fulfilment of desire for humankind:

> I compast hem a kynde crafte and kende hit hem derne,
> And amed hit in Myn ordenaunce oddely dere,
> And dyght drwry therinne, doole alther-swettest,
> And the play of paramorez I portrayed Myselven,
> And made therto a maner myriest of other:
> When two true togeder had tyghed hemselven,
> Bytwene a male and his make such merthe schulde come,
> Welnyghe pure paradys moght preve no better.[60]

[I created a natural skill for them and taught it to them secretly, set it as singularly precious in My scheme for the world, causing love, the sweetest of all pleasures, to be part of it. I Myself drew up the play of sexual love ['paramours'], and made it the most enjoyable practice of all: that when two faithful people had bound themselves together, there should be such joy between a man and his beloved that even paradise itself could scarcely improve on it.]

There is no evidence that anyone ever thought that such a claim was blasphemous or wrong; desire was a natural, *kynde*, part of being human. It is unusual to find a religious writer insisting so frankly and enthusiastically on that fact; but it is a belief that the romances made their own. The poet can therefore have God draw on secular language: 'paramorez' is itself a term borrowed from romance, from loving *par amour*—a tautology that enacts the attraction of both body and heart. Its primary usage is for any passionate love that goes beyond the mutual goodwill indicated by the clerical terminology of *maritalis affectio*, marital affection. It therefore commonly occurs in extramarital contexts, but it is also often used, as here, to describe a passion that is joyfully guilt-free.

As *Cleanness* recognizes, that sex could be intensely enjoyable was not in doubt: hence the perceived need to regulate it, especially in the pre-contraception world. 'Two true' must bind themselves together before the unconstrained play of paramours can re-create unfallen bliss, 'pure paradys'. Despite their twentieth-century reputation for promoting adultery (discussed in the next chapter), most romances, English ones in particular, reserve the lovers' sexual bliss for marriage, and any contravention of that reservation is likely to bring speedy retribution. The young lovers are usually scrupulous about not sleeping with each other before they are married, a standard most rigorously urged by the women and sometimes endorsed by authority figures who have the power of magic to back them. Oberon in *Huon of Bordeaux* and Prospero in *The Tempest* both threaten disaster if the lovers pre-empt their weddings, and in *Huon* it does indeed happen: when Huon ignores Esclarmonde's protests and effectively rapes her, she is carried off by a shipful of pagans and he is tied up and left to die of exposure (he does of course escape to marry her, many episodes later). Very occasionally, lovers intending marriage will enjoy each other before their wedding, but even that is rare. Malory's Gareth and Lyonesse try to do so, but are repeatedly thwarted by the intervention of a phantom knight created by Lyonesse's disapproving younger sister.[61] Even without such supernatural threats, pre-marital sex can lead to serious trouble. The resulting babies are often lost for an entire generation, and the same length of time may intervene before the lovers recover each other. Disaster likewise engulfs the lovers of Sidney's *Old Arcadia* at the moment when Musidorus is on the point of raping Pamela and Pyrocles makes love to Philoclea.[62] But marriage remains the aim and the norm, even in such cases as the rape of a maiden by a fairy knight in *Sir Degaré*, and even if the wedding has to wait until the child of the liaison has grown up.[63]

In a secular society in which the family was the basic unit of organization, there was good reason to celebrate sexuality, so long as it expressed itself within marriage; and that celebration received massive ecclesiastical support. The insistence on consent between the spouses for making a marriage valid was a major part of this; and the upgrading of marriage into a sacrament was in keeping with that emphasis on consensual bonding. Rather less has been heard in recent years about that sacramentalizing of sexuality than about the connection between desire and sin—and that connection was also forcefully made by Roman Catholicism, not least in the Middle Ages; St Augustine had concluded that any sexual activity, even within marriage, was inseparable from sin, since rational and divinely authorized motives of procreation could never entirely dominate over irrational desire. Even so, medieval Catholicism never made such a belief into dogma, whereas its endorsement of marriage was a matter not only of theological doctrine but of daily practice. For every celibate Catholic cleric who composed misogynist texts, there must have been at least a thousand—probably several thousand—who performed the marriage service, a single text replicated in oral form over and over again and therefore leaving no explicit record of its frequency, and which gives a very different idea of the theology of sex. The service as a whole still fell well short of an unmitigated celebration of sexuality—as the traditional Anglican version still insists, sex within marriage is justified by the begetting of children and the avoidance of the worse sin of fornication—yet the anxiety of much of its phrasing does not altogether conceal the fact that it is a form of fertility rite, and one that binds the physical with the divine. It invokes a broader cultural context that insists on sexual desire not just as a necessary means of continuing a lineage, nor even as the greatest secular happiness, but as instigated by God. The marriage service was the face that the Church turned towards the secular and sexual world, and it incorporated imagery from that greatest of erotic poems, the *Song of Songs*. It turned its allegorical meanings back to the literal and the human, as offering a model of how a husband should love his wife, in a way that sacramentalizes the body itself. The *Song of Songs* was one of the major sources for the expression of spiritual love, authorizing a language of mystical union in metaphors of the sexual; but it also authorized the expression of sexual union in metaphors of the mystical. Moreover, it has two speakers, a woman and her beloved, and both express their desire for the other frankly and unashamedly.

The dual meaning of the *Song of Songs* serves to introduce a larger cultural endorsement of women's active choice from an altogether unexpected quarter, namely religious treatises on the value of virginity—the lives of virgin martyrs, handbooks for women recluses, and the writings of women mystics. Here, as in the romances, the basic narrative of the perfect life requires that the woman should reject her father's plans for her marriage, or the approaches of various unwanted suitors, to insist on a marriage to the lover who surpasses all other lovers in both beauty and rank, Christ Himself.[64] There is no particular virtue in being put in a convent in accordance with family convenience,[65] nor is the negative wish to avoid the sinfulness of the world enough. The woman must herself make an active choice for Christ, and show the strength of her choice through adversity as great as, or greater than, the romance heroines show in remaining faithful to their own lovers. Bevis of Hamtoun's beloved Josian—a pagan princess who, true to form for Anglo-Norman heroines and their descendants, is the first of the couple to fall in love, and who actively woos him—has to keep a succession of husbands at bay by various means, including stringing up her second unwanted spouse from the rail of the bed-hangings on their wedding night.[66] The women marked for sainthood may take less drastic action to dispose of rival suitors, but that is only because Christ Himself will intervene to inflict equally unpleasant fates on them by direct miraculous intervention.

The minimum requirement for an active demonstration of the force of the woman's own will for Christ was to override the opposition of her parents: in effect, to elope.[67] The great thirteenth-century Catalan thinker and missionary Ramón Lull, whose works were widely disseminated across Europe for the next couple of centuries (his great handbook on chivalry was translated and printed by Caxton), wrote a quasi-romance named *Blanquerna* precisely to give the religious life the same appeal as secular narrative, and its deliberate closeness to romance patterning is instructive: many of the conventional memes reappear, but they are given new meanings so as to direct the readers towards finding fulfilment in God rather than within the secular world. The work is a *bildungsroman* of both its hero, Blanquerna himself, and its heroine, Natana. She has been chosen as his wife by their parents, but he insists on renouncing the world and becoming a hermit (by the end of the work, he has been elected pope: the ecclesiastical equivalent of the romance hero's becoming emperor). She expresses her passionate love for him, and offers to follow him into the wilderness; but he converts her to loving Christ instead, whereupon she escapes from her home to a convent, and, when her furious kinsfolk threaten to attack the convent and force her out, she persuades them to peace.[68] Real life did, on occasion, come surprisingly close to romance. The twelfth-century Christina of Markyate, who made a private vow of virginity as a child, had to resist intensive moral and physical pressure both from her parents and from a number of churchmen to force her into marriage, the approved social model for young women; she was compelled to adopt a number of extreme techniques of avoidance, culminating in an escape in male clothing, in order to enforce her own will for Christ. Saints can safely rely on God's intervening to prevent rape; real-life women, like secular romance heroines, have to take measures for themselves, as when Christina locked the randy bishop of Durham inside her bedroom while she got away.[69] The love of Christ, in other words, properly trumps both the love of man, and the obedience owed to one's parents. Romance develops a similar line of argument in the secular world: love of one's chosen spouse overrides filial duty, and presents it as right that it should do so.

Love for both kinds of heroines incorporates desire. Although physical sexual activity is ruled out for women under vows, it is still taken for granted that they have sexual desires: what is required is that they should be redirected towards Christ, Who is (as such writings repeatedly stress) the most handsome, the richest, and most powerful of all possible husbands, and also (as a surprising number of them stress) the most sexually fulfilling.[70] Sexuality, in the Catholic Middle Ages as in the Protestant Renaissance, was taken as a given. What mattered was what you did with it. Promiscuity was condemned in both men and women (even if with considerably more vigour for the latter). What a woman with a religious vocation has to do is very explicitly to sublimate her sexuality, to choose Christ as her sexual partner rather than a man. A post-Freudian age reads this as a form of sexual repression, but it is quite clear from the texts themselves that the writers regarded it as the highest form of fulfilment: how could one have a better lover than Christ? 'Lover', moreover, on the model of the *Song of Songs*, was taken in a more literal, embodied, sense than our modern, supposedly liberated, sensibilities are happy with. *Hali Meithhad*, 'holy maidenhood', an early thirteenth-century treatise encouraging young women to reject earthly marriage in favour of the vocation of an anchoress, describes the final union of the woman with her beloved Christ after death in terms of unashamed sexual consummation: 'blessed is His spouse, whose virginity is unspotted when He sheds His seed into her'.[71] This is a spiritual love that represents itself as fully embodied, such as now demands some effort of imagination in comprehending its cultural power. The effort is particularly great because such a synthesis was not only dismantled but condemned by the Reformation, with its rejection of a physically incarnational theology in favour of a theology of the text;[72] and the modern world has largely inherited, often subconsciously, that intense distrust of the expression of spirit in terms of the body, regarding the result as confusion rather than fusion. In the Middle Ages, despite the division between the theological primacy given to virginity and the secular primacy given to procreation, spiritual longing existed in close symbiosis with the desirability of female desire expressed in the romances.[73]

The authors of the religious treatises for women wrote so that their readers might pattern their lives on the models they presented: not, in the case of saints' lives, necessarily literally, but at least with the same absolute commitment to God. *Admiranda non imitanda*, the recognition that some examples of pious heroism should be wondered at rather than imitated, was a useful saving principle, and applied no doubt to Josian's short way with her husband too. The fact that pious authors sometimes looked to romance for their imagined scenarios is an indication of how the secular genre was acknowledged to influence women's desires and self-images: the famous allegory in the *Ancrene Wisse* of the soul as a lady besieged by her foes within her castle, and rescued by her wooer Christ, takes as its premiss that the anchoresses for whom it is written (that is, women living a life of enclosure under vows but without belonging to a religious community of nuns) will identify with such a lady.[74] There is a further close correlation between many of the lives of virgin saints and the romances, not just in that the young women in both have to repel rival suitors, but that those suitors are often represented as heathen tyrants: romance heroines as various as the Fere of *Ipomadon* and Percyvell of Galles' beloved need defence against pagan kings who aim to compel their submission by force. Whereas the romance tyrants, like the foe of the *Ancrene Wisse*, rarely get closer to the ladies than to besiege their castles, those in saints' lives typically try to impose their will by a direct attack on the bodies of the nubile young maidens they desire, stripping them naked and torturing them. The graphic description devoted to this has frequently been attacked by modern critics as authorized pornography,[75] but the equation is problematic. Quite apart from the very different cultural meanings for both nakedness (with its strong symbolic association with innocence, emphasized in pictures of virgin martyrdoms by the brightness of the saint's body compared with the other figures and the background) and for the infliction of pain (with its associations with the Passion), the element of potential pornographic fantasizing through such images is strictly controlled by both hagiographers and artists. Rival suitors and torturers are alike on their way to damnation; and they are always presented as in some sense 'other'. The pictures make that particularly clear by the ugliness of the men surrounding the heroine, just as the men who attack the lady in romance are often represented as in some way monstrous. The pressure from romance actively discourages identification with a heathen villain or would-be rapist, or with the intense voyeurism of their gaze.

The Catholic cult of virginity might seem to entail a break-point at the Reformation in the link between such discourses and romance, but any disruption of memetic replication takes place only over a long time-scale. Elizabethan England was only a generation, or the width of the Channel, away from a fully Catholic culture, and those ways of thinking, its imagery, and its books did not disappear with the Act of Settlement. Many of these images and patterns of narrative accordingly continue in the new religious context. Spenser makes explicit both the innocence of nakedness and the beastliness of voyeuristic lust in his analogous stories of Serena, stripped for the 'sordid eyes' of the satyrs whose desire to ravish her is thwarted initially only by the decision to sacrifice her instead; and of Una, the 'heavenly virgin' who is rescued from Sansloy's attempted rape by another troupe of satyrs, but they are impelled by the revelation of her unveiled beauty, not, like her attacker, to the feeding of their 'fiery lustfull eye', but to the adoration of Truth.[76] The secular surface of Spenser's narrative never conceals his models in hagiographic legend: the resonances of such episodes with the lives of virgin saints would still have have been familiar to his readers. On occasion he states as much, as when he describes Florimell's resistance to Proteus' attempts to seduce her away from her true love (first offering her kingdoms, then assailing her in hideous form with 'sharpe threates') as making her worthy of a 'crowne of heavenly praise with saints above' (III. viii. 40–2). Martyrdom, moreover, continued to hold a fascination even on the Reformation stage. The scenes in *Pericles* of Marina in the brothel, secular as they are, bring with them connotations from the legend of St Agnes, who was condemned to such a fate by the pagan whose advances she had refused, but with even direr consequences for her would-be clients; her story was among those retained as historical in Foxe's *Ecclesiasticall Historie*, and so had continuing currency in the great Protestant marty-

rology.[77] In 1620, Massinger and Dekker took the further step of drama-
tizing the death of St Dorothy, as *The Virgin Martyr*. Here, her persecu-
tors are clownish villains, presented not as types of evil but rather as the
butt of satire, comic figures in the classical sense as defined by Sidney:
characters represented 'in the most ridiculous and scornefull sort that
may be; so as it is impossible that any beholder can be content to be such
a one'.[78] Dorothy also proclaims the sublimated sexuality characteristic
of Catholic spirituality focused on the virgin martyr: she has chosen a
lover who surpasses any other, and He in turn 'languisheth to death' for
her.[79]

One of the great defining moments of the Reformation was when the
ex-monk Martin Luther married a former nun. It marked a redefinition
of the perfect life, from rejection of the world and the flesh to the uncon-
tested sacramentalizing of the secular: earthly marriage was no longer
second best, but the institution in which the highest Christian life could
be practised. Spenser famously redefines the Chastity represented by
Britomart, the title knight of Book III, from virginity to faithful love. The
move is evidently to some extent a product of the Reformation, an active
rejection on Spenser's part of Roman Catholic doctrines of perfect
celibacy in favour of an ideal of marriage. Yet the Protestant shift in ideo-
logy reinforced the whole romance ideal that cast married love as the
model of chaste faithfulness; medieval writers of romance were to an
extent writing against the dominant cultural model of their age, whereas
Spenser can write in accord with his. Faithful love with marriage as its
aim makes a statement in favour of England's own reformed theological
(and therefore political) ideals. Romance therefore has the potential to lie
at the heart of a Protestant national literature, just as marriage lies at the
heart of the genre. If outside the *Faerie Queene* it does not often do so,
that is perhaps the consequence of a larger cultural shift, from an
assumption that literature exists to express an age or a nation's ideology
to an assumption that it speaks with an individual voice at odds with the
institutional requirements of Church and state.

EROTIC THOUGHT: SPENSER AND SIDNEY

That that spectrum of good love did indeed embrace both human and
divine is the underlying principle of the *Faerie Queene*, and in particular
of Books III and IV. Here, Spenser presents an array of love in all its
variations: divine and cosmic and human, good and bad, natural and

unnatural; promiscuity and virginity, the right attraction between virtues and the dangerous attraction between vices, the seduction of the virtuous away from their true natures. The dividing point comes not between physical and spiritual love, but between love inspired by God and lust that sets the soul on a wrong path. Where medieval presentations of similar ideas had to work against a multiplicity of competing discourses, Spenser had on his side not only the Reformation theology of God-given sexuality, but also the Neoplatonic theories of how the soul might rise to God by using earthly love and beauty as stepping-stones towards higher things. What might appear simple when expressed in the abstract, however, becomes much more ethically complex in practice, and the acting out of such principles in fictional examples brings those complexities to the fore. None of Spenser's characters has an easy or assured road to the fulfilment of love, and Sidney's numerous love-smitten characters in the *Arcadia* exemplify anxiety at least as much as they exemplify love. Spenser starts from the position that earthly love is the highest human good, and has divine approval; the *Arcadia* reads like an extended debate as to whether that is true. Sidney goes well beyond most romance writers, English or continental, in the subtlety of his exploration of the links between sexuality and ethics. In both versions of the *Arcadia*, but most markedly in the revision, he shows that even the men and women who fashion themselves according to the cultural norms of virtue have their self-images broken and re-formed by desire; the potential for good and evil inherent in sexuality does not divide out easily between heroes and villains. Providing a thread through such complexities, however, in both the *Arcadia* and the *Faerie Queene*, runs the continuing meme of the 'passionate and pure' young woman, who sets her choice on a man on whom she gazes.

Spenser offers, as the lead protagonist in the large cast of his books of Love and Friendship, not a knight but a woman acting the role of a knight: a maiden seeking the man she loves. The choice follows almost inevitably from the long-standing English portrayal of the feisty heroine, the agent of her own choices in life and love, as the generically central figure of love-romance, not least stories of the founding of dynasties. Although her immediate predecessor is Ariosto's Bradamante, another maiden knight who in turn has the Grisandol of the prose *Merlin* in her background, Spenser is concerned to make Britomart's British derivation clear by what she says as well as by what she is called. Her very first speech offers a declaration of belief in love as free choice, for both partners: an idea that takes further the Church's insistence on the consent of both bride and bridegroom for a valid marriage. As the culmination of this primary speech, the affirmation carries a particular weight.

> Ne may love be compeld by maisterie;
> For soone as maisterie comes, sweet love anone
> Taketh his nimble wings, and soon away is gone.

III. i. 25

The passage is itself a quotation from the *Franklin's Tale*, where Chaucer has his Franklin make the same point, in a story that insists on the importance of mutual respect within marriage:

> Love wol nat been constreyned by maistrye.
> Whan maistrie comth, the God of Love anon
> Beteth his wynges, and farewel, he is gon![80]

The quotation is so precise as to indicate that it was meant to be recognized, and so to bring its original context with it. It is an ideal of behaviour within a relationship as well as of choice of partner. Chaucer's emphasis falls on the former: his lines are in context a warning about the effect on a loving wife of a bullying husband. Spenser shifts the emphasis to the second meaning, though without leaving the first behind. Chastity, faithful married love, is for Spenser effectively defined as the free and unconstrained direction of a woman's will towards the man of her choice, or, by extension, of a man's towards a woman, both in the selection of a partner and in the maintenance of that love. He roots that definition in the native tradition of romance, in the father of English poetry.

As a maiden warrior, Britomart offers the most extensive exploration of how the contrasting possibilities of action for men and women in love can be brought together in a single figure. In keeping with his practice throughout the poem, Spenser introduces her first in action, so that the effect of what she represents is made clear before she is given a name, or indeed a gender. That opening action is a typically male one, the unhorsing of Guyon, the knight of temperance. Far from virtue being opposed to evil here, what Spenser is demonstrating in the overthrow is a hierarchy of virtue: good love, allegorically speaking, is stronger than dispassionate temperance, and can rightly overcome it. That she does so with a magic lance makes the same point as the arrows of the God of Love: love carries its own supra-human power that is stronger than will or reason. That, for St Augustine, had been what was wrong with it; in Britomart, Spenser insists on its rightness. Only after her credentials have been

established in these terms is she introduced to the readers (the characters
continue to think of her as a fellow knight for some time longer):

> Even the famous Britomart it was,
> Whom straunge adventure did from Britaine fet,
> To seeke her lover (love farre sought alas,)
> Whose image she had seene in Venus looking glas.
>
> III. i. 8

Britomart is not a fairy queen, with her traditional freedom from normal
moral constraints; she is not a fay of any kind. She is a young woman who
has seen 'her lover'—the man who is to be her husband, but, more par-
ticularly, the man with whom she has fallen in love and to whom she has
dedicated her sexuality—in a mirror. The 'looking glas' is at once an alle-
gorization of loving at first sight, since a mirror offers nothing except
sight; and of the growth into self-awareness consequent on falling on
love, which Spenser develops in a long exploration of her emotions.
Rather than a formal soliloquy, he offers a long and sympathetic account
of her inarticulate feelings of bewilderment and distress that brings us
into intimate contact with her inward state of mind, in a way unique in
the whole poem.

> And if that any drop of slombring rest
> Did chaunce to still into her wearie spright,
> When feeble nature felt her selfe opprest,
> Streight way with dreames, and with fantasticke sight
> Of dreadfull things the same was put to flight,
> That oft out of her bed she did astart,
> As one with vew of ghastly feends affright:
> Tho gan she to renew her former smart,
> And thinke of that faire visage, written in her hart.
>
> III. ii. 29

For Britomart as for Lavine, or the Fere, or indeed any Petrarchan male
lover, the experience of desire is not pleasant, and Spenser does not hes-
itate to foreground its sexual element. Her 'fraile fleshly mould' is burned
by 'no usuall fire, no usuall rage' (III. ii. 37, 39), even though the object of
her desire does not so much as know of her existence. To pursue her
desire, she steals away from her father's house, to which she is the heir
(22), in the guise of a knight-errant. She would appear to be breaking just
about every patriarchal taboo on women's actions that there was; but she

carries Spenser's full approval, and all the other women of these books are implicitly or explicitly judged by comparison with her. The approval is not just a matter of the private ethics that govern personal relationships. The mirror that made her fall in love is not only Venus's, as the overpowering deity of love; it is also, as we learn later, made by Merlin, the figure who intervenes in history to fulfil the destiny that will culminate in the Tudors. He does it in traditional legend by engineering the conception of Arthur. In Spenser's addition, he sets Britomart on her quest for Arthegall so that they can become the founders of the Tudor line.

For once, Britomart's 'lover' is introduced first of all by name, not by action: Arthegall, 'equal to Arthur'. It is Britomart herself who names him (III. ii. 9), as if he were a part of her own subjectivity rather than an independent character. Arthegall is equivalent to Arthur, moreover, not just in that he takes the place that might be expected to be Arthur's as the ancestor of the Tudors, but through the parallelism—or rather the mirror imagery, reversal as well as reflection, appropriate to 'Venus looking glass'—of the ways in which Britomart falls in love with him and Arthur falls in love with Gloriana. Gloriana visits Arthur in a vision, somewhere between dream and reality (the pressed grass with its signification of her body), and he spends the rest of the poem seeking for her. His desire for her is grounded in her declaration of desire for him. Britomart sees an image of her own lover without any consciousness on his part, and embarks on her quest on her own initiative: she puts her own desire into action. Both Arthur and Arthegall are therefore the objects of female desire; but Britomart is closest to Arthur in the active role she takes in seeking that desire's fulfilment. Lesser loves in the poem have the man wooing the woman, but these two are the great love-interests that dominate the work. Britomart's desire allows for a future that will lead down to the sixteenth century; Gloriana's allows for a continuation beyond Spenser's own time, in an expression of hope in a romance happy ending that combines the fulfilment of procreative desire with the continuation of the state. There is a strong sense in which the whole of the *Faerie Queene* is structured on those two love-quests, with the implication that the consummation of both will also complete the work itself. Both are grounded in female desire.

Britomart is not so much a personification as an exemplary person, and what she exemplifies is active female desire. As such, she serves as the dominant theme of the core narrative to which all the other characters play variations. The method of the central books of the poem is to present not so much the 'continued metaphors' described in the opening Letter to Ralegh, but a 'romance of types', where the central characters represent not ideas or principles, but people who illustrate general human attitudes or tendencies with regard to love.[81] Heterosexual human relationships here are not, as they were in the opening two books, primarily a means by which Spenser expresses larger moral and political allegories: they are the major subject in their own right. The exemplary quality of the characters does not limit them to being stereotypes; as with so much of the best literature that operates with stereotypical figures, they are constantly striving towards a condition of uniqueness, just as the more highly individualized characters of other great works strive towards a condition of universality.[82] Britomart herself is the most striking example of this breaking the 'type' mould to become at the same time a unique individual. The Tudors do not emerge from a genealogical allegory, but from a desiring woman.

It does not follow that Spenser endorses women's desire as necessarily good. As with all matters of sexuality, what matters is how it is exercised, and the central books of the *Faerie Queene* function as an exploration of that. The first woman Britomart encounters, shortly after her unhorsing of Guyon marks chaste love as a superior good to temperance alone, is Malecasta, the 'ill-chaste': a desiring woman whose desire has turned into lust, the random sexual appetite for any man available. She, like Britomart, acts as her own mistress, outside male authority; but she does not control her own sexual appetites for good, and uses them to break faithful heterosexual bonds when she can. The last major woman opposed by Britomart in the poem as we have it is the Amazon Radigund, a warrior woman who uses both her sovereignty and her beauty for dominance alone, to enforce her power over men. Spenser describes such female dominance as 'a licentious libertie' contrary to the bonds imposed on women by Nature, but the issue of women's sovereignty is one that he negotiates with some anxiety. After her defeat of Radigund, Britomart reigns 'as princess' in order to exercise the true justice of restoring women to men's subjection; but the next stage of Arthegall's own quest brings him to Mercilla, a figure for Elizabeth, and therefore one of those women whose sovereignty 'the heavens' have rendered lawful.[83] Earlier, Spenser describes the 'streight lawes' that curb women's liberty as being imposed by men out of fear that women will excel them, whether in the exercise of arms or in 'artes and pollicy': a passage in justification of Britomart, but which is designed to move into a panegyric to his own queen.[84]

Spenser's embodiment in Britomart of his definition of chastity as faithful desire for one man none the less prevents her from becoming a figure for the queen on either the personal or the political level. In the 'mirrors more than one' that the poem offers to Elizabeth, Gloriana reflects her rule, Belphoebe her 'rare chastitee' in the strict sense of virginity (III Proem 5). Both are variations on Britomart's central good sexuality, and they are joined by a number of other women in these central books who offer further positive variations on women's desire. Belphoebe and her twin sister, Amoret, are begotten by the sun on a fairy, in something close to an immaculate conception.[85] They are more mythological than human: unlike the other women of the *Faerie Queene*, their life choices are made for them. Belphoebe may be fierce in defence of her virginity, but her form of life is laid down for her independently of any exercise of her own will. She has been raised by Diana in 'perfect Maydenhed', Amoret by Venus in 'goodly womanhed' (III. vi. 28). The adjectives might seem to reflect the Catholic hierarchy of dedicated virginity as superior to marriageability, but, as their twinship indicates, the distinction is not one of subordination. Belphoebe's virginity can be 'perfect' in so far as it is complete in itself, requiring nothing beyond itself; Amoret is destined—somewhere beyond the poem as Spenser left it—to find her fulfilment in a husband. It would take the ex-Catholic John Donne to insist that on her wedding night a maiden 'puts on perfection, and a woman's name', that perfection lies in what is added to virginity.[86] Spenser's narrative none the less implies something of the kind. Belphoebe's readiness to accept adoration without returning anything is criticized in the episode of Timias, based on Elizabeth's harsh treatment of Ralegh after his marriage. Amoret is a maiden who is sought by her lover rather than seeking him herself; her imprisonment by Busyrane may be a comment on the complexities of unequal desire, or the difficulties of right desire (it is one of the episodes that have resisted all attempts at definitive interpretation), and her need for rescue by Britomart indicates that the actively desiring heroine possesses something that she does not. Of all the women associated with the virtues in the central books of the work, only one, Florimell, completes her story and achieves her desire. She appears at first as if she exemplified the infinitely desirable but undesiring woman, as one man after another pursues her, from Arthur to casual rapists; but she too, like Britomart, is in fact in quest of the man she loves.

Spenser allows Britomart to cross-dress to give an emblematic representation of the active virtue of romance love. The women warriors who had preceded her in English (Grisandol of the prose *Merlin*, Ide of *Huon*) were martial virgins rather than questing lovers, but there were other models of women who had adopted a less military male disguise to find or assist the men they loved, and who helped to prepare the way for Britomart, and indeed for Shakespeare's cross-dressing heroines. *Clyomon and Clamydes*, one of the few surviving English romance plays of the 1570s, provides such a heroine, and enlarges her role from that provided for her in its source, the recent print of the fourteenth-century French *Perceforest*.[87] The heiress to the Kingdom of the Strange Marshes finds Clyomon lying exhausted and seasick on the shore, nurses him, back to health, falls in love with him and soliloquizes about it; when she is kidnapped by a rival suitor, she devises her escape so that she can seek him out in male disguise; and she arranges the scene of her revelation to him. She is the main agent in the fulfilling of their love, and the most ardent expressions of love are all hers. On this evidence, Elizabethan dramatic romance took such a woman as its generic centre, and Spenser did not need to look to any general English acquaintance with Ariosto to set the expectations of his readers.

That very establishment of a horizon, however, enables its resetting. The gender confusions in Sidney's *Arcadia* are much more disturbing, not least because they do not have any such traditional value behind them and do not acquire any inherent value of their own. The implications of gender differences are to an extent the raw material of the work, and especially in the love-tangle focused on Pyrocles—the man who disguises himself as a woman in order to get near his beloved lady (a scenario modelled on Spanish, not English, romance), but who is himself desired as a woman by her father, as a man by her mother, and as a woman whom she would like to be a man by the deeply confused Philoclea. In the revised version, for the purposes of his disguise as an Amazon, Pyrocles takes the name Zelmane, that of a woman who herself loved him and followed him in the guise of a page, but who never declared her love until she was on the point of death. She had continued to be restrained by her feminine self-effacement and modesty; he continues to behave with all the self-confidence of a man. His cross-dressing never amounts to an assumption of social gender. His aim is to place himself in a position where he can declare himself and his love; the complication is that the means he uses to do so, disguise as a woman, cuts down on his options, despite some heroic bear-slaughtering. The story is driven by the various characters' attempts to stalk or escape each other: Pyrocles perpetually trying to get time alone with Philoclea; Basilius trying to do the same with him; and

Gynecia determined to prevent either of them from succeeding. The principal desiring maiden in this part of the plot is Philoclea; but, although Sidney goes long and generously inside her mind, she is the least pro-active of all of these characters. The figure who occupies the role occupied in earlier romance by the pursuing heroine is here a woman in appearance only, Pyrocles–Zelmane.

Both the comedy of situation and Pyrocles' centrality are counterbalanced by the sympathy and detail with which Sidney presents the feelings of his desiring women. Basilius is not treated kindly at all (he is presented as something close to the conventional *senex amans* of the *Merchant's Tale* and other such fabliaux, the old man who makes a buffoon of himself through love), and Pyrocles himself has to go through the indignity of scornful mockery from Musidorus for both his subservience to love and his choice of such an ignoble disguise as that of a woman (revenged, of course, when Musidorus himself settles for playing the shepherd). Gynecia, however, is not a figure of comedy ('wit' in the following quotation of course means 'intellect'): she is

a woman of great wit, and in truth of more princely virtues than her husband; of most unspotted chastity, but of so working a mind and so vehement spirits as a man may say it were happy she took a good course, for otherwise it would have been terrible.[88]

The potentially destructive nature of her passion is evident both to Pyrocles and to herself, as she torments herself with the recognition that she is 'a plague to myself and a shame to womankind', and, more wretchedly yet, that she has no comfort except to place herself beyond shame.[89] Philoclea has none of her knowingness. Her own falling in love is presented as her first awaking to experience beyond herself—she is 'like a young fawn who, coming in the wind of the hunters, doth not know whether it be a thing or no to be eschewed'.[90] By the time she discovers, it is too late to resist. Sidney charts the growth of her desire, at first in his own authorial voice so that he can maintain the reticence of distance. She wishes that she and Zelmane might be sisters, or that one of them should be a man,

that there might succeed a blessed marriage betwixt them. But when that wish had once displayed his ensign in her mind, then followed whole squadrons of longings that so it might be . . . Then dreams by night began to bring more unto her than she durst wish by day, whereout waking did make her know herself the better by the image of those fancies.   (pp. 239–40)

Only once the sexual nature of her longings has been established does he give her her own voice, in verses and a soliloquy. Despite her belief that her desire for a woman must be both sin and shame, she finishes with a passionately willed acceptance of her love (p. 244): 'O my Zelmane, govern and direct me, for I am wholly given over unto thee.'

The *Arcadia* mounts an extended exploration of the complexity of human categories and roles across many fronts. Peasants and aristocrats are confused, not so much by Musidorus' adoption of a shepherd disguise as by the exemplary love shown by the ideal shepherds Strephon and Klaius—noblemen in disguise in the first version, but real shepherds in the revision. Gender definitions and roles are generously explored in the varying mix of masculine and feminine elements in many of the characters, in Gynecia and Pamela as much as in the cross-dressed Pyrocles. The relationship between desire and virtue is similarly complicated, by the 'princely virtue' of the would-be adulteress Gynecia, and the apparent perversion of the virgin Philoclea's love for an Amazon. The story, being a romance, ends by restoring social and ideological boundaries: Philoclea's love is not unnatural; neither Gynecia nor Basilius commits the evil of adultery; the irrational desire of the young lovers—a desire that in the first version drives Musidorus to the point of raping Pamela, and Pyrocles to overcome Philoclea's reluctance to yield to him—is finally contained within marriage. It is what the lovers have all been seeking, but too many of the dangers and disruptions along the way have had their origins within themselves for the happy ending of the plot to convey a secure sense of assured order.

'QUICK, AND IN MINE ARMS'

Shakespeare's handling of romantic love and women's desire requires discussion to itself, not so much because he is working from different models or with different ideas as because of the wide range of plays in which his 'passionate and pure' heroines are active. Many of the comedies he wrote before 1608 or so are drawn from classical models or Italian *novelle*, but, although those may provide him with plots (his 'matter', in medieval terminology), both the *sentence*, the *sens* or inner shaping that he gives to them, and his treatment of his material, are dominantly inflected by romance. 'Comedy', the dramatic term newly used in Elizabethan England for plays with happy endings, is Greek by etymology and Latin by familiar usage, and Renaissance theorists accordingly define the genre in classical terms: comedy requires low-life characters and low style, and has the aim of reforming the audience through satiric laughter. Shakespeare largely confines such elements to minor characters and subplots, and patterns almost all his comedies instead on romance. The two forms have in common a happy ending, but not a great deal else. In his romance redefinition of the genre, centre stage is taken by high-born characters, who most often speak in the high style of blank verse, and whose falling in what eventually turns out to be right love is treated as normative. Some element of family reunion and rediscovery is a widespread plot element of Roman comedy; but Shakespeare gives it an emphasis much more characteristic of the whole romance tradition. Similarly, his presentation of love in his heroines develops directly from that tradition's interest in both the outward actions and inward thoughts of the actively desiring woman, and it is her desire that keeps the plot on course towards its happy resolution.

By the time he was writing his late plays, his 'romances', he was calling overtly and directly on the full romance models of dispossession and restoration, transgression and atonement, and of an active and desiring female sexuality that has to be accepted and celebrated by the male characters of the play in order for the final happiness to be possible. These late plays none the less push very close to another generic boundary for the love-romance, that of tragedy. The closeness of the two was not a new discovery (witness the stories of Tristan and Lancelot), but Shakespeare on occasion pushed the genre over the edge: in *Romeo and Juliet*, in *Othello*. In those plays, he breaks the links between the heroine's 'passionate and pure' sexuality and the happy ending, between virtue and reward, to contemplate the bleakness of a world in which providential ordering is not in evidence. The last plays write supernatural guidance towards a final joyful closure back into the romance script.

The pattern for much of Shakespeare's comic romance is set in what may have been his very first play, *The Two Gentlemen of Verona*.[91] Its dual debt to both classical and medieval traditions is inscribed in the names of the two gentlemen themselves: Proteus, named after the changeable Greek sea-god; and Valentine, named for the favourite romance hero as well as the patron saint of lovers. The association with romance is confirmed in the second scene, when the first of Julia's suitors to be named is 'the fair Sir Eglamour'. The name would have received instant audience recognition, as the eponymous hero of a romance that maintained an inexplicable popularity from the fourteenth into the seventeenth century. Later in the play, this character (or another of the same name) enters the action, as a man who has sworn chastity in memory of his dead 'true love', and who is willing to assist the distressed Silvia in her escape from an unwanted marriage (4. 3). The disjunction between the roles assigned to him in the two scenes suggests that the resonances of the name were of more immediate concern to Shakespeare than full narrative consistency: the emotional world the play invokes is that of the native romances. So it is not surprising to find that the first soliloquy given to any of the lovers in the play is Julia's, in which she recognizes in her own actions the folly of love (1. 2. 50–65). Julia indeed has the bulk of the soliloquies in the play; when Proteus and Valentine speak alone on stage, they are much less likely to analyse how they feel than to comment on the action—Proteus on his betrayal of both his lady and his friend; Valentine on his alteration of state to that thoroughly medieval character, a forest outlaw on the model of Gamelyn (on whom more below) or Robin Hood. Neither of the women apparently initiates courtship, but both actively pursue their own choice of suitor: Julia by following Proteus in male disguise; Silvia, daughter and heiress to the duke of Milan, by first agreeing to elope with Valentine, and then, when that fails, by escaping to the forest from the unwanted marriage her father wishes to impose on her. The women's consistent faithfulness, to their lovers and to each other, likewise follows the model of the loyalty and uprightness of the earlier heroines of English romance. Valentine's attempt to hand Silvia over to his rival, by contrast, is an aberration by any conventions, and almost as gross a violation of her own freedom of choice as Proteus' attempt to rape her. 'All that is mine in Silvia I give thee', he declares, as if she were indeed a commodity, to be disposed of at his pleasure just as her father had tried to dispose of her to another suitor. That it is Julia who intervenes to claim her own right in Proteus contradicts the men's assumption that they are the owners of the women. As is emblematized by the rings they have exchanged, the contracts are mutual. The men—both the duke himself and the lovers—finally agree to the disposition of love and marriage chosen by the women.

The Two Gentlemen of Verona contains patterns of structure and event that are replicated many times over in Shakespeare's later works, but the plays and narrative poems that immediately followed it offer a broad array of variations on, and disruptions to, its generically central theme of love as ultimately controlled by women's faithfulness, rather as the various subordinate stories within the central books of the *Faerie Queene* offer variations on, and counter-models to, its Knight of Chastity. Even the barest summaries suffice to demonstrate this array; what should be emphasized is how much their presentation of women's love takes as its unspoken norm the desire of the romances. *The Taming of the Shrew* makes marriage overtly a matter of economics, and the point of the play is to show the hero riding roughshod over the woman's wishes, even if its fiction is that that is really what she wants; and the 'fiction' is emphasized—this is the one play of Shakespeare's that does not pretend to be 'really' happening, but never to be anything other than a play. *Titus Andronicus* almost defines itself as tragedy by its resistance to any romance models of loving women: it presents two female protagonists, one, the young Roman Lavinia, raped and dismembered; the other, the older Goth Tamora, sexually voracious and vengeful. The story of the original Lavinia was known to the Elizabethans from the *Aeneid*, not any derivative from the *Roman d'Eneas*, but Shakespeare's choice of name for the heroine is no less significant for being based on the more passive model of Rome's founding mother: the glory of Rome dies in her abuse as it had been founded on her predecessor's marriage. *The Rape of Lucrece* tells a similar story, in which the denial of a woman's sexual choice has political consequences as great as the *Eneas* poet's allowing of such choice. *Venus and Adonis* calls attention to the imbalance inherent in gender relationships, in which female desire, no matter how great, cannot compel the male; this goddess of love, in contradiction of the whole of western literature, does not carry all before her. Less concerned with its women's thoughts and feelings, and offering a measure of the difference between classical and romance comic patterns, is *The Comedy of Errors*, the play of Shakespeare's most closely modelled on Roman comedy. *A Midsummer Night's Dream* shows Helena and Hermia ultimately getting their own choice of partner, in the teeth of parental opposition, male capriciousness, and mis-targeted magic, but within the more questioning framework offered by Theseus' defeat of Hippolyta and Oberon's crushing of Titania's own volitions. And one comedy, *Loves Labours Lost*, sorts out a full four couples into desiring pairs but then refuses to end 'like an old play', or indeed like an old romance, by not giving Jack his Jill.

Romeo and Juliet looks initially as if it will most completely fulfil the romance model, of mutual love overriding all obstacles, and its faithfulness to such expectations for the first three acts (there is even, as in *Two Gentlemen*, a Friar Laurence) makes the disaster of the last two all the more shocking: this is a tragedy by virtue of being a romance with an unhappy ending. The mutuality of the lovers' attraction is given brilliant performative expression in the sonnet they share at their first meeting: a sonnet that is a rhetorical enactment of shared minds and shared desires, and in which the touching hands ('palm to palm is holy palmer's kiss') and the kiss itself become part of the reciprocating syntax of the action.[92] It is Juliet who speaks the most expansive of all Shakespeare's soliloquies celebrating a woman's desirable desire, the thirty lines in which she urges the sun's horses to gallop apace so that her bridegroom may 'leap to these arms, untalked of and unseen' to fulfil their 'amorous rites'.[93] (Thomas Bowdler, in his *Family Shakespeare* first published in 1807, cut it down to fifteen lines.) But *Romeo and Juliet* refuses the implied providential modelling of romance, replacing it with the sheer contingency of disaster.

Two of the great comedies of the late 1590s owe a debt to medieval sources more pervasive than the Eglamour and Robin Hood models of *Two Gentlemen*, and it is no accident that they also present two of Shakespeare's strongest heroines, both of them heiresses: Portia, of *The Merchant of Venice*; and Rosalind, of *As You Like It*. Portia's dead father extends his power over her disposition in marriage from beyond the grave, through the requirement that her suitors must win her by choosing the right casket: a story given wide dissemination through its appearance in the *Gesta Romanorum*, a collection of stories originally assembled in England in the fourteenth century and still a hot favourite in the Renaissance.[94] There, however, it is the prospective wife, not husband, who has to select the right casket, in order to win the emperor's son. The test, as the moralization appended to the story in the *Gesta* makes clear and as remains true in the play, is whether the suitors can distinguish between outward and inward value. Portia has already announced her own preference among her suitors, but she takes more of the active role of her prototype in the *Gesta* than might appear. Like those earlier romance heroines who pretend to submit meekly to their male relatives and advisers while actually engineering their decisions for them, she is not above nudging things along the way she wants them to go.[95] Bassanio might have made the right choice anyway, but it is the lady of the house who makes quite sure that he does so, and who then proceeds to engineer the trial to save the life of the friend who has made his wooing possible.

The immediate source for *As You Like It* was Thomas Lodge's pastoral romance *Rosalynde*; and Lodge's source was the Middle English *Gamelyn*, a story halfway between a Robin Hood ballad and a romance of dispossession and restoration. It had never reached print, but was preserved as an alternative Cook's tale copied into some manuscripts of the *Canterbury Tales*. *Gamelyn* itself, however, contains no love interest—no Rosalynde figure; and it has been assumed that Lodge made up that half of his story. In fact, it seems that that, too, has a medieval antecedent. The story of the young woman, dispossessed by her uncle, who flees to the countryside and there finds the suitor she had first met at the court, had figured in William Warner's bestseller *Albions England*, first published in 1586 and reprinted in a succession of later editions; and Warner had taken it from the history of England most widely disseminated in the Middle Ages and printed by Caxton, the prose *Brut*.[96] The origins of the story lie even earlier, in a legend most familiar now under the title of its independent romance version, *Havelok*. Both there and in the *Brut*, the heroine's usurping uncle forcibly marries her to the hero when he is working as a scullion, and she only later discovers his true identity as heir to the throne of Denmark and falls in love with him. Warner turns the story back into an independent mini-romance within his larger narrative. His heroine escapes from the court to the country in the guise of a milkmaid rather than be compelled to marry the kitchen knave, and she falls in love with him while he is similarly incognito in disguise as a shepherd: the story, in fact, doubles as a dispossession romance and a pastoral romance, and it is as such that Lodge adopts it. The rewriting also turns her from being the victim of a forced marriage to one of those feisty heroines who follow their own desires in marrying. Warner, like Lodge and Shakespeare, has both lovers fall in love spontaneously, and allows each of them to discover the other's true identity before they marry; but it is Shakespeare who has his heroine dominate the wooing after both lovers have fallen in love at first sight. In addition, he designs the play to offer an array of different types of love—not so much in this instance varieties of heroines, as varieties of literary love: the sub-Petrarchan art-pastoral sighings of Silvius and Phoebe, Audrey's yokel inarticulacy, Touchstone's appeal to the bird world to justify his own lust—'As pigeons bill, so wedlock would be nibbling' (3. 3. 74). The love that is presented as normative is that of Rosalind and Orlando, and the focus is on hers more than his. We encounter his stereotyped expressions of love not directly from him but through her own quicksilver reactions to the poems he has pinned to the trees. Her love is active, wooing, and both emotional and sexual: her early declaration that she sighs for her 'child's father', for the man she already imagines as her procreating husband, was censored for much of the nineteenth and early twentieth centuries into a sigh for her 'father's child', herself.[97] At the end of the play, she engineers a happy ending not only for herself and Orlando, but for all the other pairs of the play too. Her dominance is the major factor in ensuring the play's happiness: it is arguably the sunniest of all

266 The English Romance in Time

Shakespeare's comedies. By contrast, the loving and active heroine of *All's Well that Ends Well* finds a much more muted happiness, so much so as to require discussion later as an 'unhappy ending'.

The last plays present some of the most frankly desiring heroines in the whole Shakespeare canon, but the desirability of their desire often has to contend with intensely misogynist images of female sensuality (the subject of the next chapter). Miranda is both the most naïve and also the least contested of these figures: beyond Caliban's attempt to rape her, she has no knowledge of any wider social misogyny, and within the play she never has to learn it. She accordingly has no hesitation in offering herself to the man she has chosen as her husband: 'I am your wife, if you will marry me', she tells Ferdinand (*Tempest,* 3. 1. 83), and her father is sufficiently anxious over their mutual enthusiasm, despite their having done of their own volition what he had planned to bring about himself, to threaten them with perpetual wedded misery if they pre-empt the proper 'sanctimonious ceremonies'.[98] Perdita takes the frankness still further: after Juliet, she is Shakespeare's most openly desiring heroine, with her publicly spoken wish to have her lover strewn with flowers in an unashamed evocation of sexual ecstasy:

> like a bank, for love to lie and play on,
> Not like a corpse—or if, not to be buried,
> But quick and in mine arms.[99]

In some respects the lines confirm the recognition of women's desire that has dominated the first three acts of the play, but their tone and phrasing and meaning are at the far extreme from the distorted imaginings within Leontes' mind that have driven his wife to apparent death. *The Winter's Tale*, like *Cymbeline,* is deeply concerned with recuperating women's sexuality as positive, and finally with celebrating it—a celebration required if the play is to register as a romance at all, with the harmony required for its closure. There is no general claim, however, in Shakespeare's romances or in those of his medieval predecessors, that all sexuality is good. The story of Apollonius of Tyre, in all its versions from its fifth-century origins down to *Pericles,* shapes itself around a series of powerful exempla of right and wrong sexuality. The first couple to be introduced are the incestuous Antiochus and his daughter, a pair whose transgression of the natural is grotesquely magnified by the death visited on all those suitors who fail to guess the riddle they set—and indeed of any who do guess it, as Pericles' experience shows. Wrong sexuality, this time in the public domain rather than concealed within the family, is flaunted again in the episode in which Tarsia-Marina is sold to a brothel; though unlike her avatar, St Agnes, she preserves herself without any assistance from miracle or intervention from God. Yet interwoven with these episodes of the evils of wrongly used sexuality are others that insist on its inherent goodness. The other fathers of the play, Thaisa's father Simonides and Pericles himself, harbour nothing possessive, or jealous, or incestuous towards their daughters. Simonides wants nothing better than his daughter's sexual happiness with another man, and is delighted when she makes her own choice. Good love—good sexual desire— throughout the play is focused on Thaisa, the woman whom Pericles marries; or, to put it more accurately, the woman who marries him.

Thaisa herself is as forward and decisive in her choice of husband as any romance heroine. Her response to her very first sight of Pericles is to write a letter to her father, declaring that

> she'll wed the stranger knight,
> Or never more to view nor day nor light,
>
> (9. 14–15)

even while Pericles himself has barely seemed to register her existence. Simonides' response is equally decisive, and approving of her downright way of doing things:

> I like that well. Nay, how absolute she's in't,
> Not minding whether I dislike or no!
>
> (16–17)

and, after a pretence at anger with the young lovers interrupted by asides of delight, he chases them off stage with the couplet,

> It pleaseth me so well that I will see you wed,
> That with what haste you can, get you to bed.
>
> (112–13)

Their brief bliss is ended by Thaisa's apparent death in childbirth, a death which the audience, unlike Pericles, speedily learns not to be real. When they eventually meet up again, Pericles is unrecognizable after years of suffering, and she is a priestess of Diana. In a passage unique to Shakespeare, her response to the story he tells of his life is not to check his identity by means of a mole or a token (though recognition by a ring comes later), but by her sexual desire for him: if he arouses her 'sense', he is indeed the husband she has lost:

> O, let me look upon him!
> If he be none of mine, my sanctity
> Will to my sense bend no licentious ear
> But curb it, spite of seeing.

> (22. 48–51)

Her sexual instinct, in other words, will be sufficient for her to identify the man she loves; and they embrace, twice, in perhaps the most extended staging of loving physical contact required in the whole Shakespeare canon.[100] That the play is generally so exceptionally faithful to its source texts marks Thaisa's unprecedented means of recognizing her husband as being of key importance. The moment is none the less deeply faithful to the romance genre in which it is rooted. *The Winter's Tale* makes the recognition of the accused wife's virtue the condition that enables its final closure in restored order; *Pericles* makes female desire itself the agent of and authority for its ending in joy. To call it a 'happy ending' is here not enough: Shakespeare manages to achieve that hardest of all literary effects, an ending in bliss. How far that steps beyond ordinary human experience is measured by Pericles' belief, as a prelude to the vision in which Diana instructs him to visit her temple, that he can hear the music of the spheres, the music normally inaudible to humankind (as Shakespeare had noted in an earlier play) while 'this muddy vesture of decay | Doth close us in'.[101] It is as if Thaisa's faithful sexuality reverses the Fall itself.

Pericles is the play of Shakespeare's that has the least likelihood of any kind of topical reference. The story had changed remarkably little over the millennium of its existence. Shakespeare's own dramatization of the old tale—his dramatization, indeed, of the *telling* of an old tale, since the storyteller himself, in the shape of Gower, acts as its presenter—is rather a recuperation of romance itself. And with romance comes his most generous recuperation of female sexuality: of active female sexual choice as the well-directed and faithful will for good, and women's desire as desirable both to their earthly lovers and to the divine order.

CHAPTER SIX

Women on trial

Any glance at medieval and Renaissance writing about women outside
the field of romance is enough to indicate that its warm endorsement of
its heroines' sexuality had to contend with very different views. A long
history of clerical misogynist writings on one side, and vernacular fabli-
aux on the other, portrayed women as creatures of insatiable sexual
appetite, though the Latin writings interpret as a threat what the fabliaux
regard as a promise. Romances could not seal themselves off from such
attitudes. They were so deeply engrained in the culture as to be
inescapable, and the misogyny inherent in them is clearly audible as
background noise even in a genre that resists such beliefs. The romance
emphasis on women's sexuality invites antifeminist accusations from
contemporaneous thinkers who regarded virginity as the only good, or
from recent theorists not content with anything short of modern social
conditions and convictions as to the equality of women. Furthermore, it
has been argued that the 'fundamental definition' of misogyny is any
essentialist definition of woman,[1] and the generic quality of the heroine
puts her within that category.

That definition, however, itself essentializes a phenomenon that is far
more complex and nuanced than is often allowed for, and ignores the
contestations of it made from within the culture itself.[2] Many romance
writers clearly regarded themselves as entering into the wider debate on
the whole issue of women's goodness or wickedness, and they cast them-
selves in the role of the defence. Their heroines' transgression of
approved social practices in the pursuit of their own desires laid them
open to losing the sympathy of anyone in their audiences (especially, but
not only, the men among them), who might perceive such actions as
proof of women's tendency to rebellion. Scarcely any writer of romance
takes universal approval of these heroines for granted. Instead, the trans-
gressions recurrently become the nexus for competing discourses and
images of women, as the authors incorporate voices that offer resistance
to or approval of their narrative models. The rival arguments function as

a way of recognizing scepticism or anxiety on the part of male readers, sometimes in order just to relieve it, but often to mount an active refutation. The opposing positions are sometimes set out as formal intellectual debates; alternatively, the debate may be conducted implicitly, through examples and counter-examples built into the narrative. If a work is to remain within the parameters of romance, its final meaning, its *sentence*, must be one of approval: the text constitutes a kind of trial, in which the 'sentence' in the forensic sense exonerates the heroine. In some cases, debate indeed crystallizes into a trial, either in a lawcourt or on a field of battle—trial by combat.

In the set of memes at the core of these romances—the pattern most widely replicated, and to which other variations in plot are subordinate—the focus of debate shifts to an individual woman, most often a wife, who is charged with unchastity. She finds herself the exemplary model of the same debate, as to whether her sexuality follows a pattern of faithfulness or promiscuity. Her accuser is most often a man whose advances she has rejected, who aims to displace his own guilt onto her. Secular attempts at justice, especially if they are conducted by her jealous husband, may find her guilty; but providence or some earthly equivalent intervenes to prove her innocence, and to reveal the charges against her as deliberate calumny. The final outcome of the trial vindicates her claim of goodness, and identifies her accuser as the one who is guilty. Such a woman may not escape the further 'essentialist' charge, but the balance of the romances falls another way: the accusation against her carries weight because it is given credibility by culturally instilled misogynist beliefs, but her vindication amounts to a challenge to those beliefs. The fear and hatred of female sexuality implied by these stories is invariably presented as being irrational, sometimes even diabolical; and they are written to resist complicity with such beliefs, not to invite it. The motif of the falsely accused wife—the wife who is believed to be the protagonist in a story of adultery, but whose faithfulness demands a rewriting of the script—denies that the background noise of antifeminism has real content.

The general tenor of recent feminist criticism would offer a different interpretation of these stories, in which the heroine's innocence would be taken as an instance of the polarization of women into madonnas and whores, one woman's innocence confirming rather than questioning the whole structure of misogyny. The great majority of such romances, however, endow their 'madonnas' with a vibrant sexuality; and although their probity may have a heroic quality about it that puts it beyond the commonplace, it is not suggested that it is exceptional in itself. Even these stories, however, can make space for villainous as well as virtuous women, most particularly when the source of the calumny is not a rejected suitor but a mother-in-law, the woman who has been displaced by the arrival of the new wife. These characters are unequivocally evil, like the wicked stepmothers of fairytale,[3] and come to nasty ends. The issue that makes the mother-in-law a plausible danger is less one of jealousy of the younger woman's sexual hold over her son than resentment at her own loss of power and status: these women are always widows, so their sons' marriages mean marginalization, a fall from their position as the woman at the top of the court hierarchy, to a status largely dependent on sufferance. The young wife may thus be the target of either male desire or female envy. Both are dangerous, but it is the first, the accusation by a man, that immediately persuades her husband of her guilt. No husband, in these narratives, stops loving his wife because she is hated by his mother, but a word from a male subordinate carries a weight that women's accusations never do.

Antifeminism is an age-old phenomenon—Aristotle, 'the Philosopher' to the Middle Ages, gave a veneer of intellectual respectability to much wider fears of women—but the Roman Catholic emphasis on virginity as perfection provided particularly fertile ground for its growth, especially after the first millennium, when the Church began to require celibacy of all its priests. This movement helped to keep in circulation the writings of some of the Fathers of the early Church who had not only promoted the avoidance of all sexual activity but done so with a virulence against women that now looks pathological. These views never became a part of Catholic dogma, but they were none the less taken as authorizing later antifeminist discourses, written with varying degrees of seriousness but always insisting on the potential of women for replicating Eve's temptation of Adam and so separating Man (in the gender-specific sense) from God.[4] In the Middle Ages, the more extreme assertions of misogynist discourse were largely confined to a few texts that were particularly popular among clerics, not least apparently among witty young students; Chaucer may well have been representing fact by portraying his expert on misogynist writings, the Wife of Bath's fifth husband Jankin, as a former student of Oxford. Despite the recent attention given to such writings, they were never the only, or even the dominant, representation of women's sexuality, as the chapter above has argued. Even Latin works, moreover, often took the form of debate, for or against women—and although such debates operate by overt mass generalization, those generalizations pull in opposing directions.[5] Similar debates attained still

wider currency once they shifted into the vernacular and were dissemi-
nated through print, and they remained uninflected by the Reformation
approval of married clergy. A reading of the titles licensed by the
Stationers' Company in the second half of the sixteenth century shows
that debates on women constituted a substantial proportion of the read-
ing-matter of the period.[6] The vibrancy of the continuing life of the motif
of the falsely accused woman in turn testifies to the equal vibrancy of the
antifeminism that gave such narratives their point. The disproving of the
accusation, and with it the belief in women's fickleness that gives it sur-
face plausibility, also enacts a resistance to that antifeminism.

A fascination with sexuality in general and women's sexuality in
particular is shared by romance, fabliau, and the clerical discourses of
misogyny, though their portrayals differ radically. The timing of the
emergence of romance, in the century after Gregory VII began the
process of enforcing universal clerical celibacy, suggests that one element
in its rise may have been a secular backlash against the anti-sexual atti-
tudes that accompanied that imposition. Romance attitudes by contrast
embody and promote the vested interests of the great secular majority of
the population, though the genre confines its portrayal to the élite group
who have both major dynastic interests and also the leisure to devote
themselves to the development of sentiment.[7] Its authors do not invite
any sexual revolution—they accept that the public world is a male one,
even while recognizing that individual women may do rather better in it
than men; they never question the system of patrilinear descent that
made a wife's chastity a matter of crucial political and economic import;
and in a world without access to the technologies of contraception, there
could be no pretence that sexual liberation was desirable for women, even
if the whole ethical force of the culture had not been against it. There is
none the less a widely expressed resistance across all these works to any
sexual double standard, even though women are the target of much of the
prescription, and even though the definitions of the sexual standard in
question are as discrepant as they could be. The clerical texts promote
virginity for both sexes. Most romances, and English ones in particular,
demand faithfulness from their male as well as female protagonists. The
fabliaux portray (and often champion) generous unlicensed sexual activ-
ity for both men and women, and the figure most likely to receive unsym-
pathetic treatment is the inadequate husband. Wives, and more rarely
maidens, are here treated very much as sexual objects; and the only group
to emerge favourably with any degree of consistency is the young clerks
who are often cast in the role of roving lovers, and through whom the

stories are often focalized. Nicholas in the *Miller's Tale* and John and Aleyn of the *Reeve's Tale* would be the most familiar English examples of such clerical protagonists. Although many fabliaux, like Chaucer's own, were written by secular authors who worked in other genres too, clerical and fabliau discourses of women share much common ground, and the romances recognize and combat both.

Adultery is a hidden sin, and popular estimates of its frequency vary with changing cultural norms independently of whatever the facts may be. A reading of medieval fabliaux suggests a world of young women permanently on heat, and the propagandists for celibacy seem to have shared that fantasy. The Victorians, with their downplaying of women's sexual desire and the concomitant elevation of them as exemplars of purity, regarded the chaste heroine as the acme of Christian civilization. Young women of the technological twenty-first century assume that their premodernist forebears enjoyed the same attitudes to sexual liberation as they do themselves. All those, of course, are generalizations about recent as well as past eras, such as can be made only by ignoring rival attitudes in each age in turn. The fabliau view of the Middle Ages, for instance, is contradicted not only by the universal and unequivocal teaching on sexual morals from both ecclesiastical and secular sources, and by the romances themselves, but also by works such as Christine de Pizan's *Book of the City of Ladies* (itself printed in English translation in 1521), with its appeal to the everyday experience of women's faithfulness to set against the male chorus clamouring the opposite.[8] For the first time, however, advances in biochemical techniques of analysis now permit a factual picture of medieval and early modern rates of adultery to be drawn independently of such claims and counter-claims. Surnames, which were coming into use in England some seven hundred years ago, record a traceable line of paternity, or notional paternity. Mitochondrial DNA, inherited from the mother, records a traceable and factual line of maternal ancestry. Correlating one against the other therefore indicates the legitimacy rates of children born within marriage over that long period of time. A sample case study has been undertaken for a single English surname, with an estimated factor built in to allow for special circumstances such as parents' adoption of children or children's adoption of a stepfather's surname; but with that allowance, the analysis shows a remarkable 99 per cent legitimacy rate over those seven centuries.[9] It is only in the last of those centuries that contraception could have concealed the correlation between adultery and illegitimacy. Even allowing for generosity in the estimate for non-genetic acquisition of a surname, and even if the study is not taken as typical, such a degree of wifely faithfulness could not be achieved solely by oppression or male control; its result must still be read as an indication of how deeply women identified their personal integrity, their own *trouthe*, with their sexual integrity. Such identification can no less (or no more) be ascribed to cultural propaganda than can sexual liberation: both can become the self-fulfilling internalization of a contemporary paradigm of behaviour, and faithfulness has both length of endurance and multicultural breadth on its side. It is dangerous to read too much into a single case-study, even one that covers seven hundred years, and comparable research has not yet been undertaken for other European cultures. Yet it does offer striking confirmation that English romances endorse an ideal of wifely living and loving—purity quite possibly accompanied by passion—that was already in everyday practice.

THE CALUMNY ROMANCE IN TUDOR ENGLAND

Stories of falsely accused women occur throughout Europe and beyond, but they found particularly fertile ground in England, and it is possible that the particular romance form of the motif originated there.[10] This pattern of recurrence invites an explanation, just as the frequency of stories of rudderless boats correlates with an extensive coastline. Social practices and beliefs cannot be mapped with anything resembling the same precision; but one interesting correlation is with the rarity of romances of adultery in Britain. Outside Malory, the woman charged with adultery in English romance is overwhelmingly likely to be innocent. The genre is consistently associated either with courtship leading to marriage or (as in these romances of accusation) with the faithfulness of a wife within marriage: subject-matter that accords a positive voice to women's sexuality, and which insists on its compatibility with accepted ethics and social institutions.[11] The degree of social freedom allowed to women in Britain presupposes a broad male acceptance of their probity, and the justification of the accused woman offered by romance endorses such acceptance and gives it imaginative authority. A further, positive, correlation within English romance lies with the dominance in courtship narratives of active and passionate heroines. It is very easy, in a culture in which suspicion of female sexuality is so deeply engrained, to take their choosing of their own husband and their pursuit of him as evidence for the prosecution, for their readiness to desire other men too. The stories of calumny acknowledge the fear of such a connection, but ultimately deny it any substance.

Given the high value set in most cultures on women's chastity, it is inevitable that analogous stories from elsewhere should feed into the English tradition. One that was increasingly used to support the principle of the accused woman's innocence was the Biblical story of Susanna, which constitutes an apocryphal chapter (13 in the Vulgate numbering) of the Book of Daniel. Accused of adultery with a young man by the Elders whose advances she rebuffed, she is cleared only by the sagacity of Daniel, who is prepared to trust her integrity above male accusations. The story was given separate narrative treatment in Middle English and with increasing frequency in post-Reformation England, where her story was an acceptable Biblical substitute for saints' lives. Robert Greene thought it sufficiently saleable to write it in two versions: one about Susanna herself; the other substituting a lady named Isabel. It was dramatized around 1569 in Thomas Garter's *Commody of the moste vertuous and Godlye Susanna*.[12] All the versions culminate in a trial scene, in which the Susanna figure is found guilty solely on the word of her male accusers, and a providential (male) intervention is needed in order to save her. The play is acutely aware of the ease with which even the most upright of women can be calumniated, and of the evil of so doing: the Devil himself sends Ill Report, the Vice figure of the play, to betray her. It is, in other words, the work of the devil to destroy women's goodness through slander.

The meme of the falsely accused woman retained its popularity throughout the era of romance and into the novel, turning up in the most unlikely places (*What Katy Did at School*, for instance). A number of variants on the central model of the rejected suitor as accuser appear in the later Middle Ages and Renaissance. One that seems to be continental in origin, and reaches England only in the sixteenth century, is the husband's bet on his wife's chastity, most familiar now from *Cymbeline*. It was given its widest currency by one of the stories in the *Decameron*, and reached Shakespeare either directly from that or from its free adaptation *Frederyke of Jennen*, first printed in England in 1518.[13] That Shakespeare keeps the Italian context for the bet despite the British setting of his play suggests that the motif retained an alien feel to it, or at the least that he wanted to keep it alien. Another variant is not to have any external accuser at all: for the husband to generate all the suspicion himself. This too is most familiar now from Shakespeare, from Leontes in *The Winter's Tale*, but it was already familiar in the late Elizabethan era. The source for the play, Greene's *Pandosto* of 1588, takes the same form; and he used it again, this time with an urban setting, four years later in *Greene's Vision*. There, it constitutes the plot of a tale told by a dreamed persona of John Gower, as if such stories already carried something of the medieval about them—or at least, as if Greene wanted them to appear that way.

If narratives of calumniated women appeared at all old-fashioned around 1590, however, they reasserted themselves energetically over the next twenty years, and not least on the stage. Their most thoughtful practitioner, and the author to use them most extensively, is that promoter of the 'pure and passionate' heroine, Shakespeare. The motif evidently fascinated him; it may not be coincidence that he called one of his daughters Susanna. He bases five of his plays on it, plays that run the full generic gamut from comedy to tragedy but that focus centrally on romance: *The Merry Wives of Windsor, Much Ado About Nothing, Othello, Cymbeline,* and *The Winter's Tale*. The one consistent element in all these is the forcefulness with which the misguided men are condemned: it is they, and not the women, who are in the wrong. In this particular form of the antifeminist debate, Shakespeare is the chief spokesman for the defence.

He made further use of the motif in a sixth play: his Fletcher collaboration *All is True*, better known now as *Henry VIII*. As both titles indicate—this is recent history, and unlike the rest of these stories, it really happened—Tudor England had particular reason to be interested in such stories, for a reason that makes Greene's relegation of them to the medieval look like playing safe. Henry VIII had divorced one wife, Katherine of Aragon, after a trial that accused her not of unchastity but of not being a wife at all. He tried and executed two more, Anne Boleyn and Katherine Howard, after charging them with adultery: accusations of which both were found guilty. An accused queen who is not restored, like Katherine of Aragon herself, cannot look to a happy ending in this world; only God's justice can provide the reward her innocence deserves. Shakespeare accordingly incorporates a vision of such a heavenly afterlife into his own play, in which Katherine dreams shortly before her death of being crowned with heavenly garlands—a dream performed on stage rather than just recounted, so coded as true. He predicates the justice of such a reward, not only on what he has shown us of Katherine within the play, but on his modelling of her story on that of the falsely accused queen. He was not the first writer to have claimed such divine vindication for her after the failure of earthly justice: he was preceded by William Forrest, chaplain to Katherine's daughter Mary Tudor. Forrest's model was not the romances of calumny but an alternative widely known story of a wife's undeserved suffering and rejection by a near-psychopathic husband, the story of Griselda as contained in Chaucer's *Clerk's Tale*. The *Tale* itself has a happy ending, in so far as the husband takes back the wife he has pretended to divorce; but for Katherine, and therefore for Forrest and for Shakespeare, history refused to follow the model of fiction. Forrest, writing a text that was probably never intended for publication, casts Henry as a deeply imperfect husband, to a degree much more difficult for Shakespeare in writing for the Globe. The text of *All is True* indeed testifies abundantly to the difficulty of presenting both a good calumniated queen and a husband who is not a fool or a knave. Too warm a defence of Katherine of Aragon, moreover, would not only amount to an attack on the monarchal exercise of justice, but would bring Henry's second marriage, and therefore Elizabeth's legitimacy, into question.[14] Equally, too warm a defence of Anne Boleyn would call into question the operation of regal justice as it was to be exercised in her own condemnation. Yet Anne, the woman who replaces Katherine in her husband's bed and on the throne, must also be portrayed as good, and that presents even greater difficulty in a play sympathetic to the divorced wife. Anne is frequently spoken of by other characters as a woman prepared to sacrifice her morals to her ambitions, but her stage appearances are at odds with that, as if the play set out to enact the difference between defamation and inward truth. It stops with the birth of Elizabeth, therefore before Anne's own downfall; but the shadow of that hangs over the whole play, and it may too have inflected the reception of all the romances in which a queen and her baby are condemned by a powerful husband.

Elizabeth's accession tacitly confirmed her mother's status as the victim of calumny. Her claim to the throne was grounded on her mother's marital fidelity, at the very least up to the time of her birth; but, given the habit of reading loose sexual morals as an inherent tendency in a woman rather than as an individual act, what happened after that weighed in evience for her earlier life too. That Anne was indeed innocent of adultery at any point has not been seriously doubted by most modern scholars, and her guilt was far from universally believed at the time; but any sense that she might not be guilty could no more affect the verdict against her than, in the *Winter's Tale*, every other character's belief in Hermione's innocence can affect her condemnation. Archbishop Cranmer, who heard Anne's last confession, declared in distress to a confidant on the day she died that 'she who has been the Queen of England on earth will today become a Queen in heaven'.[15] Henry did not act as judge in person, as

Leontes does, but it is a distinction without a difference given his total control over the exercise of the law. He never seems to have doubted his own paternity of Elizabeth, but he did have his marriage to Anne declared null shortly before her execution, with the consequence that their daughter was declared a bastard, though she was later re-incorporated into the succession to the throne. The declaration that the marriage was invalid was not taken to affect the charges of adultery, nor the punishment to which Anne was liable. She was beheaded, at her request by a French swordsman so as to ensure the minimum of suffering; but the grimmer form of execution by burning at the stake was allowed by law, and was a real possibility. The frequent threat to burn an adulterous queen in romance may sound like a fantasy element; it was not.

Henry's matrimonial disasters are a salutary reminder that motifs familiar as fiction may take historical form too, and that what seems like fantasy, even escapist fantasy, can be dangerous or fatal when it turns into reality. *All is True* apart, Shakespeare no more overtly refers to the events of the 1520s and 1530s in his plays of falsely accused women than do the authors of such stories before that date; but those stories must have read very differently after those events than they had done before. It may not be coincidence that the most popular story of a calumniated queen written later in the century, Greene's *Pandosto*, has her die before she can be rehabilitated. Shakespeare rewrote the death to accord with the romance model when he adapted the work in the *Winter's Tale*, but Greene's variant on the conventional motif made his story powerful enough to remain in print, in various abbreviated forms, for almost as long as the parallel story of a vindicated queen in *Valentine and Orson*.[16] Yet, despite the happiness of the last act of the *Winter's Tale*, the similarities between the treatment of Hermione and the treatment of Katherine in *All is True* show Shakespeare's full consciousness of how closely historical events could match the romance stories of accused queens.

Pandosto may have been Shakespeare's direct source for the *Winter's Tale*, but there were other, older romances of calumny available to him as there had been to Greene. The fourteenth-century *Earl of Toulouse* was still being copied around 1500, and an analogous story appears in the Percy Folio *Sir Aldingar* and a traditional ballad;[17] *Sir Tryamour*, also fourteenth-century, was reprinted at least until the 1560s, and was still popular enough in the mid-seventeenth century to be recorded in the Percy Folio; and *Valentine and Orson* remained a bestseller for a couple of centuries after that. One curious feature of these works, including Shakespeare's, is their avoidance of naming the woman in the title.[18] They may be called after the husband who imagines himself wronged (*Pandosto*, the non-romance *Othello*), or the accuser (*Sir Aldingar*); the lost children (*Tryamour*, *Valentine*), or the wife's defender (*The Earl of Toulouse*), or a child who acts as her defender (the alliterative *Chevalere Assigne*, 'chevalier à cygne', and the related prose *Knight of the Swan*); or even her father (*Cymbeline*). The one exception is so illogical as to confirm the principle: 'Frederyke of Jennen' is the assumed name taken on by the Innogen figure of the story when she is in male disguise, the equivalent of Shakespeare's Fidele. The consistency of the avoidance of the woman's own name may be a way of endorsing her honour, on the principle that a woman becomes public property even by being spoken about; or it may point to the significance carried by these stories beyond the woman alone, to questions of the succession, or to the husband's growth through repentance—several of these narratives share features with the romances of atonement. Whatever man is named in the title, all the stories treat the male belief in such accusations as an aberration. It may be normal in the sense that a predisposition to such credulity is commonplace, but it is very far from normative in the sense of what *ought to be*.

The allegorical method adopted by Spenser in the *Faerie Queene* is particularly well fashioned to bring out the difference between those two, the commonplace and the normative. His narrative operates by presenting the good (such as Una), the evil (such as Duessa), and the evil disguised as good ('Fidessa'); the false accusation promotes a fourth state, the good perceived as evil (Una calumniated, by means of her promiscuous simulacrum shown to Redcrosse). When Spenser treats of such false perceptions, he sometimes writes in terms that emphasize the closeness of such falsehood to the stereotypical faithlessness of women themselves; but that closeness often seems to be deliberate strategy rather than an unconscious carrying over of preconceptions. The opening stanza of Canto iv of Book I is an example of where the most interesting reading emerges from taking the similarity as intentional, as being designed to wrong-foot the reader into an automatic antifeminist response that is then reproved. The reader—specifically the male reader predicated by Spenser in the Letter to Ralegh—is thus led to enact the process of blame and retraction that is itself the narrative subject. The stanza begins:

> Young knight, what ever that dost armes professe,
> And through long labours huntest after fame,
> Beware of fraud, beware of ficklenesse,
> In choice, and change of thy deare loved Dame.

It sounds like the conventional warning against women's unfaithfulness; but the context is the tricking of Redcrosse into believing that he has seen Una in the arms of another man, and 'change' here refers not to female changeability, but to male. The passage continues:

> Least thou of her beleeve too lightly blame,
> And rash misweening doe thy hart remove:
> For unto knight there is no greater shame,
> Than lightnesse or inconstancie in love.

Men's faithlessness, the passage suggests, is to be condemned as much as women's; and the first reason adduced by the poem for such inconstancy—by implication men's first excuse—is that they can cast the woman herself as blameworthy.

A woman's honour is fragile, 'frail' in Elizabethan English, because it is too easily subject to defamation, to 'blame'; but defamation lies in the speech of others, and there was little difficulty in destroying a woman by such means. Hamlet's notorious exclamation, 'Frailty, thy name is woman!', is followed by his insistence that even ice-cold chastity will not escape calumny.[19] The naming of women as frail was all too easy to pass off, or to receive, as the real thing. Romance, with the generic primacy it accords to women and to sexuality, and with its weighting towards the happy ending, needs to assert its own countering reality. Trial and debate were the central means by which it did so.

'I AM FALSELY AND WITHOUT CAUSE ACCUSED'[20]

A man's belief in his lady's unfaithfulness may seem to belong to a different narrative and psychological category from the motif of the woman's spontaneous and single-minded love, but many of the narratives of false accusation make clear how closely the two are related. A woman's desire for her fiancé or husband does not have the corollary that she will lust for other men too, but he himself may take it as evidence of guilt. A late example (*c.*1608) that makes the point clearly is John Fletcher's Philaster, who is asked by the heiress to the kingdom, in defiance of her father, if he will marry her. His first response, despite the fact that he claims to love her himself, is not joy, but a threat of trouble to come:

> How this passion should proceed from you
> So violently, would amaze a man
> That would be jealous.[21]

And Philaster is indeed jealous, though in this case the target of his jealousy is not only a boy whom his fiancée loves for his sake, but a boy who is in fact a woman in disguise. Feminine virtue is fragile not because of any inherent frailty in women, but because it can be so easily destroyed by the premisses of antifeminism itself. The romances accordingly ensure that their audiences are on the side of the woman before the accusation is made: her innocence and faithfulness are explicit in the narrative from the start.[22] Her downright dismissal of the approaches made by a would-be seducer in many of these stories is designed to provide further explicit evidence of her integrity that the husband, lacking a narrator's omniscience or a playwright's privileged access to private space, does not have. Yet an antifeminist culture creates the conditions in which a wife's desire for her husband can easily lead to a plausible accusation of adultery, even if that accusation is made in revenge or as a pre-emptive defence by the man whose advances she has rejected. Belief in her guilt, even within the story, is however in almost every case confined to her husband. The woman herself is surrounded by men and women who trust her probity but who lack the political power to support her, especially in those romances in which her husband is the king or emperor. He, by contrast, is all too ready to believe the lone male voices of accusation, taking their calumny as proof of loyal homosociality and confirmation of the truth of that background noise that insists on the depravity of women.

Othello gives the most extensive expression to the connection between the heroine's desire for her husband and his suspicion that she has betrayed him, and gives it tragic consequences. We are informed by Othello himself that Desdemona took the initiative in encouraging his courtship of her, and it is she who asks the Senate that they be allowed to consummate their marriage: both are Shakespeare's additions to his source, and serve to turn her into the kind of heroine familiar to English audiences, not least from his own plays.[23] Yet her insistence on following her own desires in defiance of her father is taken as *prima facie* evidence for a similar defiance of her husband, and her blithe indifference to the ethnic difference between herself and the man she loves is reformulated by Iago into evidence of unnatural sexual tastes:[24]

> Not to affect many proposèd matches
> Of her own clime, complexion, and degree,
> Whereto we see in all things nature tends.
> Foh, one may smell in such a will most rank,
> Foul disproportion, thoughts unnatural!

Sir Aldingar takes such an attitude to its extreme by having the wicked Aldingar put a leper in the queen's bed: the sexual perversion expressed in her apparent choice of partner itself becomes evidence against her. Yet *Sir Aldingar*, and the great majority of analogous stories, have the plotting and the lies revealed in time and their heroines justified. *Othello* does end with its heroine vindicated, but only when it is too late.

One thing about which *Othello* leaves us in no doubt is Desdemona's innocence. The villains, in the narratives and the plays of accusation, are the calumniators; the husbands (even Leontes, who doubles the part of husband and accuser) are treated as misled rather than wicked, and most get off comparatively lightly in the final bestowal of rewards and punishments. Only those who cause the actual (rather than apparent) deaths of their wives suffer punishments much worse than remorse: hence the suicides of Othello himself, and of Greene's Pandosto. Just one, the emperor of *The Earl of Toulouse*, is presented from the start as an unworthy husband. His empress, the beautiful and wise Dame Beulybon ('belle et bonne'), advises him rightly on several occasions when he makes both ethically and strategically wrong decisions, and his reluctance to forgive her for that[25] lays him open to believing the charge of adultery brought against her by two knights whose advances she has rejected, and who lay in her bed a young man they have murdered. (The evidence of a dead male corpse is taken throughout this literature as trumping the denials of the woman in the bed beside it: it never seems to occur to Lucrece, in Shakespeare's or any other version, that Tarquin's identical threat might not be taken as a proof of guilt.) The eponymous hero of the *Earl*, who has loved her from a distance, disguises himself as a monk in order to hear her confession and so confirm his belief in her innocence. Her worst sin, she tells him—and as he knows—is that she once gave the earl a ring. He duly undertakes a trial by combat to save her from the stake, and, although her husband is delighted with his victory, the real happy ending comes later, with his death, which enables the empress to marry the earl and for him to be elected emperor.

The alternative to a sentence of death for an accused wife is exile, for herself and her child: a scenario that makes for a bipartite romance, the first part about the calumny, the second about the chivalric adventures of the son (the *Winter's Tale* offers a variant on this, with its queen concealed rather than banished, and a daughter growing into love rather than adventures). *Sir Tryamour* and *Valentine and Orson* both follow this pattern, though whereas *Sir Tryamour* ends as soon as the family is reunited, the prose versions of *Valentine* extend the careers of the children forward to encompass the whole of their lives too. Its earlier metrical form had followed the more typical scheme of calumny and restoration,[26] expectations familiar enough for the long prose redaction to be later cut back to fit them: the Percy Folio *The Emperor and the Child* comprises a summary retelling in couplets that manages to get the introduction of the characters, the failed attempt at seduction, and the seducer's false accusation into its first twenty lines.[27] The prose *Valentine* makes the most of its expansiveness not only to continue the story beyond the reunion of the family but to spell out the implications of all these events. Its heroine is empress of Greece and the sister of King Pepin of France; her calumniator is an archbishop who also acts as the emperor's principal adviser. Her rejection of his advances is unequivocal, on grounds in which earthly and heavenly considerations make unanswerable claims:

Never please it God that the bloud of Fraunce from the which I am extraught, nor the maiestie of the puissant Emperoure, be shamed nor dishonoured by me in any maner. O false and cursed man, beholde what thou woulde do, that will dispoyle and unclothe me of myne honour, and put my body in vytuperable shame for ever, and my soule in the waye of dampnacion eternall.[28]

Just as bodily clothing is the outward sign of status, so honour is the clothing of the soul, and to be stripped of it, 'dispoyled', is a fall in the sight of both men and God. She threatens to tell the emperor, however, only if the archbishop renews his suit: a threat that gives him the opportunity to cut off danger from himself by accusing her both of adultery and of plotting her husband's death. The emperor accords the story instant belief, for 'he had his trust in hym more than in any man of the worlde' (p. 18). He assaults his wife, who is pregnant, and threatens to have her burned. Only his barons' urging of the risk of political recriminations from King Pepin makes him change his mind, to exile her instead. In the event, however, male trust is just as strong between the emperor and the king as it is between emperor and archbishop. Even though Pepin is told the story of her banishment by the faithful squire who has accompanied her into exile, he still takes her husband's part rather than his sister's, endorsed as it is by the long tradition of condemning all women in Eve:

Of as muche holde I the Emperoure more folysher, because he made not my syster dye, for by the God almighty, if I had her here at this present time, I should never reste til that I hadde made her dye an evil death . . . . Ha veray God almighty (sayd he) howe often is man deceived by woman.   (p. 35)

The empress's innocence is finally accepted only when the archbishop is defeated in full judicial combat by a merchant who had come upon him attempting to rape her as she journeyed into exile, and who later accuses him before the emperor.[29] The archbishop is defeated, and condemned to be boiled in oil; but by that time the empress's whereabouts are unknown, and her children lost—one, Valentine, to be brought up in ignorance of his lineage by King Pepin; the other, Orson, reared by a bear.

These stories of empresses and queens are almost by definition dynastic. The rediscovery and restoration of the calumniated wife are generically inseparable from the rediscovery of the lost heirs. The monarch's folly in believing his wife unfaithful potentially deprives his realm of its future stability, and the story necessarily continues until the children as well as the wife have been recovered. If the descent of the crown is not an issue, there is no need, within the narrative economy of the story, for the accused wife to be pregnant. Leontes' purposes require the exposure of Perdita as a corollary of his accusation of her mother; the purposes of the narrative require the baby to exist because of the death of Mamillius, which leaves her as the only heir. In *Cymbeline*, by contrast, Innogen is not pregnant, since, although she appears to be heiress to the crown of Britain, the rediscovery of her long-lost brothers diverts the line of descent back to them. In the related events of *Henry VIII*, the inconvenient existence of an heiress in the shape of Katherine's daughter Mary is passed over in almost complete silence, in order to allow space for the celebration of her new half-sister Elizabeth. Stories that are concerned with a prospective bride rather than a wife likewise bypass the question of succession, since there are no children in existence, and the man has the possibility of marrying someone else instead—though the generic shaping of these stories still calls for his reconciliation with the defamed woman. This is what happens to Una and Redcrosse, after Archimago has fooled him into thinking he has seen her in the arms of another man. Spenser's allegory does not require a failed seduction attempt on Una herself on Archimago's part; his desire here is to injure Una rather than seduce her, and to injure Redcrosse through her. The issue is accordingly not one of offspring, but of 'honour', in the sense of the need for outward appearance and reputation to match the truth of what lies inside; and in Una's case, importantly, it is Truth that she personifies. Calumny always threatens to write a woman out of social existence; it threatens to erase Una altogether.

Una is an heiress—the heiress to humankind, though that has a theological rather than a social or political meaning, and it is not an issue in the calumny episode. Spenser does not claim that all the daughters of Eve are recuperated by her integrity. In her standing as prospective bride rather than wife, Una has more in common with the protagonists of stories of false accusation set lower down the social scale, including those who follow her later in the *Faerie Queene*. The account of Phedon and Claribell (in II. iv) is the most detailed of these. The story is the same as that of *Much Ado About Nothing*, of the fiancée whose maidservant, dressed in her mistress's clothes, is shown to her betrothed in a compromising position with another man. Unlike Hero, however, who is finally married to Claudio after her reported death and return, Claribell is killed by her outraged lover, who then murders her calumniator too, and attempts to murder the maid.[30] Guyon's warning to him against 'intemperaunce' (II. iv. 36) is, in the circumstances, excessively mild. The stories of Una and Claribell show how easily the generic shaping of the motif of the falsely accused woman can fall either towards romance, or towards tragedy—the shaping of *Much Ado*, or of *Othello*. Greene's *Pandosto* has a tragic trajectory, with the death of the wife and the suicide of her husband after he has lived to lust incestuously for his own unrecognized daughter. The permeability of the boundary between the two genres does not necessarily require large shifts of plot. It often depends on a subordinate narrative detail that is entirely outside the woman's control: the detection of the calumny, and its timing. It is subordinate, not because it is not important to the plot, but because these romances never read like detective stories. The precise means whereby her innocence is discovered does not much matter, just as the initial evidence is usually very thin. Rationality is overridden by passion in such accusations, as the inclusion of the story of Phedon in the Book of Temperance asserts, and it takes something more than protests by either the lady or her supporters to correct the image of women in the mind of the man who thinks himself deceived. He is much more likely to be affected by an evident intervention of Providence: the oracle of the *Winter's Tale*, disbelief of which on Leontes' part is immediately followed by the death of his son; the hound that runs into the court in *Sir Tryamour* to tear the throat out of the man who had accused the queen and killed its master for his support of her;[31] or the seeming 4-year-old child, perhaps an angel, who defeats the wicked Sir Aldingar in combat.[32]

Shakespeare found the calumniated woman one of the most fertile memes in the whole of romance, but he plays numerous variations on the elements peripheral to that central figure. Only in *Cymbeline* does he have the calumny originate with an unsuccessful seducer, and that is

Iachimo, who has reasons for attempting the seduction (the bet with the husband) quite independent of any desire for Innogen herself. Other calumnies are motivated by a desire to damage the husband more than the bride or wife: Don John wants to injure the man who was instrumental in his own defeat; Iago hates Othello for reasons that go beyond his casual and unsustained mention of the possibility of his general's having slept with his own wife. Their plots require rather less material evidence than a corpse in the lady's bed: in these plays, the husband or fiancé can be persuaded of her fall from virtue with frightening ease. Claudio has the excuse of scarcely knowing Hero, but Othello runs ahead of Iago (he has to be reminded about the proof supposedly offered by the handkerchief), Posthumus is convinced of Innogen's guilt well before Iachimo reaches his punch line about the mole on her breast, and Leontes generates his own accusation without the need for any external persuasion at all. The range of variations Shakespeare plays on the false accusation, in terms both of generic shaping and of his analysis of the power dynamics that sustain the charge and the psychology of the reactions to it, is unmatched by any other writer. The one element he carries over directly and without question is the woman's innocence. The husbands' suspicions are consistently presented, as in the medieval romances, as irrational aberration. The antifeminist voices occasionally heard in authorial comments in the earlier romances are here put in the mouths of characters who are unequivocally *wrong*.

Shakespeare's most light-hearted treatment of the motif is also his first, and it largely falls outside the 'romance' category for very different reasons from the tragic shaping of *Othello*. His only comedy to have an unequivocal English location, *The Merry Wives of Windsor* (of 1597) is too local and contemporary, too middle-class, and too funny to bring romance to mind; yet both its main plot, of the overturning of Ford's conviction of his wife's unfaithfulness, and the subplot, which concerns the junior heroine's engineering her marriage to the man she loves in defiance of the rival choices made by her mother and her father, are drawn from romance models with appropriately strong English associations. It is one of Shakespeare's plays that has no known single source; its major plot line, of the clever wife fooling her husband, was widespread in Italian *novelle*, but very few such stories show the wife as faithful. The assumption of women's integrity is so rare in that tradition as to mark Shakespeare's treatment as deriving from elsewhere, and the obvious 'elsewhere' would be English romance, in keeping with the play's English setting. The treatment of the plot, by contrast, conforms not to romance models but rather to classical conventions of comedy, in its social level, its corrective ridicule of folly, and its stereotypical characters of citizens, bawd, parasite, and braggart soldier.[33]

The combination of classical comedy with a romance-style plot of false accusation was not completely new: Nicholas Udall had used it for the first formal comedy in English, *Ralph Roister Doister*, written probably in 1552 for performance before the young Edward VI by the boys of the Windsor choir school. There, the defaming of the heroine threatens to have more serious consequences for her than one ever imagines for her Windsor successors. The play's eponymous braggart-parasite, a figure not unlike Falstaff, attempts to force marriage on a rich young widow while her betrothed is away on business. Her probity is written into her very name, Christian Custance: a name that links her with another accused good woman from English tradition, the Custance (Chaucer's own form for Constance) of the *Man of Law's Tale*. Her fiancé hears rumours of what is going on, and refuses to believe her own account of her innocence when he returns. Like her namesake in Chaucer, she turns to God to help her:

> Thou didst help Susanna, wrongfully accused,
> And no less dost thou see, Lord, how I am now abused.[34]

Her reputation and marriage are saved, not by God, but by a man who is a friend of both of them, and whose assurances of her faithfulness her betrothed is happy to accept. There is never any suggestion that her future husband might be at fault in giving more credit to a male friend than to the woman he supposedly loves, or indeed in weighing the fatuous courtship of Roister Doister more heavily than her own integrity. In that particular respect, the *Merry Wives* is distinctively different: the jealous Master Ford is made the object of ridicule, the trusting Master Page is presented as admirable. In keeping with his practice in his later treatments of analogous plots, Shakespeare consistently censures the folly—increasingly, the criminal folly—of the men who cannot recognize female integrity when they see it. There is no positive evidence that he knew *Roister Doister*, and the familiar traditions behind the meme of false accusation mean that he would not have needed to. The common assumptions made by the plays concerning the good sense of women and the various kinds of folly of the men suggest that both élite and more popular audiences were receptive to such representations—that they formed part of an accepted horizon of expectation.

It was the other and nastier expectations about women that made these plots possible. The action of the *Merry Wives* shows both the easy social freedom enjoyed by its eponymous wives, and also the dependence of that freedom on the assumption that married women will use it responsibly. The wives are outraged by Falstaff's belief that they might be susceptible to his advances, quite apart from the fact that he has propositioned them with identical letters. The play turns its criticism on Falstaff, for believing that the wives' openness, their 'familar style', amounts to a 'leer of invitation' (1. 3. 40–1); on Master Ford, for his willingness—indeed, his determination—to believe that his wife will respond to those seduction attempts; and on the various unsuccessful suitors to Anne Page, for their self-deception as to their own desirability. The audience is never in the slightest doubt that Mistress Ford is well able to look after herself, but her husband's rhetoric of jealousy is none the less disturbing, not least in the way it shifts so easily from the singular to the plural, the grounding of one woman's perceived guilt in the guilt of the entire sex:

Who says this is improvident jealousy? My wife hath sent to him, the hour is fixed, the match is made. Would any man have thought this? See the hell of having a false woman! . . . Then she plots, then she ruminates, then she devises; and what they think in their hearts they may effect, they will break their hearts but they may effect. God be praised for my jealousy!   2. 2. 278–81, 294–8

That last phrase keeps the speech safely on the side of comedy, but the plays that deal with jealousy more seriously show the same shift from individual accusation to its broad misogynist context in much more dangerous ways. It takes only a few lines for Othello to move from his first conditional questioning of Desdemona's possible unfaithfulness to a condemnation of the uncontrollable appetites of 'these delicate creatures' (3. 3. 272–81), or Leontes from a conviction of his wife's adultery with Polixenes to a claim that there is

> no barricado for a belly; know't;
> It will let in and out the enemy
> With bag and baggage: many thousand on's
> Have the disease, and feel't not.
>
> *Winter's Tale* 1. 2. 205–8

And Posthumus is still more explicit in his extension of his new-found hatred of his wife and his conviction of her unchastity to the viciousness of all women:

> There's no motion
> That tends to vice in man but I affirm
> It is the woman's part.
>
> *Cymbeline* 2. 5. 20–2

The movement of these speeches is from the individual to the general, whilst the subtext runs the other way: from a pre-existent image of Woman as the source of all evil to a casting of even the most familiar and beloved of women in that image. The hatred of the whole sex leads easily enough into a hatred of all sexual activity, expressed in the ugliness of the sexual imaginings associated with these fantasies of betrayal:

> O all the devils!
> This yellow Iachimo in an hour—was't not?—
> Or less—at first? Perchance he spoke not, but
> Like a full-acorn'd boar, a German one,
> Cried 'O!' and mounted.
>
> *Cymbeline*, 2. 5. 13–17

This is language differentiated in every detail from the rhetoric of mutual love of the romances that celebrate sexuality, and where that celebration is confirmed and endorsed by its syntactic mimesis.[35] Yet these plays make clear, before we hear any of the husbands' speeches, that their rhetoric of jealousy is fantasy: language has become separated from substance, from the actuality of the chaste and faithful wife. The calumnies get their power not from any authority in an external accuser but from a programme of beliefs already instilled in the husband. The ease with which 'she' converts into 'they', the loving wife into the whole promiscuous tribe of women, shows the replication of a meme at its most dangerous. It does not matter that the casting of women as sexually insatiable is untrue: the notion is endemic, and replicates with all the speed and vigour of HIV.

The intensity of such a rhetoric of jealousy is a measure of the irrationality of these beliefs, and that irrationality makes it impossible for the women to refute the accusations against them. When Claudio accuses Hero of unchastity in *Much Ado*, he takes her blushes as evidence of hypocrisy, the 'show of truth' with which 'cunning sin' can cover itself, or alternatively as 'guiltiness, not modesty' (3. 5. 35–6, 42). Asked whom she has talked with, and required to answer 'if you are a maid', her denial— 'I talked with no man at that hour, my lord'—leads her straight into the trap Claudio has set for her:

> Why, then you are no maiden.

> 3.5.89

The immediate reaction of her father is to accept the truth of the charge made by the men—'Would the two princes lie? and Claudio lie?'—and he, as the man still responsible for her in her unwedded state, is given the strongest rhetoric of repudiation in the play, of her 'foul tainted flesh' (4.1.44). He is brought to a more moderate response by another man, the Friar; only Benedick is convinced by a woman's own conviction, Beatrice's. In the plays in which the supposedly injured husband has more power, the accused wife has no hope of redress. As in the romances of calumniated empresses—and therefore including the lost 1590s dramatizations of *Valentine and Orson*—the husband acts as both prosecutor and judge, and any legal trial the woman undergoes is an outward formality to confirm a guilty verdict decided long before. Shakespeare has Hermione sum up the hollowness of such a process at her own trial in the *Winter's Tale*:

> Since what I am to say must be but that
> Which contradicts my accusation, and
> The testimony on my part no other
> But what comes from myself, it shall scarce boot me
> To say 'Not guilty'. Mine integrity
> Being counted falsehood shall, as I express it,
> Be so received.

> 3.2.21–7

Her appeal to her own past faithfulness and obedience is indeed dismissed as another instance of the 'impudence' that made her unchaste in the first place. Katherine of Aragon's speech in defence of her wifehood at her own trial in *All is True*—a speech based on historical record—similarly asserts her integrity even while acknowledging that she has no power to affect a verdict already reached. When the nominal judges invite her to address the court, she crosses the stage to her husband and speaks to him; but he remains silent.[36] Her removal is necessary in order to make way for the birth of Elizabeth, but the play does not allow that to overwrite the injustice of the proceedings against her.

Cymbeline takes one extraordinary further step, beyond any other of these plays, in having Posthumus forgive his wife and accept her sexuality even while he still believes she is guilty. Like Phedon and Othello, he has killed her, or rather believes that he has had her killed; but he recognizes that the act was not one of justice, and that justice can only be satisfied through his own death—a worthless life for her own 'dear life'[37]—before he knows that his original verdict was wrong.

> Gods, if you
> Should have ta'en vengeance on my faults, I never
> Had lived to put on this; so had you saved
> The noble Innogen to repent, and struck
> Me, wretch, more worth your vengeance.

> 5. 1. 7–11

It looks unprecedented; but it, too, has one notable romance antecedent, in *Amadas et Ydoine*—a work that also provides the only precedent for the false insistence to the audience in the *Winter's Tale* that the heroine is indeed dead. Other characters often suffer such a misapprehension, but everywhere else, as in *Cymbeline*, it is known by the audience to be wrong. Shakespeare did not have access to *Amadas*; but that two such exceptional variations on familiar conventions should be found in a single early Anglo-Norman romance and his own romances shows how similarly two authors of intense generic alertness, writing three or four centuries apart, could widen out the horizons of their material. Ydoine is, uniquely, her own calumniator: she slanders herself on her deathbed in order to persuade the suicidal Amadas to stay alive to pray for her soul, stained as she declares it to be with the sin of an earlier affair. She maintains none the less that her only true love is for him, and it is Amadas' belief in this that is tested by the strange supernatural knight whom he encounters at her grave. The knight not only claims that he was the man she loved, but to prove it shows him on his own finger the ring that Amadas had given her:[38] an ocular proof far stronger than the handkerchief that convinces Othello. Amadas initially responds with a predictable (and in the circumstances, one feels, more justifiable than usual) outburst against the fickleness of all women. Yet despite having been persuaded by her own words of her previous bloodstained sexual history, his belief in the truth of her love for him reasserts itself, and he fights the combat of his life in defence of that. The plot details make Posthumus' bet on his wife's chastity in *Cymbeline* and his decision to have her murdered look positively plausible by comparison; but the inner *sentence* of both stories is closely similar. That a woman's active sexuality, even affairs with other men, does not necessarily deny her love or destroy her integrity; that acceptance of that is itself the greatest test of a man's love; that the passing of that test is in turn rewarded with the discovery that his beloved is chaste after all; and that all those together can fittingly call her back from the dead—in all those claims, one of the most thoughtful early romances, by an anonymous Anglo-Norman poet, and one of the last romances to be written within the same tradition, by the greatest English writer of all time, touch hands. They make what seems a surprisingly modern claim, that misogynist views of women as sexual beings may be a worse evil than aberrant female sexuality; but they also insist that women are indeed true in loving.

IF WOMEN BE A GOOD THING, OR NO

Amadas and *Cymbeline* and *The Winter's Tale* are all deeply concerned with recuperating women's sexuality as positive, and finally with celebrating it, in order to achieve the harmony of romance closure. There is no general romance claim, however, in Shakespeare or in his medieval predecessors, that all women, or all sexuality, are good. Posthumus and the whole tribe of jealous husbands condemn their wives in the name of all women, and both the narrative and the dramatic romances ground themselves on the fact that they are mistaken; but the opposite position— that all women can be justified in the name of one good one—is never argued. Romances frequently offer the same process of generalization as the rhetoric of jealousy, from the singular to the plural, one woman to the sex at large; but, unlike the rhetoric of jealousy, they do not insist that their generalizations about women's goodness are universal truths. Women's probity may be represented as normative, but it is regularly set in opposition to other images of women, or examples of women, who come much closer to justifying misogynist ideas. This might sound no different from the customary spectrum of characters in any fiction into the good and the not so good, the attractive and the unpleasant; the difference lies in the habit of generalization that these women bring with them—that both the good and the wicked are treated as arguments about the whole sex, in a manner closely reminiscent of the madonna/whore dichotomy. Not the least significant point about such arguments, however, is the ease with which women can be turned, not just into generalizations, but into male debating positions. Even in romances, such debates can become explicit; but their frequent combination of argument with exemplar makes the process rather subtler than that might sound, since the illusion of autonomy possessed by any fictional characters gives the women at least an outward form of opportunity to represent their own point of view. The declarations in favour of women's integrity as the norm moreover qualify the antifeminism inherent in the debate.

The process is exemplified by the two stories contained within *Greene's Vision*. The vision in question contains a storytelling contest between Chaucer and Gower, their stories being designed to exemplify their rival views as to the value and function of literature, for entertainment or morality; but the narrative vehicles Greene chooses to conduct the argument are tales of jealous husbands. Gower tells a calumny romance (if its social level allows such a generic label), about how a 'gentleman of good parentage' casts out his wife on unprompted false suspicion, and how his discovery of her continuing (and implausible) devotion to him reconciles them. Chaucer tells a fabliau reminiscent of the *Miller's Tale*, with a setting in and around Cambridge University, about a feisty (though never unfaithful) wife, her artisan husband, and a student. No less a personage than Solomon awards Gower the victory, in a defeat of pleasure by homiletics. The moral that receives all the emphasis in Gower's story has to do with the supreme importance of virtue in women; the husband's folly and cruelty towards his wife receive little stress. That the debate over the nature of literature fuses with a debate on the nature of women is made further explicit by the inclusion of twenty frankly antifeminist maxims, 'sentences', spoken by Chaucer, as for instance number eighteen:

Women, be they chast, be they curteous, be they constant, be they rich, renowmed, honest, wise: yet have they sufficient vanities to countervaile their vertues.[39]

What is being argued out here is a parallel between the seductions of women and the seductions of literature.[40] Chaucer, the proponent of pleasure, takes the more cynical view of women, in keeping with his fabliau story, and denies any greater value to literature. 'Moral' Gower's more romance-like model argues that literature, like women, can have ethical value. It would be attractive to be able to assert that Greene is arguing that the recuperation of women, romance, and literature, and of romance through women and of literature through romance, go together and reinforce each other—that the virtuous but suspected woman offers a counter-model to all those theorists who declared that 'poetry', fiction, was no better than lies; but it has to be acknowledged that Greene's defence of fiction is half-hearted, just as the existence of the good wife does not turn the *Vision* into a pro-feminist work. The text is none the less interesting in that it offers such testimony as to the paradigmatic quality of the debate over women's virtue, the way it can subsume or serve as a vehicle for debates of other kinds. It is also interesting, for the larger scope of this book, that in that great literary decade of the 1590s, Greene should have chosen for his defence of literature a form that belongs to the newly-emerging discourse of medievalism, the conscious revival of the past, and chosen competing generic representations of women's sexuality to fill it.

Romances did not need to look outside their own boundaries, however, to find counter-models to their good women, and the ones they contain are much more dangerous than the lively wives of fabliau. One such figure who has her own niche as a meme in romance is the wicked mother-in-law, who figures as an alternative to the unsuccessful seducer as the accuser in some romances of calumny. She can herself be regarded as a misogynist fantasy, but she is one who is as dangerous to women as to men: her target is by definition her daughter-in-law and the bond between her and her husband. Although her wickedness is presented as exceptional, the extremity of her treatment—which is much less natural-istic than that of male would-be seducers—is coloured for later readers by a knowledge of the ease with which such a categorization of old women who had outlived their social usefulness could in the seventeenth century accommodate charges of witchcraft. In these stories, however, although she may be presented as devil-inspired, her malignancy oper-ates through natural means. Her danger lies rather in her place in the heart of the household and family. The testing of her son inherent in her accusation challenges him to commit himself to belief in his wife, not in the face of homosocial assumptions of male probity, but by breaking his bonds to his mother. The husband is generally cast in a better light in these stories, in that he is at least reluctant to believe the accusations. The charges in any case commonly take a different form, not directly of unchastity, but of having given birth to a monster.[41] The mother thus avoids using the antifeminist clichés that might strike at herself too, but she opens the channel for an almost equally deep fear, to do with birth as much as adultery, though the two are closely connected: a monstrous child can be taken as a sign of an 'unnatural' conception. The wicked mother-in-law of the Knight of the Swan romances[42] abducts the queen's septuplets at birth and substitutes seven puppies, and then accuses the queen of bestiality with a dog. In *La Manekine* and Chaucer's *Man of Law's Tale*, the claim of a monstrous birth is known only to the mother-in-law and the absent husband, as she substitutes her own letters to him for those telling him of the birth of an heir. When he refuses to respond in the way she would like, she again substitutes forged messages, order-ing the wife to be cast adrift with her child. The calumny in these cases is bound to be revealed as soon as the king returns home, and he punishes his mother accordingly. The revelation of the wife's innocence in the *Knight of the Swan* is more difficult, since she herself has no idea that her true babies were stolen, and when faced with the evidence of the puppies can only plead her own knowledge of her sexual purity. The plot accord-ingly needs an intervention from Providence to resolve matters—a miraculous intervention in the secular world, though miracle and magic are not far apart in a story in which six of the infants turn into swans. The remaining child, who has been brought up by a hermit in the forest for the twelve years since his birth, does not know what a 'mother' is, let alone a sword or a horse; yet, when an angel summons him to defend his mother in combat, he overcomes the mother-in-law's experienced cham-pion, and all the bells of the cathedral close ring out spontaneously to cel-ebrate his miraculous skill.[43] The defeat of the mother-in-law, like the defeat of a male accuser, carries an endorsement by the story and by God of the rightness of the wife's sexuality.

That a mother-in-law should be jealous of her son's bride, and in par-ticular resent the usurpation of her power and status at court, gives a degree of psychological plausibility to such stories, but the romances are not greatly concerned with social motives. These older women are cate-gorized simply as evil; they are not exactly 'whores', in the modern phras-ing of the polarization of women, since their own sexuality is not an issue, but they are in the grip of the devil just as the young wives are preserved by God. The devilishness is explicit in the *Man of Law's Tale*, which con-tains two wicked mothers-in-law, the first a Saracen, the second (the calumniator of the story) a pagan. The latter is twice condemned for the specifically male vice of tyranny, and, in the rhetorical search for adjec-tives bad enough to describe her evil, 'mannysh' is first chosen, to be rejected in favour of 'feendlych':[44] her sex is not part of the accusation against her except in so far as she does not act *as* a woman—a formula-tion that assumes goodness to be a normal attribute of being female, just as 'womanly' is a virtue word (it can indeed connote *resistance* to sexual temptation).[45] The sultaness is described as being less a woman than the devil who tempted Eve—a woman only in appearance, a 'feyned wom-man', but in fact a 'serpent under femynyntee', recalling the recurrent representation of the serpent of the Fall with a woman's head.[46] This might sound like an expulsion of her from the category of women alto-gether; but Chaucer continues by connecting her to Eve, on whom the whole medieval debate on women was founded. She was chosen as his instrument by Satan because

> thou . . .
> Wel knowest to wommen the olde way!
> Thou madest Eva brynge us in servage . . .
> Thyn instrument so—weylawey the while!—
> Makestow of wommen, whan thou wolt bigile.
>
> *CT*, II. 366–71

Women, in the standard charge reproduced in these lines, are the gateway to the devil. The standard refutation is given in the *Tale*, too: Eve is counterbalanced by the Virgin, 'glorie of wommanhede' (II. 851), just as the evil of the pagan women is offset by the near-sanctity of Custance. The conflict between God and the devil is thus channelled through the debate about women. God, of course, decisively wins, but it is a story as much about the dangers of women as their virtue. Such a degree of polarization is unusual in Chaucer's work, but its causes here are generic, in the tale's closeness to the clerical discourses of hagiography. This is not only a romance but a romance on the border where it crosses into saint's life, where ethical and devotional exemplarity trump any romance push towards the individual. In contrast to most calumniated women, the various Constance figures are presented primarily as Christian women rather than wives; the *Man of Law's Tale* (in marked contrast to its more secular analogue, *La Manekine*) dismisses sex as merely an impediment to 'hoolynesse' (713). There is no reference to any particular love Custance holds towards her husband before their marriage, and though their reunion, and her realization that he played no part in having her cast adrift, brings the highest earthly bliss 'bitwix hem two' (1075), her rediscovery of her father and the restoration of the imperial line receives just as much emphasis, when she is slotted back into her place as the dynastic link between her father and her son. The story may be one of romance, but its fashioning consistently pulls it in the direction of hagiography and its accompanying ecclesiastical simplicities.

There was no need for a hagiographical bias for the devil to be invoked. Even when an older woman plays a subordinate role to a male villain in a calumny narrative, her activities may be described as devil-inspired as his are not. It happens almost as a reflex in *Frederyke of Jennen*. Here, after the character equivalent to Iachimo realizes he is going to lose the wager on the wife's chastity, he goes for help to an old woman because, as we are twice told, 'an olde woman can do that the devell hym selfe can not do'.[47]

She is the one who thinks up the trick of concealing him in a chest—though it is the man who receives a gruesome punishment at the end of the tale.

The Fall was the archetypal event that was commonly taken to mark women as tainted by the devil, but romances, including some that are less overtly committed to reaching a verdict on women's goodness, may invoke it with greater subtlety to refigure its *sentence* into something much more sympathetic to women. Heldris of 'Cornwall' first mentions Adam and Eve in *Silence* when the eponymous heroine's father describes them as the model of sacramental marriage. Later, a personified Nature and Nurture debate as to which of them is responsible for Adam's sin; Nature wins when she points out that God made Adam and Eve perfect, so it must have been the devil's nurturing of Adam that deceived him by means of the apple, 'par la pome le deçut'—Eve is left out of this part of the argument altogether.[48] Partonope of Blois goes further, when, after he has betrayed his wife's trust, he blames Adam outright for the Fall, but notes that he at least was able to keep 'hys love, hys wyffe', whereas he has lost his own—and lost her, moreover, because he was persuaded by his mother and an archbishop that she might be a devil in disguise. That the narrator was fully aware of what he was doing in this intervention in the gender debate is proved by his noting that 'olde clerkes' are fond of generalizing from a single bad woman to condemn the entire sex. The Wife of Bath was far from being the only character in the Middle Ages to be aware of the sexist bias of her culture, and of the clerical dominance in maintaining it.[49]

It was not just antifeminist discourses that were an immediate spur to debate; argument could be triggered by almost any representation of women. The passionate heroine's independence in choosing her own sexual partner can invite an antifeminist response, however firmly that choice may have marriage as its final aim, and romances often raise it as an issue at points where it is most likely to be raised in the minds of listeners or readers. Chrétien's *Cligés*, which tells with apparent full approval (explicitly in contrast with Isolde) the story of a young woman's managing to preserve her body for the man she loves even after she has been compelled to marry an emperor, closes with the statement that her skill at circumventing her official husband resulted in the strict control under which later empresses have to live. Ydoine's resourcefulness in manipulating the men around her invites recurrent denigrations of women's deceitfulness, and equally recurrent palinodes exempting the heroine herself from the general condemnation. Hue of Rhuddlan drops a series of distasteful remarks, often of a voyeuristic kind, into his *Ipomedon*, so that the desire shown by both his male and his female characters carries something of a fabliau tinge; and he ends by offering his services to any of the local ladies who care to drop around. There is none the less a curious disjunction between such statements and the treatment of the stories and characters, where the narrative tenor is strongly approving,[50] and it is the approval, not any irony towards it, that is carried through into the Middle English versions. Such comments read more like asides: a turning away from the story to make a joke to the audience, and especially to the men in the audience, perhaps to keep them on side in scenarios that risk their identifying not with the hero but with the fooled husband or the defied father. The comments recognize the anxiety, reformulate it as a topic not to be taken seriously, and deflate it in the process. At the same time, they recognize that the issue is not one that can be closed: that the debate will continue.

The Reformation made little impact on that continuing debate, or even on its terms: the same examples are repeated; the same authorities cited; the same polarization taken for granted. Almost the only change is that the denigration of women is more likely to be ascribed to 'some men' rather than to clerics in particular. This is how Sidney phrases it, when Kalander claims early in the *New Arcadia* that the princesses' excellence in 'all the gifts allotted to reasonable creatures' (a formula that itself insists on women's equal claim with men to rationality) is sufficient to counter the antifeminist arguments—though the metaphor he chooses to formulate the claim somewhat spoils the effect:

We may think they were born to show that nature is no stepmother to that sex, how much soever some men, sharp-witted only in evil speaking, have sought to disgrace them.[51]

The conflict between what those evil-speaking men say and what the princes come to believe is a theme not only for debate but for combat. The series of challengers to Amphialus in Book III of the *New Arcadia* includes one man who offers as 'the cause of his quarrel' that women are

the oversight of nature, the disgrace of reasonableness, the obstinate cowards, the slave-born tyrants, the shops of vanities, the gilded weather cocks; in whom conscience is but peevishness, chastity waywardness, and gratefulness a miracle.[52]

He is, of course, defeated; but the ideas on trial were not so easily overcome. The syntactic pattern of the passage, with its piling up of insults, shows Sidney's familiarity, not just with a tradition of antifeminist

vituperation going back over a thousand years, but with the same author-
ities who had underpinned it throughout that time. This definition of
women is a paraphrase of the views of the first- or second-century Greek
philosopher Secundus, popularized through a twelfth-century Latin ver-
sion and widely current in the vernaculars of Europe. To quote from a
text of 1530, woman is

the confusyon of man, a beaste insaciable, a continuall busynesse, a batell never
endid, mannis manciple, and to a continent man destruccyon.

The same text ascribes a further battery of definitions to St Jerome: 'The
gate of the fende, the waye of wyckednesse, the strooke of the serpente, a
noyable kynde is the woman.'[53] Sidney is still happy to present the most
virtuous and the most wicked characters in the *Arcadia*, the princesses
and Cecropia, as polarized extremes of women, but the work as a whole
sets the conventional terms of the debate at odds with the experience of
the narrative, testing theory against practice. The dual representations of
women are disputed between the heroes in the early stages of the work,
in a passage written for the first version and retained in the second. The
issue here is not so much whether essentialized woman is madonna or
whore, but whether her effect on the male subject is bad or good:

As the love of heaven makes one heavenly, the love of virtue, virtuous, so doth the
love of the world make one become worldly; and this effeminate love of a woman
doth so womanize a man that, if he yield to it, it will not only make him an
Amazon [a direct dig at Pyrocles' newly-acquired disguise, and a threat to which
Spenser has his macho hero Arthegall submit], but a launder, a distaff-spinner or
whatsoever other vile occupation their idle heads can imagine and their weak
hands perform.[54]

Pyrocles responds by bringing the debate away from abstraction: 'If we
love virtue, in whom shall we love it but in a virtuous creature?'[55] Sidney
is not content, all the same, just to oppose lovers against women-haters;
the princes' debate is shown to be inadequate, not only because their con-
clusions are simplistic, but because women live and think and feel in their
own right. They are not merely the objects of male love, or (as Gynecia
shows) summarily divisible into the good and the evil. Sidney may have
been encouraged in his exploration of such attitudes by the fact that he
was writing the work for his sister, but the romance form that he chose
was already pushing him in that direction.

The debate over women in romances matters because of the belief that fiction was persuasive: that it instructed its readers, not only by direct statement, but by the representations of the characters and actions that composed it. The contention exemplified by Chaucer's fabliau and Gower's romance in *Greene's Vision*, as to whether the function of literature was primarily entertaining or didactic, had customarily been resolved from classical times forward by the argument that its delight was merely a means to a didactic end. In medieval encyclopedic texts, poetry and fiction often appear as a branch of ethics. Any fictional, or indeed historical, characters are therefore likely to be portrayed as models to be imitated or shunned, and the tendency to generalize from women characters made them especially potent as such models. That is why the passionate heroines of romance are potentially so dangerous. Yet they are often set in opposition to other women whose ethical undesirability is much more obvious, and who by virtue of their existence underline the approval given to the independent-minded heroines. Many romances offer an array of types of women for endorsement or rejection, sometimes in extreme moral terms, but sometimes with a subtlety at odds with such absolutes.

The story of Apollonius of Tyre, in all its versions from its fifth-century origins down to *Pericles*, is the paradigmatic model of how the categories of female sexuality can be played off against each other. The story shapes itself around a series of powerful exempla of right and wrong sexuality focused on a series of women, but the 'wrong' sexuality here takes the form of excessive obedience to a father, and in turn highlights the rightness of the true heroine's independence in choosing her own sexual partner. The first couple to be introduced are the incestuous Antiochus and his daughter,[57] a pair whose transgression of the natural is grotesquely magnified by the death visited on all those suitors who fail to guess the riddle they set—and indeed of any who do guess it, as Apollonius'–Pericles' experience shows. Wrong sexuality, this time in the public domain rather than concealed within the family, is flaunted again in the late episode of the selling of women's flesh in the brothel. The contrast with Apollonius' wife-to-be helps to mark as unequivocally good the eagerness of the maiden who chooses her own husband and is prepared to defy her father to do so. The extremity of the bad examples also allows for a comparably extreme example at the good end of the spectrum, the fierce virginity of Tarsia-Marina as she resists the men who come to buy her, with its reminiscence of the legends of the virgin martyrs.[58] She finds herself as the chaste and virginal cynosure of all the lustful men of the city, and she preserves herself without any paternal protection, or assistance from miracle, or intervention from God.

Some romance heroines might seem to present especially undesirable role models, whether to young women or to their parents. The cross-dressed maidens who lead their lives as knights appear to be at the furthest extreme from the womanly obedience required of young women; the calumny romances would seem to be problematic in a different way, since they show virtue to be no defence against suspicion and ill treatment. The two issues come together in the Grisandol of the prose *Merlin* and her direct descendant Silence, both of whom are the victims of a gender-reversed calumny when a promiscuous empress or queen tries to seduce the supposed young man and accuses him/her of rape when her advances are rejected.[59] The empress of the *Merlin*, furthermore, is revealed as keeping a troupe of gigolots disguised as waiting-women; the queen of *Silence* has a lover dressed as a nun. Quite apart from their being condemned to death, these guilty women are presented as decisively unattractive in a way that insists on the loveliness of chastity, however strangely its proponents may be acting by the standards of normal social behaviour. Merlin himself, in both texts, reveals the truth about the various cross-dressings, but confesses even himself to have been deceived, since he could only be captured by a woman's wiles—in these stories, those of the maiden whose true sex he failed initially to recognize. Yet neither he nor anyone else condemns these particular wiles, and each heroine finishes up marrying the sovereign after the execution of the guilty wife. Despite his support for women at earlier points in the work, Heldris ends rather more equivocally, by insisting that good women are more worthy of praise than bad women are of blame since they have to go against their own nature to act well. He asks for approval specifically from the women in his audience for the praise he has given Silence, but although his whole narrative has been designed to insist that a woman can excel not only in her own sphere but in men's too, and therefore that the female deprivation of inheritance rights that set the story going must be reversed at the end, it avoids any revolutionary conclusions and withdraws into a model of containment.

Silence never made it into English; *Merlin* was widely known in France, but this section was not translated into English until the mid-fifteenth century, and Malory either avoided it or did not know it. English audiences were consistently more wary than continental ones of the actual practice of adultery (as distinct from a false charge of adultery) within serious secular literary forms, no matter how faithful, or how casual, the affair might be. If it appears at all, such love is most likely to make its appearance, not as a subject in itself, but as part of the whole array of different kinds of love offered, whether by intention or by virtue of sheer comprehensiveness, in the more capacious romances. All such works distinguish between good and bad kinds of sexuality, and therefore offer models of women to be followed or shunned, but the boundary is never simply aligned with marriage. The dividing line is most likely to be drawn between faithful sexual love, and casual affairs that involve no commitment of the heart; but different writers draw the ethical limits in surprisingly different ways, and there may even be no sharp division at all. The medieval term for such a comprehensive array was *distinctio*, a term that means the division of a complex whole or idea into its constituent parts; but that is not a binary division, and many romance writers recognize such a complexity both in love and in the women who embody or typify the various forms it can take.[60]

The *Morte Darthur* offers such an array of sexuality, though the comprehensiveness seems to be a consequence of the work's scope rather than being intentional on Malory's part. He presents a hierarchy of value in the various love-stories in the work, and the legalities of marriage have very little to do with it. What matters is that love should be true, singular, and faithful. There is no adverse judgement offered when Dame Lyonesse celebrates her new and immediate love for Gareth by promising to come to his bed in the hall; her younger sister's success in spoiling things is reported neutrally, though with the balance of sympathy falling towards the eager young lovers.[61] Lancelot likewise seems to be a good deal more shocked than Malory is by Elaine of Ascolat's suggestion that she should become his paramour, and Malory invents for her her moving speech in defence of earthly love. Like Spenser and the great majority of romance authors, Malory reserves his strongest disapproval for lust, physical desire without love, whether it takes the form of Gawain's sleeping with Pelleas's beloved Ettard while Pelleas waits in increasing anxiety at the gates, or Morgan le Fay's casual promiscuity.[62] Enforced sex is an evil, whether the perpetrator is a male rapist or a female seducer. Celibacy is presented as an overriding value only within the bounds of the Grail narrative, and even there much the most interesting character is Lancelot, the man who cannot quite renege on his love for the queen. Malory never commits himself to the position taken by his French Grail source, that all sex is damnable, even though he adopts all the female characters who turn out to be (male) devils in disguise. The very absoluteness of the demands of the Grail quest paradoxically helps Malory's sympathy towards love. The knights are required to leave behind their ladies of whatever marital status, and it is only the totally celibate (or the almost-totally-celibate: Bors, as we keep being reminded, has slept with a woman just once) who are going to succeed. To have a wife is just as much a disqualification on the quest as is a mistress, or indeed somebody else's wife. And so the fact that Lancelot's love is for the queen, not only married to another man but the wife of the king, would logically be no worse so far as the Grail is concerned than his liaison with Elaine of Corbin that resulted in the birth of Galahad himself. Malory accordingly never represents the fall of the Round Table as being due to Lancelot's affair with the queen; the people he consistently blames are Mordred and Agravain, the treacherous knights who speak open shame about the lovers even though they know that it will bring about the downfall of the kingdom. There is no virtue in speaking the truth when the motive behind it is malice and the results so catastrophic. 'Vertuouse love', in Malory's definition, is long-lasting love set on a single person, and Guinevere is its exemplar—'for whome I make here a lytyll mencion, that while she lyved she was a trew lover, and therefor she had a good ende'.[63]

Malory carries over much of this array of kinds of love from the *Lancelot-Grail*, but its particular inflection, and especially his refusal to separate godliness from devoted sexual attraction, is his own. Another derivative of the French prose romances, the *Orlando Furioso*, likewise presents a wide variety of kinds of love, but, as with Malory, the French and Italian writers of romance do not seem to have deliberately set out to present a full normative array of love: a comparable effect is more a contingent result of their multiplication of love-narratives. Sir Philip Sidney, by contrast, seems to have moved across from the contingent to the intentional in the course of his revision of the *Arcadia*. In the revised version, many of the digressions are precisely designed to show different kinds of sexual attraction in operation in a wider assortment of characters than would be allowed by his main narrative alone. The exemplary nature of these added love-stories is demonstrated by the inset narrative of the cynical seducer Pamphilus, found by Pyrocles tied up with garters and being pricked with bodkins by nine deceived gentlewomen led by the abandoned Dido: an episode that would seem more at home in the 'romance of types' sections of the *Faerie Queene*.[64] Where Spenser illustrates different kinds of love along a spectrum from spirituality and faithfulness to the instant gratification of lust, however, Sidney questions much more consistently how far, or whether, or when, love can be considered as a good at all. The Protestant theology of marriage does not seem to help him in the slightest, and when his princes appeal to Neoplatonic theory, they get it wrong: their immediate response to falling in love is to move downwards, Musidorus by abandoning his nobility of rank, Pyrocles his superiority of sex; and when Musidorus sings an eclogue that should be about rising upwards towards the Ideal, the poem in fact descends from an image of contemplation beyond nature to the beautiful body that encloses the 'dear soul' of a particular woman.[65] Some of these differences may be due to the political thrust of the work (if Blair Worden is right, it is an allegory of the key issues of late 1570s politics),[66] in contrast to Spenser's concern with what an ideal England might look like. Some may also be due to the two authors' different personal experiences of love: Spenser with his passionately happy marriage; Sidney with whatever complications followed from his entanglement with the married Lady Rich. The fullness of romance structure taken by the two works, however, gives both authors space to explore love to a degree that takes them beyond topical concerns, whether political or personal. Both make the exploration of the ethics of sexuality central to their romances.

The middle books of the *Faerie Queene* contain the most extensive deliberate portrayal of different kinds of love within English romance, but Spenser is not the first writer to design a work with such an intention. Chaucer was an important forerunner. The Canterbury tales between them portray a spectrum of desire from St Cecilia's adoration of Christ above her husband, through Palamon and Arcite's rarefied passion for a lady whom they regard as being on the borderline with a goddess, to the Wife of Bath's cheerful voraciousness for serial monogamy, and to the unadorned lust of the characters in the fabliaux, the 'churls' tales'. The array follows in part from the encyclopedic generic scope of the *Tales*, which brings a variety of approaches to women and to sexuality in its wake, but the deliberateness of its display of varieties of love is indicated by *The Parliament of Fowls* (a text to which Spenser makes explicit reference).[67] The work is in some ways the allegorical epitome of the *Tales*, and it makes such a variety its principal subject. The *Parliament* is a dream poem about the different mating habits of various birds, who function as an avian equivalent of humans. A dream poem is itself a generalizing form, offering a simplified schema that avoids the messy complicating detail of the real world; the choice of birds as characters in the

Parliament offers the further advantage of avoiding ethical questions altogether, since their actions are by definition natural, and Chaucer accordingly assembles them under the aegis of Nature, the 'vicaire of the almyghty Lord' (379). There is thus no judgemental attitude taken as to whether the birds follow their natures as profligate cuckoo or as aristocratic eagle, a spectrum originating with Aristotle that encompasses both ornithological accuracy and social hierarchy. The assembly of birds represents a *distinctio* of kinds of loving; but there is a larger dichotomy that Chaucer makes in the poem. Nature and the birds occupy only the second half of the dream. The first half is devoted to a different kind of desire, emblematized in the claustrophobic temple of Priapus occupied by Venus; it consists of sexuality almost entirely divorced from procreation. On its walls are painted the stories of lovers—most of them classical (Pyramus and Thisbe, Dido, Cleopatra, Troilus), but including Tristram and Isolde—whose love has been unhappy and in some way illicit, and has resulted in death. The contrast between the two loves represented in the temple and on Nature's hill is summarized in the double inscription over the gate to the park where the dream is set: one inscription warning of barrenness, 'ther nevere tre shal fruyt ne leves bere', and death; the other promising an everlasting May of health and grace (127–40).

The poem thus offers a dichotomy between two kinds of love: fatal passion, and pairing as procreation, as embodied respectively by humans and birds. Yet the distinction is not as absolute as it might appear, and not just because the justification for the birds' presence in the poem is that they offer the closest analogy in the animal world to human patterns of sexual behaviour. One of the figures painted in the temple is 'the moder of Romulus'; she is the only one to be defined as procreative, but her presence prevents any definition of the human lovers as representing sterile passion alone. Equally, the birds are not immune from death: the turtle dove is defined in terms of its faithfulness even beyond the death of its mate. The choice of lovers for the temple, including Troilus and Tristram, suggests a distinction in terms of 'courtly' as against 'natural' love; but the aristocratic birds likewise suffer, offer long service, and speak eloquently of their own desire, yet all under the aegis of Nature. Since the three eagles all seek the same female, two of them will necessarily be disappointed—potentially, therefore, becoming further trophies for the temple. Not least because of its refusal to follow easy categorizations, the work is illuminating in many ways for thinking about love in the romances. It decisively splits down the middle the modern monolithic construction of 'courtly love'. The intensity of desire portrayed in the temple leads only to death, and so is not natural—it takes place outside the dominion of Nature. Unfulfilled desire and the eagles' courtly formulation of requests for fulfilment, by contrast, are represented as appropriate for those of highest rank, and therefore as natural as the turtle-dove's (ornithologically accurate) lifelong mating, or the goose's altogether more casual attitude as to how one finds a mate.

The middle books of the *Faerie Queene*, with their multiplicity of representations of love and desire, present a similar array, interwoven rather than sequential, and so with the contrasts and differences made part of the narrative structure. Spenser's method is often to present chaste women alongside promiscuous ones, often pairing them as narrative antonyms (as the virgin Una is contrasted with the unchaste Duessa, Britomart with Malecasta), and the *Faerie Queene* can itself be read as an extended debate on the nature of women. Books III and IV are designed to portray

> in diverse minds,
> How diversely love doth his pageants play,
> And shewes his powre in variable kinds.
>
> III. v. 1

These 'variable kinds' are the variations on the central, good image of Britomart's own desire, and their function as variations is unusually explicit. Spenser makes a radical distinction between the two kinds of desire. One is the 'Love', capitalized, that catches its spark from the 'sacred fire . . . y kindled first above', and represents a choice for virtue; the other is 'filthy lust' such as is associated with an abdication from the fully human, being chosen by 'brutish minds' (III. ii. 1). It may look like that division of women into madonnas and whores, but there is no double standard: the criticisms in particular are consistently applied equally to men and women. There is an opportunistic Paridell for every adulterous Hellenore, a randy Squire of Dames for every promiscuous Malecasta, and the actions of the men are reprehended equally with the women's. Furthermore, since the human characters (as distinct from personified abstractions or figures of supernatural or mythological origin) are types rather than ideas—fictional people, not embodied concepts—their forms of life are represented as active choices, not as an allegorical given. The human women—Britomart, Malecasta, the dominating Radegund, the disdainful Briana—are shown as self-fashioning, choosing the ethical and sexual model they wish to follow. Women's independence, their freedom of choice, is therefore built into the structure of the work, for bad or, most strongly, for good; and any attempts at male control, such as the jealous Malbecco's of Hellenore, are destined to fail, not for antifeminist reasons to do with untamable female sensuality, but because the women, like the men, are made the agents of their own ethical choices. 'Do after the good', Caxton wrote in his address to his readers that prefaces his edition of the *Morte Darthur*, 'and leave the evil.' Spenser likewise writes so that his readers can imitate his characters, not only in their actions but in taking responsibility for their own forms of living and loving.

THE ADULTERY QUESTION

The meme of the falsely accused woman has the wife's innocence built into it: she is *falsely* accused. Two of the most famous romances, by contrast, those of Isolde and Guinevere, are stories in which an adulterous wife is justly accused, and others (Marie de France's *Guigemar*, the Provençal *Flamenca*) show a mistreated wife escaping from a tyrannical husband into the arms of a lover. These romances demand sympathy for their lovers; yet no reader of the episodes of the adulterous queens in *Merlin* or *Silence* would have been likely to object to their executions; and Marie herself condemned a wife's unfaithfulness in *Bisclavret*. If these responses appear contradictory, it is perhaps due to our own habits of reading the Middle Ages too simplistically. Adultery, like love, comes in an infinity of forms; yet it was so universally reprehended, by the Church, the law, and the whole political system, as well as being the most feared element in the charges against women's licentiousness, that the high profile given to such love in some romances demands analysis. No single explanation can cover the entire phenomenon, involving as it does cultural, historical, and generic variants: not only is French romance much more ready to accommodate adultery than is English (and Italian more so again), but the same phenomenon is illustrated even more generously in the later genre of the novel—fictional adultery, or its avoidance, can be a national rather than just a medieval or generic phenomenon.

Adultery was never a norm in romance in any language. It stretches the genre to its limits, or indeed breaks them. In contrast to the active desire of the maiden for the man she chooses for her husband, it makes a happy ending almost impossible, as the stories of Tristan and Lancelot bear witness. It requires attention in this chapter, not only because it is the most difficult area in which to analyse the representation of women, but because the habits of criticism set early in the twentieth century made it central to romance, and numerous attempts to deny that centrality have had little impact outside the circle of scholars most immediately involved. The particular problem arises from C. S. Lewis's notorious dictum that adultery was a *sine qua non* of courtly love, and therefore of medieval literary love: a dictum that is probably the most misleading remark ever made about medieval literature.[68] Unfortunately, it has itself become one of the most successful memes in the modern view of the Middle Ages, a kind of urban myth with an extraordinary power of replication quite regardless of its untruth. The problem lies not only in the equation of courtly love and adultery but in the very concept of 'courtly love'. The term itself is rarely found in any medieval language, and never in Middle English. Gaston Paris coined 'amour courtois' in the late nineteenth century specifically to describe the relationship of Lancelot and Guinevere in Chrétien's *Chevalier de la Charrette*, his one romance of adultery, and his term too has acquired a popular currency (a memetic replicability) out of all proportion to its actual usefulness.[69] The nearest equivalent phrases in common usage in medieval French are either simply *amors*, love, or *fin amor*, 'refined love', anglicized by Chaucer as 'fyn loving', where the 'fin' denotes the surplus of emotion over physical desire alone. Neither has any inherent connotation of adultery; Chaucer uses the English term for married love, and other writers use it for charity, godly love.[70] Although the link between adultery and courtly love has been extensively challenged, the concept itself is still often invoked in relation to the romances' representations of women, in particular to claims that the lady is denied any subjectivity—a claim that, as the previous chapter has demonstrated, is simply wrong so far as writing in England is concerned. The debate over courtly love has therefore recently been subsumed within the scholarship on misogyny, but in relation to different issues from the concerns with women's right and wrong uses of sexuality that exercised medieval authors and commentators.

   Lewis derived his odd belief about the centrality of adultery from the declaration ascribed to Marie de Champagne by Andreas Capellanus, André the chaplain, in his handbook on love, *De amore*, that it was impossible to love one's spouse. The work did not have the seminal status or dissemination that Lewis assumes, and this declaration furthermore comes at quite a late stage of the work, with none of the primacy he assigns it: most of the text up to that point, supposedly written as instruction in seduction for a young man named Walter, never mentions the marital status of the various women whose love Andreas' assorted male characters are forever seeking, and seeking with an invariable lack of success. The ladies' refutations of the men's arguments indeed give them all an air of cool good sense that goes beyond the dialectic requirements of the form. The book's conclusion in a sharply misogynistic palinode aligns it with clerical antifeminism much more than with any secular discourses of love: a context confirmed by the fact that it is written in the male linguistic preserve of Latin. The nature of Andreas' work has been called into question from all angles since Lewis wrote: as P. G. Walsh puts it, 'Controversy surrounds its title, date, author, social setting, literary frame, purpose and importance.'[71] It may have no historical connection with the court of Champagne, but rather be a mildly salacious historical novel for scholastically-trained clerics.[72] Marie de Champagne is, however, also named by Chrétien as having commissioned his *Chevalier de la Charrette*, the foundational romance of adulterous love inspired without the help or excuse of magic draughts. Chrétien describes the countess as prescribing both *matière* and *sentence* for his story, but it was certainly typical neither of her reading-matter, which tended towards the pious, nor of his own works, the rest of which all promote love within marriage.[73] His *Cligés* is, indeed, written explicitly as an anti-*Tristan* story, in which the greatest ill lies in dissociating love from marriage. Despite going through a wedding ceremony with a man she does not love, the heroine Fénice insists that 'he who has the heart, has the body'—'Qui a le cuer, cil a le cors'[74]—and, like Ydoine and Josiane, she manages to avoid ever sleeping with her husband. She at least believes that love both of the heart and body was properly shared with the one man she aims, ultimately, to marry, and it would be perverse to imagine that Chrétien or anyone else expected her love to cease at that moment.

The conclusion Andreas gives to the countess of Champagne, in which she divides love from marriage, is in any case necessitated by the particular terms of the argument, and only by them. The sexual predator involved in raising the question effectively eliminates the possibility of love between married couples by defining love at the crucial moment of his seduction routine as 'an uncontrolled desire to obtain the sensual gratification of a stealthy and secret embrace'—*furtivi et latentis amplexus*.[75] The definition is intended to rebut his latest lady's refusal of him on the grounds that she is married to a worthy husband of whom she is very fond, and he is trying to find ways around her rejection. It is this fictional pair who take to Marie de Champagne for judgement the question of whether it is possible for there to be love between a married couple, and she rules against it, not on the grounds that marital embraces need not be stealthy, but because in marriage the wife has no sexual choice. The tenets of medieval marriage held that husband and wife were under an obligation to each other to have sex: as Andreas' countess puts it, 'Married partners are forced to comply with each other's desires as an obligation, and under no circumstances to refuse their persons to each other.'[76] She is in effect expounding a paradox; the modern equivalent might be, can a husband and wife enjoy free love together? The answer in all three cases is essentially one of definition: each pair of terms—marriage and stealthy desire; marriage and free sexual choice; marriage and free love—is inherently contradictory. A few pages later, Ermengarde of Narbonne refuses to answer another question related to the love between lovers and spouses because the terms are too ambiguous to give a logically coherent answer.[77] The emphasis of the declaration against married love is not on living or feeling but on casuistic argument, a vernacular and emotional equivalent of the Latin and philosophical debates in the Schools where the whole text perhaps originated, and says little or nothing about actual practice either in real life or in literature.

The fate of Andreas' *De amore* in England confirms that the declaration for which the work is now best known was not regarded as either central or normative, and confirms, too, the preference shown by English romance for love that is ultimately circumscribed by orthodox morality. Chaucer's Franklin dismisses the notion that the 'law of love' might separate off the roles of 'lady' and 'wyf',[78] and there is no reason to think that Chaucer did not agree. It is not likely, however, that Andreas' argument underlies the dismissal, as there is no evidence for any knowledge of the Latin text in Britain in the Middle Ages. The work did eventually make its way across the Channel, but in an adaptation into French in which the advice on love to the young Walter is put into the mouth of the wise abbess Heloïse—and wisdom seems to be the point at issue in this version. The text confines itself to the first half of the first book of Andreas' original, so it stops short before the question arises of whether one can or cannot love one's spouse; the vicious antifeminism of the final book also therefore disappears. The differences are moreover far from just a matter of length. The relentless male point of view of Andreas' text is recurrently made gender-inclusive, not just by the change of instructor, but from the very first page by the redefinition of love as a mutual emotion shared by both lovers: it concerns 'les cuers des deux gens amans', and that *both* lovers are equally involved is stressed throughout.[79] The fictional recipient of the text is still a man, but the emphasis of the work has been altered to turn it into a young man's guide to winning his lady's heart (rather than, as in Andreas, her body), through a training in fine emotion. That intention is confirmed by the nature of the single surviving manuscript, a beautiful production made for the young prince Arthur, heir to Henry VII, some time before his marriage to Katherine of Aragon. It contains, in addition to this treatise, a series of *demandes d'amour* more sympathetic to women than those contained in Andreas' series of conundrums, and a further treatise of advice to princes.[80] If ever Elizabeth I had picked it out from among the books in the Royal Library, she would have found nothing in it to offend her.

Despite its distance from English ethical and generic norms, the full Latin version of Andreas' treatise and Marie's ruling within it are illuminating on one matter, and that is the importance of free sexual choice for the woman. The sophistical or legalistic point on which her decision turns is the issue of compulsion: that the husband who has his wife's body does not necessarily also have her heart, yet she has no right to refuse herself to him. The normal solution, both inside and outside romance, was not to deny the possibility of loving one's husband, but to insist that the ideal marriage was one where the wife did love her spouse—hence the ecclesiastical emphasis on consent, which may not compel the heart, but at least insists on the personal choice of partner for both men and women. Such choice, however, in practice took different forms for the two sexes. For men, with their greater social and personal freedom, it could precisely mean active personal choice, even if that choice was made in line with parental interests and for reasons of economics and status rather than love. For women, 'consent' was likely to mean no more than the right of refusal of a husband chosen for her. Although the Church set its face against enforced marriages, it was in practice extremely difficult for a daughter to resist parental compulsion, which was in any case further reinforced by the Church on the grounds of obedience. No romance heroine ever considers the possibility of simply refusing a bridegroom at the altar as a way round a parental choice of husband; and Friar Laurence in *Romeo and Juliet* similarly never thinks that a downright refusal of Paris on Juliet's part would cut any ice. At the higher aristocratic levels that concern Marie de Champagne and her court, and which are the main setting of the romances, women would be especially unlikely to be given much freedom in the choice of husband.[81] Romances notwithstanding, they were largely the passive objects of arranged marriages, and the arrangement was made by the man responsible for them, normally the father. The romances of adultery typically therefore involve a married woman and a single man. She makes her own active sexual choice independently of the husband who has chosen her and the father who has endorsed that choice, in an extreme form of resistance to male commodification of women; the man she loves likewise exercises his free sexual choice, for her. The romance authors were fully alert to such processes. In *Flamenca*, the heroine's father demands his daughter's obedience to his choice of husband, and she replies by consenting to his wish: she never, within the text, consents as such to her marriage partner, a distinction that prepares the way for her affair when her husband turns brutal on her.[82] Arthur consults Guinevere's father before he marries her, but not her. The marriage of Isolde to Mark is a matter of diplomatic negotiation conducted by men, and one, furthermore, that disrupts a love relationship that already exists—the husband, not the lover, is the third in this particular triangle. Romances show their heroines resisting the passive role laid down for them, choosing their own sexual partners regardless of their fathers' plans for them, or, in the rare extreme case, notwithstanding the existence of a husband.

Happy marriage in the real world was taken to depend not so much on passionate love, nor on the love-at-first-sight commitment of romance, as on mutual respect between the spouses: on marital affection and friendship,[83] qualities that could be achieved by active good will without the need for intervention by any god of love. That a woman has a worthy husband is often given as a forceful argument against extramarital affairs. The married lady accosted by the sex-hungry man in the *De amore* cites it as her reason for refusing him (hence the need for the sophistical Andreas to find a way around the objection); Gawain tries to keep Bertilak's over-familiar wife at bay by telling her that she has chosen ('waled', 1276) a much better man than he is; and the respect, or the lack of it, that can be accorded the husband makes the crucial difference in the *lais* of Marie de France between those where extramarital love is treated sympathetically and those where it is not. In *Guigemar* and *Yonec*, extramarital love is represented as supernaturally-bestowed compensation for good women imprisoned by jealous husbands. The unfaithful wives in *Equitan* and *Bisclavret* by contrast are unequivocally condemned, together with their lovers, even though in the latter the husband has the habit of turning into a werewolf. In each, to drive the point home, the wife's readiness to betray her husband opens the way to trying to get rid of him altogether: in *Equitan* by scalding him to death in a bath (which her lover, the king, accidentally climbs into); in *Bisclavret* by removing the clothes that enable him to turn back into human form. *Generides*, one of the romances to enjoy considerable popularity in print, opens with an announcement of the queen's adultery, and she and her paramour remain major characters throughout the narrative; they finish up defeated, but they are allowed to beseech, and be granted, forgiveness before they die. The early announcement of the affair clears the way for the wronged husband to be led by a hart to meet his own beloved, and the child born to them, Generides, in due course recovers his father's throne from the usurping wife and paramour.

It is notable how rarely 'romances' of adultery provide happy endings for the lovers. If such stories are recognizable as romances because of their focus on love, they are marginal to the genre in so far as the nature of that love prevents their achieving a final order and equilibrium within this world. The affair between Lancelot and Guinevere causes Arthur's downfall, whether that downfall is represented as the punishment for sexual transgression (as in the *Lancelot-Grail*) or as political treachery motivated by hatred of Lancelot, in which the affair is no more than an excuse (as in the *Morte Darthur*). The love at the basis of the Tristan romances cannot find any resolution for the lovers other than death, and Tristan's marriage to Isolde of the White Hands adds a second tragedy within the first: it is one of the very few stories where the hero marries someone other than the woman he loves, with disastrous results for his bride. If a wife with both a husband and a lover is in a near-impossible position, the rare wife whose husband is in love with someone else is worse off still. In Marie's *Eliduc*, the young Guilliadun falls for Eliduc without knowing that he is married, and he does not have the courage to tell her; when she discovers, after they have eloped, she faints so deeply as to appear dead. They are enabled to live ever after in 'parfit' amur' (1150) only by the wife's discovering the inanimate Guilliadun, finding a way to bring her back to life, and then withdrawing to a convent: a happy ending, in fact, achieved only through her unstinting generosity, unrewarded in this world, and the next is never explicitly mentioned. The few romances that do manage happy endings for extramarital lovers (Marie de France's *Guigemar*, the anonymous Provençal *Flamenca*, which calls itself a 'novas' rather than a romance)[84] are those in which the husband suffers from such paranoid jealousy that he imprisons his innocent wife, and an escape into the arms of a lover offers the only hope of a happy ending for her, or indeed any tolerable existence at all. Even so, a brutal husband is not enough to ensure the poetic justice of happiness for the wife. Marie's *Yonec* tells of how an imprisoned wife finds happiness with a supernatural lover who gets access to her chamber in the form of a hawk, but the husband succeeds in killing him.

In these early decades in the history of romance, the possible permu-
tations of combining the pursuit of happiness with the pursuit of more
than one spouse were enlarged by the fact that the formalities of marriage
had not so long before been more flexible than they became after the
Church imposed its own control, and there were advantages for
romance-writers in making the most of such flexibility. When Eliduc's
first wife declares that it is neither good nor becoming, 'bien ne avenant',
for a man to have two wives, and the law furthermore does not allow it
(1128–9), her becoming a nun is presented as sufficient to free her hus-
band to marry Guilliadun. There is no divorce before the new wedding,
nor is the Church in any way consulted. Ulrich von Zatzikhoven's
Lanzelet, and presumably therefore his Anglo-Norman original,[85]
secretly leaves his beloved wife Iblis (the maiden who fell in love with him
in a dream the night before she first laid eyes on him) in order to under-
take an adventure that involves overcoming a hundred knights, with the
reward of the hand of the queen of Pluris; he overcomes the knights, and
marries her. She will not allow him to leave, and he has to be rescued by
means of a trick mounted by four knights (including Gawain and
Tristan) before he can return to Iblis, after which we hear no more of his
new wife. Guinevere, in this romance, remains faithful to her husband,
and passes a magic test of fidelity to prove it; Lanzelet's status as hero
seems to derive both from his participation in a passionately happy
marriage and from his readiness to accept sexual adventures, and even a
second wife, as they offer themselves. If these episodes do indeed derive
from Anglo-Norman, they would constitute an unusual instance in
England of a double sexual standard; but neither Lanzelet, nor the
author, nor, so far as we know, the readers, found the combination of
blissful love and sexual opportunism especially troubling.

ADULTERY IN ENGLISH ROMANCE

In every medieval European language, literary adultery is in the first
instance the hallmark of fabliau rather than romance. Lanzelet's love-
adventures with every woman other than Iblis, whether bigamous or
merely promiscuous, are treated with a mild salaciousness that is less
than fully serious. The wonder one expects romance to evoke as a
response to the supernatural or the suprahuman coexists here with
amazement at what he and the various women get up to. Just as the
discourses of clerical antifeminism are allowed a voice in romance, so are

the discourses of fabliau: not necessarily to be debated or put down, but perhaps as a means of allowing for inappropriate or cynical responses from any sections of the audience who might be disinclined to docile acceptance of sentiment or human idealism such as romance usually demands. The romance concern to present faithful heterosexual love as the highest human good elides easily with the cheerful conviction of the fabliaux that sex is the main goal of all humanity, and not least the female half.

The potential closeness of romance and fabliau is exemplified by the incorporation into a number of romances, including the *Lanzelet*, of narratives that show the near-universal imperfection of women, by way of mantles that shrink or cups that spill in the hands of disobedient or unfaithful wives. When such tales are free-standing, they are more likely to be chastity tests, and are often indistinguishable from fabliau. Their affinity with clerical antifeminism is indicated by the claim in one of the earliest such texts, the Anglo-Norman *Lai du Corn*, that the author got the story from an abbot.[86] That is by no means necessarily true, but it must have carried a degree of plausibility, even if it shifts the emphasis from antifeminism to anticlericalism. Romance treatments of comparable stories often raise the standard of wifely faithfulness impossibly high: the most extreme is that a wife should never have had a single thought that she would not be happy for her husband to know. In the *Lanzelet*, where Iblis is the only one such a magic mantle fits, the other ladies of the court err at least in thought, or are inclined to grumble against their husbands.[87] This is magic that does work, though whether it serves to mark the supra-human, the exceptional, as a possibility or as an impossibility in a thoroughly fallible world is left to the reader to decide. The location of the episode immediately before Lanzelet's entanglement with the queen of Pluris invites a contrast to be made between the hero and the heroine, whether in favour of Iblis's greater perfection, or as marking different ethical or fantasy expectations of male and female protagonists.

The precise statistics attaching to such stories vary: at best they offer a hundred-to-four ratio of imperfect to good women; at worst they imply a figure closer to Solomon's claim, much cited in the Middle Ages, that there is scarcely one good woman in a thousand.[88] The tales therefore require a large number of women to be found together in one place, and so a court made a good setting, especially Arthur's: an Arthurian context fits with the magic element of the tales, and the presentation of the cup or mantle may constitute the marvel that the king requires before he will eat at major feasts. One would expect a court setting to have been attractive to a non-courtly audience, as it calls into question the women's claim to be 'ladies' rather than 'wenches', in the class-and-sexuality-specific distinction familiar from the fourteenth century forwards;[89] but although that may have encouraged the spread of such stories beyond the élite, it evidently did not hinder their acceptability within courtly romance. The longest-enduring of such stories was that of the mantle won by Caradoc's, or Craddock's, chaste wife. Widely known throughout Europe, the tale is first mentioned in England in Sir Thomas Gray's *Scalachronica* (late 1350s), as fact—he claims that the mantle is preserved at Glastonbury, refashioned into a cope. Caxton also cites its preservation as evidence for Arthur's historicity in his preface to the *Morte Darthur*, though he locates it at Dover Castle. The only full English version of the story survives from a more popular level, in the ballad-style *The Boy and the Mantle* preserved in the Percy Folio manuscript.[90] The mantle's antics—shrinking or shredding itself—reflect how seriously the ladies have 'done amiss' (l. 30), down to the slightest infringement of a strict moral code: even Craddock's sweet wife has to reproach it when it begins to 'crinkle and crowt' above her toes, for a misdemeanour most people in England would not have regarded as such:

> Shee said, 'Bowe downe, mantle,
> and shame me not for nought.
>
> 'Once I did amisse,
> I tell you certainlye,
> When I kist Craddockes mouth
> under a greene tree,
> When I kist Craddockes mouth
> before he marryed me.'
>
> 115–22

When such stories appear contextualized within a larger romance, they are subjected to a more sober critique. When Malory recounts the episode of Morgan le Fay's gift of a magic drinking-horn intended to show up Guinevere's guilt, he shifts its emphasis away from the mass female errancy it reveals towards the hatred on Morgan's part that drives her desire to damage Arthur. In the event, the horn is diverted to Mark's court, where Isode and a hundred ladies all fail to drink cleanly, only four succeeding. Mark's response, to order a mass burning of the errant women, is immediately overridden by his barons, who despite their own disgrace simply want nothing to do with any product of sorcery. 'For that horne dud never good, but caused stryff and bate', comments Malory, with typical greater concern for political stability than for matrimonial relationships. The larger drift of his whole narrative none the less leads him to add that Morgan was always 'an enemy to all trew lovers', in an acknowledgement rare for English romance other than his own that 'true' love might exist outside marriage.[91]

It is surprising, given his normal method of balancing out exempla of the loving and the lustful, to find Spenser incorporating an analogous full-scale chastity test into the *Faerie Queene*. The episode is one that eliminates the magic element, to demonstrate simply women's easy sexuality. This is the story put into the mouth of the Squire of Dames, who tells of a ratio of 12,000 seducible women to three who resist him, and one of those is a prostitute whose charges are too high. That is the only moment that elicits laughter from its auditor (hearty laughter, at that), who otherwise shows minimal reaction, though Spenser comments later that the story defames the Squire more than it does women.[92] The Squire's story is insulated from the larger tenor of the *Faerie Queene* by the fact that it is recessed within the main narrative: these women exist as fictions within a fiction, not as characters present to our eyes. The Squire first appears moreover in the grip of the giantess Argante, the embodiment of a 'sensuall desyre' 'gainst natures law' so intense as to be unslakeable even by incest and bestiality. The fact that she is female might suggest the commonplace of women's sexual insatiability; but the Squire is a victim not of women's voraciousness but of his own. He is the work's principal example of *men's* insatiable sensuality (even if, in turn, he finds women excessively compliant), and it is that that Argante represents. She, moreover, can be defeated only by a maiden knight-errant on the Grisandol or Britomart model, Palladine, named after the virgin goddess of wisdom.[93] The episode is the only one of all the diverse pageants of love and lust in the *Faerie Queene* to suggest that female promiscuity is a norm, and the rest of the work never endorses that. Elsewhere, Spenser goes so far as to offer a statistic for virtue that inverts Solomon's, one bad woman ''mongst thousands good' (III. i. 49). Even the Squire's story, moreover, stops short of any explicit mention of adultery. The many examples of loose morals in the work rarely extend to that. The primary instance is that of Hellenore with Paridell. As their names indicate, their escapade is designed to recall the archetypal adultery of Helen and Paris, but there is nothing either epic or romantic about it in Spenser's treatment: it is a shoddy affair, which is designed to satirize the jealous husband Malbecco as much as the principals in the case, even though Hellenore partakes of the sexual insatiability of antifeminist discourse (she ends by taking herself off to the satyrs for satisfaction, a way of life that receives surprisingly little explicit condemnation in the poem, however much the allegory may define it as beastly).

The broader inhospitality of English romance towards adultery is indicated by the fact that Spenser derives the stories of both the Squire and Malbecco from Ariosto; magic mantles apart, there is nothing directly comparable in any native source. Badly treated ladies who escape from imprisonment by jealous husbands into the arms of a lover scarcely get a mention in Anglo-Norman romance after Marie de France, and are effectively non-existent in Middle English. There is just one tale that follows such a pattern, the story known as *Inclusa*, 'the imprisoned woman', in *The Seven Sages of Rome*, a work of ultimately Oriental origin that reached England through various continental redactions and which remained popular through numerous printed editions.[94] Here, the lovers surpass the expectations for most such romances, both of them falling in love by dreaming of each other before they ever meet, in a doubling of the effect of the *Lanzelet*'s Iblis or Spenser's Arthur; and they manage to trick the husband into giving his own wife in marriage to her lover, in another instance of bigamy that originated before Church control was strengthened. Just as the story of the magic mantle is altered by its context, however, this tale is taken decisively away from romance by its larger setting. The plot of the *Seven Sages* tells how a wicked stepmother and the eponymous sages tell rival stories on seven successive days, the stepmother's designed to persuade the king to execute his own son, those of the boy's teachers designed to make him distrust her—and *Inclusa* is one of the latter. The one story of an unhappy lady's escape to love in Middle English owes its existence to the fact that it is an exemplary story against women.

The greater wariness towards adultery in English-language romance than in its French counterpart is illustrated by the story of the *Chatelain de Coucy*, the French version of which ends with the jealous husband feeding his unknowing wife with her lover's heart. It was rewritten in English around 1500, keeping the tragic ending but with the affair removed. The lovers insist on loving

> wyth herte and minde,
> Nat in vyce but in chastyte,

and it is only the husband's irrational jealousy that assumes that their relationship is sexual.[95] Husbands are not exempt from the requirement of faithfulness, in English in particular: the king's extramarital love in

Generides follows the revelation to him of his wife's adultery and treason, as if her actions freed him from his own commitment to a marriage vow already broken, and he and his new beloved remain passionately faithful to each other despite a long separation. The only Middle English romance before the fifteenth century to present, or to carry over from Anglo-French, a sympathetic story of an adulterous love—or rather, a love that becomes adulterous through the marriage of the heroine—is *Sir Tristrem*, the adaptation of Thomas's *Tristan*; and that survives in only one manuscript, suggesting no great interest in the story, and did not inspire imitations. The French prose *Tristan* and *Lancelot* were known and read in England, at least by some aristocrats, but their stories do not decisively enter English until Malory, and he includes nothing on the growth of love between Lancelot and Guinevere. The one British text to recount that early part of the story, the northern or Scottish *Lancelot of the Laik*, was not written until the very end of the fifteenth century. Furthermore, although the single manuscript of the text is incomplete, the small number of missing leaves strongly suggests that it would have taken the lovers no further than their first kiss.

The 'adultery' version of Arthurian romance was not unknown in anglophone Britain before Malory (there is the barest mention of it in an addition to an early fourteenth-century chronicle, and it is taken for granted in the stanzaic *Morte Arthur* of *c*.1400),[96] but the general silence seems to suggest that the whole story was regarded, in so far as it was thought of at all, as a French slander on the historical British Arthur as drawn by Geoffrey of Monmouth. In Geoffrey, Lancelot does not even exist. The early Anglo-Norman romance of Lancelot that underlies Ulrich's *Lanzelet* was perhaps written to counter Chrétien's adulterous version of Guinevere; its hero's amorous interests extend to four enthusiastic women but exclude her, and her probity is made explicit.[97] In the fifteenth century, John Harding's rhyme-royal *Chronicle*, which is unique in incorporating the story of the Grail into the historical version of Arthur derived from Geoffrey of Monmouth, not only omits the affair, but has Lancelot married to Elaine the mother of Galahad 'in very clene spousage'.[98] Harding has political as well as ethical reasons for the change, since he wrote his chronicle to encourage the king of England to pursue English claims to Scotland, which partly derived from Arthur's overlordship of the whole of the British Isles; and so he has a strong vested interest in representing Arthurian history as morally admirable. He therefore draws the story of Lancelot within the normative patterns of romance love as found in England: love as a matter of courtship leading to marriage. English Renaissance romance is even less hospitable towards adultery. Roger Ascham's famous condemnation of the Arthurian stories as 'bold bawdry' is typical of an absolute line drawn by Protestant views of marriage, one which does not allow for any gap between theological and secular discourses, let alone Malory's belief in God's sympathy for faithful lovers.

The degree of that sympathy is therefore surprising. Malory downgrades the story of Lancelot and Guinevere for much of his narrative; he borrows a tiny fraction of the French prose *Lancelot*, and the greater part of that fraction, which forms his 'Tale of Sir Lancelot', has almost nothing to do with the queen. He is also fully aware of the ills consequent on their love. To have an affair with the king's wife was high treason, and, in case anyone might have been in any doubt, it had been categorized as such in English law in the Statute of Treasons of 1352—the point being that such a sexual relationship potentially interferes with the succession. Both Guinevere and Isolde, conveniently—of necessity, so far as the stories are concerned—are childless.[99] Yet the faithfulness and strength of Lancelot's love for Guinevere override the legal categories of both adultery and treason. Lancelot maintains a rigorous and paradoxical loyalty to Arthur, always supporting him, always working to his highest good, and desperately reluctant to fight against him. In contrast to the Geoffrey-derived versions that make her a willing accomplice in Mordred's abduction of her, Malory's Guinevere similarly never acts publicly against the king.

Perhaps the best way of comprehending Malory's presentation of the love between Lancelot and Guinevere is to set aside the category of 'adultery' altogether: not because it is not an issue (very obviously, it is) but because it pre-empts too much. It puts an end to thought, just at the point where thinking ought to start. In his 'Tale of Sir Lancelot', when an unnamed damsel mentions almost for the first time in the work that there are rumours of such an affair, Lancelot responds forcefully:

And as for to sey to take my pleasaunce with paramours, that woll I refuse: in prencipall for drede of God, for knyghtes that bene adventurers sholde nat be advoutres nothir lecherous . . . And so who that usyth paramours shall be unhappy, and all thynge unhappy that is aboute them.[100]

The speech, like so many of those that comment on the affair, is Malory's own invention. It looks at first glance like a denial that any such affair exists—possibly because it has not yet started (though we are never shown its beginnings, and rumours are already rife in the Arthurian world); the obvious alternative would be for Lancelot to be making the kind of denial familiar in the mouths of politicians, one that never quite meets the point at issue. A medieval equivalent would be the oath sworn by Isolde that no man ever lay between her thighs except her husband and the man under whom she fell while he carried her ashore from a boat— that man being, of course, Tristan in disguise. Lancelot answers the charge of loving the queen with a denial that he is promiscuous, and what he says is strictly true: he is not lecherous, he does not take his pleasure with paramours (in the sense of casual mistresses; as a noun, the phrase *par amour* had lost its intensifying sense by this date), and knights-errant ought not to be adulterers. The speech is certainly intended by Lancelot to stop the damsel's loose talk, but the tenor of what he is saying may none the less be as heartfelt as it sounds. A knight-errant, a knight adventurous, should not use his wanderings as a means of getting promiscuous sexual pleasure, and Lancelot consistently resists such opportunities. The words may well be intended by Malory to make the reader think harder about the distinction between the casual sleeping with other men's wives implied by 'advoutres nothir lecherous' and his single-minded love for Guinevere. Even the damsel acknowledges that 'ye shall never love none other but hir'. Lancelot's reply is designed to mark the ethical boundary that falls not between active sexuality and celibacy, nor between love for your own wife and love for someone else's, but between promiscuity and faithfulness. His prediction of 'unhappiness' for sexual adventurers therefore does not come over as ironic, or as applicable to himself, for all our foreknowledge of what will happen.

The stories of Lancelot and Guinevere and of Tristan and Isolde are the most famous love-stories of the Middle Ages because of the strength of love represented in them; and for that to be shown, it has to be demonstrated by some kind of opposition. The course of true love, as Shakespeare's Lysander notes, never did run smooth, and especially not in fiction, for if it did there would be no story at all. There must be some obstacle, and being married to someone else—especially to the king—is one of the most awkward. Just as a knight proves his surpassing strength by fighting giants or dragons or an entire army of Saracens, not the boy next door, so love proves its invincibility by being set against every social, political, and religious taboo, and not by being reducible to convenient marriage. Adultery is the most extreme condition for showing the power of love; and it is a consequence of love, not (*pace* Lewis) the condition that makes love possible. The idea that love is irresistible is doubled in the *Tristan* story by having the lovers come together as a result of their accidental drinking of the magic love-potion: having drunk it, they are helpless against it. The drink also has the advantage of removing moral blame from them. It is not saying much for love, however, if it needs to be inspired by magic, and lovers in lyrics and romances soon start insisting that a love inspired solely by the loved one is altogether superior to a potion-inspired passion.[101] The affair between Lancelot and Guinevere is calqued on that of Tristan and Isolde, but their love is spontaneous, and its power makes the question of guilt problematic just as the potion does. Malory's damsel who notes Lancelot's faithfulness to Guinevere also suggests that maybe the queen's hold over him is due to 'enchauntement'. That is a charge that could be brought against Elaine of Corbin, at least so far as her getting Lancelot into her bed goes, but the significance of his love for Guinevere is that it comes entirely of himself.

Finally and tragically, there is no way out; an affair between a married queen and a vassal cuts off all possibilities of a happy ending. But it does not necessitate an ending in Hell, not even for the first writer to portray most of the story of Lancelot and Guinevere in that inhospitable English tradition—indeed, especially not for him. Malory does not make the morality easy for himself or his readers: in one of his largest structural interventions in his sources, he reorganizes episodes from the *Lancelot-Grail* so that the three accusations of Guinevere that threaten her with execution at the stake mark a progression from guiltlessness (she is innocent of the charge of murdering Sir Patrice), to innocence on a technicality (she has not slept with any of the wounded knights lodged in her chamber, and the charge does not extend to sleeping with Lancelot), to guilt (Lancelot has indeed been taken with her in the night, 'whether they were abed other at other maner of disportis'), and he has no option but to defend her. Whether he 'ded ryght othir wronge', the only possible right thing to do is to save her from burning.[102]

And Malory's God is on the side of the lovers. In an episode original to him, placed immediately after the section in which the lovers explicitly sleep together for the first and only time in the work, God gives Lancelot his own personal miracle, in the healing of Sir Urry. The 'good end' that Malory allows to Guinevere takes the form in this world of a retreat to a nunnery in penitence for causing the death of her 'most noble lord', but it is still an end awarded to her because of her love rather than because of her repentance.[103] Lancelot himself, who similarly abandons the world, does so primarily because she has done the same—'Sythen ye have taken you to perfeccion, I must nedys take me to perfection, of ryght.'[104] He keeps faith with her, and never repents of loving her; and he dies in the odour of sanctity. The demand for absolute chastity in the story of the Grail may have required Malory to have Lancelot unceremoniously dumped outside the chamber door when he tries to approach the Grail, but he still allows the Archbishop of Canterbury a vision of a crowd of angels heaving him up into Heaven, 'and the yates of heven opened ayenst hym'.[105] Bunyan's Faithful had to exhibit a very different kind of faithfulness unto death, and undergo a very different quest, before he achieved such an ending.

Persuasive as it is, it is not a conclusion that could be taken forward. Spenser, in his own Arthuriad, allows the occasional glimpse of other Arthurian knights (an adolescent Tristram, for instance); but there is no possible room for Lancelot, and less still for Guinevere. In this version of his biography, Arthur will marry not a Guinevere who made her sexual choice elsewhere, but the Gloriana who made her own choice of him. Spenser may have been helped in writing Guinevere out of history by the confusion of traditions about her; Holinshed, in one particularly desperate moment, goes so far as to suggest that Arthur might have married three successive women of the same name.[106] Yet the change also means that Spenser is writing himself into a dead end. It was Guinevere's unfaithfulness—with Mordred in Geoffrey, with Lancelot in the romance tradition—that opened the space for Arthur's downfall. Write Guinevere out of history, and there is no final battle; and so the whole course of British history is changed, down through the coming of the Anglo-Saxons and the Normans and so ultimately the Tudors. In his account of British history in the House of Alma, Spenser brings the story up as far as Uther Pendragon—the present moment of the poem. The rest is told later, in Merlin's prophecy. In the gap between the two histories, Guinevere and Gloriana engage in unwritten rivalry. Guinevere was the woman rightly accused of adultery. Elizabeth, Gloriana's human form, was the child of a queen executed on the same charge. Yet to substitute the virgin queen, the fairy queen, for the guilty queen of British history, meant a rewriting of history that would threaten to erase her very existence.

CHAPTER SEVEN

Restoring the rightful heir:
'If that which is lost
be not found'

The quest to discover one's inborn chivalry and true parentage; the child adrift on the open seas; the elf-queen's prophecies; the frank willingness of Melusine or Gloriana, Lavine or Britomart, to offer themselves to the man of their choice, whether an adventurer outcast from his patrimony or one who does not know what that might be, and so become the founding mother of a dynasty; the child falsely declared a bastard and lost to its true father—all these memes of romance come together in the concern of the genre with true inheritance, the rightful passing on of land and power underwritten by Providence. Only one of the motifs discussed so far in this book does not directly concern itself with this issue. When it comes to identifying the true heir, magic works. No one but the rightful successor to the throne of Britain, the unknown son of Uther Pendragon, can pull the sword from the stone. A disputed succession calls for some sign by which the rightful king can be known, whether by magic, miracle, or some recognizable natural or material proof. Its precise metaphysical status matters less than its signification: it must be a sign visibly and demonstrably beyond everyday experience, such as raises the man who bears the mark of it beyond the common run of humanity.

The insistent concern of romance with identifying the rightful king is a reflection of the fact that rightfulness does not necessarily show itself in unequivocal ways, even without the complications of the heir being brought up as a foundling of unknown parentage. A 'lost' heir required some mark of identity, some equivalent to a DNA test to prove paternity. Havelok has a light shine from his mouth when he sleeps, and also a 'kynemerk', a birthmark showing both his kinship and 'kunrik', royalty, in the form of a gold cross on his right shoulder.[1] The shoulder was the location of badges of allegiance: men who had taken a vow to go on crusade bore a cross on the shoulder of their cloak, and the angels of Richard II's Wilton Diptych wear white hart badges in the same position. Havelok's king-mark is inscribed directly on his body by God, as witnessed by the angel who explains its meaning to his bride. Valentine likewise bears 'a crosse upon my shoulder, the whiche is also yelowe as the fyne golde', that suggests to him that he must be greater than he knows.[2] Romance, however, can make sure that such markers are reliable, as history cannot. Henry III was faced with a pretender bearing 'the mark of royalty upon his shoulder', who tried to assassinate him; Perkin Warbeck backed up his claim to be Richard duke of York, the younger son of Edward IV, with three congenital marks on his body.[3]

The appearance of a man claiming to be a lost heir was, in practice, much less common than a succession of questionable legality, or a succession disputed by a known claimant. Those raised the same problems of identifying the rightful successor, and similarly required some demonstration of divine arbitration. Where the ultimate power in the state was concerned, the principles and laws of primogeniture could easily conflict with political, national, or personal issues and interests. The Hundred Years War was not in immediate origin a dynastic war, but it was increasingly justified in terms of the claim of successive English kings to be the rightful inheritors of the crown of France, a claim not surprisingly denied by the French. The laws of primogeniture might be thought to pre-empt disputes over succession, but they did not prevent, and in many cases fuelled, the sequence of problematic accessions to the English throne from the fourteenth to the sixteenth centuries. Bolingbroke's deposition of his cousin, Richard II, left both his son and grandson with claims that were repeatedly contested, culminating in full civil war. The Yorkists denied the validity of the homage sworn to Henry VI by asserting Edward IV's superior line of descent from his great-great-great-great-grandfather.[4] Richard III's usurpation diverted the crown from son to uncle, a less drastic step in terms of the linear succession than Bolingbroke's; but Henry Tudor's victory at Bosworth entailed the biggest disruption to the succession of the crown since the Norman Conquest. It was not without reason that he set about systematically eliminating every possible rival claimant. Henry VIII altered the whole history of Britain through his desperation to beget a male heir, and even after he had finally settled on naming his three legitimate (or re-legitimated) children as lineal successors, Protestant politics forced the promotion of Lady Jane Grey as a rival to Mary, and Catholic politics urged the claim of Mary Queen of Scots against Elizabeth. Elizabeth's own virginity gradually hardened from being an issue of political and diplomatic concern over potential husbands to the irrevocable fact of childlessness. 'The king shall live without an heir':[5] it was the most dangerous of all political scenarios, and the closing decades of Elizabeth's reign made it a matter of increasing anxiety.

The methods of identifying the true heir offered by romance do not immediately connect with practical politics. James VI of Scotland could not draw an immovable sword from a stone or reveal a miraculous birthmark, and it would have cut little ice if he had. The insistence of romance that there was such a thing as a *true* heir, however—that one person, and one person only, carried the right to the crown, and with it the approval of God—bore an ideological charge that might be at odds with *realpolitik* but which was very widely subscribed to, and which carried immense judicial, ethical, and theological weight. Dark Age heroes such as Scyld Scefing, whose drifting ashore as a baby is mentioned in *Beowulf*, owe part of their capacity as leader or ruler to the fact of their mysterious birth; medieval heroes may often similarly be foundlings, but they owe their potential sovereignty to the fact that they have a parentage that can be discovered. The shift happens at about the same time as the origins of romance, in the same period that primogeniture becomes the legal norm for inheritance:[6] for that norm is intended to make the same point, that there will always be one claimant whose title can be proved rightful ahead of all rivals. Romance follows to its logical and semi-miraculous conclusion the legal principle that 'Only God can make an heir', first formulated in the late eleventh century but carried through into English law.[7] The various systems that operated in central Europe, including the election of the Holy Roman Emperor, translated into romance rather more awkwardly, but the clarity of the laws of kingship developed in England and France constituted an open invitation to concordant narratives. Romance is the myth of the ideology of primogeniture.

'A myth', wrote Northrop Frye, 'is designed not to describe a specific situation but to contain it, in a way that does not restrict its significance to that one situation.'[8] Every change of ruler invited authorization or challenge from the myth of the rightful heir. Chronicles concern themselves with the evidence of reason and knowledge, the knowable past. Romances are concerned with the unfolding lives of the characters within their narratives, who have to discover the true line of descent by more providential or intuitive means. Romances, and especially genealogical romances, are also concerned with the future beyond their narratives, the present of writer and readers; and so they offer predictions of that present coded as just such providential shaping. They therefore function to authorize the present, to insist on its rightness. The density of dynastic concern in the sixteenth century—the renewed interest in London as Troynovaunt; works such as William Warner's *Albions England*, which represents all of legend and history since the pagan gods as a teleological progression towards Elizabeth; the abundance of 'prophecy' of post-Arthurian history down to the house of Tudor incorporated by Spenser into the *Faerie Queene*—may be in part a response to the doubtful legitimacy of the ruling house, the need to find a justification for it in the deep past since it was so difficult to do so from more recent times. It is not without reason that Spenser gives a fairy genealogy for his Henry VII figure; a real one would have been much too embarrassing.[9] Elizabeth I, notoriously, refused to name any heir. Whether or not the story is true of the dying queen, her power of speech gone, raising her hand to her head in a gesture of coronation when the Archbishop of Canterbury asked her if James should succeed her, it was a story that would have had to be invented. The weight given to the prophecy ascribed to Thomas of Erceldoune of the Scottish ascent of the English throne becomes more comprehensible in this context.[10] Such prophecies appeared to ground the queen's gesture far back in time, in the processes of destiny or Providence rather than in any whim of a dying woman. They provide a guarantee beyond rational human decision, a supernatural mark of identification, that could select James VI from among any other possible claimants to the crown.

The concern of romance with the rightful heir is closely bound up with the justification of the present by the past, often a legendary past about the founding of a dynasty; but it links up too with a broader principle, of the deep psychological need for children to know who their parents are, and of parents to find missing children.[11] The close connection of that principle in the Middle Ages with inheritance is the corollary of the culture-specific systems of land tenure, but the urge to know one's origins, or a parent's hope to rediscover a lost child, runs deeper than that. The identification of a child by means of a birthmark or of goods left with it is the stuff of romance, but not of romance alone. Perdita is identified by her mother's cloak and jewel with which she was exposed, Pastorella by the birthmark of 'a litle purple rose' on her breast (*FQ*, VI. xii. 18). The origins of the elder son of Cymbeline are confirmed by the mantle his mother had embroidered, his younger brother's by a 'mark of wonder', a star-shaped mole on his neck (5. 6. 366–7); both sons require such identification since in the legendary genealogies the younger succeeded the elder as king. Outside fiction altogether, the museum of the Thomas

Coram Foundling Hospital in London, founded in 1741, preserves a col-
lection of identifying mementoes left by the desperate mothers who
handed over their babies, many of them no more than scraps of cheap
ribbon, but all such items were immediately separated from the children
by the institution's authorities. From there, there was no going back. A
child is especially likely to lose its identity if it is illegitimate, though
romance, with its insistent concern with noble blood lines, is prepared to
allow such children within its remit even if it is *gentilesse* or prowess
rather than territorial inheritance that is at issue. Gawain's bastard son,
Gingelain, has nothing to inherit but the prowess of his father, which is
innate to him, but he still becomes the hero of one of the longest-lasting
of the romances, *Lybeaus Desconus*. The meme descends by linear inher-
itance from the romance to the novel: the love-child Oliver Twist, left
orphaned in the workhouse with a locket and ring, is innately good
despite all his horrific childhood experiences, and is finally recognized by
the friends and relatives of his parents even though the mementoes have
got lost along the way. Since he, and related heroes such as the foundling
Tom Jones, are illegitimate, inheritance is not a direct issue, though it can
be added in as a bonus in the hero's happy ending. Poetic justice is served
in *Tom Jones* by Tom's displacing his legitimate, but villainous, half-
brother as the chosen heir to his Allworthy uncle's estate, and his gentil-
ity of blood and character is recognized in his marriage to the daughter
of the neighbouring squire.

Romances, whether in medieval or novel form, are often notably for-
giving to the mothers of these illegitimate children—though the novel
makes forgiveness simpler by removing them from the narrative through
death at an early stage. That the mothers of both Oliver and Tom are
more important than their fathers in the network of relationships reflects
the facts of abandonment, but it also seems to bond the children more
closely with the family than male promiscuity would do; and almost all
such stories insist that the mother was expecting marriage to her lover.
Early romances, where inheritance is at issue, sometimes end with the
son presiding over the final marriage of his long-separated parents, so
endorsing the woman's role as a link in the chain of patrilineal descent.
The romances where an unknown son comes close to marrying his
mother, such as *Sir Degaré*, may well have as much to do with anxieties
over property transfer as with anxieties over incest. Degaré's heiress
mother abandons him, with a pair of gloves that will fit no woman but
herself, after she is raped by a fairy knight; when as a young man he wins
her hand in marriage, they discover their relationship to each other in the

nick of time by means of the gloves, and he in turn is recognized by his father by means of another such recognition token, a sword without a point. The son is able to preside over the long-delayed marriage of his parents, in an action that both reunites the separated family and legitimates his place in the line of inheritance. In Marie de France's *Milun*, an analogous story though without the threat of incest, the rediscovered son takes on the role of his mother's dead father to give her away in marriage to his own father, to mark how control of the family line and territory lies in his disposal.

Degaré is brought up by a hermit, a figure who falls safely within the standard character set for romance. Other foundlings may be brought up as, and by, a peasant (as is William of Palerne, after his abduction by a werewolf) or even a butcher (as is Octavian's son Florent, who had initially been carried off by an ape), but the point of their romances is that their high birth will be revealed. In the novel, this will be by superiority of character generously helped out by coincidence and the pressure for poetic justice and a happy ending; in romance, those are commonly backed up by the overt intervention of Providence, a divine order that endorses social hierarchy and the inherent superiority of noble blood. The young Helyas, the future Knight of the Swan, has his royal parentage revealed by an angel to the hermit who has raised him, together with a prophecy that 'of his lignage should descende Godfrey of Boulion, that for to agment the holy faith of God shal conquere the holy lande of Jherusalem'.[12]

Providence is especially active when the lost child is the heir to a duchy or a kingdom. The political element in the motif might none the less seem to exclude it from the realm of memes, those self-replicating burrs within the mind, to place it rather as a reflection of legal principle and political events. It was not common practice, however, to *lose* an heir. That is a distinctively romance twist, a surplus added to the normal customs of succession, and a surplus that insists, with its stress on the recovery of the true claimant, on an ideal pattern of succession. It is not surprising, therefore, that the motif is sometimes replicated in the language in which it is described, often as a kind of punning inherent in the name of the missing heir—or even, at a pinch, just his number. The Augustinian friar John Capgrave celebrated the restoration of the dispossessed Yorkist line in such terms in the dedication of his *Abbreviacion of Chronicles* to Edward IV:

He that entered be intrusion was Herry the Fourte. He that entered by Goddis provision is Edward the Fourt. The similitude of the reparacioun is ful lich the

werk of the transgression, as the Cherch singith in a preface: 'Because Adam tres-
pased etyng the frute of a tre, therfor was Crist nayled on a tre.'[13]

That particular argument could never have carried much political
weight, but the likening of the Lancastrian usurpation to the *felix culpa*,
the fault redeemed by the advent of the man who offers reparation for
transgression, witnesses to the urgency of finding a divine endorsement
for such disruptions to the succession. It also reads like an attempt to
extend to Edward not just the endorsement of Redemption history but
the kind of legitimacy of title conferred on other lost heirs by the writing
of their loss into their names. Perdita—'the lost one', gendered femin-
ine—is so called on the instruction of the seeming ghost of Hermione,
because she is 'lost for ever'; but her name also promises the fulfilment of
Apollo's prophecy, of the finding of 'that which is lost'.[14] Perdita's kin-
dred dispossessed are more likely to have the names that mark their loss
(and by generic extension, their rediscovery) rooted in the romance
language of French rather than humanist Latin. Two of the fourteenth-
century English Breton lais make the loss and recovery of the line of
descent central to their plots, and give their protagonists names to match.
Emaré, a version of the Constance story, states at the end that its Breton
version (now unknown) was entitled 'Playn d'Egarye', Egaré's lament—
Egaré, 'the lost one', being the name that Emaré, heiress to an emperor,
calls herself by after she has been cast away in an open boat from her own
country, and she keeps the name when she is cast adrift a second time
with her newborn son. Her true name is restored to her only when she is
herself restored, first to her husband, then to her father, and with that
restoration comes the safe descent of both kingdom and empire to her
son. Her change of name, and its use as a title for the Breton original,
highlights that central concern of the romance with the finding of the lost
one. The same concern is evident in *Sir Degaré*, though there the name is
baptismal: the baby's name is given him by the hermit beside whose
hermitage he is abandoned. The later versions of the story, as exemplified
by the Percy Folio text, obscure the similarity to *egaré* by calling him
'Degree', but they keep the same explanation of the name:

> Degree, to understand i-wis,
> A thing that almost lost itt is;
> As a thing that was almost lost agoe,
> Therefore he called his name soe.[15]

The true etymology may in fact be from the Anglo-Norman *deswarre*,
'destitute', and the Middle English text suggests a meaning closer to that:

> Degarre nowt elles ne is
> But thing that not never what hit is,
> Other thing that is neggh forlorn also.[16]

He is not only lost to his parents (and he will need to find them before they are reconciled and married), but lost to himself, and nearly lost altogether, 'nigh forlorn'. The *deswarre* form in turn suggests a link with the Dissawar of *Roswall and Lillian*. This is the name that the young prince, cast out from his home court to live unknown and in poverty, assumes as his alternative, self-alienated identity, 'thing that not never what hit is'. He is also dis-aware rather than unaware of his actual identity: he knows who he is, but events have forced a disjunction between that knowledge and its practice. He recovers his own name at the moment when he is restored to his parents and to his rightful place in the succession, the moment when what had been lost is found again.

The centrality of losing and finding to the motif of the missing heir appears not only in names but in statements. Perdita is the bearer of both effects, her name being given to her, so far as the narrative is concerned, quite distinctly from the prophecy that inscribes her name within it. The formulaic nature of that prophecy is indicated by the fact that it is the one element of Apollo's declaration that Shakespeare takes over word for word from Greene: 'The King shal live without an heire: if that which is lost be not founde.'[17] Something of the same idea, that loss and recovery confirm the identity of the true heir, seems to underlie the episode in *Edward III* (?1592–3) when the Prince of Wales is reported killed in battle before he turns up on stage alive and triumphant a few lines later. The episode would seem singularly redundant, except that it gives his father the chance to declare,

> As things long lost when they are found again,
> So doth my son rejoice his father's heart.[18]

The phrasing might seem to invoke the parable of the Prodigal Son, but there is nothing remotely prodigal about the Black Prince. Rather, he gains charisma and credibility as the true heir by such an association with loss, as the *filius perditus* who is rediscovered.

THE FOUNDLING AND THE FAIR UNKNOWN

A foundling in romance is always a 'fair unknown': a child whose parentage may well have been told to the reader, but is not known either to the child himself (he is typically male) or to those who raise him. As his mysterious birth indicates, he is destined to be a hero; he will frequently turn out to be a channel through whom a dynasty runs, whether baronial or royal. A fair unknown will, however, not necessarily be a foundling, though the children of both categories demonstrate their high lineage by beauty, courtesy, and exceptional prowess. The fair unknown who has not been abandoned may be brought up by his mother in ignorance of his father, as Perceval is, or not knowing that the queen at whose court he lives is his mother, like Generides. He may be fostered, as Arthur is by Sir Ector, without his parentage being revealed either to himself or his guardian; or adopted, as Lancelot is by the Lady of the Lake, who knows his parentage but for long chooses not to tell him. He may opt to hide his origins after dispossession, as the young Horn does in his exile after his father has been killed. In the later years of romance when characters are allowed to imitate their own generic memes, he may pretend anonymity in order to win a chivalric reputation independently of his blood line, as Malory's Gareth does.

The fair unknown, *le bel inconnu* or *le beau desconnu,* is most often a young man who undertakes a series of adventures in quest of his family identity. The character who gives his name to the type—the eponymous Bel Inconnu—makes his first recorded appearance in France in a late twelfth-century romance by Renaut de Beaujeu. He crossed into English, as Libeaus Desconus, in the fourteenth century, and remained a favourite long enough to be condemned by the humanists and to put in a late appearance in the Percy Folio manuscript.[19] The Libeaus figure is unknown even to himself, though his parentage shows through in his chivalric prowess: he is, it transpires, the bastard son of Gawain. His parentage is demonstrated not only by natural means but by supernatural ones too, equivalent to the material signs by which lost heirs are recognized. In Libeaus' case, he is kissed by a serpent with a woman's face, and the kiss immediately transforms the beast into the lady for whose deliverance he has been questing. She had been condemned to serpent form by enchantment until she could kiss Gawain or one of his kin. Libeaus duly marries her and so becomes lord of both her and her territories, his innate nobility confirmed by action, by recognition, and by the touchstone of magic.

Although he gives his name to the type, Gawain's son was not the first fair unknown. It was the Perceval of Chrétien's *Conte du Graal* that set the fashion for such a figure, and who ensured its power of mimetic replication. Perceval, and Le Bel Inconnu in imitation of him, are brought up outside the court and find their place within it only in the course of their romances, though both have a birthright to such belonging before they know it themselves. Chrétien's romance rapidly outgrew its initial framing as a *Bildungsroman* of a young man's maturing into personal and chivalric consciousness, and its later continuations turned it still further away from such a model; its Middle English descendant, *Sir Percyvell of Galles*, by contrast, follows the *bel inconnu* model much more closely. It loses all the additional material of Chrétien's romance, including the Grail, in order to concentrate on this theme alone, and it is constructed solely in terms of the unknown young man's processes of self-discovery. Importantly, therefore, it brings Percyvell back to his home at the end: his mother does not die, as she does in the French, but remains alive in the forest, mad with anxiety over her son, ready for him to find her and restore her to health and to himself. *Sir Percyvell*, in other words, conforms more closely than its sources to the pattern of the family romance, where rediscovery and reconciliation of parents and children constitute the recovered equilibrium of the happy ending. It is this cluster of expectations that comes to dominate such romances in England, though they often incorporate the descent of the crown as an issue, as it is not in *Lybeaus* or *Percyvell*. This concern remains constant from two of the earliest romances in English, *King Horn* and *Havelok*, down to Shakespeare's own romances in the early seventeenth century.

One of the memes of the fair unknown romances is that the hero is ignorant not only of his family identity but of his name, even if there is no particular reason why he should not know it. The Perceval of Chrétien's *Conte du Graal* has been raised by his mother, anonymous both to himself and the reader; she calls him only 'fair son', and it is not until a crucial moment in his ethical development, when he has to face the fact of his major chivalric and intuitive failure, that he names himself, by intuition but rightly. *Sir Percyvell* names its hero to the reader in the first stanza, though he knows himself only as 'myn awnn modirs childe'. Arthur, however, guesses that he is his lost nephew when he first sees him, even though the wild young man is not at this stage interested; and the king makes his name and parentage public when he knights him.[20] The English Libeaus, like the French Perceval, knows himself only as 'beufise', *beau fils* (*Percy*, 26), and he never thinks to ask his mother for more. The discovery of his family identity matters far more than any discovery of his proper name, which one might expect to be the marker of his personal identity. He continues to be known as Libeaus, the name under which Arthur knights him before he knows any other, and half the English manuscripts including Percy name him (as Gingelein) only to the audience at the start of the romance, never to himself at the end. Namelessness often appears to set a challenge for the hero's associates far more than it troubles himself. Ulrich von Zatzikhoven's Lanzelet does ask his name from the Lady of the Lake who has raised him, but she postpones telling him until he has completed his first adventures; to everyone else, he is known as 'the proud warrior from the lake, and nothing else; for some reason he is nameless'.[21] The meme of anonymity remained an expected part of such romances well into the sixteenth century. Amadis de Gaule, who had been cast adrift in a chest as a baby and rescued by fishermen, is for long known only as 'the Gentleman of the Sea'.

Women are rarely lost so comprehensively, and especially not in the Middle Ages. Their loss is more usually threatened than actual, and it is political loss that is at issue, not disappearance. The most typical situation in medieval romance is for the heiress to be faced with an undesired marriage to a deeply unsuitable husband, thereby threatening the transfer of her land to an alien, tyrannical, or even Saracen, lord—a loss to good or godly rule rather than to patrilinear succession. She is, therefore, still in possession of her land, or at least expecting its reversion. She is embedded in the territory she has the capacity to bestow, and she and her citadel together are typically under siege; the assault is made equally on her lands and herself. The knight who rescues her acquires land and lady as a single package, and her desire for him encodes his rightful entry into her patrimony.

The conventions for the heiress who has actually been dispossessed differ both from those for such threatened women, and from those for the male of species. She tends, for a start, to be less unknown than most of her male counterparts. She rarely or never becomes nameless. When such a woman is deprived of her inheritance, as happens to Goldeburh in *Havelok*, she does not usually disappear from knowledge in the way that happens to dispossessed heirs, such as Havelok himself: her identity continues to be known, whereas it is a condition of the plot that his is not. The different treatment stems partly from the premiss that a woman's place is within the protection of a household, not in the outside world of adventure: Goldeburh herself is kept under her usurping guardian's eye until he fulfils his vow to marry her to the highest and strongest man in the kingdom, which he chooses to interpret literally (as he believes; Providence has other ideas) rather than politically. Although dispossessed, she still has her being within the land whose rightful possession she embodies in her own person. An alternative way of depriving an heiress of her true inheritance is, therefore, for the villain of the story to charge her with bastardy, to enforce the loss of her dynastic identity rather than her person. Leontes inflicts both on Perdita; the Knight of the Swan acquires his territorial power through defending the heiress to the duchy of Bulloigne from just such a charge, and then marrying her. Robert Copland dedicated his 1512 adaptation of *The Knight of the Swan* to Edward duke of Buckingham, since he 'lynially is dyscended' from the couple; and the duke was far from alone in England in claiming this particular legendary ancestry. The Beauchamp earls of Warwick owned a cup reputedly made of the gold from the neck-chains of the siblings who had been turned into swans.[22]

The later sixteenth century sees a greater readiness for such stories to allow heiresses to go missing altogether, and so to assume more of the characteristics of the 'fair unknown'. Medieval examples of girl foundlings do exist—Marie de France's *Le Fresne* and its Middle English adaptation *Lai le Freine* are an obvious instance. The English version survives in a single manuscript and was never printed, its interest perhaps being depressed since inheritance is not here an issue. Girl foundlings never become a meme of Middle English romance, and it is not until the 1580s that they begin to form a tradition. Spenser goes so far as to adapt the story of *Sir Eglamour* to change its male foundling into a girl. The mothers of the babies share both a name and the opening stages of their biographies. Sir Eglamour's heiress-beloved, Cristabell, is cast adrift with her new-born son after her father has forbidden their marriage, only for the child to be carried off by a griffin and raised as a foundling. Spenser's heiress Cristabell likewise gives birth to a child after her father has forbidden her to marry the man she loves; but this time it is a daughter, who is left in the fields for a shepherd to find and take home. For all her consequent raising as a shepherdess, Pastorella's beauty and grace win the heart of Sir Calidore; she is eventually united with her parents (now married, but childless), and becomes the heir to both their lines of inheritance.[23] She is one of the models behind Perdita, who likewise enjoys a pastoral upbringing and the love of a gentleman (a prince, indeed), though her inheritance is even greater than Pastorella's. Perdita's textual ancestry is also more varied, as it includes a foundling from outside the dominant English tradition, the Chloe of Longus' late Greek romance *Daphnis and Chloe*: a work translated from French into English by Angel Day in 1587, and which influenced Shakespeare's immediate source, Greene's *Pandosto*. In keeping with his own cultural circumstances, however, Longus has little interest in any capacity of his heroine for inheritance, and pays far more attention to her sexual education.

A girl is generally of interest to patrilinear romance only if she has no brothers. Innogen earns her place as the heroine of *Cymbeline* since she is the heir presumptive after the abduction of her brothers in infancy, and her story becomes one of solely personal interest when they reappear. The *Winter's Tale* is unique in the Shakespeare canon—though much more typical of earlier romances, including the familiar *Valentine and Orson*—in that Hermione's condemnation results in the loss of the king's heirs, his son dying through 'mere conceit and fear', imaginative dread, of what his father is doing to his mother, and his daughter exposed as a result of his own deliberate act. That loss of Perdita becomes crucial to the play primarily because of her brother's death. He is unusual in romance, as in tragicomedy, for being irremediably dead—there is no symbolic return for him in the plot, as there is for Hermione—but the theatre may have offered a way around that, too. It is possible, perhaps likely, that the same boy actor played both siblings: that Mamillius does, in the most literal sense, return in the person of his sister.

Nobody knows the identity of Perdita, or of either Daphnis or Chloe, until the old shepherds who found them produce the tokens that accompanied them on their exposure as babies. Libeaus' and Perceval's mothers know who their children are, but they are not telling; and neither for many years does the Belarius of *Cymbeline*, who abducted the infants Guiderius and Arviragus and brought them up in the wilderness. For all the youngsters, nature wins out over nurture—Perdita through the innate courtesy that makes her seem 'too noble for this place' (4. 4. 159), the men by their readiness to engage in combat and their skill and courage in doing so. Malory's Tor, raised as the son of a cowherd, is taller and stronger than any of his twelve brothers, refuses to engage in labour, and drags his supposed father to the court to ask Arthur to knight him; but it still requires the supernatural insight of Merlin to declare his true parentage, as the bastard son of King Pellinore. His mother confirms that the child is not her (future) husband's son as soon as she is called on to do so:

And there she tolde the kynge and Merlion, that whan she was a mayde and wente to mylke hir kyne, 'there mette with me a sterne knyght, and half be force he had my maydynhode. And at that tyme he begate my sonne Torre.'[24]

She is however dependent on Merlin's knowledge to identify the knight in question, and Pellinore did not know that he had a son at all. At the other extreme from these, a 'fair unknown' may himself know who he is, but choose to keep everyone else in the dark. It is a role that can be adopted as a form of disguise, not by altering but by concealing one's identity. Malory's Gareth conceals his origins as Gawain's brother to spend a year in the royal kitchen, before calling in Arthur's promise to grant him a boon in the form of the quest to rescue the Lady Lyonesse. His mother, far from having tried to prevent him from embarking on a career of chivalry, as Perceval's does, is outraged to find that he has not been given proper recognition. He is finally identified to the world through the inscription of his name in gold on the helmet she had equipped him with before he left home, rather as a mother might sew nametapes onto her son's sports gear. By this time, in fact, the fair unknown is so familiar a meme that Gareth himself can be allowed a conscious knowledge of it.

Spenser's Redcrosse Knight combines many of the qualities of Perceval and Libeaus, Tor and Gareth. According to the summary of the events preceding the action of the poem in the Letter to Ralegh, he appears at court as 'a tall clownishe younge man', like all those four, and claims the boon of an adventure. That adventure, like Libeaus', takes the form of a lady accompanied by a dwarf, who requests help in raising a siege.[25] Like Libeaus and Perceval, Redcrosse discovers his own true parentage only much later. He too was a foundling, discovered by a ploughman lying in a furrow, and called 'George' from the earth (*geo-*) that to all intents and purposes might have generated him. In allegorical terms, it did so: he is, it transpires, a mortal, not a fairy, and therefore of the race created out of dust and which shall return to dust—a figure for mankind in whom lies the capacity to resist the dragon-devil. He is exceptional among foundlings in that his immediate parentage is never revealed, though Spenser has Contemplation tell him that he is sprung 'from ancient race | Of Saxon kings' (I. x. 65). St George is, in other words, true English by descent as well as by the exercise of saintly patronage. The suggestion that one's origins can be discovered by contemplation is a strange one, and perhaps should not be pushed too far; but it has the effect of turning the process of self-identification inwards, and so away from the processes of physical adventure and the personal interest of a quest for family that mark most of the fair unknowns. St George's family is the English branch of humankind.

How much the change alters the ideological balance of the foundling story is more open to question. Redcrosse's discovery in a furrow by a ploughman might appear to open out the capacity for nobility of nature to all men regardless of social rank (*Piers Plowman*, something of a best-seller in its mid-sixteenth-century editions, was known to Spenser), but the immediate specification of his royal ancestry nips any such notion in the bud. Spenser in any case sets himself a particular problem since he allegorizes nobility of character as nobility of lineage, so leaving no way open to consider the possible separation of the two. The relationship between gentility of blood and gentility of action had long been debated (Chaucer, following Boethius and Dante, repeatedly comes down on the side of virtue over descent), but it comes close to being part of the generic definition of romance—its recognizability—that it should insist that the two are interlinked. In the formulation offered by Stephen Hawes in his *Comfort of Lovers* (*c.*1511), even if 'one of the gentyll blode' should be brought up among 'yomanry':

> Though he knewe not his parentes verament
> Yet nature would werke so by entendyment
> That he sholde folowe the condycyons doubtles
> Of his true blode by outwarde gentylnes.[26]

This is far from meaning that nobility of blood necessarily results in good action. Romances contain an abundance of characters who are both noble and vicious, but they show them little sympathy or mercy: usurpers, even from the royal line, and unknightly knights regularly come to unpleasant ends. *Noblesse oblige*, and those who fail to follow its obligations are severely punished. Still more powerful as a dominant maxim, however, is that nobility will out. It is part of the political fantasy of romance that high social rank is both justified and discoverable through innate nobility even when that rank is occluded. One difference between romance and its contiguous genres is the greater readiness of other genres to allow the genuinely poor or low-born child to rise in the world through outstanding prowess or virtue and through marriage to a prince or princess.[27] The scullion Havelok must be a prince; the Squire of Low Degree must be a squire, not a scullion. Romance discovers the child to be at the very least of gentle blood, and usually noble or royal. The one exception that is allowed is in the case of a feral child whose true parentage cannot be discovered. There are plenty of instances in romance of children known to be noble who are carried off by beasts and indeed raised by them (examples known into the sixteenth century include Orson, the twin sons of Octavian, and all three sons of Sir Isumbras; Richard Johnson adds the three sons of St George), but the very mysteriousness of the origin of children recovered from animals promises heroism. As Sir Calidore puts it when he is trying to persuade the childless Matilda to take over the bawling baby he has just rescued from a bear:

> It hath oftentimes bene seene,
> That of the like, whose linage was unknowne,
> More brave and noble knights have raysed beene,
> As their victorious deedes have often showen,
> Being with fame through many nations blowen
> Then those, which have bene dandled in the lap.
>
> VI. iv. 36

The fact that its new father is named Sir Bruin gives the child an obvious, quasi-prophetic, appropriateness for the adoption: a further use for the bearsuit, which if it cannot reproduce on its own account, can none the less acquire offspring. Such children form a meme to themselves in romances, and might appear to be well within the realm of fantasy; but at least one English baronial family, the Stanleys, was quite happy to incorporate such a legend into their own genealogy, and to locate it within knowable historical time. The childless Lord Lathom and his wife supposedly adopted a baby boy recovered from an eagle's nest, and made him their heir;[28] that foundling's daughter married Sir John Stanley, who has been suggested as the patron for the *Gawain*-poet, and their descendants, as earls of Derby, became the subject of a number of poems in the Percy Folio manuscript.[29]

If mysteriousness of origins could stand in for known nobility of blood, ideas about high birth, inner virtue, and social mobility came to be differently inflected as the centuries passed. A conception of inherent nobility could cut both ways as prosperous lower gentry or even merchant families increasingly married upwards: such social elevation could be seen as undermining the link between blood and virtue, or as endorsing the rise on the grounds that it brought with it a justifying assumption of virtue, of *gentilesse* of character rather than descent. If a steward's son such as Guy of Warwick could marry an earl's daughter, or the Squire of Low Degree marry the heiress of the kingdom of Hungary, and their elevation be justified by the pre-eminence of their chivalry, then the way was open for other forms of public action to be taken to fill the requirements of high rank. That it was in practice usually wealth rather than virtue that underlay such transactions was a fact that did not need exploring, though it profited from mystifying. It was not until James VI and I turned property or income from being a qualifying condition for knighthood into a factor that rendered it compulsory regardless of either rank or gentility of character, that the 'gentleman' decisively replaced the knight as the social ideal.

There is one social rank, however, that insists on a direct and provable blood line; and that is royalty, in the person of the true heir to the kingdom. In romance, that legitimacy is shown by sovereign qualities of good rule and self-rule, by divine endorsement in the working out of the plot, and often by supernatural signs too.

THE DESCENT OF THE CROWN

The romances that tell the story of lost heirs and their recovery of their kingdoms are the clearest example of the objective of romance to promote the well-being of the realm, the common wele. They might seem to have little to say to an established sovereign, but their insistence on presenting models of good rulers, and their tendency to equate tyranny with a false claim to the crown, both promote the idea that the rightful king is also the good king. Prowess in battle, faithfulness in marriage (a consistent element of English romance, for men as much as for women), due reward of his followers, firm rule in accordance with the law, and keeping his word, all mark a kingship that carries the approval of God and the goodwill of the people. Failure in any of those can result in trouble, a suspicion that all is not well. Inability to defend the land can result in its loss; tyranny that overrides law invites rebellion; a bastard son can threaten the safe descent of the crown. The fiction of romance may be that the rightful king will be a man who enacts all those virtues, but its covert message is that a king who hopes to keep his crown would be wise to do the same. The fiction that a rightful monarch must also rule well was preserved in the repeated claim by rebellious barons that they aimed to remove the advisers who had supposedly misled him rather than himself. Romance proffers a more polarized good and evil, a simplified ethical issue in place of a complex political or legal problem. Tyrants are therefore likely to be usurpers rather than rightful inheritors; a disputed succession will have a single identifiable right outcome, a right 'issue'—a word, as Helen Hackett has pointed out, that embraces both 'outcome' and 'offspring'.[30] The dispossessed heir of romance embodies that right issue in both its senses, and proves its rightfulness by the wisdom and capability of his rule, his readiness to uphold and rule by the law.

There is a series of memes for the disappearance and return of such figures. They may be lost through their father's false suspicion and exile of their mother, like Valentine and Orson, or through the machinations of a mother-in-law, like Constance and her son. They may be displaced by a usurper, either a wicked relative or an invader. They may recover their loss through active prowess, whether directly aimed at retrieving the crown or not, or through the intervention of Providence or a divinely-guided fate or fortune without their taking much of an active role. One story outline, which itself takes on the quality of a replicable meme rather than just a repeated plot, is recurrently found in Anglo-Norman romance and remains distinct to England, and that is the return of the heir from over the sea to claim his throne: the story of Horn and his descendant Ponthus; of Henry Bolingbroke and Henry Tudor; and eventually of Charles II.[31]

The rightfulness can lodge in the man who becomes king through marriage to the heiress as well as in a male heir apparent, and especially if he himself is also the victim of wrongful dispossession. John Capgrave, the friar who tries to inscribe the accession of Edward IV into salvation history, gives an epitome for such a story—in effect, a miniature archetype for this kind of romance—in the course of his world chronicle. Benighted while hunting, the Emperor Conrad takes shelter with a hermit who is in fact an earl that he had banished. That same night the countess, who had accompanied her husband into exile, bears a child, and a voice announces to the emperor that this child will succeed him. He, scorning 'that so pore a a child schul regne aftir him', orders his servants to kill it and bring him the heart. Taking pity on the baby, they bring him instead the heart of a hare, abandoning the child in the forest to be found and raised as their own by a childless duke and his wife.

Whan the child was growe the emperour dyned with this duke, the child stood before him, and he gan remember the face of that child whech he comaunded to be slayn, desired him of the duk, led him forth, sent him to the emperesse with swech a lettir, 'That day that ye receyve this child, ordeyn for him that he be ded'. So happed the child for to slepe in a prestes hous be the weye, and the prest red the lettir, of pité he raced the clause and chaungid it into this sentens, 'That day ye receyve this child, in moost goodly hast wedde him to oure doutir'. Whan the emperour cam hom and sey that Goddis ordinauns wold not be broke, took it more at ese, specialy whan he knewe what man was his fader.[32]

Providence has to work especially hard on this one, employing directly miraculous interventions (the voice of prophecy), apparent chances (the emperor's arriving at the hermitage), and a series of co-operative individuals (the royal servants, the duke, the priest). The restoration of the earl and the reunion of the foundling with his true family are left implicit in the emperor's relief at discovering the young man's identity, by means that the story does not trouble to make explicit. What matters is God's fixing of the succession to the empire, and the need for mere mortals, even an emperor, to submit to the divine will in the matter.

Such an explicit sense of almost magical rightness, or of the supernatural or Providence acting independently of purposeful human agency, is none the less unusual—or at least in the case of men, who are expected to show their fitness for rule by their own capacity for action. Providence is most likely to make a direct intervention on behalf of either a child or a dispossessed woman, whose age or gender debars them from most such action, and the behaviour of the men falls into place around that providential shaping. Perdita's recovery accordingly happens independently of any deliberate action on her part or her father's; it is desired, and the prophecy leaves open the possibility that it may happen, but it is not something that can be pursued through human means. The bear in this play does not rescue the baby, as it does in *Valentine*, but by killing Antigonus at the same moment that his ship is lost it ensures that her whereabouts are unknown, and that she cannot be recovered by the exercise of human will. The beast's attack is the last act of irrational violence in the play. After this point, young love, patience, and penitence hold centre stage, and finally restore at least some of what Leontes has destroyed; but they do so, in terms of the characters' own intentions within the larger plot, by accident.

So far as a lost male heir is concerned, by contrast, and given the stress universal in the genre on the hero's abilities as well as his lineage, it is a very small step from God's identification of him to his own replacing of himself on the throne and proving his fitness to rule in the process. Full-scale romances accordingly often sideline any overt intervention of the divine even while implying that the pattern taken by the story is providentially guided. Arthur is defined as the rightful king while he is still a boy by the miracle of the sword in the stone, but he has to set about winning and consolidating his kingship by force of arms. Romances such as *King Horn* and its descendants down through the Renaissance open with the exile or dispossession of the hero as a child and his miraculous survival, and end with his winning back his kingship, his rightful place in society, through the exercise of his own capacities. What happens between those two events typically takes the form of a journey or quest, with all the demands that questing places on the courage, integrity, and prowess of the hero. It need not be specifically a quest for the throne that is his by right, but it is designed to show the audience that right, capability, and divine endorsement go together.

In *Havelok*, whose antecedents in legendary chronicle go back to the generation after Geoffrey of Monmouth, the heiress Goldeburh carries almost as much of the weight of the narrative as does Havelok himself, though she cannot take any part in the exercise of prowess that enables her husband to win back both her throne and his own. In her half of the story, the earl who displaces her sets out not to bypass a prophecy but to foil the consequences of a vow made to her dying father, that he will marry her to the strongest man in the kingdom. He chooses a husband who will at once fulfil the letter of his vow while, he believes, negating her political danger: the tough young Havelok, employed as a scullion in Lincoln. What neither of them knows is that Havelok is in fact the subject of an analogous narrative, being the rightful heir to Denmark; his guardian too seizes the throne, and believes (like Capgrave's emperor) that he has had Havelok murdered. The intended murderer, however, realizes who the child is when he sees the light that comes from his mouth as he sleeps and the gold cross on his shoulder, and he escapes with him to England. The same signs in due course also identify Havelok to Goldeburh and to his Danish supporters. It is however his strength in fighting, not the miraculous cross, that enables him to fulfil his prophetic dream of clasping Denmark in his arms and England in his hand, the hand by which Goldeburh has taken him in marriage. The future of their various territories is assured by their having fifteen children, all of whom become kings or queens. The development of the legend may have been influenced by the desire of the eastern areas of England with which the narrative is concerned to justify their earlier embracing of Danish rule.[33] Here, the king of Denmark does indeed acquire overlordship of the area, but he rules in right of his English wife; and the markings on his body give divine sanction to his position.

Some of the most interesting things about this romance happened to it long after its composition. The story appeared as a regular part of the prose *Brut*, where the names of the protagonists are given as Curan and Argentille.[34] In that form, it was printed by Caxton as part of his *Chronicles of England*; and it was borrowed from there by William Warner for his encyclopaedic history of Britain from the pagan gods to the Tudors, *Albions England.* The story of Curan appears in the first edition, of 1586, and again in all the later redactions that gradually extended the story forwards, ultimately to the accession of James I. Warner's version has already been mentioned as the likely source for the love-interest side of Lodge's *Rosalynde*, and so ultimately for *As You Like It*.[35] By the time of the play, the political force of the story is becoming much attenuated: in the play, we never even discover what territory Rosalind's father is duke *of.* Warner's own story enjoyed a lively afterlife independent of its original context, in verse retellings and eventually in popular ballads; a partly word-for-word version was reprinted as an 'old ballad' in 1725, under the title of 'A Song of the Strange Lives of Two Young Princes in England', by which time any suggestion of historicity was thoroughly drained out of it.[36] The versions of the story down to Warner, by contrast, all stress the political power invested in the dispossessed daughter. He himself carries this through to the point where he makes her a golden-haired beauty who could take the prize from the three goddesses in a new Judgement of Paris: a convention that defines her as an avatar of Elizabeth herself. That, however, was not a point that could be reached historically until much later in his verse chronicle, after the Tudor usurpation had been negotiated; had been turned into the romance myth of the recovery of the lost scion of the royal house.

ROMANCE AFTER BOSWORTH

Every one of the English kings from Edward II to Henry VII suffered either deposition or a disputed crown, or both. Almost all had their claim to the throne contested by someone who insisted that the incumbent sovereign was a usurper, and that he himself was the true heir dispossessed of his right. Several of those monarchs in turn declared that they themselves were just such true heirs, reclaiming what was rightfully theirs. The romance archetype of the dispossessed heir could thus be invoked either by whoever occupied the throne, or whoever wanted to displace him. It could be especially powerful if it appeared that the rightful sovereign might be returning from apparent death, on the model close to the generic heart of romance. There were persistent rumours that Edward II had not in fact been murdered at Berkeley Castle, rumours substantial enough for his brother to rebel in his cause; there is even some evidence that they may have been true.[37] There was a similar widespread belief that Richard II remained alive and had taken refuge in Scotland,[38] a belief that encouraged Henry V's ceremonial reburial of his corpse: bury a king twice, and perhaps he will stay dead. The mercy initially shown to the deposed Henry VI, who was briefly restored to his throne, showed the still greater dangers in leaving a former monarch alive; after his murder, the widespread belief in his power to work miracles, which did at least assume his death, must have come almost as a relief. Henry VII lived in fear of the remaining members of the Yorkist line, real or pretended, who might, or did, claim a prior right to the throne. Much the most dangerous of them, to whom the government assigned the identity Perkin Warbeck, claimed to be Richard duke of York, son of Edward IV and the younger of the 'princes in the Tower', who had, so he said, been spared by a repentant murderer at the time when his brother was killed; and in his case, as in Edward II's, it is impossible to be entirely certain that the story was not true.[39] The extinction of the separate Yorkist line did not mark the end of rumour. Mary Tudor found herself facing a pseudo-prophecy connected with Thomas of Erceldoune, to the effect that Edward VI had not died, but was alive and in prison and preparing to return:

> Then shal rise the joyful sice,
> For sice was lost, and sice was found,
> And sice was buried in the ground,
> And sice shal rise and wear the crown

—a 'sice' being a throw of six at dice. The same rumour was current well into Elizabeth's reign, though by her later years the same prophecy seems to have been taken as a prediction of the coming of James VI.[40]

Even without the problem of a return from death, the monarchy was recurrently contested. Every one of the fifteenth-century kings had to contend with open or planned rebellion from the descendants of Edward III—the Mortimers and the related Yorkists opposing the Lancastrian dynasty; the Lancastrians opposing the Yorkists; the Yorkists torn by self-division when Richard III deposed the uncrowned Edward V; the last Lancastrian scion defeating Richard in battle but still having to fight off a series of Yorkist pretenders. The victory of Henry Tudor at Bosworth did not at the time seem like the successful break with the troubled past that the Tudor myth insisted it was. It was itself the most traumatic scission in the lineal descent of the crown since 1066, when Harold was killed at Hastings (or, as rumours then too insisted, survived to live on as a hermit). Henry Tudor was, like both the Lancastrians and the Yorkists, a descendant of Edward III, who had by this time been dead for over a century; but in his case he came through the line of the Beauforts, the bastard children of John of Gaunt by his long-standing mistress. They had been granted legitimacy when he finally married her, but when the legitimation was renewed by Parliament under their half-brother Henry IV, they were specifically excluded from any claim to the succession. Moreover, if Henry Tudor's claim had been a dynastic one, it would have been self-cancelling, since his lineal claim came through his mother, the redoubtable Lady Margaret Beaufort, and she, being very much alive, had the prior claim to the throne, though she never pursued it for herself. He took the crown by virtue of conquest—famously, Sir William Stanley found the coronet Richard III had been wearing, under a rosebush, and crowned him with it on the field of battle—but conquest was no guarantee of right, however much one might claim (as Henry of course did) that the victory had been granted by God. He presented it indeed as a *verum Dei iudicium*, a quasi-judicial ordeal that showed the true judgement of God by direct supernatural intervention.[41] He strengthened his hold on the throne by marrying the prime Yorkist heiress, Edward IV's daughter Elizabeth; but he deliberately waited several months before doing so, to put it beyond doubt that he meant to claim the throne in his own right and not hers. When Parliament confirmed him as king, instead of outlining his claims to the title, they settled for acknowledging that he was.[42]

It was, however, not enough to be king: it was necessary to be seen as the rightful king, too. Henry's very name argued against him. The royal name Plantagenet had come to be applied to the entire line of kings since Henry II; but this new Henry was not a Plantagenet, he was a Tudor. John Fisher, in his memorial sermon for Henry's mother, recounted how St Edmund himself had bidden her to marry Edmund Tudor, thereby lending divine approval to his paternity;[43] but the fact remained that it was an outlandish surname, lacking the respectability of either English or Anglo-Norman, and further lacking in dignity when pronounced in the Welsh fashion as Tidder. His initial advance across England was not helped by the absence of a resonant royal name:

> They called him Henry Tydder, in scorn truely,
> And said, in England he shou'd wear no crown.[44]

The Welsh were commonly regarded as a wild people on the margins of civilization (and not just by the English: in France too, Perceval de Galles, Perceval of Wales, was marked as being reared beyond the reach of courtliness by his cognomen), who had been properly subjugated by the cultured English. To the Welsh, Henry could be regarded as the *mab darogan*, the son of prophecy; and Merlin, that prophet among the undead, was given wide credence in Wales and beyond. That was never going to carry much weight with the English, however, and especially since the messianic child was not a part of Merlin's or any other prophecies in general circulation in England. It was true that the Welsh were also recognized as being the last of the British, and that Henry could therefore claim to be a descendant not only of Brut, but of Cadwallader, last of the British kings; Spenser has Merlin incorporate the point in his account of the descent of the crown, noting that 'a sparke of fire' from Anglesey, the ancestral home of the Tudors, will ultimately burst into flame:

> So shall the Briton bloud their crowne againe reclame.
>
> *FQ*, III. iii. 48

He does not mention that the Yorkists, through a Mortimer marriage to a daughter of Llewellyn the Great a couple of centuries earlier, could, and did, claim exactly the same blood line. In neither case did the connection make any practical difference to a claim to the English crown. It reinforced an ancestral genealogy, the confirmation of the present by the past; but it could not in itself create any such confirmation.

It was with some reason therefore that Henry set about trying to make the fact of his kingship seem both right and necessary, and in conformity with deep cultural ideals: the ideals embodied in romances, and dynastic romances in particular. This was always secondary to more practical measures (notably the elimination of every remaining Plantagenet), but the propaganda gradually worked towards a consolidation of the new regime, until by the time of Elizabeth the whole Tudor myth was well entrenched. The best-known aspect of this campaign exploited his Welsh ancestry for its connection with King Arthur.[45] It was not possible to argue in detail for descent from him (though it was sometimes mentioned in vague terms), since Arthur had notoriously died with no legitimate son. It was indeed risky to press the lineal argument too far, since the line of descent from Uther Pendragon passed after Arthur to his eldest daughter, who had married King Lot of Lothian—a fact that was not lost on the Scots, who made it a live issue in fourteenth- and fifteenth-century historiography so as to turn on its head the English claim to the throne of Scotland.[46] The alternative legend that Arthur himself might return—that he was, in the formulation given at the end of the *Morte Darthur*, *rex quondam rexque futurus*—could be exploited to some degree but was again not anything that provided a plausible foundation for a rightful title. Henry's naming of his eldest son as Arthur may have had more to do with naturalizing the Welshness of the Tudors than with making any claim to be a returning king, though court poets were happy to note the conjunction.[47] Henry VIII instigated the painting of the Round Table at Winchester, perhaps to make a point about his own imperial ancestry to the emperor Charles V.[48] Elizabethan courtly literature made rather more of Arthur's connection with the Tudor line, though in more metaphorical fashion—on which more below.

What Henry lacked in lineage could be made up for by association, and especially by arguments concerning divine approval. It was reported that 'Henry the saint', Henry VI, had prophesied that 'the Earl of Richmond must be King of England', and Shakespeare incorporates the scene into *Henry VI* Part 3.[49] Stephen Hawes concluded his allegorical quest romance *The Example of Vertue* with a eulogy of the king that upgrades his coming from the reappearance of the red rose 'kepte ryght longe in close' to something almost messianic, 'to be our bote | After our bale sente by grete grace'; and his mother's joy at his victory over his enemies is extended from the romance analogy of the mother united with her long-lost son,

> A ioyfull metynge than bytwene
> The moder and the sone so dere,

to something more reminiscent of the joys of the Blessed Virgin.[50] The poem seems to have been completed in 1509, at the time of Henry's death: it includes a hasty coda on the next Henry's accession. Even a generation on from Bosworth, the Tudor usurpation was clearly still felt to be in need of divine sanction.

The romance model of the dispossessed heir made a quieter appearance on the Tudor scene, in the form of the commissioning by Lady Margaret Beaufort in 1489 of Caxton's translation of the French prose romance *Blanchardyn and Eglantine*. Any political point it might be making is so understated that it cannot have served much propaganda purpose in the country at large, despite its dissemination in printed form; but it was the only secular work that the pious Lady Margaret ever commissioned, and the choice seems likely to have been driven by political analogy rather than just a desire for entertainment.[51] It tells the story of how Blanchardin, son of the king of Frise, leaves home to pursue a life of chivalry, falling in love with Eglantine in the course of it. During his absence, the kingdom is overrun by Saracens, and the king himself captured. Blanchardin eventually drives them out, is recognized as the true heir, succeeds his father, and marries his beloved. The events are all romance commonplaces, but they also have the potential to be mapped onto the events of Henry's own life: his strategic retreat from England to Brittany is dignified by association with Blanchardin's leaving home for the exercise of prowess; the Yorkist tenure of the throne parallels the abeyance of rightful rule in Frise; the imprisonment of Henry VI matches that of Blanchardin's father; and Henry's own battling for, and winning of, the crown offer an analogy for the hero's restoration to the true line of succession. These parallels gain a sharper specificity, however, from the one significant change that Caxton makes to his source. In the French, the heroine is known consistently by her byname, *la pucelle orgueilleuse d'amours*, the maiden proud in love. Caxton names her emphatically as early as his dedication to Lady Margaret, as Eglantine.[52] And the eglantine, French *englantier*, was not just a flower of general appropriateness for a heroine: the similarity of the word to 'England' or 'Angleterre' led on occasion to the equation of the eglantine with the country, and not least with the English rose.[53] Blanchardin's winning of Eglantine can thus become a reflection of Henry's marriage to the English princess, the 'lily-white rose' in the 'glorious garden' of England, Elizabeth of York.[54] The romance itself symbolizes Eglantine as just such a flower, as the hero walks in a garden and sets his eyes on a rose

that of flagraunt odoure and of beaulte passed all the other; wherfore upon her he dyde arrest his eyen, and said in this maner, 'Ha, noble rose, preelect and chosen byfore all other flouris that ben about the, how be it that they be right fayre, thou puttest into my remembraunce thurgh the fayrnes that I see in the, the right perfyt and excellent beaulte of myn owne goode lady.'[55]

The fact that the romance was not composed for the occasion, but pre-existed the events it could be taken to parallel, increases its political value: the biography of the romance hero who recovers his throne and marries the princess brings with it all the confirming ideologies of royal self-representation without their even having to be invented for the occasion.

The ability of a text to acquire a topical weight unforeseen by its original author is demonstrated even more strikingly in the case of *Oliver of Castille*, a French prose romance translated into English by Henry Watson in 1518, and printed by Wynkyn de Worde, who had been the printer to Lady Margaret until her death in 1509. Its co-hero, who, like the first Tudor prince of Wales, is named Arthur, has a right to the crown of England through his marriage to the heiress to the throne. At the end of the narrative, however, when the king dies, his cousin, the duke of Gloucester, seizes the crown.

Wherfore [Arthur] sente in to Englande for to knowe and it were by the consente of the noblemen of the countree, and for to knowe yf that he sholde not be receyved for kynge as reason wolde. It was answered to hym naye.[56] Wherfore he assembled a grete company of folke, and with grete puyssaunce came and descended in Englande, and dyde so much by force of armes, after dyvers grete batajlles, that he that sayd hym kynge was taken and put in pryson, where as he never yssued oute after. After he made hym to be crowned kynge as reason wolde, and the Englysshemen receyved hym for theyr lord.[57]

A reader in 1518 could not but have made the equation with a more recent usurping duke of Gloucester, for all that he had been a part of the story since it was first composed in France in the mid-fifteenth century; and with that equation comes the strong implication that the more recent usurpation too had happened without the consent of the nobles, who welcomed the new king in accordingly. Even more overtly than *Blanchardyn*, the episode suggests that Henry's taking of the throne was a restoration of the rightful line, not a violent disruption of it. In one significant other way, however—a way that perhaps underlay the post-ponement of the translation until after Henry's death—it offered a much more undesirable analogy, for Arthur claims the throne in right of his wife. By 1518, that was no longer a live issue, since Henry VIII was safely on the throne, inheriting in his own person the claims of both his father and his mother. Henry VII would not have wanted any romance model that suggested he reigned by any right but his own.

It was, therefore, outside court circles that a rather different romance account of the Tudor takeover took place—one that dealt directly with the historical personages involved, even if it gave a fictional spin to what happened, and which made Henry much less of a central figure. The protagonist this time is not the dispossessed Tudor prince but the dis-possessed Yorkist princess. The text in question is *Lady Bessy*: a ballad-style romance preserved both among the papers of the Elizabethan antiquary John Stow and in the Percy Folio manuscript, but which on internal evidence is likely to go back at least to the early sixteenth cen-tury.[58] It is one of the poems in the Percy Folio written to celebrate the Stanley family (descendants of the foundling in the eagle's nest), and to promote, or invent, the part they played in national history. The poem recounts the events of 1484–5 as engineered by Elizabeth of York herself, who is far from being the passive object of dynastic marriage. She dis-covers that she is herself the subject of a prophecy that she will become queen (the fact that she is literate is mentioned with some awe—a measure of the poem's distance from the highly cultured royal court):

> Shee tooke a booke in her hande,
>   And did read of prophecye,
> How shee shold be Queene of England,
>   But many a guiltelesse man first must dye.
>
> *Percy*, iii. 327 (165–8)

She accordingly determines to marry Henry Tudor, and enlists a reluctant Lord Stanley's help in sending an envoy from herself to him in exile, along with three mule-loads of treasure to assist him in an invasion—'to bring her love over the sea', in the time-honoured fashion for a returning English heir.[59] In comprehensive contradiction of historical fact, she is present to watch the aftermath of the battle of Bosworth, scornfully mocks the corpse of her uncle Richard, and promptly marries Henry:

> Great solace it was to see,
> I tell you, masters, without lett,
> When the red rose of mickle price
> And our Bessye were mett.
> A Bishopp them marryed with a ringe,
> They two bloods of hye renowne.
> Bessye sayd, 'Now may wee sing,
> Wee tow bloods are made all one.'
>
> *Percy*, iii .363 (1063–70)

And the Stanley brothers crown them jointly on the spot. This is history rewritten as romance, with Elizabeth of York in the role of both the dispossessed heiress and the desiring woman; Henry Tudor is merely her knight in shining armour. Lady Margaret Beaufort had promoted the Tudor claim on the romance model of the prince denied his right of succession; a provincial ballad-maker reworked the same events to turn them into a Yorkist romance of a dispossessed princess.

Henry's marriage to Elizabeth, when he eventually got round to it, was not the end of the story. The self-styled Richard duke of York, Perkin Warbeck, appeared to have the perfect biography for a fair unknown: escaping from the assassination planned for him by the tyrant usurper through the miraculous softening of the heart of the murderer, wandering as an unrecognized exile, finally being recognized by his own inherent nobility and by certain tokens on his body. He was supported over several years by his putative aunt, Margaret of Burgundy, and treated as what he claimed to be by various of the crowned heads of Europe. James IV of Scotland gave him a close relative of his, Lady Katherine Gordon, in marriage. Romance, however, celebrates those whom God or fortune or history favours, and Warbeck was not one of those, whatever his real identity: he was hanged in 1499, a long eight years after he had appeared on the political scene. The depth of the threat he offered to the Tudor dynasty may be measured by the fact that it was not until after the Stuarts were safely on the throne, and the question of what had happened to the

Plantagenets had receded into the distant past, that the episode became a subject of discussion, and indeed controversy, among historians and antiquarians.[60] It was a story well worth dramatizing, as John Ford realized, though not as either romance or comedy; his play was printed in 1634 under the title of *The Chronicle Historie of Perkin Warbeck: A Strange Truth*—a title that tacitly acknowledges the resistance of history to happy endings, and paradoxically calls attention to the impossibility of being quite sure what the 'truth' was. Warbeck's claims are strenuously denied by Ford's Henry VII, but its hero never admits to being anything but what he claims to be. His consistent nobility and the steadfast love for him of Lady Katherine—both historically attested—offer an endorsement to his claim that neither history nor the play disentangles.[61]

As the regime established itself, the myth it had created to disguise the fact of usurpation began to look increasingly plausible. By the time the house of Tudor had been in power for a century, the propaganda surrounding Henry's granddaughter could take as fact that God must indeed have endorsed the entry of the dynasty, must have given that *verum iudicium* at Bosworth. With the challenges to Henry VII and the troubles attending on the succession to Henry VIII safely in the past, the Tudors could be represented as the providential happy ending for the realm after the curse of the deposition of Richard II had worked itself out. That, too, could appear as a *felix culpa*, an event of apparent disaster that God could yet turn to a greater good. 'England hath long been mad, and scarred herself', but that dark night of the nation can now be turned to sunny prosperity through the descendants of the red and white roses. This is how Shakespeare has Henry represent it at the end of *Richard III*:

> O, now let Richmond and Elizabeth,
> The true succeeders of each royal house,
> By God's fair ordinance conjoin together,
> And let their heirs—God, if his will be so –
> Enrich the time to come with smooth-faced peace,
> With smiling plenty, and fair prosperous days.
>   ... Peace lives again.
> That she may long live here, God say 'Amen'.

> 5. 8. 29–34, 40–1

By the end of the speech, Henry's voice is indistinguishable from that of a chorus, or of the playwright. It offers a pseudo-prediction, an endorsement by the past of the present of dramatist and audience; and in this present, Elizabeth I and peace are effectively synonymous. It sounds like the end of history, and an end not in apocalypse but in blessing. But Elizabeth was ageing, with no heir named, and the fear that the queen and peace would die together was becoming increasingly insistent.

DANGEROUS VIRGINITY

The potent mix of the ardently desiring virgin, dynastic succession, and the ending of romance in the harmony of rightful monarch and state became explosive in late Elizabethan England. What was needed was for Elizabeth to become what Donald Maddox has called a 'mega-mother', like Melusine: the foundress of a great dynasty whose children would bear the mark of their originator.[62] The continental courtly model of wooing, in which the man pined for a distant and unresponsive lady— the model found in many of the troubadour poets and given massive currency by Petrarch—might have evident advantages as an image for the relationship of an unmarried queen and her courtiers, but the very fact that it had been found so useful for the lyric and the sonnet is an indication of its weaknesses in a political context. It is static; it has no opportunity for expanding into narrative; and its existence depends on the infinite deferral of fulfilment. The succession to the English throne demanded a story that moved forward, that promised a future in the form of offspring, and which guaranteed that future before the queen reached the limit of her mortality. There is an evident impossibility in writing a foundational romance for a virgin queen. It is an easy matter for Spenser to write of her 'great auncestry' (*FQ*, II, Proem 4), even to cast her as a fairy and potential foundress; it is much harder for him to realize that potential, to carry that ancestry forwards to a great posterity. The story of England threatens to turn into the story of a missing heir, not shaped as a romance but bringing all the horrors of a disputed succession. The heir to Elizabeth is not lost and awaiting recovery, but not there at all.

The experiences of the young princess had offered closer analogues for being reshaped as a romance, and specifically a romance of dispossession, for she herself had come close to losing both her birthright and her life. Her dynastic identity was threatened when she was declared a bastard by her father; she was imprisoned by her sister, in imminent danger of execution. The parallels between Anne Boleyn's history and that of queens and empresses falsely accused of adultery have been outlined in the previous chapter. Elizabeth would scarcely have known her mother, and never went out of her way to recall her memory, but on her deathbed she still wore on her finger a locket-ring that contained portraits of both Anne Boleyn and herself.[63] Although Elizabeth never became a foundling, never left the land she came so energetically to embody, the troubles of her early life could be made conformable without too much stretching to the romance of loss and recovery. William Warner's move to mirror her in the person of Argentille, his Goldeburh figure in *Albions England*, demonstrates how the parallels could work, as he reshapes his heroine's story to recall Elizabeth's dangerous life before her accession. She disguises herself as a milkmaid to avoid her usurping uncle's plots to render her politically safe: a state of life, according to Foxe's *Ecclesiasticall Historie* and recycled in Thomas Heywood's *If You Know not Me, You Know Nobody*, that the princess Elizabeth had sighed for while she was in exile from the court at Woodstock.[64] Even while Argentille is in disguise, she is described as worthy to defeat the goddesses in the Judgement of Paris—a confirmation of Argentille-Princess Elizabeth's inherent ability to rule even when her royal identity is still unknown, and an especially fashionable compliment to Elizabeth at the time Warner was writing (George Peele had made the same equation a couple of years earlier in his *Arraignment of Paris*, a play written for presentation before the queen). Warner's declared intention to shape English history as a necessary progression towards the House of Tudor, and Elizabeth in particular, turns his Argentille into not just a figure modelled on the queen, but a kind of historical prototype or figure for her, rather as Old Testament characters and episodes prefigure their fulfilment in the New. Such a reading of history enables him to make connections without committing himself to the precision of allegory, though his handling of his heroine's choice of husband is none the less interesting. His Argentille is committed by history to marrying, though on her own terms. By the time Warner was writing, any possibility of matrimony for the queen was past. He accordingly rewrites his heroine's marriage as the first great step on the way to uniting the various little kingdoms into what was at this time first named England. Elizabeth had once kept over-pressing enquiries about her marital intentions at bay by claiming that she was married to her people; Argentille's marriage becomes an act of unification for England itself.[65]

If it was possible to cast the young princess retrospectively as the recovered heiress, the very fact that Elizabeth was not married, and by the 1580s was clearly not going to be married, made for difficulties in finding parallels in romance heroines for her present state, whether on the courtly or Petrarchan model, or as the actively desiring heroine, or as the founding mother. She could be celebrated as Diana, goddess of chastity, but a lady of romance who is inviolably chaste is something of a contradiction in terms. She could be incorporated into the tradition of the Nine Women Worthies—a more fluid group than the male set, sometimes consisting solely of Amazons, sometimes including great Old Testament women such as Deborah—but there was not much that could be done with such a *topos* other than list them. The problem was compounded for the courtiers and poets seeking an English role to cast her in by the rather small number of ladies familiar from the native romance tradition who were the objects rather than the initiators of wooing (she being the object of their own adoration), but even when such heroines announced their reluctance to admit suitors (like Felice, or Eglantine, or Chaucer's Emily), their major function in their romances was to have their desire for independence or virginity overridden. One solution eventually adopted at Elizabeth's court was to find an English princess who was yet adored in the full continental fashion, in the form of the Oriana of *Amadis de Gaule*. Oriana was the daughter and heiress to a king of England by the name of Lisuarte: an evident impossibility in historical terms, and therefore avoiding all the awkward implications of history. It is true that Amadis does eventually win her (and is indeed granted her sexual favours), but the sheer length of the romance made the deferral of desire before that point was reached *seem* pretty infinite.

Another solution was to associate her, not with the heroines of romance, but with the greatest of British heroes: the returned Arthur. The comparison was helped by the belief, inscribed by Foxe into his *Ecclesiasticall Historie*, that Arthur had helped to defend the true Church against the pagan Saxons, just as Elizabeth defended the true Church of England against papist superstition. Sir George Buck insisted that 'hir coming was foretold by the tale of the return of K. Artur as some and not absurdly interpret it'.[66] Other writers, most particularly Spenser, interwove her history with Arthur's in more complex ways. He claims in the Proem to Book II that

> Thy name, O soveraine Queen, thy realme and race,
> From this renowned Prince derived are,

but that is not true in the simple sense of descent: one of Spenser's purposes in writing, indeed, seems to be to make up for the lack of literal children of both Arthur and Elizabeth by rewriting history into a marriage between them—a marriage that would presumably bear another kind of symbolic fruit. In addition to the fairy genealogy he invents for the Tudors' precursors, he has Merlin predict an alternative genealogy, equally fictional but human, in which Britomart, the royal warrior heiress who inscribes Britain in her name, and Arthegall, 'Arthur's equal' and his half-brother, will found a dynasty in the wake of Arthur's own death that will restore the suppressed line of Brut and ultimately culminate in Elizabeth.[67] Arthegall himself, in this new-created legend, is like the Redcrosse Knight a changeling in reverse, not a fairy child left in the place of a mortal baby, but a human child stolen by a fairy and raised as such. He too will in due course need to learn his true ancestry and 'take the crowne, that was his fathers right' from Constantius, the man who according to the Geoffrey of Monmouth tradition had succeeded Arthur. By a small but skilful intervention in the legendary chronicle genealogy, Spenser thus inserts Arthegall and Britomart into the line of descent of the British, and so ultimately the Tudor, crown.

Merlin ends his prophecy at the point where 'a royall virgin' reigns over a realm at peace, who will extend her 'white rod' over 'the Belgicke shore' to strike at Spain (III. iii. 49), in a predicted European conquest to parallel Arthur's own. Spenser can go no further, but he, like Merlin, knows that there will be a future, even if Merlin is not telling:

> But yet the end is not. There Merlin stayed.
>
> III. iii. 50

Spenser cannot recount the events of Arthur's reign as history, because in the time-frame of the poem it has not yet happened; nor can he give it as prophecy, because in this new account of the British hero, it is not going to happen. He will not marry a woman who will betray him either to a vassal or a usurper, Lancelot or Mordred, and so help cause the collapse of the kingdom in civil war. Replace Guinevere as Arthur's wife with a woman who will remain faithful, and his fall will be written out of history; but delete that fall, and the very course of history that ultimately produces Elizabeth will not happen. The prophecies, both inside and outside the poem, will not 'come out'.

Marry Arthur to Gloriana, however—a desiring Gloriana, at that—and a lineal succession becomes possible; or at least in theory. Gloriana's seeking out of Arthur provides a way for Spenser to reconcile Elizabeth's own virginity with the strong impulse of romance to locate its happy ending in the active sexual choice of the heiress heroine, the woman who can bestow rule and a kingdom together with her own person. The Fairy Queen's love for the British prince promises a way through the blank wall of the future, a means to shift the progress of history onwards towards romance. Spenser combines this with a recognition of the fact of the queen's inviolable virginity by offering her Belphoebe as an alternative 'mirrour' (III, Proem 5). Belphoebe, child of an immaculate conception, repels all suitors; Gloriana initiates her own chosen lover's quest. The two roles offered here for Elizabeth in relation to love both lie in the determination of the woman, and none of her various avatars in the poem is a woman who merely responds to a man's wooing. Belphoebe's perfect virginity is, however, a political dead end. Gloriana's desire by contrast allows for a future for Spenser's own sixteenth-century England, just as Britomart allows for a future that will lead down to the sixteenth century. That Elizabeth herself is part of the fictional posterity of Britomart and Arthegall is one way to draw as optimistic and laudatory the line of descent created in the poem, but its future beyond her has to remain uncertain. What will happen next may be as inscrutable as the mind of this or any other fairy queen, but it is the only way that Spenser has to save the romance happy ending that combines the fulfilment of procreative desire with the continuation of the state. So far as the real world of the poet and his readers was concerned, it was too late; and it is impossible to guess, from the unfinished state of the poem, what solution he was going to offer. There is nothing in the Letter to Ralegh that gives any kind of clue; the suggestion there, indeed, is that the last book will look backwards rather than forwards, to the start of all the quests. One wonders if Spenser were waiting for Elizabeth's death so that he could find out what *did* happen to the succession, who the missing heir would turn out to be, and shape his poem to fit. He was, after all, twenty years younger than she was.

The *Faerie Queene* offers abundant testimony, all the more eloquent for being unstated, to the impossibility of imagining just how that next heir might be identified, and still more covertly to the dangers of speaking any such imaginings. The fracas over the commissioning of a revival of *Richard II* by the Earl of Essex's followers on the eve of his rebellion was to demonstrate the dangers of representing even a historically attested disputed succession. Plays designed for presentation before Elizabeth concentrated on the virtues of the present moment, without looking to the future. Peele's *Arraignment of Paris*, by opting to cast her as quasi- or super-goddess, implies an illusory timelessness. *The Misfortunes of Arthur*, by Thomas Hughes and other gentlemen of Gray's Inn who acted it before her in 1587, uses Arthur not as a medium for eulogizing her, but as a contrast: far from being a romance, this is a revenge play, in which

Uther's sexual misdemeanours in tricking his way into Igerne's bed and Arthur's in begetting Mordred on his own sister are visited in terrible form on the realm in the shape of civil war. A coda eulogizes the queen by reading her virgin state as a metonymy for peace, the inviolability of her body as an emblem for the inviolate land.[68]

If Elizabeth's virginity was an inevitable topic of allusion within court plays, it was one that Shakespeare tended to steer clear of in her own lifetime. Only one of his plays, *A Midsummer Night's Dream*, makes a direct allusion to it (in its description of the 'fair vestal'), and that is not known to have been presented to her. *The Merry Wives of Windsor*, which was probably written with some kind of court performance in mind (it includes a panegyric to Windsor Castle and the Knights of the Garter),[69] has its pseudo-fairy queen (Mistress Quickly in disguise) lead her fairies in an attack on 'unchaste desire' in the person of Falstaff, and in its main plot has its Windsor wife successfully rebut her husband's suspicions of her unfaithfulness; but both are so thoroughly integrated into the action as to make any allusiveness superfluous. If Elizabeth did indeed see it, it must have been a relief to her to watch a play that took women's faithfulness as a premiss, and treated the fairy queen as a joke.[70] *Loves Labours Lost*, written some three years earlier and which claims performance before the queen on its quarto title page, is equally indirect in its allusiveness. This may none the less be the one play in which Shakespeare responds to the problem that caused Spenser so much anxiety, the queen's refusal to fit the role of desiring and fertile romance heroine. He does not take the escape route of celebrating her virginity—a *topos* that by the mid-1590s both queen and playwright may have been feeling had been done to death. The highest ranking of the four ladies who are wooed by the men of Navarre is the heiress to the throne of France; after the announcement of the death of her father in the final scene, her new position as queen regnant gives her the right to choose her own husband free of constraint, but she does not do so. Instead, she postpones her decision for a year, beyond the end of the play: an ending found in Shakespeare's reading only in Chaucer's taxonomy of natural desire in the *Parliament of Fowls*, where the formel eagle likewise postpones her own mating beyond the end of the poem.[71] The play closes with the songs of the cuckoo and the owl, the birds of spring and winter. They do, in a way, adumbrate the cycle of the seasons; but their order, with winter following spring, does not insist on an inevitable fertility. The heroine presented before Elizabeth is a queen who will not settle for marriage and posterity before the end of the action. The future of the dynasty inherent in the princess's accession to the throne remains a blank, a question both unanswered and barely asked.

Dynastic continuity in its romance form does not become a major public theme, acted on the public stage, until Shakespeare's last plays, when the posterity of the English crown itself seemed assured and the anxiety attendant on an uncertain succession had been removed. All but one of his last six plays present the safe negotiation of a succession crisis involving an heiress. Even in *Pericles*, which does not emphasize the question of succession, the rediscovery and marriage of Marina tacitly ensure the future of the royal line, and Miranda likewise represents the true line of inheritance of the usurped duchy of Milan. Perdita is heiress to Sicily, and her recovery not only ensures the future of the kingdom but completes the working out of the oracle that had declared her mother guiltless of adultery, that same charge that had destroyed Elizabeth's mother. None of the late plays is a political allegory of Elizabethan or Jacobean politics, but it may not be coincidence that *Cymbeline*, with its restoration of a male line consequent on the discovery of the king's missing sons, seems to have been the one that was written with James I most strongly in mind.[72] *The Winter's Tale* and *The Tempest* negotiate their political crises not only by the recovery of the missing heiress but by her marriage to the heir of a potentially hostile line, so that she both absorbs the rival dynasty and is absorbed in it: a faint but telling analogy of the relationship of female-ruled England and male-ruled Scotland across the Stuart accession. These two plays also offer strong central images of positive female sexuality, the desirable desire that promises to make the heroine the founding mother of a future line—that promises a happy issue, in both senses of the word.[73]

Almost the last of Shakespeare's plays, *All is True/Henry VIII* closes with its focus on Elizabeth herself and her own successors. The customary promise of abundant children from the heroine's marriage is displaced in the case of the newborn heiress onto the future fruitfulness of her country, and onto her own multiplication in good deeds, the procreation that traditionally befitted the virgin.[74]

> All princely graces
> That mould up such a mighty piece as this is,
> With all the virtues that attend the good,
> Shall still be doubled on her.

> 5. 4. 25–8

Henry Tudor's prophecy of peace under his heirs at the end of *Richard III* is now repeated:

> In her days every man shall eat in safety
> Under his own vine what he plants, and sing
> The merry songs of peace to all his neighbours.
>
> 5. 4. 33–5

Divine endorsement is evident in her Church Settlement, by which 'God shall be truly known'. She will be a Gloriana at the head of a new fellowship of men noble of soul, for whom mere lineal honour is secondary:

> Those about her
> From her shall read the perfect ways of honour,
> And by those claim their greatness, not by blood.
>
> 5. 4. 36–8

And the fertility will continue under her successor, here represented not as her progeny but as her resurrection, a phoenix arising from her maiden ashes.[75] In this 'oracle of comfort' (5. 4. 66), dynastic continuity and the happy ending for the state are achieved by more splendid mythological means than active sexual choice or the normal processes of procreation ever managed.

It was a magnificent piece of royal propaganda; a pity that the theatre burned to the ground during a performance. At around the same time, Sir Walter Ralegh, writing his *History of the World* during his long imprisonment in the Tower while he awaited execution, presented a rather more disillusioned version of the Tudor myth. The dominant factor of the Tudor dynasty, for him, was the childlessness of the heirs of Henry VIII: a childlessness that he read as divine retribution for Henry's wars against James V, when he had used 'his sharpest weapons to cut off, and cut down those branches, which sprang from the same root that himself did'.[76] The Stuarts still inherited the throne of England by divine dispensation, but of a rather different kind from that envisaged by the prophetic Cranmer: by retribution rather than by grace.

CHAPTER EIGHT

Unhappy endings: 'The most accursed, unhappy, and evil fortuned'

A chapter on unhappy endings in a book on romance might appear to be a contradiction in terms, a denial of its own generic premisses. 'Unhappy' is an especially strong word in Middle English, carrying a meaning close to 'accursed', or fated to misery. Unhappy endings make as strong a statement about the malevolence inherent in the scheme of things as happy endings make about providential ordering. They are therefore different from mere death. In the age of faith in which romance developed, the same qualities that define the chief characters as hero and heroine also promise their entry to Heaven, and a number of stories end with a happy-ever-after in the next world rather than this. The simultaneous natural deaths of Bevis, his wife Josiane, and his horse Arundel are presented as the culminating marvel of their story, not as a breach of generic decorum. An unhappy ending challenges faith more radically.

The happy ending is perhaps the feature of romance most held against it. It smacks too much of fantasy, wish-fulfilment, and escapism. There is a widespread modern assumption both that romance and realism are antonyms, and that realism is nasty (as in clichés such as 'harsh realism'); romance must therefore be both unrealistic, and unrealistically pleasant. In so far as 'realism' in the twenty-first century has an informal literary and generic meaning, it emphasizes the gruesome, the unpleasant, and the doomed. The bulk of most romances, however, is devoted to the undergoing of hardship, and a surprising number—numerically a minority, but including some of the most famous—finally opt for bleak fate over benevolent Providence. Those that do have happy endings rarely take them for granted. The difference between romance and realism lies more in the treatment of time and place, social class and motif, the location of point of view or experiential centre, than in outcome. It needs only a small alteration of structure to frustrate the happy ending. In its typical form, romance follows the cycle of experience from equilibrium through disaster to a recovered and better order, or the cycle of life from growth through death to rebirth. The upward movement is powerful enough to pull even a myth such as that of Orpheus and Eurydice with it, to allow Sir Orfeo to bring his wife back from the land of the dead. Refigure that cycle as the wheel of Fortune, and romance starts with the downward movement, but follows the wheel upward again. But while a literary structure can stop the wheel at any moment—with the protagonist at the bottom for tragedy, at the top for romance—time and event will move things on. Happiness is not inherently less realistic or more illusory than misery, but both are subject to time, and romance acknowledges that. It is especially likely to do so if its subject-matter is close to history, or if an author chooses to follow the progress of the cycle through to death or repeated misfortune.[1] The resurrections of romance, the returns from an encounter with what should by all human logic be fatal, are presented as exceptional, even as miracle; and that in itself acts as a covert reminder that the miracle may not happen—as with the families separated in the concentration camps of the Second World War and reunited decades later. Romance concentrates on the survivors, but as they live out its narratives they do not know what will happen to them, and audience expectations and hopes can be destroyed along with the hero.

Romance emerges from secular epics or legendary histories that do not offer any expectation of happiness at their conclusion. The origins of the three great 'matters' of romance, of Rome (including Troy), France, and Britain, all predate the emergence of the genre, and all include a strong element of disaster. The stories of Hector and Roland and Arthur are carried forward into the age of romance from a period when narrative bore no expectations of concluding bliss. Legendary history, like factual history, always moves on beyond its moments of recovery and stasis; the building of Troy is followed by its fall, the founding of the Round Table by Mordred's insurrection and the last battle. Germanic epic or French *chanson de geste* may offer more of a single completed narrative than history, but the completion is likely to lie in the death of the hero. Romance assimilated such stories rather than rejecting them, altered their emphasis more than their content. Tasso, working out a theory of epic for a sixteenth-century culture bred on romance, called on poets to reject stories 'that are sad, such as the death of the paladins and the rout at Roncesvalles. No Greek or Latin ever wrote a heroic poem to celebrate the defeat of the Athenians or Spartans.'[2] For him, the Charlemagne romances that transmitted the story of Roland–Orlando to his own age were opposed to classical epic, not because of their lack of Aristotelean unified structure or their frequent incredibility, but because of their readiness to admit disaster.

Once the generic norms for romance were established, they invited exploitation and resistance, and writers from the high Middle Ages forwards (Chaucer, Malory, Shakespeare) responded by producing works designed to question their own generic assumptions in ways that are more disturbing than the early legends. It had been a remarkable generic achievement of romance to justify the happy ending by the trials and hardships its protagonists underwent in the course of the action: Orfeo's final bliss is built on the foundation of his ten hard years in the wilderness after he refuses to carry on normal living without the woman he loves. It was, however, an achievement that demanded questioning, and the very suffering that lay at the heart of such romances invited a following through into full-scale tragedy. The result is a shaking loose of the genre from its customary grounding in a providential and poetic justice. God does not necessarily support the good, and an arbitrary or maleficent fate can appear to have at least as much control over what happens.

All those possibilities that had characterized the raw material of the earliest romances, of history and tragedy and destiny, recur forcefully in the shift of romance into prose in the fifteenth century, and English prose romance incorporates an exceptionally high proportion of such stories.[3] The change of medium brought with it a change in expectations, towards those raised by the prose of factual chronicle, and so invited the inclusion of disasters of the kind associated with both the legendary and the real past and the present. Coupled with the strong self-consciousness of a genre now passing into its fourth century, the resistance of history or real life to obvious or immediate providential outcomes helped to alter the norms of romance, to open it up to new and less reassuring areas of human experience. Even a writer who seems to have chosen romance *because* it promised a happy ending endorsed by God, Edmund Spenser, could find the history he was living through too resistant.

'History is what hurts', wrote Fredric Jameson. 'It is what refuses desire and sets inexorable limits to individual as well as collective praxis, which its "ruses" turn into grisly and ironic reversals of their overt intention.'[4] Romance had grounded itself on the opposite: the pursuit and fulfilment of desire, the questing knight's refusal to accept limits, the rewarding of good intention. It also typically offered the inverse of such tragic ironies—a 'romance irony' in which, for instance, Goldeburh's enforced marriage to the strongest man in the kingdom turns out to be the short step to the restoration of both herself and her husband to their crowns. But if history pressured the genre from outside, writers became increasingly ready to apply the same pressure from within. Every one of the memes described in the previous chapters of this book can result in some 'grisly and ironic reversal' of its overt intention. The 'echo chamber of motifs' that in George Steiner's formulation constitutes the essence of literature does not always resonate harmoniously,[5] and the discords are all the more troubling for the music they recall even while denying it.

The extent and depth of the process is demonstrated by the prose version of *Valentine and Orson*, translated into English shortly after 1500 from a French original written some twenty years earlier. There is no doubt about *Valentine*'s credentials as a romance. Although it touches history at a few points (its theatre of battle, for instance, is largely the Mediterranean; its villains the Turks, whose advance by the later fifteenth century presented an urgent and continuing threat to Christian Europe), it is essentially unashamed fantasy. Its fourteenth-century metrical original told of a falsely accused empress, foundling children, a combat with a giant, loving women, and a happy ending in the reuniting of the family and in marriage for the sons. But just as *Sir Orfeo* inverts the trajectory of the original myth, so the prose *Valentine* inverts the trajectory of the romance into its opposite. It starts off like the early story, and indeed intensifies the fantasy elements: it adds a Green Knight, a dwarf enchanter, a dragon, and a flying horse operated by a pin in its head. More significantly, it extends the story beyond the original ending so that what was once the stable moment of achieved bliss becomes a brief high point before a plunge down to disaster. It had long been a practice to use the events of the second half of the structure of romance to comment on the first half; here, the commentary implicit in those events serves to undermine or destroy every one of the elements that had made the moment of bliss possible.[6]

The destructive processes are hinted at even within the first part of the story. King Pepin, who finds and raises Valentine, is furnished not only with a legitimate heir, but with two bastards who plot against their father's foundling. Valentine's initial urge to find his mother gradually turns into an obsessive questing that is never satisfied, even when he has found the immediate objects of his desire, first his mother, then his father, the emperor of Greece. 'Desire', indeed, becomes an insistent repetition in the text, and rarely for good. His determined initial search for identity is superseded by an eagerness to assume new roles and disguises that ultimately take over from their ostensible purposes. The love interests of the story likewise go badly wrong, not because the women fall short of the standards expected of the desiring heroine, but because the brothers do not show any equivalent trust and faithfulness. Fezon falls in love with Orson, the brother raised by a bear, even when he is still in the shape of a wild man without speech, but that is not enough to persuade him that her love is genuine. He goes on to test her faithfulness, since, he claims,

women were of suche a nature that for a lytell thynge they chaunged theyr thoughtes and promyses, and broke theym falsly.[7]

Fezon fully lives up to her passionate assertions of fidelity and stability, but Orson, having married her, goes on to fail the very standards that she has set. In the final section of the work, he seduces the maiden Galazye on the poor excuse that 'he knewe not whether Fezon was dead or not' (p. 300). Only after Galazye has become pregnant does he inform her that he cannot marry her because he is married already. She retreats into a convent, and the plot impasse is resolved by Fezon's conveniently dying of grief when she hears of her husband's unfaithfulness. Valentine's own record in faithfulness is little better. He initially promises marriage to Pepin's daughter so long as his birth proves him worthy of her:

For by the fayth of my body if God will that I be of a place come that is any thyng worth or of valoure of extraction for to have you. I shall never have to spouse nor wyfe other than you. (p. 85)

In fact, he appears never to think of her again, falling in love with another lady, Clerimond, spending most of the romance pursuing her, and eventually marrying her. Other major characters are given unexpectedly violent ends. The faithful magician Pacolet is stabbed to death by an enemy king he has tricked. Worst of all, the climax to the prose version lies not in the reunion of parents and sons, which happens with no special highlighting halfway through, but in Valentine's killing of his father.

The killing of the emperor is in fact a chivalric act that goes wrong: both he and Valentine are disguised as Saracens in the crucial battle. Orson, who had been fighting alongside the emperor, realizes from hearing Valentine's battle-cry

that it was his brother that hade slayne his father, so he threw downe his shelde and hys spere, and lyfte up hys helme. After he cryed in weping, brother

Valentyne evill prowesse have you doone, for to daye you haue slayne the father
that engendred you.   (p. 308)

From this moment on, there is no question of this story's being just an
unusually capacious romance: it has turned into its own dark opposite.
Nearer the start of the work, the plots of King Pepin's bastards had been
frustrated; at the end, they too kill their father, and his queen—by
poison, a form of murder that was regarded in the Middle Ages with
particular abhorrence as being close to witchcraft. Valentine suggests that
perhaps his action was in retribution for his readiness to adopt Pacolet's
magic textbook, but the narrative does not pick up the idea, and the
deeper causes for the incident are left in the hands of malign Fortune
rather than divine justice. Valentine's lament when he has discovered
what he has done is one of the most powerful moments in the whole
work:

I am above all the other the moost cursed, unhappy, and evil fortuned. Alas death
where arte thou that thou comest not and take me for I am not worthy that the
earthe susteyne me, nor that none of the elementes lende me nourisshinge whan
that I haue commytted suche a dede before god detestable, and to the men
abhomynable . . . it is not reason that I live ani more upon the earth, nor that I be
put in the nombre of knightes.   (pp. 308–9)

His ensuing penance may be acceptable to God, but it does not alter the
fact that the trajectory of this romance not only leads to a series of parri-
cides but also locates their causes outside divine control. In the versions
current after the Reformation, Protestant theology required the penance
to be de-emphasized, so sidelining both Valentine's atonement and God
still further.

Elsewhere, much of the force of the rediscovery of parents by children
is to enable a smooth succession in the passing on of the throne from
father to rightful heir, and that is what happens in the early version. In the
prose, that process of right inheritance is impossibly compromised.
Valentine does, indeed, take on the rule of the empire, but he soon aban-
dons it to Orson and embarks on a life of penance as a hermit in the
wilderness. Only a few pages after he has married Clerimond, and with
no child conceived, he breaks in half their wedding ring, ostensibly to
serve as a recognition token, but she never knowingly sees him alive
again. Part of the penance prescribed for him by the pope is that he is not
to speak for seven years: just as the wild Orson, at the start of the story,
had been unable to speak, so Valentine must now commit himself to
dumbness as punishment for sin. The story had opened with the empire

threatened with being left without heirs when the emperor casts off his wife; the birth of twin sons, even in the forest, would seem to promise, within the world of romance, a double insurance against a problematic succession. Yet Orson too abdicates as emperor to become a hermit in the woods, so retreating to the wilds into which he was first born. Both the empire and the realm of France are thus left in jeopardy at the end of the story, in the hands of regents while the infant heirs of both Pepin and Orson are incapable of government—perhaps the most unstable of all political conditions. The closing sentences of the narrative assure us that the children, like Valentine and Orson themselves, make it safely to 'the blysse that never shall have ende' (p. 327), but that in itself insists how far the emphasis of the work has moved from any ideas of a providential ordering within *this* world. *Valentine* moves more towards the patterns of hagiography, where God's will is made manifest only in a rejection of secular values and ideals, and anything resembling bliss is excluded from the worlds of time and space, or of chivalry and love; but it is not hagiography, and although the value of the secular is denied, nothing substantial is offered to replace it. At the moment when romance is shifting from the medieval to the early modern, desire overreaches, love is undermined by the protagonists' endemic cynicism about women, magic is condemned, and the reunion of father and child gives way to parricide.

   Valentine is far from unique in its readiness to challenge the expectations of a happy ending, though the comprehensiveness of its attack on its own motifs is exceptional. The rest of this chapter revisits the memes discussed in this book to illustrate how they can be used not to endorse the providential structures underlying the happy ending but to call them into question.

QUESTING TOWARDS DEATH

The first free-standing adventure in Malory's *Morte Darthur*—the first, that is, to take anyone other than Arthur himself as protagonist—is the account of Balin and Balan, the brothers who kill each other. Both the position of the tale and the way Malory handles its content make it paradigmatic for the whole work as it is not in the French, where it is positioned well inside the Vulgate cycle. Its landscape, of a one-way road to death, has been described earlier: the inscribed cross, the old man who exists only to call out a warning before vanishing, the horn sounding the death of the quarry.[8] Balin is left in no doubt where his quest is taking him.

'Me repentyth', said Balyn, 'that ever I cam within this countrey; but I maye not torne now ageyne for shame, and what aventure shalle falle to me, be it lyf or dethe, I wille take the adventure that shalle come to me.'[9]

No knight is ever certain of returning from his quest; every one is undertaken on the premiss that the knight will take the adventure that will fall to him, be it life or death. Others who have taken on the same quest earlier may have failed and indeed died, but by convention they are the lesser characters, whose lives fall outside the focus of the immediate narrative. The knight-errant at the focus of the story may not know what the outcome will be, but the audience or reader has a saving knowledge of the expectations of romance. As Balin witnesses, however, that privileged generic knowledge may be wrong. This time, his premonitions are right, and the repeated expression of them forces the readers' expectations away from their own desire for the hero's success to a realization of impending doom as inexorable as Balin's own. The fact that the combatants are brothers ensures that neither of them has a congenital advantage in prowess, so neither can win; and the fact that they do not recognize each other ensures that they will fight to the death. Balan suspects for a moment that his opponent may indeed be his brother, as if fate may yet look kindly on them; but he has just exchanged his shield for one supposedly better, so that an ironic reversal of Balin's intention, a tragic irony, prevents their reconciliation. They fight with 'grete blood shedynge', until

Atte last Balan, the yonger broder, withdrewe hym a lytel and leid hym doune. Thenne said Balyn le Saveage,
   'What knyghte arte thow? For or now I found never no knyght that matched me.'
   'My name is,' said he, 'Balan, broder unto the good knyght Balin.'
   'Allas!' sayd Balyn, 'that ever I shold see this day,' and therwith he felle backward in a swoune.
   Thenne Balan yede on al four feet and handes, and put of the helme of his broder, and myght not knowe hym by the vysage, it was so ful hewen and bledde; but whan he awoke he sayd,
   'O, Balan, my broder! Thow hast slayne me and I the, wherfore alle the wyde world shalle speke of us bothe.' (i. 89–90) (II. 18)

Malory is a master at writing scenes of disaster, and the episode is one of the most compelling in the whole *Morte Darthur*. Its power lies in more than just the writing, however. The 'Book of Balyne le Saveage' functions in the work as a kind of book of prophecies: a large proportion of what is to happen later is explicitly predicted in the course of the tale. Some of those prophecies are of high chivalric acts, such as the combat between Lancelot and Tristram; but another predicts that Lancelot will use Balin's 'unhappy' sword to 'sle the man in the worlde that he lovith beste', Sir Gawain.[10] And, over and beyond those specific predictions, there is an increasing sense that the whole work will similarly be modelled on the disaster of this tale: that the history of Arthur and his knights will take the same road towards an inevitable end where brother will slay brother, and where great slaughter rather than great achievement will brand their fame.

Not every quest that goes wrong does so quite so spectacularly, but the structure of the knight-errant romance gave plenty of scope for frustrating expectation.[11] Some failing on the part of the hero was an expected part of that structure, but at an early point. The quest gives him the time and space to make up for failure, or to atone for wrongdoing. But not all quests function in that way, and wrongdoing can mark the hero not only to the end of his adventures but proleptically for the rest of his life. Lancelot never achieves the Grail, for all his refusal to abandon the quest even when he has been told that his sin will prevent him from success. Malory, in contrast to his French source, treats his failure with more admiration than the Grail knights' success, but the *Lancelot-Grail* itself is uncompromising in its insistence that his adultery is responsible for the downfall of the Round Table. Other works challenge the expectations of the characters within the work and its readers more subtly, by not fulfilling them rather than by denying them. *Sir Gawain and the Green Knight* is perhaps the prime example from the whole field of European romance. Gawain, like Balin, takes on the adventure that falls to him— falls not by chance, but by his active acceptance—whether for life or death, and he and his fellow knights strongly suspect that this one is going to be fatal. He finds neither the death that he fears nor the success that either an English Gawain romance or his own achievement would seem to promise. Like the archetypal romance hero, he goes to encounter death, and comes back alive; but in his own eyes at least he has failed. The sash that he wears as a 'token of untrawthe' may be taken as a badge of honour and of fellowship by his fellow knights, but he himself declares that he will wear it as a reminder of his weakness for the rest of his life,

> For mon may hyden his harme bot unhap ne may hit.   (2512)

'Unhap' is in the first instance a verb, 'unfasten'; but it strongly invokes the noun, 'misfortune'.[12]

Sir Gawain tells of one of the first adventures to befall Arthur's court, undertaken by its most upright representative; he fails, and the court with him. The poem is written on the assumption of the audience's familiarity with the conventions and the personalities of Arthurian romance (the king's requirement for a marvel before eating at a great feast, or Morgan le Fay), and that extends to the longer story, when 'unhap' does indeed befall the Round Table, and more disastrously.

Such failure risks compromising the highest secular and aristocratic ideologies of the Middle Ages. Writers of romance very rarely, however, allow such stories to suggest that those values are mere delusions. A work such as *Sir Gawain* does not question the worth of the ethical system by which its hero tries to live, but, in common with other romances from the high Middle Ages forwards, it does question whether such ideals are achievable in a fallen world. Earlier or simpler romances allow their heroes to aim for perfection even after they have sinned, and indeed to achieve it: Guy of Warwick dies in the odour of sanctity. So does Lancelot, whether despite or because of his refusal ever to renounce his love for Guinevere. *Sir Gawain* maintains the genre's concern with perfectibility, but denies that it is possible. It is still deeply concerned with issues of sexuality and faith, courtesy, courage, the love of life, and *trouthe*—all the more so, indeed, in that Gawain is a failure in his own eyes, and challenges his readers as to whether he is in theirs. Spenser's choice of genre makes the same assertion, of the centrality of ethics and the need to aim for perfection, and the same qualification, that perfection is not achievable within this world; but in the *Faerie Queene*, the attempt to combine the romance drive towards perfectibility with an openness to the processes of history in a society that is very far from perfect repeatedly opens up deeper fissures in the romance structure.

The blankness of the dynastic future would have made concluding the work difficult, if not impossible. For an Elizabethan writing in the 1590s, genealogical romance can produce the Tudors, but no guarantee of a safe or peaceful transition to any future true heir. The work offers to rewrite the past, to create an Arthur who will have a different biography from the one that eventuated in civil war and the collapse of the kingdom, but the past cannot be rewritten. The first generation of romances had made themselves recognizable as a distinct genre by differentiating themselves from epic and history, and there are deep problems in recombining them. The whole project of the romance-epic of the *Faerie Queene* is justified by its engagement with history, with the unfolding present of the world in which, and for which, it is written. Transposed to an allegorical Faerie Land, its Britain would seem to have the potential to realize the golden world that the brazen world of history denies. Yet the brazen or fallen world persistently denies any final possibility of achievement. The ending to every book has something problematic about it; the quests become increasingly unsatisfactory. Moments of closing equilibrium are never more than temporary, if they are achieved at all. The prospects for the whole work, were Spenser ever to have finished it, achieved his quest, look increasingly threatening. The Redcrosse Knight succeeds in killing the dragon, but his old enemies Duessa and Archimago promptly reappear. Instead of settling down with his bride Una, he is recalled to the world of questing against continuing evil: Holiness and Truth will not achieve lasting union this side of the Apocalypse, even in Elizabeth's Anglican England. Guyon cannot transform the mind as well as the body of every man whom Acrasia has turned into a beast, and the book ends with a frank acknowledgement of his failure to do any more for the man who prefers to forget 'the excellence | Of his creation' and keep his 'hoggish mind' (II. xii. 87). The happy ending originally given to Book III in its 1590 edition, with the reunion of Scudamour and Amoret—the happy ending, therefore, that the first readers of the poem found as its conclusion—was cancelled for the 1596 version, where the narrative continues through another three books without ever bringing them back together. Book IV does indeed end with two weddings, but neither of those relates to either of the major love-quests of the centre of the poem, Scudamour's or Britomart's, and those, like Arthur's for Gloriana, remain incomplete. Book V, the book of Justice, chooses Ireland as its exemplar, and although there is no doubt that the country offers itself as a strenuous test-case for political justice, neither Elizabethan policy nor the longer processes of history have been able to resolve its trials and hardships into a peaceful conclusion. Book VI, with its topic of courtesy and its closing pastoral interlude, looks an altogether gentler prospect, but it offers some of the most shocking events of the whole poem. Calidore does achieve his quest, in that he manages to bind the Blatant Beast of slander for the space of five stanzas; but its containment is an impossibility within Spenser's own world, where it now ranges at liberty, causing 'more mischiefe and more scathe' (VI. xii. 39) than ever it did before. Pastorella has half the conventional romance biography in that she discovers her true parents, but she, like so many of the other women of the work, remains separated from her love. What shocks most deeply in this last book is the destruction of the shepherd world, the nearest thing in the whole work to a good, or at least an innocent, society. Elsewhere in the work, good may have a hard time in resisting evil, but it keeps up that resistance, or is at least capable of rescue. The pastoral world is one to which wickedness, ambition, and monsters are unknown. The one inhabitant who has had contact with the corrupt society of the court has turned his back on it for the perfect contentment of the countryside. But this is not Eden, and innocence has no defence against the general massacre inflicted by the brigands. Its virtues are, in Milton's phrase, 'fugitive and cloistered', and in a fallen world that is not enough.

The pressures of time and change make themselves increasingly felt within the completed parts of the work, and Spenser admits as much in the *Mutability Cantos*, published a decade after his death. These acknowledge the impossibility of ever reaching a conclusion, a happy ending, within a universe governed by mutability. The word itself had entered the written record of English in Chaucer's work, first in the discussions of fortune in his translation of Boethius, then in *Troilus and Criseyde*, where again it is a marker for the instability of Fortune, the world of chance on the very edge of, if not beyond, the direct guidance of Providence.[13] Spenser's close attention to Chaucer must have added a further impulsion for him to give consideration to the same processes of change within his own work. In Chaucer's two major individual narrative poems, *Troilus and Criseyde* and the *Knight's Tale*, he sets the processes of rise and downfall associated with the wheel of Fortune in direct conflict with subject-matter that would seem to promise romance. For all that *Troilus* is one of the greatest love-narratives in the English language, with a legendary hero of high chivalry and prowess, it announces in its very first stanza that it will reverse the structure of romance, taking its protagonist 'fro wo to wele, and after out of joie'. The *Knight's Tale* is premised on the fact that the rise of one man on the wheel of Fortune necessitates the fall of another. It poses radical questions about the metaphysical operations that control human life, that frustrate intention and anything resembling just reward. Chaucer makes his two protagonists, the cousins Arcite and Palamon, effectively indistinguishable—much more so than in his source. There is no reason in terms of poetic justice why one should end the narrative dead, and the other with his desired bliss in the form of marriage to the lady of his adoration. The tale becomes part of a larger debate across the whole of the *Canterbury Tales* about the validity of happy or sad endings. The Knight interrupts the Monk's tragedies, with their threatened interminability of catastrophe, with a plea for a more balanced presentation of the human condition, one that allows for the 'joye and greet solas' of good fortune as well as the 'greet disese' of its opposite.[14] It is a small but significant theorization of the model of his own tale, and one that indicates that Chaucer was not adapting Boccaccio's *Teseida* just because it was there, but because it could play a part in that debate between romance and tragedy, or between a world governed by Providence and a world governed by Fortune or the stars. His rewriting, as Barbara Nolan has noted, excludes 'any hint of Christian transcendence'.[15] It is open to question whether the *Knight's Tale* is a romance at all—'romance' is in any case a word Chaucer uses only rarely, and the tale is described within the text as a 'noble storie' (*CT*, I. 3111)—but it has all the qualifying attributes of exoticism, love and chivalry, aristocratic characters and ideals, to set its audience's expectations, just as much as any work central to the genre. The death of Arcite would cease to carry its full force, indeed, without those audience expectations. As with *Troilus*, it is resistance to the very generic model it invokes that gives the narrative its power.

The resistance in the *Knight's Tale* focuses on the metaphysics of suffering. In this world, as the two young knights lament, whatever 'governance' there may be seems to torment rather than protect the innocent (I. 1313–14), and in this story those miseries do not lead to any later happiness for one of the lovers. The tale is set in a pagan world, so the standard answers of faith—that God's purposes must be believed to be for good, however much that good may not be apparent—are not available to the characters themselves. Theseus is allowed some degree of Boethian revelation at the end, but the only comfort he can offer is that it may be best to die young and famous; there is no evidence that either the dying lover or the one who is to marry Emily would agree. Theseus' determination that one must make a virtue of necessity has something in common with the romance imperative of taking the adventure that will fall to you, but 'necessity' forecloses on the freedom of action that the knight-errant must exercise. Equally, the capriciousness of the gods—the planetary gods, therefore with a continuing influence even within a Christian world—is presented as the immediate cause for the lack of providential ordering, or of poetic or any other kind of justice. There is no sense here that aspiration, metaphorical questing, will ever move towards pilgrimage, a journey towards God, and given that the characters are pagans, they have no possibility of doing so. When the old Egeus offers an image of pilgrimage, it is one without hope:

> This world nys but a thurghfare ful of wo,
> And we been pilgrymes, passynge to and fro.
> Deeth is an ende of every worldly soore.
>
> I. 2847–9

That is not the end of the tale, and Theseus' assertion of a 'feyre cheyne of love' that binds the universe (i. 2988) and Palamon and Emily's marriage and ensuing 'blisse' are still to come; but the shaping of the tale is such as to make its conclusion in happiness singularly arbitrary. There is no metaphysical principle, no access to any belief system, to offer any secure reassurance. And when Shakespeare, in collaboration with John Fletcher, turned his attention to the tale, it was that absence of providential ordering that he seized on.[16]

The practice of referring to Shakespeare's last plays as romances is well established; even *Henry VIII* can be assimilated under the same heading, given its strong providential shaping and the focusing of that Providence through the birth of an heiress. His final play is however much more equivocal. *The Two Noble Kinsmen*, like its source, offers itself for recognition as a romance: a story of two young knights of high prowess who fall in love with the same woman. Throughout the play, however, the authors home in on the elements Chaucer had made problematic, and intensify them. Love is presented not as an ideal but as an obsession. Same-sex friendship is called into question, except when its object (Emilia's childhood friend) is dead. The play's strong women speak of exercising their strength outside the action in terms of a martial acquaintance with slaughtered babies, and within it they are consistently cast as victims rather than agents. The lovers, for all their declarations of adoration, reveal themselves as callous sexual predators.[17] The play, like the *Tale*, starts with the disruption of Theseus' wedding procession by three mourning queens whose husbands are unburied and unavenged, but the scene as dramatized contains a marked predictive quality for the play as a whole. It opens with a song to Hymen, in which the birds of ill omen are enjoined to be absent; but whatever is symbolized by the 'boding crow' immediately appears in the shape of the queens dressed in black, and death remains a threatening presence throughout the play. Shakespeare enlarges the bare mention in the *Tale* of how the young knights are found and condemned to prison; and he uses this new scene, at the end of Act I, to bring forward Egeus' lines on life as a thoroughfare of woe, and to give them to Theseus. Now, however, the image has shifted significantly, from one that can resonate with ideas of spiritual pilgrimage, for its Christian audience if not for the characters, to something altogether bleaker:

> This world's a city full of straying streets,
> And death's the market-place where each one meets.

> 1. 5. 15–16

Chaucer's Arcite laments that a man trying to find happiness in life is like a drunkard unable to find his way home; Shakespeare's Theseus suggests that there is no home to be found, that life is a nightmare city where the streets themselves turn errancy into error. In this darker Jacobean world, any possibility of pilgrimage, of spiritual striving, of quest, is replaced by a barren mercantilism where death is the only commodity on offer, the only end-point with nothing beyond. Ancient Athens and contemporary London fuse into a single city of mortality.

This, it should be remembered, is Shakespeare's very last play. After the wonder of the romances, their reunions and near-miraculous resurrections and recoveries, their prophesied workings out of all things for good, he ends his career in the bleakness of a medieval romance that goes wrong.

EXPOSURE ON THE SEAS

In the conventional accounts of the child exposed on the seas, he or she is preserved by God for some great future: for sanctity or empire. Greatness, however, need not take the form of goodness. By an altogether more ironic process of Providence, or by a more malignant fate, the child who is preserved may be the ultimate traitor. The Middle Ages offered two such figures: Judas Iscariot, and Mordred.

Judas is not a figure one associates with the heroes of either romance or tragedy, but the biography recorded for him in the *Golden Legend* incorporates many of the same memes. It is a compelling story, and was still circulating in the eighteenth century in a popular print.[18] After his mother dreams that she will bear a son so evil that he will cause the downfall of his people, she and her husband determine to dispose of the child. They are reluctant to kill him, so, in the earliest Middle English version,

> hii beseye tham that hii made . a barel atte laste
> Ther inne hii dude this luther chyld . and amydde the se hyt caste.[19]

[They finally decided to prepare a barrel, and they put this evil child in it and cast it into the sea.]

The barrel containing the baby is found by a childless queen as she 'pleide bi the stronde' (31) and she raises him as hers, but after she bears a son of her own she taunts him with being a foundling. Judas kills his foster-brother, flees to Jerusalem, and unwittingly kills his father in a quarrel and marries his mother. So far, the story is close to that of Oedipus; but Judas still has the key part of his history to come. When he and his mother/wife discover the truth about themselves, she suggests he should go to Jesus to receive forgiveness for his sins, and his following of Christ leads to his great betrayal. There is of course ultimately a providential pattern behind all this—*the* providential pattern, since the betrayal enables the Passion and Redemption of mankind. Like the Fall, the betrayal has something of the quality of a *felix culpa*, a sin that brings about a far greater good. Judas's suicide, however, excludes him from participating in that good, or from sharing in the redemption offered to sinners who do not despair of God's mercy. Even in the theological interpretations of the Biblical story, there is a black irony in this, intensified in the legend. He is unquestionably a sinner, but not all his sins, especially the incest, are committed deliberately or with any intention of the will. The sense left by the full legend is that fate has it in for him rather than that the purposes of God are made manifest in him. He appears as *sacer*, that Latin word that covers the man set apart by the gods for worse as well as for the better. Judas is tainted from before his birth: in Middle English terms, unhappy.

It may have been with the legend of Judas in mind that Malory revised the account of Mordred's infancy that he found in the *Merlin*. Mordred in this tradition is himself a child of unwitting incest between Arthur and his half-sister, and his conception sparks prophetic omens of the doom that will follow. Arthur dreams that griffins and serpents will burn and slay all the people of his land, and Merlin expounds both what he has done and what the consequences will be:

> Ye have done a thynge late that God ys displesed with you, for ye have lyene by youre syster and on hir ye have gotyn a childe that shall destroy you and all the knyghtes of youre realme.   (Malory, i. 44 (I.20))

Like Judas's parents after his mother's dream, Arthur attempts to frustrate fate, and with an equal lack of success. In the French, he orders all the children born in May to be sent to him, but the ship carrying Mordred is wrecked, and he is the sole survivor. Arthur considers killing the babies he has gathered up, but instead he follows a visionary instruction to set them adrift in a pilotless boat so that Christ may save or destroy them. In the event, they all come ashore safely, and are raised by Arthur's own care. Malory makes the episode much more deadly. There is no separate voyage and shipwreck for Mordred; instead, Malory combines the two journeys into one, in the course of which all the babies except Mordred suffer the fate that should, by the logic of the story and of legal or romance convention, belong only to the child of polluted birth. After the children have been collected,

all were putte in a shyppe to the se; and som were foure wekis olde and som lesse. And so by fortune the shyppe drove unto a castelle, and was all to-ryven and destroyed the moste party, save that Mordred was cast up. (Malory, i. 55 (I. 27))

In this new version, Arthur is cast in the far from heroic role of Herod, but the real point of the changes focuses on Mordred rather than the king. In this new massacre of the innocents, it is as if Judas, not Christ, were the only one to survive.

For Mordred, as for Judas, this is only the beginning of the story, but Mordred's story does not have any redemptive final coda. Judas's career leads to his murder of his unknown father and incest with his mother, the Crucifixion, the downfall of the Jews, and his own death and damnation, but God's larger plans for salvation history still operate. Mordred, with a full knowledge of what he is doing, goes on to attempt (or to achieve, depending on the version) an incestuous relationship with his father's wife, to kill his father, and to destroy the realm; but this is, in Malory's somewhat obscure phrase, the 'morte Arthure saunz gwerdon', the death of Arthur with no recovery, no payback, no compensatory result in good.[20] Mordred is the traitor within the house, as Christ is betrayed by one of his own followers. The survivor from the boat becomes, in Arthur's words in the final battle, 'the traytoure that all thys woo hath wrought'. Lucan warns the king against fighting him, 'for he ys unhappy': that word again that indicates almost an infectious state of disaster, or an open passage through which 'thys wycked day of Desteny' has entrance. Arthur refuses to hold back, and Mordred's final action is to inflict a mortal wound on 'his fadir, kynge Arthur': the one time in the whole *Morte Darthur* when that collocation is used. The baby protected by God throughout exposure on the seas should come back to reunite his family and ensure the succession. Mordred's survival instead fulfils a different prophecy, given in full in the *Merlin*: that 'the fader sholde sle the sone, and the sone sle the fader, and the londe of the grete breteigne abide withouten heir and lordles'.[21]

DIABOLIC MAGIC

'Magic that doesn't work' is the most telling kind of romance magic, a means of turning wonder and admiration onto the characters. Magic that does work is as likely to be diabolical as helpful, and increasingly so as romance moved into the sixteenth century. The *Faerie Queene* may allow Britomart a magic lance and Arthur a magic sword and shield, but they none the less have to fight largely by their own natural courage, faithfulness, and prowess against enemies equipped with powers of shapeshifting or vanishing, conjuration, invulnerability to wounds, and witchcraft, or against hellish monsters with poisoned teeth. Magic and the supernatural increasingly inspire fear and horror rather than wonder. Magic, like fairies, has too much of an association with the devil to be comfortable.

It might be expected that the passage of time from what are customarily known as the Dark Ages to the Enlightenment would show a progressive downgrading and dismissal of magic, but this is far from being straightforwardly the case. It is true that the category of the marvellous, defined as natural phenomena that lie beyond rational explanation, shrank over the centuries as experiment and exploration explained or disproved them. The miraculous too took a severe battering at the Reformation, with the denial of the capacity of saints or their relics to intervene in the normal processes of the created world, and a resistance to any belief that even God would intervene other than through natural processes. The supernatural, however—the realm of phenomena beyond the reach of scientific analysis, and not directly under the control of God—in many ways increased its hold, partly through claims for the divine potential of hermetic and Neoplatonic magic, but partly through an increasing conviction that the only remaining source of the supernatural, when the miraculous and the fairy were eliminated through the exercise of reason, was the devil.[22] Roman Catholicism offered a way to resist such diabolical interventions, through exorcism or pious charms, even the sign of the cross. Rational Protestantism rejected all such defences as superstition, and in doing so, as Keith Thomas has argued, made magic much more threatening than it had been in the Middle Ages.[23] Although witchcraft was condemned and witches (male or female) occasionally punished, they were not perceived as a major social threat in the Middle Ages, in life or in literature. Even Morgan le Fay is more of a nuisance than a diabolic Other, and she is much less dangerous than the entirely non-supernaturally-powered Mordred. The stepmother of *William of Palerne*, who uses her 'coninge of wicchecraft' to turn her stepson into a werewolf, is forgiven and accepted back into the life of the court as soon as he re- transforms him.[24] The first English statute against witchcraft was passed only in 1542, and the great age of witch-hunting, with witches cast as agents of the devil, was contemporary with the increasing impetus of the scientific revolution, in the seventeenth century.[25]

The anxieties that made magic appear so ominous were none the less already stirring before the recognized Catholic means of keeping it at bay were removed, and they are reflected in its treatment in a number of romance texts from the fifteenth century forwards. The text that inspired the witch-hunts of continental Europe, the *Malleus Maleficarum*, is a Catholic work that narrowly predates the Reformation. Its publication in 1486 altered the whole balance of how magic and enchantment and their practitioners were regarded, redefining all such practices as sorcery. Magic in earlier romance rarely invites rejection: it frequently appears as neutral, even as a good thing. Wonder-working rings that help the hero are a simple bonus. They operate on the edge of marvel, those unexplained powers of nature; if a lodestone can turn towards the north, why should another stone not have comparable virtues of a different kind? The emphasis falls on the power of the talisman, not on the means that brought it into being. There was an idea around in the Middle Ages that it might be possible to entrap a devil in a ring to give it magical powers, but it seems to have been floated as an intellectual possibility rather than as a theological proscription.[26] A hero may, like Partonope of Blois, fear that the self-propelling boat on which he finds himself is the work of the devil, but he is wrong. Later romances do not always take such a comforting view.

Two of the most widely known of the early printed prose romances, *Valentine and Orson* and *The Four Sons of Aymon* (which, like *Valentine*, was both abundantly reprinted and dramatized in the sixteenth century), show the transition in progress from the acceptance of magic to its demonization, as the helpful magic that has sustained the heroes in their many adventures is finally rejected. Maugis, the magician cousin of the Four Sons, becomes a hermit, and there is a strong sense that Christianity is foreclosing on magic. *Valentine and Orson*, specifically in its fifteenth-century prose recasting discussed above, makes the process still more explicit; it may not be coincidental that the composition of the French version was almost exactly contemporary with the *Malleus Maleficarum*, though direct influence is unlikely.[27] The earlier episodes of the text employ the more benevolent kinds of magic, such as a speaking bronze head that gives helpful instructions to the heroes, and the marvellous mechanical horse. The horse's creator, the dwarf Pacolet, is introduced as if he were a benevolent agent of good, the practitioner of magic that helps the heroes when natural means fail. Over the course of the work, however, he is transformed into something much more suspect. Valentine's Saracen enemies themselves acquire the assistance of an enchanter, named Adramayne, who has long been known to Pacolet, and they are presented not as contrasting but as equivalent. Both have been trained in the same techniques, perhaps even the same school, of 'nygromancy',[28] and both are masters of the art. Pacolet is initially happy to host Adramayne, and they compete with each other in producing entertainments for the company. When their enmity becomes apparent, Adramayne at first succeeds in outwitting Pacolet, but the dwarf speedily gets his revenge. He disguises himself (with a little magic help) as a woman, gets access to Adramayne's tent, and after casting him into an enchanted sleep he beheads him. He likewise puts the rest of the Saracen army to sleep, and invites in the Christians to slaughter the lot. His actions thus benefit the Christians, but they are not godly: there is no distinction made between his own arts and those of his pagan counterpart, and the fact that the narrative regularly refers to Adramayne as 'fals' does not disguise that. As the work progresses, Pacolet's methods become increasingly suspect. He plays the same trick of putting an army to sleep ready for slaughter in contradiction of an oath of Valentine's, in an action acknowledged as treasonable; he raises the devil to discover whether a castle can be taken.[29] Finally he becomes too clever for his own good, and is stabbed to death by a king he has tricked into Valentine's hands. Valentine takes his magic tables, 'in whyche was wryten all the secretes of hys arte', from his bosom, 'the whyche', the narrative adds, 'dyd him good servyse afterwarde' (p. 282). But that is not how the plot itself goes. After his accidental killing of his father in battle, his own explanation for the deed is to blame his readiness to trust magic:

Never please it God that I plaie more with suche arte, for it is dampnable. And he that tought it me dyed unhappely at the laste, and I beleve that for this sinne I have slain my father.   (p. 311)

A romance that starts out with all the wide-eyed acceptance of enchantment as a legitimate element of its own generic form turns to attack and reject it as diabolic.

Although *Valentine* recognizes some of the same anxieties that went into the creation of the *Malleus Maleficarum*, there is one important exception. The romance does not manifest the terror of women as channels of diabolic communication evident in its notorious contemporary. Its heroines, indeed, generally show considerably more probity than the men, and magic and enchantment are presented as male skills. None the less, its sixteenth-century readers came to it from a cultural background in which fears of sorcery and witchcraft were steadily increasing. For all its elements of fostering bears, foundlings recovered, and innocence vindicated, *Valentine* marks the end of an age of innocent wonder.

Such an extreme reaction against magic provides a useful context for considering the Elizabethan literary magicians, not least Spenser's Archimago, discussed earlier, and Marlowe's Dr Faustus. Faustus's urge to damnation marks the play for tragedy, but the suspicion of magic even in so hospitable a genre as romance underlines the danger of what he is doing. The diabolic nature of his magic is never in question, since it is acted out on stage; but in one crucial sense that too is magic that does not work. As Mephistopheles calmly informs him, it is not his conjuration that has summoned him from Hell, but the fact of his abjuration of God. The *frisson* one expects to follow from the summoning up of the devil turns into the grimmer fascination of seeing someone choose their own damnation, just as wonder shifts from the magical to the human. The tricks Faustus plays with his newly acquired powers have often been regarded as disappointing, but although their frequent quality of practical joke has some precedents in Merlin and Pacolet, their diabolic operation makes them far more dangerous. His flight through the air in a dragon-drawn chariot (unstageable, even by elastic Elizabethan standards of imaginative audience participation) is not cognate with Alexander's cunning invention of a griffin-drawn flying-machine, but an overt transgression of the limits of knowledge allowed to humankind by God, and retribution follows accordingly. The late medieval Valentine rejects magic only after irremediable disaster has struck, but he spends the last years of his life in penitence, and dies in the odour of sanctity. The Renaissance Dr Faustus does neither, despite his last-second offer to burn his books.

FAIRIES AND FATES

Fairies, even more than magic, smacked of the devil. However careful authors might be to distinguish the fairies of their own texts from the altogether more suspect sort still widely believed to be at loose in the world, the very qualities that marked them as supernatural also marked them as dangerous, whether those qualities were strict judgement, capriciousness, their ability to alter the laws of the physical world, or the power of prophecy. Thomas of Erceldoune is returned to middle-earth by his elf-queen just before the devil comes to carry him off as part of the tribute due to him from her country. Few of the supernatural beings of medieval romance are as benevolent as the fairy godmothers of fairytales, and even godmothers are prepared to turn vicious towards the enemies of their protegées. Otherworld generosity, in the romances, is usually performed in the interests of the giver, and lasts only as long as those interests are protected. Morality in the human sense is rarely an issue. If Oberon insists that Huon should stay chaste before marriage, it comes over more as a taboo from an area outside reason than as an ethical or Christian prohibition. Often, the same figures who offer rewards initiate disaster. This may, as in *Sir Launfal*, amount to a trial of faithfulness that he is allowed to pass, but fairies do not bring any assurance of a providential outcome. Equally, their powers of prophecy are amoral. Bliss and catastrophe are foretold without distinction, whether they might take the form of due reward or due punishment or of something outside justice altogether.

Having a fairy mother as your foundress can therefore cut both ways. *Richard Cœur de Lion* preserves the legend that the wife of Henry II was a fairy of the devilish variety, whose true nature was unmasked when she was forced to attend Mass. The legend offers a retrospective explanation for the towering and unconventional personality of Eleanor of Aquitaine (though she is given a different name and biography in the text); for Richard's exceptional savagery, of a kind to be wondered at rather than imitated (his byname supposedly derives from his tearing the heart out of a lion that attacked him; the romance describes his fondness for eating roast Saracen); and perhaps also for the inadequacies of her youngest son, the future King John, whom she dropped as she made her final disappearance through the church roof.[30] Although the whole English royal dynasty descended from herself and Henry (the Plantagenet name was derived from his badge), the legend of the demon wife does not seem to have been called on to explain what happened to their later descendants—not even when it was printed under the Tudors by Lady Margaret Beaufort's own printer, Wynkyn de Worde. The story of Melusine, by contrast, seems to have been recorded to do just that. Ancestral romance can not only incorporate the illustrious and semi-magical origins of a family but also account for the disasters that may afflict it over the course of history, so shifting their cause from personal responsibility to a godless predestination. The house of Lusignan suffered a series of disasters in the later fourteenth century, with the loss of Poitou to the English in the

Hundred Years War, and the Lusignan king of Armenia's loss of his crown in 1375.[31] The writing of the legend of Melusine in France in the 1390s thus takes cognizance both of the illustrious origins that could be claimed for the line, and of its less than illustrious present.

The story of *Melusine*'s fairy taboos and prohibitions, the dangers accompanying sexual access to the women, has already been told. An alternative way to tell the same story is to concentrate on how the disasters that befall the Lusignan line are grounded in a series of double predictions of the future, prophecies or promises of either wish-fulfilment or disaster, that are to be governed by the actions of the male protagonists.[32] Wealth and honour await the king of Albany if he does not see his fairy wife Pressine in childbed. Instead, his unthinking entry into her room compels her to leave him, lamenting bitterly; and in due course her daughters take revenge on him by shutting him inside a mountain. This in turn leads Pressine to tell them that their action has prevented their release from the world of the fairies, and to give them each a 'gift', or a curse, Melusine's being that she should turn every Saturday into a serpent from the waist down. Her deliverance will depend on whether or not her husband will keep his word not to look at her then.[33] Melusine accordingly offers Raymondin two alternative prophecies on their wedding night: a future of unalloyed happiness if he keeps his word; or, if not, that 'bothe you and your heyres shall fall litil and litil in decaye and fro your estate' (p. 57). Even while he keeps his oath, having a fairy for a wife has drawbacks: each of her ten sons bears a 'mother-mark',[34] not an enhancing king-mark but a congenital deformity. The eldest, for instance, has a large, squat face, one red and one blue eye, and ears 'as grete as the handlyng of a fan'.[35] For the older sons, who turn out well, this figures as a sign of their exceptionalness without its counting against them. They become leaders of the Christian resistance against the Turks and win kingdoms and dukedoms, but the younger sons have rather different fates. One is so saintly that he opts to become a monk, but that so infuriates his brother Geoffrey 'with the great tooth' that he burns the monastery, and his brother and his fellow monks with it. In the case of the youngest, three-eyed, son, the aptly named Horrible, his moral deformities are so extreme (by the age of 4, he has killed two wet-nurses) that his parents arrange to have him murdered. Things are, in other words, going wrong with the family even before Raymondin breaks his oath. That diverts the course of the future from its predicted good to its predicted trouble. He is devastated by what he has done, and speaks a long lament regretting the loss of 'my joye, al my comfort and myn hoop . . . my swete and entierly beloved lady'.[36] She herself has to abandon husband and family and the castle of Lusignan she had founded, to wander in the shape of a flying serpent until the Day of Judgement. For her, this is an outcome far worse than death. The greatest blessing she desired, it transpires, would have been ordinary mortality. Without the breaking of the taboo, she

> hadd lyved the cours natural as another woman; and shuld have be buryed, aftir my lyf naturel expired, within the chirche of Our Lady of Lusynen, where myn obsequye and afterward my annyversary shuld have be honourably and devoutely don.   (p. 316)

In contrast to Launfal, whose grief at the loss of his own fairy mistress after he has broken her taboo ultimately leads to his return to her favour and perpetual life with her in fairyland, Raymondin has no way to recover either his own loss or hers. He becomes a hermit, 'for to pray god that it playse hym to give allegeaunce [=alleviation] to my lady my wyf' (p. 335), but his prayers are unavailing against her fairy mother's curse. Melusine's last appearance is in her serpent form, at the moment of his death, when she utters a cry so dolorous that it threatens to make the fortress of Lusignan fall.

The loss of Armenia is presented as the long-term effect of Pressine's curse on another of her daughters, who is banished there to a castle where she is to preside over the adventure of the sparrow-hawk. A knight who can watch it for three days and nights without sleeping can have any gift he chooses, except only herself. Anyone who persists in asking for her as his reward 'shalbe infortunate unto the ninth lynee, and shul be putt from their prosperitees' (p. 16). In due course, a descendant of Melusine's third son, himself king of Armenia, does just that. Furious, she tells him that she is Melusine's sister, his request therefore incestuous, and that as a consequence of his forbidden desire he himself will, like Raymondin, suffer 'decay', and his heirs 'grete myschief' and exile to the ninth generation.

> And wete it wel that his heyres after his decesse were not fortunat, but unhappe in al their actes.   (pp. 367–8)

Divine retribution, including the visiting of the sins of the fathers on the children, was a well-recognized explanation for the unhappiness of life. *Melusine* insists that there can be other principles of retribution at work with which God has nothing to do.

By the time the romances of Melusine reached Middle English, around 1500, the precision of their historical and prophetic messages must have been inaudible to most of their readers. Historical prophecy is much more telling when it relates to one's own nation and time. It is an inherently apocalyptic mode of discourse, and so encouraged by disaster (as in the claims made on the internet that the events of 9/11 had been predicted by Nostradamus), though there can be prophecies for good too, as the prophecies of the Stuart rule of Britain demonstrate. The difference between hopeful and ominous prophecies is in any case not always clear, prophecy being closely related to irony, appearing to say one thing while actually meaning another. It specializes indeed in those 'grisly and ironic reversals' of Jameson's formulation. The 'goddesses of destinie, or else some nymphs or feiries' who prophesy Macbeth's kingship to him in Holinshed's *Chronicle* predict the fulfilment of his desires for the crown,[37] and Shakespeare makes that fulfilment the basis of his tragedy. For his Macbeth, the further prophecy of the descent of the Stuart line through Banquo's son Fleance adds to his miseries, however much it may have pleased James I. The processes of both history and Providence promise that the future monarchical line will spring from the boy who escapes death when his father is killed. In the longer term beyond the confines of the drama, *Macbeth* promises romance, but that is not the focus of the play.

The most prophetic of the fairies of medieval romance, the lady of *Thomas of Erceldoune*, finally reached print in 1652, in the anthology *Sundry Strange Prophecies of Merlin, Bede, and Others*. The text is very close to the earliest form to be recorded, in the Thornton manuscript of *c.*1440. Its prophecies, however, are given a coda that takes them on beyond the standard ending, and they are very grim indeed. This part of the text may well originally have been a free-standing one, but the 1652 print runs it on from its *Thomas* in the same double-column verse format with no new heading, in a way that suggests not only that its readers would take the two texts as one but that the compiler of the anthology may have found them in that form. It can be dated, as can many prophecies, by the point where accurate but lightly coded 'prediction' of what is already known gives way to fabrication, though in this instance that is made more complicated by the fact that it seems to have been overwritten, extended, and re-interpreted as the years went by. Its correct, retrospective 'prophecies' cover the Reformation and the dissolution of the monasteries, the short reign of 'I' in 1553 (the text helpfully adds dates), followed by 'the marvellous M' (Lady Jane Grey and Mary); and it gives a warning about the power of 'aliens', the Spanish,

> Until E do reign again,
> In whose time many shal turn from the faith

—'the faith' being Roman Catholicism. This looks at first glance like a prophecy about Elizabeth, and was apparently so taken by the redactor or editor of this composite text; but the 'reign *again*' is more specific, and identifies it as one of the rumours about the return of Edward VI.[38] The rest of the text is entirely fabrication, and of a particularly frightening kind. The year 1597 will bring in

> great dearth and murder,
> Neighbour against neighbour shal fight,
> The brother with the brother in armour dight.
> The father against the son you shal see.

1598 promises 'terrible' war, and a power struggle between (or perhaps invasion by) three kings. The next year, 'many shal die with sorrow and pain'. In 1600

> Ladies shal waile that ever they were born . . .
> Fortune shal turn up al that earst was down,
> And then the layity shal wear the crown;
> Then to study take thy tombe,
> It draws neer the day of doom.

> (p. 28)

The text, in fact, prophesies the death or removal of the queen, itself a treasonous act, and follows that with civil war and all the horrors of apocalypse. With texts such as this at large in the country, one sees why the government found prophecy to be so dangerous a mode.

By 1652, when it was published, the critical years were safely in the past, and the ban on the printing of prophecies had been lifted. Prophecy had indeed become one of the dominant modes of political discourse in the Civil War era, and not just by the godly; as the whole collection of texts in *Sundry Strange Prophecies* indicates, Merlin and Thomas and others were riding high on the revival. The year was a particularly active one for prophecy, encouraged by an eclipse of the sun and the millenarian events that seemed to be happening all around.[39] Part of the attraction of the text must have lain in its chiming in with a widespread popular sense that the world was coming to a crisis or to an end. The elf-queen has a role to play not only in the 1440s but in Richard Cromwell's antipapal propaganda most of a century later, and under Oliver Cromwell a century after that. The prophecies she utters, however, are increasingly doom-laden.

At their simplest, love stories that turn out wrong do so because circumstance or fate is not on the side of the lovers. A strong and loving heroine does not always act as a predictor of a happy outcome, whether for the whole romance or just for herself. Tristan and Isolde share their separation from each other and a tragic death just as they share their desire. Very few of Malory's desiring women find happiness. Elaine of Corbin is not, as the French tries to make her, a symbol of the Virgin, contented in her conception of Galahad, but a woman who aches with desire for a man who loves someone else. His Elaine of Astolat dies from unrequited love with a passionate defence of her desire in the sight of God. Stories of this kind, however, rarely spring a surprise at the end. The impossibility of a happy ending is built into the narrative from early on, and the romance elements gain extra poignancy from the reader's sense that all cannot be well, that the hopes and desires of the lovers will finally be frustrated. Such an exploitation of convention may run counter to the generic norm, but it does not altogether undermine the basic principles of romance love. The women's desire is still approved, even though the situations in which they exercise it make a final fulfilment impossible. Like the knights-errant who knowingly ride towards death, these women accept the challenge of loving and all its consequences, and do so without hesitation or repentance.

More disturbing are those romances that offer unhappy endings to their stories by locating themselves with varying degrees of explicitness within the discourses of misogyny. The 'desirable desire' of romance was always an attitude chipped out of such attitudes, and defined itself in resistance to them. That resistance in turn invites counter-opposition from the antifeminist ideology it rejects. Antifeminism was so well established by the time of the rise of romance that writers could jump either way, whether in the twelfth century or the seventeenth. The less than good can be recuperated: Medea, who in most treatments of her legend is one of the most anxiety-inducing of women—determined to obtain the man she wants, skilled in magic and necromancy, and ultimately the murderess of her own children—is given the full heroine treatment in several texts, including Raoul le Fèvre's fifteenth-century version and Caxton's translation, where she is rewarded for her love for the perfidious Jason by marriage and a happy ending.[40] The good can be rendered suspect: Lavinia, little more than a cipher in Virgil, but whose desire for Eneas in the early French *Roman d'Eneas* helped to set up the expectations for romance heroines, is recast as nothing more than a metonymy for bloodshed in the *Faerie Queene*, her marriage to Aeneas being described as

> Wedlock contract in bloud, and eke in blood
> Accomplished.
>
> III. ix. 42

Desirable desire threatened to be an unstable category, that could be constructed temporarily but that needed constant renewal.

As has been noted, it is not uncommon for a writer to incorporate some degree of antifeminism within a romance, if only to acknowledge audience anxiety and so to help neutralize it. Chrétien's *Cligés* both celebrates its Fenice, and notes that her deception of her husband in favour of the man she loves resulted in the close sequestration of later empresses. Hue's *Ipomedon* alternates its sympathetic focalization through its heroine with sly or titillating comments inviting voyeurism or sniggers— comments, interestingly, that are cut from the Middle English versions. Ulrich von Zatzikhoven endorses the desire of Iblis for the knight she dreams of, the as yet unknown Lancelot, but treats the queen Lancelot marries as a *femme fatale* who should be abandoned as soon as possible. These romances none the less follow the logic of their central heroines through to a happy ending. Altogether more disturbing are those narratives that upgrade the suspicion of women's sexuality to the point where the expectations of romance are broken down. If the authorial stance supports this suspicion, such stories are likely to move outside the ambit of romance altogether, into diatribe or fabliau, and so invoke a different set of expectations. Others keep their authorial focus centred in romance and its ideals of womanliness, but allow the male protagonist to give his own suspicions of women such loose rein as to incur disaster. The heroine's desire is set in opposition to a determinedly mistrustful man, who refuses to respond to the probity of her love even though it is endorsed by the narrative, and who persists in his refusal in despite of all generic pressure. These last categories, where the happy ending is foiled because the principles that make love-romance operative are themselves betrayed, become increasingly common from the later fifteenth century forward. Orson's behaviour is a striking example, when he seduces the trusting Galazye on the excuse that his loving and faithful wife might be dead, and refuses to marry her when she is pregnant on the grounds that she might still be alive after all. His behaviour is so transgressive that later English versions of the story toned it down (but not, interestingly, the post-medieval French versions). Earlier texts that told similar stories were more ready to break free altogether from romance; later ones insist much more that they are indeed romances, and therefore that the idealizing expectations of the genre should be revised downwards to belittle or condemn women, or at least to give up hope of any reward for their desires. A series of works written either side of 1600 will illustrate this shift: Richard Johnson's parody romance *Tom a Lincoln*, its first part printed *c.*1599 and its second *c.*1607,[41] and Shakespeare's *All's Well that Ends Well*, of *c.*1603.

Richard Johnson made his money, like tabloid writers, by never underestimating the tastes of his readers. His most famous work, *The Seven Champions of Christendom*, was one of the works that became a staple of the chapbook market, like *Valentine* itself, and was still being rewritten as an adventure story for boys in the twentieth century. He also produced collections of broadside-type ballads that converted high cultural capital into cheap but attractive commodity: his *Garland of Golden Roses*, for instance, includes simple retellings of both the *Wife of Bath's Tale* and *Clerk's Tale*, for those for whom Chaucer's *Works* and language were too expensive and too difficult. *The Pleasant Historie of Tom a Lincolne, the Red Rose Knight, for his Valour and Chivalrie, surnamed The Boast of England* seems designed to appeal both to the worst tastes of sophisticated readers for its unrelenting over-the-top treatment of every romance motif and meme that ever existed, and to the less sophisticated for the density of its hair-raising adventures. Tom is the bastard son of King Arthur and the fair Angelica, daughter of the earl of London. He is abandoned to be raised by shepherds; proves his valour through the inherent prowess he shows on various voyages; and is desired (successfully) by both the queen of a country 'called by the name of the Fayerie-Land' inhabited solely by women,[42] who commits suicide when he abandons her, and the daughter of Prester John, with whom he elopes. So much occupies the first part of the work. Its sequel, like the last part of *Valentine*, sets itself to blight all the motifs that had constituted its first part. That Johnson chooses to write like this at all shows how familiar the 'unhappy' treatment of romance was, and how fully conscious even populist writers were of the way a bipartite structure could be used not just to comment on but to dismantle itself.

The Second Part of the Famous Historie of Tom a Lincolne opens with King Arthur's dying confession of how he had seduced Angelica and that the Red Rose Knight is, in fact, their son. The consequences of the revelation are dire. His widowed (unnamed) queen determines to be revenged on Angelica; Angelica is reclassified as a strumpet, and is devastated by her loss of honour; the Red Rose Knight is devastated at discovering himself to have been 'begot in wantonnesse, and borne a bastard';[43] and Prester John's daughter, Anglitora, to whom he is now married, is so disgusted that she sails off for home with their son, named the Black Knight, and a blackamoor slave. The rest of the work is devoted to dealing with each of these initiatory plot elements. The queen sends Angelica seven different means of being put to death, from which she chooses poisoned robes; the report of her patience in dying so troubles the queen's conscience that she has all the messengers executed, and then hangs herself from her bedpost with 'a girdle of pure Arabian silke' (p. 666). Anglitora's ship arrives at the castle of a lord with whom she immediately starts an affair, made easier by the fact that her son gets lost while hunting and spends seven years in the forest, his hair growing long and shaggy and his nails becoming so talon-like that they enable him to climb trees. The slave, upset by his mistress's adultery, sets off to find the Red Rose Knight, but is shipwrecked, and saved by the Knight himself, who is the only survivor on another ship that has been seven years at sea and whose other occupants have all eaten each other. They make their way to the castle of his wife and her paramour, where she, recognizing him despite his palmer's attire, chokes him by stuffing the jewels she had once given him down his throat, and disposes of the corpse in a dunghill. She also has the slave buried up to the waist in the earth, where he eats the flesh of his own arms before being found by the Black Knight, who has been led back to the castle by the ghost of his father demanding revenge. He kills his mother, regrets his actions and laments over her, and is comforted only by the arrival of his half-brother, son of the Red Rose Knight and his fairy queen, with whom, after more hectic adventures, he returns to England, and, with the encouragement of an ageing Sir Lancelot, builds Lincoln cathedral.

For all its rip-roaring adventures, the second part of *Tom a Lincoln* was right to drop the 'Pleasant' from its title: it is hard to overstate its unpleasantness. The distastefulness focuses relentlessly on its attitude to its women. They are all lustful, vengeful, and sadistic, and are sadistically punished for it. The first part is gentler, with Angelica's yielding to the king and the desire of both the fairy queen and Anglitora being treated with superficial sympathy; the last two are both allowed pillow soliloquies, in the best tradition of desiring heroines. The whole work, however, is deliberately designed to titillate its male readers, and perhaps less intentionally to play to male hatred of women; it could scarcely provide its female readers with any self-image other than loathing. The fairy queen and all her country of ladies are desperate for men (they had slaughtered all the original male inhabitants), and Tom's accompanying hundred knights are snapped up by a hundred of her own followers. The myth of women's sexual insatiability is given a strong showing, most particularly in the misdemeanours of the previously loving Anglitora in the sequel. All the evil in the work is carried out by women: the murderous widowed queen, the adulterous and bloodthirsty wife. The men's transgressions are never held against them; the women's virtues are never credited to them. The only good woman in the whole double work is the heroine of a story-within-the-story told in the first part. This concerns a young maiden, 'daughter to a country gentleman', who falls in love with a thoroughly intertextual Valentine, son of the emperor of Greece. She too pines for him in soliloquy, but his mother scorns the lowness of her rank and attempts to have her poisoned. She is saved because the physician who has been ordered to dispense the poison substitutes a sleeping-draught; and, in this story, love is triumphant (she joins Diana's nymphs, he becomes a shepherd, etc.), and when they return to court even the queen is brought to approve of their marriage. But it is only a story, and therefore, by implication, a mere fantasy compared with the unrelenting wickedness of the 'real' women of the main plots. For all the work's qualities as spoof, there is no suggestion that the antifeminism is other than genuine: that is, it does not show any trace of satirizing misogyny itself. This is the real thing. Johnson deploys it precisely to destroy the ideology of romance, in a way that shows both how deeply that is dependent on the strong and faithful heroine and how thoroughly he disbelieves in such a creature. Replace her with her opposite, the woman whose passions for sex and revenge are alike uncontrolled, and the other elements of romance—the chivalry and the exoticism and the magic—lose all their meaning. *Tom a Lincoln* is not so much romance as pornography.

All's Well that Ends Well, written between the two parts of Johnson's *History*, dismantles romance in much subtler ways. It is unusual in that it fulfils almost every surface requirement of the genre, including the conversion of a failing hero and a closing marriage, without fulfilling its substance. Its title could be applied to almost every romance ever written in which a happy ending follows from hardship and trial, including Shakespeare's own, but it would fit *Cymbeline* or the *Winter's Tale*, or indeed *A Midsummer Night's Dream* or *As You Like It*, much better than this play. The story contains the loving and faithful heroine who pursues her chosen man until she gets him, an announcement of death overcome in apparent resurrection, an insistence on the priority of virtue over birth, recognition tokens, and a quasi-prophecy that appears impossible of fulfilment but which finally brings together husband, wife, and child. It is possible to produce Shakespeare's play as the romance that all these elements suggest, but neither directors nor critics have usually been persuaded. The ready acceptance given to it as a 'problem play' demonstrates how widely the insubstantiality of its outward form is recognized. Its outline is closely faithful to its source story, from Boccaccio's *Decameron* by way of William Painter's novella collection, but that provides a happy ending unshadowed by doubt.[44] The play's recasting of its short and uncomplicated fairytale-type original is consistently designed to heighten the elements that resonate with English romance tradition, to reproduce its memes, and to set expectations that it finally refuses to endorse. For its original audience, coming to it with a familiarity with that tradition, the disparity between what they are led to expect and what they are given must have struck still more sharply than it does modern audiences. Shakespeare adapts the story towards romance even while he rejects its generic trajectory.

The one respect in which the grounding of the plot is unusual for English, though it shares it with *Tom a Lincoln*'s inset story, is that the woman is of lower rank than the man (it is one respect in which its Italian original shows through). The reverse is much the more commonplace situation, where men such as Guy, or Amadas, or the Squire of Low Degree win aristocratic wives through the strength of their love and the exercise of prowess. In all those cases, their inherent *gentilesse*, nobility of character, is sufficient to justify their winning the ladies they love. Disparity of rank is what Bertram most holds against Helena, but the play goes to some lengths to deny the validity of the objection, and not only by the king's offer to her of lands and titles. The heart of the argument, and one insisted on over and over again from the first scene forwards, is the supremacy of inherited and innate virtue over inherited title—the same argument that holds good for the non-aristocratic lovers of high-born ladies. Helena inherits from her father not only the medical skills that enable her to heal the king, but her 'honesty' (that is, the quality that gives substance to honour), to which she adds virtues of her own: 'she derives her honesty and achieves her goodness' (1. 1. 42–3). Bertram inherits his father's looks and his land, but the injunction that he should also inherit his goodness remains no more than a pious hope (1. 1. 58–61). The question of the nature of true nobility is raised again and again in the play, the king's speech on the subject reiterating all the familiar arguments with the added trenchancy given by the immediate situation:

> That is honour's scorn
> Which challenges itself as honour's born
> And is not like the sire; honours thrive
> When rather from our acts we them derive
> Than our foregoers.

2. 3. 134–8

The argument is given emblematic form in the exchange of Bertram's ring for Diana's chastity, both of them a jewel, an honour, 'bequeathèd down from many ancestors' (4. 2. 45, 48). This may turn chastity into a commodity, but it also commodifies honour, and it is the woman's virtue that comes out of the exchange untainted. Helena, taking Diana's place, gives him another ring that the king had given her, a gift he had accompanied by a promise that he would always help her at need (5. 3. 85–7). Recognized by the king in the last scene, this ring acts like a naturally-functioning talisman; but it cannot make her husband love her.

Helena expresses her desire in the classic way for heroines from Lavine forward, in soliloquy. She phrases it in the way most familiar in the sixteenth century as an expression of male desire, in terms of the eyes and heart, but medieval heroines had been doing the same thing for centuries: the Melior of *William of Palerne*, for instance, in its verse and presumably also its printed prose version, soliloquizes about how

> I have him portreide and paynted in mi hert withinne,
> That he sittus in mi sight, me thinkes, evermore.[45]

Helena imagines how she might

> see him every hour, to sit and draw
> His archèd brows, his hawking eye, his curls,
> In our heart's table.

1. 1. 92–4

Like so many earlier romance heroines, she determines to act to get the man she wants—and given the familiarity of English romance tradition, it is likely to be such heroines that the audience would think of when she makes her decision:

> Who ever strove
> To show her merit that did miss her love?

1. 1. 222–3

But the opposition to her lies solely in her husband, not in adverse cir-
cumstances or parental opposition. As in a number of other romances
where the princess loves a man of lower rank, the older generation
favours the marriage (examples include the Simonides figure in all the
versions of *Apollonius* including *Pericles*, and the king in *The Squire of
Low Degree*). The countess of Roussillon calls on her own experience to
insist on the naturalness of the young woman's desire, and she is not a
figure whose words we are invited to doubt:

> This thorn
> Doth to our rose of youth rightly belong.
> Our blood to us, this to our blood is born;
> It is the show and seal of nature's truth,
> Where love's strong passion is impressed in youth.
>
> 1. 3. 125–9

Helena's powers of healing recall those of other wise or skilled heroines,
from Guigemar's lady forward. She is protected from any suspicion of
witchcraft by the fact that her cure for the king is based on a recipe
bequeathed to her by her father, and she describes it as 'the help of
heaven' more than 'the act of men' (2. 1. 152). Both her initial decision
to seek to win Bertram through the king, wagering her life against her
failure, and her refusal to give up the quest after he abandons her, bring
her within the remit of the king's generalized words as he sends his sol-
diers off to war, as if she were a lady-errant, a Britomart seeking her
love:

> When
> The bravest questant shrinks, find what you seek,
> That fame may cry you loud.
>
> 2. 1. 15–17

Helena does not need to show physical courage on the field of battle, but
she pursues her quest with an almost theological hope in the possibility
of a happy ending even after Bertram has set his impossible conditions.

> The time will bring on summer,
> When briers shall have leaves as well as thorns,
> And be as sweet as sharp . . .
> Time revives us.
> All's well that ends well; still the fine's the crown.
>
> 4. 4. 31–3, 34–5

Mutability, she believes, will be change for good, the upward movement of the wheel. By the time the title maxim is repeated in the closing lines of the play, it has been refashioned into a thicket of subjunctives and conditionals.

A hard-to-win mistress, like Guy's Felice, will come to recognize the innate nobility of her suitor and finally give him unstinting love and faithfulness. Bertram does not. The play makes clear that his refusal goes against all principles of reason and natural desire—every other young man within the king's disposal is eager to marry Helena—and of self-advancement too, though he hopes to get away with fooling the king into thinking that Helena has left him. The assumption of modern culture that he should not be pressured into an unwelcome marriage is allowed for in the play, though it is constrained by political realism. The king declares to her that she has 'the power to choose', but the young men whose marriages are 'in [his] bestowing' have no power to refuse (2. 3. 54–7). The statement goes against all principles of mutual consent as requisite for marriage, and Helena's own initial response to Bertram's rejection of her is to accept it. The logic of the story, however, the expectations it so insistently creates, are not on his side. A beautiful, virtuous, and desiring young woman who carries the potential for wealth and titles can be rejected only by a man incapable of recognizing the desirability of that virtue and that desire: incapable, in fact, of romance in the full generic sense. He also creates his own double 'prophecy', in setting the condition for her return that he believes is impossible but which she determines to fulfil. She does indeed get the ring from which he swears he will never be parted, and become pregnant with his child. In the source novella, Giletta carries on her affair with her husband until she is sure she is pregnant. Helena makes love with Bertram once only, as if her conviction of her own desire were enough to assure her of the first-night conception that marks desiring heroines. The lack of deep reciprocity inherent in the bed-trick— the disguise of love as casual sex—is however carried through into Bertram's reluctance to acknowledge the consequences of his own demands, when she appears to him with the child he has fathered.[46] He does ask 'pardon' (5. 3. 310), but given that he never otherwise speaks to either Diana or Helena in this scene, only to the king, then he seems to be asking for remission of punishment rather than reconciliation. He does promise good behaviour, when there is absolutely no alternative left, but since he is a habitual liar, both to his women and to his king, his qualified declaration of love at the end does not carry conviction. The king's response is to protest too much, both in his own person—

> All yet seems well; and if it end so meet,
> The bitter past, more welcome is the sweet

5. 3. 334–5

—and as Epilogue:

> All is well ended if this suit be won.

Ep. 2

This is not a disaster romance; Helena does not end up dead, the heir to Roussillon is born or about to be born, and Bertram has got a better wife than ever he deserved. But where Shakespeare had shown himself, and was to show himself again, one of the writers most able to create a sense of bliss at the end of romance, here he opts for scepticism and a veneer of poetic and providential justice so thin as to invite the eye to see straight through it.

ACCUSATION

All's Well may have been written next in time to Shakespeare's other work that most disrupts the expectations of love-romance, and does so even more violently. *Othello* uses a plot that he had already developed into two comedies, and that was to drive two of his romances: the woman falsely accused. It had always been a meme that shadowed tragedy particularly closely, and there is less strain imposed on the plausibility of the story by letting such a plot fall over the edge into disaster than by pulling it back within the parameters of romance. In the Garden of Eden, the devil had seduced Eve into eating the apple: an act widely associated with the loss of sexual innocence. Polixenes suggests just such a connection in the *Winter's Tale*, as an immediate prelude to Leontes' conviction that his wife is adulterous.[47] No matter how much love and integrity women may display, men will still believe that they have listened to the serpent. And in the postlapsarian world in which women are made subject to their husbands, it is men who hold the power: both the political power of judgement, and the physical power to commit murder.

Othello was presented to audiences already familiar with the idea that innocence might not be sufficient protection against unwarranted jealousy. Bellaria, the equivalent figure to Hermione in Greene's *Pandosto*, dies as a consequence of her husband's accusation of her, and there is neither a rehabilitation of her in her lifetime nor a resurrection. The story was immensely popular, becoming one of England's long-time bestsellers under the title *Dorastus and Fawnia,* and preserving with it the awareness that wifely guiltlessness is not always vindicated.[48] Bellaria is not, however, a major figure in the way that Hermione or Desdemona is, and romance had always allowed that minor characters are disposable. The fact that Hermione and Desdemona are leading figures within their plays should qualify them for survival: a pattern that Shakespeare makes true for Hermione as he had done for Hero in *Much Ado,* but not for Desdemona.

The accused woman who dies was not altogether without precedent in pre-Elizabethan romance, quite apart from historical figures such as Anne Boleyn. *The Knight of Curtesy and the Fair Lady of Faguell* is one of the latest of the metrical romances, written probably around 1500; the sole surviving printed copy dates from the mid-1550s, and it was still a title with economic potential in the 1570s. The romance is based on a French original, but where the French makes the eponymous wife a partner in an adulterous relationship, the English insists that the love between the lady and the Knight of Courtesy is chaste, innocent, 'as children that together are kynde'.[49] Determined to get him killed, her jealous husband despatches him on crusade to Rhodes, the focus of Christian resistance to the Turkish advance in the later fifteenth century. He survives a fight with a dragon, but is mortally wounded in a combat against impossible odds against the Saracen besiegers of the city. His last act is to ask his page to return to Faguell with his heart, and give it to his lady. The page, however, presents it to the lord. He, believing his suspicions confirmed, orders the heart to be well spiced and cooked, and stands over his wife while she unsuspectingly eats it. On his telling her what she has done, she refuses all further earthly food: since her body has become the grave to her lover, she too must die. She confesses and takes the sacrament, and insists to her husband that she is his 'true wedded fere'. He does at last believe her, but it is too late for a happy ending in this world, though the poem ends with a strong implication that the Lord to whom she prays for mercy on her soul will indeed grant her 'the joye of Paradyse' (502). The end of the story may be deeply gruesome, but it does maintain the values of romance: in their very different circumstances, both lovers die thinking of the other and remaining true to that love.

Desdemona is guiltless not just of adultery, but even of loving anyone but her husband. With her determination to marry the man on whom she has set her heart and her unashamed desire for the consummation of her marriage, Shakespeare models her, like Helena, on the heroines of

English romance and of his own romantic comedies more than on his Italian source.[50] By all rights she should be the female lead in just such another comedy. Instead, the play relegates the processes of her and Othello's courtship to retrospective summary, so that what might elsewhere be the triumphant conclusion becomes the starting-point of the action. From here, the only way for the wheel to turn is downwards, and Shakespeare stops it at the bottom. The same actions and responses that are presented at the start as proof of her love become the evidence against her: her rebellion against her father's authority; her readiness to desire a Moor. Even the 'magic' handkerchief acts against her: she rightly describes herself as 'most unhappy in the loss of it',[51] and 'unhappy' carries much of that additional force that it bore in Middle English. The play was originally known as *The Moor of Venice*, a formulation indistinguishable as to genre from *The Merchant of Venice*, with its rescue of its eponymous protagonist from death, and its couples, including the young woman who has escaped from her father's house to marry the man she loves, set for happy marriage. It may well be that the original audience of *Othello* expected the story to follow its romance structure through to the end: to have Iago's plot revealed in time, the handkerchief confirm itself as a metonymy for love and faithfulness, even for Desdemona's momentary revival after her suffocation to be a genuine return to life. Poetic justice demands no less, and romance often allows more, making space for penitence and forgiveness; but not here. Othello imagines the ending for Desdemona that the *Knight of Courtesy* promises, of the salvation of his guiltless wife's soul; but the corollary of that is that

> This look of thine will hurl my soul from heaven,
> And fiends will snatch at it.

> 5. 2. 281–2

He may suggest that Iago is a devil incarnate, but he also sees no alternative for himself but damnation.[52]

FROM FAMILY ROMANCE TO FAMILY TRAGEDY

Discovering his parentage does not help a foundling if his name is Oedipus. The recovery of a lost child may appear to be quintessential romance, but it also forms the plot of the play chosen by Aristotle as the quintessential tragedy. The reunion of mother and long-lost son is tainted by the discovery of his killing of his father and his incestuous relationship with her, and their own children are polluted by their birth. The myths of the Christian tradition offer almost as little comfort as the Greek. The first act of the first couple is to lose Paradise; the first act of their children is for one brother to kill another.

Mordred and Valentine and Balin bear witness to the readiness of romance to incorporate all such motifs, and to incorporate them for their tragic potential, not for disaster avoided. There are romances where the same plot elements can be pulled back from the brink. Even incest is redeemable in the legend of Gregorius, the child of brother–sister incest who was exposed on the water and returns not only to marry his mother but to repent and become both pope and saint.[53] Father and son can recognize each other in the nick of time, as Degaré and his fairy father do. Brothers can do the same: Ipomedon recognizes his long-lost brother in mid-combat. The intensity of the relationships within a family, and the intensity of the accompanying emotions, can produce the most powerful effects of bliss at the end of a romance, of overwhelming rightness and completeness—the emotion symbolized at the end of *Pericles* by his hearing of the music of the spheres. But, as Lorenzo points out at the end of the *Merchant of Venice*, we are not in fact capable of hearing it while we are enclosed in 'this muddy vesture of decay'.[54] The same intensities produce the particular pain of tragedy: not just its suffering, but the sense that *this is not how things ought to be*.

The two works that may be the earliest of the Middle English prose romances are also family tragedies. *The Siege of Thebes* and *The Siege of Troy*, composed some time after 1422 and copied in sequence in the same manuscript, are brief retellings of Lydgate's substantial poems on the same subjects, his *Siege of Thebes* and *Troy Book*.[55] Their categorization as romance, despite the 'unhappy' nature of their narratives, stems from their treatment of their material, not least their promotion of the secular values of chivalry and, in the *Troy*, love (Jason and Medea, Paris and Helen, and Achilles and Polyxena all receive concentrated attention; Medea, heir to her father, falls for Jason in the best fashion of medieval desiring heroines, and is treated with consistent sympathy). Their aristocratic characters, their settings distant in space and time, and their readiness to incorporate magic (such as the detailed account of the five charms given by Medea to enable Jason to overcome the beasts that bar his way to the Golden Fleece) are all typical generic markers for romance. *Thebes* does open with the birth prophecy of Edippes' 'infortunat destony', but the following events stress romance patterns whenever they can. The servant ordered to take the baby into the forest and kill it refuses to do so since it is 'so faire and wel shapen'. The foundling is discovered and raised by a king, as a romance foundling should be. In an attempt to keep the morality of the story orthodox, the author insists that the child was 'ful of wicked and cursed condicions', and makes his killing of his father an act of fury; but he then goes on to kill 'an horrible beest a monstre, called a Spinx', in the best tradition of knights-errant. His marriage to his mother is recognized as being unwitting and therefore 'innocent', and his reaction to discovering what he has done is not tearing out his eyes but weeping them out. The arrangement between his sons to alternate ruling his kingdom results in the younger setting out as a knight-errant, and undergoing some Malory-style adventures. The siege of Thebes is an affair of high chivalry, conducted by 'ful grete renowned' warriors who fill the whole country 'with bright baners and harneys, that hit was mervelouse to se'.[56] But the pollution of the brothers' birth must work itself out, and their killing of each other is presented as inevitable:

Hit preved well there of theym two, that weren so horribly goten ayenst al nature and ordenaunce, for as clerkes seyn, blode to touche blode, bringeth forthe corrupt frute.   (p. 269)

When the relationships within a family become too close, parricide and fratricide will follow. *Troy* does not have to concern itself with incest, but it opens with an uncle's attempt to kill his nephew (the story of Jason), and its key word becomes 'treason': treason within the family and the palace, between knights when chivalry fails, and finally within Priam's chivalric affinity as Antenor and Eneas arrange for the betrayal of the city. The text closes, not with a prediction of the great future awaiting Eneas' descendants, but with another warning of disaster:

And alwey the ende of every tresoun and falsenes to sorwe and myschef at the last. (p. 285)

The romance elements of the great legendary-historical stories are given generous treatment, but the trajectories of their narratives lead elsewhere.

The same tension between romance treatment and inevitable catastrophe is at its most powerful in the *Morte Darthur*. Malory's ending is so overwhelming, and so familiar, that it is easy to overlook how golden Arthur's world had seemed to other writers in the fifteenth century. Even John Lydgate, not known for his idealism, delivers some high panegyrics on him, as being

> Hedspryng of honour, of largesse cheef cisterne,
> Merour of manod, of noblesse the lanterne,

who sets up the Round Table as the best means of upholding the 'comoun proffit' of the realm, and whose knights show every Christian virtue.[57] His time was everything that Lydgate's own present is not, when men and women loved only for 'trouthe and honeste'.[58] Lydgate follows Geoffrey of Monmouth and the historical tradition in having Arthur die at the height of his conquests, in battle against his rebel nephew, and that is the version of his story most commonly found in Middle English, where the processes of historical movement alone cause his downfall.[59] The *Lancelot-Grail* adds Mordred's incestuous birth and Merlin's prophecies of disaster to come, and it is that version that Malory chooses to follow. Despite his reworking of the casting adrift of the infant Mordred to turn him more into a Judas figure, the threat of impending disaster disappears from sight for most of the work, while the quests and adventures of the greatest fellowship of knights occupy the foreground. Combat throughout most of the work is presented as admirable, a test of prowess, named knight against named knight, in a process of conferring honour through renaming—*renommée*, 'renown'. Opponents who are hostile to King Arthur are defeated and either killed or brought within the fellowship. From the middle of the *Tristram*, however, an altogether more disturbing element enters the narrative, in which fellows of the Round Table actively hate each other and carry that hatred through into murder. The treacherous death of the 'good knight' Lamorak, struck from behind by Mordred while fighting alone against Gawain and three of his brothers, marks the symbolic moment when the fellowship begins to break from within.[60] Malory avoids describing the murder directly, recording it only through the horrified reactions of various other knights (Gareth among them) as they themselves hear about it.

The brothers' action can, however, still be placed morally, as an act against chivalry, a betrayal of knightliness. Their placing on the chivalric roll of honour becomes one not of fame but of infamy. Much harder to assimilate within any kind of romance pattern is the tragic irony of Lancelot's killing of Gareth in the course of his rescue of Guinevere from the threat of the stake. Although Gareth does not have the seniority to refuse Arthur's order to escort her (unlike Gawain, he is 'yonge and full unable to say you nay'), he shows his unwillingness by not bearing arms. He is, therefore, not only defenceless against Lancelot's attack but without the easy recognizability conferred by his shield.

And as they were unarmed, [Lancelot] smote them and wyst nat whom that he smote, and so unhappely they were slayne.   (Malory, iii. 1183 (XX. 9))

Malory has made Gareth one of the co-heroes of his work, creating for him a biography that demonstrates why, as Gawain recalls in bewilderment, 'he loved sir Launcelot of all men erthly'.[61] The French *Mort Artu* presents the disasters of the last book as the consequence of Lancelot's adultery, but Malory never condemns his love for Guinevere, and so holds back from justifying what happens in terms of divine punishment.[62] From the death of Gareth forwards, the *Morte Darthur* moves beyond moral or providential explanation. If there is any principle at work, it is the wheel of Arthur's final dream, that whirls upside down and tips him from his throne into 'an hydeous depe blak watir' full of serpents (iii. 1233 (XXI. 3)). God may allow the soul of the dead Gawain to appear to him in a coda to the same dream to warn him against fighting the next day, but no metaphysical explanation is offered for the adder that comes out of a 'lytyll hethe-buysshe' as the armies face each other and so causes the onset of the battle on 'this unhappy day' (iii. 1235 (XXI. 4)). We are not told what side the knight belongs to who draws his sword to kill it, and it does not matter. The conventional combat of named knights, with its implicit promise of victory for the most righteous, now becomes a universal carnage:

And thus they fought all the longe day, and never stynted tylle the noble knyghtes were layde to the colde erthe. And ever they fought stylle tyll it was nere nyght, and by than was there an hondred thousand leyde dede uppon the downe. (iii. 1236 (XXI. 4))

The knights of the Round Table and their desire for 'worship' are alike obliterated in the anonymity of slaughter.[63] This may be the Day of Destiny, in Malory's phrase, but it is not a divinely-controlled Day of Judgement.

What Malory is portraying, with full consciousness, in these last sections of his work, is civil war: the kind of war defined not by deeds of high chivalry but by the severance of what should be the closest of bonds, father with son, and brother with brother. Completing his work towards the end of the Wars of the Roses, he draws a direct comparison between the events of his own age and of Arthur's:

Lo ye all Englysshemen, se ye nat what a myschyff here was? For he that was the moste kynge and nobelyst knyght of the worlde, and most loved the felyshyp of noble knyghtes, and by hym they all were upholdyn, and yet myght nat thes Englyshemen holde them contente with hym. Lo thus was the olde custom and usayges of thys londe, and men say that we of thys londe have nat yet loste that custom.   (iii. 1229 (XXI. 2))

Shakespeare epitomizes the horrors of civil war in the emblematic scene in *Henry VI* Part 3 where a father kills his son and a son his father. The familiarity of the emblem is demonstrated from a ballad on the Wars of the Roses still current in the eighteenth century:

> Fathers unkind their Children kill'd,
> And Sons their Fathers slew;
> Yea, Kindred fought against their Kind,
> And not each other knew.[64]

Civil war, whether of Mordred against Arthur or Lancastrians against Yorkists, encapsulates family tragedy, the breaking of the bonds that should be most sacred.

'The moste party of all Inglonde hylde wyth sir Mordred', Malory announces, and Mordred is at once a rebel, a son who tries to depose his own father and marry his wife, a regicide, and a parricide. When Arthur returns to oppose the rebellion, Mordred is there to try to prevent 'hys owne fadir to londe uppon the londe that he was kynge over'. And when Arthur insists on encountering him as the last act of 'thys wycked day of Desteny', the horror of Mordred's inflicting a fatal wound on the man who is both his king and his father is intensified by the gruesome way in which he does it.

> And whan sir Mordred saw kynge Arthur he ran untyll hym with hys swerde drawyn in hys honde, and there kyng Arthur smote sir Mordred undir the shylde, with a foyne of hys speare, thorowoute the body more than a fadom. And whan sir Mordred felte that he had hys dethys wounde he threste hymselff with the myght that he had upp to the burre of kyng Arthurs speare, and ryght so he smote hys fadir, kyng Arthure, with hys swerde holdynge in both hys hondys, uppon the syde of the hede, that the swerde perced the helmet and the tay of the brayne. (iii. 1237 (XXI. 4))

Arthur may set out for Avalon in the barge, but Bedivere finds a 'tumbe newe gravyn' at Glastonbury the next day, and it is the king's corpse that Lancelot finds when he inters the dead Guinevere beside him. And on the battlefield itself, pillagers—presumably more of those unnamed Englishmen who held with Mordred—come to kill off the wounded and strip the corpses of their riches. There may be one more moment of wonder, in the arm that emerges from the lake to catch Excalibur and draw it under the water, but the removal of the sword from the world marks the end of the age of marvels.

Spenser may have tried to restore the marvellous by setting the young Arthur at large in Faery Land, but a return to more historical Arthurian material picked up the demythologized nation that Malory had set in place at the end of his work. *The Misfortunes of Arthur*, written by Thomas Hughes and acted before the queen by the gentlemen of Gray's Inn in 1587, turns Arthurian romance into a full-scale Senecan revenge tragedy, plus dumbshows. The whole action is watched over by the ghost of Gorlois, the duke of Tintagel whose likeness Uther took on in order to sleep with his wife and beget Arthur. The play is premissed on the temporal outline of Geoffrey of Monmouth's biography of Arthur (he has spent nine years abroad in pursuit of his imperial ambitions, and the play begins with his return home after hearing of Mordred's attempted usurpation), but it incorporates the incestuous begetting of Mordred from the romance tradition. As 'The Argument to the Tragedy' makes clear, indeed, every crime, and especially every sexual crime, is made worse than in its original. Uther makes love to Igerna before killing Gorlois, so making their love technically adulterous and Arthur a bastard outside the official possibility of legitimation. Mordred's mother is not just Arthur's half-sister but his twin sister, whom he seduces knowingly rather than unwittingly.[65] Guenevara is not only having a willing affair with Mordred, as Geoffrey of Monmouth suggests she did ('O mischiefe, O lewd life, O filthy dayes', as another Arthurian promoter put it),[66] but considers murdering her husband on his return. The Chorus represents the ensuing war as a replay of Theban tragedy:

> In Thebes the rotte and murreine would not cease
> Till Laius broode had paide for breach of lawes:
> In Brytain warres and discord will not stent
> Till Uther's line and offspring quite be spent.[67]

The final battle is described in the classic terms for civil war: of brother killing brother, and father and son killing each other:

> The brethren broach their blood; the sire his sonnes,
> The sonne again would prove by too much wrath,
> That he, whom thus he slew, was not his sire.
>
> IV. ii. 170–2

And Conan, the play's approximate equivalent to Bedivere, draws the contemporary moral:

> When perhaps our childrens children read
> Our woefull warres displaid with skilfull pen,
> They'l thinke they heere some sounds of future facts,
> And not the ruines olde of pompe long past.
>
> IV. iii. 29–32

To an audience in 1587, the lines are both a warning against present rebel-
lion (it was the year in which the danger of Mary Queen of Scots was
finally removed), and a reminder of the Wars of the Roses, brought to an
end by the advent of the Tudor dynasty. In this play, it is made explicit
that Uther's line dies out with Arthur and Mordred: Gorlois's curse ends
with them. It closes by looking forward to a distant future, the present of
the performance, when a Virgin shall come from Heaven, clean of all the
sexual impurity that has caused such havoc in the play, and restore peace
to Britain.

It is the inevitable way in the late sixteenth century of pulling a
romance rabbit out of a very black hat. What is interesting is how the hat
itself has changed colour, and shape. Hughes and his collaborators set out
to erase every association of Arthur with romance. There are no marvels,
no acts of prowess, no love, no faithfulness: just a heaping up of sin upon
sin and blood upon blood, to the accompaniment of platitudinous
choruses about the advantages of a quiet life and low station. Given the
continuing widespread belief in Arthur's essential historicity and in his
status as Britain's own Worthy, the demythologizing of the narrative, its
revised status as a warning about failed kingship, retribution, and civil
war, is extraordinary. The potential for most of such an interpretation
had been there since Geoffrey himself (though he casts Mordred merely
as Arthur's nephew); it took the disillusioned eyes of student lawyers of
the Elizabethan age to realize it in textual form.

There is one last legendary romance that was recast as a tragedy a few
years later, but which gave a less obvious invitation to such treatment: the
story of King Lear. In Geoffrey's version, Leir is the ninth-generation
descendant of Brut and eponymous founder of the city of Leicester. The
basis of the story is already in place in the *History of the Kings of Britain*:
the love-test and the ensuing division of the kingdom; the marriage of the
plain-speaking Cordelia to the king of Gaul; the other daughters' mis-
treatment of their father; Cordelia's invasion of Britain to restore him to
his throne. In this 'historical' account, the restoration is successful, and
Cordelia in due course succeeds him. It is a mixture of foundation
romance (for the city) and a variant on the restoration of the true king,
though for this early date there is no need for primogeniture to trump
ethical right to the succession. Only in the sequel does any element of
tragedy enter the story, when the widowed Cordelia is deposed by her
nephews and commits suicide in prison. The story appears to have been
turned into an independent romance by the late thirteenth century, when
it is named in a list of Anglo-Norman lais, and it was familiar in romance

contexts in the fourteenth.⁶⁸ It was widely known in the Elizabethan age, being retold by Holinshed, Spenser, William Warner, and others, and dramatized in the 1590s as *The True Chronicle History of King Leir*. All consistently follow the romance outline of Leir's own story, and the early play intensifies that. Its events are safely governed by a Christian Providence; prayers and invocations to God regularly punctuate the action, and are divinely answered. Its king of Gallia comes to Britain in disguise, and falls in love at first sight with the destitute Cordella before he knows who she is; she reciprocates his love while she believes him to be a palmer. Leir dreams that his elder daughters stab him, and that Cordella brings him back to life by pouring balsam into his wounds. The daughters do, indeed, attempt to have him assassinated, but the murderer, forcefully helped by thunder and lightning and other effects sent directly by God, decides to spare him. Cordella and her husband go on an outing to the seaside, disguised as country folk, and there meet up unrecognized with her father, who has crossed to France. The play ends with the defeat of the sisters, and Leir's expression of thanks to all those who have remained loyal to him.

The ways in which Shakespeare converts this romance material into tragedy are too well known to need detailed analysis. For the first audience, familiar with the story, and presented with what the quarto text calls the 'True Chronicle History' of King Lear rather than the 'Tragedy' it became in the Folio, their belief in the possibility of a happy ending may well have lasted until the final few minutes of the play. The known story of Lear promises an ending like that Shakespeare was to give *Pericles* and *Cymbeline* and the *Winter's Tale*, where father and daughter rediscover each other in a powerful invocation of harmony and a promise of a better future. The subplot that he adds, in which a bastard brother plots against his legitimate sibling, is one that he had tried out in *Much Ado About Nothing*, with the villain being unmasked before the damage he had caused was irreparable. He had indeed already written one entire play with plot materials closely similar to those of *Lear*, in the romance-based *As You Like It*. There, the configurations of family foreshadow those of the tragedy, with the three sons of Sir Roland de Boys, of whom the youngest is the most virtuous, standing in for the three daughters, and Duke Frederick's deposition of his brother approximating to Edmund's disinheriting of Edgar. The dispossessed are exiled from the court to the countryside, but it is a timeless (or at least clock-free) Forest of Arden, a Warwickshire version of the great Forest of Ardennes that occupies the landscape of adventure romance. The landscape into which the dispossessed of *Lear* are driven is nature at its harshest, stormbound and devoid of shelter. Rosalind and Celia take along their court fool to be a comfort to them in their banishment (1. 3. 130); he is a figure who properly belongs in comedy, but in *Lear* the Fool's faithfulness to the king becomes indistinguishable from the agony of conscience, of knowledge of foolish action that cannot be recalled or undone. The comedy ends with the reconciliation of brother with brother, the reunion of father and daughter, the restoration of the true ruler, and four marriages under the aegis of Hymen (and whether Hymen is presented as a 'real' theophany, like Jupiter in *Cymbeline*, or a pageant arranged by Rosalind, does not greatly matter). The tragedy ends with the breaking of marriages, brother killing brother and sister sister, the father dying on his beloved daughter's corpse, the extinction of the royal line, and no evidence that the gods so much as exist.

Shakespeare's *Lear* is almost as great a contrast to the earlier *Leir* as it is to *As You Like It*. Disguise becomes more a matter of stripping down, of becoming 'unaccommodated man' in a testing out of the minimum requirement for humanity, rather than playful holidaying. There are no scenes of falling in love or intimacy between Cordelia and the man she marries. The storm is not an act of divine protectiveness but a macrocosmic representation of psychic agony. The restoration of the king to his throne and Cordelia's succession never happen. The wheel of Fortune that casts the king down and lifts him back up is now a 'wheel of fire', a machine of torture, and its downward movement is not offset by any final rise. Cordelia, Kent, and Edgar may believe in beneficent gods, but Shakespeare's version abandons the Christian framework of *Leir*, and the new plotting holds back from endorsing any such belief. The recovery of the mad Lear may be like a resurrection, but it is not one that he wants: 'You do me wrong to take me out o' th' grave.' And his dying belief, if that is what it is, that Cordelia still lives, is delusion.[69]

Romance did not give way to tragedy without a fight. At just about the same time as Shakespeare was turning the story of Lear from romance to tragedy, an anonymous author was turning *Valentine and Orson* from tragedy back to romance. *The Emperor and the Child*, preserved in the Percy Folio, reverts to the medium of the earliest form of the story, verse, and its original shape, in which the calumny of the empress and the loss of the babies are corrected and restored in a closing family reunion:

> And soe att lenght, in spight of ffortunes happ.
> They lived in joy, and feared no after clappe.[70]

As a concluding couplet, it is strikingly close to the one inflicted on *King Lear* by Nahum Tate, in 1681. The absence of any poetic justice or divine endorsement of the good in Shakespeare's play threatened to make it intolerable; Samuel Johnson was famously appalled by it.[71] Tate's adaptation, which put back into the story everything that Shakespeare had taken out, and more besides, held the stage for almost two hundred years. Tate's reversion to an outline closer to Geoffrey, in which Cordelia wins the battle, was by this date made not for reasons of legendary-historical accuracy but for generic propriety. His Lear opts not to take back his throne but to become a hermit, along with Kent; and since the King of France is eliminated from the cast list, Cordelia is free to marry Edgar. The play ends with a triumphant affirmation of everything Shakespeare had shaped his play to avoid, as Edgar assures his bride,

> Whatever storms of fortune are decreed,
> That Truth and Virtue shall at last succeed.[72]

But this is no longer an age of faith, and the claim is altogether too easy: a piece of stage machinery, not an affirmation of hope against the odds. It was the difficulty of bringing truth and virtue to success that had given romance much of its force. It was not a characteristic evident in the everyday world. God might reward such things in Heaven, but if they were to be realized on earth, they needed both providential support and the exercise of heroism, exceptional courage and faithful love. Over the centuries, human perfectibility, then divine Providence, then the ideals themselves were falling out of belief.

Appendix: Medieval Romance in English after 1500

This appendix lists all those works originating between 1138 and 1400, or transmitting material of similar date, that were current in English or Scottish dialects of English after 1500, as evidenced by prints, further manuscripts, adaptations, and allusions. Full details of modern editions and criticism cited here by name can be found in the Bibliography.

Fuller accounts of the Middle English romances, including plot summaries, are given in J. Burke Severs, *A Manual of the Writings in Middle English* 1050–1350 I: *Romances* (New Haven, 1967). Plot summaries of all longer fictional prose narratives in English to 1558 are given in Appendix 2 of *Beware the Cat by William Baldwin: The First English Novel*, ed. William Ringler, jr, and Michael Flachmann (San Marino, 1988).

The information is organized as follows:

Heading Italicized headings indicate romance titles, roman type indicates subject area (e.g., stories of the Trojan founding of Britain appear under 'Brut'; the various redactions of the story of Horn appear under 'Horn'). The title given is that by which the romance is most commonly known, except that 'Sir' is omitted.

Edition Major modern individual editions are indicated by 'ed.' plus the editor's name; anthologies containing the work are indicated by the name of the editor only. For full details, see the Bibliography. Titles are given in cases of possible confusion.

Origin/source 'Source' indicates a translation or close adaptation of a known text; 'origin' indicates a looser relationship to an original, or a more general field. Known ownership of source texts in England is noted, in particular the manuscript presented to Margaret of Anjou on her marriage to Henry VI, London, British Library Royal MS 15 E VI.

Date/MS Summary information about the likely date of composition of the Middle English text and the number and (where of interest) date range of its surviving medieval manuscripts. Information from Severs, *Manual*, Vol. 1: *Romances*, and Guddat-Figge, *Catalogue*. Inclusion in the earliest surviving anthology of Middle English romances, the Auchinleck manuscript (Edinburgh, Advocates Library MS 19.2.1), of *c*.1340, is noted.

16th–17th c currency. Summary information about the number and dates of surviving late manuscripts and printed editions of the original texts or close adaptations down to *c.*1660, largely drawn from the *Short-Title Catalogue* (*STC*) and, where it contains material of significantly different date from the surviving copies, the *Stationers' Registers* (*SR*); place of publication is London unless otherwise stated. It should be remembered that numerous entire editions have been lost, and the prints noted here do not give anywhere near a complete account of what was available; many of the known editions survive only as fragments of a single copy. Individual late manuscripts are noted as follows:

Banyster: manuscripts copied in 1564 by Edward Banyster (Oxford, Bodleian Library, MS Douce 261 and London, British Library, Egerton MS 3132A) (see Seymour, 'MSS Douce')

Percy Folio: the last great manuscript anthology to include romances, the Percy Folio manuscript (London, British Library MS Add. 27879; edited by Hales and Furnivall), compiled *c.*1648.

Adaptations, dramatizations, etc. Indicates survival of medieval material in forms substantially different from the original texts, such as plays, broadside and traditional ballads, and other rewritings. Information about dramatizations is taken from Harbage, *Annals of English Drama 975–1700*, 3rd edn., rev. by Sylvia Stoler Wagonheim, unless otherwise noted.

Allusions. Selected references indicating the popularity of named romances after 1500. The degree of selection necessarily varies with the density of allusion, subject areas such as Arthur, Brutus, and Guy of Warwick being impossible even to adumbrate.

Abbreviations:

Complaynt	list of current romances in *Complaynt of Scotland, c.*1550, ed. Stewart, p. 50 [anonymous, but possibly by Robert Wedderburn].
Cox	list of books (possibly fictional) in *Robert Langham: A Letter*, ed. Kuin, p. 53, and Appendix G [the author may be William Patten rather than Robert Laneham or Langham: see O'Kill, 'Printed Works'].
Crosse	list of works for censure in Henry Crosse, *Vertues Commonwealth* (1603), ed. Grosart, pp. 102–3.
Dering	list of works for censure in Edward Dering, *A Brief and Necessary Instruction . . .* (1572).
Hyrd	list of English romances added to Vives' continental list by Richard Hyrd *Instrvction of a Christen woman* (written *c.*1530, printed 1541): see pp. 37–8 above.
Kirkman	works recommended by Francis Kirkman, 'To the Reader', in *The Famous and Delectable History of Don Bellianis* (1673)
Meres	Francis Meres' list of works for censure in *Palladis Tamia* (1598), in *Elizabethan Critical Essays*, ed. by G. Gregory Smith, ii.308

Nashe	list of works for censure in *Anatomie of Absurditie* (1589), *Works*, ed. McKerrow i.11
Rowlands	list of reading of the eponymous 'Melancholie Knight', 1615.

Albina and her sisters

Origin?	early 14th c Anglo-Norman *Des Granz Geans*
Date/MS history	no independent Middle English version, but incorporated into chronicles from 14th c
16th–17th c currency	chronicles, including 1543 print of Harding, Holinshed

Alexander

numerous versions in Middle English and Scots: see Severs, *Manual*, nos. 64–70
French prose included in BL Royal 15 E VI

Kyng Alisaunder

Edition	ed. by Smithers
Origin	Anglo-Norman *Roman de toute chevalerie*
Date/MSS history	early 14th c; four MSS including Auchinleck
16th–17th c currency	print *c.*1525, *STC* 321

Alexander Buik (Scottish)

Edition	ed. R. L. G. Ritchie, Scottish Text Society 12, 17, 21, 25
Sources	French *Fuerre de Gadres* and *Voeux du Paon* (13th–early 14th c)
Date/MS history	1438; no MS extant
16th–17th c currency	print Edinburgh *c.*1580 (*STC* 321.5)

Apollonius of Tyre

Edition	in Archibald, *Apollonius* (also generous bibliography of versions)
Origin	probably Greek by way of 5th–6th c Latin; other Latin texts include Godfrey of Viterbo's *Pantheon* and later versions of the *Gesta Romanorum* (rare in manuscript)
Date/MSS history	one MS of Old English version, one of late 14th c version Gower, *Confessio amantis* (*c.*1390) (from Godfrey)
16th–17th c currency	*Kynge Apollyn of Thyre* (*STC* 708.5, 1510) (from French *Gesta*)
	Gesta Romanorum (Latin; continental printings from *c.*1475); prints from *c.*1502–57 (*STC* 21286.3–21287; not in later editions)
	Gower, *Confessio amantis*, 3 edns. 1483–1554
	Lawrence Twine, *The Pattern of Painfull Adventures*, SR July 1576 (ii. 301); surviving edns. 1594, 1607 (*STC* 709–10) (from Latin *Gesta*)

George Wilkins, *The Painfull Adventures of Pericles* (STC 25638.5, 1608)

Dramatization   Shakespeare [?and others], *Pericles*, ?1608

Arthur (legendary history)
Origin   Geoffrey of Monmouth (Latin, 1138)
Middle English versions   Layamon's *Brut*, early 13th c
abundant in chronicles, including Harding (mid-15th c verse)
Arthur, late 14th c verse interpolation in Latin chronicle, one MS
Alliterative *Morte Arthure* (ed. Benson, Hamel), c.1400, one MS
Malory, *Tale of Emperor Lucius* in *Morte Darthur* (from alliterative *Morte*)
16th–17th c currency   Latin abridgement of Geoffrey 1585 (*STC* 20109)
chronicles including Harding (printed 1543), Holinshed (three edns., 1577–85)
Leland, *Assertio*, 1544 (trans. Robinson 1582)
Adaptations   Lloyd, *Nine Worthies*, 1584; extended as ballad in Percy Folio
tragedy of Arthur in 1610 edition of *Mirror for Magistrates*
Dramatization   Hathway's *Arthur, King of England*, 1598 (lost; content unknown)
Uther Pendragon, 1597 (lost)
Hughes, *Misfortunes of Arthur*, 1587 (Vulgate-influenced)
Allusions   numerous, including opening lines of ballad in *Complaynt*
Robert Chester, *Love's Martyr*, 1601
Thomas Heywood, *Troia Britanica*, 1609
Drayton, *Poly-Olbion*, 1612/1620
see also, Merlin

Arthur (Vulgate Cycle-derived)
Editions   Stanzaic *Morte Arthur* ed. Benson, *Death of King Arthur*
Malory, *Le Morte Darthur*: (manuscript-based), ed. by Vinaver; (Caxton-based) ed. Spisak; Cowen
Sources   French *Lancelot-Grail*
English ownership of various parts through 14th–15th c
Date/MS history   Stanzaic *Morte Arthur*, c.1400; one late 15th c MS
Malory, completed 1469–70; one MS; printed by Caxton 1485

16th–17th c currency	6 edns. of Malory 1485–1634 (*STC* 801–6)
Allusions	numerous, including Cox, Kirkman; condemnations by Ascham, Dering, Nashe, Meres, Baxter (1578), Florio (1603), Crosse, Rowlands
	extensively in Spenser, *Faerie Queene*
	Jonson, *Prince Henries Barriers*, 1610
Adaptations/dramatizations	1539 court masque of Arthur and his knights (John Heywood; lost)
	Leicester's Kenilworth entertainments, 1575
	Gosson suggests dramatizations pre-1582
	Hughes, *Misfortunes of Arthur*, 1587 (also historical)
	Hathway's *Arthur, King of England*, 1598 (lost; possibly legendary history)
see also, Grail, Merlin, Lancelot, Tristram	

Arthur of Little Britain

Edition	ed. E. V. Utterson
Source	early 14th c French prose *Artus de Bretagne*
Date/MS history	no Middle English versions, no MSS known
16th–17thc currency	trans. by Lord Berners before 1533; three? prints *c.*1560–1581 (*STC* 807–8)
Allusions	*Complaynt*; Underdowne's 1570 preface to *Aethiopian Historie*; Nashe
	Kirkman notes as rare, 1673

Bevis of Hamtoun

Editions	ed. E. Kölbing, EETS E.S. 46, 48, 65; Herzman *et al.*
Source	13th c Anglo-Norman *Boeve de Hamton*
Date/MSS history	*c.*1300; 7 MSS (of two versions) including Auchinleck, to late 15th c
16th–17thc currency	numerous prints from *c.*1500 to 1711 (*STC* 1987–96; Wing H2160; and see Fellows, '*Bevis redivivus*')
Adaptations	chapbook versions from late 17th c
	parts reworked by Spenser, Bunyan
Allusions	numerous, inc. *Complaynt*, Cox, Peele, Shakespeare, Jonson, Rowlands, Kirkman
	condemnations by Hyrd, Dering, Nashe, Meres, Crosse, Arthur Dent (*Plaine Mans Path-way*, 1601)

Blanchardyn and Eglantine

Edition	ed. L. Kellner, EETS E.S. 58
Source	15th c French prose redaction of 13th c romance
Date/MS history	no Middle English version prior to Caxton's translation, printed 1490 (*STC* 3124)

| 16th–17th c currency | adapted by Thomas Pope Goodwine, prints 1595, 1597 (*STC* 3125–6) |
| Allusions | Meres |

Brutus
Origin	Geoffrey of Monmouth
Date/MSS history	1138; numerous later chronicle versions
16th–17th c currency	chronicles including Holinshed; Spenser, *Faerie Queene* 'Defence of Brutus' 1593 (*SR* ii. 627) Thomas Heywood, *Troia Britanica*, 1609
Dramatization	Day and Chettle, *Conquest of Brute I & II* (1598; lost)
Allusions	extensive and various; London as Troynovaunt

The Carle off Carlile, see under Gawain

Charlemagne
Origin	mid-13th c French metrical *Fierebras* included in BL Royal 15 E VI
Middle English versions	*The Sowdone of Babylone* (*c*.1400, one MS); two other redactions both entitled *Sir Firumbras* (late 14thc, one MS each)
Printed version	Book 2 of Caxton's translation *Charles the Grete*, 1485, from Bagnyon's French prose *Fierebras*, 1478 (*STC* 5013) (ed. by Herrtage)
Adaptations	*The Twelve Peers of France* (lost; 'old' in August 1586, *SR* ii. 453)

Ariosto's *Orlando Furioso* and its Renaissance derivatives (Harington's translation, 1591; play, 1591) are distantly related to this material; the MS play *Charlemagne* (*c*.1604) is independent of both traditions.
see also, *Four Sons of Aymon*; *Huon of Burdeux*

Chaucer: the romances of the *Canterbury Tales*
Editions	*Riverside Chaucer*, ed. by Larry D. Benson; numerous
Date/MS history	*c*.1380–1400; numerous MSS
16th–17th c currency	five edns., 1477–1526 (*STC* 5082–6); *Works*, six edns. 1532–1602 (*STC* 5068–81), 1687
Allusions	numerous: see Spurgeon

Franklin's Tale
Origin	Italian (Boccaccio, probably *Decameron*)
Dramatization	Francis Beaumont and Nathan Field, *The Triumph of Honour*, 1612
Allusion	quoted *Faerie Queene* III. i. 25

Knight's Tale
Source	Italian, Boccaccio's *Teseida*
Dramatizations	Richard Edwards, 1566
	anonymous, 1594
	Shakespeare and Fletcher, *Two Noble Kinsmen*
Allusions	Wyatt, *Satire* 1; A *Midsummer Night's Dream*; Jonson, *Bartholomew Fair*

Man of Law's Tale (Constance)
Origin	Anglo-Norman, Trevet's *Chroniques*
Modernization	Thomas Alsop, *Fair Custance*, STC 538.5 (*c*.1525)
Dramatization	Dekker and others, *Fair Constance of Rome* (1600)

Sir Thopas
Origin	original, based on Middle English romance
Imitations	Dunbar; Drayton
Allusions	Wyatt, *Satire* 1; Spenser, *Faerie Queene*, *View*; Drayton, *Eglogues*

Squire's Tale
Origin	no known source, but reworking of French romance motifs
Adaptations/completions	Spenser, *Faerie Queene*; John Lane (1615, rev. 1630; unpublished)
Allusions	inc. Milton, *Il Penseroso*

Wife of Bath's Tale
Origin	probably English folktale
Dramatization	Fletcher, *Women Pleas'd* (1620)
Adaptations	Richard Johnson, ballad 1612
Allusions	numerous to the Wife and the Prologue, less common to her Tale (see Cooper, 'Shape-shifting')

Chaucer, *Troilus and Criseyde*
Editions	ed. B. A. Windeatt; *Riverside Chaucer*, ed. Benson; numerous
Origin/source	12th c French of Benoit de St-Maur, by way of 13th c Latin of Guido delle Colonne, to Boccaccio's *Il Filostrato* (Italian, 14th c)
Date/MSS history	*c*.1385; sixteen MSS
Other medieval versions	included in Lydgate's *Troy Book*
16th–17thc currency	edns. 1483, 1517, 1526 (*STC* 5094–6); *Works*, six edns. 1532–1602 (*STC* 5068–81), 1687
	Lydgate's *Troy Book* printed 1513, 1555 (*STC* 5579–80)
Translation	Kinaston's Latin translation of Books 1–2, 1635 (*STC* 5097–97.3)

Dramatizations	?Cornish, 1516; Grimald, 1540s (both lost)
	(with other sources: see Troy) Shakespeare, *Troilus and Cressida*
Adaptations	ballads 1566, 1581 (*SR* i.300, ii.394)
Allusions	numerous, including Turberville 1569; Gascoigne 1575; Sidney 1581
	see Spurgeon

Constance, see Gower; Chaucer, *Man of Law's Tale*

Degaré

Editions	ed. by Schleich (repr. Jacobs, *Later Versions*); French and Hale; Laskaya and Salisbury
Origin	no known source, but traditional materials
Date/MS history	early 14th c, 4 MSS to *c*.1500 including Auchinleck
16th–17th c currency	four editions from *c*.1512 to *c*.1565 (entitled *Sir Degore*) (*STC* 6470–6472.5)
	Banyster
	Percy Folio

The Earl of Toulouse

Editions	Fellows; French and Hale
Origin	no known literary source
Date/MS history	4 MSS to *c*.1500
Later currency	no known prints, but analogue in Percy Folio *Sir Aldingar* and later traditional ballads (Child no. 59, ii. 33–48)

Eger and Grime

Editions	ed. Caldwell (parallel texts); French and Hale (Percy)
Origin	no known source
Date/MS history	15th c allusions, but no extant medieval MSS
16–17 c currency	record of 1577 edn. (no copies extant)
	Percy Folio
	extant prints from 1669, 1687, 1711
Allusions	from 15th c; *Complaynt*

Eglamour of Artois

Editions	ed. F. E. Richardson, EETS O.S. 256; Hudson
Origin	no single source known; traditional material
Date/MS history	mid-14th c; five MSS to early 16th c
	acted at St Albans 1444 ('Eglemour and Degrebelle', lost)

16th–17th c currency	six edns. from *c.*1500 to *c.*1565 (*STC* 7541–7544.5); licence transferred 1581–2 (*SR* ii. 405)
	Banyster
	Percy Folio
Allusions	Cox; Shakespeare, *Two Gentlemen*
Adaptations	Rowlands (parody)
	influence on Percy Folio ballad *Sir Lionel* and later oral versions (Child no. 18, i. 208–15)

Four Sons of Aymon

Edition	ed. O. Richardson, EETS E.S. 44–5
Source	French prose redaction of *c.*1400 (printed *c.*1480) of late 12th c *chanson de geste, Renaut de Montauban* included in BL Royal 15 E VI
Date/MS history	no English versions before Caxton's translation, printed *c.*1489
16–17 c currency	licence transferred 12 March 1581–2, 22 Feb 1598–9 (*SR* ii. 408, iii. 137, 139)
Dramatization	acted 1603, 1624 (lost)
Allusions	*Complaynt*; North, *Diall of Princes* (1557); Cox, Dering, Nashe, Meres, Rowlands
	Kirkman notes as rare, 1673

Gamelyn

Editions	French and Hale; Sands
Origin	no known source; related to English folktales and Robin Hood ballads
Date/MSS history	later 14th c; survives as spurious 'Cook's Tale' in 25 MSS of *Canterbury Tales*
16th–17th c currency	mid–17th c MS (Ashmole)
	not printed until 1721
Adaptation	Thomas Lodge, *Euphues Golden Legacy* (*Rosalynde*), source of *As You Like It*

Gawain

Golagros and Gawain

Edition	Hanks
Origin	loose adaptation from First Continuation of 12th c *Perceval*
Date/MSS history	late 15th c; no known MSS
16th–17th c currency	one print, Edinburgh 1508 (*STC* 11984)
Allusion	*Complaynt*

The Grene Knight

Editions	Hanks; Speed
Origin	free tail-rhyme retelling of *Sir Gawain and the Green Knight*
Date/MS history	15th c; no surviving MSS; possible reference by John Paston, 1470
16th–17th c currency	no extant prints; Percy Folio

A Jeast of Sir Gawayne

Edition	Hanks
Origin	loose adaptation from First Continuation of 12th c *Perceval*
Date/MS history	late 15th c; no medieval MS
16th–17th c currency	prints from *c.*1528 to *c.*1540 (*STC* 11691a.3–.7); *SR* 1557–8 (i. 79)
	Banyster
Allusion	? Cox ('Sir Gawain')

Sir Gawain and the Carl of Carlisle

Edition	Hanks
Origin	no source known, but includes beheading motif as in *Gawain and the Green Knight*
Date/MS history	*c.*1400, one MS
16th–17th c currency	adaptation, *The Carle off Carlile*, probably early 16th c; no prints extant; Percy Folio (also ed. by Hanks)

Sir Gawain and the Green Knight, see Grene Knight

The Turke and Gowin

Edition	Hanks
Origin	no source known, but includes beheading motif as in *Gawain and the Green Knight*
Date/MSS history	*c.*1500; no extant MS
16th–17th c currency	no prints extant; Percy Folio

The Wedding of Sir Gawain and Dame Ragnell

Editions	Hanks; Shepherd
Origin	folktale; some influence from *Wife of Bath's Tale*
Date/MSS history	mid–15th c; one MS, *c.*1500
16th–17th c adaptation	*Marriage [Wedding] of Sir Gawain*, Percy Folio (also Hanks, Shepherd)

Generides

Editions	ed. Furnivall (couplet); ed. Wright, EETS o.s. 55, 70 (stanzaic)
Origin	possibly French, but no known source
Date/MS history	couplet version ?late 14th c, one MS; rhyme royal version

	?early 15th c, one MS
16th–17thc currency	three prints of rhyme royal version, *c.*1500–08 (*STC* 11721–21.7)
	licence transferred 1568–9 (*SR* i. 389)
Allusions	Hyrd

Gower, *Confessio amantis*

Edition	ed. G. C. Macaulay
Origin	multiple; see also Apollonius
Date/MS history	1390s; numerous 15th c manuscripts
16th–17th c currency	3 edns. 1483–1554; licence transferred 1582–3, 1594 (*SR* ii. 405, 651)
Dramatization/allusion	*Pericles*

Grail

| 16th–17th c currency | incorporated into Harding's 15th c *Chronicle*, printed 1543 (*STC* 12766.7–12767) |

see, Joseph of Arimathea; Malory. Henry Lovelich's translation of the *History of the Holy Grail* was not known later.

Guy of Warwick

Editions	early versions, ed. Zupitza, EETS E.S. 42, 49, 59 (repr. 1966); 15th c version, ed. Zupitza EETS ES 25–6 (repr. 1987)
Source	Anglo-Norman *Gui de Warewik*
Other medieval versions	French prose (not trans. into Middle English) included in BL Royal 15 E VI
Date/MS history	five MSS of various versions from *c.*1300 (earliest in Auchinleck)
16th–17th c currency	prints 1500–*c.*1565 (*STC* 12540–2); ed. Schleich Percy Folio (including adaptations)
Dramatizations	?1593 (extant as *The Tragical History of Guy of Warwick*, printed 1661); 1618 (anon.); 1620 (Day and Dekker) (see p. 93 above)
Adaptations	Richard Lloyd, *Nine Worthies* 1584 ballad, *SR* 1592 (ii. 601) Drayton, legend in *Poly-Olbion* verse by John Lane (1621 , MS only) verse by Samuel Rowlands (1609; numerous prints to *c.*1680 (*STC* 21378–80, Wing R2084–6; prose redaction printed to 19th c)) further broadside and chapbook versions
Allusions	numerous, including Hyrd, Dering, Meres, Rowlands Spenser, *Faerie Queene* (Guyon); Shakespeare; Jonson

For bibliography, see Richmond

Havelok

Editions	ed. by G. V. Smithers; French and Hale, Herzman *et al.*, Sands, Shepherd, Speed
Origin	English legend, but first surviving text Anglo-Norman
Date/MS history	late 13th c; two 14th c MSS
Other medieval versions	chronicles, especially prose *Brut*
16th–17th c currency	prints of prose *Brut* from 1480 (*Chronicles of England, STC* 9991–4)
	as legend of origin for Grimsby (Camden)
Adaptations	William Warner, *Albions England* (edns. from 1586 to 1612), from chronicles

Helyas, see *Knight of the Swan*

Horn

Editions	*King Horn*, ed. Hall; Fellows, French and Hale, Herzman *et al.*, Sands
	Horn Childe and Maiden Rimnild, ed. Mills
Origin	probably English, but first surviving text Anglo-Norman
Date/MSS history	*King Horn*, early 13th c, 3 MSS all *c.*1300
	Horn Child, early 14th c, Auchinleck only
16th–17th c currency	no prints
Adaptations	ballad *Hind Horn* (Child 17)
	see also *King Ponthus*

Huon of Burdeux

Edition	ed. S. L. Lee, EETS E.S. 43, 50
Origin	15th c French prose redaction of late 12th c *chanson de geste*
MS history	no Middle English version
16th–17th c currency	translated by Lord Berners, *c.*1515
	editions from *c.*1515–1601 (*STC* 13998.5–99) (see Boro)
	inventory of 3rd earl of Essex, 1646 (Davis p. 30)
Dramatization	before 1593 (lost)
Allusions	Spenser, *FQ*, II. i. 6; Cox, Nashe, Meres, Florio (1603)

Ipomadon (tail-rhyme)/*Ipomydon* (couplets)/*Ipomedon* (prose)

Editions	ed. Eugen Kölbing (all versions)
	ed. Rhiannon Purdie (tail-rhyme), EETS O.S. 316
	ed. Ikegami (couplet, including print)
Source	Anglo-Norman of Hue de Rotelande (Rhuddlan), *c.*1190
Date/MS history	three Middle English translations (14th c tail-rhyme; 15th c couplet; mid-15th c prose); one MS of each, all 15th c

| 16–17 c currency | two prints extant, 1522, 1527 (couplet version, *STC* 5732.5, 5733) |
| Allusions | Hyrd, *Complaynt* |

Isumbras

Editions	ed. by Schleich; Hudson; Mills
Origin	no single known source
Date/MS history	early 14th c; eight MSS to *c*.1500
16–17 c currency	five edns. from *c*.1530 to *c*.1565 (*STC* 14280.5–14282; Severs, *Manual*)
	Banyster
	SR 15 Jan. 1581–2, ii. 405
Allusions	Cox; *Cobler of Caunterbury* (1590); Drayton, *Eglogues* (1593)

John de Reeve

Edition	*Percy*
Origin	folktale motif of 'king in disguise'
Date/MS history	*c*.1400 (1377–1461); no medieval MS extant
16th–17th c currency	Percy
Allusions	from *c*.1500; *Complaynt*
Analogues	*King Edward and the Shepherd* (late 14th c; one 15th c MS, no post-1500 circulation; in French and Hale)
	Rauf Coilyear (see below)
	for plays, see Barton, 'The King Disguised'
	for ballads, see Child 273 (v. 67–87)

Joseph of Arimathea

Editions	alliterative poem and prints ed. W. W. Skeat, EETS O.S. 44
Origin	*Estoire del Saint Graal* (opening section of French prose *Lancelot-Grail*, early 13 c); English ownership 14th–15th c
Medieval versions	mid–14th c alliterative version, one MS
	various chronicles, in particular John Capgrave's mid–15th c *Nova legenda Angliae*
16th–17th c currency	Capgrave printed 1516 (*STC* 4601)
	prints of two prose and one verse versions of the legend, all deriving from Capgrave: *Lyfe of Joseph of Arimathy*, *c*.1511 (*STC* 14806); *De Sancto Joseph*, 1516 (in *STC* 4602); *The Lyfe of Joseph of Arimathia* (verse), *c*.1520 (*STC* 14807)
	chapbook version current to late 18th c

King Ponthus and the Faire Sidone

Edition	ed. by F. J. Mather, jr, *PMLA* 12 (1897)
Source	French prose rewriting (*c.*1390) of Anglo-Norman *Horn* (one MS probably copied in England)
	also included in BL Royal 15 E VI
Date/MSS history	mid-15th c; two MSS
16th–17th c currency	(?different translation) printed *c.*1509–11 (*STC* 20107, 20107.5, 20108); also 1548 (Scanlon); licensed 15 Jan. 1581–2 (*SR* ii. 405)

The Knight of Courtesy and the Fair Lady of Faguell

Editions	ed. E. McCausland; Hazlitt
Origin	13th c French *Chronique du Châtelain de Couci*; romance by Jakemes
Date/MSS history	?15th c; no known MSS
16th–17th c currency	one print extant, ?1556 (*STC* 24223)
Allusions	Cox

The Knight of the Swan

Editions	*Cheualere Assigne*, ed. H.H. Gibbs, EETS E.S. 6; French and Hale, Speed
Origins	redaction of story from French Godefroy of Bouillon cycle
	included in BL Royal 15 E VI
Date/MS history	late 14 c; one late 15 c MS
16th–17th c currency	extended prose version, *Helyas, Knight of the Swan,* three prints 1512–c. 1560 (*STC* 7571–2) (from French prose; in Thoms)

Lancelot

Origin	French Prose *Lancelot* (English ownership in 14th and 15th c)
Middle English versions	see Arthur: romance developments
	late 15th c northern *Lancelot of the Laik*
Middle English allusions	Auchinleck *Anonymous Short Metrical Chronicle*, *c.*1331
	Chaucer, *Nun's Priest's Tale*
16th–17th c currency	see Arthur: romance developments
Adaptations	Thomas Deloney, *Sir Lancelot of Dulake*, 1603 [Lancelot and Tarquin]: numerous prints as broadside ballad; Percy Folio
	legend of combat at Knock Castle, near Manchester, to 18th c.

Allusions	*Complaynt* (text in question not identified)
	Florio (1603); Rowlands
	character in Middleton's *Chinon of England,* Johnson's *Tom a Lincoln*

Launfal/Landeval/Lam(be)well

Editions	*Launfal* ed. Bliss; Fellows; French and Hale; Laskaya and Salisbury; Sands; Shepherd
	Landeval, in Bliss's edn.; ed. by Kittredge ('*Sir Launfal*'); Shepherd
Origin	late 12th c [Anglo-]French (Marie de France)
Date/MS history	*Landeval,* early 14th c, one late 15th c MS; *Launfal,* later 14 c, one 15 c MS
16th–17thc currency	*Sir Lamwell,* 1548–60 (*STC* 15187–87.5); licence transferred 1557–8 (*SR* i. 79)
	Percy Folio (*Sir Lambewell*)
allusions	Cox

Lybeaus Desconus

Edition	ed. by Maldwyn Mills, EETS O.S. 261
Origin	possible Anglo-Norman original; only continental version now known
	late 12th c French, *Le bel Inconnu* by Renaut de Beaujeu
Date/MSS history	late 14th c; 5 MSS
16th–17th c currency	no prints surviving; Percy Folio
Allusions	Hyrd, Crosse

Malory, see Arthur

Melusine

Edition	ed. by A. K. Donald, EETS E.S. 68
Origin	late 14th c prose of Jean d'Arras
Date/MSS history	*c.*1500, one MS
16–17th c currency	printed *c.*1510 (*STC* 14648)
	one early 16 c MS of translation of metrical version by Coudrette (ed. Skeat, *Romauns of Partenay*)
Allusions	Hyrd (Vives' list); William Holme (1537/72: see p. 176)

Merlin: birth

Edition	*Of Arthour and of Merlin,* ed. O. D. Macrae-Gibson, EETS 268, 279
Origin	Vulgate cycle *Merlin* (English ownership in 15th c)
Date/MSS history	before 1300; four MSS from Auchinleck to late 15th c

16th–17th c currency	*The byrth and prophecye of Marlyn* 1510, 1529 (*STC* 17841–41.3)
	Percy Folio
Dramatization	*The Birth of Merlin* (dramatization, ?1608) (ed. Tucker Brooke, *Shakespeare Apocrypha*)
Allusions	Rowlands

[Neither Lovelich's early 15th c metrical *Merlin* (ed. Kock), nor the mid–15th c prose translation (ed. Wheatley) was current after 1500.]

Octavian

Editions	*Octovian*, ed by F. McSparran, EETS O.S. 289; Hudson; Mills
Origin/source	probably 12th c French
Date/MS history	mid–14th c; southern version, two 15th c MSS; northern version, one late 15th c MS
16th–17th c currency	print *c*.1505 (*STC* 18779)

Oliver of Castile

Edition	ed. by G. Orgelfinger
Origin	mid-15thc French prose incorporating traditional motifs
Date/MS history	no Middle English versions
16th–17thc currency	trans. by Henry Watson printed 1518 (*STC* 18808); licence transferred 1581–2 (*SR* ii. 408)
Allusions	Cox, Dering, Meres

Orfeo

Editions	ed. by A. J. Bliss; French and Hale; Laskaya and Salisbury; Sands; Shepherd; Speed
Origin	possibly French, but no source extant
Date/MS history	early 14th c; three MSS, Auchinleck to *c*.1500
16th–17th c currency	*King Orphius* (Scottish, *c*.1586; ed. Stewart)
Ballad	*King Orfeo* (Child i. 317–29)
Allusion	? *Complaynt* ('Opheus kyng of Portingal')

Paris and Vienne

Edition	ed. E.M. Leach, EETS O.S. 234
Source	15th c French prose
Date/MS history	no English version prior to Caxton's translation (1485)
16th–17th c currency	three or four edns. 1485–1505 (*STC* 19206–8)
	licence transferred 8 Aug. 1586 (*SR* ii. 453)
Adaptation	by Matthew Mainwaring 1628, 1632 (*STC* 17201–2)
	licence assigned May 1638 (*SR* iv. 394)
Dramatization	acted by boys of Westminster School 1572

Partonope of Blois

Edition	ed. A. Trampe Bödtker, EETS E.S. 109
Origin	12th c French
Date/MS history	15th c; five MSS of couplet version, one of abbreviated quatrain version
16th–17th c currency	likely to have been printed but no edns. extant
allusions	Hyrd

Perceforest

Origin	mid-14th c French; no Middle English version
16th–17th c currency	numerous French printed edns.
Dramatization	*Clyomon and Clamydes* (1570s; printed 1599, *STC* 5450a; ed. Littleton)

Rauf Coilyear

Editions	ed. S. J. Herrtage, EETS E.S. 39; ed. E. Walsh; Speed
Origin	folktale ('king in disguise')
Date/MS history	late 14th–15th c; no extant MSS, though listed in Asloan MS (1515)
16th–17th c currency	printed St Andrews, 1572 (*STC* 5487)
Allusions	from 1500; *Complaynt*
Analogues	see *John the Reeve*, above
	for plays, see Barton, 'The King Disguised'
	for ballads, see Child 273 (v. 67–87)

Richard Cœur de Lyon

Edition	ed. Karl Brünner, *Der mittelenglische Versroman über Richard Löwenherz* (Vienna, 1913)
Origin	chronicle-type material, though treatment probably original
Date/MS history	c.1300; nine MSS (two fragmentary), Auchinleck to late 15th c
16th–17th c currency	two prints extant, 1509, 1528 (*STC* 21007–8)
	licence transferred 1568–9 (*SR* i. 389)

Robert the Devil

Edition	Hazlitt prints both early 16th c versions
Origin	12th c French *Robert le diable*
Date/MS history	no extant Middle English MS
Medieval adaptations	*Sir Gowther*, c.1400 (two MSS) (edition with important study of *Robert* by K. Breul (Oppeln, 1886); also Mills)

16th–17th c currency	prose version printed 1500, 1517 (*STC* 21070–1)
	metrical version, 1510 (*STC* 201071.5); also Banyster (Egerton)
Adaptation	Thomas Lodge, *Robert Second Duke of Normandy* (1591)
Allusions	*Complaynt*

Robert of Sicily

Edition	French and Hale; Foster
Origin	unknown, but widespread folktale type
Date/MS history	10 MSS, *c.*1375–*c.*1500
Medieval dramatization	1447–53 (lost)
16th–17th c dramatizations	1529; Latin, 1623 (both lost)

Roswall and Lillian

Edition	ed. O. Lengert, *Englische Studien* 16, 17
Origin	no known source, but influenced by *Ipomedon*
Date/MS history	probably 15th c; no surviving MSS
16th–17th c currency	prints from 1663 to 1775
Adaptations	ballad 'Lord of Lorn' (*SR* 6 Oct 1580, and ref. that year by Guilpin) inc 'Disaware', version included in Percy Folio (i. 180–98)

Seven Sages of Rome [Seven Wise Masters]

Editions	ed. K. Campbell; ed. K. Brunner, EETS O.S. 191
Origin	Oriental, by way of 12th c Latin and early 13th c French
Date/MS history	nine MSS of various texts, from Auchinleck to early 16th c Scots and English
16th–17th c currency	printed as *The Seven Wise Masters*, editions from 1493 to 1576 (*STC* 21298–21299.3)
	adaptation of early print 1653, numerous editions to early 18th c
	Scots version by John Rolland 1568, six extant editions 1578–1635 (*STC* 21254–57.7)
	other versions (short texts deriving from early print) 18th–19th c
	[see Campbell's edition]
Dramatization	Chettle and others, 1600 (lost)
Allusions	Cox

Sir Gawain and the Green Knight, see *The Grene Knight* under Gawain, above

Squire of Low Degree [Undo your Door]

Editions	French and Hale; Sands
Origin	no known source, but traditional materials

Date/MSS history	not traceable before printing, but may be 15th c
16th–17th c currency	two prints extant, *c.*1520, 1560 (*STC* 23111–12)
	Percy Folio
Allusions	Cox; Nashe; Spenser; Shakespeare (*Henry V*, 5.1)

Thomas of Erceldoune

[The following information relates to the narrative versions; prophecies ascribed to Thomas without any narrative frame are not covered, though they had an even more extensive dissemination and afterlife.]

Editions	ed. James A. H. Murray, EETS O.S. 68; ed. Ingeborg Nixon
Origin	traditional material but original
Date/MSS history	? 14th c; three surviving 15th c MSS
16th–17th c currency	one 16th c MS (*c.*1525; ed. Murray)
	printed 1652 (ed. Nixon)
Adaptations	*Prophisies of Rymour*, two MSS from *c.*1529 (Virgin for elf-queen)
	prints of redaction of *Prophisies*, 1603, 1615
	current as chapbook to early 19th c
	ballad, *Thomas Rymer*

Torrent of Portyngale

Edition	ed. E. Adam, EETS E.S. 51
Origin	no known source, but traditional materials
Date/MS history	*c.*1400; one late 15th c MS
16th–17th c currency	*c.*1505–10 (*STC* 24133, 24133.5)
Allusion	? *Complaynt* ('Opheus kyng of Portingal')

Tryamour

Editions	Fellows; Hudson
Origin	no known source, but traditional material
Date/MSS history	late 14th c; two MSS (one missing)
16th–17th c currency	five prints *c.*1503–65 (*STC* 24301.5–24303.3)
	Percy Folio
Allusions	Cox; Rowlands
	secondary hero in Middleton's *Chinon of England*

Tristram

[The 12th c Anglo-Norman *Tristan* of Thomas of Britain is represented in Middle English by a late 13th c version surviving only in Auchinleck; there are numerous allusions to the story in Middle English, but the transmission to the Renaissance comes by way of the Prose *Tristan*, an amalgam of the 12th c versions with the model of the Prose *Lancelot*.]

Editions	see Malory
Source	13th c French Prose *Tristan* (15th c English ownership)
Date/MS history	see Malory
Dramatization	*Tristram of Lyons*, 1598 (lost)
Allusions	Nashe; Spenser; character in Middleton's *Chinon of England*

Troy

Origin	ultimately Homer, by way of Dictys (4th c) and Dares (6th c; metrical version by Joseph of Exeter, 12 c) 12th c French *Roman de Troie* of Benoit de St Maur; 13th c Latin prose redaction by Guido delle Colonne
Date/MS history	various Middle English redactions from *c.*1300, none directly transmitted after 1500 (see Severs, *Manual*, nos. 72–6) Lydgate, *Troy Book* (1420) *The Recuyell of the Historyes of Troye*, trans. Caxton (*c.*1475) from Raoul le Fevre's French prose version of Guido
16th–17th c currency	Lydgate's *Troy Book* printed 1513, 1555 (*STC* 5579–80); modernization 1614 (*STC* 5581) English version of Dares by Thomas Paynell (via French), 1553 (*STC* 6274.5) 3 edns. of Caxton's *Recuyell*, 1475–1553 (*STC* 24571.3–24572) rev. as *The auncient historie of the destruction of Troy* by William Fiston, ?*SR* June 1591 (ii. 586), edns. 1596 to 1738 (*STC* 15379–82)
Dramatizations	*Troilus and Criseyde* (?1603) (from *Recuyell* and Chaucer) Thomas Heywood, *Life and Death of Hector*, *The Iron Age* (from Lydgate)

Turke and Gowin, see under Gawain

Valentine and Orson

Edition	ed. Dickson, EETS O.S. 204
Origin/source	15th c French prose redaction of lost ?14th c French original
Date/MSS history	no Middle English version
16th–17th c currency	three prints extant, *c.*1510–*c.*1565 (*STC* 24571.3–24572) licence transferred Aug. 1586 (*SR* ii. 453) abbreviated version 1637 and numerous later reprints
Dramatizations	pageant for coronation of Edward VI, 1549 plays 1595, 1598 (Hathway and Munday) (both lost)

Adaptations	couplet version in Percy Folio, *The Emperor and the Child*
	chapbook and other short versions from 17th to 19th c
Allusions	North, *Diall of Princes* (1557); Sidney ('Pacolet's horse', *Apologie*); Kirkman

Wedding of Sir Gawain, see under Gawain

William of Palerne

Edition	ed. G. H. V. Bunt
Source	early 13th c French (also 15th c French prose)
Date/MSS history	*c.*1355; one MS
16th–17th c currency	prose version (probably from the Middle English alliterative poem) printed *c.*1515, *STC* 25707.5 (fragment ed. Bunt, pp. 328–31)
	16th c Irish version of English prose
Allusions	Hyrd

Ysumbras, see *Isumbras*

Ywain and Gawain

Editions	ed. Friedman and Harrington, EETS O.S. 254; ed. Mills; ed. Braswell; Shepherd
Source	12th c French *Yvain* of Chrétien de Troyes
Date/MS history	early 14th c; one early 15th c MS
16th–17th c currency	no prints known
Allusion	*Complaynt* ('Syr Euan arthours knycht')

Notes

INTRODUCTION

1. 'An enterlude of Valentyne and Orsson, plaid by hir maiesties Players' was licensed in 1595 to Thomas Gosson and Raffe Hancock; licensing for publication commonly occurred some years after the initial composition of a play, so the dramatization may itself date from some years earlier. The licence was transferred to William White in 1600 (*SR*, iii.159). A second dramatization was made by Richard Hathwaye and Anthony Munday for Henslowe in 1598. Some of the playbooks of the Queen's Men (and conceivably the bearsuit too) passed to the Chamberlain's Men, Shakespeare's company. See also Helen Cooper, 'The Strange History of *Valentine and Orson*', in *Tradition and Transformation in Medieval Romance*, ed. Rosalind Field (Cambridge, 1999), pp. 153–68, especially pp. 163–4; and, for a sample bearsuit, *Henslowe's Diary*, ed. R. A. Foakes, 2nd edn. (Cambridge, 2002), p. 319.
2. Arthur Dickson, *Valentine and Orson: A Study in Late Medieval Romance* (New York, 1929), p. 286.
3. John Forster, *The Life of Charles Dickens* (first published 1872–4), ed. A. J. Hoppé, rev. edn. (London, 1969), i.301. The reference is not, as might be thought, to *The Two Gentlemen of Verona*.
4. *A Contextual Study and Modern-spelling Edition of Mucedorus*, ed. Arvin H. Jupin (New York and London, 1987), I.i, opening stage direction in the original version (first printed in 1598; the additions made to the third quarto of 1610 included an explanatory opening scene before the bear, and some further stage business involving it; these are printed by Jupin in an appendix). The episode is derived from Sidney's *Arcadia*, and gives the hero an opportunity of exercising his prowess. By the time of the 1610 publication, the play belonged to the King's Men. It was probably written *c*.1590, but the order of composition of the plays containing bears is uncertain, as there are no reliable dates for either this, the anonymous *Valentine and Orson* licensed in 1595, or *Locrine* (see note 5 below). The anonymous play of *Valentine* may not be the earliest, though its justification for including a bear is rather stronger than for most of them.
5. *The Lamentable Tragedy of Locrine*, ed. Jane Lytton Gooch (New York and London, 1981), composed between 1585 and 1595, specifies a 'Bear or any other beast' (plus a lion) in its opening emblematic dumbshow; the mention of a bear may have been an acknowledgement of an existing bearsuit. The spectral bear figures in John Day and William Haughton's lost *Cox of Collumpton* (1599), the plot of which is known through a summary by Simon Forman: see the account in John Pitcher, '"Fronted with the Sight of a Bear": *Cox of Collumpton* and *The Winter's Tale*', *Notes and Queries* 239 (1994), 47–53.
6. The phrase 'mouldy tale' (referring specifically to *Pericles*) is Ben Jonson's, from the 'Ode to Himself' written after the failure of *The New Inn* in 1629—*Pericles* being

another example of the long popularity of romance drama, still in the repertory twenty years after its composition (*Ben Jonson: The Complete Poems*, ed. George Parfitt (Harmondsworth, 1975), No. XXXIII; and cf. Leah Scragg, *Shakespeare's Mouldy Tales* (London and New York, 1992, p. 1). The literary ancestry of the bear of the *Winter's Tale* has been much debated: Pitcher, ' "Fronted with the sight of a bear" ', gives a summary. He favours its function as an avenging sprite, on the model of the bear in *Cox of Collumpton*. The need for a bearsuit would remain unaffected by the particular symbolic use made of the bear itself. The arguments that real bears were used after 1609 remains tenuous: see, for instance, Barbara Ravelhofer, ' "Beasts of Recreation": Henslowe's White Bears', *ELR* 32 (2002), 287–323, especially pp. 298–9, 304.

7. 'A poetics describing literary competence would focus on the conventions that make possible literary structure and meaning: what are the codes or systems of convention that enable readers to identify literary genres, recognize plots . . . and pursue the kind of symbolic interpretation that allows us to gauge the significance of poems and stories?' (Jonathan Culler, *Literary Theory: A Very Short Introduction* (Oxford, 1997), p. 62).

8. The idea of the meme was put forward by Richard Dawkins in *The Selfish Gene* (Oxford, 1976), pp. 206–7, and has been extensively developed by Susan Blackmore, *The Meme Machine* (Oxford, 1999). Romance motifs fulfil precisely her criteria of replication with fidelity, fecundity, and longevity. The romance itself would be the meme vehicle or 'memeplex' (see pp. 63–6).

9. The transmission of medieval English romance into the Tudor age was first extensively studied by Ronald S. Crane, *The Vogue of Medieval Chivalric Romance during the English Renaissance* (1919; repr. Norwood, Pa, 1977). Later studies include Jean Wilson, *Spenser's Treatment of Romance Themes in the Faerie Queene* (Ph.D., Cambridge, 1974); Velma Bourgeois Richmond, *The Popularity of Middle English Romance* (Bowling Green, OH, 1975); Andrew King, *The Faerie Queene and Middle English Romance: The Matter of Just Memory* (Oxford, 2000), esp. pp. 29–42; and Michael L. Hays, *Shakespearean Tragedy as Chivalric Romance* (Cambridge, 2003), esp. pp. 27–65. Hays estimates that there were some 85,800 copies of romances printed before 1560, and 185,600 printed 1561–1610 (though most of the latter were new works influenced by the fashion for Spanish romances, not the medieval corpus).

10. *John Bunyan: Grace Abounding and The Pilgrim's Progress*, ed. Roger Sharrock (London, 1966), Author's Apology, pp. 139, 144. For his youthful reading, see *A Few Sighs from Hell*, in *The Miscellaneous Works of John Bunyan*, Vol. 1, ed. T. L. Underwood and Roger Sharrock (Oxford, 1980), p. 333.

11. To give two examples: after the Bible, *The Pilgrim's Progress* was the book most likely to be taken to the trenches by soldiers in the First World War; and it forms the ethical backbone of Louisa May Alcott's *Little Women*, a level of explicit allusion that she could assume would be understood by her readers. The work had been popular in New England from the moment of its publication, as Bunyan notes in his introductory poem to the 'Second Part' (ed. Sharrock, l. 275). His disappearance from modern culture is comparably measured by the work's excision from film and television adaptations of her novel.

12. Vladimir Propp, *Morphology of the Folktale*, trans. Laurence Scott, 2nd edn., rev. Louis A. Wagner (Austin and London, 1968); Susan Wittig, *Stylistic and Narrative*

Structures in the Middle English Romances (Austin and London, 1978). Propp identifies the recurrent characters and their functions within folktale; Wittig's aim is to identify and analyse the various levels of motif—the syntagm and syntagmeme, motifeme and allomotif, type-scene, and type-episode—in terms of their homologousness and the degree of substitutability within each class, on a model drawn from tagmemic linguistics, 'based on the concept of selection from a paradigm of choices and substitution within an established matrix' (p. 6). Her concern is thus to parse the language of motifs rather than to consider their meanings within particular texts or their change over time. The present book by contrast is concerned to demonstrate the *non-substitutability* of motifs.

13. Margaret Schlauch, *Chaucer's Constance and Accused Queens* (New York, 1927). Other studies concentrating on continuity more than change include Charles Ross's *The Custom of the Castle from Malory to Macbeth* (Berkeley, 1997); and, largely outside romance, John Kerrigan's anthology *The Motives of Woe: Shakespeare and the 'Female Complaint'* (Oxford, 1991), and Götz Schmitz's more historically nuanced *The Fall of Women in Early English Narrative Verse* (Cambridge, 1990).

14. Anne Barton's 'The King Disguised: Shakespeare's *Henry V* and the Comical History', reprinted in her *Essays: Mainly Shakespearean* (Cambridge, 1994), takes the motif back to the Robin Hood ballads, but the romances that provide the fullest narrative comparisons remain unexplored (for details, see Appendix, s.v. *John de Reeve, Rauf Coilyear*). On boats, see David Quint, 'The Boat of Romance and Renaissance Epic', in *Romance: Generic Transformation from Chrétien de Troyes to Cervantes* ed. Kevin Brownlee and Maria Scordilis Brownlee, (Hanover and London, 1985), pp. 178–202, and pp. 133–5 below.

15. D. F. McKenzie, *Bibliography and the Sociology of Texts*, 2nd edn. (Cambridge, 1999), p. 29. A similar point is forcefully made in connection with romance by Jean Radford, in her introduction to *The Progress of Romance: The Politics of Popular Fiction* (London and New York, 1986), pp. 8–9, and by Stephen Knight in his study of the changing ideological uses of Arthurian material, *Arthurian Literature and Society* (London, 1983).

16. Northrop Frye, *The Secular Scripture: A Study of the Structure of Romance* (Cambridge, Mass., 1976).

17. Northrop Frye, in the Foreword to *Unfolded Tales: Essays on Renaissance Romance*, ed. George M. Logan and Gordon Teskey (Ithaca and London, 1989), p. ix.

18. Gordon Teskey, in his Introduction to Logan's and his *Unfolded Tales*, has noted that works such as the *Faerie Queene* and Shakespeare's late plays are not classical with romance elements, but 'whole romances in which some classical elements have managed to survive by adapting themselves, like parasites, to the larger organism in which they are enclosed' (p. 9): a formulation that provokes the thought that those 'classical elements' have become memes in the minds of later critics.

19. The advice to Arthur on good kingship was translated in the late fifteenth century in the northern *Lancelot of the Laik* (ed. Alan Lupack (Kalamazoo, 1994), ll. 1314–542). There is no Middle English translation of the Lady of the Lake's instruction, though copies of the prose *Lancelot* are known to have been owned in England (see note 84 below). Malory omits Lancelot's youth, but he substitutes a

comparable summary of the duties of knighthood in the oath taken by the
Knights of the Round Table, which is apparently modelled on the oath of the dub-
bing ceremony for Knights of the Bath (*The Works of Sir Thomas Malory*, ed.
Eugène Vinaver, 3rd edn., rev. by P. J. C. Field, 3 vols. (Oxford, 1990), i. 120 (Book
III, chapter 15 in Caxton's edition))); for the oath of the Order of the Bath, see
Viscount Dillon, 'A Manuscript Collection of Ordinances of Chivalry of the
Fifteenth Century', *Archaeologia* 57:1 (1900), 27–70 (text on pp. 67–8). For a dis-
cussion of how the *Lancelot* in particular was used in the fashioning of real-life
knights, see Elspeth Kennedy, 'The Knight as Reader of Arthurian Romance',
Culture and the King: The Social Implications of Arthurian Legend, ed. Martin B.
Shichtman and James P. Carley (Albany, 1994), pp. 70–90.

20. Hans Robert Jauss, *Towards an Aesthetic of Reception*, trans. Timothy Bahti
(Brighton, 1982), pp. 22–5, 79, 88–9. Fredric Jameson reaches a similar conclusion
through a consideration of the social mechanism by which such a 'horizon' is
established, in his 'Magical Narratives: Romance as Genre', *New Literary History*
7 (1975–6), 135–63: 'Genres are essentially contracts between a writer and his read-
ers; or rather . . . they are literary *institutions*, which like other institutions of social
life are based on tacit agreements or contracts' (p. 135).

21. Among the most powerful, though making transhistorical assumptions that this
book does not altogether share, are those of Northrop Frye, outlined in *An
Anatomy of Criticism: Four Essays* (Princeton, 1957), 'The Mythos of Summer:
Romance', pp. 186–206, and elaborated in *The Secular Scripture*; Jameson offers a
critique and development, 'Magical Narratives'. A more pragmatic approach to
specifically medieval romance, also closely followed here, is that offered by Ad
Putter in his 'Historical Introduction' to *The Spirit of Medieval English Popular
Romance*, ed. Ad Putter and Jane Gilbert (Harlow, 2000), pp. 1–2: 'The resem-
blances shared by the overwhelming majority of romances are very broad . . . We
can spare ourselves the trouble of agonizing needlessly about problems of
definition if we accept that we have inherited the word "romance", with all its
vagueness, from those who talked before us . . . "romaunce" never was a precise
generic marker.' The Brownlees' introduction to *Romance: Generic
Transformation from Chrétien de Troyes to Cervantes*, pp. 1–12, makes the further
important point that no genres, romance high among them, remain static across
time and historical change, as the essays of the book cumulatively demonstrate.
Attempts to produce rigorous definitions (such as that of John Finlayson, who
argues in his 'Definitions of Middle English Romance' (*Chaucer Review* 15
(1980–1), 44–62, 168–81), that the term should be restricted to stories of knights
achieving great feats of arms in a series of adventures for no reason other than an
increase in their renown, go against those inherited expectations, and appear cor-
respondingly restrictive. More satisfying, because grounded in medieval evidence,
are two articles by Paul Strohm, '*Storie, Spelle, Geste, Romaunce, Tragedie*: Generic
Distinctions in the Middle English Troy Narrative', *Speculum* 46 (1971), 348–59,
and 'The Origin and Meaning of Middle English *Romaunce*', *Genre* 10 (1977),
1–20. A more detailed analysis of the varieties of Middle English romance is given
by Kathryn Hume, 'The Formal Nature of Middle English Romance', *Philological
Quarterly* 53 (1974), 158–80.

22. Many romance writers include some kind of comment on how their works are to
be read such as indicates just this kind of generic self-consciousness; the pro-

logues of Chrétien de Troyes are among the most famous examples, but a very high proportion of romances, in English as well as French, include some kind of horizon-setting as part of their introductory material, often by reference to other earlier works or heroes such as place the new work in a context of existing literature on which it can build. Michel Zink stresses the element of self-consciousness: 'Le roman est définissable précisement parce qu'il est tard venu et parce qu'il est le fruit d'une activité deliberé' ('Chrétien et ses contemporains', in *The Legacy of Chrétien de Troyes*, ed. (Norris J. Lacy, Douglas Kelly, and Keith Busby (Amsterdam, 1987), i.5–32 (p. 6)). More broadly, the links to Chaucer's *Canterbury Tales* often provide some kind of generic commentary on the tale just told, and form perhaps the most extended series of definitions of vernacular genres. The genre that most insistently identifies itself is the Breton lai, a kind of mini-romance, where an opening statement of genre is its primary defining feature.

23. The point is made by Alastair Fowler, that genres should be regarded 'not as permanent classes but as families subject to change' (*Kinds of Literature: An Introduction to the Theory of Genres and Modes* (Oxford, 1982), p. v.

24. The concept is developed by Ludwig Wittgenstein, *Philosophical Investigations*, trans. by G. E. M. Anscombe (Oxford, 1953), pp. 31–2 (a passage that includes the invaluable advice: 'Don't think, but look!'). The idea has been taken up by a number of genre critics, including Fowler, *Kinds of Literature*, pp. 40–3; and, with reference to romance, by Putter, *Spirit*, p. 2.

25. *Reliquiae Antiquae*, ed. Thomas Wright and J. O. Halliwell, 2 vols. (London, 1841), i.252.

26. The point is forcefully argued by Hays, *Shakespearean Tragedy as Chivalric Romance*; and see the last chapter of this book.

27. Stanley Wells, 'Shakespeare and Romance', in *Later Shakespeare*, ed. J. R. Brown and Bernard Harris, Stratford-upon-Avon Studies 8 (1966), 49–79 (p. 49).

28. The classic work on the relationships and differences between epic and romance is W. P. Ker's *Epic and Romance*, first published in 1897; Zink, 'Chrétien' p. 7, argues that the romance is in fact closer to the saint's life than to the *chanson de geste*.

29. *Ipomedon: Poème de Hue de Rotelande*, ed. A. J. Holden (Paris, 1979), ll. 28–30 ('Si le Latin n'est translatez, | Gaires n'ie erent entendanz; | Por ceo voil [jeo] dire en romanz'), and ll. 10,557–9 (quoted).

30. He also indicates that his imagined audience, and presumably his real one, is gender-inclusive, since he adds a rather mischievous invitation to the ladies to drop in on him.

31. *Of Arthour and of Merlin*, ed. O. D. Macrae-Gibson, Early English Text Society 268, 279 (1973, 1979), Auchinleck version, ll. 23–4.

32. See S. H. Cavanaugh, *A Study of Books Privately Owned in England 1300–1450*, PhD. thesis, University of Pennsylvania (1980). For women's ownership of French romances, see Carol M. Meale, '. . . alle the bokes that I haue of latyn, englisch and frensch: Laywomen and their books in late medieval England', in *Women and literature in Britain 1150–1500*, ed. Meale, (Cambridge, 1993), pp. 128–58, esp. pp. 139–41.

33. For a recent summary of the debate, see Putter's Introduction to *Spirit*, pp. 7–15, where he adduces evidence that points unequivocally to both manuscript transmission as the norm and memorial transmission as a genuine, and by

436 Notes to pages 12–14

no means uncommon, phenomenon. There is evidence that a number of the seventeenth-century Percy Folio romances were recorded from memorized recitations of printed versions: see S. G. St Clair-Kendall, *Narrative Form and Mediaeval Continuity in the Percy Folio Manuscript: A Study of Selected Poems*, Ph.D. thesis, University of Sydney (1988), pp. 14, 24. The stories that were taken up by romance-writers may sometimes have had an earlier existence in oral form; and oral versions were sometimes developed out of romances, as seems to have happened in the case of some traditional ballads (e.g., 'Hind Horn', from a version of *Horn and Rimenhild* similar to that found in the Auchinleck manuscript, and 'King Orfeo', deriving probably from the version of *Sir Orfeo* recorded in a Scottish manuscript of *c.*1583 (*The English and Scottish Popular Ballads*, ed. Francis James Child, 5 vols. (1882–98, repr. New York, 1965), i. nos. 17, 19; Marion Stewart, ' "King Orphius" ', *Scottish Studies* 17 (1973), 1–16).

34. Chrétien de Troyes, *Erec et Enide*, ed. Mario Roques (Paris, 1981), ll. 1–22; *Le Chevalier de la Charrette*, ed. Mario Roques (Paris, 1978), l. 26; Chaucer, *Canterbury Tales*, I.798, VII.946–58 (hereafter *CT*; *The Riverside Chaucer*, general ed., Larry D. Benson (Boston, 1987)).

35. *Knight's Tale*, *CT*, I.1347–53; cf. also the ending of the *Franklin's Tale*, V.1621–4. The fictional audience of pilgrims never takes up the question.

36. For the broad cultural background to medieval debate literature, see Thomas L. Reed, jr, *Middle English Debate Poetry and the Aesthetics of Irresolution* (Columbia, Mo., and London, 1990).

37. As recorded in the Percy Folio manuscript (*Bishop Percy's Folio Manuscript: Ballads and Romances*, ed. John W. Hales and Frederick J. Furnivall, 3 vols. (London, 1868), ii.338–89, ll. 7–8; hereafter *Percy*). The text probably derives from one of the sixteenth-century printed editions, surviving from *c.*1500 to 1565 and possibly continuing later (see *Sir Eglamour of Artois*, ed. Frances E. Richardson, EETS 256 (1965), pp. xiii–xiv). The other romances to use an almost identical couplet are *Sir Degrevant* (9–10) (no prints known) and *Sir Isumbras* (7–8) (printed editions surviving from *c.*1530 to *c.*1565). See the appendix to this book for details of all the Middle English romances still current after 1500.

38. Prologue 5–8, *William Shakespeare: The Complete Works*, general eds., Stanley Wells and Gary Taylor (Oxford, 1986).

39. Telling or reading older romances (specifically *Guy of Warwick* and *The Four Sons of Aymon*) is marked as a country rather than a courtly pastime as early as 1579, in the anonymous *Cyuile and Vnciuile Life* (sig. Hivr); but both were still being acted on the London stage in the seventeenth century, and although chapbooks were increasingly regarded as country reading, that seems to have been more because there was less competing élite reading in the countryside than because there was any shortage of them in the towns. On seventeenth- and eighteenth-century chapbook reading, see Margaret Spufford, *Small Books and Pleasant Histories* (London, 1981); and John Simons, 'Romance in the eighteenth-century Chapbook', in Simons (ed.), *From Medieval to Medievalism* (Basingstoke, 1992), pp. 122–43.

40. See *Pericles, Prince of Tyre*, ed. Doreen DelVecchio and Antony Hammond (Cambridge, 1998), pp. 16–18, and on its qualities of storytelling, pp. 27–34. In contrast to most earlier critics and editors, they urge the evident 'single creative imagination' behind the play.

41. John G. Cawelti, *Adventure, Mystery, and Romance: Formula Stories as Art and Popular Culture* (Chicago, 1976), pp. 10–12.

42. *Sir Orfeo* ll. 51, 53–4, in *Middle English Metrical Romances*, ed. Walter Hoyt French and Charles Brockway Hale (New York, 1964).

43. An example of both unhelpful detail and voyeurism occurs in the Anglo-Norman *Ipomedon*, where the blazon of the beauty of La Fière continues beyond the parts of her anatomy visible to an onlooker (*Ipomedon*, ed. Holden, ll. 2211–70). The stanzaic Middle English version, which usually follows the original closely, cuts the whole passage.

44. Even more explicitly later in the poem: 'Up roos the sonne, and up roos Emelye', I.2273.

45. *Winter's Tale* 4.4.156–9.

46. See further Chapter 5 below, 'Desirable desire'.

47. *CT*, VII.2869–72, 3160–2 (quoted).

48. Thomas Hoccleve, 'Of my lady, wel me rejoise I may', in *Hoccleve's Works: The Minor Poems*, ed. by Frederick J. Furnivall and I. Gollancz, rev. Jerome Mitchell and A. I. Doyle, EETS E.S. 61, 73, rev. repr. (1970), pp. 311–12; Sidney, 'What length of verse can serve': it appears in different contexts in the *Old* and *New Arcadia*. William A. Ringler, jr, discusses the history of such poems in his edition, *The Poems of Sir Philip Sidney* (Oxford, 1962), pp. 12, 384. Donne, 'The Anagram', in *John Donne: The Complete English Poems*, ed. A. J. Smith, corr. edn. (Harmondsworth, 1976), pp. 96–7.

49. As happens in Thomas Hughes's *The Misfortunes of Arthur*, a play contemporary with the writing of the *Faerie Queene*: see further pp. 404–5 below.

50. Almost every Anglo-Norman romance (some twenty in all) had a Middle English descendant. Two probably had English versions that are now lost (*Waldef* and *Fouke le Fitz Waryn*); so far as is known, two were not given English versions (*Amadas et Ydoine*, though it was widely known and cited; and the *Protheselaus* of Hue de Rotelande). See Susan Crane, *Insular Romance* (Berkeley and Los Angeles, 1986), p. 6.

51. I use 'insular' in the sense, not of being written in Britain, but of being written in any language within England. The Scottish romance tradition does not get under way until the fifteenth century, in keeping with the country's separation from Angevin domination; the Welsh tradition has a still more distinct history, though there are strong connections, of a kind still not fully understood, between the romances of Chrétien de Troyes and some of the stories of the *Mabinogion*.

52. The *Historia* has a pro-British and anti-English agenda that may itself have served as a kind of legitimation for the Norman Conquest, most particularly for the Breton knights who followed William the Conqueror to England and who were given lands on the Welsh Marches: see Stephen Knight, *Arthurian Literature and Society* (London and Basingstoke, 1983), pp. 38–67.

53. Edmund Spenser, *The Faerie Queene*, ed. A. C. Hamilton, 2nd edn. (London, 2001), II. x. 9, 13 (Brutus), II. x. 27–32 (Leir); hereafter *FQ*. A more extended account of the Trojan ancestry of Britain is given at III. ix. 38–51.

54. *Perceforest*, a prose romance probably composed c.1330–40 under Hainault patronage and possibly brought to England by Edward III's queen Philippa of Hainault, was twice printed complete in the sixteenth century in France, and an excerpted story printed four times; it provided the plot for some early Elizabethan

plays, most particularly *Clyomon and Clamydes*. The Lear section is edited by Jane H. M. Taylor, *Le Roman de Perceforest*, Part I (Geneva, 1979), ch. 8, ll. 1075–1283. The Anglo-Norman *Leir* is mentioned in a list of titles of lays and romances in Shrewsbury School MS 7: see Elizabeth Archibald, 'The Breton Lay in Middle English', in *Medieval Insular Romance: Translation and Innovation*, ed. Judith Weiss, Jennifer Fellows, and Morgan Dickson (Cambridge, 2000), pp. 55–70.

55. See Ad Putter, 'Finding Time for Arthurian Romance: Mediaeval Arthurian Literary History', *Medium Ævum* 63 (1994), 1–16, on how these individual romances were given a chronological placing within the linear history of Geoffrey's model of Arthur.

56. See further *Honour and Shame*, ed. J. G. Peristiany (London, 1965).

57. Like Geoffrey, Chrétien may have been greatly elaborating on a pre-existing story. The term 'courtly love', or rather the French '*amour courtois*', was coined by Gaston Paris in 1883 to describe the kind of love found in the *Chevalier de la Charrette* ('Etudes sur les romans de la table ronde. Lancelot du Lac II: *Le Conte de la Charrette*', *Romania* 12 (1883), p. 523); it has proved one of the most burr-like of all memes, part of its faithful replication including the false notion that it is itself a medieval idea. For further discussion, see pp. 307–10 below.

58. Paris, Bibliothèque nationale de France, MSS fr 794 (the Guiot MS); fr 375; and fr 1450, which contains the *Roman de Troie*, the *Roman d'Eneas*, and Wace's *Brut* with Chrétien's Arthurian romances inserted into it (with the prologues removed to smooth the transitions). See Sylvia Huot, *From Song to Book: The Poetics of Writing in Old French Lyric and Lyrical Narrative Poetry* (Ithaca and London, 1987), pp. 21–8.

59. She informs us that her *Fables* are based on an English original. There would of course have been little point in designating her as being 'of France' if she still lived there.

60. Thomas was writing some time between 1150 and 1200, most likely in the 1170s. For a parallel text and translation (by Stewart Gregory and Ian Short) of what survives of his *Tristan*, including the most recently discovered fragment, see *Early French Tristan Poems*, Vol. 2, ed. Norris J. Lacy (Cambridge, 1998), pp. 3–183. The missing parts of his text can be extensively reconstructed from the Norse version composed in 1226 by one Friar Robert, *Tristrams Saga ok Ísöndar*, which is more concise than Thomas's original but otherwise appears to follow it very closely (text and trans. by Peter Jorgensen in *Norse Romance*, Vol. 1: *The Tristan Legend*, ed. Marianne E. Kalinke (Cambridge, 1999)); and also from Gottfried von Strassburg's more elaborate *Tristan* (*c.*1210; editions include that by Gottfried Weber, *Gottfried von Strassburg: Tristan* (Darmstadt, 1967). There is a translation by A. T. Hatto, together with most of the surviving fragments of Thomas, for Penguin Classics (Harmondsworth, 1960)). There is also a Middle English adaptation of the late thirteenth century, though it is more useful as supporting rather than direct evidence as to Thomas's text: *Sir Tristrem*, in *Lancelot of the Laik and Sir Tristrem*, ed. Alan Lupack (Kalamazoo, Mich., 1994). The differences of Thomas from the archetype of the *Tristan* story can partly be gauged through other early retellings not mediated through him, in particular those of Béroul, in Anglo-Norman, and Eilhart von Oberge, in German (both writing 1170–90).

61. The point should not need any references, since a glance at any range of romance texts provides the evidence; the conviction to the contrary, still widely held, goes

back to C. S. Lewis's seductive, and profoundly misguided, *The Allegory of Love*, first published in 1936 and frequently reprinted. The combined dominance of the model of Tristan and Isolde and its calque of Lancelot and Guinevere has tended to overshadow the more socially acceptable forms of romance love narratives. See also pp. 307–14 below.

62. See Bernard O'Donoghue, *The Courtly Love Tradition* (Manchester, and Totowa, NJ, 1982).

63. For the complicated textual history of the French romance and its derivatives, see pp. 155–6 below. The English *Floris* is not known to have been printed in the Renaissance, but it is now one of the most widely anthologized of the medieval romances (including French and Hale, pp. 823–55; and *Middle English Verse Romances*, ed. Donald B. Sands (New York, 1966), pp. 279–309).

64. The idea of there being three 'materes' of romance, 'de France et de Bretaigne et de Rome la grant', originates with Jehan Bodel's *La Chanson des Saisnes* (ed. Annette Brasseur (Geneva, 1989), lines 6–7). Bodel is dismissive of the matter of Britain by comparison with that of France; English romance largely inverted the comparison. There were a good number of adaptations of Charlemagne romances into Middle English, but those known in the sixteenth century (*Huon of Bordeaux, The Four Sons of Aymon*) were recent translations, besides being among the most hostile to Charlemagne himself.

65. The relationships between the lost prototype story, the Anglo-Norman *Romance of Horn*, the Middle English *King Horn* and *Horn Childe*, and the later ballads of 'Hind Horn' do not allow for easy untangling: for a summary, see Maldwyn Mills's Introduction to his edition of *Horn Childe and Maiden Rimnild* (Heidelberg, 1988), pp. 44–50. T. B. W. Reid urges the priority of an English version in his Introduction to *The Romance of Horn by Thomas*, ed. by Mildred K. Pope, ANTS 9–10, 12–13 (Oxford, 1955, 1964), 2.19–20. The most detailed edition of *King Horn* is that by Joseph Hall (Oxford, 1901); more accessible are the various recent anthologies of romance that include it (e.g., Sands, from which citations here are taken; *Of Love and Chivalry: An Anthology of Middle English Romance*, ed. Jennifer Fellows (London, 1993)). The ballad 'Hind Horn' appears in Child, *Ballads*, i. no. 17.

66. See Paul A. Scanlon, 'A Checklist of Prose Romances in English 1474–1603', *The Library*, 5th s. 32 (1978), 143–52, and, on the manuscript version, Carol M. Meale, 'The Politics of Book Ownership: The Hopton Family and Bodleian Library Digby MS 185', in *Prestige, Authority and Power in Late Medieval Manuscripts and Texts*, ed. Felicity Riddy (Woodbridge, 2000), pp. 103–22. The manuscript version of the Middle English (which may have been known to the Tudor redactor) is ed. F. J. Mather, jr, '*King Ponthus and the Faire Sidone*', PMLA 12 (1897), pp. i–150. Three printed editions are known, from *c*.1509 to 1511 (STC 20107, 20107.5, 20108); an entry in the *Stationers' Register* for 15 January 1548 (ii.405) suggests that there may have been one or more later editions, now lost. The French prose *Ponthus*, tentatively ascribed to Geoffroi de la Tour Landry, probably dates from the late fourteenth century; it appears as one of the items included in the manuscript presented by the earl of Shrewsbury to Margaret of Anjou on her marriage to Henry VI, British Library MS Royal 15 E VI.

67. For editions, see *Le Lai d'Haveloc and Gaimar's Haveloc Episode*, ed. Alexander Bell (Manchester, 1925); and for the Middle English, *Havelok*, ed. G. V. Smithers

(Oxford, 1987), and various anthologies of romance including those edited by D. B. Sands and by W. H. French and C. B. Hale.

68. See p. 354 below.

69. Facsimile with Introduction by Derek Pearsall and I. C. Cunningham, *The Auchinleck Manuscript: National Library of Scotland Advocates' MS 19.2.1*, Intro. (London, 1979). It was still finding scholarly or antiquarian readers in the later sixteenth century, as evidenced by marginal annotations.

70. The Percy Folio manuscript is London, British Library, Add. MS 27879; for an edition, see n. 37. There are 99 surviving manuscripts containing romances, but half the traditional canon of romance can be found in just ten of those, usually in anthologies that also contain historical and/or religious material: see Gisela Guddat-Figge, *Catalogue of Manuscripts Containing Middle English Romances* (Munich, 1976), pp. 18–54.

71. *Lanval* was printed in the version known most often as *Landevall* (ed. by George Lyman Kittredge, '*Launfal*', *American Journal of Philology* 10 (1889), 1–33; see *STC Lamwell*, 15187–15187.5, of 1548 and 1560). This derives from the earliest of the Middle English translations, and is the closest to Marie. It appears in the Percy Folio under the name *Sir Lambewell*. Thomas Chestre adapted it in the later fourteenth century for his *Sir Launfal*, an expanded version put into tail-rhyme rather than couplets. Hue's *Ipomedon* was translated into English three times, in tail-rhyme, couplets, and prose; it was the couplet version that was printed, the first edition perhaps dating from 1505 (ed. Tadahiro Ikegami as the second volume of his edition of *The Lyfe of Ipomydon*, Seijo English Monographs 21, 22 (Tokyo, 1983, 1985)). On the setting-copy, see Carol M. Meale, 'Wynkyn de Worde's Setting-Copy for *Ipomydon*', *Studies in Bibliography* 35 (1982), 156–71. All three English texts are edited by Eugen Kölbing, *Ipomedon in drei englischen Bearbeitungen* (Breslau, 1889).

72. *Guy and Amarant / Guy and Colbrande*, a medieval version of the Guy legend; *Merline*; *Eglamore*; *Sir Degree*; *Sir Lambewell* (*Landevale*). The manuscript contains one further fourteenth-century romance, *Libius Desconus*, 'Le Beau Desconus', the Fair Unknown; it was almost certainly printed, though no copies survive. Other of the Percy romances are fifteenth-century in origin, including a tail-rhyme retelling of *Sir Gawain and the Green Knight* entitled *The Grene Knight*, and a Gawain romance that uses some of the same motifs, *The Turke and Gowin*.

73. Susan Crane points out, however, that neither romance praises a patron, or mentions the family currently holding the title (*Insular Romance*, p. 16). *Guy* in particular was none the less treated later as if it were an ancestral romance: it became one, even if it were not written as such. On the Albinis, see M. Dominica Legge, *Anglo-Norman Literature and its Background* (Oxford, 1963), pp. 156–61, and Judith Weiss, 'The Date of the Anglo-Norman *Boeve de Haumtone*', *Medium Ævum* 55 (1986), 237–41.

74. On the later history of *Bevis*, see Jennifer Fellows, '*Bevis redivivus*: The Printed Editions of *Sir Bevis of Hampton*', in *Romance Reading on the Book*, ed. Jennifer Fellows, Rosalind Field *et al.* (Cardiff, 1996), pp. 250–68. For a full account of the dissemination of the legend of Guy, see Velma Bourgeois Richmond, *The Legend of Guy of Warwick* (New York and London, 1996).

75. *FQ*, I. xi. 29–53: see also King, *The Faerie Queene and Middle English Romance*, pp. 129–45.

76. The connection between Guy and Spenser's Guyon was noted as evident by John Lane, in 1617 (Richmond, *Legend of Guy*, p. 219), and there is no reason not to take him as typical. See further King, *The Faerie Queene and Middle English Romance*, pp. 161–2, and pp. 95–6 below. Guy's ancestry of the earls of Warwick was taken up by Robert Dudley, earl of Leicester, younger brother of the Elizabethan earl of Warwick (see Richmond, *Legend*, pp. 189–90). The *Golden Legend* also defines 'Guyon' as 'holy wrestler': see Hamilton's note to *FQ*, I. x. 65–6.

77. An early allusion to *Bevis* occurs in the dispute between Peter and Horner in the first quarto of *Henry VI* Part 2 (*The First Part of the Contention*, sig. D2r, in *Shakespeare's Plays in Quarto: A Facsimile Edition*, ed. Michael J. B. Allen and Kenneth Muir (Berkeley, Los Angeles, and London, 1981), p. 56): 'with downright blowes, as Beuys of South-hampton fell upon Askapart'. The simile is cut in the Folio text and modern editions: it would follow 2.3.96. Besides the couplet discussed below, there is a further allusion in *Henry VIII* (originally entitled *All is True*) 1.1.36–8, when the Duke of Norfolk notes of the Field of the Cloth of Gold, 'Former fabulous story | Being now seen possible enough, got credit | That *Bevis* was believed.' Allusions to *Guy* are made by the Bastard Faulconbridge in *King John* 1.1.225 (to Guy's opponent 'Colbrand the Giant') and by the porter's man in *Henry VIII* 5.3.22 (to Sir Guy and Colbrand)).

78. William Copland's edition of *c*.1565, sig. Gir; and both texts of *Lear*, Quarto 11.126–7, Folio 3.4.131–2. By the time of Thomas East's 1585 edition, 'dere' was modernized into 'chere' (sig. Diir). See also *The Romance of Sir Beues of Hamtoun*, ed. Eugen Kölbing, EETS E.S. 46 (1885), p. 74, ll. 85–6. There was no need, as has been suggested, for Shakespeare to have used a 1503 edition (see Hays, *Shakespearean Tragedy*, p. 28).

79. Nashe was particularly scathing: 'Who is it, that reading Bevis of Hampton, can forbeare laughing, if he marke what scambling shyft he makes to ende his verses a like? I will propound three or foure payre by the way for the Readers recreation. *The Porter said, by my snout,* | *It was Sir Bevis that I let out*' ('The Anatomie of Absvrditie', in *The Works of Thomas Nashe*, ed. R. B. McKerrow, corr. by F. P. Wilson, 5 vols. (Oxford, 1958), i. 26).

80. The surviving text is entitled *The Tragical History, Admirable Atchievments and various events of Guy earl of Warwick*; it was printed in 1661, but dates from the very early 1590s, perhaps 1593. See Helen Cooper, 'Guy of Warwick, Upstart Crows and Mounting Sparrows', in *Shakespeare, Marlowe, Jonson*, ed. J. R. Mulryne and Takashi Kazuka (Aldershot, 2004). Details are also given there of the other possible dramatizations (one entered in the Stationers' Registers in 1620 as being by John Day and Thomas Dekker; one, probably different, performed at an Islington inn in 1618; and possibly one current around 1580, if the details of Stephen Gosson's account of the kind of drama that he despised can be trusted).

81. *The Complete Works of Samuel Rowlands*, intro. Edmund W. Gosse (Glasgow, 1880), Vol. 3; the latest printing of the prosification appears to have been in the Carisbrooke Library volume of 1889.

82. Samuel Richardson, *Pamela; or, Virtue Rewarded*, ed. Peter Sabor (Harmondsworth, 1980), p. 206. Pamela's own name comes from Sidney's *Arcadia*.

83. The connection is important for the dating of the romance (probably completed 1330–40); see *Perceforest* Part I, ed. Taylor, pp. 22–7, and Part IV, ed. Gilles Roussineau, I. xii–xiii.

84. Known owners include the earl of Warwick, who gave a substantial number of books to the abbey of Bordesley in 1305; Isabella, wife of Edward II, whose copies may have been those recorded as still being in the royal library at the end of the fourteenth century; Thomas of Woodstock, earl of Gloucester; and Elizabeth Woodville (or possibly her brother) and her daughters (see Madeleine Blaess, 'L'Abbaye de Bordesley et les livres de Guy de Beauchamp', *Romania* 78 (1957), 511–18; Susan H. Cavanaugh, 'Royal Books: King John to Richard II', *The Library*, 6th ser. 10 (1988), 304–16; Carol M. Meale, 'Manuscripts, Readers and Patrons in Fifteenth-century England: Sir Thomas Malory and Arthurian Romance', *Arthurian Literature* 4 (1985), 93–126); and Roger Middleton, 'Manuscripts of the *Lancelot-Grail Cycle* in England and Wales: Some Books and their Owners', in *A Companion to the Lancelot-Grail Cycle*, ed. Carol Dover (Cambridge, 2003), pp. 219–35).

85. The first Middle English work to incorporate the affair and the incest is the metrical *Morte Arthur* of c.1400, based on the Vulgate *Mort Artu*, though it manages to give both a very low profile by comparison with the French (Mordred's own incestuous pursuit of his uncle's/father's wife receives much more stress). The Alliterative *Morte Arthure*, of around the same date, follows Geoffrey. The earliest implied reference to the affair in English appears to be a legend of origin for the caves of Nottingham Castle, found in a unique interpolation in the Auchinleck manuscript text of a metrical chronicle, which describes Lancelot as having them excavated to hide Guinevere from Arthur: an account that presupposes a knowledge of his rescue and abduction of her, and which can be dated c.1331 (*An Anonymous Short English Metrical Chronicle*, ed. Ewald Zettl, EETS OS 196 (1935), Auchinleck additions 1071–90 (pp. 70–1); Helen Cooper, 'Lancelot, Roger Mortimer, and the Date of the Auchinleck Manuscript', in *The Key of All Remembrance*, ed. A. J. Fletcher (forthcoming); Elizabeth Archibald, 'Lancelot as Lover in the English Tradition before Malory', in *Arthurian Studies in Honour of P. J. C. Field*, ed. Bonnie Wheeler (Cambridge, 2004), pp. 199–216).

86. For the circulation of the French Arthurian prose romances in Italy, see Daniela Delcorno Branca, *Tristano e Lancillotto in Italia* (Ravenna, 1998); and for their influence on Ariosto, her *Orlando Furioso e il Romanzo cavalleresco medievale* (Florence, 1973).

87. Richard Cooper provides an analysis and bibliography of printed French romances in ' "Nostre Histoire renouvelée": The Reception of Romances of Chivalry in the Renaissance', in *Chivalry in the Renaissance*, ed. Sydney Anglo (Woodbridge, 1990) pp. 175–238; their progression from manuscript to print can be followed in Brian Woledge's *Bibliographie des romans et nouvelles en prose français antérieures à 1500* and its *Supplement* (Geneva, 1954, 1975). Rabelais made them a subject of satire in the 1530s, casting Lancelot as a horse-flayer and Valentine and Orson as bath attendants (Cooper, Nostre Histoire' p. 189), but their popularity continued for centuries in shortened versions in the *Bibliothèque bleue*.

88. It is generally assumed to be Greek in origin, though its earliest extant text is in Latin. It is the only romance to appear in Old English; versions appear in Gower's *Confessio amantis* and in the course of the *Gesta Romanorum* (in a translation that itself went through numerous printed editions); and a further translation, *King Apollyn*, was printed c.1510. For the later sixteenth-century versions, see Vol. 6 of

Geoffrey Bullough's *Narrative and Dramatic Sources of Shakespeare*, 8 vols. (London and New York, 1957–75). For a history and edition of the story, see Elizabeth Archibald, *Apollonius of Tyre: Medieval and Renaissance Themes and Variations* (Cambridge, 1991).

89. Its history is discussed in the parallel-text edition of the manuscript and prints by James Ralston Caldwell, *Eger and Grime* (Cambridge, Mass., 1933), pp. 6–42, esp. p. 10.

90. O. Lengert, 'Die schottische Romanze "Roswall and Lillian"', *Englische Studien* (1892), 16.321–56 (an account of the prints and an edition of the text), and 17.341–77 (annotation). The five known prints include just one from south of the border, from Newcastle, undated. The romance borrows a number of motifs from *Ipomedon*, probably from one of its Middle English translations rather than from Hue's Anglo-Norman; the printed text might be too late as a source.

91. *Saint Augustine: Confessions*, trans. R. S. Pine-Coffin (Harmondsworth, 1961), i.13 (pp. 33–4).

92. On Guy's lion, see Andrea Hopkins, *The Sinful Knights*, pp. 74–5, citing a sermon in British Library MS Harley 7322, f. 49 (it was none the less too good a story to pass over, and Spenser borrows from it for the fatal wounding of Una's lion, *FQ*, I. iii. 41–4). Religious texts that offered themselves as a substitute for the wickedness of reading romances included the *South English Legendary*, William of Nassington's translation of the *Speculum vitae*, the sermon collection known as the *Mirror*, and the *Cursor mundi*, which gives the fullest listing of the stories of which it disapproves (ed. Richard Morris, Vol. 1, EETS O.S. 57 (1874), prologue 1–26).

93. *Hoccleve: Minor Poems*, ed. Furnivall and Gollancz, p. 14, ll. 193–8. 'Vegece of the aart of Chivalrie' is the popular military handbook by Vegetius, *De re militari*.

94. *A very frvteful and pleasant boke callyd the Instrvction of a Christen woman*, cap. 5; there were numerous editions in the sixteenth century. For Vives' original, see *De institutione foeminae Christianae* (Antwerp, 1524), sig. Ciiiv.

95. The ballad version tells only a fraction of the story, and is not evidently descended from Middle English: see Child, *Ballads*, v. 175, no. 300, 'Blancheflour and Jellyflorice'.

96. The prose redaction of the original alliterative romance, printed *c.*1515, is now known only from one double leaf (ed. G. H. V. Bunt in *William of Palerne*, pp. 328–31).

97. From *The Scholemaster* (published in 1570, six years after his death), in *Roger Ascham: English Works*, ed. William Aldis Wright (Cambridge, 1904, repr. 1970), p. 230. His animus is particularly directed against the *Morte Darthur*.

98. 'Anatomie of Absvrditie', *Works of Nashe*, ed. McKerrow, i.11; Henry Crosse (1603) accuses 'lazie monkes, and fat-headed friers, in whom was noght but sloath and idlenes' of acting as agents of Satan in so occupying 'Christian wits in Heathens foolery' (*Vertue's Commonwealth*, ed. Alexander B. Grosart (Manchester, 1878), p. 99). For a conspectus of sixteenth- and seventeenth-century condemnations (and, just occasionally, defences) of chivalric romance, see Alex Davis, *Chivalry and Romance in the English Renaissance* (Cambridge, 2003), pp. 7–19.

99. M. C. Seymour, 'MSS Douce 261 and Egerton 3132A and Edward Banyster', *Bodleian Library Record* 10 (1980), 162–5; the Douce manuscript contains *Isumbras, Degaré, The Jest of Sir Gawain*, and *Eglamour*; the Egerton contains *Robert the Devil.*

100. *Robert Langham: A Letter*, ed. R. J. P. Kuin (Leiden, 1983), p. 53. The author was in fact probably not Robert Langham (or Laneham), but William Patten; Langham indeed seems to have tried to have the work suppressed (see Brian O'Kill, 'The Printed Works of William Patten (c.1510–c.1600)', *Transactions of the Cambridge Bibliographical Society*, 7 (1977), 28–45; and David Scott, 'William Patten and the Authorship of Robert Laneham's *Letter* (1575)', *ELR* 7 (1977), 297–306). The element of fictionality about the authorship in turn raises the question of the fictionality of Captain Cox, but the list of his books must have been recognizably plausible whether it were true or invented. The eight early romances from the list are *Bevis*, *Sir Eglamour*, *Sir Tryamour*, *Sir Lamwell* (i.e., *Launfal*), *Sir Isumbras*, *Sir Gawain* (which could be one of several texts), and two texts of c.1500, *The Squire of Low Degree* and *The Knight of Courtesy and the Fair Lady of Faguell*. The prose romances are 'King Arthur's book' (presumably Malory), *Huon of Bourdeaux*, *The Four Sons of Aymon*, *Oliver of Castile*, and also *The Seven Wise Masters* (otherwise known as *The Seven Sages of Rome*). Ben Jonson makes a reference to his library as late as his 1624 *Masque of Owls* (l. 27; in *Ben Jonson*, ed. C. H. Herford and Percy and Evelyn Simpson, 11 vols., corr. edn. (Oxford, 1954), vii 781–6).

101. So Robert Ashley (born in 1565, writing in 1614): 'Memini me dum puer essem . . . magistri me in officio continerent, si forte in manus meas incideret libellus aliquis qui fictas et futiles fabellas contineret qualia de Bevisio Hamtonensi Guidone Warwicensi historia Valentini et Orsoni vita Arthuri Regis Britaniae et equitum orbicularis mensae circumferuntur, ac huiusmodi portentis ac monstris qualia aut nunquam extiterunt, aut certe supra omnem fidem futilia ac vana per otiosos monachos de eis addita (ad irretiendam plebeculam et voluptate inescandam conficta in superiore seculo) . . .' (Ronald S. Crane, 'The Reading of an Elizabethan Youth', *Modern Philology* 11 (1913–14), 1–3 (p.3): 'I remember how when I was a boy and my masters kept me hard at work, if by chance some book fell into my hands that contained some fabulous and useless fictions such as were told about Bevis of Hamtoun or Guy of Warwick, or the history of Valentine and Orson, or the life of Arthur king of Britain and his knights of the Round Table, or portents and monsters of a kind that never existed, or else indeed were useless and vain things surpassing all belief added in by monks with nothing better to do (made up in an earlier age to entrap the ignorant common man and ensnare him with pleasures)', he would abandon play, sleep, and work to read them. (The Latin word order allows for a scornful pun: tales 'such as were circulating about the Round Table . . .'.)

102. They were taken sufficiently seriously at the popular level for the *Seven Champions* to be dramatized in the seventeenth century (the surviving text dates from 1635), to remain a chapbook favourite through the nineteenth, and to appear in boys' versions in the twentieth; for the first five editions of *Tom a Lincoln* to be comprehensively read to pieces; and for *Chinon* to be dramatized in 1595, assuming that the story was the same as that of the prose romance first entered for publication in 1599. The sense they give of deliberately going over the top may be illusory: as with some modern paperback fiction (such as the novels entered for the Bad Sex Awards), a certain level of sophistication in the reader can incur a reaction presumably unintended by the author. *Tom* and its 1607 sequel look much the most deliberate: see pp. 389–91 below.

103. *The Melancholie Knight* (1615), in *Works of Rowlands*, ed. Gosse, ii.27–9 (double-numbered as pp. 33–5).
104. Samuel Butler, *Hudibras*, ed. John Wilders (Oxford, 1967), i.447–50; the work was first published in 1663, with a note on the title page that it was 'written in the time of the late Wars' (probably in fact in the late 1650s, p. xlvi).
105. See Larry D. Benson, 'The Tournament in the Romances of Chrétien de Troyes and *L'Histoire de Guillaume le Maréchal*', in *Chivalric Literature*, ed. Larry D. Benson and John Leyerle (Kalamazoo, 1980), pp. 1–24.
106. The nude gymnastic exercises of the Latin *Apollonius* mystified later writers; Gower represents them as a 'game' played naked (*Confessio amantis*, 8682–94), Twine's *Pattern of Painefull Adventures* (1576) has its hero play tennis (Bullough, *Narrative and Dramatic Sources*, vi. 387, 435). Conversion into a tournament emphasizes the assimilation of *Pericles* into the model of chivalric quest.
107. Extensive discussions of these issues can be found in Maurice Keen, *Chivalry* (New Haven and London, 1984), pp. 18–82, and Richard Barber, *The Knight and Chivalry*, rev. edn. (Woodbridge, 1995), pp. 3–46.
108. *Sir William Segar: The Book of Honor and Armes (1590) and Honor Military and Civil (1602)*, facsimile intro. Diane Bornstein (Delmar, NY, 1975); *Honor Military*, p. 60. The second work is in effect an expanded edition of the first. Segar was promoted through the various posts of herald, becoming Garter King of Arms in 1603, so had a professional interest in the rituals of chivalry.
109. Lull's *Libre del ordre de cavayleria* became a pan-European bestseller; its Scots version was made by Gilbert Hay; its English by Caxton (as *The Book of the Ordre of Chyvalry*, ed. by Alfred T. P. Byles, EETS OS 168 (1926)). The Lady of the Lake, instructing the young Lancelot before he departs for King Arthur's court, con-centrates solely on the symbolism of armour as the defence of the Church (*Lancelot*, ed. Alexandre Micha, 9 vols. (Geneva, 1978–83), vii.xxia; trans. S. Rosenberg, in *Lancelot-Grail: The Old French Arthurian Vulgate and Post-Vulgate in Translation*, ed. Norris J. Lacy, 5 vols. (New York: Garland, 1992–7), ii. 59–60). A further widely disseminated set of interpretations is given in the anonymous *Ordene de chevalerie* (before 1250), which purported to describe how Saladin had asked the captive Hugh, count of Tiberias, for a demonstration of how a knight was created. See further Keen, *Chivalry*, pp. 6–11.
110. Segar, *Honor Military*, pp. 51–2. A comparable process of backdating, this time between the 1590 and 1602 versions of his work, occurs when the description of the ceremony for creating knights is redated from 1020 to 'about the yeere of Christ 500, neere which time King Arthur reigned in England' (p. 53; compare *Book of Honor*, V. 4 (pp. 8–9 of new pagination)).
111. Arthur B. Ferguson, *The Chivalric Tradition in Renaissance England* (Cranbury, NJ, and London, 1986) pp. 13, 17, 25–6, 107–25.
112. Segar, *Honor Military*, heading to II. 7 (p. 60).
113. Lawrence Stone, *The Crisis of the Aristocracy 1558–1641* (Oxford, 1965), pp. 71–9.
114. Robert Anton, *Moriomachia* (London: Simon Stafford, 1613), sig. B1v; the 'fayry champion' is in fact a transformed cow. Alex Davis calls attention to the passage, *Chivalry and Romance*, p. 44, in a discussion of the crisis of knighthood.

1. John Milton, *Areopagitica* (1644), in *John Milton: Selected Prose*, ed. C. A. Patrides (Harmondsworth, 1974), p. 213.
2. See p. 31 and note 76 above.
3. Of whom Lancelot is the 'best breathed': Malory, i. 266 (VI. 8).
4. The point is elaborated with regard to romance forms from Ariosto to Keats by Patricia A. Parker in her *Inescapable Romance* (Princeton, 1979): ' "Romance" is characterized primarily as a form which simultaneously quests for and postpones a particular end, objective, or object' (p. 4). Her term for this postponement is 'dilation'.
5. Monica Fludernik, *Towards a 'Natural' Narratology* (London and New York, 1996), p. 22. She also notes how rare such duplicity is in folktales; it is the more sophisticated romance authors, working in a tradition already well established and understood, who produce such complexities of plotting.
6. See, for instance, 'On Transience' and 'Those Wrecked by Success', in *The Standard Edition of the Complete Psychological Works of Sigmund Freud*, ed. James Strachey, 24 vols. (London: Hogarth Press, 1957–74), xiv. 303–7, 316–31.
7. The story of the young man who has to marry the hag who tells him what women most desire appears first in the late fourteenth century, in Gower as well as Chaucer, and may have folktale antecedents; but the place they gave it within romance was confirmed by its reappearance in the following century as *The Wedding of Sir Gawain and Dame Ragnell* (ed. Thomas Hahn in *Sir Gawain: Eleven Romances and Tales* (Kalamazoo, 1995), pp. 41–80).
8. Caroline Walker Bynum, *Metamorphosis and Identity* (New York, 2001), p. 23; the following quotation is from p. 30.
9. Reto R. Bezzola, *Le Sens de l'aventure et de l'amour* (Paris, 1947), p. 83.
10. The heraldic device of St George first appears in the later thirteenth century, a few decades after the invention of the Grail legend: see Olivier de Laborderie, 'Richard the Lionheart and the Birth of a National Cult of St George in England', *Nottingham Medieval Studies* 39 (1995), 37–53, esp. pp. 41–2. I have not found an early source for the statement that he was sometimes claimed to be a descendant of Joseph of Arimathea (e.g., by Samantha Riches, *St George: Hero, Martyr and Myth* (Stroud, 2000), p. 20), though it would link the two bearers of the arms. Malory summarizes the legend of the white or silver shield (they are the same, 'argent', in heraldic terminology) with the red cross, as developed originally in the *History of the Holy Grail* of Robert de Boron and repeated in his immediate source, the French *Quest of the Holy Grail* (cf. Malory, ii. 880–1 (XIII.10–11)); Galahad is the bearer of the shield within his main narrative. John Harding's *Chronicle*, printed with Grafton's continuation in 1543, also summarizes the history of the shield (*The Chronicle of Iohn Harding*, ed. Henry Ellis (London, 1812), ch. lxxviii, pp. 133–4). Spenser further mentions the legend of Joseph of Arimathea's role as disciple to the English, II. x. 53.
11. Steven Gunn, 'Chivalry and the Politics of the Early Tudor Court', in *Chivalry and the Renaissance*, ed. Anglo, pp. 107–28 (p. 110).
12. *FQ*, I. x. 60, and see pp. 193–4 below. Redcrosse's raising by a ploughman supplies a link with Langland's promotion of true religion in the person of a

ploughman; *Piers Plowman* was printed in Edward VI's reign as a proto-Protestant work. Johnson's *Seven Champions of Christendom* is edited by Jennifer Fellows (London, 2003); there is summary of its St George biography in Riches, *St George*, pp. 180–1. Riches also notes the casting of St George in Protestant opposition to a papal dragon, p. 153.

13. In *Stephen Hawes: The Minor Poems*, ed. Florence W. Gluck and Alice B. Morgan (EETS 271, 1974); it was first printed in 1509 and went through at least two more editions. The poem takes the form of a dream vision with a first-person narrator, who is named as Youth in the list of contents and is renamed as Virtue from line 1540 onwards; see further pp. 102–3 below.

14. Carol V. Kaske, 'How Spenser Really Used Stephen Hawes in the Legend of Holiness', in *Unfolded Tales*, ed. Logan and Teskey, pp. 119–36.

15. *Sir Gawain and the Green Knight*, ed. J. R. R. Tolkien and E. V. Gordon, 2nd edn. rev. by Norman Davis (Oxford, 1967), ll. 54, 86 (taking 'childgered', with the editors, as 'boyish' rather than 'childish'; 'child' did not have pejorative connotations in Middle English, and is often used for a young hero).

16. The text survives only in the Percy Folio manuscript (ii. 56–77; also ed. Hahn, *Sir Gawain*, pp. 309–35), so its dating and its relationship to *Sir Gawain and the Green Knight* cannot be established with accuracy. Sir John Paston lists a romance entitled *The Grene Knyght* in an inventory of books of the late 1470s, which might or might not be this version. On Herbert and his determination to do justice to his white lace, see *The Life of Edward, First Lord Herbert of Cherbury*, ed. J. M. Shuttleworth (London and New York, 1976), pp. 38, 42–3; and Davis, *Chivalry and Romance*, pp. 140–1.

17. The account closely follows the activities of earlier Arthurian fair unknowns, such as Libeaus Desconus and Gareth (see below, p. 337, and Malory, i. 293–7 (VII. 1–2)). Guyon also makes mention of the episode, II. i. 19.

18. *Lybeaus* was adapted into Middle English from French in the late fourteenth century; it was still popular enough in the seventeenth to appear in the Percy Folio manuscript. See further pp. 331–3 below.

19. Curiously, supposedly sexually liberated post-modern Britain and the United States are much less tolerant of sexual infidelity in those in authority than was the case in the Middle Ages. Modern literature, by contrast, generally operates by much looser standards than life, whereas romance set stricter demands than many princes followed in practice.

20. Northrop Frye, *The Great Code* (London, 1982), p. 43.

21. 1 Cor. 15:21–2, Bishops' Bible version (the most widely disseminated of the late sixteenth-century translations), adopted by the King James editors (*New Testament Octapla*, ed. Luther A. Weigle (New York, 1962)).

22. From God's speech explaining the providential scheme of salvation, spoken immediately preceding the Annunciation (the first moment when the Fall begins to move towards the Redemption) in *The Towneley Plays*, ed. Martin Stevens and A. C. Cawley, EETS S.S.13 (1994), Vol. 1: Text, play 10, ll. 31–4.

23. Ed. Tolkien and Gordon, 625–6, 2509. On the contemporary significance of *trouthe*, see Richard Firth Green, *A Crisis of Truth* (Philadelphia, 1999).

24. There is no evidence for any intermediate source, though the radical rethinking of the story indicates that the author was not working with a copy of Chrétien's

text in front of him. It is edited by Maldwyn Mills, *Ywain and Gawain, Sir Percyvell of Gales, The Anturs of Arthur* (London, 1992); also in French and Hale, pp. 531–603.

25. Ed. Mills, ll. 5 and 7; *CT*, VII. 915–16.

26. Rosemond Tuve, *Allegorical Imagery* (Princeton, 1966), p. 363.

27. See Judith Weiss, 'Structure and Characterisation in *Havelok the Dane*', *Speculum* 44 (1969), 247–57, esp. pp. 247–8.

28. *Clyomon and Clamydes*, ed. Betty J. Littleton (The Hague, Paris, 1968); its outside dates are 1570–83 (pp. 30–3). Its main story had already been separately printed in France in 1542, but the author knew and used the whole romance, which had gone through a number of printed editions (pp. 38–9). See also Littleton's discussion of the problems of turning episodic romance into coherent drama, p. 55.

29. See Helen Cooper, *Oxford Guides to Chaucer: The Canterbury Tales* 2nd edn. (Oxford, 1996), pp. 67–8, 73–5. On *The Two Noble Kinsmen*, see pp. 374–5 below.

30. The last performance of the Coventry mystery plays, just a few miles from Stratford, took place when Shakespeare was 15; Kendal managed to continue with its cycle until *c.* 1610.

31. *Pericles*, scene 1.104, 65, 72 (the Wells–Taylor numbering incorporates Gower's prologue), scene 2.77.

32. 5.1. 17–28. Although he avoids harming anyone from Italy, this is the first point at which he makes it clear that he does not intend to maroon his particular enemies on the island. Productions have traditionally presented a gentler Prospero, but the text would seem to favour a change of heart at this point.

33. See further pp. 112–13 below.

34. See further pp. 171–2 below.

35. There was not even any single medieval term for 'map'; 'mappa mundi' itself could refer simply to a list of place-names, such as monasteries (Evelyn Edson, *Mapping Time and Space* (London, 1997), p. 132). The first maps after the Romans to use spatial co-ordinates, and therefore to have a practical function, were coastal maps for the use of sailors.

36. The few medieval maps designed as journey aids sometimes took the form of strip-maps, itineraries arranged spatially; Matthew Paris, the thirteenth-century polymath who experimented with most contemporary kinds of mapping, produced such a map, with place-names marked a day's journey apart (Edson, *Mapping Time*, pp. 121–2).

37. Erich Auerbach, *Mimesis: The Representation of Reality in Western Literature*, trans. Willard Trask (1953; repr. New York, 1957), ch. 6, 'The Knight Sets Forth', esp. pp. 112–13.

38. *Mandeville's Travels*, ed. P. Hamelius, EETS OS 153 (1919), pp. 109, 180; *The Boke of Duke Huon of Bordeux*, ed. S. L. Lee, EETS ES 40, 41, 43, 50 (1882–7; 2-vol. reprint, 1973, 1998), ch. cviii, pp. 369–71; *FQ*, II. xii. 7–8. Huon's island prevents anyone drawn to it from leaving (he himself escapes by griffin); Spenser's wrecks everyone caught within its field of attraction.

39. For a full discussion, see Corinne J. Saunders, *The Forest of Medieval Romance* (Cambridge, 1993).

40. The point is made by Helen Moore, in her forthcoming *Amadis in English*.

41. Andrew King stresses this continuity in *The Faerie Queene and Middle English Romance*, pp. 48–52, 161–2, and *passim*; and see also Jacqueline Simpson, *British Dragons* (London, 1980), pp. 80–90 (ch. 5, 'You Can See it There Still').

42. Northrop Frye, *A Natural Perspective* (New York, 1965), p. 65. The chapter in which the term occurs, entitled 'The Return from the Sea', is a powerful discussion of the romance elements in the play.

43. See Bullough, *Narrative and Dramatic Sources*, viii. 238–45, 275–98; and the edition for the Oxford Shakespeare by Stephen Orgel (Oxford, 1987), pp. 31–6 and appendices B and D. Stephen Greenblatt offers an extended discussion of the play's links with the New World through William Strachey's *True Reportory of the Wracke and Redemption of Sir Thomas Gates* in *Shakespearean Negotiations* (Oxford, 1988), pp. 142–63.

44. See below, pp. 227–8.

45. *Les Romans de Chrétien de Troyes II: Cligés*, ed. Alexandre Micha (Paris, 1982), ll. 28–33.

46. A denial of Trojan origins for France landed someone in the Bastille as late as the eighteenth century: see George Huppert, *The Idea of Perfect History* (Urbana, 1970), pp. 75–7.

47. See, for instance, Edson, *Mapping Time*, plates VI and VII (the Psalter and Hereford maps).

48. 'And also', he adds as an afterthought, 'I was not worthi' (*Mandeville's Travels*, ed. Hamelius, p. 202).

49. The story made its way from Latin to French to Sir Gilbert Hay's Scots *Buik of Alexander the Conqueror*, of *c*.1460, ed. John Cartwright, Scottish Text Society (Edinburgh, 1986–), ll. 14458–16314.

50. See the chapter on 'Flyaway Islands and False Voyages 1100–1492', in Samuel Eliot Morison, *The European Discovery of America: The Northern Voyages* AD 500–1600 (New York, 1971), pp. 81–105.

51. Geoffrey, in his *Life of Merlin*, describes Morgen's home as 'insula pomorum que Fortunata vocatur' (*Life of Merlin: Geoffrey of Monmouth, Vita Merlini*, ed. Basil Clarke (Cardiff, 1973), l. 908, and his note on p. 147 on the connection of Isidore's *fortunatorum insulae*, 'the island of the blessed women', with the text's island of apples / Avalon).

52. Such a voyage was proved possible by Tim Severin's re-enactment of it in a replica leather boat in 1976–7: see his *The Brendan Voyage* (London, 1978). Translations of the Irish and Latin forms of the legend, together with the Middle English texts from the *South English Legendary* and the *Golden Legend*, are collected by Denis O'Donaghue, *Lives and Legends of Saint Brendan the Voyager* (1893; repr. Felinfach, 1994).

53. Caroline Walker Bynum emphasizes the medieval stress on non-appropriative wonder in her *Metamorphosis and Identity*, pp. 38–75.

54. See further Mary W. Helms, *Ulysses' Sail* (Princeton, 1988), pp. 211–20.

55. Ariosto's *Orlando Furioso* was published in 1532, Tasso's *Gerusalemme Liberata* in 1575.

56. 'Solo un ovile sia, solo un pastore' (Ludovico Ariosto, *Orlando Furioso*, ed. Lanfranco Caretti (Turin, 1966) XV. 26, and see also 21–7); Sir John Harington, 'it was but a vaine conceit of some idle head' (*Ludovico Ariosto's Orlando Furioso*, ed.

Robert McNulty (Oxford, 1972), p. 166, sidenote to his xv. 18—his abbreviation of the text indicates his impatience with the whole section).

57. Edward Fairfax, *Godfrey of Bulloigne*, ed. Kathleen M. Lea and T. M. Gang (Oxford, 1981), xv. 31. Neither 'knight' nor 'wondrous' is present in the original: Tasso's equivalent terms are merely 'uom' and 'incognito' (*Torquato Tasso: Gerusalemme Liberata*, ed. Lanfranco Caretti (Milan, 1979)).

58. *Orlando Furioso*, cantos 6 and 7; he leaves for the return journey across Asia in canto 10.

59. Fairfax's term, *Godfrey*, ed. Lea and Gang, xiv. 75, xv. 62. See xiv. 70 for the location in the Fortunate Isles.

60. Fairfax, *Godfrey*, vi. 43. A further link between Morgan and this series of enchantresses lies in Ariosto's making Morgana into Alcina's sister and fellow-conspirator.

61. The classic study is by Irving A. Leonard, *Books of the Brave* (1949; repr. Berkeley and Los Angeles, 1992). Popular titles included not only *Amadis de Gaule* and its offspring but others of earlier origin, including versions of *Floris and Blanchefleur*, *Partonope*, *Robert the Devil*, *Renaud of Montauban* (*The Four Sons of Aymon*), and *Oliver of Castille* (pp. 104–20). See also Jennifer Goodman, *Chivalry and Exploration* 1298–1630 (Woodbridge, 1998), esp. pp. 149–67 on Cortes.

62. Segar, *Honor Military*, pp. 58–9.

63. *FQ*, II Proem 2–3; and the end of Ralegh's *Discovery of . . . Guiana*, *Sir Walter Ralegh: Selected Writings*, ed. Gerald Hammond (Harmondsworth, 1986), p.123 (see also the discussion in Louis Adrian Montrose, ' "Shaping Fantasies": Figurations of Gender and Power in Elizabethan Culture', *Representations* 1 (1983), 61–94, esp. pp. 76–7).

64. Quoted in Morison, *European Discovery*, p. 629.

65. 'God knows, I never knew what sorrow meant till now' (letter to his wife on the death of their son on their voyage to Guiana, 1618); and he ascribes the deaths of Drake and Hawkins to heartbreak 'when they failed of their enterprise' (*Ralegh: Selected Writings*, ed. Hammond, pp. 277–8).

66. Bunyan, *Pilgrim's Progress*, ed. Sharrock, title page; summary of the journey from Part 2, pp. 383–4; pp. 264–5, echoing the Song of Songs.

67. See further pp. 269–72 below.

68. Malory, ii. 912 (XIV. 6).

69. Malory, i. 88 (II. 17).

70. 'The "Uncanny" ' ('Das Unheimliche', 1919), in *Freud: Works*, ed. Strachey, xvii. 219–52. Freud elaborates his definition into 'that class of the frightening which leads back to what is known of old and long familiar' (p. 220). *Eger and Grime* in many ways offers a more detailed fit with his category of the uncanny than the story he takes as his paradigm, E. T. A. Hoffmann's *The Sand-Man*.

71. The surviving texts present the romance in two somewhat different forms (one as found in the Percy Folio manuscript; the other in print), but apart from the ending (where the prints add a coda in which Eger's wife leaves him and enters a nunnery after he confesses to his deception of her) the differences are no greater than those that sometimes obtain between different manuscript versions of essentially the same romance in the Middle Ages. Neither version of *Eger* shows signs of extensive modernization. Caldwell's edition prints the two texts in parallel; French and Hale print the Percy version, pp. 671–717.

72. l. 1864 in Caldwell's edition of the printed text.
73. *Eger*, ed. Caldwell, ll. 887–90.
74. Fairfax's translation, *Godfrey*, ed. Lea and Gang, p. 88. Tasso is making a distinction between 'imitation', which concerns itself with outward and visible action, and 'allegory', which is concerned with what can be signified but not directly represented through such action.
75. *Chroniques de Jean Molinet*, ed. J-A. Buchon (Paris, 1828), i. 16–17, 'Autre Prologue'.
76. *Ancrene Wisse*, Part 4, 'on temptations' (various edns.; e.g. ed. J. R. R. Tolkien, EETS 249 (1962), trans. Hugh White, *Ancrene Wisse: Guide for Anchoresses* (Harmondsworth, 1993).
77. Jocelyn Wogan-Browne, *Saints' Lives and Women's Literary Culture c.*1150–1300 (Oxford, 2001), p. 139.
78. Malory, i. 280 (VI. 15).
79. Chrétien, *Chevalier de la Charrette*, ed. Roques, 3118–28. Many manuscripts of the prose *Lancelot* removed the lions altogether, presumably because the scribes found the episode baffling; they are retained in that used by H. Oskar Sommer (*The Vulgate Version of the Arthurian Romances*, Washington, 1900–16, iv. 201), but appear only in the variants in Micha's edition (iii. xxxviii.48 bis; compare ii. xxxviii–xxxix).
80. Malory's version, ii. 1014 (XVII. 14).
81. *Pilgrim's Progress*, ed. Sharrock, pp. 175–6. Compare also the episode in the Valley of the Shadow of Death when Christiana sees 'something yonder upon the road before us, a thing of a shape such as I have not seen. . . . An ugly thing, child; an ugly thing . . .', which vanishes when it is encountered by Mr Great-heart ('The Second Part', p. 338).
82. Malory, ii. 931–4 (XV. 5–6).
83. Malory, ii. 892 (XIII. 17).
84. Hopkins gives a useful account of the doctrine of penitence in so far as it affects the romances in her *Sinful Knights*, pp. 32–69.
85. It is edited by Maldwyn Mills, *Six Middle English Romances* (London, 1973), pp. 125–47.
86. *Robert the Devil* was a pan-European bestseller, but appears in England only in early printed texts in both verse and prose. Modern editions are scarce—the verse is edited by W. Carew Hazlitt, *Remains of the Early Popular Poetry of England* (4 vols., London, 1864–6), i. 218–63; the prose in William J. Thoms, *Early English Prose Romances*, rev. and enl. edn. (London, 1907), pp. 167–206. The verse romance was one of those copied by the Elizabethan recusant Edward Banyster (see p. 38 above). Lodge's version is discussed below. The story enjoyed particularly wide currency in France both before and after the age of print: its popularity was confirmed by its appearance in the *Bibliothèque bleue*, and Meyerbeer composed an opera on the subject in 1831. *Sir Gowther* (no early printings) is closely derived from *Robert the Devil*, but originated in England: text in Mills, *Six Romances*, pp. 148–68, or a fully scholarly edition by Karl Breul (Oppeln, 1886).
87. *Robert of Sicily* is edited by Hazlitt, *Remains*, i. 276–87, and French and Hale, pp. 933–46; a dramatized version composed in the reign of Henry VII was revived

at Chester in 1529 (Hazlitt, i. 265–6; Alfred Harbage, *Annals of English Drama 975–1700*, rev. S. Schoenbaum, 3rd edn. rev. Sylvia Stoler Wagonheim (London and New York, 1989), p. 14). Despite its popularity in the Middle Ages (with ten surviving manuscripts, including the Vernon manuscript, a huge volume of vernacular texts possibly composed for reading in a convent), no early prints are known. Two versions of the English *Alexius* (long and short redactions of the same text) are edited by Carl Horstmann, *Altenglische Legenden*, Neue Folge (Heilbronn, 1881), pp. 174–88.

88. See p. 37 above.

89. Langham, *A Letter*, ed. Kuin, p. 53; *The Complaynt of Scotlande* (1549), ed. James A. H. Murray, EETS E.S. 17–18 (1872–3), p. 63; Nashe, *The Anatomie of Absurditie*, *Works*, ed. McKerrow, i. 11, or in *Elizabethan Critical Essays*, ed. G. Gregory Smith (London, 1904), i. 323; Francis Meres, *Palladis Tamia*, ibid., ii. 308; and for the dramatization, Harbage, *Annals*, sub anno 1603: it may have been a revival of an older play.

90. *The Famous, true and historicall life of Robert second Duke of Normandy*, in *The Complete Works of Thomas Lodge*, intro. Edmund W. Gosse, 4 vols. (1883; repr. New York, 1963), ii. 19–20.

91. See p. 37 above.

92. *Pilgrim's Progress*, ed. Sharrock, Apology, p. 144.

93. *Pilgrim's Progress*, ed. Sharrock, p. 390.

94. *Guy of Warwick: Fifteenth-century Version*, ed. Zupitza, ll. 272 ff., 7125 ff.; or in the printed version, *Guy of Warwick nach Coplands Druck*, ed. Gustav Schleich (Leipzig, 1923), ll. 440–50, 6085–92. Successive couplets look backwards and forwards, rather on the model of the comparisons of salvation history and salvation itself: here, Guy repents of his past seeking of glory on bloody chivalric quests,

> And all for the love of that maye,　　[maid
> That he travelde fore nyght and day,　[laboured
> And not for god, his creatowre,
> That had done hym that honowre.
> ed. Zupitza, 7139–42

95. Longleat MS 249b; see Richmond, *Legend of Guy*, pp. 189–90.

96. Richard Lloyd, *Briefe Discourse of the . . . Actes and Conquests of the Nine Worthies* (London, 1584).

97. *The Famous History of Guy Earle of Warwicke*, in Samuel Rowlands, *Complete Works*, ed. Edmund Gosse (Glasgow, 1880), iii. 59.

98. The play contains a clown named Sparrow, 'a high minded lofty mounting sparrow' who is, as he notes, a 'bird of Venus', and who was born at Stratford-upon-Avon in Warwickshire. The wording is reminiscent of Greene's notorious attack on Shakespeare as an 'upstart crow', of 1592: see Cooper, 'Guy of Warwick'. The play itself was not printed until 1661.

99. In the Chorus preceding Act 2, Guy is approved for fighting against God's enemies, 'not in Deanes and Chapters lands at home', and for his lack of concern with splitting the Church over the hot topic of clerical vestments, 'He doth not strike at Surplices and Tippits, | (to bring an Oleo in of Sects in Sippits)' (*The Tragical History of Guy*, sig. B1v).

100. *Tragical History*, sig. F1v–F2.

101. For a discussion of the marital and penitential models offered by the two texts, see Neil Cartlidge, *Medieval Marriage: Literary Approaches, 1100–1300* (Cambridge, 1997), pp. 99–106. Cartlidge makes the persuasive point that *Guy*'s popularity is partly due to its being 'so free of moral anxiety' (p. 105).

102. The early fourteenth-century Auchinleck manuscript contains not only the romance of Guy and a chronicle account of him but also a homiletic work in the form of a long sermon supposedly composed for the penitent Guy by a hermit, the *Speculum Gy de Warwike*: a unique triple-genre representation of a hero in a single collection (Richmond, *Legend of Guy*, p. 54).

103. '. . . that right worthie Guy earle of Warwike, who (as some writers have recorded) fought with a mightie giant of the Danes in a singular combat, and vanquished him' (Raphael Holinshed, *Chronicles of England, Scotland and Ireland* (1807–8; repr. with intro. by Vernon F. Snow, New York, 1965) i. 688).

104. *Poly-Olbion*, Song XII, ll. 147, 272–3 (in vol. 4 of *The Works of Michael Drayton*, ed. J. William Hebel (5 vols., Oxford, 1961)).

105. 'And by cause that he [the knight] be wel horsed and hyhe is by cause he may be sene fro ferre. And that is the sygnefyaunce, that he oughte to be made redy to doo al that whiche behoveth to thordre of chivalrye more than another man' (Caxton's translation of Lull's *Book of the Ordre of Chivalry*, ed. Byles, p. 84, modern punctuation supplied).

106. Lewis, *Allegory of Love*, p. 338.

107. Rosemond Tuve, 'The Red Crosse Knight and Medieval Demon Stories', in *Essays by Rosemond Tuve: Spenser, Herbert, Milton*, ed. Thomas P. Roche, jr (Princeton, 1970), pp. 39–48.

108. *Mandeville's Travels*, ed. Hamelius, p. 187.

109. *Gerald of Wales: The Journey through Wales*, trans. Lewis Thorpe (Harmondsworth, 1978), I. i. (p. 76).

110. Malory i. 88 (II. 17); *Pilgrim's Progress*, ed. Sharrock, p. 180.

111. Malory, ii. 863 (XIII. 5).

112. Malory, ii. 1015, 1029 (XVII. 15, 20).

113. Malory, ii. 1034–5 (XVII. 22).

114. Malory, ii. 883 (XIII. 12).

115. Malory, ii. 984 (XVII. 2); and see pp. 132–3 below. Hawes has his protagonist encounter a more overtly allegorical test in the shape of a narrow bridge with the inscription

> No man this brydge may over go
> But he be pure without neglygence
> And stedfast in goddes byleve also.
> Yf he be ygnoraunt and do not so
> He must nedys into this water fall
> Over the heed and be drowned with all.
> *Example of Vertue*, 1276–81

116. Malory, ii. 1011 (XVII.13).

117. *Le Roman de la rose*, ed. Daniel Poirion (Paris, 1974), ll. 21,587–694.

118. Tasso, *Gerusalemme Liberata*, ed. Caretti, xv. 62. Fairfax, for whom pilgrimages were acceptable only when spiritual, cuts the image.

119. *The Book of the Love-Smitten Heart (Le Livre du cuers d'amours espris) by René of Anjou*, ed. and trans. Stephanie Viereck Gibbs and Kathryn Karczewska (New York and London, 2001), pp. 6–7, 230–1; and Jean de Meun further figures among the list of love-poets, pp. 173–81.
120. Jerome's treatise *Adversus Jovinianum* enjoyed a *succès de scandale* throughout the Middle Ages, especially among clerics, for its attack on sexuality, women, and marriage.
121. Kaske, 'How Spenser Really Used Hawes', p. 126.
122. Hawes, *Minor Poems*, ed. Gluck and Morgan, plates 8 and 9.
123. Anne Lake Prescott, 'Spenser's Chivalric Restoration: From Bateman's *Travayled Pylgrime* to the Redcrosse Knight', *Studies in Philology* 86 (1989), 166–97; she includes many of the woodcuts.
124. La Marche's text, written in 1483, is edited and translated by Carleton W. Carroll, *Le Chevalier deliberé (The Resolute Knight)* (Tempe, 1999). Bateman, like Lewkenor, in fact used Hernando de Acuña's Spanish translation *El Caballero determinado* as his immediate source. Another work deriving from La Marche's, the 1572 imitation *Le Voyage du chevalier errant* by the Carmelite Jean Cartigny, did keep its 'knight' in its English translation, William Goodyear's *The Wandering Knight* of 1581.
125. *FQ*, I. xii. 19, 40–1, and Hamilton's discussion.

CHAPTER 2

1. *The History of Don Quixote of the Mancha, translated from the Spanish of Miguel de Cervantes by Thomas Shelton, 1612, 1620*, intro. James Fitzmaurice-Kelly (4 vols., London, 1896), iii. 21–2 (Part 2, ch. 1).
2. There may, of course, be some element of symbolism about these boats, but they are always in the first instance real material ships—even the ship named Faith of the Grail Quest, on which see p. 101 below. The symbolism can become overt, as when Tristan and Isolde in the prose *Tristan* travel on a self-propelling magic ship known as 'la Nef de Joie' (E. Löseth, *Le Roman en Prose de Tristan* (Paris, 1890), §323–35); or it may operate simply by association, as between the providentially guided boat and the Church (on which see, in particular, V. A. Kolve, *Chaucer and the Imagery of Narrative* (Stanford and London, 1984), pp. 297–358). In the version of the Grail Quest found in the prose *Tristan*, the material boat that carries Galaad, Perceval, and Bohort is expounded as an allegory of the Church (Löseth, *Roman de Tristan*, §512–13).
3. *Don Quixote*, trans. Shelton, iii. 217–22 (Part 2, ch. 29).
4. The phrase is used by Tasso, *Rinaldo*, ed. Michael Sherberg (Ravenna, 1990), vii. 83. The major study of this kind of boat is by David Quint, 'The Boat of Romance and Renaissance Epic', in *Romance: Generic Transformations*, ed. Brownlee, pp. 178–202.
5. The oldest known example of exposure on the water, of the third millennium BCE, is the myth of Sargon, a baby abandoned on the Euphrates in a pitch-covered basket: see Otto Rank, *The Myth of the Birth of the Hero*, trans.

F. Robbins and Smith Ely Jelliffe (New York, 1952), pp. 12–13; and Donald R. Redford, 'The Literary Motif of the Exposed Child', *Numen* 14 (1967), 209–28. For the appearance of the motif worldwide, see Carolyn Hares-Stryker, 'Adrift on the Seven Seas: The Mediaeval Topos of Exile at Sea', *Florilegium* 12 (1993), 79–98, esp. pp. 80–4.

6. R. W. Chambers, *Beowulf: An Introduction*, 3rd edn. (Cambridge, 1959), pp. 70–80. Later chroniclers incorporate the legend (William of Malmesbury notes that his boat came *sine remige*, without any oarsman: *Willelmi Malmesbiriensis De gestis regum anglorum libri quinque*, ed. W. Stubbs, Rolls Series 90–1 (1887; repr. Wiesbaden, 1964), i. 121), but sometimes make nonsense of his mysterious origin by giving his genealogy; Holinshed indeed traces it back to Noah (*Chronicles*, i. 663).

7. James Hornell, 'The Curraghs of Ireland', *Mariner's Mirror* 23 (1937), 74–83, 148–75, esp. pp. 74–7.

8. Fergus Kelly, *A Guide to Early Irish Law* (Dublin, 1988), pp. 219–20; and J. R. Reinhard, 'Setting Adrift in Medieval Law and Literature', *PMLA* 56 (1941), 33–68 (p. 48). A single ox-hide would make a boat a little over 1 metre wide and under 2 metres long: see Hornell, 'Curraghs', 78, 154–61.

9. Fiacha, son of father-daughter incest, is described as having been set adrift in a text of *c.*1168: see Reinhard, 'Setting Adrift', p. 37.

10. *The Ancient, Famous and Honourable History of Amadis de Gaule* (London, 1619); quotations from pp. 11–12 (Book I ch. 2). The *Amadis* motif is closely imitated in the anonymous *Heroicall Adventures of the Knight of the Sea* (1600), sig. D2r–3r.

11. Reinhard, 'Setting Adrift', p. 43.

12. *The Pleasant Historie of Tom a Lincolne*, in *Early English Prose Romances*, ed. Thoms, p. 622; there is also a modern edition, *R.I., The Most Pleasant History of Tom a Lincolne*, ed. Richard S. M. Hirsch (Columbia, SC, 1978), pp. 23–4. The father who casts his daughter adrift in *Torrent of Portyngale*, one of the Middle English romances that made the transition to print, suffers the same punishment (ed. E. Adam, EETS E.S. 51 (1887), ll. 2122–48). Interestingly, none of these fatal instances makes use of the 'neither sail nor oar' formula, though the absence of equipment from the boats is implied.

13. The point is made forcefully by Partonope after he has entered an unmanned ship that sails off with him, by comparison with being lost in the forest: *Partonope de Blois*, ed. A. Trampe Bödtker, EETS E.S. 109 (1912), ll. 789–809—a lament that culminates with the line, 'Butte God allone he may me save'.

14. Holinshed, *Chronicles*, i. 687 (Book VI ch. xx, *sub anno* 934). His source, William of Malmesbury, describes the boat as without oarsman and devoid of oars, *remige et remigio vacuam* or *sine remige et remigio vacuam* (*Willelmi Malmesbiriensis*, i. 156). There is disagreement among the early chroniclers as to whether Edwin died from exposure rather than drowning himself, a divergence of traditions that is itself a strong indicator of suicide: see Alexander Murray, *Suicide in the Middle Ages: The Violent against Themselves* (Oxford, 1998), pp. 48–9.

15. Lady Mary Wroth, *Urania*, in *An Anthology of Seventeenth-Century Fiction*, ed. Paul Salzman (Oxford, 1991), p. 38.

16. *The Tempest*, 1.2.154; on the echoes of Holinshed's account of Edwin, see Helen Cooper, 'Prospero's Boats: Magic, Providence, and Human Choice', in

Renaissance Essays for Kitty Scoular Datta, ed. Sukanta Chaudhuri (Calcutta and Oxford, 1995), pp. 160–75, esp. pp. 169–71.

17. The play was first printed in 1661 under the names of John Webster and William Rowley, but the ascription to Webster at least is probably libellous. Its only modern edition is none the less in *The Dramatic Works of John Webster,* ed. William Hazlitt (London, 1857), Vol. 4; quotation from I. i. The plot owes something not only to Shakespeare's last plays and various Elizabethan pastoral romances (the lovers come to land separately and both lodge with shepherds) but also to the story of Havelok and Goldboru, under their alternative names of Curan and Argentille, as retold in William Warner's *Albions England:* see below, p. 265.

18. *Livy,* ed. and trans. B. O. Foster, Loeb Classical Library, 14 vols. (Cambridge, Mass., and London, 1952), i.16–25 (I. iii. 10–vi.3; quotations from pp. 18, 19, I. iv. 3).

19. Holinshed, *Chronicles,* i.435.

20. *Anonymous Short English Metrical Chronicle,* ed. Zettl, ll. 283, 290; Redford, 'Setting Adrift', pp. 59–60. The story originated in Anglo-Norman (*Des grants Geanz,* ed. Georgina Brereton (Oxford, 1937)), and (unusually) was translated from the vernacular into Latin. The story exists in various forms, with the daughters originating from Greece or Syria, succeeding or not in the murder of their husbands, and being condemned by their father or the surviving husband; the setting adrift is common to all versions. See further Lesley Johnson, 'Return to Albion', *Arthurian Literature* 13 (1995), 19–40; and James P. Carley and Julia Crick, 'Constructing Albion's Past: An Annotated Edition of *De Origine Gigantum'*, *Arthurian Literature* 13 (1995), 41–114.

21. *Sir Eglamour,* ed. Richardson, l. 883.

22. Bullough, *Narrative and Dramatic Sources,* viii.166–7; Sicily and Bohemia are inverted in the *Winter's Tale.* Greene's account is closely paraphrased in seventeenth-century rewritings: e.g., *Fortune's Tennis Ball; or, The Most Excellent History of Dorastus and Fawnia,* by 'S. S. Gent', ed. James O. Halliwell (London, 1859), p. 11: Fawnia is placed in a 'little boat . . . neither rudder, nor | A sayl to guide it', which is tied to a ship, towed out to sea, and the cord cut. The work was entered in the Stationers' Registers in 1656, but the earliest surviving copy dates from 1672.

23. Ariosto, *Orlando Furioso,* ed. Caretti, xxxvi.60–1; unusually, the mother comes to land before giving birth, but dies in the process.

24. It may also underlie the indirectness of Prospero's reply to Miranda that he is indeed her father (viz. that he had his wife's assurance on the subject), though few Shakespearean men give a simpler answer to such a question (*Tempest,* 1. 2. 56–7; cf. *Much Ado,* 1. 1. 100; *King Lear,* 1. 1. 8–9).

25. See p. 29 above.

26. *Romance of Horn,* ed. Pope, ll. 58–114; ll. 74 quoted, 'N'i ot tres n'avirum, guvernail ne struman'. For a translation, see *The Birth of Romance: An Anthology,* trans. Judith Weiss (London, 1992).

27. Copies or fragments of three printed editions survive from c.1509 to 1511; the licence to print the work was transferred on 15 January 1582, along with the highly popular *Sir Eglamour* (*SR,* ii.405). The only modern edition follows the largely independent version preserved in a mid-fifteenth century manuscript, *'King Ponthus and the Faire Sidone'*, ed. F. J. Mather, jr, *PMLA* 12 (1897), i–150.

One of the surviving manuscripts of the French prose original was probably copied in England (*Le Roman de Ponthus et Sidoine*, ed. Marie-Claude de Crécy (Geneva, 1977) p. ix); the text was also included in the manuscript presented to Margaret of Anjou on her wedding to Henry VI, British Library Royal 15 E.VI.

28. De Worde print of 1511, sig. Av^v (modernized punctuation); for the original, see *Ponthus*, ed. de Crécy, p. 8—though it appears that this English translator added the detail of the 'two or three' holes.

29. 'Or les guarisset cil ki salvat Moïsan, | Quant fud jecté petit al flum del desruban' (*Romance of Horn*, ed. Pope, ll. 72–6); cf. Exodus 1:15–2:10. The Biblical etymology given for Moses' name, 'because I drew him out of the water', underlines the significance of his discovery.

30. *Man of Law's Tale, CT* II.485–7. The analogy is found in a high proportion of texts of rudderless boats, both hagiographic and secular, including (for instance) Hartmann von Aue's *Gregorius* and the legend of St Kentigern.

31. 'Withouten mast, other myke, other myry bawelyne, | Kable, other capstan to clyppe to her ankres, | Hurrok, other hand-helme hasped on rother, | Other any sweande sail to seche after haven' (*Cleanness*, ll. 417–20, *The Poems of the Pearl Manuscript*, ed. Malcolm Andrew and Ronald Waldron rev. edn. (Exeter, 1987)).

32. *The Northern Legendary*, in *Altenglische Legenden*, ed. Horstmann, pp. 81–8 (ll. 104–6); cf. 'withouten ster and ore', *Magdalena*, in his *Sammlung altenglischer Legenden* (Heilbronn, 1878), pp. 148–62, l. 174.

33. *The Golden Legend; or, Lives of the Saints Englished by William Caxton*, ed. F. S. Ellis, 7 vols. (London, 1900), iv.76.

34. *The Lives of St Ninian and St Kentigern*, ed. Alexander Penrose Forbes (1874; repr. Lampeter, 1989), pp. 167–8: 'iuxta morum Scottorum confecto, sine omni remigio . . . "Confidit in Christo, liberet illam si valet de manu mortis, et de periculo maris"' (cf. Matthew 27:43).

35. *Die mittelenglische Gregoriuslegende*, ed. Carl Keller (Heidelberg, 1914), pp. 44, 51 (quotations from two manuscripts). The legend is best known through Hartmann von Aue's *Gregorius* and its recasting for a modern readership by Thomas Mann as *Der Erwählte* (trans. as *The Holy Sinner*).

36 This is the argument of Elizabeth Archibald, *Incest and the Medieval Imagination* (Oxford, 2001), p. 232.

37. Whitley Stokes, 'The Voyage of the Húi Corra', *Révue Celtique* 14 (1893), 22–69; they initially take oars, but ship them in order to commit themselves more completely to God.

38. *The Tripartite Life of St Patrick*, ed. Whitley Stokes, Rolls Series 89 (London, 1887), ii. 286–9; and see T. M. Charles-Edwards, 'The Social Background to Irish Peregrinatio', *Celtica* 11 (1976), 43–59 (48–50). An anti-providential, and therefore anomalous, instance of the punishment of a criminal by a saint is told of St Edmund, who condemned a murderer, his hunstman Bern (Beorn), to be cast adrift in the boat 'which nouther hadde oore, seil nor mast' in which his own victim of murder through exposure, a Danish king, had been washed up on the English coast; Bern not only survives, but on coming to land in Denmark, persuades Bern's sons that it was Edmund who killed their father (Lydgate's *Life of St Edmund* Book II, l. 247 quoted; ed. Horstmann, *Altenglische Legenden*, pp. 376–440).

39. 'The Voyage of Snedgus and MacRiagla', ed. Whitley Stokes, *Révue Celtique* 9 (1888), 14–25.
40. The passage is quoted and discussed by Charles-Edwards, 'Social Background', pp. 48–9.
41. Victor Turner, 'The Center out There: Pilgrim's Goal', *History of Religions* 12 (1972), 191–230 (p. 214).
42. 'Deus enim adiutor noster est et nautor et gubernator atque gubernat. Mittite intus omnes remiges et gubernaculum. Tantum dimittite uela extensa et faciat Deus sicut uult de seruis suis et de sua naui' (*Navigatio Sancti Brendani Abbatis from Early Latin Manuscripts*, ed. Carl Selmer (Notre Dame, 1959), cap. 6, p. 12 (and cf. also pp. 39, 40; see also *Lives of the Saints*, trans. J. F. Webb (Harmondsworth, 1965), pp. 37, 51). The passage appears in the Irish *Life*, but not the Middle English versions: see also p. 74 above. One of the hermits encountered by Brendan on an otherwise uninhabited island had also been brought there by boat without his control, and it returns empty to Ireland after leaving him there. See also Tim Severin, *The Brendan Voyage*; and, for a testimony to the continuing fascination of Brendan's 'wonders of the deep', C. S. Lewis's *Voyage of the Dawn Treader* (London, 1954).
43. *Huon of Bordeux*, ed. Lee, pp. 435–6, 439–43. Brendan's fruit provides miraculous sustenance; Huon takes apples that restore youth.
44. *Philippe de Rémi: Le Roman de la Manekine*, ed. and trans. Barbara N. Sargent-Baur (Amsterdam and Atlanta, 1999). It survives in a single manuscript, but it was more widely known than that alone would indicate. A prose redaction was made in the fifteenth century. There were two Philippes, father and son; Sargent-Baur dates the romance to *c*.1230 and ascribes it to the father, though the issue is still disputed. Philippe wrote another romance, *Jehan et Blonde*, which is largely set in England; it may possibly have been written for the earls of Oxford, whose supposed ancestress is the heroine of the story.
45. *Philippe: Manekine*, ed. Sargent-Baur, ll. 921, 1067–8; also 1081, 1190, 3989–90, 4222, 4784–5, 5047–9, 7150. Contrast 5433–4, 6819–20, 7889–90 for well-equipped ships.
46. 'Dix puet bien restorer tout, | Toutes pertes et tous tormens', ibid., 8568–9.
47. They are surveyed by Schlauch, *Chaucer's Constance*, pp. 12–61.
48. *Emaré*, in *Six Middle English Romances*, ed. Mills, ll. 271–5 (275 quoted), 335, 593, 683.
49. Brendan's voyage is dated to 565–73 (Webb, *Lives of the Saints*, p. 18); counting back from 584, the year Trevet gives for Constance's death, her second voyage would have taken place from 564 to 569 (*Trivet's Life of Constance*, ed. Margaret Schlauch, in *Sources and Analogues of Chaucer's Canterbury Tales*, ed. W. F. Bryan and Germaine Dempster (1941; repr. Atlantic Highlands, NJ, 1958).
50. 'Saunz sigle e sauntz neviroun', *Trivet's Life*, ed. Schlauch, in Bryan and Dempster, p. 168; *CT* II.439–41.
51. The surviving fragments are edited by Franklin B. Williams, 'Alsop's *Fair Custance*: Chaucer in Tudor Dress', *ELR* 6 (1976), 351–68.
52. Ann Thompson, *Shakespeare's Chaucer: A Study in Literary Origins* (Liverpool, 1968), pp. 30–1. Despite the similarity of the title to Alsop's version, the appearance of a major new edition of Chaucer's works in 1598 makes it most likely that the source was the *Man of Law's Tale* itself.

53. Geoffrey of Monmouth, *Life of Merlin*, ed. Clarke, l. 929–3 (Clarke's translation of line 931), and the note on Barinthus, pp. 165–6. In this text, Morgen herself is not in the boat; for the development of the episode, see p. 185 below.

54. The unsteered boat was probably part of the original Tristan story; it is retained in Eilhart von Oberge's *Tristant*, but its currency in western Europe is indicated by its illustration on a tile from Chertsey Abbey (reproduced in Roger Sherman Loomis, *Arthurian Legends in Medieval Art* (New York and London, 1938), fig. 48); the fragmentary accompanying inscription reads 'sans gouvernail', 'without a rudder' (p. 47).

55. See further p. 161 below.

56. 'Sanza vela e sanza remi e sanza neuno sopra sagliente' (*Il Novellino*, ed. Guido Favati (Genoa, 1970), lxxxii, p. 318.

57. See, for instance, the delightful collection put together by C. Grant Loomis in *White Magic: The Folklore of Christian Legend* (Cambridge, Mass., 1948), pp. 90–1, and notes pp. 202–3; rather more than half his examples (culled from the *Acta Sanctorum*) have British or Breton connections. The full versions of the legends in the *Acta* almost all use some form of the 'neither sail nor oar' phrasing.

58. Ariosto, *Orlando Furioso*, xxxix. 26–8; Gilbert H. Doble, *The Saints of Cornwall* (1923–44; repr. Felinfach, 1997), i. 89. St Hya had a considerable cult in Cornwall, though the first surviving written version of her legend dates from as late as 1300. There is some good maritime engineering behind the legends, as Ariosto notes, the wooden frame of a ship being constructed on a design analogous to that of the veins of a leaf.

59. John of Glastonbury, *The Chronicle of Glastonbury Abbey*, ed. James P. Carley, trans. David Townsend (1985; repr Woodbridge, 2001), pp. 48–51 (p. 48 quoted); *The History of the Holy Grail* cap. 4, trans. Carol J. Chase, *Lancelot-Grail*, ed. Lacy, i. 120 (quoted).

60. Ecclesiastes 7:27–8; the verses were so widely quoted in the Middle Ages as to make any wife of Solomon's wicked by mental reflex, whatever the gist of the story. She also constructs a bed for the ship, in an interesting analogue for the bed of Solomon's work, 'l'ovre Salemun', that Marie de France's Guigemar finds on board his own magic ship (*Guigemar*, l. 172, in *Marie de France: Lais*, ed. A. Ewert (Oxford, 1944)).

61. Malory, ii. 915 (XIV.8).

62. Malory, ii. 990 (XVII.5): it is found and entered by Pelles (misnamed in the text as Pelleas) when he is hunting 'toward Irelonde'. After transferring back to their own vessel, the companions next come to land in the marches of Scotland, locations that confirm the Celtic connections of unsteered boats.

63. Malory, ii. 984–5 (XVII.2).

64. As Lancelot notes after he has been directed to it later by a dream: Malory, ii.1011 (XVII.13).

65. Malory, ii. 1003 (XVII.11).

66. Malory, ii. 1013 (XVII.13).

67. *Rinaldo*, trans. John Hoole (London, 1792), ll. 615–20; Tasso, *Rinaldo*, ed. Sherberg, vii. 83–4.

68. Tasso, *Gerusalemme*, ed. Caretti, and Fairfax's translation, *Godfrey of Bulloigne*, ed. Lea and Gang, xiv. 56–7.

69. Fairfax, *Godfrey*, ed. Lea and Gang, xv. 3–4, 9, 40.
70. See p. 75 above; and Quint, 'The Boat of Romance', pp. 180–1.
71. Malory recounts one such episode, from the prose *Merlin*, when a ship is left by Morgan as a trap for Arthur, Uriens, and Accolon when they (like Guigemar and Partonope) lose themselves while hunting (i. 137–40 (iv. 6–8)). A more benevolent example occurs in the French *Floriant et Florete* (ed. Harry F. Williams (Ann Arbor, 1947), l. 790 ff.): this is unsinkable, and goes wherever the hero tells it.
72. Fairfax, *Godfrey*, ed. Lea and Gang, p. 90.
73. *FQ* II. xi. 4, xii. 3, 5, 15, 21, 29, 37.
74. The classic statement of such an equation is that of Max Weber, *The Protestant Ethic and the Spirit of Capitalism*, trans. T. Parsons, intro. A. Giddens (London, 1992), pp. 113–25.

CHAPTER 3

1. e.g. 'many a terible monster made of broune paper' complained of by Stephen Gosson in his *Playes Confuted in Five Actions* (facsmile intro. Arthur Freeman (New York and London, 1972), sig. C6r), or the giant Colbron in *The Tragical History of Guy of Warwick* (probably dating from the early 1590s).
2. *Of Arthour and of Merlin*, ed. Macrae-Gibson, ll. 7448, 8186, 8481. Fragments of two sixteenth-century printed editions survive, from which the version in the Percy Folio derives; these versions end at an earlier point in the story, before the birth of Arthur.
3. George Peele, *The Old Wives Tale*, ed. Patricia Binney (Manchester, 1980), l. 169, dating from c.1590. The man is, admittedly, enchanted from being a young man into being old, but that is not very marvellous on stage.
4. *Der mittelenglische Versroman über Richard Löwenherz*, ed. Karl Brunner (Vienna, 1913), ll. 1637–46; and see also *Sir Eglamour*, ed. Richardson, ll. 616–21. In technical astrological terminology, a talisman is distinguished from an amulet by its inscription with signs of power; such inscriptions are very unusual in romance, perhaps because of their association with demonology, and I use the words in their non-technical sense, as synonyms.
5. Malory, i. 54, 140–51 (I. 25, IV. 8–14). He omits the recovery of the scabbard promised (but never recounted) in his source, the French prose *Suite du Merlin* (*Merlin*, ed. Gaston Paris and Jacob Ulrich, SATF (Paris, 1886), ii. 222, trans. Martha Asher, *Lancelot-Grail*, ed. Lacy, iv. 268).
6. See p. 69 above.
7. *The Travels of Marco Polo*, trans. R. E. Latham (Harmondsworth, 1958), p. 226. The 1579 translation by John Frampton, interestingly, omits the last sentence: catching a unicorn in the lap of a virgin had crossed the boundary between the possible and the mythical in the intervening centuries (*The Most Noble and Famous Travels of Marco Polo*, ed. N. M. Penzer, 2nd edn. (London, 1937), pp. 103–4).
8. *Gervase of Tilbury: Otia Imperialia, Recreation for an Emperor*, ed. and trans. S. E. Banks and J. W. Binns (Oxford, 2002), pp. 558–9. See also Bynum, *Metamorphosis*, pp. 48–54, for comparable ideas in authors from Aristotle to Augustine and Roger Bacon.

9. The point is argued for an earlier period by Adrienne Mayor, *The First Fossil Hunters: Palaeontology in Greek and Roman Times* (Princeton, 2000).

10. e.g., on the origins of the spark that makes Arcite's horse rear and throw him, 'what envious flint, | Cold as old Saturn and like him possessed | With fire malevolent', *Two Noble Kinsmen*, 5.6.61–3. In contrast to the source, the gods do not appear in person in this play: it is the only one of Shakespeare's late plays where their existence is not 'proved' by a stage appearance or a true oracle, most of which he adds to his sources.

11. Ibid., 5.3.1; for the prayers for virginity, 5.3.24–32 (an apparent preference over being given to the knight who best loves her), and Chaucer, *Knight's Tale*, *CT*, I. 2304–21, which gives a higher profile to her preference for maidenhood.

12. *Beues of Hamtoun*, ed. Kölbing, ll. 1393–400 and variants (p. 77).

13. J. R. R. Tolkien, *Farmer Giles of Ham* (London, 1949), p. 12.

14. *Percy*, ii. 56–77; also ed. Hahn, *Sir Gawain*, pp. 309–35.

15. *Orlando Furioso*, vi. 67 (fraud, Ariosto's 'frodo'), xxii. 67–73, in Sir John Harington's translation.

16. Malory, iii. 1216–20 (XX. 21–2). Gawain is the protagonist in the sections of *Of Arthour and of Merlin* where his increase of strength is mentioned (ll. 4778–806, 8130–50), but the first of those passages starts by noting that it is already past noon.

17. Bynum, *Metamorphosis*, pp. 72–3.

18. *CT*, V. 115–27; *Valentine*, ed. Dickson, p. 170 (cap. xli); *Don Quixote*, Part 2, chs. 73–4, trans. Shelton, Part 2, chs. xl–xli, iv. 18–33. An early version of the material that follows appeared in Helen Cooper, 'Magic that does not work', *Medievalia et Humanistica* 7 (1976), 131–46.

19. Chrétien, *Chevalier de la Charrete*, ed. Roques, ll. 2335–55.

20. *Amadas et Ydoine*, ed. John R. Reinhard (Paris, 1926), l. 2318 (2007–302 for the whole episode); there is a translation by Ross G. Arthur, *Amadas and Ydoine* (New York and London, 1993). The romance dates from 1190 to 1220, and survives in one complete French manuscript and two Anglo-Norman fragments. It was, however, much more widely known than those figures indicate, especially in England, though it is not known to have been translated into Middle English (see p. 475 n. 18 below). A copy was among the books given to Bordesley Abbey in 1305 by Guy Beauchamp (Blaess, 'L'Abbaye de Bordesley').

21. *Huon of Bordeux*, ed. Lee, pp. 113–14 (cap. xxxvi).

22. *Les romans de Chrétien de Troyes IV: Le Chevalier au Lion (Yvain)*, ed. Mario Roques, CFMA (Paris, 1965), ll. 2947–3011, 3086–127.

23. Ibid., ll. 2597–615, 2769–79.

24. *Ywain and Gawain*, ed. Mills, lines 1527–40; Chrétien, *Chevalier au Lion*, ed. Roques, ll. 2602–15.

25. 'It es ful mekyl ogains the right | To cal so fals a man a knight . . . Traytur untrew and trowthles!' (ed. Mills, 1611–12, 1626).

26. *King Horn*, ed. Sands, lines 567–80 (my italics). The effect threatens to be spoiled by the next lines: 'And Sire Athulf, thy brother, | He shal have another'—presumably meaning 'another ring', not 'another ring like the one I am giving you'. The poet has the tact not to mention this one again.

27. Out of innumerable examples, one might select the newly betrothed Guinevere's kissing Arthur as she arms him with each piece of his armour, at which 'Merlin

bad Arthour the king | Thenche on that ich kisseing | When he come into bataile', which with additional incitement from Merlin he duly does (*Of Arthour and of Merlin*, ll. 8681–3, 8821–30, 9239–6).

28. It lasts indeed into the seventeenth century, with or without a (non-magic) ring to embody the idea. In *Eger and Grime*, the phrase itself become a recognition token when Grime has to repeat back to the lady with whom he has fallen in love the words she had spoken to him on their first meeting: 'In press think on your paramour: | I will not bid you think on me, | Think on your love wherever she be' (ed. Caldwell, chapbook text ll. 1412–14 (cf. Percy 902–4); also 1470, 1803–4, 1863–4, and Percy 1003–4). It is, of course, she that he thinks of. The formula is just occasionally used with the genders reversed: Rowlands's Guy leaves his wife with the words, 'Here is my ring, this memory receive, | And swear the same, to make thee think on me' (ed. Gosse, iii. 59).

29. *Floris and Blancheflour*, ed. Sands, ll. 374–8. Compare lines 1213–19 in the French source, the 'roman aristocratique' version, *Le Conte de Floire et Blancheflor*, ed. Jean-Luc Leclanche (Paris, 1980).

30. Ed. Sands, ll. 966–79; cf. *Floire*, ed. Leclanche, ll. 2793–4, 2806–18.

31. In his Preface to the French translation of Erich Köhler, *L'Aventure chevaleresque*, trans. Éliane Kaufholz (Paris, 1974), p. xii.

32. None of the discussions of the complex relationships between any lost prototype story, the Anglo-Norman *Romance of Horn*, the Middle English *King Horn* and *Horn Childe*, and the later ballads of *Hind Horn* takes the ring into account—not even the best of them, Mills's Introduction to his edition of *Horn Childe*, pp. 44–55.

33. *King Horn*, ed. Joseph Hall (Oxford, 1901), text O (Bodleian Library, MS Laud Misc. 108); the couplet would be expected to follow l. 588.

34. *The Romance of Horn*, ed. Pope, ll. 2055–9; trans. Weiss, *The Birth of Romance*, p. 48.

35. *Horn*, ed. Pope, 3165–79; trans. Weiss, pp. 73–4.

36. *King Ponthus*, ed. Mather, ch. xxi (p. 62).

37. Child, *Ballads*, no. 17 (i. 187–208); *Horn Childe*, ed. Mills, 565–73.

38. See the rings motifs in Stith Thompson, *Motif-Index of Folk Literature*, rev. edn. (Copenhagen, 1955–8), D 1076, D 1310.4.1, D 1344.1, H 433.1, H 94, and H 94.4, though as several of Thompson's citations are to the *Horn* romances the argument becomes somewhat circular. The indirect bestowal of prowess found in *King Horn* does not, however, feature under any of his headings: a further indication of the poet's distance from popular literature. Child cites numerous analogous folktales that use the ring solely as a recognition token (*Ballads*, i. 195–200).

39. Chrétien, *Erec et Enide*, ed. Roques, l. 22.

40. See p. 8 of the Introduction to Leclanche's edition, the critical notes on ll. 2811–14 and 2937–8, and the textual notes to ll. 1213–19 and 2987–8 (where each lover is trying to die before the other, but, in one manuscript, 'l'anel ne pooit soffrir', and in the other, 'Li autres [i.e., the onlookers] nel voloit soffrir'). 'Aristocratique' and 'populaire' imply an excessively polarized view of different audiences; the alternative appellations of 'roman idyllique' and 'roman d'aventures' are in some ways less misleading, though, as the following account

indicates, the non-functioning magic of the 'aristocratic' version never becomes popular in either the general or the social sense.

41. See Gaston Paris's account of the relationship between the various versions in *Romania* 28 (1890), 439–47, in a review of the first volume of Vincenzo Crescini's edition of the Italian *Cantare di Fiorio e Biancifiore* (Bologna, 1889, 1899, repr. 1969) (see i. 437–40); later discussions have not always improved on that. Paris does not, however, specifically consider the protective ring in drawing up his scheme of relationships.

42. See Crescini, *Cantare*, i. 438, and *Florés Saga ok Blankiflúr*, ed. Eugen Kölbing (Halle, 1896), xxiii (p. 74).

43. *Floire et Blancheflor: seconde version*, ed. Margaret M. Pelan (Paris, 1975), ll. 651–6, and 995–1208 for the combat (in which any special properties in the sword are not mentioned).

44. See *Cantare*, ed. Crescini, i. 437–40, and ii. stanzas 23–4, 36, 91, 132–4.

45. 'Assai gli aiutasse l'anello': *Filocolo* in *Boccaccio: Opere I*, ed. Salvatore Battaglia (Bari, 1938), p. 427. The ring does not, however, fulfil an additional promise: it was supposed to make its wearer lovable as well as protecting him or her from fire and water (p. 274), but the emir figure does not find Fiorio at all lovable.

46. *Gottfried von Strassburg: Tristan*, ed. Gottfried Weber (Darmstadt, 1967), ll. 15791–890, 16333–402.

47. *Tristrams saga ok Ísöndar*, ed. and trans. Peter Jorgensen, in *Norse Romance I: Tristan*, ed. Kalinke, chs. 61–3 (pp. 153–61); *Sir Tristrem*, ed. Lupack, ll. 2399–2424, 2468. Both versions (and presumably therefore also Thomas: this section of his text has not survived) end the account of Petit-creiu by having him become a skilful hunting dog. Gottfried's substitution of a different future for the dog suggests that the disabling of the magic may originate with him. In all the Celtic analogues for the dog, the magic works: see Gertrude Schoepperle, *Tristan and Isolt*, 2nd edn. (New York, 1960), pp. 322–5, and, on the whole episode in *Tristan*, Louise Gnädinger, *Hiudan and Petitcreiu* (Zürich, 1971), pp. 26–8.

48. The balance of evidence suggests that it was Gottfried, not Thomas, who first invented this outcome; but even if it were present in Thomas, its omission in the other adaptations would run true to form for non-functioning magic.

49. Boccaccio tells the story twice, in the *Filocolo* (Book IV qu. iv, ed. Battaglia, pp. 311–25; it forms part of one of the long digressions inserted into the story of Floris), and again in the *Decameron* (10,5, ed. Vittore Branca, 2nd edn. (Turin, 1984)). The outline of the story is the same in both versions, though the first is considerably longer. The *Filocolo* has generally been cited as Chaucer's source, but the evidence is, in fact, much stronger for the *Decameron*: see Helen Cooper, 'The Frame', in *Sources and Analogues of the Canterbury Tales*, Vol. 1, ed. Robert M. Correale and Mary Hamel (Cambridge, 2002), pp. 1–22, especially pp. 7–13.

50. Aurelius had thought of that earlier, with his prayer to the sun and moon to change their courses—itself an indication of how mammoth an intervention in the natural order would be required: see p. 141 above. A sufficiently high tide would last at most an hour or two, not a week or two.

51. *The Triumph of Honour*, stage direction after ii. 175. The play is part of the *Four Plays, or Moral Representations, in One*, for which Fletcher's collaborator (who may have been responsible for this play) may have been Nathan Field (ed. Cyrus

464 Notes to pages 160–7

Hoy in *The Dramatic Works in the Beaumont and Fletcher Canon*, general editor Fredson Bowers, 10 vols. (Cambridge, 1966–96), viii. 247–67).

52. *Sir Gawain*, ed. Tolkien and Gordon, ll. 2354–7. The fifteenth-century tail-rhyme version of the story preserved in the seventeenth-century Percy Folio manuscript, *The Grene Knight*, states that the white lace (its equivalent of the green girdle) has nothing to do with Gawain's survival, and the lady's account of it falls just short of claiming that it is actually magic (ed. Hales and Furnivall, ii. 56–77, lines 484–5, 395–402).

53. *Sir Gawain*, ed. Tolkien and Gordon, ll. 626, 2030–6, 630.

54. The commonest metaphorical usage of 'weave' had to do with constructing an argument or a discourse, though it could mean 'entangle', *MED* 'weven' 5a. 'Spell' was similarly a neutral word, normally meaning 'speech' or 'story' (s.v. spel).

55. Malory, i. 18 (I. 8).

56. Hyrd adds it to Vives' original list of romances, as being especially popular in England; such popularity strongly suggests that it was printed, even though no traces of any printed editions survive.

57. *Partonope de Blois*, ed. Bödtker, ll. 5913–35.

58. *The Siege of Troy*, 'Zwei mittelenglische Prosaromane: *The Sege of Thebes* and *The Sege of Troy*', ed. Friedrich Brie, *Anglia*, 130 (1913), 40–52, 269–85 (corrected quotation from p. 274).

59. Bödtker's marginal note to l. 1659. The word most often used in the original French text is 'engien', skill or skilful device (see, for instance, i. 1385 in *Partonopeus de Blois*, ed. Joseph Gildea (Villanova, 1967)).

60. Malory, i. 10 (Caxton, I. 2).

61. *Othello*, 3. 3. 271.

62. *Othello*, 3. 3. 291–2. Taylor and Wells insert the stage direction '*He puts the napkin from him. It drops*' between the lines, though neither the Quarto nor the Folio spell out the action; early readers of both occasionally marked it in for themselves. In Cinthio's original, Iago steals the handkerchief from Desdemona's girdle after distracting her attention (Bullough, *Narrative and Dramatic Sources*, vii. 246–7); there is nothing corresponding to the 'magical' history of the handkerchief, which is Shakespeare's own addition to his source—another example of equivocal magic's appearance through individual invention rather than replication.

63. *CT*, V. 1125, 1184, 1272.

64. Ariosto, *Orlando Furioso*, ed. Caretti, vii.70–2, 8.2.

65. *FQ*, I. vii. 33–6 (a description that promises considerably more than the shield ever delivers), and IV. viii. 42; Arthur continues the battle without the shield's apparently having any effect on his enemy. The shield is based on Ruggiero's, described on p. 142 above.

66. The combat against Pyrocles, *FQ*, II. viii. 20–2, 30, 49; against Maleger, II. xi. 40–1.

67. *FQ*, I. i. 12, 14; v. 9; vii. 2, 19. Both Sansfoy and Duessa believe that the armour is enchanted, I. ii. 18, iv. 50, v. 22. When his armour does shine with light from 'heaven' in his fight with the dragon (I. xi. 4), at the narrative level it is the sun that causes it, not supernatural intervention.

68. *The Romaunce of the Sowdone of Babylone*, ed. Emil Hausknecht, EETS E.S. 38 (1881), ll. 1183–98.

69. Ibid., ll. 2299–318.
70. See further, pp. 379–80 below.
71. See further, p. 179 below.
72. *Partonope*, ed. Bödtker, l. 847.
73. The long version followed here (at over 12,000 lines, one of the longest romances in Middle English) follows the structure of the thirteenth-century French original; there was also an abbreviated version (itself derived from a shorter French text) that explains everything in order, starting with the lady and her education and only then going on to Partonope. Only the opening of the short English text survives; it is printed by Bödtker as an appendix, *Partonope*, pp. 481–8. See also the entry in Severs, *Manual*, i. 149–51.
74. Shakespeare is indeed careful to distinguish them from ghosts or devils: see *Midsummer Night's Dream* 3. 3. 382–9.
75. *Tempest*, 5. 1. 60–1, and cf. also 3. 3. 66–8; *Tragical History of Guy*, Act 2.
76. *Tempest*, 5. 1. 25–8; and see p. 164 above.

CHAPTER 4

1. On the whole question of why Spenser should have chosen a 'fairy' medium for his work, see Matthew Woodcock, *Fairy in the 'Faerie Queene'* (London, 2004).
2. The romance also appears in the list of books owned by Captain Cox, in *Robert Laneham's Letter*. For *Lanval*, see *Marie de France: Lais*, ed. Ewert, pp. 58–74; *Landeval* is edited by George Lyman Kittredge, 'Launfal', in *American Journal of Philology* 10 (1889), 1–33; *Sir Launfal* is widely anthologized, including Sands, pp. 201–32; *Sir Lambewell* appears in the *Percy Folio*, i.142–64. *Landeval* represents the earliest of the Middle English translations, and is the closest to Marie; it is also the immediate source of the Renaissance print (*Sir Lamwell*: see Kittredge's edn., pp. 2–20), and is effectively represented by *Sir Lambewell*. Thomas Chestre adapted *Landeval* for his *Sir Launfal*, an expanded version put into tail-rhyme rather than couplets, and this is the Middle English version most extensively referred to in this chapter.
3. A basic core of prophecies appears in British Library MS Harley 2253, *c*.1340 (f.127r; see the facsimile edn. N. R. Ker, EETS OS 255 (1965), and *The Romance and Prophecies of Thomas of Erceldoune*, ed. James A. H. Murray, EETS O.S. 68 (1875), pp. xviii–xix). No narrative setting is provided, but Thomas is named in the heading. The first reference to the romance comes in the course of a complaint about the corruption of English-language texts in general and romances in particular in the introduction to Robert Mannyng of Brunne's *Chronicle* (completed in 1338), where 'Erceldoun' is attacked between tail-rhyme romances and *Sir Tristrem*, (ed. Idelle Sullens (Binghamton, NY, 1996), l. 94; a reference to 'Thomas' a few lines later is not to Thomas of Erceldoune, but apparently to the Thomas who composed the original Anglo-Norman *Tristan*).
4. All the surviving fifteenth- and sixteenth-century manuscript texts of the romance, plus several of the prophecies-dominated texts, are edited by Murray. The traditional part of the text in the 1652 *Sundry Strange Prophecies of Merlin*,

Bede . . ., printed by Matthew Walbancke, which is a modernization of a form of
the early Thornton text, is included in William P. Albrecht's *The Loathly Lady in
"Thomas of Erceldoune"* (Albuquerque, 1954), pp. 80–94; and also as Appendix IV
in Part 2 of *Thomas of Erceldoune*, ed. Ingeborg Nixon (Copenhagen, 1980–3),
which updates but does not replace Murray's edition.

5. The earliest identifiable text of the ballad, traceable back to 1700 or before, is text
E of Child's *Thomas Rymer* (*Ballads*, no. 37, Additions and Corrections 4.454–5;
main texts i. 317–29); it is also printed by Nixon, *Thomas*, Appendix 1. Murray
prints two of the later texts, pp. liii–v. E. B. Lyle, 'The Relationship between
Thomas the Rhymer and *Thomas of Erceldoune*', *Leeds Studies in English* NS 4
(1970), 23–30, suggests that an early form of the ballad may underlie the
romance.

6. The legend of Melusine was well known in France and on the European mainland
generally, partly through the prose version (begun in 1387) of Jean d'Arras, and
more widely through Coudrette's metrical version (*c.*1403), both of which were
printed and translated into various languages. The prose version survives com-
plete in English in a single manuscript of *c.*1500 (*Melusine* ed. A. K. Donald, EETS
E.S. 68 (1895)), and in printed form only as a fragment printed *c.*1510 by De
Worde. The rhyme royal *Romance of Partenay* (ed. W. W. Skeat, EETS O.S. 22,
(revised edn. (1899)) was less well known in England than the prose; it survives in
a single manuscript, and is not known to have been printed. For Hyrd, see
pp. 37–8 above; for the allusion, 'More mystical than Melusine or any nimph
alive', see Wilfride Holme, *The Fall and Evill Successe of Rebellion* (written 1537,
published 1572), sig. I.ivr.

7. *Huon* itself went through an uncertain number of reprints to 1601, and had been
dramatized by 1593, when Henslowe recorded three performances (*Henslowe's
Diary*, ed. Foakes, p. 20). Greene used Oberon as the presenter of his *James IV* of
*c.*1590. *A Midsummer Night's Dream* is generally dated to 1595; Jonson's *Masque of
Oberon* was performed in 1611.

8. Ovid, *Metamorphoses*, iii. 173; xiv. 382, 438. He also uses it once for Latona, mother
of Apollo and Diana (vi. 346).

9. The confusion of the seasons caused by the quarrel between Titania and Oberon
also picks up on Proserpina's resonances as goddess of the spring and summer
and Diana's as moon goddess (the moon being, as Titania's speech on the subject
notes, the governess of floods): *A Midsummer Night's Dream*, 2.1.88–117.

10. See, for instance, *Melusine*, ed. Donald, p. 5; Spenser, *Teares of the Muses*, 31, and
FQ, VI. x. 7, 17.

11. Arthur Golding's translation, *Ovid's Metamorphoses*, ed. John Frederick Nims
(Harmondsworth, 2000), vii. 265–6, translating Ovid's vii. 197–8; *Tempest*, 5.1.33,
36–8.

12. He also imports the woodland-dwelling satyrs, though they occupy a niche rather
closer to wodewoses, wild men, who seem to have been regarded as 'Other' in that
they were not human, and marvellous in that they were unusual, but not as
supernatural: a modern analogy might be Bigfoot or the yeti.

13. For a summary of Celtic fairy mythology and further bibliography, see Bernhard
Maier, *Dictionary of Celtic Religion and Culture*, trans. Cyril Edwards
(Woodbridge, 1997), s.v. *síd*, *Tuatha Dé Danann*. On the medieval French usage

of fairies, see Laurence Harf-Lancner, *Les Fées au Moyen Age: Morgan et Mélusine* (Paris, 1984); and Kathryn S. Westoby, 'A New Look at the Role of the Fée in Medieval French Arthurian Romance', in *The Spirit of the Court*, ed. Glyn S. Burgess and Robert A. Taylor (Cambridge, 1983), pp. 373–85. The name Oberon itself is connected with the Germanic king of the dwarfs Alberich.

14. See in particular Rachel Bromwich, 'Celtic Dynastic Themes and the Breton Lays', *Etudes Celtiques* 9 (1960–1), 439–74. Sigmund Eisner's claim that the myth underlies Chaucer's *Wife of Bath's Tale* (*A Tale of Wonder* (Wexford, 1957)), has been refuted by J. K. Ballard, 'Sovereignty and the Loathly Lady in English, Welsh and Irish', *Leeds Studies in English* 17 (1986), 41–59.

15. For an outline of beliefs about the origins and nature of fairies, see Minor White Latham, *The Elizabethan Fairies* (New York, 1930), pp. 41–8, and C. S. Lewis, *The Discarded Image* (Cambridge, 1964), pp. 122–38. *Huon of Bordeaux* distinguishes between its fairies, who operate by their own rules but promote virtue, and a further group of supernatural beings consisting of angels who fell as far as the earth because of their sympathy for Lucifer but who still hope for divine forgiveness (ed. Lee, ch. 155 (pp. 592–3)).

16. *Thomas of Erceldoune*, ed. Murray, Lansdowne MS, ll. 143–50.

17. *Richard Cœur de Lion*, ed. Brunner, ll. 188–94, 207–34. The episode is found in only one of the two versions of the romance: see John Finlayson, '*Richard, Cœur de Lyon*: Romance, History, or Something in Between?', *Studies in Philology* 87 (1990), 156–80. See also p. 382 below.

18. For a eucharistic test, see e.g., Marie de France, *Yonec*, ll. 145–90 (*Lais*, ed. Ewert), after the lady's future lover has arrived in her chamber in a locked tower in the form of a bird. Oberon, in *Huon of Bordeaux*, insists 'I am a man as other be', apparently on the basis that his father was human (Julius Caesar, to be precise), despite having full fairy powers including extended life (ch. 23, ed. Lee, pp. 69, 71). Melusine claims at the end that her children are born 'of a mortal woman, and not of a serpent, nor as a creature of the fayry'—though the 'as' seems to make a distinction between her fairy descent from her mother and the human descent from her father, the latter being passed on to her children (*Melusine*, ch. 46, ed. Donald, p. 320).

19. *The Progresses and Public Processions of Queen Elizabeth*, ed. John Nichols, 3 vols. (1823; repr. New York, n.d.), ii. 212–13, reprinting Churchyard's *A Discourse of the Queenes Majestie's Entertainment in Suffolk and Norfolk* (1578).

20. *Thomas of Erceldoune*, ed. Murray, ll. 93, 201–22.

21. *Thomas Rymer*, ed. Child, *Ballads*, i. 325, C stanzas 11–13.

22. *Thomas of Erceldoune*, ed. Murray, ll. 157–60, quoting the sixteenth-century Lansdowne MS; the phrasing is closely similar in all versions. The appearance of the term 'middle-earth' in *Thomas* may be the first usage to distinguish the mortal world from the Otherworld of fairy rather than Heaven and Hell (though Layamon uses 'middel-aerde' in close conjunction with supernatural water-creatures in the *Brut*, l. 10848 (*Laȝamon: Brut*, ed. G. L. Brooke and R. F. Leslie, 2 vols. EETS 250, 277 (1963, 1978))).

23. They are on the northern slopes of the Eildon Hills, south-east of Melrose in the Scottish borders; an inscribed stone marks the spot where Thomas met his lady, grid ref. NT 564 337.

24. *Sir Thopas, CT*, VII. 757; and for the heat of the day, e.g., *Sir Launfal*, ed. Sands, l. 220, and the Renaissance *Sir Lambewell*, Percy i, l. 55 (reading 'underntide' for Bishop Percy's emendation to 'eventide'); *Sir Orfeo*, ed. Sands, ll. 41–2, 51–2, 109–10, 157; and Malory, i. 253, 256 (VI. 1, 3) where Lancelot is cast into a seven-hour enchanted sleep while sleeping under an apple-tree at noon.

25. *Sir Lambewell*, Percy i, ll. 53–4; cf. also *Sir Launfal*, ed. Sands, ll. 280–1 (Her fadir was King of Fairie I Of Occient ['the west'], fere and nyghe).

26. *Melusine*, ed. Donald, p. 27; for her mother's parallel encounter, p. 7.

27. *CT*, III.990; *FQ*, VI. x. 11.

28. *Progresses of Queen Elizabeth*, ed. Nichols, iii. 118. Aureola also brings the queen greetings from the fairy king Auberon.

29. *Huon*, ed. Lee, pp. 63, 75.

30. *Thomas of Erceldoune*, ed. Murray, ll. 217–20 (Lansdowne MS).

31. *Huon*, ed. Lee, pp. 596, 605; *FQ*, I. x. 55–6.

32. *Sir Orfeo*, ed. Sands, ll. 349–52.

33. *Huon*, ed. Lee, p. 71.

34. *Richard*, ed. Brunner, ll. 76, 60–72.

35. It is not, however, found in the only complete surviving pre-Reformation version of texts of this group, *Landeval*.

36. *Sir Lambewell*, Percy i, l. 534; cf. 'She might me of my balis bete, I Yef that lady wolde', *Sir Launfal*, ed. Sands, ll. 971–2.

37. See the 1603 'Prophecie of Thomas Rymour', in *Thomas of Erceldoune*, ed. by Murray, p. 48, ll. 31–45, 73–4, and the early sixteenth-century *Prophisies of Rymour*, ibid., pp. 52–3, ll. 19–38. Texts that contain the affair between Thomas and the elf-queen limit the likeness to a mis-identification, for obvious reasons (*Thomas of Erceldoune*, ll. 85–92; *Thomas Rymer*, ed. Child, *Ballads*, i. 323–5, stanzas 3–4 of all versions).

38. See Helen Hackett, *Virgin Mother, Maiden Queen: Elizabeth I and the Cult of the Virgin Mary*, rev. edn., Basingstoke, 1996) on the whole phenomenon, and pp. 142–3 for a discussion of the closest Spenser comes in the *Faerie Queene* to inviting adoration of her (II. ii. 41)—though as 'th'Idole of her makers great magnificence', not as the Virgin.

39. *Ulrich von Zatzikhoven: Lanzelet*, ed. Wolfgang Spiewok (Greifswald, 1997), l. 180; there is a translation by Kenneth G. T. Webster, *Ulrich von Zatzikhoven: Lanzelet*, rev. Roger Sherman Loomis (New York, 1951), though Loomis's notes drastically overstate the Celticism of the text. That it had an Anglo-Norman original is shown by some details of names and vocabulary, as well as by Ulrich's claim that his source copy had been taken to Austria by the English knight Hugh de Morville when he was acting as hostage for Richard the Lionheart (ll. 9323–41; this may or may not have been the same man who was involved in the murder of Thomas Becket, see Loomis's introduction, p. 5). Ulrich's version probably dates from c.1210–20 (ed. Spiewok, p. xv).

40. *Lancelot*, ed. Micha, vii: via; trans. *Lancelot-Grail*, ed. Lacy, ii. 11 (quoted), 12.

41. Malory, i. 52, 125 (I.25, IV.1). In the glosses to Spenser's *Shepheardes Calender*, E. K. identifies 'Ladyes of the lake' as nymphs, as if classical demi-gods were more intellectually acceptable than water-fairies (gloss to *Aprill* 120).

42. *Life of Merlin*, ed. Clarke, ll. 908–40; and see also Clarke's entry on Morgen, pp. 203–6. Morgen is not herself in the boat that fetches Arthur in this account.

43. Etienne de Rouen, *Draco Normannicus*, ii. 1161–3, in *Chronicles of the Reigns of Stephen, Henry II and Richard I*, Vol. 2, ed. Richard Howlett, Rolls Series (London, 1885), pp. 585–762.

44. Layamon was apparently working from the *Life* for this scene, since she is not mentioned in Geoffrey's *History of the Kings of Britain* or in Wace's Anglo-Norman version, and he gives no hint of any kinship to Arthur.

45. 'And ich wulle varen to Avalun, to vairest alre maidene, I to Argante there quene, alven swithe sceone; I and heo scal mine wunden makien alle isunde' (ed. Brooke and Leslie, Caligula MS, 14277–9; and 14290–1, quoted). There is a parallel translation in *Laȝamon's Arthur*, ed. and trans. W. R. J. Barron and S. C. Weinberg (Harlow, 1989).

46. Quoted by Louis Adrian Montrose, ' "Shaping Fantasies": Figurations of Gender and Power in Elizabethan Culture', *Representations* 1 (1983), 61–94 (p. 83).

47. *Arthur of Little Britain*, trans. by John Bourchier, Lord Berners, ed. E. V. Utterson (London, 1814), pp. 297–300; it is one of the romances most frequently noted as still being read in Elizabeth's reign. Proserpyne also acts as patroness to Arthur, giving him a shield and sword. Spenser may have known it, but the parallels cited by e.g., Sarah Michie, '*The Faerie Queene* and *Arthur of Little Britain*', *Studies in Philology* 36 (1939), 105–23, overstate the case for her being the original of Gloriana.

48. By I. M., perhaps Gervase Markham; it gets a first mention in the *Stationers' Registers* in February 1595–6, but the first surviving edition is from 1612 (*STC* 17844). Morgue is a benevolent fairy, sister of Artus, and mother of Mervine. The fairies here are very much under the control of God

49. *Sir Gawain and the Green Knight*, ed. Tolkien and Gordon, l. 2452; see their note to the line for other uses of the title in Gerald of Wales and one manuscript of the Prose *Lancelot*, and Micha's edition of *Lancelot*, i. xxii (p. 305). The idea that she is derived from the Celtic goddess Morrigan, although still popular among those interested in the occult, has been discredited by modern scholarship: see, for instance, Rachel Bromwich's conclusion in her 'Note on Modron and Morgain la Fée', that Morgan's association with the *Morrígan* 'can be dismissed as too remote to be credible' (Bromwich, (ed.), *Troiedd Ynys Prydein: The Welsh Triads* (Cardiff, 1978), p. 461).

50. Avalon in all these texts is a much more mysterious place than Glastonbury, with which it is elsewhere identified; as in its reappearance in *Melusine*, it is not somewhere within the normal geographical world (see p. 210 below). Malory does not at first commit himself that it is Arthur who is buried in the Glastonbury tomb, but Lancelot sees his corpse when he opens it to inter Guinevere beside him.

51. The earlier couplet version is edited as *A Royall Historie of the Excellent Knight Generides*, ed. Frederick J. Furnivall (Roxburghe Club, 1866; repr. New York, 1971), and the rhyme-royal *Generydes* (the form in which it was printed) by W. Aldis Wright, EETS O.S. 55, 70 (1878). The work is coupled with *Partonope* by Richard Hyrd in his list of the most popular English romances (pp. 37–8 above), and it was still of sufficient interest in 1568–9 for its licence for printing to be transferred.

52. 'The Prophecie of Thomas Rymour' in *The Whole Prophesie of Scotland* (1603), in *Thomas of Erceldoune*, ed. Murray, p. 48, l. 8.

53. Bullough, *Narrative and Dramatic Sources*, vii. 494–5, quoting *The Chronicle of Scotland*. William Warner, in the Scottish additions incorporated into the 1606 edn. of his metrical history of England, identifies them first simply as 'fairies', then as 'Weird-Elfes' (*Albions England (1612)*, facsimile (Hildesheim and New York, 1971), pp. 376–7).

54. For instance, in *Kyng Alisaunder*, ed. G. V. Smithers, EETS O.S. 227 (1952), l. L 5708 (B 6975), though in a context which claims the prophecy to be specious.

55. 'I am of god, and my byleve is as a Catholique byleve oughte to be . . . Make you no doubte of me but that I am of god,' *Melusine*, ed. Donald, ch. 6, pp. 31–2.

56. *Melusine*, ed. Donald, pp. 30–3, 38–9, 299, 317–18; and see pp. 383–4 below. Depictions show her looking like a mermaid: see, for instance, the illustrations on pp. 159 and 170 in *Melusine of Lusignan: Founding Fiction in Late Medieval France*, ed. Donald Maddox and Sarah Sturm-Maddox (Athens, Ga., and London, 1996).

57. *Huon*, ed. Lee, p. 73.

58. *The Whore of Babylon*, 'Lectori' and IV. iii. 69, in *Thomas Dekker: Dramatic Works*, ed. Fredson Bowers, 3 vols. (Cambridge, 1953–8), ii. 491–584. The work was licensed in 1607, but was performed before its licensing, and may have been written some years earlier (pp. 493–4).

59. *The Tragedy of King Lear*, 3. 2. 95–6, 81–90.

60. It appears in numerous manuscripts, some of them Chaucerian, and in all the printed editions of Chaucer to 1598; quoted from the preface of Thynne's 1532 edn.

61. Trans. from *Thomas of Erceldoune*, ed. Murray, pp. xviii–xix (from BL Harley MS 2253).

62. Ariosto, *Orlando Furioso*, ed. Caretti, iii. 9–20; *FQ*, III. iii. 25–49.

63. See, for instance, R. R. Davies, *The Revolt of Owain Glyn Dŵr* (Oxford, 1995), pp. 90, 335–6.

64. The Tudor print covers the first part of *Of Arthour and of Merlin* (ed. by O. D. Macrae-Gibson, EETS 268, 279 (1973, 1979)). Fragments of two sixteenth-century printed editions survive, enough to show that their text closes before the birth of Arthur. The prints were probably the basis for the text in the Percy Folio (i. 422–96). The story was attractive enough in the early seventeenth century to earn a very free dramatization, *The Birth of Merlin* (conjecturally *c*.1608, but first published in 1662 with an attribution to Shakespeare and Rowley; ed. C. F. Tucker Brooke in *The Shakespeare Apocrypha* (Oxford, 1908)).

65. See the chapter on 'Ancient Prophecies' in Keith Thomas, *Religion and the Decline of Magic* (1971; Harmondsworth, 1973), pp. 461–514, esp. pp. 470–3; and Howard Dobin, *Merlin's Disciples* (Stanford, 1990).

66. See Sharon L. Jansen, *Political Protest and Prophecy under Henry VIII* (Woodbridge, 1991), esp. pp. 63–90, where she also gives a good edition of the text, and pp. 157–60 for the manuscript dates. The text has some overlap with *Thomas of Erceldoune* (see below for its unusual iconography of a horseback Blessed Virgin) but is essentially a new work. Its *terminus post quem* of 1513 is set by the accurate 'prediction' of the battle of Flodden; the text also cites 1531 as the date when various of its other prophecies will be fulfilled (ll. 608–15), but nothing particular turned out to happen that year. The 'Marlin' form of Merlin's name is also found in both Malory and the print of *The byrth and prophecye of Marlyn*. For the singing of 'a song of Thomas Ersholedon and the quene of ffeiree' that included prophecies of the battles of Stoke and Flodden in a gentry house in Cheshire in

1520, see Lesley Coote and Tim Thornton, 'Merlin, Erceldoune, Nixon: A Tradition of Popular Political Prophecy', *New Medieval Literatures* 4 (2001), 117–37 (p. 124).

67. *Prophisies of Rymour*, ed. Murray, l. 111; the phrase is effectively a memetic formula for civil war (see further pp. 385–6 below).

68. Jansen, *Political Protest*, pp. 1–4, 57–61; Thomas, *Religion and the Decline of Magic*, p. 475–8.

69. Ibid., pp. 482–3.

70. Neither Albrecht nor Nixon print this part of the text, which continues on the next leaf from where the received text ends: see n. 4 above, and, for further discussion, pp. 385–6 below.

71. *FQ*, I. i. 1–2. The description of St George in the 1603 'Prophecie of Thomas Rymour' is not quite so close in phrasing to Spenser as the earlier manuscripts, but the description of him and St Andrew notes that 'two croces on there brestes they bare' (ed. Murray, p. 48, l. 16; cf. 'on his brest a bloudie Crosse he bore', *FQ*, I. i. 2). His shield by contrast portrays his emblem of a dragon, the ultimate enemy overcome by the saint according to both his legend and Spenser.

72. Malory, i. 244 (V. 12); *The Chronicle of Iohn Harding*, ed. Ellis, ch. 82, p. 145.

73. Without knowing of these prophecies, A. Kent Hieatt argues for such a plan on Spenser's part in a second set of books of the *Faerie Queene* on the political virtues: see 'The Passing of Arthur in Malory, Spenser and Shakespeare: The Avoidance of Closure', in *The Passing of Arthur: New Essays in Arthurian Tradition*, ed. Christopher Baswell and William Sharpe (New York and London, 1988), pp. 173–92.

74. So noted in the entry for *STC* 17841.7.

75. 'The Prophecie of Thomas Rymour', ll. 235–48, in *Thomas of Erceldoune*, ed. Murray, p. 51. The four lines beginning 'A French wife . . .' had already appeared in another Thomas-related prophecy (p. xxxvi).

76. It could apply to a putative son of James V and Mary of Guise (their only child was in fact a daughter, Mary Queen of Scots). Murray notes an eighteenth-century suggestion that it refers to John duke of Albany, a cousin of James IV (p. xxxiv), but he was only of the eighth generation.

77. John Colville, in his *Oratio funebris exequiis Elizabethae* (Paris, 1604), where he gives a Latin translation of Rymer's lines: see *Original Letters of Mr John Colville 1582–1603*, ed. David Laing (Edinburgh, 1858), pp. xxxvi–xxxvii; and John Spottiswood, *The History of the Church of Scotland 1655* (facsimile, Menston, 1972), p. 47, under the year 1279 (Thomas's approximate date).

78. *The Magnificent Entertainment given to King James*, ll. 31–8, in *Dekker: Works*, ed. Bowers, Vol. 2; Dekker wrote up the whole series, and probably designed this opening 'device', though it was not in the event performed.

79. Malory, ii. 1059 (XVIII.8); she is identified as Nenive, not therefore as the Lady of the Lake who gave Excalibur to Arthur, though Malory does not always keep the differences exact.

80. *Huon*, ed. Lee, p. 72.

81. Ibid., pp. 76–8, 111, 155–60.

82. *The Famous Historie of Chinon of England by Christopher Middleton*, ed. William Edward Mead, EETS O.S. 165 (1925), pp. 27–30. Oberon is here named as 'Oberam'.

83. *Lanval, Marie de France: Lais*, ed. Ewert, ll. 21–2; *Sir Launfal*, ed. Sands, ll. 28–36; *Sir Lambewell, Percy*, i. 144–5, ll. 17, 21.
84. *CT*, IV. 2227, 2220–1, 2035–41.
85. See *Sources and Analogues of Chaucer's Canterbury Tales*, ed. Bryan and Dempster, pp. 341–50.
86. Genesis 3:16; and on Oberon, see, for instance, E. Talbot Donaldson's discussion in *The Swan at the Well: Shakespeare reading Chaucer* (New Haven and London, 1985), pp. 44–8.
87. Malory, i. 172 (IV. 23 [24 in some editions]).
88. For white fairy horses, see e.g. *Tydorel*, in *Les Lais anonymes des XIIe et XIIIe siècles*, ed. Prudence Mary O'Hara Tobin (Geneva, 1976), pp. 207–26, and the horses that can outstrip any other in *Le Lai de l'Espine* (ibid., pp. 255–88) and in *Pwyll Lord of Dyved* in the *Mabinogion* (trans. Jeffrey Gantz (Harmondsworth, 1976), p. 52). Bells on the bridle are also a common attribute, e.g., on the dapple-grey horse ridden by Thomas's lady.
89. *Amadas et Ydoine*, ed. Reinhard, ll. 5584–622 (trans. Arthur, pp. 100–115).
90. See the Percy Folio *The Turke and Gawain* and *The Carle of Carlisle* (*Percy*, i. 88–102, iii. 275–94; *Sir Gawain: Eleven Romances*, ed. Hahn, pp. 337–91). The Green Knight of *The Grene Knight* is not very enchanted in the first place, and just changes his clothes before his final encounter with Gawain (ll. 442–4, *Percy*, ii. 74; or ll. 441–3, ed. Hahn, p. 326).
91. See Maier, *Dictionary of Celtic Religion*, s.v. *geis*, for definitions, summary history, and bibliography.
92. The hag is a mortal woman under a spell in Gower's 'Tale of Florent' in the *Confessio amantis* (*The English Works of John Gower*, ed. G. C. Macaulay, EETS E.S. 81–2 (1900–1), i. 1407–1861), the fifteenth-century *The Wedding of Sir Gawain and Dame Ragnell*, and the Percy Folio *Marriage of Sir Gawain* (the latter two are edited by Hahn in *Sir Gawain: Eleven Romances*).
93. *Melusine*, ed. Donald, pp. 110–13. She gives further advice to her next two sons when it is their turn to leave home.
94. *Lancelot*, ed. by Micha, vii. xxia (trans. in *Lancelot-Grail*, ed. Lacy, ii. 59–60). Partonope's Melior, while she is still in fairy mode, gives him similar but briefer instruction: *Partonope*, ed. Bödtker, ll. 1852–65, 2404–22—both passages ending with the injunction in which he fails, not to attempt to see her.
95. *FQ*, VI. x. 27; Sidney, *Apology for Poetry*, in *Elizabethan Critical Essays*, ed. Smith, i. 157.
96. *Robert Langham: A Letter*, ed. Kuin, pp. 40–1. The text of the Lady of the Lake's speech is given in Gascoigne's more official version of events, *The Princely Pleasures at Kenelworth Castle* (*The Complete Works of George Gascoigne*, ed. John W. Cunliffe, 2 vols. (1907; repr. New York, 1969), ii. 93–4 (or, see Nichols, *Progresses*, i. 431, 491–2)). Elizabeth had given Kenilworth to Leicester only in 1563. For a recent discussion, see Davis, *Chivalry and Romance*, pp. 73–97.
97. Malory, i. 52–3, iii. 1240 (I.25, XXI.5).
98. Etienne, *Draco*, ii. 1165–1208, ed. Howlett, *Chronicles*.
99. *Huon*, ed. Lee, pp. 599–603.
100. *The Alchemist* (1610), in which Dol Common acts Dapper's 'aunt of Faerie' (*Ben Jonson*, ed. Herford and Simpson, Vol. V, I. ii. 149). For a comparable fraud regarding the fairy king, see *The Fary Knight; or, Oberon the Second*, attrib. to

Thomas Randolph (?1622–4) (ed. (from manuscript) Fredson Thayer Bowers (Chapel Hill, 1942)). One of the more extensive series of real-life frauds was recorded in *The severall notorious and lewd Cousenages of John West and Alice West, falsely called the King and Queene of Fayries* (1613), repr. in *Fairy Tales, Legends and Romances illustrating Shakespeare and other early English Writers*, ed. W. C. Hazlitt (London, 1875), pp. 223–38; Alice West would claim that the fairies, most often the fairy queen, were particularly desirous of giving treasure to a selected individual, but up-front payment was required for a banquet or other preparations for the bestowing of the gift. Only one of their frauds involved a claim of sexual attraction, when Alice's companion made an apprentice 'beleeve the queene of fayries did most ardently doat upon him' (p. 237).

101. Dekker, *Whore*, ed. Bowers, II. i. 236–42.
102. See Donald Maddox, *Fictions of Identity in Medieval France* (Cambridge, 2001), pp. 178–85.
103. *Melusine*, ed. Donald, p. 12.
104. Ibid., p. 368; and see p. 384 below. The story also appears in *Mandeville's Travels*, ed. Hamelius, pp. 97–8, though without the Melusine connection.
105. *Lanval*, in *Marie de France: Lais*, ed. Ewart, ll. 71–4: 'Sire Lanval, ma dameisele, | Que tant est pruz e sage e bele, | Ele nus enveie pur vus; | Kar i venez ensemble od nus!'
106. *Sir Lambewell*, ll. 83–6 (*Percy* i).
107. *FQ*, I. xii. 41, *Mutabilitie Cantos*, viii.1–2.
108. *Graelent*, l. 317, in *Les Lais anonymes*, ed. Tobin, pp. 83–125. The poem was written on the continent but was circulated within the ambit of Anglo-Norman (p. 89). Its story is very close to that of *Lanval / Launfal*.
109. *Thomas of Erceldoune*, ed. Murray, Thornton text ll. 129–36.
110. Dame Tryamour's father is 'King of Fairie' and Thomas's fairy mistress has a 'lord', but neither figure has any role in the narrative, or seems to have any influence or control over his daughter or lady (*Sir Launfal*, ed. Sands, l. 280; *Thomas of Erceldoune*, ed. Murray, l. 229, though she expresses alarm at the thought that he might discover their affair). Richard Cœur de Lion's mother is unusual in that she is given in marriage to King Henry by her own father, but, despite his fairy coding, he identifies himself as king of Antioch.
111. A possible exception would be the prohibition laid on Thomas of Erceldoune by his elf-queen that once he is in his own country he is to speak to no one but her, which seems intended to prevent her husband's discovering their relationship through any careless talk; she will say that she took away his power of speech before bringing him to the Otherworld (*Thomas of Erceldoune*, ed. Murray, ll. 223–32).
112. See the note to 2. 1. 158–64 in Peter Holland's edn. of the play (Oxford, 1994).
113. See Helen Cooper, *Pastoral: Mediaeval into Renaissance* (Ipswich, 1977), pp. 196–210.
114. Montrose describes the play as both 'personally and politically inimical' to Elizabeth (' "Shaping Fantasies" ', p. 82).

CHAPTER 5

1. Germaine Greer, *Shakespeare* (Oxford and New York, 1986), p. 109.
2. Michel Foucault, *The History of Sexuality*, trans. Robert Hurley (Harmondsworth, 1981), i. 78.
3. See Archibald, *Apollonius of Tyre*, for its history. The name Thaisa (Thaise) first appears in Gower's version of the story, but it is used for Apollonius/Pericles' daughter (who is normally named Tarsia); his wife remains anonymous in most early versions.
4. This is the manuscript poem 'The Question Answer'd', in *Poetry and Prose of William Blake*, ed. Geoffrey Keynes (London, 1932), p. 100.
5. *Legend of Good Women*, l. 544, describing Queen Alceste, who gave her life for her husband's.
6. See for instance, Bullough, *Narrative and Dramatic Sources*, vi. 394 (Gower, *Confessio amantis* Book viii. 980–1), 444 (Twine); *Pericles*, 10. 9–11 (chorus to 3.1 in editions with act divisions). The wedding-night conception is part of the plot of *Guy*, so likewise figures in both the medieval and the printed versions: see, for instance, Schleich's edn. of the print, l. 6073–5.
7. John Gillingham, 'Love, Marriage and Politics in the Twelfth Century', reprinted in his *Richard Cœur de Lion: Kingship, Chivalry and War in the Twelfth Century* (London and Rio Grande, 1994), pp. 243–55; Sir Frederick Pollock and F. W. Maitland, *The History of English Law before the Time of Edward I*, 2nd edn., (Cambridge, 1911), ii. 260–313, 414–21; F. M. Powicke, *Henry III and the Lord Edward* (Oxford, 1947), ii. 788–90. Stricter practices of primogeniture meant that political power was less likely to be diverted away from an heiress towards a cadet male line (e.g., of her father's younger brothers). Complications arose where there were two daughters, and those too are recognized in some romances, including Chrétien's *Yvain*. See further Knight, *Arthurian Literature*, pp. 47–51, 58–9, 68–104.
8. See R. Howard Bloch, *Etymologies and Genealogies: A Literary Anthropology of the French Middle Ages* (Chicago, 1983), pp. 73, 78–9.
9. R. Howard Bloch, *Medieval Misogyny and the Invention of Western Romantic Love* (Chicago and London, 1991), pp. 186–96; and Joan M. Ferrante, *Woman as Image in Medieval Literature* (New York and London, 1975), pp. 11–13, who notes a concomitant decline in positive images of women in the thirteenth century.
10. See Judith Weiss, 'The Wooing Woman in Anglo-Norman Romance'; and Rosalind Field, 'Romance as History, History as Romance', both in *Romance in Medieval England*, ed. Maldwyn Mills, Carol Meale and Jennifer Fellows (Cambridge, 1991), pp. 149–61, 163–73. The actual amount of intermarriage between Normans and aristocratic Englishwomen was low: see Michael Wood, *In Search of England* (London, 1999), p. 15.
11. Twenty Norman baronies descended in the female line before 1130 (Jane Martindale, 'Succession and Politics in the Romance-Speaking World c.1000–1140', in *England and her Neighbours 1066–1453*, ed. Michael Jones and Malcolm Vale (London, 1989), pp. 19–41); twenty-one peerages continued through marriage to an heiress between 1439 and 1504 (J. M. Lander, *Conflict and Stability in Fifteenth-century England* (London, 1977), p. 170).

12. William Brenchley Rye, *England as Seen by Foreigners in the Days of Elizabeth and James I* (London, 1865), pp. 90, 260–2.
13. See Gillingham, 'Love, Marriage', for examples.
14. See p. 145 above, and the accompanying note as to the provenance of the romance. A comparable example of a woman's fixing male arrangements for her choice of husband in accord with her own wishes occurs in *Ipomadon*, where the Fere promises her barons to follow her uncle's advice in her choice of husband, but agrees with him a scheme for a tournament which she trusts Ipomadon will win.
15. See p. 455 n. 12 above.
16. Colin Richmond, *The Paston Family in the Fifteenth Century: The First Phase* (Cambridge, 1990), pp. 47–63.
17. *Sir Isumbras*, ll. 745–50, ed. Mills, *Six Romances*; Peter Day, *Dictionary of Religious Orders* (London, 2001), s.v. Hatchet.
18. See pp. 201–3 above. The lovers are cited in the early thirteenth-century 'Luve Ron' of Thomas of Hales (in *English Lyrics of the XIIIth Century*, ed. Carleton Brown (Oxford, 1932), no. 43, ll. 65–72, where they figure alongside Paris, Helen, Tristram, and Isolde as *ubi sunt* examples), and in texts across the fourteenth century from *Cursor mundi* through *Emaré*, *Sir Degrevant*, and *The Parliament of the Three Ages* to Gower's *Confessio amantis*. They are embroidered on the first corner of Emaré's marvellous cloth, as exemplifying 'love that was so trewe', the other corners depicting Tristram and Isolde, Floris and Blancheflower, and the emir's daughter who embroidered it and the sultan's son whom she loves (*Emaré*, 121–68, ed. Mills, *Six Romances*).
19. Ann Rosalind Jones, 'Mills and Boon meets Feminism', in *The Progress of Romance*, ed. Radford, pp. 194–218 (esp. 198–9, 204).
20. From Caxton's heading to his translation, *Caxton's Blanchardyn and Englantine, c.1489*, ed. Leon Kellner, EETS E.S. 58 (1890), p. 3.
21. Mary Carruthers, 'Afterword' to 'The Wife of Bath and the Painting of Lions', in *Feminist Readings in Middle English Literature: The Wife of Bath and all her Sect*, ed. Ruth Evans and Lesley Johnson (London and New York, 1994), pp. 39–44 (42). For the feminist argument for the composition, circulation, and meaning of such texts as solely homosocial constructions, see Sheila Fisher and Janet E. Halley: 'For a male author to write women in these periods was to refer not to women, but to men—to desire nor relationship with women, but relationship to the traditions of male textual activity, and, by extension, of male social and political privilege' (Introduction ('The Lady Vanishes') to their collection *Seeking the Woman in Late Medieval and Renaissance Writings: Essays in Feminist Contextual Criticism* (Knoxville, 1989), p. 4).
22. The Wife herself may want dominance, but her *Tale* offers a model in which marital bliss follows on the husband's recognition of, and trust in, his wife's ability to make her own choices. Several other tales, including the *Franklin's Tale* and *Melibee*, make a comparable point. *Melibee* shows a wife creating such a role for herself within the larger role of obedience to her husband; the declaration about love's freedom in the *Franklin's Tale* is taken up as a key text by Spenser (on which see p. 253 below).
23. *Le Roman de Silence*, ed. Lewis Thorpe (Cambridge, 1972), l. 2497–656 (l. 261 quoted; for a translation, see the parallel-text edition by Sarah Roche-Mahdi,

Silence (East Lansing, 1992)). 'Cornüalle' could alternatively designate an area of Brittany or a small French town in Maine-et-Loire, but the only connection offered by the text itself is with the British Cornwall (l. 2697). Heldris shows no close knowledge of the area, however, and he was not apparently a denizen of Cornwall: the dialect of the poem is northern French rather than Anglo-Norman (see Thorpe's Introduction to his edition, pp. 15–16).

24. Gayle Rubin, 'The Traffic in Women: Notes on the "Political Economy" of Sex', in Rayna R. Reiter (ed.), *Towards an Anthropology of Women* (New York and London, 1975), pp. 157–210.

25. Chaucer, *Troilus*, IV. 182.

26. *House of Fame*, 256–95; Legend of Dido in *Legend of Good Women*.

27. *King Horn*, ed. Sands, ll. 281–96, 341–50.

28. *Roswall*, ed. Lengert, ll. 373–6.

29. So Troilus's eyesight goes 'depe' as it lands on Criseyde, and her look in turn fastens a 'fixe and depe impressioun' in 'his hertes botme' (*Troilus*, I. 272, 295–8). It was believed that sight involved beams or rays travelling out from the eye, and back from that object through the observer's eye to his heart. The 'impression' made by sight on the heart was therefore literal. The physicality of these rays gives rise to such images as Donne's lovers' eyebeams being 'twisted ... upon one double string' as they gaze into each other's eyes ('The Ecstasy' 7–8, in *John Donne: Poems*, ed. Smith, p. 53). For a full account of the physiological and optical theories underlying sight and falling in love in the Middle Ages, see Norman Klassen, *Chaucer on Love, Knowledge and Sight* (Cambridge, 1995).

30. Chaucer, *Troilus*, I. 267–308, 400–20 (quotations from 416–20), translating Petrarch's Sonnet 132.

31. This correlates with the lady's inaccessibility, taken to have its origins in the poetry addressed by the Provençal troubadours to a feudal *donna*; but it proved much too useful as a literary device to abandon.

32. *Eneas*, ed. J. J. Salverda de Grave (Paris, 1925, 1929), ll. 8057–61 (p. 215 in the translation by John A. Yunck, *Eneas* (New York and London, 1974)).

33. *Eilhart von Oberge: Tristrant und Isalde*, ed. and trans. Danielle Buschinger and Wolfgang Spiewok (Greifswald, 1993), 2508–719; *Eilhart von Oberge's Tristrant*, trans. by J. W. Thomas (Lincoln, Nebr., and London, 1978), pp. 75–7.

34. Ed. and trans. by Ian Short in *Early French Tristan Poems*, ed. Lacy, ii. 176–83, esp. ll. 30–71. The soliloquy is cut in both the Norse and Middle English versions of Thomas.

35. *Gottfried: Tristan*, ed. Weber: the whole passage runs from ll. 11707 to 12043. See, in particular, 11968–12012 (the punning on 'lameir'); 11707, 11787–8, 11817–18 quoted. For a translation, see *Gottfried von Strassburg: Tristan*, trans. A. T. Hatto (Harmondsworth, 1960), pp. 195–6.

36. ll. 4240–48 in Ulrich's version; she also addresses a soliloquy to love, 'minne', 4372–406. On the Anglo-Norman origin of the romance, see p. 468 n. 39 above.

37. For the date, see the introduction to *Guillaume de Palerne*, ed. Alexandre Micha (Geneva, 1990). Wooing women were starting to become less frequent in French by this date; but the poem had a female dedicatee, the countess Yolande, daughter of count Baudouin IV of Hainault, and the author may therefore have opted for a representation that was moving out of fashion in his own culture.

38. In his list of additional titles of reprehended works in his translation of Vives, see pp. 37–8 above. The prose version of *William* was printed around 1515. Bunt prints the surviving fragment in his edition of the poem, *William of Palerne*, pp. 328–31.

39. Ed. Bunt, ll. 451–7. A leaf containing the opening of the soliloquy is missing from the single manuscript, but it still runs for 140 long alliterative lines (433–570)—longer, therefore, than the 140 shorter lines of the original French (ed. *Guillaume*, Micha, ll. 829–969).

40. The editor of Hue's text, A. J. Holden, goes so far as to call it 'une composition comique' on the grounds of its bawdiness, satire and effrontery (*Ipomedon*, pp. 53–4); but those elements are almost entirely confined to the narratorial frame, and affect the story only indirectly. Susan Crane offers a more nuanced reading, in which she recognizes the balance of the work between the sophisticated reassessment of romance ideals and the ironic narrative voice, which she compares to Jean de Meun (*Insular Romance*, pp. 160–5, 171).

41. The classic analysis of the male gaze in film is Laura Mulvey's 'Visual Pleasure and Narrative Cinema', reprinted in her *Visual and Other Pleasures* (Basingstoke, 1989), pp. 14–26. Her comments on the male gaze in the cinema (by characters, camera, and audience), that they make the woman 'an object of sexual stimulation through sight', is precisely inverted in the romances; and they call into question too her statement that 'the male figure cannot bear the burden of sexual objectification' (pp. 18, 19).

42. See ll. 4694–5 and 5287–8 of the tail-rhyme version, *Ipomadon*, ed. Rhiannon Purdie, EETS OS 316 (2001); for a full list of examples, see Bartlett Jere Whiting, *Proverbs, Sentences and Proverbial Phrases from English Writings mainly before 1500* (Cambridge, Mass.: Harvard University Press, 1968), W275.

43. See William Calin, 'The Exaltation and Undermining of Romance: *Ipomadon*', in *The Legacy of Chrétien de Troyes*, ed. Lacy, Kelly, and Busby, ii. 111–24, esp. p. 121.

44. E. D. Blodgett, for instance, claims that in courtly romance, the lover 'is the subject of a language that generates the figure of the Lady, who is continually redesigned as the speaker's apostrophe' (Introduction, *The Romance of Flamenca*, (New York and London, 1995), p. xxiv). There are areas of romance where this holds good (one could indeed define 'courtly' romances as those where it does), but it is more generally true of medieval lyric and of the whole Petrarchan tradition than of the whole corpus of romance.

45. *Huon*, ed. Lee, p. 628 (cap. clxi).

46. *Eliduc*, ll. 300–5 (and see the whole context, 273–538), in *Marie de France: Lais*, ed. Ewert; cf. also 327–8, 'La pucele ki l'ot veü I Vodra de lui fere son dru', 'when she saw him, the maiden wished to make him her lover'. 'Curage', translated as 'heart', was adopted into Middle English with a strong sexual association (cf. the twitterpated birds in the General Prologue to the *Canterbury Tales*, I. 11, and Criseyde's being 'slydynge of corage', *Troilus* V. 825). *Eliduc* is exceptional among romances in that the man is already married: it is the husband, not the wife, who falls in love with someone else, in a kind of *Dr Zhivago* scenario where all three parties carry the author's and readers' sympathy. Marie resolves it by having the wife become a nun in an act of emotional magnanimity, to allow her husband and his new beloved to marry. Such an ending may reflect the less rigid attitude to divorce obtaining before the twelfth century.

47. *Hadewijch: The Complete Works*, trans. Mother Columba Hart OSB (London, 1980), Vision 7 (p. 281). See also letter 9, on how the Beloved and his earthly lover will 'penetrate each other in a way that neither of the two distinguishes himself from the other. But they abide in one another in fruition, mouth in mouth, heart in heart, body in body, and soul in soul, while one sweet divine nature flows through both and they are both one thing through each other, but at the same time remain two different selves—yes, and remain so forever' (p. 66). Michael Camille notes that the only male body fully open to the female gaze is that of Christ, *The Medieval Art of Love: Objects and Subjects of Desire* (London, 1998), pp. 35–6.

48. *The Book of Margery Kempe*, ed. Barry Windeatt (Harlow, 2000), chs. 35–6 (ll. 2951–2 quoted). Margery's readiness to put words into Christ's mouth might be regarded as a reversal of the ventriloquism of male authors in regard to their female characters, though it is, of course, a characteristic of mystical writings generally.

49. 'Li oel d'esgarder se refont, | cil qui d'amor joie refont | et le message au cuer anvoient, | mes molt lor plest quanque il voient' ('the eyes, which are the well-spring of the joy of love and send its message to the heart, renewed themselves with looking, for everything they saw pleased them greatly'): *Chrétien: Erec et Enide*, ed. Roques, ll. 2037–40.

50. Malory, ii. 332 (VII. 21).

51. *Jehan et Blonde de Philippe de Rémi*, ed. Sylvie Lécuyer (Paris, 1984), ll. 4740–831. Compare also Hue's rather startling description of the wedding night of Ipomedon and La Fière: 'Chescun de cez ad ben gardé | A autre sa virginité, | Or se entreaiment tan par amur | Ke il se entrefoutent tute jur' (each had so well kept their virginity for the other that now they loved each other with such desire that they fucked each other all day long) (ed. Holden, ll. 10513–16).

52. Malory, ii. 645 (X. 38–9).

53. Malory, ii. 803 (XI. 7).

54. 'And yf ye were nat, I myght have getyn the love of my lorde sir Launcelot' (Malory, ii. 806 (XI. 9)).

55. Malory, ii. 1091 (XVIII. 19).

56. Malory, ii. 1093 (XVIII. 19)

57. See in particular Hugh White, *Nature, Sex, and Goodness in a Medieval Literary Tradition* (Oxford, 2000), ch. 3: *Natura Vicaria Dei*, pp. 68–109; and for the quotation, Chaucer, *Parliament of Fowls*, 379. A personified Nature first enters vernacular poetry in the *Roman d'Eneas*: see Yunck's note to his translation, *Eneas*, p. 133, to l. 3915 (ed. Salverda de Grave).

58. H. A. Kelly has argued that private vows such as they have exchanged constituted a valid marriage in medieval canon law (*Love and Marriage in the Age of Chaucer* (Ithaca, 1975), pp. 59–67); but they never appear to regard themselves as married, or speak of themselves in those terms. Despite the 'woodbine' simile, and in keeping with the Petrarchan shaping of Troilus, most of the description of their love-making (the most erotic poetry yet written in English) is focalized through him: see in particular ll. 1247–53, and the abundance of speech given to him compared to Criseyde's brief interjections.

59. Larry D. Benson, 'The Occasion of *The Parliament of Fowls*', in *The Wisdom of Poetry*, ed. L. D. Benson and Siegfried Wenzel (Kalamazoo, 1982), pp. 123–44. There is no confirming evidence from within the text.

60. *Cleanness*, 697–704, in *The Poems of the Pearl Manuscript*, ed. Andrew and Waldron. The lines are not free of anxiety about all sexual activity, however, as they form part of a condemnation of homosexual activity.

61. Malory, i. 332–6 (VII. 22–3); the sister acts to preserve their honour rather than their virtue, though Malory implies that there may be a touch of jealousy in her motives too.

62. *Sir Philip Sidney: The Countess of Pembroke's Arcadia (The Old Arcadia)*, ed. by Jean Robertson (Oxford, 1973), pp. 201–2, 242–3, 306; hereafter *Old Arcadia*. The printed versions never allow the lovers to go beyond 'virtuous wantonness' (*Sir Philip Sidney: The Countess of Pembroke's Arcadia*, ed. Maurice Evans (Harmondsworth, 1977), iii. 38 (p. 652); hereafter *New Arcadia*.

63. For *Sir Degaré*, see *The Middle English Breton Lays*, ed. Anne Laskaya and Eve Salisbury (Kalamazoo, 1995), pp. 89–14, and *Percy*, iii. 16–48; there are prints surviving from *c.*1512 to 1560 in addition to the Percy text. Compare also *Torrent of Portyngale*.

64. See Jocelyn Wogan-Browne, *Saints' Lives and Women's Literary Culture c.1150–1300* (Oxford, 2001), esp. pp. 95–106.

65. There is of course no necessary disjunction between a woman's free choice to enter a convent and family wishes: as Wogan-Browne notes, 'The free will of young women is a prestige symbol for their male kin, since it denotes a political and economic mastery so complete . . . that young women's choices can be afforded' (*Saints' Lives*, p. 85).

66. *Beues of Hamtoun*, ed. Kölbing, ll. 3216–24 (Auchinleck text; 2863–7, Chetham MS).

67. The great majority of the most popular legends of virgin martyrs follow the outline given here, including those of St Margaret of Antioch, St Katherine of Alexandria, St Barbara, St Agnes, and St Agatha.

68. Ramón Lull, *Le Livre de Evast et de Blaquerne*, ed. A. Llinarès, Publications de l'Université de Grenoble 47 (Paris, 1970), Book I (Natana's love) and II. i (her escape) (for a translation, see *Blanquerna*, trans. E. Allison Peers (London, 1926), chapters VI, XX).

69. *The Life of Christina of Markyate*, ed. and trans. C. H. Talbot, rev. edn. (Oxford, 1987), pp. 42–3. On the impossibility of raping a saint, see Corinne J. Saunders, *Rape and Ravishment in the Literature of Medieval England* (Cambridge, 2001), pp. 120–51; there are, however, very rare exceptions when the woman is required to give birth to a more famous male saint, in which case her unwillingness can help to prove her own sanctity—St Non, mother of St David, being a case in point.

70. For more detailed discussion, see the analysis of the 'bridal' model of holy virginity in Sarah Salih, *Versions of Virginity in Late Medieval England* (Cambridge, 2001), pp. 10 (where she describes holy virginity as 'a culturally specific organisation of desires'), 12–13, 66–74. I would want to modify her analysis of 'Virgins and Romance' (pp. 57–66) in so far as it flattens romance into a single patriarchal/misogynist model. Cartlidge, *Medieval Marriage*, offers an extensive expoloration of the relationship between secular and religious models of love.

71. 'Eadi is his spuse, hwas meithhad is unwemmet hwen he on hire streoneth' (*Hali Meiðhad*, ll. 28–9, in *Medieval English Prose for Women*, ed. by Bella Millett and Jocelyn Wogan-Browne (Oxford, 1990), p. 34); my translation. 'Streoneth'

indicates the act of procreation; Millett and Wogan-Browne's translation stresses the result—'begets offspring'. The first editor of the text, in the 1860s, classed this sentence among the 'coarse and repulsive passages' for which he used Latin in his parallel-text modern English translation (*Hali Meidenhad*, ed. Oswald Cockayne, EETS OS 18 (1866), Foreword and p. 38; most library sets of the EETS have substituted the less eccentric revised edition by F. J. Furnivall published in 1922).

72. See Michael O'Connell, *The Idolatrous Eye: Iconoclasm and Theater in Early-Modern England* (New York and Oxford, 2000), for a thoughtful study of the distinction and its effect on artistic and dramatic representation.

73. How absolute the division between the two kinds of love was depended on the text in question and the writer's agenda: there was a widespread recognition that the chastity of virginity, chaste widowhood, and virtuous marriage itself consituted a spectrum—see for instance the Tree of Charity episode in *Piers Plowman* (B-text xvi. 65–82, in *William Langland: The Vision of Piers Plowman*, ed. A. V. C. Schmidt, 2nd edn. (London, 1995)), and Wogan-Browne, *Saints' Lives*, p. 83.

74. *Ancrene Wisse*, Part 7; in *Medieval English Prose for Women*, ed. Millett and Wogan-Browne, pp. 112–14.

75. See for instance Kathryn Gravdal, *Ravishing Maidens: Writing Rape in Medieval French Law and Literature* (Philadelphia, 1991), pp. 22–5; Simon Gaunt, *Gender and Genre in Medieval French Literature* (Cambridge, 1995), pp. 196–233; and, for a more nuanced reading, Jocelyn Wogan-Browne, 'The Virgin's Tale', in *Feminist Readings in Middle English Literature*, ed. Evans and Johnson, pp. 165–94.

76. *FQ*, VI. viii. 40–3 (a passage where Spenser's blazon of Serena's naked beauty constitutes a bold and arguably not fully successful attempt to enact the distinction between the voyeuristic and the marvelling gaze); and I. vi. 4–19 (quotations from 4 and 5). Una finally is 'content to please their feeble eyes' (19), to be the subject of the satyrs' gaze, as the implied symbolism of the exposed virgin as witness to God is brought to the allegorical surface.

77. John Foxe, *Ecclesiasticall Historie*, 3rd edn. (London, 1576), p. 95. Foxe also recounts the rather similar legend of Theodora, pp. 63–4.

78. Sir Philip Sidney, *Apologie for Poetry*, in *Elizabethan Critical Essays*, ed. Smith, i. 176–7; *The Virgin Martyr*, in Dekker, *Works*, ed. Bowers, iii. 365–465 (see in particular Act IV. ii). The play was licensed for the Red Bull in 1620, entered in the *Stationers' Register* on 7 December 1621, and first published in 1622. Like all saintly martyrs, Dorothea does not in fact feel pain at her martyrdom.

79. *The Virgin Martyr*, II. iii. 85–7, IV. iii. 151 (spoken most immediately about her guardian angel figure, but it is made clear that he is a stand-in for Christ).

80. *CT*, V. 764–6.

81. For the phrase and how the practice fits into Spenser's other varieties of allegory, see Graham Hough, *A Preface to The Faerie Queene* (London, 1962), pp. 105–8.

82. Cawelti, *Adventure, Mystery*, p. 12; and see pp. 14–15 above.

83. *FQ*, V. v. 25, vii.42.

84. *FQ*, III. ii. 1–3.

85. *FQ*, III. vi. 7; compare the frequent analogy for the conception of Christ whilst Mary's virginity remained intact as the sun passing through glass, though Spenser

goes on to discuss the generative power of the sun within Nature. A comparison with the Annunciation is also suggested earlier (vi. 3), in the comment that Belphoebe's 'birth was of the wombe of morning dew'; the dew on Gideon's fleece was a recognized prefiguration of the conception of Christ.

86. 'An Epithalamion made at Lincoln's Inn', Donne, *Poems*, ed. Smith, pp. 133–5, refrain line.

87. *Cleomon and Clamydes*, ed. Littleton, in particular scenes viii, xi, xv, xx, xxiii. The play was first printed in 1599; for the date, see pp. 30–3, and for its difference from its source, pp. 38–49. Littleton assumes the greater freedom of the heroine to mark a shift to an Italian model, and marks the difference between her and her courtly original by calling her a 'new woman' (p. 39); but she conforms much more strikingly and consistently to the native English tradition—not a new woman, but the continuing reincarnation of a conception of the heroine that always remained fresh.

88. Sidney, *New Arcadia*, ed. Evans, I. 3 (p. 76).

89. Ibid., I. 14 (p. 150); II. i (pp. 213–14).

90. Ibid., II. 4, p. 238. Helen Hackett, in *Women and Romance Fiction in the English Renaissance* (Cambridge, 2000), pp. 116–29, also discusses the emergence of Sidney's heroines into subjecthood, though she finds the most striking examples at the time of their imprisonment, in Book III of the *New Arcadia*.

91. This at least is the chronology accepted by Stanley Wells and Gary Taylor in their Oxford edn. External evidence for the dating of the early plays is lacking.

92. *Romeo and Juliet*, 1. 5. 92–105.

93. Ibid., 3. 2. 1–31; 7–8 quoted.

94. Copies survive from thirteen editions of the *Gesta* in English published between c.1502 and 1640 (STC 21286.2– 21290a). The casket story is no. 66 in *The Early English Versions of the Gesta Romanorum*, ed. Sidney J. H. Herrtage, EETS 33 (1879), pp. 294–306, 'Ancelmus the Emperor'; the story is reprinted, without the moralization, in Bullough, *Narrative and Dramatic Sources*, i.511–14.

95. Bassanio is the only suitor to be provided with an accompanying song while he makes his choice; and, although the degree of emphasis given to it will vary with individual productions, the song gives him some pretty clear hints that the lead casket is the one to go for, in the warning that 'fancy' engendered by the eyes alone gets you nowhere, and the rhyme words 'bred—head—nourishèd'.

96. Caxton gave it the title *Chronicles of England*; most of it is based on Geoffrey of Monmouth, but this particular story is an interloper. See further p. 343 below, and Helen Cooper, 'The Elizabethan *Havelok*', in *Medieval Insular Romance*, ed. Weiss, Fellows, and Dickson, pp. 169–83. Warner's work is most easily accessible in the facsimile of the 6th edn., *William Warner: Albions England* (1612) (Hildesheim and New York, 1971); the work was enlarged in almost every edition it went through, but the 'Havelok' section had been included from the start (Book IV, ch. 20). The Havelok character is in fact given the alternative name he bears in the chronicle tradition, Curan; texts that tell his story sometimes use one name, sometimes the other, or sometimes both, one as his true name and the other as the name he carries while his identity is unknown.

97. The alteration was made by Thomas Bowdler in his *Family Shakespeare*, reprinted throughout the nineteenth century, and held the stage for longer than that.

98. *Tempest*, 1. 2. 422–3, 3. 1. 93–5, 4. 1. 14–22.
99. *Winter's Tale*, 4. 4. 130–2. Thomas Bowdler cuts this, too, though doing so would seem to assume a recognition of Elizabethan terminology of orgasm on his readers' part such as would make the need for sparing their sensibilities redundant.
100. They first take hands (so that she can see the ring), 22. 58–61, an unproblematic stage action between male actors; then kiss (64–5), a rarer move; and then additionally have a long embrace, the closeness of which is indicated by the description of her as 'buried' within his arms (65).
101. Pericles, 21. 210–21; Merchant of Venice, 5. 1. 64–5.

CHAPTER 6

1. Bloch, *Medieval Misogyny*, p. 6.
2. See Alcuin Blamires, *The Case for Women in Medieval Culture* (Oxford, 1997).
3. And indeed of *Cymbeline*, where the 'stepdame false' has no name of her own, being identified rather as a 'crafty devil' or simply the 'wicked queen' (1. 6. 1, 2. 1. 49, 5. 4. 464). Stepmothers are however, likely to be younger than mothers-in-law, so the rejection of the aged operates to different degrees for the two groups.
4. For an anthology of such writings, see Alcuin Blamires's anthology, *Woman Defamed and Woman Defended* (Oxford, 1992).
5. See the 'Defence' section of Blamires's *Woman Defamed*.
6. The quantity is summarized in Francis Lee Utley, *The Crooked Rib* (Columbus, 1944), and Linda Woodbridge, *Women and the English Renaissance* (Brighton, 1984); for the proportion, see the *Registers* themselves.
7. Hence the personification of Idleness (Leisure) as the gatekeeper to the Garden of Mirth in the *Roman de la Rose*. The only medieval literary mode that found room for peasant love was French *bergerie* writings, where the famously undemanding life of watching sheep and the coexistence of shepherds and shepherdesses allowed space for just such sentiment (see Cooper, *Pastoral*, ch. 2. Shepherding in England was a male occupation).
8. Christine opens the work by contrasting 'the natural behavior and character of women' with the 'lies' universally told by male authorities; Lady Reason then attacks her for doubting her direct experience of the first in the light of the second (*Christine de Pizan, The Book of the City of Ladies*, trans. Earl Jeffrey Richards (New York, 1982), pp. 4, 6 (I. i. 1. I. ii. 2); *La Città delle Dame*, ed. Patrizia Caraffi and Earl Jeffrey Richards (Milan, 1998), pp. 42, 44, 46). For Brian Anslay's *Boke of the Cyte of Ladyes*, see STC 7271.
9. The research, given wide press coverage, was undertaken by Bryan Sykes and Catherine Irven on his own surname, 'Surnames and the Y Chromosome', *American Journal of Human Genetics* 66 (2000), 1417–19. The 99% figure can be alternatively expressed as only one child in a hundred per generation having no legitimate paternity (or at least strongly acknowledged paternity: it does not distinguish between legitimate children and the children of unmarried mothers who are given the father's surname, for instance within a stable but unofficially sanctioned relationship, or between children conceived to the same parents outside or inside marriage).

10. Schlauch, *Chaucer's Constance*, pp. 64–5; the book gives a full account of the dissemination of the whole motif.

11. The scarcity of Middle English fabliaux might be taken as further evidence of the same phenomenon (Chaucer had to look to continental models for his own), but there are a number in Anglo-Norman: a fact that may do no more than reflect the comparatively high survival rates for the more prestigious language, but may equally reflect a resistance on the part of the married secular English-speaking population of England—ordinary people, in other words—to buy into this particular aspect of international high or clerical culture.

12. The Susanna corpus is surveyed by Götz Schmitz, *The Fall of Women in Early English Narrative Verse* (Cambridge, 1990), pp. 155–69. For Greene, see *The Myrrour of Modestie* and *Francescos Fortunes*, in *The Life and Complete Works of Robert Greene*, ed. A. B. Grosart, 12 vols. (1881–3; repr. New York, 1964), iii. 1–42, viii. 111–229 (for the Isabel section, see 144–64). The play is edited as *The Most Virtuous and Godly Susanna by Thomas Garter*, ed. B. Ifor Evans and W. W. Greg (Oxford, 1937). It was entered in the *Stationers' Registers* early in 1569, but the surviving print dates from 1578. It is discussed as a forerunner to Shakespeare's plays of calumniated women by Joyce H. Sexton, *The Slandered Woman in Shakespeare* (Victoria, BC, 1978), pp. 39–49.

13. For a discussion of the medieval origins of the motif and for texts of both tales, see Bullough, *Narrative and Dramatic Sources*, viii. 12–16, 50–63 (*Decameron* 2,9), 63–78 (1560 edition of *Frederyke*); Shakespeare may have used both stories. On the increasing emphasis on the woman in medieval French romances of the wager, which she sees as a step towards the 'feminist interpretation of romance', see Roberta L. Krueger, 'Double Jeopardy: The Appropriation of Woman in four Old French Romances of the "Cycle de la Gageure"', in Fisher and Halley (eds), *Seeking the Woman*, pp. 21–50 (p. 45).

14. The danger was made explicit by Pope Pius V, who in 1570 excommunicated Elizabeth and declared her deposed (so inviting her Catholic subjects to rebel against her), and his successor Gregory XIII, who encouraged plans to assassinate her.

15. Diarmaid MacCulloch, *Thomas Cranmer* (New Haven and London, 1996), p. 159.

16. On its later history, see Lori Humphrey Newcomb, 'The Triumph of Time: The Fortunate Readers of Robert Greene's *Pandosto*', in *Texts and Cultural Change in Early Modern England*, ed. Cedric C. Brown and Arthur F. Marotti (Basingstoke and New York, 1997), pp. 95–123.

17. *The Earl of Toulouse* itself is not known to have been printed. The analogous story underlying *Sir Aldingar* first appears in written form in William of Malmesbury's *De gestis regum anglorum*, from where it is taken over by Vincent of Beauvais and Matthew Paris: see Paul Christopherson, *The Ballad of Sir Aldingar: Its Origin and Analogues* (Oxford, 1952), pp. 18–21. Here it is told about Gunhild, sister of Hardicanute. For the later texts, see nn. 31–2 below.

18. The only exceptions are some 'rudderless boat' stories that incorporate calumny: *La Manekine* in French, Thomas Alsop's *Fair Custance*, and the lost play *Fair Constance of Rome* (see pp. 126–8 above).

19. *Hamlet*, 1. 2. 146, 3. 1. 138–9.

20. *The Knight of the Swanne*, in *Early English Prose Romances*, ed. Thoms, p. 756.

21. *Philaster*, I. i. 94–6, in *Beaumont and Fletcher*, gen. ed. Bowers, Vol. 1.
22. Posthumus' comment on Innogen's sexual restraint would fall into this category (2. 5. 9–10); its interpretation as meaning that the marriage has not been consummated would fall so far outside audience expectation as to need a stronger statement, especially as his choice of words as to how she 'prayed me oft forebearance' does not suggest 'always'. The opposing argument has been put most intelligently by Anne Barton, ' "Wrying but a little": Marriage, Law and Sexuality in the plays of Shakespeare', in her *Essays, Mainly Shakespearean*, pp. 3–30.
23. *Othello*, 1. 3. 163–5, 250–7; contrast Cinthio's *Gli Hecatommithi*, in Bullough, *Narrative and Dramatic Sources*, vii.242–3.
24. 1. 3. 292–3, 3. 3. 209, and 3. 3. 234–8 (quoted).
25. 'Hyt was sothe the lady sayde— I Therfore hym lykyd ylle', ll. 158–9, ed. Fellows in *Of Love and Chivalry*, pp. 231–65.
26. The original French verse romance is lost, but its contents can be reconstructed from a number of derivative versions in other languages: see Dickson, *Valentine: A Study*.
27. *Percy*, ii. 390–9.
28. *Valentine and Orson*, ed. Dickson, p. 15.
29. The shorter printed versions current from the seventeenth century, and aimed at a wider market than the full romance, highlight the role of the merchant and blacken the archbishop still further.
30. The deaths are Spenser's own addition; his source (Ariosto's story of Ginevra, *Orlando Furioso* v. 5–74) has Ginevra vindicated in a trial by combat. The renaming of the woman as 'Claribell'—a name close to such romance heroines as the Christabelle of *Sir Eglamour* and the Desonelle of *Torrent of Portyngale*—suggests a desire on Spenser's part to imply a setting closer to home.
31. *Sir Tryamour*, ed. Fellows, *Of Love and Chivalry*, pp. 147–98, ll. 528–64; *Percy*, ii. 78–135, ll. 547–70. 'Providence' might be accused of being too kindly a reading of the episode: a more cynical interpretation would see the testimony of a dog as outweighing that of a woman (though the creature is directly avenging the murder of his master rather than the defaming of the queen).
32. *Sir Aldingar*, *Percy*, i. 165–73. In one of the ballad versions, a knight volunteers to be the queen's champion, a non-supernatural outcome that brings the story closer to *The Earl of Toulouse* (Child, *Ballads*, no. 59, ii. 33–48).
33. It is one of the few plays of Shakespeare to be designated as a 'comedie' on the title-page of its quarto edition; his only play to incorporate the word into its title, *The Comedy of Errors*, is his most closely imitative of Latin comedy in both structure and plot.
34. *Ralph Roister Doister*, v. iii. 11–12, in *Three Sixteenth-century Comedies*, ed. Charles W. Whitworth (London, 1984); it was first printed c.1567. Cf. *CT*, II. 639–40: 'Immortal God, that savedest Susanne I From false blame . . .'
35. See p. 239 above.
36. *All is True*, 2. 4. 10–54.
37. *Cymbeline*, 5. 3. 116.
38. See also pp. 201–3 above for further discussion of this episode.
39. *Greenes Vision*, in *The Life and Complete Works in Prose and Verse of Robert Greene*, ed. A. B. Grosart (1881–6; repr. New York, 1964), xii. 201–81 (pp. 222–3).

40. Carolyn Dinshaw explores the analogy extensively in *Chaucer's Sexual Poetics* (Madison, Wis., 1989).
41. *Octavian* (mid-fourteenth century, printed *c.*1505) is an exception, in that the mother-in-law arranges for a young man to be placed alongside the empress in her bed.
42. The fourteenth-century alliterative *Chevelere Assigne* and the Tudor print of the prose *Knight of the Swanne*, both derive from the Godfrey of Bulloigne cycle of French *chansons de geste*.
43. *The Romance of the Cheuelere Assigne*, ed. H. H. Gibbs, EETS ES 6 (1868), ll. 272–3: a detail omitted from the prose.
44. *CT*, II. 696, 779, 782–3.
45. The heroine of *Frederyke of Jennen* is 'so womanly in her behavoure' that the man who has bet that he can seduce her does not dare to proposition her (Bullough, *Narrative and Dramatic Sources*, viii. 66); in Hoccleve's 'Tale of Jereslaus' Wife', a story of a series of attempted seductions and false accusations, the wife dismisses the seneschal who seeks her sexual favours with a 'wommanly nay' (Hoccleve, *Minor Poems*, ed. Furnivall and Gollancz, pp. 140–73, l. 77).
46. *CT*, II. 358, 360; the woman-headed serpent in the Garden of Eden makes its first appearance in Peter Comestor's late twelfth-century *Historia scholastica*, from where it rapidly entered iconography.
47. Bullough, *Narrative and Dramatic Sources*, viii. 68; see also p. 66.
48. Heldris, *Silence*, ed. Thorpe, ll. 1701–24, 6033–80 (6080 quoted).
49. *Partonope*, ed. Bödtker, ll. 6471–5, 6759–94. The authorial comments (carried over from the French original) are partly self-serving, in that the real or fictional claim of the author is that his lady does not reciprocate his love; but the argument against generalization can hardly be ironic, given the wide documentation of its truth. On the Wife, see *CT*, III. 688–96.
50. The question of antifeminism in Hue's *Ipomedon* is given a nuanced discussion by Crane, *Insular Romance*, pp. 158–73. Hue makes the sexuality more aggressive and the antifeminism more overt in his *Prothesilaus*, though that was never so popular, and never translated into English (possibly as a consequence): see Judith Weiss, 'A reappraisal of Hue de Rotelande's *Protheselaus*', *Medium Ævum* 52 (1983), 104–11.
51. *New Arcadia*, ed. Evans, p. 76. The metaphor of the stepmother may well have been so commonplace as to pass unnoticed by both Sidney and his readers.
52. Ibid., p. 501.
53. *The Dialogues of Creatures Moralysed*, ed. Gregory Kratzmann and Elizabeth Gee (Leiden and New York, 1998), p. 239. The Secundus quotation is given at fuller length in Blamires, *Woman Defamed*, p. 100: 'man's undoing, an insatiable animal, perpetual trouble and non-stop combat, man's daily ruin, a storm in the home, an impediment to peace of mind, the wreck of a weak-willed man, instrument of adultery, expensive war, the very worst creature and heaviest burden, hateful snake, human property'. *Mulier est hominis confusio* ('man's undoing', 'confusyon of man') decisively entered English literature in Chauntecleer's misapprehension of it in the *Nun's Priest's Tale* as 'womman is mannes joye and al his blis' (*CT*, VII. 3164–6).
54. *Old Arcadia*, ed. Robertson, p. 20; *New Arcadia*, ed. Evans, p. 134.

55. Ibid., p. 22 (*Old*), p. 136 (*New*).
56. From the close of Caxton's preface to the *Morte Arthur*.
57. In all the English versions other than Shakespeare's, the daughter is initially the unwilling victim of paternal rape; he is unusual in removing any degree of sympathy for her.
58. See pp. 250–1 above.
59. For the mid-fifteenth century Middle English version, see *Merlin*, ed. Henry B. Wheatley, Vol. I part II (EETS O.S. 21), rev. edn. (1877), chapter XXIII (pp. 420–37); this section is also included in *Prose Merlin*, ed. John Conlee (Kalamazoo, 1998), pp. 224–41. The episode forms the last section of Heldris's *Silence*.
60. On *distinctio* as 'normative array', see Judson Boyce Allen and Theresa Anne Moritz, *A Distinction of Stories* (Columbus, OH, 1981), p. 86. They offer the idea as a principle of narrative structure and unity, contrasting with the Aristotelean idea of organic unity, but widely used in medieval—and, one should add, Renaissance—works.
61. Malory, i. 323–4 (VII. 21–2).
62. Malory, i. 168–9 (IV. 23), Gawain and Ettarde; i. 145–6 (IV. 11), i. 256 (VI. 3), ii. 643 (X. 38), Morgan.
63. Malory, iii. 1120 (XVIII. 25).
64. Sidney, *New Arcadia*, ed. Evans, ii. 18 (pp. 334–44).
65. 'O sweet woods the delight of solitariness', in the Eclogues to Book II (ed. Evans, pp. 433–4).
66. Blair Worden, *The Sound of Virtue* (New Haven and London, 1996).
67. In the description of Nature in the *Mutability Cantos*, VII. vii. 9.
68. Lewis, *Allegory of Love*, esp. pp. 2, 32–43.
69. In *Romania* 12 (1883), p. 523. It was Lewis's 1936 *Allegory of Love* that gave the term the status it held for much of the twentieth century. The criticisms of Lewis's position have been many and various: see, for instance, *The Meaning of Courtly Love*, ed. F. X. Newman (Albany, New York, 1968); in particular John F. Benton, 'Clio and Venus: An Historical View of Medieval Love', pp. 19–42; and, for a more recent discussion, David Burnley, *Courtliness and Literature in Medieval England* (London, 1998), pp. 148–75. For an excellent and varied selection of medieval texts with an Introduction that raises all the necessary questions, see *The Courtly Love Tradition*, ed. Bernard O'Donoghue (Manchester, 1982).
70. See Burnley, *Courtliness*, pp. 152–62.
71. P. G. Walsh in his edition and translation, *Andreas Capellanus on Love* (London, 1982), p. 1. He notes that 'De amore' is the commonest title; the more familiar 'De arte honeste amandi' (used for instance by J. J. Parry to entitle his translation 'The Art of Courtly Love') is based on a single manuscript where 'honeste' is added above the line in a different hand. The rendering of 'honeste' as 'courtly' is in any case tendentious (and Lewis-derived).
72. For a recent summary of the scholarly debate, see Alastair Minnis, *Magister Amoris: The Roman de la Rose and Vernacular Hermeneutics* (Oxford: Oxford University Press, 2001), pp. 9–10. John F. Benton's study of the literary culture of the court of Champagne found no likely 'Andreas', nor any evidence to support any non-fictional basis for the promotion of 'courtly love' or for the existence of

courts of love. He did, however, find a good deal to indicate that marriage was regarded at the court of Champagne with approval and as normative, and that Marie's literary tastes leaned towards the religious ('The Court of Champagne as a Literary Center', *Speculum* 36 (1961), 551–91).

73. Interestingly, Chrétien himself did not finish the *Chevalier de la Charrette*; its conclusion (which reads more like the conclusion to an episode than to a completed narrative) was written by another poet.

74. *Cligés*, ed. Micha, l. 3123.

75. *Andreas*, ed. Walsh, i. 6 (pp. 146–7; Walsh's translation).

76. Ibid., pp.156–7. In those rare cases where a couple opted for married celibacy, the Church required that both parties should agree; Margery Kempe, for instance, has some difficulty in persuading her husband to accord with her own wish for such a marriage, but she takes it for granted that his agreement is necessary (*The Book of Margery Kempe*, ed. Windeatt, chs. 9–11).

77. *Andreas*, ed. Walsh, ii. 7. ix (pp. 258–9).

78. *CT*, V.796–8.

79. *Two Late Medieval Love Treatises*, ed. Leslie C. Brook (Oxford, 1993), Heloïse's *Art d'amour*, p. 35. The manuscript is preserved in the British Library, Royal MS 16.F.II.

80. The *demandes d'amour* constitute the second of the *Two Late Medieval Love Treatises*, ed. Brook.

81. If most aristocratic women did not initiate marriage, their right to refusal of consent was none the less important. The treaty setting out the terms under which the child Isabella of France was handed over to Richard II not only gave her the right to withdraw from the marriage before its consummation, when she reached the age of puberty, but set out the financial arrangements to be followed if she did so wish. This does not mean it would have been easy, but the detail indicates that it was considered a real possibility.

82. 'Por vos plas, ieu i consen,' 'since it's what you want, I consent' (*Flamenca*, ed. and trans. Blodgett, l. 284). The description of the wedding night, interestingly, is told from the man's point of view, not in the terms of mutuality employed for lovers (323–42).

83. Despite some classical pronouncements that friendship was possible only between men, a number of authors argued that marriage could be a compelling form of friendship. Aquinas described it as *maxima amicitia* (quoted by Benton, 'Clio and Venus', p. 21); and for sample medieval and Renaissance vernacular instances, see Chaucer's *Franklin's Tale*, *CT*, V. 762, and *The Flower of Friendship* by Edmund Tilney, Elizabeth's Master of the Revels, an entire work devoted to arguing the case for marriage as the highest form of friendship (ed. Valerie Wayne (Ithaca, 1992)).

84. *Flamenca*, ed. Blodgett, pp. xii, xxi. The work is incomplete in the single manuscript, but it seems to be heading irreversibly towards a happy ending for the wife and her lover.

85. On the work's Anglo-Norman source, see p. 468 n. 39 above. The allusions to Chrétien's Arthurian romances are too deeply embedded in the work to have been added by Ulrich, though he may have known them on his own account. For the episodes cited below, see in particular Ulrich, *Lanzelet*, ed. Spiewok, ll. 215–48 for

Iblis's dream and her subsequent lying awake, and 5178 for Guinever's passing the test of the 'Eren steine', the stone of honour that will not tolerate falsehood.

86. It appears in the famous Bodleian Library, Oxford, MS Digby 86; Robert Biket, *Le Lai du Corn*, ed. E. T. Erickson, ANTS 24 (Oxford, 1973).

87. Ed. Spiewok, ll. 5679–6228.

88. Ecclesiastes 7.28–9. On its widespread medieval use, see Blamires, ed., *Woman Defamed*.

89. Chaucer comments on it in the *Manciple's Tale*, *CT*, IX. 212–22; for a later pointed contrast, see Beaumont's *Knight of the Burning Pestle*, Act II. 292–3, in *Beaumont and Fletcher*, gen. ed. Bowers, vol. 1.

90. *Percy*, ii. 301–11 (quoted); Child, *Ballads* no. 29 (i. 257–74). Child gives a full account of the tales of both the mantle and the drinking-vessel in his introduction (the text contains both).

91. Malory, i. 430 (VIII. 34).

92. *FQ*, III. vii. 55–60, viii.44.

93. *FQ*, III. vii. 37, 49, 52. The later statement that Argante 'did in feminine | And filthie lust exceede all woman kind' (III. xi. 4) does however use her to denigrate women even while superficially distinguishing her from them. Spenser's choice of name for her has no connection with Layamon's use of it for his Morgan figure.

94. The stories contained in the *Seven Sages* vary from version to version, but this one is found in all the English texts in both manuscript and print: see *The Seven Sages of Rome*, ed. Killis Campbell (Boston and London, 1907), pp. xxxiv–lxvi, and for the text, ll. 3235–726.

95. *The Knight of Curtesy and the Fair Lady of Faguell*, ed. E. McCausland (Northampton, Mass., 1922), ll. 46–7; also in Hazlitt (ed.), *Remains*, ii. 65–87. It survives in a single printed copy of *c*.1556, which the electronic *STC* describes as a second edition. There are two possible French sources, the *Chronique du Chatelain de Coucy*, included in McCausland's edn., and *Le Roman du Castelain de Couci et la Dame de Fayel par Jakemes*, ed. M. Delbouille (Paris, 1936), both thirteenth-century; there is also a French prose version of the fifteenth century. The *Chronique*, like the English but in contrast to the French romance, keeps the affair platonic. See also p. 397 below.

96. The earliest reference to the affair in English occurs in a unique addition to the Auchinleck manuscript version of the *Anonymous Metrical Chronicle*, ed. Zettl, A 1071–98, pp. 70–1, in which a foundation legend for the caves in Nottingham Castle rock is created by having Lancelot carve them out to hide Guinevere after he has rescued her from the stake. The passage seems to have been inspired by the arrest of Mortimer at Nottingham late in 1330: see Cooper, 'Lancelot, Roger Mortimer'.

97. Numerous allusions to Chrétien's Arthurian romances indicate knowledge of his work on the part of either the Anglo-Norman author or Ulrich himself. One of the episodes, but with the love interest removed, concerns Lanzelet's rescue of Ginover from abduction: this constitutes the whole plot of the *Chevalier de la Charrette*, but some form of the story, with Gawain as hero, pre-existed Chrétien too.

98. *Chronicle of Iohn Harding*, ed. Ellis, p. 131 (ch. 76, misnumbered as 77).

99. See Ruth Morse, 'Sterile Queens and Questing Orphans', *Quondam et Futurus* 2:2 (1992), 41–53.

100. Malory, i. 270–1 (VI. 10).

101. Examples are widespread across Europe, but see, for instance, Chrétien de Troyes's lyric 'D'Amors, qui m'a tolu a moi', in which the lover insists that 'fins cuer et bone volentez' create a stronger love than the poison drunk by Tristan (in *Les Chansons courtoises de Chrétien de Troyes*, ed. Marie-Claire Gérard-Zai (Frankfurt, 1974); Heinrich von Veldeke's 'Tristrant mūste āne sīne danc', in O'Donoghue, *Courtly Love Tradition*, pp. 218–19; and *Amadas et Ydoine*, ll. 81–2 of the Anglo-Norman fragment.

102. Malory, iii. 1165, 1171 (XX. 3, 6).

103. Malory, iii. 1120, 1252 (XVIII. 25, XXI.9).

104. Malory, iii. 1253 (XXI. 9).

105. Malory, iii. 1258 (XXI. 12).

106. *Holinshed's Chronicles*, i. 580. He also questions whether Guinevere was unfaithful at all, suggesting that both her marriage to Mordred and indeed any 'incontinencie and breach of faith to hir husband' are slanders; but that was scarcely enough to make her plausible as a national heroine.

CHAPTER 7

1. *Havelok*, ed. Sands, ll. 604 (and note), 1262–3, 2139–45.

2. *Valentine*, ed. Dickson, p. 85.

3. *Matthew Paris: Chronica Maiora*, ed. Henry Richards Luard, Rolls Series 57, 7 vols. (London, 1872–83), iii. 497–8; Ann Wroe, *Perkin: A Story of Deception* (London, 2003), pp. 119–20.

4. From Edward III through his second son Lionel; his daughter, Philippa; her son Roger, earl of March; his daughter, Anne; and her son, Richard, duke of York, Edward IV's father. There was a shorter line of descent through Edward III's fourth son, but that was a cadet line to the Lancastrians, who were descended from John of Gaunt, the third son.

5. *Winter's Tale*, 3. 2. 134–5.

6. The tightening of the principles of primogeniture into rules with the force of law took place predominantly in the twelfth century; Donald Maddox notes the tendency to enhance genealogies with fiction at this period, describing it as a 'distinct propensity to alloy biology with mythology' (*Fictions of Identity*, pp. 171, 176).

7. Formulated *c*.1090 as that a king 'fieri non possit nisi a Deo', the principle was picked up by Bracton: see Ernst Kantorowicz, *The King's Two Bodies* (Princeton, 1957), pp. 330–1. English kings were also 'elected' by acclamation, and in the later Middle Ages endorsed by Parliament, but that was a *post hoc* procedure confirming an implicit true kingship.

8. Frye, *The Great Code*, p. 46; and see p. 182 on the contrasting of past-directed causality and future-directed typology.

9. *FQ*, II. x. 70–5.

10. See p. 195 above.

11. Freud powerfully links the psychological and the literary in his 'Family Romances', *Works*, ed. Strachey, ix. 237–41.

12. *The Knight of the Swanne*, in *Early English Prose Romances*, ed. Thoms, p. 726.
13. *John Capgrave's Abbreuiacion of Chronicles*, ed. Peter J. Lucas, EETS 285 (1985), p. 9.
14. *Winter's Tale*, 3. 3. 32, 3. 2. 135. The naming is original to Shakespeare, who found her in *Pandosto* merely as 'Fawnia'.
15. *Percy*, iii.16–48, ll. 213–16.
16. In *The Middle English Breton Lays*, ed. Laskaya and Salisbury, ll. 255–7. On the etymology, see Nicolas Jacobs, 'Old French "Degaré" and Middle English "Degarre" and "Deswarre"', *Notes and Queries* 17 (1970), 164–5.
17. *Pandosto*, ed. by Bullough, *Narrative and Dramatic Sources*, viii. 169; *Winter's Tale*, 3. 2. 134–5.
18. *King Edward III*, ed. Giorgio Melchiori (Cambridge, 1998), 5. 1. 87–8; for the date, see pp. 3–5. The New Cambridge Shakespeare series includes the play on the grounds, increasingly widely accepted, that at least part of it is by Shakespeare.
19. *Lybeaus Desconus* may have been written by Thomas Chestre, the early/ mid-fourteenth-century author of *Sir Launfal* and *Octavian*: see Maldwyn Mills's Introduction to his edition (EETS O.S. 261 (1969)). No print survives, but the accuracy of the Percy text (ed. Hales and Furnivall, ii. 404–99) and an allusion of 1603 strongly indicate publication. Skelton lists it among other romances known to have been printed in *Philip Sparrow* (ll. 649–50, in *John Skelton: The Complete English Poems*, ed. by John Scattergood (Harmondsworth, 1983); before 1505?).
20. *Sir Percyvell*, ed. Mills, ll. 506, 1094; 545–76, 1107–8; 1572–647.
21. 'Niht anders me, | wan der stolze degen vonme Sê. | Er ist durch neizwas namelôs', Ulrich, *Lanzelet*, ed. Spiewok, ll. 2293–5; trans. Webster, p. 56.
22. *Knight of the Swanne*, ed. Thoms, pp. 753–6, and the 'Prologue of the Translatour' from the original print. The fifteenth-century antiquarian John Rous claimed to have drunk from the Beauchamp cup (Antonia Gransden, *Historical Writing in England II* (London, 1982), p. 324). The Bohuns also carried a swan badge in sign of their descent, adopted by Henry V through his Bohun mother.
23. *FQ*, VI. ix. 14, xii. 3–22.
24. Malory, i.101 (III. 3). The 'milkmaid' detail is specific to English; French texts, here and widely elsewhere, make such a victim of a countryside rape or seduction a shepherdess.
25. Malory is less close as an analogue at this point: the dwarf in 'The Tale of Sir Gareth' is Gareth's own, who brings him his armour after he has been granted the adventure. Spenser is unlikely to have known the Perceval story, as *Percyvell* is not known to have been printed, and his *enfances* do not figure in Malory. On the parallels with 'Gareth', see the opening of Paul R. Rovang's *Refashioning 'Knights and Ladies Gentle Deeds'* (Madison and London, 1996), pp. 23–8.
26. ll. 116–19, in Hawes, *Minor Poems*, ed. by Gluck and Morgan, pp. 93–122.
27. So, for example, Ine, who became king of Wessex in 688; a twelfth-century account, written at the very start of the romance era, has him called from the plough to the throne by revelation from God. He proposes marriage to the queen of the region north of the Humber, Aethelburgh, in order to unite their kingdoms, but she scornfully rejects the idea of marriage to a peasant; in a move more characteristic of early romance, she is won over by sheer sexual desire when he visits her incognito. See *A Brief History of the Bishopric of Somerset from its*

Foundation to the year 1174, in *Ecclesiastical Documents*, ed. Joseph Hunter, Camden Society Old Series 8 (London, 1840); and Tony Davenport, 'Chronicle and Romance: The Story of Ine and Aethelburgh', in *Cultural Encounters in Medieval English Romance*, ed. Corinne Saunders (Cambridge, 2004).

28. For its fullest development, see 'The Stanley Poem' written by Thomas Stanley, bishop of Sodor and Man, around 1562 (printed in *The Palatine Anthology*, ed. James Orchard Halliwell (London, 1850), pp. 208–71 (pp. 217–21)). The Eagle and Child inn in Oxford, which dates from around 1650, memorializes the legend; it is a medieval, not a classical, eagle and child.

29. See Ad Putter, *An Introduction to the Gawain-poet* (London, 1996), pp. 34–6.

30. The point is made by Helen Hackett, *Women and Romance Fiction*, pp. 154–5, in relation to Shakespeare's last plays.

31. See, in particular, Rosalind Field, 'The King over the Water: Exile-and-return in Insular Tradition', in *Cultural Encounters*, ed. Saunders.

32. Capgrave, *Abbreuiacion of Chronicles*, ed. Lucas, p. 97 (under the years 1010–29).

33. See Thorlac Turville-Petre, '*Havelok* and the History of the Nation', in *Readings in Medieval English Romance*, ed. Carol Meale (Cambridge, 1994), pp. 121–34.

34. In other versions, Havelok is sometimes the name given to Curan's father, or Curan and Havelok are the two names the hero bears in his own identity and after his dispossession; Goldeburh would seem to be a revaluing upwards of the merely silver Argentille. G. V. Smithers's edition of the romance outlines the numerous early versions of the story and gives a table of the names (pp. xvi–xxi). The chronicle texts, in contrast to the Middle English romance version, do not fashion the stories of hero and heroine as parallels.

35. See p. 265 above.

36. *A Collection of Old Ballads* (possibly ed. by Ambrose Phillips; 3 vols. (London, 1723–5)), iii. 1–10. This supplements the other later versions described in Cooper, 'The Elizabethan *Havelok*'.

37. For a survey of the evidence, see Ian Mortimer, *The Greatest Traitor: The Life of Sir Roger Mortimer* (London, 2003), pp. 244–64.

38. On these rumours, and comparable stories across Europe, see Simon Walker, 'Rumour, Sedition and Popular Protest in the Reign of King Henry IV', *Past and Present* 166 (2000), 31–65.

39. This is the central thesis of Ann Wroe's *Perkin*; and see n. 54 below.

40. The prophecies are discussed by Thomas, *Religion and the Decline of Magic*, pp. 498–501; and see *Thomas of Erceldoune*, ed. Murray, p. 63. The quotation is from the coda at the end of the Thomas prophecies found in the 1652 printing of the elf-queen version, *Sundry Strange Prophecies*, p. 27. Albrecht and Nixon omit these lines from their texts of this version; they are on a new page after the end of the medieval part of the prophecy, but they follow with no other break from the preceding text and in the same double-column verse format (which is unique to *Thomas* in the volume). The coda seems to date from the middle of Mary's reign ('Sice, that was lost in three, | Shall come again in six only', i.e., 1553 and 1556), but the print adds a 1596 date for the 'sice's' return. See further pp. 385–6 below.

41. Michael K. Jones and Malcolm G. Underwood, *The King's Mother* (Cambridge, 1992), p. 69.

42. Francis Bacon succinctly summarized his difficulties in his *History of the Reign of King Henry VII*, though even he avoids mentioning the complication of his still living mother (ed. Brian Vickers (Cambridge, 1998), pp. 7–10).

43. Jones and Underwood, *The King's Mother*, pp. 37–8. She in fact outlived her son by a few months, so the sermon indicates a continuing anxiety over the succession even in the next generation.

44. From *The Most Pleasant Song of Lady Bessy*, discussed further below (ed. by J. O. Halliwell, Percy Society 20 (1847), p. 34; and see also Ian Baird, 'Some Missing Lines in *Lady Bessy*', *Library*, 6th ser., 5 (1983), 268–9). The lines quoted come from a later seventeenth-century manuscript, now untraceable, which seems to preserve some authentic details not found in the earlier texts.

45. See Sydney Anglo, 'The *British History* in Early Tudor Propaganda', *Bulletin of the John Rylands Library* 44 (1961), 17–48, and the qualifications to that in his *Images of Tudor Kingship* (London, 1992), pp. 40–60.

46. See Robert Huntington Fletcher, *The Arthurian Materials in the Chronicles*, 2nd edn., rev. by Roger Sherman Loomis (New York, 1966), pp. 241–9. The tradition runs from John of Fordun (1385) to Hector Boece (1527) and his translators.

47. Pietro Carmeliano, Giovanni de' Giglis and Bernard André all made the comparison, though in phrasing drawn as much from Virgil's Fourth Eclogue (the 'Messianic' prophecy) as romance: see Anglo, '*British History*', pp. 29–30.

48. Martin Biddle, *King Arthur's Round Table* (Woodbridge, 2000), pp. 425–73.

49. Sir George Buck, *History of King Richard III*, ed. Arthur Noel Kincaid (Gloucester, 1979), p. 38; *Henry VI Pt 3*, 4. 7. 65–76. Buck, still in 1618 an ardent Yorkist, holds it against Henry Tudor that he illegitimately pre-empted what Providence would have arranged for him anyway; contrast *FQ*, III. iii. 25 on the need for 'mens good endevours' to 'guide the heavenly causes' to the outcome that would happen regardless.

50. ll. 2053–71, in Hawes, *Minor Poems*, ed. Gluck and Morgan, pp. 68–9.

51. See Jones and Underwood, *The King's Mother*, pp. 181–2; Helen Cooper, 'Romance after Bosworth', in *The Court and Cultural Diversity*, ed. Evelyn Mullally and John Thompson (Cambridge, 1997), pp. 149–57.

52. She is completely unnamed in the original French metrical romance; the prose romance does, in fact, once give her her proper name, deep within the narrative (see *Blanchardyn*, ed. Kellner, p. 36), contrary to my discussion of the work in 'Romance after Bosworth', pp. 151–2. The prominence given to her name by Caxton is none the less original, and presumably also intentional.

53. 'The eglantine, by which I mean England' as the chronicler Jean Molinet put it, in the course of his account of Perkin Warbeck ('l'englentier, par qui j'e[nt]ens Engleterre': *Chroniques*, ed. Buchon, v. 49); for English examples, see Anglia as looking 'like eglantine' in Holme, *Fall and euill Successe*, sig. I.iii v, and Gorges' use of the eglantine as 'the Albion flowre' to symbolize Elizabeth (*The Poems of Sir Arthur Gorges*, ed. Helen Easterbrook Sanderson (Oxford, 1953), no. 100).

54. From the lyric 'In a gloryus garden grene', ed. Rossell Hope Robbins, *Historical Poems of the XIVth and XVth Centuries* (New York, 1959), pp. 93–4. It is preserved in a court songbook, so the equation of its 'queen' with Elizabeth of York seems inevitable; but it is still odd that it should be the Yorkist rose that is described as

ruling 'by rightwise law', a claim that would not have pleased Henry. Ann Wroe's suggestion that it refers to Perkin Warbeck, the supposed Richard of York, seems too subversive for the manuscript context (*Perkin*, p. 449).

55. *Blanchardyn*, ed. Kellner, pp. 122–3.

56. i.e., the usurpation was not 'by the consente of the noblemen of the countree'.

57. *The Hystorye of Olyuer of Castylle*, ed. Gail Orgelfinger (New York, 1988), pp. 206–7.

58. See *Percy*, iii. 319–63; Stowe's copy is printed with the later seventeenth-century manuscript by Halliwell, *The Most Pleasant Song*. In so far as the story has a hero, it is Humphrey Brereton of Malpas, Elizabeth's envoy; the Breretons were in the Stanley affinity, and the poem may have originated in their household. The poem borrows from *Bosworth Field*, also preserved in the Percy Folio (3. 233–59), which treats the claims of Richard and Henry with exceptional even-handedness, and which appears to date from before Sir William Stanley's execution in 1495; *Lady Bessy* includes a reference to that at the end. See Cooper, 'Romance after Bosworth', pp. 154–6.

59. Percy text, l. 440, but similar lines are recurrent: see 188, 600, 604, 620, 752. The plotting for Elizabeth's marriage to Henry was in fact carried out by Lady Margaret Beaufort; there is no evidence outside this poem for the princess's personal involvement.

60. Bacon, in his *Life of Henry VII*, declared that Henry's actions (or failure to act) 'hath so muffled it that it hath left it almost as a mystery to this day' (ed. Vickers, p. 96); Thomas Gainsford, in his *True and Wonderful History of Perkin Warbeck* (1618), came down firmly on the side of impersonation; and Sir George Buck in his *History of King Richard III* argued passionately for his being what he claimed to be.

61. The play does not make mention of the confession that Warbeck signed after his capture, except in so far as he persistently refuses to confirm such an identity (*John Ford: Three Plays*, ed. Keith Sturgess (Harmondsworth, 1970)). Ford used Gainsford and Bacon as his sources.

62. Donald Maddox, *Fictions of Identity*, pp. 172, 177–86 (he offers the term specifically for those rare women who start a dynasty from nothing). On the less beneficent mother-marks of Melusine's children, see p. 383 below.

63. It was on display in the 2003 'Elizabeth' exhibition at the National Maritime Museum, Greenwich.

64. See Cooper, 'The Elizabethan *Havelok*'; Foxe, *Ecclesiasticall Historie*, p. 1987; and Thomas Heywood, *If You Know not Me, You Know Nobody; or, The Troubles of Queen Elizabeth* (1605) (Oxford, 1934), ll. 1184–90. Compare also her remark in a speech to Parliament in 1576, on her intention of remaining single: 'If I were a milkmaid with a pail on my arm, whereby my private person might be little set by, I would not forsake that poor and single state to match with the greatest monarch' (J. E. Neale, *Elizabeth I and her Parliaments* (London, 1953), p. 366).

65. See the last eight lines of Warner, *Albions England*, Book IV, ch. 20; and Anne Somerset, *Elizabeth I* (London, 1991), pp. 99–100.

66. From his *Commentary on the Book of Domus Dei*, quoted in Buck, *History of King Richard III*, ed. Kincaid, p. xxxii.

67. *FQ*, II. x. 70–6, III. iii. 26–49; and see also Bart van Es, *Spenser's Forms of History* (Oxford, 2002), pp. 164–96.

68. Ed. by J. W. Cunliffe in *Early English Classical Tragedies* (Oxford, 1912); and by Brian J. Corrigan (New York, 1992), though his claim that its source is the alliterative *Morte Arthure* is certainly wrong—heavy alliteration is typical of mid-Elizabethan poetry. The play is discussed further below, pp. 404–5.

69. *Merry Wives* 5. 3. 55–72 (from the Folio text). It was probably written for the feast of the Order of the Garter held in April 1597, and may have been acted at the feast at Whitehall preceding the installation of the new knights at Windsor. The Arden edition by H. J. Oliver (London, 1971) assembles what is known or conjectured about the play (pp. xliv–xlix), and later editors and critics have concurred. The title page of the 1602 quarto makes the claim that it had been acted before the queen; it is a 'bad quarto', most likely a memorial reconstruction (pp. xiii–xxxvii), but there is no particular reason to doubt its claim.

70. Commentary on the play's relation to Elizabeth has been largely focused through its Garter connections: see Giorgio Melchiori, *Shakespeare's Garter Plays* (Newark, 1994).

71. On the possibility that Shakespeare 'learned from Chaucer's *Parlement* a certain plotting of poetic language and history', see Theresa M. Krier, 'The Aim was Song: From Narrative to Lyric in the *Parlement of Foules* and *Love's Labour's Lost*', in *Refiguring Chaucer in the Renaissance*, ed. Krier (Gainesville, 1998), pp. 165–88 (p. 166 quoted).

72. See Emrys Jones, 'Stuart Cymbeline', *Essays in Criticism* 11 (1961), 84–99.

73. Hackett notes that the double meaning is especially common in the *Winter's Tale* (*Women and Romance Fiction*, pp. 154–5).

74. Multiplying in good deeds was the preferred Catholic exegesis of Genesis 1:28, God's instruction to 'be fruitful, and multiply'.

75. On the wider use of phoenix imagery for the unbroken line of kingship, see Kantorowicz, *The King's Two Bodies*, pp. 385–95; and for Elizabeth herself, Elkin Calhoun Wilson, *England's Eliza* (1938; repr. New York, 1966), pp. 23, 27, 244 and facing plate (the Phoenix Jewel).

76. *History of the World*, 2nd edn. (London, 1617), Preface, sig. B2r. On the implications for historiography of reading everything as part of a divine plan, see Arthur B. Ferguson, *Clio Unbound: Perception of the Social and Cultural Past in Renaissance England* (Durham, NC, 1979), esp. p. 18.

CHAPTER 8

1. See the discussion in Hayden White, 'Historical Text as Literary Artefact', in his *Tropics of Discourse* (Baltimore, 1978), pp. 84–92.

2. Torquato Tasso, *Discourses on the Heroic Poem*, trans. Mariella Cavalchini and Irene Samuel (Oxford, 1973) p. 50.

3. Helen Cooper, 'Counter-Romance: Civil Strife and Father-killing in the Prose Romances', in *The Long Fifteenth Century: Essays for Douglas Gray*, ed. Helen Cooper and Sally Mapstone (Oxford, 1997), pp. 141–62. The late fifteenth-century prose *Siege of Jerusalem*, which has as its central events not just the destruction of the city but the cannibalism to which its starving inhabitants resort, has none of the idealizing markers of courtesy or love or adventure that set audience expectations for romance, and is, therefore, not considered here.

4. Fredric Jameson, *The Political Unconscious* (Ithaca and London, 1981), p. 102.
5. George Steiner, 'Roncevaux', in *The Return of Thematic Criticism*, ed. Werner Sollers (Cambridge, Mass., 1993), p. 299.
6. See p. 58 above; and, for a more extensive discussion of the transformation of the romance, Helen Cooper, 'The Strange History of *Valentine*', pp. 153–68.
7. *Valentine*, ed. Dickson, p. 163.
8. See p. 81 above.
9. Malory, i. 89 (II. 17).
10. Malory, i. 89, 91 (II. 18, 19).
11. See further, Elspeth Kennedy, 'Failure in Arthurian Romance', *Medium Ævum* 60 (1991), 16–32.
12. The strength of the pun is emphasized by the manuscript reading 'non' (for the editors' 'mon'): no one may conceal his failure without misfortune. The verb 'hitte' is not normally intransitive in Middle English, so the attractiveness of translating the phrase as 'lest disaster strike' is a false friend; but it can carry the meaning 'come true' or 'be verified' (*MED* 'hitten', 3c).
13. Boethius' Philosophy explains that randomness increases with distance from the centre, God; cf. *Knight's Tale*, *CT*, I. 3007–10, where Theseus argues that although the natural world takes its origin from something perfect and stable, it 'descend[s] so til it be corrumpable'.
14. *CT*, VII. 2771–4.
15. Barbara Nolan, *Chaucer and the Tradition of the 'Roman antique'* (Cambridge, 1992), p. 248.
16. For more extensive discussion, see Helen Cooper, 'Jacobean Chaucer: *The Two Noble Kinsmen* and other Chaucerian Plays', in Krier (ed.), *Refiguring Chaucer*, pp. 189–209.
17. 1. 3. 35–85 for the debate on heterosexual versus same-sex love; 1. 3. 18–22 on the Amazons' experience of war; and 3. 3 for the lovers' joking about the women they have seduced and ruined.
18. Thomas Gent, an Irishman who set up a publishing business in York, wrote a verse life of Judas that devotes six pages to the casting adrift (*Judas Iscariot* (York, 1772), reprinted in *Yorkshire Chap-books*, ed. Charles A. Federer, 1st ser. (London, 1889), pp. 205–10; Gent probably wrote it some decades earlier (p. 11)).
19. *The South English Legendary*, ed. Charlotte d'Evelyn and Anna J. Mill, EETS O.S. 236 (1956), pp. 692–7, ll. 23–4. The legend originated in Latin in the twelfth century; it was most widely disseminated through the legend of St Matthias, who took his place as apostle after the Betrayal, in the *Golden Legend* of Jacobus de Voragine. It also appears in Middle English in Judas's introductory monologue to the *Suspensio Judae* in the Towneley cycle of mystery plays. Thomas Gent adds the detail that the baby carries a double birthmark of a cross and a gibbet (in *Yorkshire Chap-Books*, ed. Federer, p. 206).
20. The phrase is the linking colophon at the end of Vinaver's section 7, which he uses as a heading for the final section: see iii. 1154. Caxton omits the phrase.
21. From the anonymous mid-fifteenth-century translation, *Merlin*, ed. Wheatley, p. 579. The kin-killing is a synecdoche for civil war as well as being a specific reference to Mordred: see further p. 403 below.
22. On the rival interpretations of magic as divine or devilish, see John S. Mebane, *Renaissance Magic and the Return of the Golden Age* (Lincoln, Nebr., and London,

1989). Fairies were interpreted by the witch-hunters as devils rather than as a separate order outside the human, angelic, and diabolic.

23. This is the driving argument of his *Religion and the Decline of Magic*.

24. *William of Palerne*, ed. Bunt, l. 120. She turns into an attractive character at the end, reassuring her de-wolfed stepson that he needn't be ashamed of his nakedness because he is all that a man should be, bathing him 'curtesli', and being greeted as 'swete lady hende' by William (4443–80).

25. For the development of English legislation, see Thomas, *Religion and the Decline of Magic*, pp. 521–34.

26. *Gervase of Tilbury: Otia Imperialia*, ed. Banks and Binns, pp. 118–19. He also insists that precious stones have intrinsic virtues that can be enhanced by God through consecration, pp. 614–19.

27. The French text was first printed in 1489, having been composed probably within the dozen or so years before that. Direct influence from the *Malleus* even on its later English readers is highly unlikely, as the work remained little known in England (Thomas, *Religion and the Decline of Magic*, p. 523).

28. *Valentine*, ed. Dickson, pp. 142 (Pacolet at the 'scole of tollette', Toledo), 168 (Adramayne 'had learned so wel the arte of tollette').

29. *Valentine*, ed. Dickson, pp. 255–7 (Valentine's anxiety is less about the treachery itself than its being ascribed to him); p. 272.

30. *Richard Cœur de Lion*, ed. Brunner, ll. 188–234.

31. The Armenian episode is emphasized in the French metrical version of the romance composed early in the fifteenth century, a few years after the prose; for its political context, see Laurence Harf-Lancner's Introduction to her modernization of this text, *Coudrette: Le Roman de Melusine* (Paris, 1993), pp. 26–35. My discussion here follows the briefer version appended to the prose romance. The metrical text was also translated into English, as the *Romance of Partenay*; see in particular ll. 5619–28, 5682–91 (ed. Skeat).

32. See Maddox, *Fictions of Identity*, p. 178.

33. *Melusine*, ed. Donald, p. 15.

34. The term is Donald Maddox's, *Fictions of Identity*, p. 178.

35. *Melusine*, ed. Donald, pp. 64–5.

36. Ibid, p. 298.

37. See pp. 187–8 above.

38. *Sundry Strange Prophecies*, p. 27; and see also, p. 345 above.

39. See Antonia Fraser, *Cromwell our Chief of Men* (London, 1973), pp. 400–33.

40. William Caxton, *The History of Jason translated from the French of Raoul Lefevre*, ed. John Munro, EETS E.S. 111 (1913), p. 198. She promises not to practise any more 'enchantemens ne none other malefices' unless she tells him first.

41. These are the dates of their entry in the *Stationers' Register*; no copies survive from before the sixth (1631) impression (*STC* 14684).

42. Ed. Thoms, *Early English Prose Romances*, p. 621 (the *Pleasant Historie* is on pp. 603–54, the *Second Part* on pp. 655–90).

43. *Tom a Lincolne*, Part II, ed. Thoms, p. 657.

44. It is probably taken from Novel 38 in William Painter's *Palace of Pleasure*, (1st edn. (1566); Bullough prints the 1575 edn., *Narrative and Dramatic Sources*, ii. 373–96), though there is a possibility that he used a French translation of Boccaccio's story. The subplot is apparently his own invention.

45. *William of Palerne*, ed. Bunt, ll. 445–6; the corresponding section of the printed version does not survive. The continuing familiarity of such a motif in the heroine's mouth is proved by its reappearance in *Tom a Lincoln* (p. 630, Valentine's lover; p. 644, Anglitora).

46. In the Painter, she presents her husband with the twins she has borne, and he recognizes them as his because 'they were so like hym' (Bullough, ii. 396). The play text implies that she is just pregnant, since she presents him with his letter and ring but not explicitly any baby; but the stage presence of a baby is not ruled out.

47. *Winter's Tale*, 1. 2. 69–88.

48. See Newcomb, 'The Triumph of Time'.

49. *The Knight of Curtesy*, ed. McCausland, l. 48; cf. also 87–96. It appears among the books listed in the mid-1570s in Robert Langham's *Letter*. On its sources, see note 95 on p. 488. The core motif of the eaten heart is most widely known through Boccaccio's story of Guiscardo and Sigismonda, though the *Knight of Curtesy* shows no influence from it; the Boccaccio does, however, probably underlie the ballad of *Lady Diamond* (Child, *Ballads*, no. 269, v. 29–38), in which the lady eats the heart of the kitchen-boy who has made her pregnant.

50. Cinthio's *Gli Hecatommithi*, possibly by way of a French translation: see Bullough, *Narrative and Dramatic Sources*, vii. 194.

51. 3. 4. 100; and see p. 163 above.

52. The Folio reading 'Iudean' in 5. 2. 356, indicating Judas Iscariot as the traitor who destroyed someone of infinite worth, in place of 'Indian', the ignorant man who cannot recognize value when he sees it, would fit attractively with this line of argument; but since 'Indian' scans and 'Iudean' does not, the Folio reading is overwhelmingly likely to be simply the result of a turned *n*.

53. See pp. 121–2 above.

54. 5. 1. 64.

55. From Bodleian MS Rawlinson D 82, a paper manuscript without watermarks; the handwriting probably dates from after 1450. In Friedrich Brie's edn. ('Zwei mittelenglische Prosaromane', *Anglia*, 130 (1913), 40–52, 269–85), *Thebes* runs from pp. 47–52, 269–72; *Troy* from pp. 272–85.

56. Quotations up until the last from Brie's edn., pp. 47–52; 'with bright baners . . .' from p. 270.

57. John Lydgate, *Lydgate's Fall of Princes*, ed. H. Bergen, EETS E.S. 121–4 (1924–7), Vol. 3, viii. 2703–870 (2855–6, 2759 quoted).

58. *Lydgate's Reson and Sensuallyte*, ed. Ernst Sieper, EETS E.S. 84 (1901), ll. 3140–210; Lydgate has Diana choose Arthur's court as the exemplum of good love.

59. The argument that the Alliterative *Morte Arthure* punishes Arthur for his *hubris*, his overweening pride, does not receive any significant support from the text. In contradiction of the general moral emphasis of Lydgate's *Fall of Princes*, Arthur's is one of the very few falls ascribed solely to envious Fortune.

60. Malory, ii. 698–700 (X. 58).

61. Malory, iii. 1183 (XX. 9).

62. Guinevere blames their love for 'the deth of the most nobelest knyghtes of the worlde' and commits herself to a life of religious penance (Malory, iii. 1252 (XXI. 9)), but even she does not claim that it was God's punishment.

63. The French treatment is very different, describing the battle as a series of long-drawn-out individual combats. Malory is here following the ballad-like stanzaic

Morte Arthur (in *King Arthur's Death*, ed. L. D. Benson, rev. by Edward E. Foster, 3rd edn. (Kalamazoo, 2000), ll. 3358–83).

64. 'The Union of the Red Rose and the White', in *A Collection of Old Ballads*, ed. Phillips, ii. 106–14.

65. *Early English Classical Tragedies*, ed. John W. Cunliffe (Oxford, 1912), pp. 217–97, p. 224; and see also III. iv. 21, 'I made my sister bad'—and by Elizabethan conventions of twinhood he could hardly have failed to recognize her anyway. The original text as printed includes a number of variant speeches written by other members of Gray's Inn, which substituted for some of Hughes's.

66. Richard Robinson's 1582 translation of the antiquary John Leland's 'O scelera: o mores: o corrupta tempora', in his 1544 *Assertio inclytissimi Arturii*, ed. W. E. Mead, EETS O.S. 165 (1925), as part of the issue titled for Middleton's *Chinon of England*; see pp. 63, 129.

67. From the Chorus that closes Act I, ll. 21–4.

68. See p. 24 and n. 54.

69. Quotation from 4. 6. 38 of the Folio 'Tragedy' text (21. 43 of the Quarto 'History': Wells and Taylor print the texts in sequence). Lear's 'Look there!', inviting performance as a belief that she still breathes, appears only in the Folio.

70. *Percy*, ii. 390–9 (ll. 183–4 quoted).

71. From his concluding note on *Lear* in his edition of Shakespeare: 'Since all reasonable beings naturally love justice, I cannot easily be persuaded, that the observation of justice makes a play worse . . . I was many years ago so shocked by Cordelia's death, that I know not whether I ever endured to read again the last scenes of the play till I undertook to revise them as an editor' (*Johnson on Shakespeare*, ed. Arthur Sherbo (New Haven, 1968), ii. 704).

72. Nahum Tate, *The History of King Lear*, ed. James Black (Lincoln, Nebr., 1975), V. vi. 159–60.

Bibliography

Anonymous works are listed by title; anthologies are listed under the surname of the editor. For further information on individual romances contained within anthologies, see Appendix.

PRIMARY

Alexander. The Prose Life of Alexander, ed. J. S. Westlake, EETS O.S. 143 (1913).
—— see also Hay; *Kyng Alisaunder.*

Alsop, Thomas, *Fair Custance*, in Franklin B. Williams, 'Alsop's *Fair Custance*: Chaucer in Tudor Dress', *ELR* 6 (1976), 351–68.

Amadas et Ydoine: Roman du XIIIe siècle, ed. John R. Reinhard, CFMA (Paris: Honoré Champion, 1926).

Amadas and Ydoine, trans. Ross G. Arthur (New York and London: Garland, 1993).

Amadis de Gaule: see Munday.

Andreas Capellanus on Love, ed. and trans. P. G. Walsh (London: Duckworth, 1982).
—— see also Brook.

An Anonymous Short English Metrical Chronicle, ed. Ewald Zettl, EETS OS 196 (1935).

Anton, Robert, *Moriomachia* (London: Simon Stafford, 1613).

Apollonius of Tyre: see [secondary], Archibald.

Ariosto, Ludovico, *Orlando Furioso*, ed. Lanfranco Caretti, 2nd edn. (Turin: Einaudi, 1992).
—— see also Harington.

Arthur, ed. F. J. Furnivall, EETS O.S. 2 (1864).

Arthur. Of Arthour and of Merlin, ed. O. D. Macrae-Gibson, EETS 268, 279 (1973, 1979).

Arthur of Little Britain, trans. John Bourchier, Lord Berners, ed. E. V. Utterson (London: White, Cochrane, 1814).

Ascham, Roger, *Roger Ascham: English Works*, ed. William Aldis Wright (Cambridge: Cambridge University Press, 1904, repr. 1970).

The Auchinleck Manuscript: National Library of Scotland Advocates' MS 19.2.1, intro. Derek Pearsall and I. C. Cunningham (London: Scolar Press in association with the National Library of Scotland, 1979).

Augustine, *Saint Augustine: Confessions*, trans. R. S. Pine-Coffin (Harmondsworth: Penguin, 1961).

Bacon, Francis, *The History of the Reign of King Henry VII and Selected Works*, ed. Brian Vickers (Cambridge: Cambridge University Press, 1998).

Baldwin, William, *Beware the Cat by William Baldwin: The First English Novel*, ed. William Ringler, jr, and Michael Flachmann (San Marino: Huntington Library, 1988).

Bateman, Stephen, *The Trauayled Pylgrime* (London: H. Denham, 1569).

Beaumont, Francis, and Fletcher, John, *The Dramatic Works in the Beaumont and Fletcher Canon*, general editor Fredson Bowers, 10 vols. (Cambridge: Cambridge University Press, 1966–96).

Benson, L. D. (ed.), *King Arthur's Death* (1974; repr. Exeter: Exeter University Press, 1986).

Berners: see *Arthur of Little Britain, Huon of Bordeaux*.

Bevis of Hamton: The Romance of Sir Beues of Hamtoun, ed. Eugen Kölbing, EETS E.S. 46, 48 65. (1885, 1886, 1894) (also 1-vol. reprint, Kraus, New York: 1978).

——*Syr Beuis of Hampton* (London: W. Copland, ?1565).

——*Syr Beuis of Hampton* (London: T. East, ?1585).

Biket, Robert, *Le Lai du Corn*, ed. E. T. Erickson, Anglo-Norman Text Society 24 (Oxford: Blackwell, 1973).

Blake, William, *Poetry and Prose of William Blake*, ed. Geoffrey Keynes (London: Nonesuch Press, 1932).

Blamires, Alcuin (ed.), with Karen Pratt and C. W. Marx, *Woman Defamed and Woman Defended: An Anthology of Medieval Texts*, (Oxford: Clarendon Press, 1992).

Blanchardyn and Eglantine, see *Caxton's Blanchardyn*.

Boccaccio, Giovanni, *Decameron*, ed. Vittore Branca, 2nd edn. (Turin: Einaudi, 1984).

——*Opere I*, ed. Salvatore Battaglia, Scrittori d'Italia 167 (Bari: Laterza, 1938).

Bodel, Jean, *La Chanson des Saisnes*, ed. Annette Brasseur, TLF, 2 vols. (Geneva: Droz, 1989).

Bowdler, Thomas (ed.), *The Family Shakespeare* (London, 1807).

Braswell, Mary Flowers (ed.), *Sir Perceval of Galles and Ywain and Gawain* (Kalamazoo: TEAMS, 1995).

Brendan, see *Navigatio*; O'Donaghue.

Brie, Friedrich (ed.), 'Zwei mittelenglische Prosaromane: *The Sege of Thebes* und *The Sege of Troy*', *Anglia* 130 (1913), 40–52, 269–85.

Brook, Leslie C. (ed.), *Two Late Medieval Love Treatises*, Medium Ævum Monographs, 16 (Oxford: Society for the Study of Mediæval Languages and Literature, 1993).

Brooke, C. F. Tucker (ed.), *The Shakespeare Apocrypha* (Oxford: Clarendon Press, 1908).

Brown, Carleton (ed.), *English Lyrics of the XIIIth Century* (Oxford: Clarendon Press, 1932).

The Brut; or, The Chronicles of England, ed. Friedrich W. D. Brie, EETS O.S. 131, 136 (1906, 1908).

Bryan, W. F., and Dempster, Germaine (eds), *Sources and Analogues of Chaucer's Canterbury Tales* (1941; repr. Atlantic Highlands, NJ: Humanities Press, 1958).

Buck, George, *History of King Richard III,* ed. Arthur Noel Kincaid (Gloucester: Alan Sutton, 1979).

Bullough, Geoffrey (ed.), *Narrative and Dramatic Sources of Shakespeare,* 8 vols. (London: Routledge and Kegan Paul; New York: Columbia University Press, 1957–75).

Bunyan, John, *The Miscellaneous Works of John Bunyan,* ed. T. L. Underwood and Roger Sharrock (Oxford: Clarendon Press, 1980).

Bunyan, John, *The Pilgrim's Progress and Grace Abounding,* ed. Roger Sharrock (London: Oxford University Press, 1966).

Butler, Samuel, *Hudibras,* ed. John Wilders (Oxford: Clarendon Press, 1967).

Il Cantare di Fiorio e Biancifiore, see *Fiorio.*

Capgrave, John, *John Capgrave's Abbreuiacion of Chronicles,* ed. Peter J. Lucas, EETS 285 (1985).

Caxton, William, *Caxton's Blanchardyn and Eglantine, c.*1489, ed. Leon Kellner, EETS E.S. 58 (1890).

—— *The Book of the Ordre of Chyualry Translated by William Caxton,* ed. A. T. P. Byles, EETS O.S. 168 (1926).

—— *Christine de Pisan: The Book of the Fayttes of Armes and of Chyvalrye,* ed. A. T. P. Byles, EETS O.S. 189 (1932).

—— *The Golden Legend; or Lives, of the Saints Englished by William Caxton,* ed. by F. S. Ellis, Temple Classics, 7 vols. (London: J. M. Dent, 1900).

—— *The History of Jason translated from the French of Raoul Lefevre,* ed. John Munro, EETS E.S. 111 (1913).

—— *The Right Pleasant and Goodly History of the Four Sons of Aymon,* ed. Octavia Richardson, EETS E.S. 44, 45 (1884–5).

—— *Paris and Vienne Translated from the French and Printed by William Caxton,* ed. M. Leach, EETS O.S. 234 (1957).

Cervantes, Miguel de: see Shelton.

Chatelain de Coucy: see Jakemes; *Knight of Curtesy.*

Chaucer, Geoffrey, *The Riverside Chaucer,* general ed. Larry D. Benson (Boston: Houghton Mifflin, 1987; Oxford: Oxford University Press, 1988).

Chevelere Assigne: The Romance of the Cheuelere Assigne, ed. Henry H. Gibbs, EETS E.S. 6 (1868).

Child, Francis James (ed.), *The English and Scottish Popular Ballads,* 5 vols. (1882–98; repr. New York: Dover, 1965).

Chrétien de Troyes: Arthurian Romances, trans. by William W. Kibler (Harmondsworth: Penguin, 1991).

Chrétien de Troyes, *Les Chansons courtoises de Chrétien de Troyes*, ed. Marie-Claire Gérard-Zai (Frankfurt and Berne: Lang, 1974).

—— *Les Romans de Chrétien de Troyes I: Erec et Enide*, ed. Mario Roques, CFMA (Paris: Champion, 1981).

—— *Les Romans de Chrétien de Troyes II: Cligés*, ed. Alexandre Micha, CFMA (Paris: Champion, 1982).

—— *Les Romans de Chrétien de Troyes III: Le Chevalier de la Charrette*, ed. Mario Roques, CFMA (Paris: Champion, 1978).

—— *Les Romans de Chrétien de Troyes IV: Le Chevalier au Lion (Yvain)*, ed. Mario Roques, CFMA (Paris: Champion, 1965).

—— *Les Romans de Chrétien de Troyes V–VI: Le Conte du Graal (Perceval)*, ed. Félix Lecoy, 2 vols., CFMA (Paris: Champion, 1975) .

Christina of Markyate: The Life of Christina of Markyate, a Twelfth-century Recluse, ed. and trans. C. H. Talbot, rev. edn. (Oxford: Clarendon Press, 1987).

Christine de Pizan, *The Boke of the Cyte of Ladyes*, trans. Brian Anslay (London: Henry Pepwell, 1521).

—— *The Book of the City of Ladies*, trans. Rosalind Brown-Grant (Harmondsworth: Penguin, 1999).

—— *Book of Fayttes of Armes*: see Caxton, *Christine*.

—— *La Città delle Dame*, ed. Patrizia Caraffi and Earl Jeffrey Richards (Milan: Luni Editrice, 1998).

Cyuile and Vnciuile Life (London: R. Jones, 1579).

Clyomon and Clamydes, ed. Betty J. Littleton, Studies in English Literature 35 (The Hague and Paris: Mouton, 1968).

Colville, John, *Original Letters of Mr John Colville 1582–1603*, ed. David Laing (Edinburgh: Bannatayne Club, 1858).

The Complaynt of Scotland (c.1550) by Mr Robert Wedderburn, ed. A. M. Stewart, Scottish Text Society (Edinburgh, 1979).

Coudrette: Le Roman de Mélusine, intro. and trans. Laurence Harf-Lancner (Paris: Flammarion, 1993).

Coudrette: *Le Roman de Mélusine ou histoire de Lusignan par Coudrette*, ed. Eleanor Roach, Bibliothèque française et romane (Paris: Klincksieck, 1982).

Crosse, Henry, *Vertue's Commonwealth by Henry Crosse (1603)*, ed. Alexander B. Grosart (Manchester: privately printed, 1878).

Cunliffe, John W. (ed.), *Early English Classical Tragedies* (Oxford: Clarendon Press, 1912).

Cursor mundi I, ed. Richard Morris, EETS O.S. 57 (1874).

Dekker, Thomas: *The Dramatic Works of Thomas Dekker*, ed. Fredson Bowers, 3 vols. (Cambridge: Cambridge University Press, 1953–8).

Degrevant: see *Sir Degrevant*.

De origine gigantum: James P. Carley and Julia Crick, 'Constructing Albion's Past: An annotated Edition of *De origine gigantum*', *Arthurian Literature* 13 (1995), 41–114.

Dering, Edward, *A Briefe and Necessary Instruction* (London: J. Awdely, 1572).

Des grants Geanz, ed. G. E. Brereton, Medium Ævum Monographs 2 (Oxford: Basil Blackwell, 1937).

The Dialoges of Creatures Moralysed, ed. Gregory Kratzmann and Elizabeth Gee (Leiden and New York: E. J. Brill, 1998).

Donne, John, *John Donne: The Complete English Poems*, ed. A. J. Smith, corr. edn. (Harmondsworth: Penguin, 1976).

Drayton, Michael, *The Works of Michael Drayton*, ed. J. William Hebel, 5 vols. (Oxford: Shakespeare Head Press, 1961).

Eger and Grime, ed. James Ralston Caldwell, Harvard Studies in Comparative Literature 9 (Cambridge, Mass.: Harvard University Press, 1933).

Eglamour: see *Sir Eglamour of Artois*.

Eilhart von Oberge: Tristrant und Isalde, ed. and trans. Danielle Buschinger and Wolfgang Spiewok, WODAN 27 (Greifswald: Reinecke Verlag, 1993).

Eilhart von Oberge's Tristrant, trans. J. W. Thomas (Lincoln, Nebraska, and London: University of Nebraska Press, 1978).

Eneas, roman du XIIe siècle, ed. J. J. Salverda de Grave, CFMA 44, 62 (Paris: Champion, 1925, 1929).

Eneas: A Twelfth-Century French Romance, trans. John A. Yunck (New York and London: Columbia University Press, 1974).

Etienne of Rouen, *Draco Normannicus*, in Howlett (ed.), *Chronicles of the Reigns of Stephen, Henry II and Richard I*, ii. 585–762.

Fairfax, Edward (trans.), *Godfrey of Bulloigne*, ed. Kathleen M. Lea and T. M. Gang (Oxford: Clarendon Press, 1981).

Federer, Charles A. (ed.), *Yorkshire Chap-books*, 1st ser. (London: Elliot Stock, 1889).

Fellows, Jennifer (ed.), *Of Love and Chivalry: An Anthology of Middle English Romance*, Everyman (London: J. M. Dent, 1993).

Fiorio e Biancifiore: Il Cantare di Fiorio e Biancifiore, ed. Vincenzo Crescini, Scelta di curiosità di letterarie inedite o rare 233, 249 (1889; repr. Bologna: Commissione per i testi de lingua, 1969).

Flamenca: The Romance of Flamenca, ed. and trans. E. D. Blodgett (New York: Garland, 1995).

Fletcher, John: *The Dramatic Works in the Beaumont and Fletcher Canon*, general editor Fredson Bowers, 10 vols. (Cambridge: Cambridge University Press, 1966–96).

Floire et Blancheflor: Le Conte de Floire et Blancheflor, ed. Jean-Luc Leclanche, CFMA (Paris: Champion, 1980).

Floire et Blancheflor: seconde version, ed. Margaret M. Pelan, Association des publications près les Universités de Strasbourg (Paris: Ophrys, 1975).

Florés Saga ok Blankiflúr, ed. Eugen Kölbing, Altnordische Saga-Bibliothek 5 (Halle: Max Niemeyer, 1896).

Floriant et Florete (ed.), Harry F. Williams (Ann Arbor: University of Michigan Press, 1947).

Forbes, Alexander Penrose (ed.), *The Lives of St Ninian and St Kentigern* (1874; repr. Lampeter: Llanerch, 1989).

Ford, John, *Three Plays*, ed. Keith Sturgess (Harmondsworth: Penguin, 1970).

Forster, John, *The Life of Charles Dickens*, ed. A.J. Hoppé (revised edn., London: Dent, 1969).

Foster, Edward E. (ed.), *Amis and Amiloun, Robert of Cisyle, and Sir Amadace* (Kalamazoo: TEAMS), 1997).

Four Sons of Aymon: see Caxton, *Right Pleasant and Goodly History*.

Foxe, John, *Ecclesiasticall Historie*, 3rd edn. (London: John Day, 1576).

French, Walter Hoyt, and Hale, Charles Brockway (eds.), *Middle English Metrical Romances* (New York: Russell and Russell, 1964).

Garter, Thomas, *The Most Virtuous and Godly Susanna by Thomas Garter*, ed. B. Ifor Evans and W. W. Greg (Oxford: Malone Society Reprints, 1936 for 1937).

Gascoigne, George, *The Complete Works of George Gascoigne*, ed. John W. Cunliffe, 2 vols. (1907; repr. New York: Greenwood Press, 1969).

Gawain: see *Sir Gawain and the Green Knight*; Hahn.

Generides: A Royal Historie of the Excellent Knight Generides, ed. Frederick J. Furnivall (Roxburghe Club, 1865; repr. New York: Burt Franklin, 1971).

Generydes: A Romance in Seven-line Stanzas, ed. W. Aldis Wright, EETS O.S. 55, 70 (1878).

Gent, Thomas, *Judas Iscariot*, in Federer (ed.), *Yorkshire Chap-books*.

Geoffrey of Monmouth: The History of the Kings of Britain, trans. Lewis Thorpe (Harmondsworth: Penguin, 1966).

Geoffrey of Monmouth, *Life of Merlin: Geoffrey of Monmouth, Vita Merlini*, ed. Basil Clarke (Cardiff: University of Wales Press, 1973).

Gerald of Wales: The Journey through Wales and The Description of Wales, trans. Lewis Thorpe (Harmondsworth: Penguin, 1978).

Gervase of Tilbury: Otia Imperialia, Recreation for an Emperor, ed. and trans. S. E. Banks and J. W. Binns (Oxford: Clarendon Press, 2002).

Gesta Romanorum: The Early English Versions of the Gesta Romanorum, ed. Sidney J. H. Herrtage, EETS 33 (1879).

Golden Legend: see Caxton.

Golding, Arthur, *Ovid's Metamorphoses: The Arthur Golding Translation of 1567*, ed. John Frederick Nims (Harmondsworth: Penguin, 2000).

Gorges, Arthur, *The Poems of Sir Arthur Gorges*, ed. Helen Easterbrook Sanderson (Oxford, 1953).

Gosson, Stephen, *Playes Confuted in Five Actions by Stephen Gosson*, facsmile with a preface by Arthur Freeman, 'The English Stage: Attack and Defence 1577–1830' (New York and London: Garland, 1972).

Gottfried von Strassburg: Tristan, ed. Gottfried Weber (Darmstadt: Wissenschaftliche Buchgesellschaft, 1967).

Gottfried von Strassburg: Tristan, trans. A. T. Hatto, Penguin Classics (Harmondsworth, 1960).

Gower, John, *The English Works of John Gower,* ed. G. C. Macaulay, 2 vols., EETS E.S. 81–2 (1900–1).

Greene, Robert, *The Life and Complete Works in Prose and Verse of Robert Greene,* ed. Alexander B. Grosart, 12 vols. (1881–3; repr. New York: Russell and Russell, 1964).

Gregorius: Die mittelenglische Gregoriuslegende, ed. Carl Keller (Heidelberg: Carl Winter, 1914).

Gui de Warewic, roman du XIIIe siècle, ed. Alfred Ewert, CFMA 74–5 (Paris, 1932–3).

Guillaume de Palerne, ed. Alexandre Micha, TLF (Geneva: Droz, 1990).

Guy of Warwick: The Romance of Guy of Warwick, ed. Julius Zupitza, EETS E.S. 42, 49, 59 (1-vol. repr., 1966) .

Guy of Warwick: The Romance of Guy of Warwick: Fifteenth-century Version, ed. Julius Zupitza, EETS E.S. 25, 26 (1-vol. repr., 1966).

Guy of Warwick nach Coplands Druck, ed. Gustav Schleich, Palaestra 139 (Leipzig: Mayer und Müller, 1923).

Guy of Warwick: The Tragical History, Admirable Atchievments and Various Events of Guy Earl of Warwick (London: Vere and Gilbertson, 1661).

Hadewijch: The Complete Works, trans. Mother Columba Hart (London: SPCK, 1980).

Hahn, Thomas (ed.), *Sir Gawain: Eleven Romances and Tales,* TEAMS (Kalamazoo: Western Michigan University Press, 1995).

Halliwell, James Orchard (ed.), *The Palatine Anthology* (London: privately printed, 1850).

Harding, John, *The Chronicle of Iohn Harding,* ed. Henry Ellis (London: Rivington *et al.,* 1812).

Harington, John, *Ludovico Ariosto's Orlando Furioso translated into English Heroical Verse by Sir John Harington (1591),* ed. Robert McNulty (Oxford: Clarendon Press, 1972).

Harley 2253: *Facsimile of British Museum MS Harley 2253,* intro. N. R. Ker, EETS OS 255 (1965).

Havelok: Le Lai d'Haveloc and Gaimar's Haveloc Episode, ed. Alexander Bell (Manchester: Manchester University Press, 1925).

Havelok, ed. G. V. Smithers (Oxford: Clarendon Press, 1987).

Hawes, Stephen, *Stephen Hawes: The Minor Poems,* ed. Florence W. Gluck and Alice B. Morgan, EETS 271 (1974).

Hay, Sir Gilbert, *The Buik of King Alexander the Conqueror,* ed. John Cartwright, Scottish Text Society, 3 vols. (Edinburgh, 1986–90).

—— *The Prose Works of Sir Gilbert Hay,* Vol. 3. ed. Jonathan A. Glenn, Scottish Text Society (Edinburgh, 1993).

Hazlitt, W. Carew (ed.), *Fairy Tales, Legends and Romances illustrating Shakespeare and other early English Writers* (London: Frank and William Kerslake, 1875).

—— (ed.), *Remains of the Early Popular Poetry of England,* 4 vols. (London: John Russell Smith, 1864–6).

Heldris of Cornuälle, *Le Roman de Silence: a thirteenth-century verse romance by Heldris de Cornuälle*, ed. Lewis Thorpe (Cambridge: W. Heffer, 1972).
—— *Silence: A thirteenth-century French Romance*, ed. and trans. Sarah Roche-Mahdi (East Lansing: Colleagues Press, 1992).
Henslowe, Philip: *Henslowe's Diary*, ed. R. A. Foakes, 2nd edn. (Cambridge: Cambridge University Press, 2002).
Herbert, Edward, *The Life of Edward, First Lord Herbert of Cherbury*, ed. J. M. Shuttleworth (London and New York: Oxford University Press, 1976).
The Heroicall Adventures of the Knight of the Sea (London: William Leake, 1600).
Herzman, Ronald B., Drake, Graham, and Salisbury, Eve (eds.), *Four Romances of England: King Horn, Havelok the Dane, Bevis of Hampton, Athelston* (Kalamazoo: TEAMS, 1999).
Heywood, Thomas, *If You Know not Me, You Know Nobody; or, The Troubles of Queen Elizabeth*, Malone Society Reprints (Oxford: Oxford University Press, 1934).
Hoccleve's Works: The Minor Poems, ed. Frederick J. Furnivall and I. Gollancz, rev. by Jerome Mitchell and A. I. Doyle, EETS E.S. 61, 73 rev. repr. (London, 1970).
Holinshed, Raphael, *Chronicles of England, Scotland and Ireland* (1807–8; repr. with intro. by Vernon F. Snow, New York: AMS Press, 1965).
Holme, Wilfride, *The Fall and Evill Successe of Rebellion* (London: H. Binneman, 1572).
Horn: The Romance of Horn by Thomas, ed. Mildred K. Pope and T. B. W. Reid, Anglo-Norman Text Society 9–10, 12–13 (Oxford: Basil Blackwell, 1955, 1964).
Horn Childe and Maiden Rimnild, ed. Maldwyn Mills, Middle English Texts 20 (Heidelberg: Carl Winter Universitätsverlag, 1988).
—— see also *King Horn*.
Horstmann, Carl (ed.), *Altenglische Legenden*, Neue Folge (Heilbronn: Henninger, 1881).
—— *Sammlung altenglischer Legenden* (Heilbronn: Henninger, 1878).
Howlett, Richard (ed.), *Chronicles of the Reigns of Stephen, Henry II and Richard I*, Rolls Series (London, 1885).
Hudson, Harriet (ed.), *Four Middle English Romances: Sir Isumbras, Octavian, Sir Eglamour of Artois, Sir Tryamour* (Kalamazoo: TEAMS, 1996).
Hue de Rotelande, *Ipomedon: Poème de Hue de Rotelande*, ed. A. J. Holden, Bibliothèque française et romane 17 (Klincksieck: Paris, 1979).
Hughes, Thomas, *The Misfortunes of Arthur*, ed. Brian Jay Corrigan (New York and London: Garland, 1992).
Hunter, Joseph (ed.), *Ecclesiastical Documents*, Camden Society, OS 8 (London, 1840).
Huon of Bordeaux: The Boke of Duke Huon of Burdeux, Done into English by John Bourchier, Lord Berners, ed. S. L. Lee, EETS ES 40, 41, 43, 50 (1882–7; 2-vol. repr., 1973, 1998).

Hyrd, Richard, *A very frvteful and pleasant Boke callyd the Instrvction of a Christen woman* (London: T. Berthelet, 1541).

Ipomadon, ed. Rhiannon Purdie, EETS OS 316 (2001).

Ipomedon in drei englischen Bearbeitungen, ed. Eugen Kölbing (Breslau: Wilhelm Koebner, 1889).

Ipomedon: see Hue de Rotelande.

Ipomydon: The Lyfe of Ipomydon, ed. Tadahiro Ikegami, 2 vols., Seijo English Monographs 21–2 (Tokyo: Seijo University, 1983, 1985).

Isumbras: Sir Ysumbras, ed. Gustav Schleich, Palaestra 15 (Berlin: Mayer and Müller, 1901).

Jacques de Lalaing: Le livre des faits de Jacques de Lalaing, ed. Kervyn de Lettenhove, *Oeuvres de Georges Chastellain* 8 (Brussels, 1866).

Jakemes, *Le Roman du Castelain de Couci et la Dame de Fayel par Jakemes*, ed. M. Delbouille, SATF (Paris, 1936).

Jean d'Arras: Melusine, ed. Louis Stouff (1932; repr. Geneva: Slatkine, 1974).

John of Glastonbury: *The Chronicle of Glastonbury Abbey: An edition, Translation and Study of John of Glastonbury's 'Cronica sive Antiquitates Glastoniensis Ecclesie'*, ed. James P. Carley, trans. David Townsend (1985; repr. Woodbridge: Boydell and Brewer, 2001).

Johnson, Richard, *R. I., The Most Pleasant History of Tom a Lincolne*, ed. Richard S. M. Hirsch (Columbia, SC: University of South Carolina Press, 1978).

—— *The Seven Champions of Christendom*, ed. Jennifer Fellows (Aldershot: Ashgate, 2003).

Johnson, Samuel, *Johnson on Shakespeare*, ed. Arthur Sherbo, The Yale Edition of the Works of Samuel Johnson 8 (New Haven and London: Yale University Press, 1968).

Jonson, Ben, *Ben Jonson*, ed. C. H. Herford and Percy and Evelyn Simpson, 11 vols. (corr. edn., Oxford: Clarendon Press, 1954).

—— *Ben Jonson: The Complete Poems*, ed. George Parfitt (Harmondsworth: Penguin, 1975).

Joseph of Arimathie, ed. W. W. Skeat, EETS O.S. 44 (1871).

Kempe, Margery, *The Book of Margery Kempe*, ed. Barry Windeatt (London and New York: Longman, 2000).

Kerrigan, Joh (ed.), *Motives of Woe: Shakespeare and the 'Female Complaint', A Critical Anthology* (Oxford: Clarendon Press, 1991).

King Alexander: see Alexander; Hay; *Kyng Alisaunder*.

King Apollyn: The Romance of Kynge Apollyn of Thyre, facsimile intro. Edmund William Ashbee (London: privately printed, 1870).

King Horn, ed. Joseph Hall (Oxford: Clarendon Press, 1901).

'*King Orphius*', ed. Marion Stewart, *Scottish Studies* 17 (1973), 1–16.

King Orphius, Sir Colling, The Brother's Lament, Little Musgrave, ed. Marion Stewart and Helena M. Shire (Cambridge: Ninth of May, 1976).

King Ponthus: The Noble History of King Ponthus (London: Wynkyn de Worde, 1511).

'*King Ponthus and the Faire Sidone*', ed. F. J. Mather, jr, *PMLA* 12 (1897), pp. i–150.

—— see also *Ponthus*.

Kirkman, Francis, *The Famous and Delectable History of Don Bellianis* (London: Thomas Johnson, 1673) .

The Knight of Curtesy and the Fair Lady of Faguell, ed. E. McCausland, Smith College Studies in Modern Languages 4:1 (Northampton, Mass.: Smith College, 1922).

Kyng Alisaunder, ed. G. V. Smithers, EETS O.S. 227, 237 (1952, 1957).

Lady Bessy: The Most Pleasant Song of Lady Bessy, ed. J. O. Halliwell, Percy Society 20 (1847).

Laȝamon, see Layamon.

Lais: see Tobin.

La Marche, Olivier de, *Le Chevalier deliberé (The Resolute Knight)*, ed. and trans. Carleton W. Carroll (Tempe: Medieval and Renaissance Texts and Studies, 1999).

—— see also Bateman; Lewkenor.

Lancelot ed. Alexandre Micha, TLF, 9 vols. (Geneva: Droz, 1978–83).

Lancelot do Lac: The Non-cyclic Old French Prose Romance, ed. Elspeth Kennedy, 2 vols. (Oxford: Clarendon Press, 1980).

Lancelot of the Laik: see Lupack.

Lancelot-Grail: The Old French Arthurian Vulgate and Post-Vulgate in Translation, ed. Norris J. Lacy, 5 vols. (New York: Garland, 1992–7).

Landeval, ed. George Lyman Kittredge, 'Launfal', *American Journal of Philology* 10 (1889), 1–33.

Laneham, Robert, see Langham.

Langham, Robert, *Robert Langham: A Letter*, ed. R. J. P. Kuin, Medieval and Renaissance Texts 2 (Leiden: E. J. Brill, 1983).

Langland, William, *William Langland: The Vision of Piers Plowman*, ed. A. V. C. Schmidt, Everyman 2nd edn. (London: J. M. Dent, 1995).

Laskaya, Anne, and Salisbury, Eve (eds.), *The Middle English Breton Lays*, TEAMS (Kalamazoo, Michigan: Medieval Institute Publications, 1995).

Launfal: Sir Launfal, ed. A. J. Bliss (London: T. Nelson, 1960).

—— see also *Landeval*.

Layamon, *Laȝamon: Brut*, ed. G. L. Brooke and R. F. Leslie, 2 vols., EETS 250, 277 (1963, 1978).

Layamon, *Laȝamon's Arthur*, ed. and trans. W. R. J. Barron and S. C. Weinberg (Harlow: Longman, 1989).

Lefevre, Raoul, see Caxton, *History of Jason*.

Leland, John, *Assertio inclytissimi Arturii*, ed. W. E. Mead, EETS O.S. 165 (1925) (issued with Middleton, *Chinon*).

Lewis, C. S., *The Voyage of the Dawn Treader* (1952; repr. Harmondsworth, Penguin, 1965).

Lewkenor, Lewes, *The Resolved Gentleman* (London: Richard Watkins, 1594).

Livy, ed. and trans. B. O. Foster, Loeb Classical Library, 14 vols. (Cambridge, Mass.: Harvard University Press; London: Heinemann, 1952) .

Lloyd, Richard, *A Briefe Discourse of the most renowned Actes and right valiant Conquests of those puisant Princes, called the Nine Worthies* (London: R. Warde, 1584).

Locrine: The Lamentable Tragedy of Locrine, ed. Jane Lytton Gooch (New York and London: Garland, 1981).

Lodge, Thomas, *The Complete Works of Thomas Lodge*, intro. Edmund W. Gosse, 4 vols. (1883; repr. New York: Russell and Russell, 1963).

Lull, Ramón, *Blanquerna*, trans. E. Allison Peers (London: Jarrolds, 1926).

—— *Le Livre de Evast et de Blaquerne*, ed. A. Llinarès, Publications de l'Université de Grenoble 47 (Paris, 1970).

—— see Caxton, *Book of the Ordre of Chyualry*; Hay, *Prose Works*.

Lupack, Alan (ed.), *Lancelot of the Laik and Sir Tristrem* (Kalamazoo, Michigan: Medieval Institute Publications, 1994).

Lybeaus Desconus, ed. Maldwyn Mills, EETS O.S. 261 (1969).

Lydgate, John, *Lydgate's Fall of Princes*, ed. H. Bergen, EETS E.S. 121–4 (1924–7).

—— *Lydgate's Reson and Sensuallyte*, ed. Ernst Sieper, EETS E.S. 84 (1901).

—— *The Minor Poems of John Lydgate* Part II, ed. H. N. MacCracken, EETS O.S. 192 (1934, repr. 1961).

The Mabinogion, trans. Jeffrey Gantz (Harmondsworth: Penguin, 1976).

Malory, Thomas, *The Most Ancient and Famous History of the Renowned Prince Arthur* (London, 1634).

—— *The Works of Sir Thomas Malory*, ed. Eugène Vinaver, 3rd edn. rev. P. J. C. Field, 3 vols. (Oxford: Clarendon Press, 1990).

Mandeville, Sir John, *Mandeville's Travels*, ed. from Cotton Titus C.XVI by P. Hamelius, EETS OS 153–4 (1919, 1923).

Mannyng, Robert, *Robert Mannyng of Brunne: The Chronicle*, ed. Idelle Sullens (Binghamton, NY: Medieval and Renaissance Texts, 1996).

Marco Polo, *The Most Noble and Famous Travels of Marco Polo, edited from the Elizabethan Translation of John Frampton*, ed. N. M. Penzer, 2nd edn. (London: Charles Black, 1937).

—— *The Travels of Marco Polo*, trans. R. E. Latham (Harmondsworth: Penguin, 1958).

Marie de France: Lais, ed. A. Ewert (Oxford: Blackwell, 1944).

M[arkham], I[ervase], see *Mervine*.

Marlowe, Christopher, *Doctor Faustus: A- and B- Texts*, ed. David Bevington and Eric Rasmussen, Revels Plays (Manchester: Manchester University Press, 1993).

Martorell, Joanot, and de Galba, Martì Joan, *Tirant lo Blanc*, trans. by David H. Rosenthal (London: Picador, 1984).

Matthew Paris: Chronica Maiora, ed. Henry Richards Luard, Rolls Series 57, 7 vols. (London, 1872–3).

Melusine, ed. A. K. Donald, EETS E.S. 68 (1895).

———— see Coudrette; Jean d'Arras; Partenay.

Merlin: La Suite du Roman de Merlin, ed. Gilles Roussineau (Geneva: Droz, 1996).

Merlin, ed. Henry B. Wheatley, EETS O.S. 10, 21, 36, 112 (1865–99; repr. 1987, 2000).

Merlin: Prose Merlin, ed. John Conlee, TEAMS (Kalamazoo, Michigan: Medieval Institute Publications, 1998).

Mervine: The most famous and renowned Historie, of that woorthie and illustrious knight Meruine, Sonne to that rare and excellent Mirror of princely Prowesse, Oger the Dane (London: R. Blower, 1612).

Middleton, Christopher, *The Famous Historie of Chinon of England by Christopher Middleton*, ed. William Edward Mead, EETS O.S. 165 (1925).

Millett, Bella, and Wogan-Browne, Jocelyn (eds.), *Medieval Prose for Women: Selections from the Katherine Group and Ancrene Wisse* (Oxford: Clarendon Press, 1990).

Mills, Maldwyn (ed.), *Six Middle English Romances*, Everyman (London: Dent, 1973).

———— (ed.), *Ywain and Gawain, Sir Percyvell of Gales, The Anturs of Arthur*, Everyman (London: J. M. Dent, 1992).

Milton, John, *John Milton: Selected Prose*, ed. C. A. Patrides (Harmondsworth: Penguin, 1974).

Molinet, Jean, *Chroniques*, ed. J-A. Buchon, 5 vols. (Paris: Verdière, 1828).

La Mort le roi Artu, ed. Jean Frappier, TLF, 2nd edn. (Geneva: Droz, 1954).

———— trans. James Cable, *The Death of King Arthur* (Harmondsworth: Penguin, 1971).

Morte Arthur (anonymous) see Benson.

Mucedorus: A Contextual Study and Modern-spelling Edition of Mucedorus, ed. Arvin H. Jupin, The Renaissance Imagination 29 (New York and London: Garland, 1987).

Munday, Antony (trans.), *The Ancient, Famous and Honourable History of Amadis de Gaule* (London: N. Okes, 1619).

Nashe, Thomas, *The Works of Thomas Nashe*, ed. R. B. McKerrow, corr. by F. P. Wilson (Oxford: Blackwell, 1958).

Navigatio Sancti Brendani Abbatis from Early Latin Manuscripts, ed. Carl Selmer (Notre Dame: University of Notre Dame Press, 1959).

The New Testament Octapla, ed. Luther A. Weigle (New York: Nelson, 1962).

Nichols, John (ed.), *The Progresses and Public Processions of Queen Elizabeth*, 3 vols. (1823; repr. New York: Burt Franklin, n.d.).

Norse Romance Vol. I: *The Tristan Legend*, ed. Marianne E. Kalinke, Arthurian Archives III (Cambridge: D.S. Brewer, 1999).

Il Novellino, ed. Guido Favati (Genoa: Fratelli Bozzi, 1970).

Octovian, ed. Frances McSparran, EETS 289 (1986).

O'Donaghue, Denis (ed.), *Lives and Legends of Saint Brendan the Voyager* (1893; repr. Felinfach: Llanerch Press, 1994).

Of Arthour and of Merlin, see *Arthur.*

Oliver of Castile: The Hystorye of Olyuer of Castylle, ed. Gail Orgelfinger (New York and London: Garland, 1988).

Orfeo: Sir Orfeo, ed. A. J. Bliss 2nd edn. (Oxford: Clarendon Press, 1966).

Ovid, *Metamorphoses,* ed. Frank Justus Miller, Loeb Classical Library, 2 vols. (London: Heinemann; Cambridge, Mass.: Harvard University Press, 1944).

—— see also Golding.

Palatine Anthology, see Halliwell.

Partenay: The Romans of Partenay, ed. W. W. Skeat, EETS O.S. 22, rev. edn. (1899).

Partonope de Blois, ed. A. Trampe Bödtker, EETS E.S. 109 (1912).

Partonopeus de Blois: A French Romance of the Twelfth Century, ed. Joseph Gildea (Villanova: Villanova University Press, 1967).

Pearl: The Poems of the Pearl Manuscript ed. Malcolm Andrew and Ronald Waldron, rev. edn. (Exeter: Exeter University Press, 1987).

Peele, George, *The Old Wives Tale,* ed. Patricia Binney, Revels Plays (Manchester: Manchester University Press, 1980).

Perceforest: Le Roman de Perceforest, TLF (Geneva: Droz): Part I, ed. Jane H. M. Taylor (1979); Part III, ed. Giles Roussineau, 3 vols. (1988, 1991, 1993); Part IV, ed. Giles Roussineau, 2 vols. (1987) .

Percy Folio: Bishop Percy's Folio Manuscript: Ballads and Romances, ed. John W. Hales and Frederick J. Furnivall, 3 vols. (London: Trübner, 1868).

Philippe de Rémi, *Jehan et Blonde de Philippe de Rémi,* ed. Sylvie Lécuyer, CFMA (Paris: Champion, 1984) .

Philippe de Remi: Le Roman de la Manekine, ed. and trans. Barbara Sargent-Baur (Amsterdam and Atlanta: Rodopi, 1999).

[Phillips, Ambrose] (ed.), *A Collection of Old Ballads,* 3 vols. (London: J. Roberts, 1723–5).

Ponthus: Le Roman de Ponthus et Sidoine, ed. Marie-Claude de Crécy, TLF 475 (Geneva: Droz, 1977).

——see also *King Ponthus.*

Ralegh, Walter, *The History of the World,* 2nd edn. (London: W. Burre, 1617).

—— *Sir Walter Ralegh: Selected Writings,* ed. Gerald Hammond (Harmondsworth: Penguin, 1986).

Randolph, Thomas, *The Fary Knight; or, Oberon the Second, a manuscript play attributed to Thomas Randolph,* ed. Fredson Thayer Bowers (Chapel Hill: University of North Carolina Press, 1942).

Rauf Coilyear: The Taill of Rauf Coilyear, ed. S. J. Herrtage, EETS E.S. 39 (1882).

—— *The Tale of Ralph the Collier: An Alliterative Romance,* ed. Elizabeth Walsh, RSCJ (New York, Berne: Peter Lang, 1989).

René of Anjou, *The Book of the Love-Smitten Heart (Le Livre du cuers d'amours espris) by René of Anjou,* ed. and trans. Stephanie Viereck Gibbs and Kathryn Karczewska (New York and London: Routledge, 2001).

Richard Cœur de Lyon: Der mittelenglische Versroman über Richard Löwenherz, ed. Karl Brunner (Vienna: Wilhelm Braumüller, 1913).

Richardson, Samuel, *Pamela; or, Virtue Rewarded*, ed. Peter Sabor (Harmondsworth: Penguin, 1980).

Robbins, Rossell Hope (ed.), *Historical Poems of the XIVth and XVth Centuries* (New York: Columbia University Press, 1959).

Le Roman de la rose, ed. Daniel Poirion (Paris: Garnier-Flammarion, 1974).

Roswall and Lillian, ed. O. Lengert, 'Die schottische Romanze "Roswall and Lillian" ', *Englische Studien* 16 (1892), 321–56, 17 (1892), 341–77.

Rous, John, *History of the Earls of Warwick*, ed. T. Hearne, with *Historia vitae et regni Ricardi II* (Oxford, 1729).

Rowlands, Samuel, *The Complete Works of Samuel Rowlands*, intro. Edmund W. Gosse, 3 vols. (Glasgow: Hunterian Club, 1880).

S.S., Gent., *Fortune's Tennis Ball; or, The most excellent History of Dorastus and Fawnia*, ed. James O. Halliwell (London: Thomas Richards, 1859).

Salzman, Paul (ed.), *An Anthology of Seventeenth-Century Fiction* (Oxford: Oxford University Press, 1991).

Sands, Donald B. (ed.), *Middle English Verse Romances* (1969; Exeter: Exeter University Press, 1987).

Segar, William, *Sir William Segar: The Book of Honor and Armes (1590) and Honour Military and Civil (1602)*, facsimile intro. Diane Bornstein (Delmar, NY: Scholars' Facsimiles and Reprints, 1975).

The Seven Sages of Rome, ed. Killis Campbell (Boston: Ginn & Co., 1907).

—— ed. Karl Brunner, EETS O.S. 191 (1933).

Shakespeare, William, *The Complete Works*, general editors Stanley Wells and Gary Taylor (Oxford: Clarendon Press, 1986).

—— *Shakespeare's Plays in Quarto: A Facsimile Edition of Copies Primarily from the Henry E. Huntington Library*, ed. Michael J. B. Allen and Kenneth Muir (Berkeley, Los Angeles, and London: University of California Press, 1981) .

[Shakespeare, William], *King Edward III*, ed. Giorgio Melchiori, New Cambridge Shakespeare (Cambridge: Cambridge University Press, 1998).

—— *The Merry Wives of Windsor*, ed. H. J. Oliver, Arden Shakespeare (London: Methuen, 1971).

—— *A Midsummer Night's Dream*, ed. Peter Holland, Oxford Shakespeare (Oxford: Oxford University Press, 1994).

—— *Pericles, Prince of Tyre*, ed. Doreen DelVecchio and Antony Hammond, New Cambridge Shakespeare (Cambridge: Cambridge University Press, 1998).

—— *The Tempest*, ed. Stephen Orgel, Oxford Shakespeare (Oxford: Oxford University Press, 1987).

Shelton, Thomas (trans.), *The History of Don Quixote of the Mancha, translated from the Spanish of Miguel de Cervantes by Thomas Shelton, 1612, 1620*, intro. James Fitzmaurice-Kelly, The Tudor Translations 13–16, 4 vols. (London: David Nutt, 1896).

Shepherd, Stephen H. A. (ed.), *Middle English Romances* (New York and London: W. W. Norton, 1995).

Sidney, Philip, [*The New Arcadia*:] *Sir Philip Sidney: The Countess of Pembroke's Arcadia*, ed. Maurice Evans (Harmondsworth: Penguin, 1977).

—— *Sir Philip Sidney: The Countess of Pembroke's Arcadia (The Old Arcadia)*, ed. Jean Robertson (Oxford: Clarendon Press, 1973).

—— *The Poems of Sir Philip Sidney*, ed. William A. Ringler, jr (Oxford: Clarendon Press, 1962).

The Siege of Jerusalem in Prose, ed. Auvo Kurvinen, Mémoires de la Société Néophilologique de Helsinki 34 (Helsinki: Société Néophilologique, 1969).

Siege of Thebes and *Troy*: see Brie, ed., 'Zwei mittelenglische Prosaromane'.

Silence: see Heldris of Cornuälle.

Sir Degrevant: The Romance of Sir Degrevant, ed. L. F. Casson, EETS O.S. 221 (1949).

Sir Eglamour of Artois, ed. Frances E. Richardson, EETS 256 (1965).

Sir Gawain and the Green Knight, ed. J. R. R. Tolkien and E. V. Gordon, 2nd edn. rev. by Norman Davis (Oxford: Clarendon Press, 1967).

Sir Gowther, ed. Karl Breul (Oppeln: Georg Maske, 1886).

Sir Tristrem: see Lupack .

Skelton, John, *John Skelton: The Complete English Poems*, ed. John Scattergood (Harmondsworth: Penguin, 1983).

Smith, G. Gregory (ed.), *Elizabethan Critical Essays* (London: Oxford University Press, 1904).

The South English Legendary, ed. Charlotte d' Evelyn and Anna J. Mill, EETS 235–6 (1956).

Sowdone of Babylon: The Romaunce of the Sowdone of Babylone, ed. Emil Hausknecht, EETS E.S. 38 (1881).

Speed, Diane (ed.), *Medieval English Romances* (Sydney: Department of English, University of Sydney, 1987).

Spenser, Edmund, *The Faerie Queene*, ed. A. C. Hamilton, text ed. Hiroshi Yamashita and Toshiyuki Suzuki, 2nd edn. (Harlow: Longman, 2001).

—— *The Shorter Poems*, ed. Richard A. McCabe (Harmondsworth: Penguin, 1999).

Spottiswood, John, *The History of the Church of Scotland 1655*, facsimile (Menston: Scolar Press, 1972).

Stationers' Registers: Edward Arber, *A Transcript of the Registers of the Company of Stationers of London*, 1554–1640 (vols. 1–4, London, 1875–7; vol. 5, Birmingham, 1894).

Sundry Strange Prophecies of Merlin, Bede, Beckett (London: Matthew Walbancke, 1652).

Tasso, Torquato, *Discourses on the Heroic Poem*, trans. Mariella Cavalchini and Irene Samuel (Oxford: Clarendon Press, 1973).

—— *Torquato Tasso: Gerusalemme Liberata*, ed. Lanfranco Caretti (Milan: Mondadori, 1979).

——— *Torquato Tasso: Rinaldo*, ed. Michael Sherberg, Classici Italiani Minori 16 (Ravenna: Longo, 1990).

——— *Rinaldo: A Poem in XII Books from the Italian of Torquato Tasso*, trans. John Hoole (London: J. Dodsley, 1792).

——— see also Fairfax.

Tate, Nahum, *The History of King Lear*, ed. James Black (Lincoln, Neb.: University of Nebraska Press, 1975).

Thomas, *Tristan*, see *Tristan*.

Thomas of Erceldoune: The Romance and Prophecies of Thomas of Erceldoune, ed. James A. H. Murray, EETS O.S. 68 (1875).

Thomas of Erceldoune, ed. Ingeborg Nixon, Publications of the Department of English, University of Copenhagen 9, 2 parts (Copenhagen: Akademisk Vorlag, 1980–3).

——— see also *Sundry Strange Prophecies*.

Thoms, William J. (ed.), *Early English Prose Romances*, rev. and enlarged edn. (London: Routledge, 1907).

Tilney, Edmund, *The Flower of Friendship: A Renaissance Dialogue contesting Marriage*, ed. Valerie Wayne (Ithaca, NY: Cornell University Press, 1992).

Tobin, Prudence Mary O'Hara (ed.), *Les Lais anonymes des XIIe et XIIIe siècles*, Publications romanes et françaises 143 (Geneva: Droz, 1976).

Tolkien, J. R. R., *Farmer Giles of Ham* (London: George Allen and Unwin, 1949).

——— *The Lord of the Rings* (London: George Allen and Unwin, 1954).

Torrent of Portyngale, ed. E. Adam, EETS E.S. 51 (1887).

The Towneley Plays, ed. Martin Stevens and A. C. Cawley, EETS S.S.13–14 (1994).

The Tragical History of Guy of Warwick, see *Guy*.

The Tripartite Life of St Patrick, ed. Whitley Stokes, Rolls Series 89 (London, 1887).

Tristan: Early French Tristan Poems, ed. Norris J. Lacy, 2 vols., Arthurian Archives I–II (Cambridge: D. S. Brewer, 1998).

——— see also Lupack; *Norse Romance*.

Troiedd Ynys Prydein: The Welsh Triads, ed. Rachel Bromwich (Cardiff: University of Wales Press, 1978).

Ulrich von Zatzikhoven: Lanzelet, ed. Wolfgang Spiewok, WODAN 71 (Greifswald: Reinecke-Verlag, 1997).

Ulrich von Zatzikhoven: Lanzelet, trans. Kenneth G. T. Webster, rev. Roger Sherman Loomis, Records of Civilization, Sources and Studies 47 (New York: Columbia University Press, 1951).

Valentine and Orson, ed. Arthur Dickson, EETS O.S. 204 (1937).

Vives, see Hyrd.

'*The Voyage of the Húi Corra*', ed. Whitley Stokes, *Révue Celtique* 14 (1893), 22–69.

'*The Voyage of Snedgus and MacRiagla*', ed. Whitley Stokes, *Révue Celtique* 9 (1888), 14–25.

The Vulgate Version of the Arthurian Romances, ed. H. Oskar Sommer, 7 vols. (Washington DC: Carnegie Institute, 1900–16).

Wace's Roman de Brut: A History of the British, ed. and trans. Judith Weiss, Exeter Medieval English Texts and Studies (Exeter: Exeter University Press, 1999).

Warner, William, *Albions England* (London: G. Robinson/R. Ward, 1586).

—— *William Warner: Albions England* (1612), Anglistica and Americana 131 (Hildesheim and New York: Georg Olms, 1971).

Watson, Henry, see *Valentine and Orson*.

Webb, J. F. (trans.), *Lives of the Saints* (Harmondsworth: Penguin, 1965).

Webster, John, *The Dramatic Works of John Webster*, 4 vols. (London: John Russell Smith, 1857).

Wedderburn, Robert, see *Complaynt*.

Weiss, Judith (trans.), *The Birth of Romance: An Anthology* (London: Dent, 1992).

Whitworth, Charles W. (ed.), *Three Sixteenth-century Comedies*, New Mermaids (London: Ernest Benn, 1984).

William of Malmesbury: *Willelmi Malmesbiriensis De gestis regum anglorum libri quinque*, ed. W. Stubbs, Rolls Series 90–1 (London, 1887).

William of Palerne: An Alliterative Romance, ed. G. H. V. Bunt (Groningen: Boema's Boekhuis, 1985).

Wright, Thomas, and Halliwell J. O. (eds.), *Reliquiae Antiquae*, 2 vols. (London: William Pickering, 1841).

Wroth, Lady Mary, *Urania*, in Salzman (ed.), *Anthology of Seventeenth-Century Fiction*, pp. 1–208.

Ysumbras: see *Isumbras*.

Ywain and Gawain, Sir Percyvell of Galles, The Anturs of Arthur, ed. Maldwyn Mills (London: J. M. Dent, 1992).

Ywain and Gawain, ed. A. B. Friedman and N. T. Harrington, EETS O.S. 254 (1964).

SECONDARY

Ackerman, R. W., *An Index of the Arthurian Names in Middle English*, Stanford University Publications in Language and Literature (Stanford: Stanford University Press; London: Oxford University Press, 1952).

Albrecht, William P., *The Loathly Lady in 'Thomas of Erceldoune'*, University of New Mexico Publications in Language and Literature 11 (Albuquerque: University of New Mexico Press, 1954).

Allen, Judson Boyce, and Moritz, Theresa Anne, *A Distinction of Stories: The Medieval Unity of Chaucer's Fair Chain of Narratives for Canterbury* (Columbus, Ohio: Ohio State University Press, 1981).

Anglo, Sydney, 'British History in Early Tudor Propaganda', *Bulletin of the John Rylands Library* 44 (1961–2), 17–48.

—— (ed.), *Chivalry in the Renaissance* (Woodbridge: Boydell Press, 1990).

Anglo, Sydney, *Images of Tudor Kingship* (London: Seaby, 1992).

Archibald, Elizabeth, *Apollonius of Tyre: Medieval and Renaissance Themes and Variations* (Cambridge: D. S. Brewer, 1991).

—— *Incest and the Medieval Imagination* (Oxford: Clarendon Press, 2001).

—— 'The Breton Lay in Middle English', in Weiss, Fellows, and Dickson (eds.), *Medieval Insular Romance: Translation and Innovation*, pp. 55–70.

—— 'Lancelot as Lover in the English Tradition before Malory', in Wheeler (ed.), *Arthurian Studies*, pp. 199–216.

Auerbach, Erich, *Mimesis: The Representation of Reality in Western Literature*, trans. Willard Trask (1953; repr. New York: Doubleday Anchor, 1957).

Baird, Ian, 'Some Missing Lines in *Lady Bessy*', *Library* 6th ser., 5 (1983), 268–9.

Ballard, J. K., 'Sovereignty and the Loathly Lady in English, Welsh and Irish', *Leeds Studies in English* 17 (1986), 41–59.

Barber, Richard, *The Knight and Chivalry*, rev. edn. (Woodbridge: Boydell Press, 1995).

—— 'Malory's *Le Morte Darthur* and Court Culture', *Arthurian Literature* 12 (1993), 133–55.

Barron, W. R. J., *English Medieval Romance* (London and New York: Longman, 1987).

Barton, Anne, *Essays, Mainly Shakespearean* (Cambridge: Cambridge University Press, 1994).

Baswell, Christopher, and Sharpe, William (eds.), *The Passing of Arthur: New Essays in Arthurian Tradition* (New York and London: Garland, 1988).

Bennett, Josephine Waters, *The Evolution of the Faerie Queene* (1942; repr. New York: Burt Franklin, 1960).

Benson, Larry D., *Malory's Morte Darthur* (Cambridge, Mass.: Harvard University Press, 1976).

—— 'The Tournament in the Romances of Chrétien de Troyes and *L'Histoire de Guillaume le Maréchal*', in Benson and Leyerle, *Chaivalric Literature*, pp. 1–24.

—— 'The Occasion of *The Parliament of Fowls*', in *The Wisdom of Poetry*, ed. Benson and Wenzel, pp. 123–44.

—— and Leyerle, John (eds.), *Chivalric Literature* (Kalamazoo: Medieval Institute, 1980).

—— and Wenzel, Siegfried (eds.), *The Wisdom of Poetry* (Kalamazoo: Medieval Institute, 1982).

Benton, John F., 'The Court of Champagne as a Literary Center', *Speculum* 36 (1961), 551–91.

Bezzola, Reto R., *Le Sens de l'aventure et de l'amour (Chrétien de Troyes)* (Paris: La Jeune Parque, 1947).

Biddle, Martin, *et al.*, *King Arthur's Round Table: An Archaeological Investigation* (Woodbridge: Boydell Press, 2000).

Blackmore, Susan, *The Meme Machine* (Oxford: Oxford University Press, 1999).

Blaess, Madeleine, 'L'Abbaye de Bordesley et les livres de Guy de Beauchamp', *Romania* 78 (1957), 511–18.

Blamires, Alcuin, *The Case for Women in Medieval Culture* (Oxford: Clarendon Press, 1997).

Bloch, R. Howard, *Etymologies and Genealogies: A Literary Anthropology of the French Middle Ages* (Chicago and London: Chicago University Press, 1983).

—— *Medieval Misogyny and the Invention of Western Romantic Love* (Chicago and London: Chicago University Press, 1991).

Boro, Joyce, 'The Textual History of *Huon of Burdeux*: A Reassessment', *Notes and Queries* 246, 48 (2001), 233–7.

Bossuat, Robert, Pichard Louis, and Renaud de Lage, Guy (eds.), *Dictionnaire des lettres français: Le Moyen Age*, rev. by Geneviève Hasenohr and Michel Zink (Paris: Fayard, 1992).

Branca, Daniela Delcorno, *Orlando Furioso e il Romanzo cavalleresco medievale*, Saggi di lettere italiane 17 (Florence: Leo S. Olschki, 1973).

—— *Tristano e Lancillotto in Italia: Studi di letteratura arturiana*, Memoria del Tempo 11 (Ravenna: Longo, 1998).

Brewer, Derek (ed.), *Studies in Medieval English Romances: Some New Approaches* (Cambridge: D. S. Brewer, 1988).

Bromwich, Rachel, 'Celtic Dynastic Themes and the Breton Lays', *Études celtiques* 9 (1960–1), 439–74.

Brown, Cedric C., and Marotti, Arthur F. (eds.), *Texts and Cultural Change in Early Modern England* (Basingstoke: Macmillan; New York: St Martin's Press, 1997).

Brown, J. R, and Harris, Bernard (eds.), *Later Shakespeare*, Stratford-upon Avon Studies 8 (1966).

Brownlee, Kevin, and Brownlee, Maria Scordilis, *Romance: Generic Transformation from Chrétien de Troyes to Cervantes* (Hanover and London: University Press of New England for Dartmouth College, 1985).

Brundage, James A., *Law, Sex and Christian Society in Medieval Europe* (Chicago: University of Chicago Press, 1987).

Bullough, Vern L., and Brundage, James A. (eds.), *Handbook of Medieval Sexuality* (New York: Garland, 1996).

Bunt, Gerritt H. V., *Alexander the Great in the Literature of Medieval Britain*, Medievalia Groningana 14 (Groningen: Egbert Forsten, 1994).

Burgess, Glyn S., and Taylor, Robert A. (eds.), *The Spirit of the Court: Selected Proceedings of the Fourth Congress of the International Courtly Literature Society* (Cambridge: D. S. Brewer, 1985).

Burnley, David, *Courtliness in Medieval Literature* (London and New York: Longman, 1998).

Bynum, Caroline Walker, *Metamorphosis and Identity* (New York: Zone Books, 2001).

Cadden, Joan, *Meanings of Sex Difference in the Middle Ages: Medicine, Science and Culture* (Cambridge: Cambridge University Press, 1993).

Calin, William, *The French Tradition and the Literature of Medieval England* (Toronto: Toronto University Press, 1994).

—— 'The Exaltation and Undermining of Romance: *Ipomadon*', in Lacy *et al.* (eds.), *The Legacy of Chrétien de Troyes*, Vol. 2, pp. 111–24.

Camille, Michael, *The Medieval Art of Love: Objects and Subjects of Desire* (London: Laurence King, 1998).

Carruthers, Mary, 'Afterword' in Evans and Johnson (eds.), *Feminist Readings in Middle English Literature*, pp. 39–44.

Cartlidge, Neil, *Medieval Marriage: Literary Approaches, 1100–1300* (Cambridge: D. S. Brewer, 1997).

Cavanaugh, Susan H., *A Study of Books Privately Owned in England 1300–1450*, PhD thesis, University of Pennsylvania (1980).

—— 'Royal Books: King John to Richard II', *The Library* 6th ser., 10 (1988), 304–16.

Cawelti, John G., *Adventure, Mystery, and Romance: Formula Stories as Art and Popular Culture* (Chicago: University of Chicago Press, 1976).

Chambers, R. W., *Beowulf: An Introduction*, 3rd edn. (Cambridge: Cambridge University Press, 1959).

Charles-Edwards, T. M., 'The Social Background to Irish *Peregrinatio*', *Celtica* 11 (1976), 43–59.

Chaudhuri, Sukanta (ed.), *Renaissance Essays for Kitty Scoular Datta* (Calcutta and Oxford: Oxford University Press, 1995).

Christopherson, Paul, *The Ballad of Sir Aldingar: Its Origin and Analogues* (Oxford: Clarendon Press, 1952).

Cooper, Helen, *Oxford Guides to Chaucer: The Canterbury Tales*, 2nd edn., Oxford: Clarendon Press, 1996).

—— *Pastoral: Mediaeval into Renaissance* (Ipswich: D. S. Brewer, 1977).

—— 'Counter-Romance: Civil Strife and Father-killing in the Prose Romances', in Cooper and Mapstone (eds.), *The Long Fifteenth Century*, pp. 141–62.

—— 'The Elizabethan *Havelok*: William Warner's First of the English', in Weiss *et al.* (eds.), *Medieval Insular Romance*, pp. 169–83.

—— 'The Frame', in Correale and Hamel (eds.), *Sources and Analogues of the Canterbury Tales*, pp. 1–22.

—— ' Good Advice on Leaving Home in the Romances', in Riddy and Goldberg (eds.), *Youth in the Middle Ages*, pp. 101–21.

—— 'Guy of Warwick, Upstart Crows and Mounting Sparrows', in Mulryne and Kozuka (eds.), *Shakespeare, Marlowe, Jonson*.

—— 'Jacobean Chaucer: *The Two Noble Kinsmen* and other Chaucerian Plays', in Krier (ed.), *Refiguring Chaucer*, pp. 189–209 .

—— 'Lancelot, Roger Mortimer, and the Date of the Auchinleck Manuscript', in Fletcher and D'Arcy (eds.), *The King of All Good Remembrance*.

—— 'Magic that does not work', *Medievalia et Humanistica* 7 (1976), 131–46.

—— 'Prospero's Boats: Magic, Providence, and Human Choice', in Chaudhuri (ed.), *Renaissance Essays for Kitty Scoular Datta*, pp. 160–75.

—— 'Romance after Bosworth' in *The Court and Cultural Diversity*, ed. Mullally and Thompson, pp. 149–57.

—— 'The Strange History of *Valentine and Orson*', in Field (ed.), *Tradition and Transformation*, pp. 153–68.

—— and Mapstone Sally (eds.), *The Long Fifteenth Century: Essays for Douglas Gray* (Oxford: Clarendon Press, 1997).

Cooper, Richard, '"Nostre Histoire renouvelée": The Reception of Romances of Chivalry in the Renaissance', in Anglo (ed.), *Chivalry in the Renaissance*, pp. 175–238.

Coote, Lesley, and Tim Thornton, 'Merlin, Erceldoune, Nixon: A Tradition of Popular Political Prophecy', *New Medieval Literatures* 4 (2001), 117–37.

Correale, Robert M., and Hamel Mary (eds.), *Sources and Analogues of the Canterbury Tales*, Vol. 1 (Cambridge: D. S. Brewer, 2002).

Crane, Ronald S., *The Vogue of Medieval Chivalric Romance During the English Renaissance* (1919; repr. Norwood, Pa: Norwood Editions, 1977).

—— 'The Reading of an Elizabethan Youth', *Modern Philology* 11 (1913–14), 1–3.

—— 'The Vogue of *Guy of Warwick* from the Close of the Middle Ages to the Romantic Revival', *PMLA* 30 (1915), 125–94.

Crane, Susan, *Insular Romance: Politics, Faith, and Culture in Anglo-Norman and Middle English Literature* (Berkeley and Los Angeles: University of California Press, 1986).

Culler, Jonathan, *Literary Theory: A Very Short Introduction* (Oxford: Oxford University Press, 1997).

Dawkins, Richard, *The Selfish Gene* (Oxford: Oxford University Press, 1976).

Davenport, Tony, 'Chronicle and Romance: The Story of Ine and Aethelburgh', in Saunders (ed.), *Cultural Encounters*.

Davies, R. R., *The Revolt of Owain Glyn Dŵr* (Oxford: Oxford University Press, 1995).

Davis, Alex, *Chivalry and Romance in the English Renaissance* (Cambridge: D. S. Brewer, 2003).

Day, Peter, *Dictionary of Religious Orders* (London and New York: Burns and Oates, 2001).

Dean, Christopher, *Arthur of England: English Attitudes to King Arthur and the Knights of the Round Table in the Middle Ages and the Renaissance* (Toronto and London: University of Toronto Press, 1987).

Dickson, Arthur, *Valentine and Orson: A Study in Late Medieval Romance* (New York: Columbia University Press, 1929).

Dillon, Viscount, 'A Manuscript Collection of Ordinances of Chivalry of the Fifteenth Century', *Archaeologia* 57:1 (1900), 27–70.

Dinshaw, Carolyn, *Chaucer's Sexual Poetics* (Madison, Wis.: University of Wisconsin Press, 1989).

Dobin, Howard, *Merlin's Disciples: Prophecy, Poetry, and Power in Renaissance England* (Stanford: Stanford University Press, 1990).

Doble, Gilbert H., *The Saints of Cornwall*, 4 vols. (1923–44; repr. Felinfach: Llanerch Press, 1997).

Donaldson, E. Talbot, *The Swan at the Well: Shakespeare Reading Chaucer* (New Haven and London: Yale University Press, 1985).

Dover, Carol (ed.), *A Companion to the Lancelot-Grail Cycle* (Cambridge: D. S. Brewer, 2003).

Edson, Evelyn, *Mapping Time and Space* (London: British Library, 1997).

Edwards, A. S. G. (ed.), *Middle English Prose: A Critical Guide to Major Authors and Genres* (New Brunswick: Rutgers University Press, 1984).

Eisner, Sigmund, *A Tale of Wonder: A Source Study of the Wife of Bath's Tale* (Wexford: John English, 1957).

Evans, Ruth, and Johnson, Lesley (eds.), *Feminist Readings in Middle English Literature: The Wife of Bath and all her Sect* (London and New York: Routledge, 1994).

Fellows, Jennifer, Field, Rosalind, Rogers, Gillian and Weiss, Judith (eds.), *Romance Reading on the Book: Essays on Medieval Narrative presented to Maldwyn Mills* (Cardiff: University of Wales Press, 1996).

Fellows, Jennifer, '*Bevis redivivus*: The Printed Editions of *Sir Bevis of Hampton*', in Fellows *et al.* (eds.), *Romance Reading on the Book*, pp. 250–68.

Ferguson, Arthur B., *The Chivalric Tradition in Renaissance England* (Cranbury, NJ, and London: Associated University Presses, 1986).

—— *Clio Unbound: Perception of the Social and Cultural Past in Renaissance England* (Durham, NC: Duke University Press, 1979).

Ferrante, Joan M., *Woman as Image in Medieval Literature from the Twelfth Century to Dante* (New York and London: Columbia University Press, 1975).

Fewster, Carol, *Traditionality and Genre in Middle English Romance* (Cambridge: D. S. Brewer, 1987).

Field, Rosalind, 'The King over the Water: Exile-and-Return in Insular Tradition', in Saunders (ed.), *Cultural Encounters*.

—— 'Romance as History, History as Romance', in Mills, Fellows, and Meale (eds.), *Romance in Medieval England*, pp. 163–73.

—— (ed.), *Tradition and Transformation in Medieval Romance* (Cambridge: D. S. Brewer, 1999).

Finlayson, John, 'Definitions of Middle English Romance', *Chaucer Review* 15 (1980–1), 44–62, 168–81.

—— '*Richard, Cœr de Lyon*: Romance, History, or Something in Between?', *Studies in Philology* 87 (1990), 156–80.

Fisher, Sheila, and Halley, Janet E. (eds.), *Seeking the Woman in Late Medieval and Renaissance Writings: Essays in Feminist Contextual Criticism* (Knoxville: University of Tennessee Press, 1989).

Fletcher, A. J., and M.-A. D'Arcy (eds.), *The Key of All Good Remembrance* (forthcoming).

Fletcher, Robert Huntington, *The Arthurian Material in the Chronicles*, 2nd edn. rev. Roger Sherman Loomis (New York: Burt Franklin, 1966).

Fludernik, Monica, *Towards a 'Natural' Narratology* (London and New York: Routledge, 1996).

Foucault, Michel, *The History of Sexuality*, trans. by Robert Hurley (Harmondsworth: Penguin, 1981).

Fowler, Alastair, *Kinds of Literature: An Introduction to the Theory of Genres and Modes* (Oxford: Clarendon Press, 1982).

Fraser, Antonia, *Cromwell our Chief of Men* (London: Weidenfeld & Nicolson, 1973).

Freud, Sigmund, *The Standard Edition of the Complete Psychological Works of Sigmund Freud*, trans. from the German under the general editorship of James Strachey, 24 vols. (London: Hogarth Press, 1957–74).

Frye, Northrop, *An Anatomy of Criticism: Four Essays* (Princeton: Princeton University Press, 1957).

—— *The Great Code: The Bible and Literature* (London: Routledge & Kegan Paul, 1982).

—— *A Natural Perspective: The Development of Shakespearean Comedy and Romance* (New York: Columbia University Press, 1965).

—— *The Secular Scripture: A Study of the Structure of Romance* (Cambridge, Mass.: Harvard University Press, 1976).

Gaunt, Simon, *Gender and Genre in Medieval French Literature* (Cambridge: Cambridge University Press, 1995).

Gillingham, John, *Richard Cœur de Lion: Kingship, Chivalry and War in the Twelfth Century* (London and Rio Grande: Hambledon Press, 1994).

Gnädinger, Louise, *Hiudan and Petitcreiu: Gestalt und Figur des Hundes in der mittelalterlichen Tristandichtung* (Zürich: Atlantis, 1971).

Goodman, Jennifer R., *Chivalry and Exploration 1298–1630* (Woodbridge: Boydell Press, 1998).

Gransden, Antonia, *Historical Writing in England II: c.1307 to the Early Sixteenth Century* (London: Routledge & Kegan Paul, 1982).

Gravdal, Kathryn, *Ravishing Maidens: Writing Rape in Medieval French Law and Literature* (Philadelphia: University of Pennsylvania Press, 1991).

Green, Richard Firth, *A Crisis of Truth: Literature and Law in Ricardian England* (Philadelphia: University of Pennsylvania Press, 1999).

Greenblatt, Stephen, *Learning to Curse: Essays in Early Modern Culture* (New York and London: Routledge, 1990).

—— *Shakespearean Negotiations: The Circulation of Social Energy in Renaissance England* (Oxford: Clarendon Press, 1988).

Greer, Germaine, *Shakespeare* (Oxford and New York: Oxford University Press, 1986).

Guddat-Figge, Gisela, *Catalogue of Manuscripts Containing Middle English Romances*, Münchener Universitätschriften 4 (Munich: Wilhelm Fink, 1976).

Gunn, Steven, 'Chivalry and the Politics of the Early Tudor Court', in Anglo (ed.), *Chivalry and the Renaissance*, pp. 107–28.

Hackett, Helen, *Virgin Mother, Maiden Queen: Elizabeth I and the Cult of the Virgin Mary*, rev. edn. (Basingstoke: Macmillan, 1996).

—— *Women and Romance Fiction in the English Renaissance* (Cambridge: Cambridge University Press, 2000).

Hanning, Robert W., 'The Social Significance of Twelfth-century Chivalric Romance', *Medievalia et Humanistica*, 3 (1972), 3–29.

Harbage, Alfred, *Annals of English Drama 975–1700*, rev. S. Schoenbaum, 3rd edn. rev. Sylvia Stoler Wagonheim (London and New York: Routledge, 1989).

Hares-Stryker, Carolyn, 'Adrift on the Seven Seas: The Mediaeval Topos of Exile at Sea', *Florilegium* 12 (1993), 79–98.

Harf-Lancner, Laurence, *Les Fées au Moyen Age: Morgan et Melusine* (Paris: Champion, 1984).

Hays, Michael L., *Shakespearean Tragedy as Chivalric Romance: Rethinking Macbeth, Hamlet, Othello, King Lear* (Cambridge: D. S. Brewer, 2003).

Helms, Mary W., *Ulysses' Sail: An Ethnographic Odyssey of Power, Knowledge, and Geographical Distance* (Princeton: Princeton University Press, 1988).

Hibbard, Laura A., *Mediæval Romance in England: A Study of the Sources and Analogues of the Non-cyclic Metrical Romances*, rev. edn. (New York: Burt Franklin, 1960).

Hieatt, A. Kent, 'The Passing of Arthur in Malory, Spenser and Shakespeare: The Avoidance of Closure', in Baswell and Sharpe (eds.), *The Passing of Arthur*, pp. 173–92.

Hopkins, Andrea, *The Sinful Knights: A Study of Middle English Penitential Romance* (Oxford: Clarendon Press, 1990).

Hornell, James, 'The Curraghs of Ireland', *Mariner's Mirror* 23 (1937), 74–83, 148–75.

Hough, Graham, *A Preface to The Faerie Queene* (London: Duckworth, 1962).

Hume, Kathryn, 'The Formal Nature of Middle English Romance', *Philological Quarterly* 53 (1974), 158–80.

Huot, Sylvia, *From Song to Book: The Poetics of Writing in Old French Lyric and Lyrical Narrative Poetry* (Ithaca and London: Cornell University Press, 1987).

Huppert, George, *The Idea of Perfect History: Historical Erudition and Historical Philosophy in Renaissance France* (Urbana: University of Illinois Press, 1970).

Jacobs, Nicolas, *The Later Versions of 'Sir Degarre': A Study in Textual Degeneration*, Medium Ævum monographs 18 (Oxford: Society for the Study of Mediæval Languages and Literature, 1995).

—— 'Old French "Degaré" and Middle English "Degarre" and "Deswarre"', *Notes and Queries* 17 (1970), 164–5.

Jameson, Fredric, *The Political Unconscious: Narrative as a Socially Symbolic Act* (Ithaca: Cornell University Press; London: Methuen, 1981).

—— 'Magical Narratives: Romance as Genre', *New Literary History* 7 (1975–6), 135–63.

Jansen, Sharon L., *Political Protest and Prophecy under Henry VIII* (Woodbridge: Boydell Press, 1991).

Jauss, Hans Robert, *Towards an Aesthetic of Reception*, trans. Timothy Bahti (Minneapolis: University of Minnesota Press; Brighton: Harvester, 1982).

Johnson, Lesley, 'Return to Albion', *Arthurian Literature* 13 (1995), 19–40.

Jones, Ann Rosalind, 'Mills and Boon meets Feminism', in Radford (ed.), *The Progress of Romance*, pp. 194–218.

Jones, Emrys, 'Stuart Cymbeline', *Essays in Criticism* 11 (1961), 84–99.

Jones, Michael, and Vale, Malcolm (eds.), *England and her Neighbours 1066–1453: Essays in Honour of Pierre Chaplais* (London and Ronceverte: Hambledon Press, 1989).

Kantorowicz, Ernst, *The King's Two Bodies: A Study in Medieval Political Theology* (Princeton: Princeton University Press, 1957).

Kaske, Carol V., 'How Spenser Really Used Stephen Hawes in the Legend of Holiness', in Logan and Teskey (eds.), *Unfolded Tales*, pp. 119–36.

Keen, Maurice, *Chivalry* (New Haven and London: Yale University Press, 1984).

Kelly, Fergus, *A Guide to Early Irish Law* (Dublin: Dublin Institute for Advanced Studies, 1988).

Kelly, Henry Ansgar, *Love and Marriage in the Age of Chaucer* (Ithaca: Cornell University Press, 1975).

Kennedy, Edward Donald, 'John Hardyng and the Holy Grail', *Arthurian Literature* 8 (1989), 185–205.

Kennedy, Elspeth, *Lancelot and the Grail: A Study of the Prose Lancelot* (Oxford: Clarendon Press, 1986).

—— 'Failure in Arthurian Romance', *Medium Ævum* 60 (1991), 16–32.

—— 'The Knight as Reader of Romance', in Shichtman and Carley (eds.), *Culture and the King*, pp. 70–90.

Ker, W. P., *Epic and Romance: Essays on Medieval Literature* (London and New York: Macmillan, 1897).

King, Andrew, *The Faerie Queene and Middle English Romance: The Matter of Just Memory* (Oxford: Clarendon Press, 2000).

Klassen, Norman J., *Chaucer on Love, Knowledge and Sight*, Chaucer Studies 21 (Cambridge: D. S. Brewer, 1995).

Knight, Stephen, *Arthurian Literature and Society* (London and Basingstoke: Macmillan, 1983).

Köhler, Erich, *L'Aventure chevaleresque: Idéal et réalité dans le roman courtois*, trans. Éliane Kaufholz (Paris: Gallimard, 1974).

Kolve, V. A., *Chaucer and the Imagery of Narrative: The First Five Canterbury Tales* (Stanford: Stanford University Press; London: Edward Arnold, 1984).

Krier, Theresa M. (ed.), *Refiguring Chaucer in the Renaissance* (Gainesville: University of Florida Press, 1998).

Krueger, Roberta L. (ed.), *The Cambridge Companion to Medieval Romance* (Cambridge: Cambridge University Press, 2000).

Krueger, Roberta L., 'Double Jeopardy: The Appropriation of Woman in four Old French Romances of the "Cycle de la Gageure"', in Fisher and Halley (eds.), *Seeking the Woman*, pp. 21–50.

Laborderie, Olivier de, 'Richard the Lionheart and the Birth of a National Cult of St George in England: Origins and Development of a Legend', *Nottingham Medieval Studies* 39 (1995), 37–53.

Lacy, Norris J. (ed.), *The New Arthurian Encyclopedia* (Chicago and London: St James Press, 1991).

—— Kelly, Douglas and Busby, Keith (eds.), *The Legacy of Chrétien de Troyes*, 2 vols. (Amsterdam: Rodopi, 1987–8).

Lander, J. M., *Conflict and Stability in Fifteenth-century England* (London: Hutchinson, 1977).

Latham, Minor White, *The Elizabethan Fairies: The Fairies of Folklore and the Fairies of Shakespeare* (New York: Columbia University Press, 1930).

Legge, M. Dominica, *Anglo-Norman Literature and its Background* (Oxford: Clarendon Press, 1963).

Leonard, Irving A., *Books of the Brave* (1949; repr. Berkeley and Los Angeles: University of California Press, 1992).

Lewis, C. S., *The Allegory of Love: A Study in Medieval Tradition* (Oxford: Oxford University Press, 1936).

—— *The Discarded Image* (Cambridge: Cambridge University Press, 1964).

Logan, George M., and Teskey, Gordon (eds.), *Unfolded Tales: Essays on Renaissance Romance* (Ithaca and London: Cornell University Press, 1989).

Loomis, C. Grant, *White Magic: The Folklore of Christian Legend*, Medieval Academy of America Publications 52 (Cambridge, Mass.: Mediæval Academy of America, 1948).

Loomis, Laura Hibbard: see Hibbard.

Loomis, Roger Sherman, *Arthurian Legends in Medieval Art* (New York: Modern Language Association of America; London: Oxford University Press, 1938).

Löseth, E., *Le Roman en prose de Tristan*, Bibliothèque de l'École des hautes Études 82 (Paris: Emile Bouillon, 1890).

Lyle, E. B., 'The Relationship between *Thomas the Rhymer* and *Thomas of Erceldoune*', *Leeds Studies in English*, 4 (1970), 23–30.

MacCulloch, Diarmaid, *Thomas Cranmer: A Life* (New Haven and London: Yale University Press, 1996).

Maddox, Donald, *Fictions of Identity in Medieval France* (Cambridge: Cambridge University Press, 2001).

—— and Sturm-Maddox, Sarah (eds.), *Melusine of Lusignan: Founding Fiction in Late Medieval France* (Athens, Georgia, and London: University of Georgia Press, 1996).

Maddox, Donald, 'Lévi-Strauss in Camelot: Interrupted Communication in Arthurian Feudal Fictions', in Shichtman and Carley (eds.), *Culture and the King*, pp.35–53.

Maier, Bernhard, *Dictionary of Celtic Religion and Culture*, trans. Cyril Edwards (Woodbridge: Boydell Press, 1997).

Martindale, Joan, 'Succession and Politics in the Romance-Speaking World c.1000–1140', in Jones and Vale (eds.), *England and her Neighbours*, pp. 19–41.

Matheson, Lister M., 'The Arthurian stories of Lambeth Palace Library MS 84', *Arthurian Literature* 5 (1985), 70–91.

Mayor, Adrienne, *The First Fossil Hunters: Palaeontology in Greek and Roman Times* (Princeton: Princeton University Press, 2000) .

McCash, June Hall (ed.), *The Cultural Patronage of Medieval Women* (Athens, Ga: University of Georgia Press, 1995).

McCoy, Richard C., *The Rites of Knighthood: The Literature and Politics of Elizabethan Chivalry* (Berkeley, Los Angeles, and London: University of California Press, 1989).

McKenzie, D. F., *Bibliography and the Sociology of Texts*, 2nd edn. (Cambridge: Cambridge University Press, 1999).

Meale, Carol M. (ed.), *Readings in Medieval English Romance* (Cambridge: D. S. Brewer, 1994).

—— (ed.), *Women and Literature in Britain* 1150–1500, Cambridge Studies in Medieval Literature 17 (Cambridge: Cambridge University Press, 1993).

—— '. . . alle the bokes that I haue of latyn, englisch and frensch: Laywomen and their Books in late medieval England', in Meale (ed.), *Women and Literature*, pp. 128–58.

—— 'Caxton, de Worde, and the Publication of Romance in late medieval England', *The Library*, 6th ser., 14 (1992), 283–98.

—— 'Manuscripts, Readers and Patrons in Fifteenth-century England: Sir Thomas Malory and Arthurian Romance', *Arthurian Literature* 4 (1985), 93–126.

—— 'The Politics of Book Ownership: The Hopton Family and Bodleian Library Digby MS 185', in Riddy (ed.), *Prestige, Authority and Power*, pp. 103–31.

Mebane, John S., *Renaissance Magic and the Return of the Golden Age: The Occult Tradition and Marlowe, Jonson, and Shakespeare* (Lincoln, Nebraska, and London: University of Nebraska Press, 1989).

Melchiori, Giorgio, *Shakespeare's Garter Plays: Edward III to Merry Wives of Windsor* (Newark: University of Delaware Press; London and Toronto: Associated University Presses, 1994).

Michie, Sarah, '*The Faerie Queene* and *Arthur of Little Britain*', *Studies in Philology* 36 (1939), 105–23.

Middle English Dictionary, ed. Hans Kurath and Robert E. Lewis (Ann Arbor: University of Michigan Press, 1954–99).

Middleton, Roger, 'Manuscript of the *Lancelot-Grail Cycle* in England and Wales: Some Books and their Owners', in Dover (ed.), *A Companion to the Lancelot-Grail Cycle*, pp. 219–35.

Mills, Maldwyn, Meale, Carol and Fellows, Jennifer (eds.), *Romance in Medieval England* (Cambridge: D. S. Brewer, 1991).

Minnis, Alastair, *Magister Amoris: The Roman de la Rose and Vernacular Hermeneutics* (Oxford: Oxford University Press, 2001).

Montrose, Louis Adrian, ' "Shaping Fantasies": Figurations of Gender and Power in Elizabethan Culture', *Representations* 1 (1983), 61–94.

Moore, Helen, *Amadis in English: A Study in the Reception of Romance* (forthcoming).

Morison, Samuel Eliot, *The European Discovery of America: The Northern Voyages AD* 500–1600 (New York: Oxford University Press, 1971).

Morse, Ruth, 'Sterile Queens and Questing Orphans', *Quondam et Futurus* 2:2 (1992), 41–53.

Mortimer, Ian, *The Greatest Traitor: The Life of Sir Roger Mortimer, 1st Earl of March* (London: Cape, 2003).

Mullally, Evelyn, and Thompson John, *The Court and Cultural Diversity: Selected Papers from the Eighth Triennial Congress of the International Courtly Literature Society 1995*, ed. Evelyn Mullally and John Thompson (Cambridge: D. S. Brewer, 1997).

Mulryne, J. R, and Kozuka, Takashi, eds, *Shakespeare, Marlowe, Jonson: New Directions in Biography* (Aldershot: Ashgate, 2004).

Mulvey, Laura, *Visual and Other Pleasures* (Basingstoke: Macmillan, 1989).

Murray, Alexander, *Suicide in the Middle Ages: The Violent Against Themselves* (Oxford: Oxford University Press, 1998).

Neale, J. E., *Elizabeth I and her Parliaments* 1559–1581 (London: Jonathan Cape, 1953).

Newcomb, Lori Humphrey, 'The Triumph of Time: The Fortunate Readers of Robert Greene's *Pandosto*', in *Texts and Cultural Change in Early Modern England*, ed. Brown and Marotti, pp. 95–123.

Newman, F. X. (ed.), *The Meaning of Courtly Love* (Albany, NY: State University of New York Press, 1968).

Nolan, Barbara, *Chaucer and the Tradition of the 'Roman Antique'* (Cambridge: Cambridge University Press, 1992).

O'Connell, Michael, *The Idolatrous Eye: Iconoclasm and Theater in Early-Modern England* (New York and Oxford: Oxford University Press, 2000).

O'Donoghue, Bernard, *The Courtly Love Tradition* (Manchester: Manchester University Press; Totowa, NJ: Barnes and Noble, 1982).

O'Kill, Brian, 'The Printed Works of William Patten (c.1510–c.1600)', *Transactions of the Cambridge Bibliographical Society* 7 (1977), 28–45.

Paris, Gaston, 'Études sur les romans de la table ronde. Lancelot du Lac II: *Le Conte de la Charrette*', *Romania* 12 (1883), 459–534.

Parker, Patricia A., *Inescapable Romance: Studies in the Poetics of a Mode* (Princeton: Princeton University Press, 1979).

Payer, Pierre J., *The Bridling of Desire: Views of Sex in the Middle Ages* (Toronto: University of Toronto Press, 1993).

Pearsall, Derek, 'The English Romance in the Fifteenth Century', *Essays and Studies*, 29 (1976), 56–83.

Peristiany, J. G. (ed.), *Honour and Shame: The Values of Mediterranean Society* (London: Weidenfeld & Nicholson, 1965).

Pitcher, John, ' "Fronted with the Sight of a Bear": *Cox of Collumpton* and *The Winter's Tale*', *Notes and Queries* 239 (1994), 47–53.

Pollock, Frederick, and Maitland, Frederic William, *The History of English Law before the Time of Edward I*, 2nd edn. (Cambridge, 1911).

Powicke, F. M., *Henry III and the Lord Edward: The Community of the Realm in the Thirteenth Century* (Oxford: Clarendon Press, 1947).

Prescott, Anne Lake, 'Spenser's Chivalric Restoration: From Bateman's *Travayled Pylgrime* to the Redcrosse Knight', *Studies in Philology* 86 (1989), 166–97.

Propp, Vladimir, *Morphology of the Folktale*, trans. Laurence Scott, 2nd edn., rev. Louis A. Wagner (Austin and London: University of Texas Press, 1968).

Putter, Ad, *An Introduction to the Gawain-poet* (London and New York: Longman, 1996).

—— 'Finding Time for Arthurian Romance: Mediaeval Arthurian Literary History', *Medium Ævum* 63 (1994), 1–16.

—— and Gilbert Jane (eds), *The Spirit of Medieval English Popular Romance* (London and New York: Longman, 2000).

Quint, David, 'The Boat of Romance and Renaissance Epic', in Brownlee and Brownlee (ed.), *Romance: Generic Transformations*, pp. 178–202.

Radford, Jean (ed.), *The Progress of Romance: The Politics of Popular Fiction* (London and New York: Routledge, 1986).

Rank, Otto, *The Myth of the Birth of the Hero: A Psychological Interpretation of Mythology*, in Segal (intro.), *In Quest of the Birth of the Hero*.

Ravelhofer, Barbara, ' "Beasts of Recreation": Henslowe's White Bears', *ELR* 32 (2002), 287–323.

Redford, Donald R., 'The Literary Motif of the Exposed Child', *Numen* 14 (1967), 209–28.

Reed, Thomas L., jr, *Middle English Debate Poetry and the Aesthetics of Irresolution* (Columbia, Missouri, and London: University of Missouri Press, 1990).

Reinhard, J. R., 'Setting adrift in Medieval Law and Literature', *PMLA* 56 (1941), 33–68.

Reiter, Rayna R. (ed.), *Towards an Anthropology of Women* (New York and London: Monthly Review Press, 1975).

Riches, Samantha, *St George: Hero, Martyr and Myth* (Stroud: Sutton Publishing, 2000).

Richmond, Colin, *The Paston Family in the Fifteenth Century: The First Phase* (Cambridge: Cambridge University Press, 1990).

Richmond, Velma Bourgeois, *The Legend of Guy of Warwick* (New York and London: Garland, 1996).

—— *The Popularity of Middle English Romance* (Bowling Green, OH.: Bowling Green University Press, 1975).

Riddy, Felicity (ed.), *Prestige, Authority and Power in Late Medieval Manuscripts and Texts* (Woodbridge: York Medieval Press, 2000).

—— and Goldberg, Jeremy (eds.), *Youth in the Middle Ages* (Woodbridge: York Medieval Press, 2004).

Ross, Charles, *The Custom of the Castle from Malory to Macbeth* (Berkeley, Los Angeles, and London: University of California Press, 1997).

Rovang, Paul R., *Refashioning 'Knights and Ladies Gentle Deeds': The Intertextuality of Spenser's Faerie Queene and Malory's Morte Darthur* (Madison, Teaneck: Fairleigh Dickinson University Press; London: Associated University Presses, 1996).

Rubin, Gayle, 'The Traffic in Women: Notes on the "Political Economy" of Sex', in Reiter (ed.), *Towards an Anthropology of Women*, pp. 157–210.

Rye, William Brenchley, *England as Seen by Foreigners in the Days of Elizabeth and James I* (London: John Russell Smith, 1865).

St Clair-Kendall, S. G., *Narrative Form and Mediaeval Continuity in the Percy Folio Manuscript: A Study of Selected Poems*, Ph.D. thesis, University of Sydney (1988).

Salih, Sarah, *Versions of Virginity in Late Medieval England* (Cambridge: D. S. Brewer, 2001).

Saunders, Corinne J., *The Forest of Medieval Romance: Avernus, Broceliande, Arden* (Cambridge: D. S. Brewer, 1993).

—— *Rape and Ravishment in the Literature of Medieval England* (Cambridge: D. S. Brewer, 2001).

—— (ed.), *Cultural Encounters in Medieval English Romance* (Cambridge: D. S. Brewer, 2004).

Scanlon, Paul A., 'A Checklist of Prose Romances in English 1474–1603', *The Library*, 5th ser. 32 (1978), 143–52.

Schlauch, Margaret, *Chaucer's Constance and Accused Queens* (New York: New York University Press, 1927).

Schmitz, Götz, *The Fall of Women in Early English Narrative Verse* (Cambridge: Cambridge University Press, 1990).

Schoepperle, Gertrude, *Tristan and Isolt: A Study of the Sources of the Romance*, 2nd edn. rev. by Roger Sherman Loomis (New York: Burt Franklin, 1960).

Scott, David, 'William Patten and the Authorship of Robert Laneham's *Letter* (1575)', *ELR* 7 (1977), 297–306.

Scragg, Leah, *Shakespeare's Mouldy Tales: Recurrent Plot Motifs in Shakespearean Drama* (London and New York: Longman, 1992).

Segal, Robert A. (intro.), *In Quest of the Birth of the Hero* (Princeton: Princeton University Press, 1990).

Severin, Tim, *The Brendan Voyage* (London: Hutchinson, 1978).

Severs, J. Burke, *A Manual of the Writings in Middle English 1050–1350* I: Romances (New Haven: Connecticut Academy of Arts and Sciences, 1967).

Sexton, Joyce H., *The Slandered Woman in Shakespeare*, English Literary Studies 12 (Victoria, BC: University of Victoria, 1978).

Seymour, M. C., 'MSS Douce 261 and Egerton 3132A and Edward Banyster', *Bodleian Library Record* 10 (1980), 162–5.

Shichtman, Martin B., and Carley, James P. (eds.), *Culture and the King: The Social Implications of Arthurian Legend* (Albany: State University of New York Press, 1994).

A Short-Title Catalogue of Books printed in England, Scotland, and Ireland 1475–1640, comp. A. W. Pollard and G. R. Redgrave, 2nd edn. rev. and enlarged W. A. Jackson, F. S. Ferguson, and Katharine F. Pantzer, 3 vols. (London: Bibliographical Society, 1976–91).

Simons, John, 'Romance in the Eighteenth-century Chapbook', in Simons (ed.), *Medieval to Medievalism*, pp. 122–43.

Simons, John (ed.), *From Medieval to Medievalism* (Basingstoke, 1992).

Simpson, Jacqueline, *British Dragons* (London: Batsford, 1980).

Sollers, Werner (ed.), *The Return of Thematic Criticism*, Harvard Studies in English 18 (Cambridge, Mass.: Harvard University Press, 1993).

Somerset, Anne, *Elizabeth I* (London: Weidenfeld & Nicolson, 1991).

Spiegel, Gabrielle M., *Romancing the Past: The Rise of Vernacular Prose Historiography in Thirteenth-century France* (Berkeley: University of California Press, 1993).

Spufford, Margaret, *Small Books and Pleasant Histories: Popular Fiction and its Readers in Seventeenth-century England* (London: Methuen, 1981).

Spurgeon, Caroline, *Five Hundred Years of Chaucer Criticism and Allusion*, Chaucer Society 48–50, 52–6 (London: Oxford University Press, 1914–25).

Stock, Brian, *The Implications of Literacy: Written Language and Models of Interpretation in the Eleventh and Twelfth Centuries* (Princeton: Princeton University Press, 1983).

Stone, Lawrence, *The Crisis of the Aristocracy 1558–1641* (Oxford: Clarendon Press, 1965).

Strohm, Paul, 'The Origin and Meaning of Middle English *Romaunce*', *Genre* 10 (1977), 1–20.

—— '*Storie, Spelle, Geste, Romaunce, Tragedie*: Generic Distinctions in the Middle English Troy Narrative', *Speculum* 46 (1971), 348–59.

Sykes, Bryan, and Irven, Catherine, 'Surnames and the Y Chromosome', *American Journal of Human Genetics* 66 (2000), 1417–19.

Thomas, Keith, *Religion and the Decline of Magic* (1971; Harmondsworth: Penguin, 1973).

Thompson, Ann, *Shakespeare's Chaucer: A Study in Literary Origins* (Liverpool: Liverpool University Press, 1978).

Thompson, Stith, *Motif-Index of Folk Literature*, rev. edn. (Copenhagen: Rosenkilde and Bagger, 1955–8).

Turner, Victor, 'The Center Out There: Pilgrim's Goal', *History of Religions* 12 (1972), 191–230.

Turville-Petre, Thorlac, '*Havelok* and the History of the Nation', in Meale (ed.), *Readings in Medieval English Romance*, pp. 121–34.

Tuve, Rosemond, *Allegorical Imagery: Some Medieval Books and Their Posterity* (Princeton: Princeton University Press, 1966).

—— *Essays by Rosemond Tuve: Spenser, Herbert, Milton*, ed. Thomas P. Roche, jr (Princeton: Princeton University Press, 1970).

Utley, Francis Lee, *The Crooked Rib: An Analytical Index to the Argument about Women in English and Scots Literature to the End of the Year* 1568 (Columbus: Ohio State University Press, 1944).

van Es, Bart, *Spenser's Forms of History* (Oxford: Oxford University Press, 2002).

Walker, Simon, 'Rumour, Sedition and Popular Protest in the Reign of King Henry IV', *Past and Present* 166 (2000), 31–65.

Weber, Max, *The Protestant Ethic and the Spirit of Capitalism*, trans. Talcott Parsons, intro. Anthony Giddens, 2nd edn. (London: Allen and Unwin, 1976).

Weiss, Judith, 'The Date of the Anglo-Norman *Boeve de Haumtone*', *Medium Ævum* 55 (1986), 237–41.

—— 'A Reappraisal of Hue de Rotelande's *Protheselaus*', *Medium Ævum* 52 (1983), 104–11.

—— 'Structure and Characterisation in *Havelok the Dane*', *Speculum* 44 (1969), 247–57.

—— 'The Wooing Woman in Anglo-Norman Romance', in Mills, Fellows, and Meale (eds.), *Romance in Medieval England*, pp. 149–61.

—— Fellows, Jennifer and Dickson, Morgan (eds.), *Medieval Insular Romance: Translation and Innovation* (Cambridge: D. S. Brewer, 2000).

Wells, Stanley, 'Shakespeare and Romance', in Brown and Harris (eds.), *Later Shakespeare*, 49–79.

Westoby, Kathryn S., 'A New Look at the Role of the Fée in Medieval French Arthurian Romance', in Burgess and Taylor (eds.), *The Spirit of the Court*, pp. 373–85.

Wheeler, Bonnie (ed.), *Arthurian Studies in Honour of P. J. C. Field* (Cambridge: D. S. Brewer, 2004).

White, Hayden, *Tropics of Discourse: Essays in Cultural Criticism* (Baltimore and London: Johns Hopkins University Press, 1978).

White, Hugh, *Nature, Sex, and Goodness in a Medieval Literary Tradition* (Oxford: Oxford University Press, 2000).

Whiting, Bartlett Jere, *Proverbs, Sentences and Proverbial Phrases from English Writings Mainly Before 1500* (Cambridge, Mass.: Harvard University Press, 1968).

Williams, Franklin B., 'Alsop's *Fair Custance*: Chaucer in Tudor Dress', *ELR* 6 (1976), 351–68.

Wilson, Elkin Calhoun, *England's Eliza* (1938; repr. New York: Octagon Books, 1966).

Wilson, Jean Lesley, *A Consideration of Spenser's Treatment of Romance Themes in the Faerie Queene in the light of Elizabethan Attitudes to Romance*, Ph.D. thesis, University of Cambridge, 1973.

Wittgenstein, Ludwig, *Philosophical Investigations*, trans. G. E. M. Anscombe (Oxford: Blackwell, 1953).

Wittig, Susan, *Stylistic and Narrative Structures in the Middle English Romances* (Austin and London: University of Texas Press, 1978).

Wogan-Browne, Jocelyn, *Saints' Lives and Women's Literary Culture c.1150–1300: Virginity and its Authorizations* (Oxford: Oxford University Press, 2001).

—— 'The Virgin's Tale', in Evans and Johnson (eds.), *Feminist Readings in Middle English Literature* (London and New York: Routledge, 1994), pp. 165–94.

Woledge, Brian, *Bibliographie des romans et nouvelles en prose français antérieures à 1500* and *Supplement* (Geneva: Droz, 1954, 1975).

Wood, Michael, *In Search of England: Journeys into the English Past* (London: Viking, 1999).

Woodbridge, Linda, *Women and the English Renaissance: Literature and the Nature of Womankind, 1540–1620* (Brighton: Harvester, 1984).

Woodcock, Matthew, *Faerie in the Faerie Queene: Renaissance Elf-Fashioning and Elizabethan Myth-Making* (Aldershot: Ashgate, 2004).

Worden, Blair, *The Sound of Virtue: Philip Sidney's Arcadia and Elizabethan Politics* (New Haven and London: Yale University Press, 1996).

Wroe, Ann, *Perkin: A Story of Deception* (London: Cape, 2003).

Zink, Michel, 'Chrétien et ses contemporains', in Lacy, Kelly, and Busby (eds.), *Legacy of Chrétien de Troyes*, i. 5–32 .

Index

adultery 28, 270, 273, 274–6, 281, 307–22, 404
advice to princes 56
Agnes, St 250
Alain de Lille 241, 244
Albina 115–16, 411
Alexander 6, 74; romances of 411
Alexander III, Pope 222
Alexis, St 89, 94
allegory 10, 83–6, 99 104, 242–3; magic in 164–5; see also *Quest of the Holy Grail*
Alsop, Thomas 128, 415
Amadas et Ydoine 145, 201–3, 223–5, 237, 291–2; Ydoine 297
Amadis de Gaule 28, 35, 38, 39, 71, 110, 334; Oriana 355
ancestral romance 120, 353
Ancrene Wisse 84, 249
Andreas Capellanus 308–12; *De amore* in England 310–11
Angevin empire 22, 26
Anglo-Saxon Chronicle 123
Anonymous Short English Metrical Chronicle 115, 422, 442 n. 85
Anton, Robert 44
Apollonius of Tyre 35, 266, 300–1; conspectus of versions 411–12; Apollonius 121; *see also* Shakespeare, *Pericles*
Ariosto, Ludovico 34, 75–6; *Orlando Furioso* 28, 54, 117, 131, 303, 414; magic in 142, 164; as source for Spenser 191, 252, 318
Aristotle 271, 398
arms, symbolic 42, 51, 102, 104, 165, 205; magic lance 253; magic sword and scabbard 138, 143, 165; sword as recognition token 329; *see also* shield
Arthur, King 22, 347, 355; legend of 24, 342; conspectus of romances 412–13; campaign against Rome 194; as 'fair unknown' 55, 332; death 129, 185, 186, 347, 403; *see also* Guinevere; Hughes; Malory; *Morte Arthur*; *Morte Arthure*; *Of Arthour and of Merlin*
Arthur of Little Britain 185, 413

Ascham, Roger 38, 320
Ashley, Robert 444 n. 101
Athelstan 112, 114
Auchinleck manuscript 30, 409, 413, 416, 419, 420, 423–7 *passim*, 453 n. 102
Auerbach, Erich 69
Augustine, St 37, 246

Bacon, Francis 492 n. 42, 493 n. 60
Banyster, Edward 38, 410
barca aventurosa 107, 129, 133–5; *see also* rudderless boats
Barinthus 124, 129
Bateman, Stephen 103–4
bears 432 n. 6; abduction by 284, 339; bearsuits 1, 8, 229; on stage 1–2, 137; in *Winter's Tale* 342; see also *Valentine and Orson*
Beaufort, Lady Margaret 346, 348–9, 382, 493 n. 59
beauty of heroine 15–20
Beowulf 6, 108, 326
Berners, John Bourchier, Lord 35; see also *Arthur of Little Britain*; *Huon of Bordeaux*
Bevis of Hamton 30, 38, 142, 247, 413; Bevis 361; printed editions 3, 36; used by Bunyan 3, 32, 90–1; used by Shakespeare and Spenser 31–2
Biket, Robert 315
Blake, William 221
Blanchardyn and Eglantine 225, 348–9, 413–14
Boccaccio, Giovanni: *Decameron*, as source of *All's Well* 392; of *Franklin's Tale* 157; of *Frederyke of Jennen* 275; and *Knight of Curtesy* 497 n. 49; *Il Filocolo* 156
Bodel, Jean 439 n. 64
Boleyn, Anne 276–8, 353–4
Bowdler, Thomas 264, 482 n. 99
Boy and the Mantle 316
Brendan, St 74, 124–5
Brut, prose 265, 343, 420; *see also* Layamon, Wace

Brutus (Brut) 24, 115, 414
Buck, George 355, 493 n. 60; quoted 348
Bunyan, John, 3, 32, 68, 98, 102; and *Bevis* 32, 90–1; Christian 78, 85, 99–100; Faithful 323
Butler, Samuel, *Hudibras* 40
Bynum, Caroline Walker 49, 143
Byrth and Prophecye of Marlyn 191, 424; see also *Of Arthour and of Merlin*

Camoens 75
Capgrave, John 329–30, 341–2, 421
Carle of Carlisle 418, 472 n. 90
Catherine of Aragon, *see* Katherine
Caxton, William 34, 343, 348–9; Preface to *Morte Darthur* 307, 316; see also *Four Sons of Aymon*; *Golden Legend*; Lefevre; Lull, *Book*; *Paris and Vienne*
Cervantes, Miguel de, *Don Quixote* 39, 106–8
Charlemagne 56; romances 6, 363, 414; see also *Huon of Bordeaux*; *Sowdone of Babylone*
Chatelain de Coucy 318; see also *Knight of Curtesy*
Chaucer, Geoffrey:
    afterlife of writings 128, 158–9, 174, 374–5, 414–16
    women in 16–20, 304
    Canterbury Tales:
        Franklin's Tale 27, 141, 157–8, 253, 475 n. 22
        Knight's Tale 12, 16–17, 48, 64, 141, 372–5
        Man of Law's Tale 116–17, 127–8, 294, 295–6; Constance 287
        Merchant's Tale 19, 174, 176, 200
        Nun's Priest's Tale 19–20, 422, 485 n. 53
        Squire's Tale 138
        Tale of Sir Thopas 19–20, 48–9, 138, 180, 235; elf-queen 141, 174
        Wife of Bath's Prologue 297
        Wife of Bath's Tale 48–9, 181, 204–5, 214–15, 226
    Parliament of Fowls 243, 304–6, 358
    Troilus and Criseyde 18–19, 21, 48, 227, 230, 242, 372
    see also Greene, *Greene's Vision*
Chestre, Thomas 440 n. 71, 490 n. 19; see also *Sir Launfal*
Chevelere Assigne 279; see also *Knight of the Swan*
Chrétien de Troyes 12, 26–7, 43, 73; *Chevalier de la Charrette* 26, 28, 84, 102, 145, 308–9, 438 n. 57; *Cligés* 233,

297, 309; *Conte du Graal (Perceval)* 21, 46, 60–2, 100, 332–3; *Erec et Enide* 56, 185, 239; *Yvain (Chevalier au Lion)* 87, 102, 146–8, 204
Christina of Markyate 248
Christine de Pizan 273
Churchyard, Thomas 179
Cleanness 119–20, 244–5
Clyomon and Clamydes 64, 258, 425
Colville, John 195
Complaynt of Scotland 90, 410
condemnations of romance 37–9, 90, 410–11, 441 n. 79
Constance 127–8; see also Chaucer, *Man of Law's Tale*
Cortes 76
courtly love 26, 308; see also love, terminology for
Cox, Captain, see Laneham, Robert
Cox of Collumpton 431 n. 5
cross-dressing, female to male 279, 281, 301; male to female 258–60, 299, 301; see also women warriors
Crosse, Henry, *Vertue's Commonwealth* 410, 443 n. 98
crusades 42, 99
Cyuile and Unciuile Life 436 n. 39

Dante 34, 70
Day, Angel 335
Dekker, Thomas 128; 'Magnificent Entertainment' 196–7; *Virgin Martyr* 251; *Whore of Babylon* 189, 190, 209
Deloney, Thomas 422
Dering, Edward 410
Des grants Geanz 411, 456 n. 20
Dialoges of Creatures Moralysed [1530], quoted 299
Dickens, Charles, 1; *Oliver Twist* 328
Donne, John 20, 257, 476 n. 29
Drayton, Michael 95, 412, 415, 419, 421

Earl of Toulouse 278–9, 416
Edmund, St 457 n. 38
Edward II 344
Edward IV 325, 329
Edward VI 1, 345
Eger and Grime 36, 58, 82, 416, 462 n. 28
eglantine, as symbol of England 349
Eilhart von Oberge 232, 459 n. 54
Elaine of Ascolat 130–1, 240

Elizabeth I 179, 187, 257, 277–8, 323, 353–5,
    492 n. 53; and fairy queen 22, 181; and
    Shakespeare 216–17, 352, 358, 359–60;
    at Kenilworth 207–9; sexuality 185,
    211; virginity 96, 325–6; death 195,
    327; *see also* Dekker, *Whore*; Spenser,
    Faerie Queene, Gloriana
Elizabeth of York 346, 349; see also *Lady
    Bessy*
Emaré 126–7, 330, 475 n. 18
Emperor and the Child 283, 407–8, 429
enchanters 157, 164, 166–7, 171–2, 379–81;
    enchantresses 18, 79–80, 129–35, 145,
    160–4; *see also* Merlin; Morgan;
    witchcraft
Eneas, Roman de 25–6, 72; Lavine 227–8,
    231–2, 388
English language 7, 11–12
Erasmus 223
Esplandian 76
Etienne of Rouen 185, 208
eucharistic test 179, 203, 382
exposure: at sea 108–10, 112–14, 117–19,
    120–3, 335, 375–7; on land 335, 341, 389

'fair unknown' 55, 331–40; see also *Lybeaus
    Desconus*
Fairfax, Edward 75, 79; *see also* Tasso
fairies: frauds involving 209, 472–3 n. 10;
    rationalized 184, 186–7; traditions of
    177–84, 188, 381–2
fairy mistress 22, 141, 173, 175, 178, 211–15,
    389; *see also* Chaucer, *Tale of Sir
    Thopas*; Gloriana; *Melusine*; *Sir
    Launfal*; *Thomas of Erceldoune*
fairytale, distinguished from romance 143
Fall 79–80, 89, 244, 297; Eve 271, 283,
    295–6, 297, 396; Paradise 399; *see also*
    salvation history
Field, Nathan 158–9
Fielding, Henry, *Tom Jones* 328
Fisher, John 346
Flamenca 307, 312, 313
Fletcher, John: *Philaster* 280–1; *Triumph of
    Honour* 158–9; *Women Pleas'd* 415;
    see also Shakespeare, *Two Noble
    Kinsmen*
Floire et Blancheflor 28, 155–6
Floris and Blauncheflour 28, 38, 56, 150–1;
    conspectus of versions 155–6
Ford, John 352
forest 70
Forrest, William 276–7

Foucault, Michel 219
Four Sons of Aymon 39, 89–90, 167, 379, 417
Foxe, John 250–1, 354, 355
Frederyke of Jennen 275, 279, 296–7
Freud, Sigmund 48; uncanny 82
Frye, Northrop 5, 57, 72, 326

Gamelyn 36, 264, 417
Garter, Thomas 275
Gawain 6, 34, 142–3; conspectus of
    romances 417–18; see also *Sir Gawain
    and the Green Knight*
gaze 238–9; female 19, 234, 236–7; male 17,
    250
geis 204, 210
Generides 38, 186, 312–13, 318–19, 332,
    418–19
Gent, Thomas 495 n. 18
gentilesse 9, 328, 392; gentility 338–40
Geoffrey of Monmouth 27, 412, 414;
    History of the Kings of Britain 23–4,
    405; *Life of Merlin* (*Vita Merlini*) 74,
    129, 184; 'Prophecies of Merlin' 191
George, St 42, 46, 51; and prophecy 193–4,
    196
Gerald of Wales 99
Gervase of Tilbury 140; cited 379
Gesta Romanorum 264, 411, 442 n. 88
Gloriana, *see* Elizabeth I; Spenser, *Faerie
    Queene*, Gloriana
Godfrey of Bulloin, *see* Fairfax; *Knight of
    the Swan*; Tasso
Golagros and Gawain 417
Golden Legend 121, 375, 441 n. 76
Golding, Arthur 177
Gottfried von Strassburg 156–7, 233
Gower, John 127, 411, 419, 442 n. 88; *see
    also* Greene, *Greene's Vision*
Graelent 213
Grail, quest of 53, 85–6, 100–1; see also
    Chrétien de Troyes, *Conte*; *History of
    the Holy Grail*; Perceval; *Quest of the
    Holy Grail*
Gray, Sir Thomas 316
Greek romance 35
Greene, Robert: *Greene's Vision* 276,
    293–4; *Pandosto* 87, 116–17, 276,
    278–9, 285, 331, 396–7 (afterlife 456
    n. 22); Susanna stories 275
Greer, Germaine 218, 220
Gregory, St (Gregorius) 121–2, 399
Grene Knight 142, 418, 440 n. 72, 464 n. 52,
    472 n. 90

Grisandol 252, 301
Guillaume de Lorris, see *Roman de la Rose*
Guinevere 312, 323, 461–2 n. 27; in *Sir
  Orfeo* 199–200; in *Lanzelet* 314, 319;
  see also Lancelot; Malory, Guinevere
Guy of Warwick 89, 98, 370; ancestor of
  earls of Warwick 31, 93; and Guyon
  31, 95–6; fathered by St George 51
Guy of Warwick 30, 38, 92, 419; later know-
  ledge 31–3, 92–3; see also *Tragical
  History of Guy*

Hadewijch 238
Hali Meithhad 248
Harding, John 194, 319, 411, 412, 419, 446
  n. 10
Harington, John 75; see also Ariosto
Hartmann von Aue 457 nn. 30, 35
Havelok 29, 64, 334, 343, 420; Havelok 324;
  later versions 343–4; see also Warner
Hawes, Stephen: *Comfort of Lovers* 338;
  Example of Vertue 51, 102–3, 348, 453
  n. 115
Hay, Sir Gilbert 445 n. 109, 449 n. 49
heir, recovery of 114–15, 127, 324–31, 340–3,
  348; from over sea 117, 341, 351
heiress 222–3, 225, 227, 229, 284, 334–6,
  351, 354, 359; see also Elizabeth of
  York; Warner
Heldris of Cornuälle 226, 297, 301
Henry II 25
Henry III 325
Henry VI 344, 348
Henry VII (Tudor) 71, 191, 192, 325, 341,
  344–52
Henry VIII 35, 192, 276–8, 325, 347
Herbert of Cherbury, Lord 52
Heywood, Thomas 354, 412, 414, 428
History of the Holy Grail 132, 419, 421
Hoccleve, Thomas 20, 37, 485 n. 45
Holinshed's *Chronicles*: Albina 115, 411;
  Arthur 412; Brutus 24, 414; Edwin
  112; Guinevere 323; Guy of Warwick
  95; Macbeth 187–8, 385; Scyld 455
  n. 6
Holme, Wilfride 423, 466 n. 6, 492 n. 53
Horn 332, 341; conspectus of romances 29,
  117–18, 153–5, 420; *Hind Horn* (ballad)
  36, 154–5; see also *King Horn*; *King
  Ponthus*
Hue de Rotelande 11, 29, 478 n. 51;
  Ipomedon 19, 30, 235–6, 297–8, 437
  n. 43; see also *Ipomadon*

Hughes, Thomas 357–8, 404–5, 412, 413
Huon of Bordeaux 76, 245, 420; Clariette
  237; Huon 69, 125, 139, 145–6 (in
  Spenser 198); Oberon 176, 181–2, 189,
  197–8, 208, 467 n. 18
Hya, St 131
Hyrd, Richard 37–8, 176, 216, 235, 410

incest 34, 121–2, 328, 398–400, 403–4
Ine 490 n. 27
instruction 6–7, 56, 205–6
interlacing 53–4, 63
Ipomadon 225, 235–6, 420–1, 475 n. 14; *Lyfe
  of Ipomydon* 38; see also Hue de
  Rotelande
Irish Laws 109
Irish pilgrims of the sea 122–4; see also
  Brendan, St
iudicium Dei 110, 130, 132, 346

James I (VI) 43, 195–6, 327, 339, 359;
  prophecy of 188–9, 195, 345
Jameson, Frederic 363–4
Jason, see Lefevre; Medea
Jauss, Hans-Robert 8
Jeast of Sir Gawayne 418
Jerome, St 103
John of Glastonbury 131–2
John de Reeve 421
Johnson, Richard 39, 338, 389, 415; *Seven
  Champions of Christendom* 51; *Tom a
  Lincoln* 111, 138, 389–91, 423, 497 n. 45
Johnson, Samuel 408
Jonah 119
Jonson, Ben: *Alchemist* 209; knowledge
  of romances 413, 415, 419, 444
  n. 100
Joseph of Arimathea 131–2, 421
Judas 122, 375–6

Katherine of Aragon 37, 311; see also
  Shakespeare, *Henry VIII*
Kempe, Margery 238, 487 n. 76
Kenilworth entertainments 207, 209, 211,
  413
Kentigern, St 121, 457 n. 30
King Alexander, see Alexander
King Apollyn, see under *Apollonius*
king in disguise 4, 421, 425
King Edward III 331
King Edward and the Shepherd 421
King Horn 149–50, 153–4, 342, 420;
  Rimenhild 228; see also Horn

king-mark 324–5, 343
King Orphius 424
King Ponthus and the Faire Sidone 29, 38,
  118, 154, 422
Kirkman, Francis 410
Knight of Curtesy 318, 397, 422
Knight of the Swan 294–5, 335, 422; Helyas
  329
knighthood 41–4, 84; social context 55

Lady Bessy 350–1; quoted 346
Lady of the Lake 184, 205, 332; at
  Kenilworth entertainments 207; *see
  also* Malory, Lady
Lai du Corn, see Biket
Lai le Freine 335
La Marche, Olivier de 43, 104; *see also*
  Bateman; Lewkenor
Lancelot 34, 468 n. 24; conspectus of
  romances 422–3; in Harding 319–20;
  little known in England 6, 34, 319;
  education 6, 205; encounters with
  lions 84–5; as 'fair unknown' 332; on
  Grail quest 86, 101, 369; and
  Guinevere 26, 133, 313, 320–3, 442 n.
  85; death 322–3, 370
Lancelot, Prose 6, 42, 85, 184, 422
Lancelot-Grail 33–4, 205, 369, 401; English
  adaptations 412, 421, 423; *see also*
  Malory; *Merlin,* Prose; *Quest of the
  Holy Grail*
Lancelot of the Laik 56–7, 319, 422, 433
  n. 19
Landeval, see Sir Launfal
Lane, John 32, 415, 419, 441 n. 76
Laneham [Langham], Robert, *Letter:*
  authorship 410, 413, 444 n. 100; Cox,
  Captain 38–9, 90; romances cited in
  410, 444 n. 100
Langland, William, *Piers Plowman* 338,
  447 n. 12, 480 n. 73
Layamon, *Brut* 185, 412
Lefevre, Raoul 387–8
legitimacy rates 273–4
le Goff, Jacques 152
Leicester, Robert Dudley, earl of 207, 209,
  441 n. 76
Leir 24, 405; *see also* Shakespeare,
  King Lear; Tate; *True Chronicle
  History*
Leland, John, *Assertio inclytissimi Arturii*
  412
Leon, Ponce de 76

Lewis, C. S. 4, 95, 308; *Allegory of Love*
  438–9 n. 61, 486 n. 69; Narnia books
  4 (*Voyage of the Dawn Treader* 74,
  458 n. 42)
Lewkenor, Lewes 43
Libeaus [Libius] Desconus see *Lybeaus
  Desconus*
Lloyd, Richard 93, 412, 419
loathly lady 178, 204–5, 214
Locrine 431 n. 5
Lodge, Thomas 36; *Robert the Devil* 90,
  426; *Rosalynde* 264–5
Lollardy 90; Wycliffism 37
Longus, *Daphnis and Chloe* 35, 335–6
love, language of 239, 289; terminology for
  221, 245, 308, 321, 438 n. 57
Lovelich, Henry 419, 424
Lull, Ramón, *Blanquerna* 247–8; *Book of
  the Order of Chivalry* 42, quoted 453
  n. 105
Luther, Martin 251
Lybeaus [Libeaus, Libius] Desconus 38, 55,
  328, 332–4, 423, 440 n. 72
Lydgate, John 400–1, 457 n. 38; *Troy Book*
  399, 415

Mabinogion 27, 437 n. 51, 472 n. 88
Macbeth 187, 385
Maddox, Donald 353
magic, and astrology 140–1; distinct from
  marvel and miracle 139–41; non-
  functioning 144–55, 159–60; problems
  of 141–3; suspicions of 164–72; test of
  chastity 314–16; *see also* arms;
  enchanters; ring; shield
Malleus maleficarum 379
Malory, Sir Thomas 33–4, 38, 45
  Morte Darthur 24, 412–13
    *see also under individual entries
  disaster in 400–3
  *Grail quest in 63, 85–6, 100–1, 132–3,
    369
  shame culture in 83
  topography 71, 81
  women 302–3, 387
  Alysaunder and Alys 239
  *Arthur, death 403, 469 n. 50
  Balin 81, 99–100, 367–9
  Elaine of Ascolat 130–1, 240
  Elaine of Corbin 239–40
  Excalibur 138, 143
  Gareth 236, 239, 245, 332, 337
  *Guinevere 197, 320–3

Malory, Sir Thomas (*cont.*):
  Morte Darthur:
    *Lady of the Lake 184, 197, 201, 208
    *Lancelot 320–3, 468 n. 24
    *Merlin 191
    *Mordred 376–7, 403
    *Morgan 161, 316–17
    *Perceval 78–9
    Tor 336
Mandeville, Sir John 69, 74, 99, 473 n. 104
Manekine, see Philippe de Rémi
Marco Polo 139–40
Margaret of Anjou, manuscript for 409,
  439 n. 66, 457 n. 27
Marie de Champagne 26, 308–11
Marie de France, *Lais* 27, 312–14; *Bisclavret*
  307; *Deux Amants* 148–9; *Eliduc*
  237–8, 313; *Guigemar* 129–30, 186, 394,
  459 n. 60; *Lanval* 30, 198, 211, 423 (*see
  also Sir Launfal*); *Le Fresne* 335; *Milun*
  329; *Yonec* 467 n. 18
Markham, Gervase 185
Marlowe, Christopher, *Doctor Faustus* 381
marriage, consent required for 222, 252–3,
  311–12, 395; sacrament 241; theology
  of 246
Martorell, Joanot, see *Tirant lo Blanc*
Mary [Tudor] 345
Mary Hamilton 109
Mary Magdalene, St 120–1
matter of England 29, 117
'matters' of romance 29, 362
Medea 161, 172, 387–8
Melusine 38, 71, 175–6, 423; fairy prohibi-
  tions in 210–11, 215, 382–4; good
  advice in 205; Melusine 181, 188–9,
  197, 467 n. 18
memes 3, 21; and courtly love 308; of lost
  heirs 340–1; of rudderless boats 106
Meres, Francis 410, 413, 417, 419, 420, 424
Merlin 160, 167, 423–4; as prophet 189–92,
  346–7, 385–6; *see also* Geoffrey of
  Monmouth, *Vita Merlini*; Morgan;
  Spenser, *Faerie Queene*, and prophecy
Merlin, Prose 185–6, 191, 376; Grisandol
  252, 301; later versions 11, 33, 423–4
  (English quoted 377); see also *Of
  Arthour and of Merlin*
Mervine 185
middle-earth 467 n. 22
Middleton, Christopher 39, 40, 198, 423, 428
Mills and Boon 218–19, 225
Milton, John 45, 77, 87, 415

Mirror for Magistrates 412
misogyny 132, 269, 271–3, 281, 298–9,
  308–9, 315, 387–91; fears of women
  169; *see also* sexuality
Molinet, Jean, *Chroniques* 84
Monty Python and the Holy Grail 21
Mordred 34, 122, 358, 376–7, 403–5
Morgan le Fay 76, 134, 378; early history
  74, 184–5; in Malory 316–17; in prose
  romances 185–6; in *Sir Gawain and
  the Green Knight* 160–2
Morte Arthur (stanzaic) 319, 412, 442 n. 85
Morte Arthure (alliterative) 412, 442 n. 85,
  497 n. 59
Moses 108, 118–19
Mucedorus 2
Munday, Antony, see *Amadis de Gaule*
mystics 238, 241

naming 126, 330–1; of fairy monarchs 176;
  anonymity 333–4
Nashe, Thomas 38, 411, 441 n. 79
Nature 241–5, 305–6
Nicuesa, Diego de 111, 114
Nine Worthies 93; Nine Women Worthies
  355
Noah 119–20
Novellino 131

Oberon 176, 198, 467 n. 13; see also *Huon*;
  Randolph; Shakespeare, *Midsummer
  Night's Dream*
Octavian [*Octovian*] 30, 424, 485 n. 41;
  Florent 250
Oedipus, legend of 398–400
Of Arthour and of Merlin 30, 33, 423–4, 460
  n. 2, 461–2 n. 27, 470 n. 64; giants in
  137; quoted 11
Oliver of Castile 349–50, 424
Ordene de chevalerie 445 n. 109
Order of the Bath 52, 434 n. 19
Order of the Garter 33, 51, 52, 494 n. 69;
  Knights 358
Ovid 172, 176–7, 232; Pyramus story 38

Painter, William 392
Paris, Gaston 308
Paris and Vienne 38, 424
Partenay 423, 466 n. 6; see also *Melusine*
Partonope of Blois 38, 297, 425; boat in 130,
  455 n. 13; magic in 160–1, 167–70;
  Melior as fairy 186, 215–16, 297, 425,
  472 n. 94

Paston, Margaret 224
Patrick, St 122
Peele, George, *Arraignment of Paris* 354,
    357; *Old Wives Tale* 137, 166
penitential romance 87–98; romances of
    atonement 279
Perceforest 24, 33, 64, 258, 425
Perceval 18, 78–9, 90, 134; *see also*
    Chrétien, *Conte*; *Quest*; *Sir Percyvell*
Percy Folio manuscript 30, 36, 350, 410,
    416–19 *passim*, 422–9 *passim*; *Birth of
    Merlin* [*Of Arthour and of Merlin*]
    423–4, 470 n. 64; *Boy and the Mantle*
    316; *Emperor and the Child* 283,
    407–8, 429; *Grene Knight* 142, 418, 440
    n. 72, 464 n. 52, 472 n. 90; *Guy*
    romances 32, 419, 440 n. 72; *Libius
    [Lybeaus] Desconus* 332–4, 423, 440
    n. 72, 490 n. 19; *Sir Aldingar* 278–9,
    282, 285, 416; *Sir Degree [Degaré]*
    330–1, 416; *Sir Lambewell*, quoted 183,
    199, 211; Stanley poems 339, 350;
    Turke and Gawain [Gowin] 203, 418,
    440 n. 72; *see also Eger and Grime*;
    Lady Bessy; *Sir Eglamour*; *Sir Launfal*;
    Sir Tryamour
Petrarchan love 19, 230, 236, 353
Philippa, Queen 224
Philippe de Rémi, *Jehan et Blonde* 239, 458
    n. 44; *Manekine* 125–6, 294
pilgrimage 84, 98–9, 102; at sea 123–4
Ponthus, see *King Ponthus*
primogeniture 225, 325–6; inheritance
    practices 222–3
prophecy 113, 187–96, 329, 350, 385–7; of
    Stuarts 188–9, 195–6, 327; of Tudors
    187, 188, 192, 327
Prophisies of Rymour 192–4; *see also*
    Thomas of Erceldoune, as prophet
Propp, Vladimir 4
Pullman, Philip 8

quest 41, 45–50, 53, 58, 67; allegorical 84,
    99–105; and exploration 74–7; one-
    way 98–9, 124, 133, 367–9
Quest of the Holy Grail, Prose 25, 62, 63,
    78–9, 85–6, 100–1, 132–3, 419; *see also*
    Chrétien de Troyes, *Conte*; Grail;
    Perceval

Ralegh, Walter 76–7, 257, 360; *see also*
    Spenser, Letter to Ralegh
Randolph, Thomas 472–3 n. 100

Rauf Coilyear 425
readership 7, 10–14, 38–9, 152–3; women
    219, 226; *see also* instruction
recognition tokens 327–9
Reformation 35; condemnation of
    romance 38–9; continuity across 250,
    298; effect on romance 5, 90–2, 96–7,
    98, 110, 135, 251, 320, 366, 378; and
    prophecy 192, 194; and spiritual love
    249
Renaut de Beaujeu 332, 423
René of Anjou 102
resurrections 10, 57–8, 170–1, 344–5, 360,
    362, 407
Richard II 243, 325, 344; marriage contract
    487 n. 81
Richard Cœur de Lyon 30, 138, 425: mother
    179, 182–3, 382, 473 n. 110
Richardson, Samuel 114–15
ring, [non-]magic 138, 145–8, 149–51,
    153–6, 164, 202, 462 n. 28
Robert the Devil 36, 89, 425–6
Robert of Sicily 89, 426
Roman de la Rose 17, 102, 482 n. 7
romance, continuity of 5–6, 30–3, 35–6, 39;
    definition 8–10, 24–5, 218, 222; history
    of 22–40; structure of 57–67, 87;
    topography of 70–81, 111, 135–6; *see
    also* ancestral romance; condemna-
    tions; penitential romance; reader-
    ship; Reformation
romans antiques 25–6, 43
Romulus and Remus 108, 114–15
Roswall and Lillian 36, 228–9, 331, 426
Rowlands, Samuel, *Guy of Warwick* 32, 93,
    95, 462 n. 28; *Melancholie Knight*
    39–40, 411
Rubin, Gayle 227
rudderless boats 101, 106–23, 126–9, 133; see
    also *Quest*; *Partonope*; Shakespeare,
    Tempest

saints' lives 249–51; *see also* Agnes;
    Brendan; Dekker, *Virgin Martyr*;
    Edmund; Mary Magdalene
salvation history 5, 57–8, 87–9, 125–6, 352,
    376; Redemption 119, 330; *see also* Fall
Schlauch, Margaret 4
Secundus 299
Segar, William 42, 43
sentence and matter (*sens* and *matière*) 12,
    49, 101, 148–9, 152, 155, 260; *see also*
    allegory

Seven Sages of Rome 318, 426
sexuality 103, 219–21, 241; dangers of
78–80, 244, 404–5; exemplary models
132, 300–2, 304–7; female desire
231–8, 248–9, 254–5; approval 222,
359; fear 202–3, 221, 269, 274, 288–9,
292–3, 390–1; theories of conception
222
Shakespeare, William:
knowledge of romances 31, 72, 261, 264–5,
412, 413, 415–16, 417, 419, 427, 428
All's Well that EndsWell 391–6
As You Like It 21, 170, 264–6, 406–7
Comedy of Errors 263
Cymbeline 98, 284, 285–6, 288–9, 290–2,
327
and James I 359
Milford Haven 71
sources 275
Henry VI part 3 348, 403
Henry VIII 276–8, 284, 290, 359–60
King Lear 9, 406–8
Fool's prophecy 189–90
poor Tom 31
Loves Labours Lost 263, 358
Merchant of Venice 264, 399
Merry Wives of Windsor 177, 286–8, 358
Midsummer Night's Dream 143, 216–17,
263
fairies in 170, 174, 177, 178, 201
Much Ado about Nothing 285–6, 289–90
Othello 162–4, 261, 281–2, 286, 396–8
Pericles 13–14, 97–8, 266–8
structure 64–6
tournament 42
Marina 250, 359
Thaisa 220, 300–1
see also *Apollonius*
Rape of Lucrece 263
Richard II 357
Richard III 352
Romeo and Juliet 261, 263–4, 311
sonnets 20, 234
Taming of the Shrew 263
Tempest 77, 117, 177, 245, 359
setting 72, 111
structure 66–7
Gonzalo 118
Miranda 266
Prospero 110, 112–13, 170–2
Titus Andronicus 263
Two Gentlemen of Verona 261–2
Two Noble Kinsmen 141, 374–5

Venus and Adonis 263
Winter's Tale 87, 97, 116–17, 170–1, 282,
336
bear 2, 342
Hermione 290, 396–7
Perdita 17–18, 266, 327, 330, 331, 335,
359
see also *King Edward III*
shame culture 25, 54, 83
Shelton, Thomas, *Don Quixote* 39
shield, magic 142, 165; pentangle on 52,
59–60, 160; red cross on 51, 193;
Trinity on 103; Virgin on 95–6
Sidney, Philip 20, 43, 251, 429; *Arcadia*
(*New*) 34, 42, 47, 62, 252, 258–60;
Arcadia (*Old*) 245; representations of
women 298–9, 303
Siege of Jerusalem 494 n. 3
Siege of Thebes 399–400
Siege of Troy 399–400
Silence, see Heldris of Cornuälle
Sir Aldingar 278–9, 282, 285, 416
Sir Degaré 30, 246, 328–9, 330–1, 416
Sir Eglamour of Artois 13, 30, 106, 116–17,
335, 416–17; known to Shakespeare
261; *see also* Rowlands, *Melancholie
Knight*
Sir Firumbras 414
Sir Gawain and the Carl of Carlisle 418
Sir Gawain and the Green Knight 13, 21,
47–8, 50–3, 80, 142, 369–70, 418; girdle
159–60; opening 73; shame culture
83; structure of 59–60, 64; Bertilak
203–4; Gawain 54–5; guide 69; lady
18, 312; Morgan 186
Sir Gowther 89, 425
Sir Isumbras 30, 88–9, 98, 224, 421
Sir Launfal 79, 181, 183, 198–200, 211; con-
spectus of versions 175, 423;
Tryamour 473 n. 110
Sir Orfeo 16, 63–4, 181, 182, 204, 209, 424;
Orfeo 362, 363; ballad 36; see also
King Orphius
Sir Percyvell of Galles 26, 60–2, 333
Sir Tristrem 234, 319; see also *Tristan*
Sir Tryamour 278–9, 282, 285, 427
Song of Roland 25, 54
Song of Songs 241, 246–7
Sowdone of Babylone 166–7, 227, 414
Spenser, Edmund 363
knowledge of *Bevis* 31; of Chaucer
414–15; of *Eglamour* 335; of *Guy* 31;
of Hawes 103

Faerie Queene 10, 13, 34, 54, 63, 71, 104, 370–2
and hagiography 250
magic in 165–6
and prophecy 191, 193–4, 347, 356–7
Arthur, education of 206
Cleopolis 182
Gloriana 173–4, 183–4, 187, 189, 257, 323; and Arthur 55–6, 96, 181, 212, 255, 355–7
Book I 50, 70, 105, 212; representation of women 279–80, 284–5; Redcrosse Knight 51–2, 89, 96–7, 165, 193–4, 337–8; Serena 250
Book II 79–80, 134–6; chronicles in 24, 323; read by Milton 45; Guyon 31, 95–6; Phedon and Claribell 285
Book III-IV 47, 251–8, 306–7, 317–18; Trojan history 388; Britomart 228, 252–7, 356; Garden of Adonis 242–3
Book VI 181, 206–7, 339; Pastorella 17, 327, 335
Letter to Ralegh 7, 52, 55–6, 279, 337
Mutabilitie Cantos 105
Spottiswood, John 195
Squire of Low Degree 338, 339, 394, 426–7
Stanley family 339, 350, 493 n. 58
Stow, John 350
Sundry Strange Prophecies [1652] 192, 385–7, 465–6 n. 4; quoted 345; *see also* Thomas of Erceldoune, as prophet
Susanna 275, 287
swan cup 335; see also *Knight of the Swan*

Tasso, Torquato 34, 362–3; *Gerusalemme Liberata* 75–6; Armida 79–80, 102, 134–5; *Rinaldo* 133–4
Tate, Nahum, *King Lear* 408
Thomas, see *Horn; Tristan*
Thomas Coram Foundling Hospital 327–8
Thomas of Erceldoune 178, 181–2, 473 n. 111; as prophet 188–9, 190–1, 192–5, 345; conspectus of texts 175, 427; *Thomas of Erceldoune* 179–80, 181–2, 183, 213–14; (ballad) *Thomas the Rhymer* 36, 183; see also *Sundry Strange Prophecies*
Thracian Wonder 112
Tilney, Edmund 487 n. 83
Tirant lo Blanc 32
Tolkien, J. R. R. 4; *Farmer Giles of Ham* 142; *Lord of the Rings* 46, 80–1

Torrent of Portyngale 224, 427; Torrent 116–17
tournaments 41–2
Towneley Plays, quoted 58
Tragical History of Guy of Warwick 93–4, 166, 441 n. 80; Oberon in 176
translatio imperii 26, 72–5, 227
Trevet, Nicholas 127
Tristan 9, 25, 38, 313, 321–2; early versions 27–8, 129; Prose 33, 319, 427–8, 454 n. 2; Isolde 232–3, 312; Petit-Creiu 156–7; see also *Sir Tristrem*
Tristram 427–8
Troy, romances of 25–6, 399–400, 428
True Chronicle History of King Leir 406–7
Tudor dynasty 187, 347–8, 352, 370, 405; prophecies of 191–6, 346–7
Turke and Gawain [*Gowin*] 203, 418, 440 n. 72, 472 n. 90
Tuve, Rosemond 63, 97

Udall, Nicholas, *Ralph Roister Doister* 287
Ulrich von Zatzikhoven, *Lanzelet* 184, 314, 315, 319, 388; Iblis 233; Lanzelet 334
unicorns 139–40

Valentine and Orson 89, 167, 278–9, 282–4, 325; later versions 1, 36, 39, 283, 290, 407–8, 428–9; unhappy ending 9, 364–7, 379–81; Orson 388–9
Vives, *see* Hyrd
Vulgate Cycle, see *Lancelot-Grail*

Wace, *Roman de Brut* 24, 26
Warbeck, Perkin 325, 345, 351–2, 493 n. 54
Warner, William, *Albions England* 327, 470 n. 53; as source for *As You Like It* 265; story of Havelok in 29, 343–4, 354, 420
Warwick, earls of 335; see also *Guy of Warwick*; Leicester
Watson, Henry, see *Oliver of Castile; Valentine and Orson*
Wedderburn, Robert, see *Complaynt*
Wedding of Sir Gawain and Dame Ragnell 418, 446 n. 7
Whole Prophesie of Scotland 194–5; *see also* Thomas of Erceldoune, as prophet
William of Malmesbury 455 nn. 6, 14, 483 n. 17
William of Palerne 38, 234, 329, 378, 429; Melior 229, 234–5

witchcraft 160–2, 366, 378–81; sorceresses
   145; 'weird-elfes' 470 n. 53; *see also*
   enchanters, enchantresses
Wittig, Susan 4
Wolfram von Eschenbach, *Parzival* 100
women warriors 53, 224, 252, 257–8, 317
Worde, Wynkyn de 30, 349, 382

Worden, Blair 304
Wroth, Lady Mary 112
Wyatt, Thomas 415

Ywain and Gawain 26, 429; Alundine 204;
   Ywain 50–1, 146–8; *see also* Chrétien,
   Yvain